THE CAMBRIDGE HANDBOOK OF GENERATIVE AI AND THE LAW

This handbook offers an important exploration of generative AI and its legal and regulatory implications from interdisciplinary perspectives. The volume is divided into four parts. Part I provides the necessary context and background to understand the topic, including its technical underpinnings and societal impacts. Part II probes the emerging regulatory and policy frameworks related to generative AI and AI more broadly across different jurisdictions. Part III analyses generative AI's impact on specific areas of law, from non-discrimination and data protection to intellectual property, corporate governance, criminal law, and more. Part IV examines the various practical applications of generative AI in the legal sector and public administration. Overall, this volume provides a comprehensive resource for those seeking to understand and navigate the substantial and growing implications of generative AI for the law.

Mimi Zou leads the School of Private and Commercial Law at the University of New South Wales (UNSW), Australia, and is a Visiting Fellow at the University of Oxford. She has advised the UK government, World Economic Forum, and G7 on responsible AI and data governance and legal technology. Zou founded Oxford's first deep tech and law innovation lab and co-edited *Contracting and Contract Law in the Age of AI* (2022) with Martin Ebers and Cristina Poncibò.

Cristina Poncibò is Full Professor of Comparative Private Law in the Law Department at the University of Turin and an Affiliate of Collegio Carlo Alberto. Her work spans over 140 publications, focusing on the intersection of science, technology, and law. She regularly contributes to international conferences and, in 2022, co-edited *Contracting and Contract Law in the Age of Artificial Intelligence* (Hart) with Martin Ebers and Mimi Zou.

Martin Ebers is President of the Robotics & AI Law Society. He teaches IT Law at the University of Tartu. A prolific author with 20 books and over 120 articles to his name, he has also presented at more than 100 international conferences. Ebers is a leading voice in shaping European legal frameworks for emerging technologies and co-edits the Beck/Hart/Nomos Commentary on the EU's AI Act with Mimi Zou.

Ryan Calo co-directs the Tech Policy Lab at the University of Washington School of Law and co-founded the Center for an Informed Public. His research on law and emerging technology is widely published and cited. A frequent speaker at high-profile events, he has testified before the US Senate on technology policy issues.

The Cambridge Handbook of Generative AI and the Law

Edited by

MIMI ZOU

University of New South Wales

CRISTINA PONCIBÒ

University of Turin

MARTIN EBERS

University of Tartu

RYAN CALO

University of Washington

CAMBRIDGE
UNIVERSITY PRESS

CAMBRIDGE
UNIVERSITY PRESS

Shaftesbury Road, Cambridge CB2 8EA, United Kingdom

One Liberty Plaza, 20th Floor, New York, NY 10006, USA

477 Williamstown Road, Port Melbourne, VIC 3207, Australia

314–321, 3rd Floor, Plot 3, Splendor Forum, Jasola District Centre, New Delhi – 110025, India

103 Penang Road, #05–06/07, Visioncrest Commercial, Singapore 238467

Cambridge University Press is part of Cambridge University Press & Assessment,
a department of the University of Cambridge.

We share the University's mission to contribute to society through the pursuit of
education, learning and research at the highest international levels of excellence.

www.cambridge.org
Information on this title: www.cambridge.org/9781009492584

DOI: 10.1017/9781009492553

When citing this work, please include a reference to the DOI 10.1017/9781009492553

First published 2025

Cover image: "Codes" Gray and Black abstract watercolor painting by Bruce Black, 2020

A catalogue record for this publication is available from the British Library

Library of Congress Cataloging-in-Publication Data
NAMES: Zou, Mimi, 1985- editor | Poncibò, Cristina editor | Ebers, Martin, 1970- editor | Calo, M. Ryan editor
TITLE: The Cambridge handbook of generative AI and the law / edited by Mimi Zou, University of New South Wales, Sydney; Cristina Poncibò, University of Turin; Martin Ebers, University of Tartu, Estonia; Ryan Calo, University of Washington.
OTHER TITLES: Cambridge handbook of generative Artificial intelligence and the law
DESCRIPTION: Cambridge, United Kigndom ; New York, NY : Cambridge University Press, 2025. | Series: Cambridge law handbooks | Includes bibliographical references and index. | Summary: "This volume is for lawmakers, lawyers, business leaders, and curious minds interested in the legal and regulatory implications of generative AI as the fast-evolving technology is transforming our world. It offers clear and nuanced insights into the challenges of AI for the law, helping readers navigate this complex landscape"– Provided by publisher.
IDENTIFIERS: LCCN 2025007716 (print) | LCCN 2025007717 (ebook) | ISBN 9781009492584 hardback | ISBN 9781009492553 epub
SUBJECTS: LCSH: Artificial intelligence–Law and legislation–Untied States | Artificial intelligence–Law and legislation
CLASSIFICATION: LCC KF390.5.C6 C36 2025 (print) | LCC KF390.5.c6 (ebook) | DDC 343.7309/998–dc23/eng/20250306
LC record available at https://lccn.loc.gov/2025007716
LC ebook record available at https://lccn.loc.gov/2025007717

ISBN 978-1-009-49258-4 Hardback

Contents

Figures

Tables

List of Contributors

Bruce Boyden, Associate Professor of Law, Marquette University Law School, USA

Wanru Cai, LLM Graduate, Waseda University, Japan

Ryan Calo, Lane Powell & D. Wayne Gittinger Professor of Law, University of Washington, USA

Riccardo de Caria, Associate Professor of Law, University of Turin, Italy

Gabriele Cifrodelli, PhD Researcher, CREATe, University of Glasgow, UK

Jérôme De Cooman, Research Professor Premier Assistant, Law School, University of Liege, Belgium

Massimo Durante, Full Professor of Philosophy of Law and Legal Informatics, University of Turin, Italy

Martin Ebers, Associate Professor of IT Law, University of Tartu, Estonia

Lilian Edwards, Professor of Law, Innovation and Society, University of Newcastle, UK

Stefano Faraoni, Teaching Fellow in Law, University of Birmingham, UK

Jason Allen Grant, Associate Professor of Law, Singapore Management University, Singapore

Peter Henderson, Assistant Professor, Princeton University, USA

Hiroki Habuka, Research Professor, University of Kyoto, Japan

Sebastian Hallensleben, VDE Association for Electrical, Electronic & Information Technologies, Germany

Zijie Huang, PhD Scholar in Electrical and Electronic Engineering, University of Bristol, UK

Francesca Lagoia, Associate Professor in Legal Informatics, University of Bologna, Italy, and Part-time Professor at Professor at European University Institute, Florence, Italy

Ellen Lefley, Senior Lawyer, JUSTICE, UK

Rūta Liepiņa, Research Fellow, ALMA-AI Research Institute, University of Bologna, Italy

Marco Lippi, Associate Professor in Computer Engineering, University of Florence, Italy

Jane Loo, Senior Research Associate, Centre for AI & Data Governance, Singapore Management University, Singapore

Tom Melham, Professor of Computer Science, University of Oxford, UK

Hans-Wolfgang Micklitz, Professor for Economic Law, European University Institute, Florence, Italy

Patrick O'Malley, Associate Professor of Law, Universidad de Navarra, Spain

Ugo Pagallo, Professor of Jurisprudence, University of Turin, Italy

Przemysław Pałka, Assistant Professor of Law, Jagiellonian University, Krakow, Poland

Sylvia Papadopoulo, Associate Professor, Department of Private Law, University of Pretoria, South Africa

Ludovica Paseri, Postdoctoral Researcher in Philosophy of Law and Legal Informatics, University of Turin, Italy

Beatrice Panattoni, Postdoctoral Researcher in Criminal Law, Temporary Professor, University of Verona, Italy

Cristina Poncibò, Professor of Comparative Private Law, University of Turin, Italy

Christoph Rademacher, Professor of Law, Waseda University, Japan

Teresa Rodriguez de las Heras Ballell, Full Professor of Commercial Law, Charles III University of Madrid, Spain

Hannah Ruschemeier, Junior Professor of Public Law, FernUniversität in Hagen, Germany

Joséphine Sangaré, PhD Researcher, CREATe, University of Glasgow, UK

Giovanni Sartor, Professor, Department of Legal Studies, University of Bologna, Italy and also Professor at European University Institute, Florence, Italy.

David U. Socol de la Osa, Assistant Professor, Hitotsubashi Institute for Advanced Study, Japan

James Stewart, Senior Lecturer, Science, Technology and Innovation Studies, University of Edinburgh, UK

Igor Szpotakowski, Lecturer in Intellectual Property Law, University of Leeds, UK

Sophie Weerts, Associate Professor of Public Law, Swiss Graduate School of Public Administration, University of Lausanne, Switzerland

Elana Zaide, Assistant Professor, University of Nebraska School of Law, USA

Lu Zhang, Assistant Professor, School of Journalism & Communication, China University of Political Science and Law, China

Mimi Zou, Professor and Head of School of Private & Commercial Law, University of New South Wales, Australia

Foreword

*Michael Kirby The Hon AC CMG**

As I write the Foreword to this Handbook, the announcement has been made in Sweden that the 2024 Nobel Prize in Physics has been awarded to scientists John Hopfield (USA) and Geoffrey Hinton (UK/Canada) for their 'foundational discoveries and inventions that enable machine learning with artificial neural networks'. The Laureates built on each other's research to help establish foundations for machine learning and artificial intelligence (AI). Moreover, the 2024 Nobel Prize in Chemistry has been awarded to AI scientists Demis Hassabis (UK) and John Jumper (US/UK) of Deepmind. The award recognises their development of an AI model 'AlphaFold2' to 'solve a 50-year-old problem: predicting proteins' complex structures'. The world is now full of publications about the likely impact of this technology on humanity. At the heart of the debates are the question of 'AI safety' and 'X-risk'. This Handbook is an outstanding legal text about the building of responses, supported by law, to these two existential human dilemmas.

The dilemmas are at once intriguing and concerning. They have enormous implications for the law. *The Cambridge Handbook on Generative AI and the Law* is published at a crucial juncture, as we grapple with a technology that promises to revolutionise not just our legal systems, but human society and the world at large.

In my thirty-five years as a judge, I encountered numerous complex problems that tested the boundaries of existing legal rules. Yet none quite compares with the far-reaching challenges posed by generative AI. This technology, with its ability to mimic human intellectual output across a spectrum of activities, presents us with a new frontier in legal thought and practice.

The editors have assembled an impressive group of scholars and experts to navigate this still substantially uncharted territory. The contents of the Handbook impressed me by both the breadth and depth of the issues the authors have addressed. From the foundational explanations of AI technology, written for a newcomer, to the nuanced discussions of its impact in various legal domains, the Handbook serves as both a primer for the newcomer and an exploration of the subject for those with knowledge of the burgeoning materials already published on this topic.

What particularly resonates with me is the recurring theme of balance. Balance between innovation and regulation. And balance between the potential benefits of AI and the protection of fundamental rights. This tension is not unfamiliar to inquisitive members of the legal profession and its academy. Indeed, it lies at the heart of many landmark cases that have shaped

* Justice of the High Court of Australia (1996–2009); Chair of the OECD Expert Group on Trans Border Data Barriers and the Protection of Privacy (1968–70); Gruber Justice Prize (Washington, 2010, jointly).

our jurisprudence when confronted by earlier technology. Still, it is the scale and pace at which generative AI is developing that magnify the challenge in the current age.

The contributions in this Handbook provide its readers with a strong foundation. As judges and lawyers, we must understand not just the legal implications of generative AI. We must also seek familiarity with its technical underpinnings and societal impacts. The warnings about computational manipulation and the potential for 'unnatural selection' are particularly concerning. They remind us that our legal frameworks must evolve to address not just the obvious, direct consequences of new technologies, but also the subtle, far-reaching effects that such innovations have on individuals, corporations, communities and markets.

The exploration of various regulatory approaches across different jurisdictions highlights the global nature of the challenge that we face. As I reflect on my own experiences, I am reminded of how often we looked to international approaches when dealing with novel legal issues. In the realm of generative AI, such cross-border learning and cooperation will be more crucial than ever. Yet the mind of the lawyer is still commonly shaped by jurisdiction. Lawyers are trained to think in terms of their own jurisdictions. The internet has already challenged us to consider cross-border impacts of technology. Now, generative AI obliges us to think, even more deeply, in terms of universal and global challenges.

The examination of generative AI's impact on specific areas of law – from non-discrimination and data protection to intellectual property and criminal law – is particularly illuminating. These chapters underline the pervasive nature of AI's influence and the need for a holistic approach to legal adaptation. Judges often have to interpret and apply laws in contexts unforeseen by the law's drafters. The challenge with generative AI is that it may require us to rethink how we apply some of our most long-standing legal concepts and principles to the world of AI; but also re-fashion to make new.

There are potential applications of AI in legal analytics and even in judicial decision-making. Chapter 25 on the right to a human judge, viewed through the lens of human dignity, raises anew ancient questions about the essence of justice and the role, legitimate and illegitimate, of human judgement in our legal systems.

To my colleagues in the legal profession – practitioners, scholars and jurists alike – I commend this Handbook to open their minds and advance their thinking. The issues explored will undoubtedly shape the future of our profession and of the administration of justice. Benjamin N. Cardozo once said: 'The law, like the traveler, must be ready for the morrow. It must have a principle of growth.' The advent of generative AI presents us with an unprecedented opportunity – and responsibility – for growth of such a kind. This Handbook serves as an invaluable guide in the journey many have already begun. It offers insights, raising critical questions and proposing thoughtful approaches to the astonishing challenge.

I congratulate the publisher and editors of this Handbook, as well as the individual contributors. This volume is not just a compilation of scholarly work. It is a roadmap for the future of law. It will spark robust discussions, inform policy decisions and guide us all on the new journey of the law into the world of generative AI. That journey has already begun. In this book are some keys for this new kingdom.

Preface

As generative AI continues to revolutionise various sectors of society, the *Cambridge Handbook of Generative AI and the Law* brings together leading scholars and experts to examine the challenges and opportunities presented by generative AI within diverse legal contexts and jurisdictions. It covers a wide range of important and timely topics that reflect the multifaceted, far-reaching potential and risks associated with the development and deployment of technology. The various contributions in this volume analyse how existing legal and regulatory frameworks may address the attendant risks and challenges as well as offer innovative solutions to fill the relevant gaps and limitations in the law.

It is important to note that the landscape of generative AI capabilities is evolving at an unprecedented pace, with new models and applications emerging frequently, often outpacing our ability to fully analyse their legal implications. As one of our contributors, Tom Melham, remarked in Chapter 1: 'any account of the frontier would quickly be out of date'.

Additionally, in the process of compiling the chapters from July 2023 to May 2024, the European Union's AI Act was in the final stages of enactment. Consequently, some references to the Act in the chapters may be outdated by the time of publication of this Handbook. Readers should be aware that the final version of the AI Act may differ from the drafts discussed in these chapters, and some analyses may require updates in light of the Act's final form. Nevertheless, the principles and challenges discussed in relation to the AI Act remain valuable for understanding the broader regulatory landscape surrounding generative AI.

As we stand at the crossroads of technological innovation and legal adaptation, this volume contributes significantly to academic experts', policymakers', and practitioners' conversations on how to harness the power of generative AI while safeguarding fundamental rights, promoting fairness, and upholding the rule of law in our increasingly AI-driven world.

This preface provides a brief overview of each chapter. However, it can only offer a glimpse into the deep and rich analyses our authors have conducted on these diverse topics.

PART I

Part I offers a multidisciplinary examination of generative AI's impact on technology, society, and the law. A common thread running through these chapters is the recognition of both the immense potential and significant challenges posed by this rapidly evolving technology, and the need for collaboration across disciplines to effectively navigate its legal implications.

In Chapter 1, Tom Melham, a computer scientist, sets the stage by explaining key concepts of generative AI. Melham provides a useful definition of AI as 'the capability of a machine to imitate intelligent human behaviour'. The fundamental nature of modern generative AI is to imitate or mimic 'the intellectual productions of humans', ranging from everyday conversation to creative works. His technical account provides a contextual understanding of the pressing legal questions and regulatory challenges arising from generative AI.

In Chapter 2, Zijie Huang, another computer scientist, examines the advancements in the development of different types of generative AI models and their applications in recent years. Huang emphasises the importance of developing trustworthy and responsible generative AI, highlighting the need to balance innovation with ethical considerations.

The ethical dimension of generative AI is further spotlighted in Chapter 3 by Ludovica Paseri and Massimo Durante, who propose a dual approach to analysing generative AI's impact: normative and epistemological. Their analysis reveals the complex interplay between how generative AI functions and its broader societal implications, particularly in relation to legal epistemology.

The potential for misuse and manipulation emerges as another significant concern. Stefano Faraoni's Chapter 4 presents a stark warning about the unprecedented capabilities of generative AI in computational manipulation. Faraoni critiques the existing weaknesses in the EU's legal frameworks to protect individual autonomy in the face of increasingly sophisticated generative AI-driven computational manipulation.

Economic implications of generative AI are explored in Jerome De Cooman's Chapter 5, which applies a Darwinian lens to examine the potential market distortions in the art world. This unique perspective highlights how generative AI could lead to 'unnatural selection' in creative markets, potentially undermining human artists and traditional notions of copyright and value.

These contributions in Part I reveal the interdisciplinary nature of the challenges posed by generative AI. From computer science and ethics to economics and law, addressing the implications of this technology requires a holistic approach that draws on diverse fields of expertise.

PART II

The contributions in the second part of our Handbook explore the different approaches to generative AI regulation and governance that have emerged at national and international levels, as well as industry self-regulation, and the challenges they present.

In Chapter 6, Ugo Pagallo examines the regulation of generative AI, foundation AI, and large language models (LLMs) within the context of the EU's AI Act. Pagallo highlights several potential risks associated with these technologies, including discrimination, information hazards, and environmental harm. He also points out the limitations of current regulatory attempts, including issues of competitiveness, legal certainty, and the need for frequent revisions to keep pace with technological advancements.

This theme is further developed in Chapter 7 by Teresa Rodriguez de las Heras Ballell, which maps the liability cases for generative AI within the EU legal framework. Ballell's analysis focuses on testing the liability rules provided in the draft Artificial Intelligence Liability Directive and the Revised Product Liability Directive, assessing their sufficiency and effectiveness in addressing generative AI challenges.

The challenge of establishing clear liability for foundation model developers and deployers is a key focus of Peter Henderson's Chapter 8. Henderson points out the difficulties in meeting scienter requirements and creating proof under many existing statutes and torts in US law. He also highlights potential constitutional protections for AI-generated speech and the possibility of legal challenges to regulatory agencies' authority over AI systems.

In Chapter 9, Lu Zhang and Mimi Zou provide insight into China's regulatory approach to generative AI, highlighting the tension between addressing potential risks and promoting industry growth. The authors carefully analyse the provisions of China's vertical Interim Measures for the Management of Generative AI Services, which primarily target content safety and security risks while aiming to foster industry development.

In Chapter 10, Jason Grant Allen and Jane Loo offer an overview of Singapore's evolving AI governance framework. They describe Singapore's 'soft touch' approach, which emphasises collaboration between government and industry, clear responsibility structures, and the importance of public trust in AI. The authors highlight Singapore's proactive stance in developing initiatives like the AI Verify Toolkit and participating in international collaborations.

The importance of international cooperation efforts in generative AI governance is the focus of Hiroki Habuka and David U. Socol de la Osa's Chapter 11. They analyse the G7's Hiroshima AI Process and the resulting Comprehensive Policy Framework as a significant step towards international alignment on principles for safeguarding individual rights and enhancing trust in AI systems.

In Chapter 12, Sebastian Hallensleben looks at the role of international standardisation in generative AI governance, and the relationship between regulation and standardisation in the EU. Hallensleben notes that while AI standardisation efforts are well underway, specific work on generative AI standards is still in its early stages. He suggests potential areas of future standardisation, including test methods, performance metrics, and standards for marking AI-generated content.

Moving from public regulation to private ordering, Chapter 13 explores self-regulation in the generative AI landscape. Its authors, Igor Szpotakowski, Joséphine Sangaré, Lilian Edwards, Gabriele Cifrodelli, and James Stewart, examine the terms and conditions, privacy policies, and other instruments used by model providers to govern their relationships with users. The chapter highlights a common paradigm where providers disclaim ownership of outputs while also avoiding liability, positioning themselves as 'neutral intermediaries' in a manner reminiscent of earlier platform regulation debates.

The contributions in Part II point to the need for adaptive regulatory approaches in light of the fast-paced technological advancements in and the global nature of generative AI development and deployment. The analyses of different national approaches (United States, China, Singapore) and multilateral efforts (European Union, G7) underscore the need for coordinated global governance. Overall, the chapters in this part collectively highlight the multifaceted governance challenges facing policymakers, regulators, and all stakeholders as they attempt to harness the potential of generative AI while mitigating its risks.

PART III

This part comprises contributions concerning the multifaceted implications of generative AI across various domains of law, including non-discrimination law, data protection, privacy, intellectual property (IP), competition, consumer, corporate governance, and criminal law.

In Chapter 14, Ricardo de Caria highlights a crucial gap in the EU's AI Act: the disconnect between provisions addressing discrimination and those regulating generative AI. This observation raises important questions about the effectiveness of current legislation in addressing potential discriminatory outputs from generative AI models. The author's conclusion that the

AI Act has not brought significant innovation in this area suggests a potential blind spot in EU regulation. There is a pressing need to fill this regulatory gap considering the growing public concerns about bias in AI systems.

Hannah Ruschemeier's contribution in Chapter 15 delves into the tension between data protection laws and the 'data-hungry' nature of generative AI, particularly LLMs. This tension exemplifies the broader challenge of balancing individual privacy rights with technological advancement. The author's analysis of the interplay between generative AI and data protection within the European legal framework provides valuable insights into the complexities of applying existing regulations to rapidly changing technologies. The chapter raises important questions about the feasibility of strict data protection in the age of LLMs and the potential need for a more nuanced approach to data governance.

Offering a transatlantic perspective, Elana Zeide in Chapter 16 examines the limitations of traditional US privacy frameworks in addressing the challenges posed by generative AI. The author calls for a fundamental reorientation of privacy protection, shifting from individual control to collective conceptions and from reactive to proactive governance. The proposed paradigm shift, emphasising responsible innovation, is particularly relevant given the rapid advancement of generative AI.

Chapter 17 tackles the IP issues around generative AI for IP laws in the United States. In this chapter, Bruce Boyden focuses on whether AI-generated creations should be legally treated similarly to or differently from human-made works across various IP domains. This raises fundamental questions about the nature of creativity and authorship in the digital age. Boyden explores whether AI systems truly 'learn' or merely copy, whether they function as user-controlled tools or independent agents, and how existing legal doctrines should be applied or adapted. We are urged to avoid 'magical thinking' about AI but remain 'open to the possibility' that it 'may pose serious doctrinal or practical conundrums' under IP laws.

Christopher Rademacher and Wanru Cai in Chapter 18 offer a valuable comparative analysis of copyright law in Japan and China, particularly in relation to generative AI. The authors' exploration of how these countries balance content owners' rights with national policy goals of technological advancement provides insight into different approaches to AI regulation. The chapter's focus on the fundamental questions of training data use and copyright ownership in AI-generated content in two East Asian jurisdictions highlights the global nature of the challenges raised in Boyden's chapter.

In Chapter 19, Sylvia Papadopoulos examines the impact of generative AI on market structures and competition law, providing an analysis of recent legal developments in this area and the challenges posed by GenAI to traditional business models and antitrust laws. Papadopoulos emphasises the need for balancing innovation with market competitiveness and fairness.

Chapter 20, by Christina Poncibò, explores the intricate relationship between consumer protection and generative AI, focusing on the concept of 'hypersuasion' in algorithmic consumer interactions. She concludes that current legal instruments in the EU fail to comprehensively govern the power dynamics in algorithmic consumer interactions, highlighting a critical gap in consumer protection.

Patrick O'Malley, in Chapter 21, examines the impact of generative AI on corporate governance, highlighting the need for directors and officers to adapt to new technological, legal, and ethical challenges. The author's focus on the responsibilities of top management in ensuring the safe and ethical use of AI tools raises important questions about liability and accountability in the age of AI. The chapter's emphasis on the human and moral element in corporate governance is particularly relevant given the potential for AI to automate decision-making processes.

In Chapter 22, Beatrice Panattoni explores the complex intersection of generative AI and criminal law, raising important questions about moral agency, responsibility, and guilt in AI-related harms. The author's examination of how AI changes criminal affordances and the potential need for criminal law involvement in AI-related harms provides a thought-provoking perspective on an emerging legal challenge. The chapter's exploration of preserving the concept of guilt when the *actus reus* is delegated to generative AI raises fundamental questions about criminal liability in the age of AI.

The chapters in Part III highlight, to varying degrees, some of the limitations of existing legal concepts and frameworks in addressing the challenges posed by generative AI across different areas of law. Several authors grapple with the tension between fostering technological advancement and protecting individual rights, market fairness, and societal values. How to achieve this balance remains a central challenge across diverse legal fields.

PART IV

Generative AI is being deployed across a variety of sectors, including the legal sector. In this final part of the Handbook, contributors examine how practical applications of this technology are reshaping the landscape of legal services and public administration – from automating legal tasks such as document generation to potentially writing court decisions. However, with these advancements come complex ethical, regulatory, and societal issues.

In Chapter 23, Rūta Liepiņa, Francesca Lagioia, Marco Lippi, Przemysław Pałka, Hans-Wolfgang Micklitz, and Giovanni Sartor delve into the transition from predictive to generative AI in legal analytics, focusing on the enhancement of AI systems such as CLAUDETTE through LLMs. They explore how LLMs can be leveraged for consumer empowerment and privacy protection use cases to demonstrate the opportunities and shortcomings of LLMs vis-à-vis earlier AI approaches. They further note that new obligations under the AI Act and related EU legislation will significantly affect how such technology will be deployed.

Martin Ebers, in Chapter 24, addresses the critical questions arising from the use of LLMs in legal practice. By examining recent incidents and potential risks, he explores the ethical and professional obligations of lawyers using these technologies. His comparative analysis of US and EU law and model rules gives a succinct view of the regulatory challenges and potential solutions in integrating LLMs into legal services.

In Chapter 25, Ellen Lefley and Mimi Zou examine how the use of generative AI in courtrooms may impact the right to a fair trial, as enshrined in Article 6 of the European Convention of Human Rights. In this context, they argue for an interpretation of Article 6 that takes seriously the principle of human dignity, with implications for the role of human judges in justice systems that will increasingly deploy and even rely on AI. Their analysis prompts us to consider the intrinsic value of human judgement and empathy in legal decision-making processes.

Finally, Sophie Weerts in Chapter 26 broadens the scope to examine the deployment of generative AI in public administration. By comparing the regulatory approaches of the United States and the European Union, she illuminates the key legal issues and administrative values at stake. This exploration provides valuable insights into how different jurisdictions are navigating the integration of AI technologies into governance structures.

These chapters paint a picture of a legal sector in flux, grappling with the transformative potential of generative AI that could improve access to legal services and justice for more people, while striving to uphold fundamental principles of our legal system. Part IV invites us to contemplate the future of legal practice and public administration, while providing a more nuanced understanding of the interplay between human expertise and generative AI capabilities in these contexts.

CONCLUDING REMARKS

Overall, the Handbook paints a picture of generative AI as a transformative force with significant implications for the law, demanding careful consideration and proactive governance. As generative AI continues to evolve, the legal and regulatory frameworks surrounding it must likewise adapt, guided by principles of accountability, trustworthiness, and the protection of human agency. I am very grateful to my co-editors and contributors for making this Handbook possible. Given the pace of change, I have no doubt that we will need a second volume very soon!

– Mimi Zou

PART I

Understanding Generative AI from Multidisciplinary Perspectives

1

Generative AI

An Introduction

Tom Melham

Artificial intelligence (AI) is notoriously hard to define, but a useful shorthand description is *the capability of a machine to imitate intelligent human behaviour*.[1] One merit of this definition is that it makes no reference to the underlying technology; this is under constant and rapid development, and far too varied to encapsulate neatly as the defining characteristic of AI. This terse definition also avoids questions about whether our machines really are intelligent. Whether they *think*. Most importantly, this definition is a salutary reminder, in the context of the astonishing performance of modern *generative artificial intelligence* (GAI) – the subject of this research handbook in its connections with law. It reminds us that this is technology that generates outputs that look like – that *mimic* – the intellectual productions of humans, from everyday speech to creative literary works.

Of course, artificial intelligence has many potential and practical applications, beyond just mimicry of human intelligence. Artificial intelligence technologies are widely looked to for practical solutions to specific problems in particular application domains, such as disease diagnosis, personalised education, electronic retail, risk management, or fraud detection in finance – and many more. The European Union Artificial Intelligence Act (EU AI Act) is therefore rightly concerned with the regulation of a very broad range of both AI applications and technologies. Accordingly, the Act defines an 'AI system' to mean 'a machine-based system designed to operate with varying levels of autonomy, that may exhibit adaptiveness after deployment and that, for explicit or implicit objectives, infers, from the input it receives, how to generate outputs such as predictions, content, recommendations, or decisions that can influence physical or virtual environments'.[2]

The contrast between these two definitions illuminates a distinction that is commonly made between the two principal aims of artificial intelligence research. The first is so-called artificial general intelligence (AGI). The pursuit of AGI aims at creating machines that have an intelligence equal to humans – that can learn intellectual skills across a broad or even an unlimited range of human intellectual activities. It can learn to play chess, but also compose a poem, solve

[1] Paraphrased from 'artificial intelligence'. Meriam-Webster.com, 2024. www.merriam-webster.com/dictionary/artificial%20intelligence, 2 June 2024.

[2] The Artificial Intelligence Act, Regulation of the European Parliament and of the Council laying down harmonised rules on artificial intelligence and amending Regulations (EC) No. 300/2008, (EU) No. 167/2013, (EU) No. 168/2013, (EU) 2018/858, (EU) 2018/1139, and (EU) 2019/2144 and Directives 2014/90/EU, (EU) 2016/797 and (EU) 2020/1828, Art. 3, para. 1.

a puzzle, or work out some legal reasoning. There are no examples of AGI in existence today – but the optimistic pursuit of AGI is a widespread mindset among AI researchers and in the tech industry. It is sometimes explicit in published objectives or aspirations, but also commonly betrayed by a tendency to yield to our human predisposition to anthropomorphise.[3] Some researchers or commentators also posit artificial intelligence that is self-aware, conscious, or sentient – about which there is a great deal of discussion and speculation.[4] In this chapter, we will leave this controversial topic aside – though should sentient artificial intelligence ever be achieved, this will present many obvious challenges to ethics and law.[5]

The second principal aim of artificial intelligence research is applied, or 'narrow', artificial intelligence. This is artificial intelligence designed to do a specific task – one narrow, specific task that usually requires human intelligence, but which we can 'train' the computer to do, typically using a significant quantity of data and special 'learning' algorithms. A famous example is AlphaGo, which can play the complex game of Go as well as the most accomplished human master.[6] That is all it can do, but it does that extremely well.

There are also two broad technical approaches to achieving artificial intelligence, whether general or applied. The first is so-called *symbolic* or *logical* artificial intelligence. This is the kind of artificial intelligence that represents the substance of focus for the artificial intelligence algorithm – whether it be knowledge, a virtual world, some goals, or rules governing simulated actions – in explicitly *symbolic* form. Abstract, usually structured, explicit representations of entities, their properties, and the relationships between them. Symbolic AI has a long history and was the dominant paradigm of AI research from the 1950s to the mid 1990s. And it is still useful today; for example, AlphaGo incorporates significant components of symbolic AI.

The second technical approach could, in very general terms, be called *statistical AI*. This is artificial intelligence that is based on something resembling a *statistical model* of the domain of interest. A characteristic example is an AI system that generates a decision outcome for a particular case in hand, based on a statistical summary of decisions that have been made in the past. Example applications include automation of a wide range of decision-based government services.[7] This approach to AI has been in the ascendant throughout the twenty-first century, animated by the remarkable successes of *machine learning* with *deep neural networks*.[8] Statistical AI is also the approach that underpins much of the generative artificial intelligence that is explored in this handbook, and therefore the focus of this introductory chapter.

Research in generative artificial intelligence has a long history, going back – in many different forms – to the founding of the modern field of artificial intelligence in the 1950s. By the early 2020s, powered by 'deep learning' with neural networks, highly capable generative AI had been developed that can produce many forms of intellectual output – including text in natural language (such as English), but also many other forms of output such as images, videos, music,

[3] N. Epley, A. Waytz, and J. T. Cacioppo, 'On seeing human: A three-factor theory of anthropomorphism', *Psychological Review*, 114(4), pp. 864–886.

[4] P. Butlin et al., 'Consciousness in Artificial Intelligence: Insights from the Science of Consciousness', *arXiv Computing Research Repository*, arXiv:2308.08708 [cs.AI], 22 August 2023.

[5] K. Mindaugas, 'Legal framework for the coexistence of humans and conscious AI', *Frontiers in Artificial Intelligence*, 6, 20 September 2023.

[6] D. Silver et al., 'Mastering the game of Go with deep neural networks and tree search', *Nature*, 529, pp. 484–489, 27 January 2016.

[7] V. J. Straub et al., 'AI for bureaucratic productivity: Measuring the potential of AI to help automate 143 million UK government transactions', *arXiv Computing Research Repository*, arXiv:2403.14712 [cs.CY], 18 March 2024.

[8] Y. LeCun, Y. Bengio, and G. Hinton, 'Deep learning', *Nature*, 521, pp. 436–444, 27 May 2015; T. J. Sejnowski, *The Deep Learning Revolution* (The MIT Press, 2018).

or computer code. But it is no exaggeration to say that the introduction of the *transformer* model by researchers at Google Brain in 2017 revolutionised the field of generative AI for production of natural language outputs in particular.[9] The invention of transformers initiated a period of very rapid development of AI for natural language tasks, exemplified by a series of language 'models' of unprecedented capability and versatility being developed and released by researchers, technology companies, and creators of open-source AI software. We provide a brief sketch to introduce the transformer architecture later in this chapter.

A ground-breaking advance was the introduction of the 'Generative Pre-trained Transformer 3' (GPT-3) by the US technology company OpenAI and released for early testing in spring 2020.[10] GPT-3 was significantly larger than all other transformer models to date; it was trained on around 500 billion so-called tokens, which for our purposes here can be thought of as words of text. Most of this text was harvested by computers from the internet, with some filtering applied. GPT-3 represents its learning as a predictive statistical model with around 175 billion *parameters* – numerical values embedded within the model software that determine the model's operation and outputs.

This scaling up in size gave GPT-3 unprecedented capability for language processing, very significantly beyond what existing models could do at the time. GPT-3 and its successors produce written text in ordinary English – and other languages – of such a high quality and apparent meaningfulness that it is often difficult to tell if it has been written by a human or a machine. The following years saw an explosion of research and development for such so-called large language models – as well as huge commercial interest worldwide.

It is entirely natural to suppose that there may be many opportunities for the use of such generative AI in legal applications. Legal knowledge, whether black letter law or arcane legal expertise, and the articulation of law in textual form – as texts in natural language – are in some sense central to the enterprise of law. And the importance of text to legal knowledge aligns well with the strength of generative AI embodied in large language models. The emergence of highly capable generative AI also poses many legal issues and questions, including consequences for intellectual property, contracts and licenses, liability, data protection, use in specific sectors, potential harms, and of course ethics, policy, and regulation of the technology.

This research handbook discusses many of these issues in depth, and this chapter is intended to support these discussions by providing a very basic sketch of generative artificial intelligence from a technical perspective. The focus here will be on generative AI for natural language, though other forms of generative AI – for example for images or videos – also exist, are increasingly capable, and have specific legal issues.

It is, of course, impossible to provide a full account in this chapter of the highly technical, mathematical foundations of generative AI. Nor would it be helpful to delineate the state of the art at the time of writing. Technical progress in generative artificial intelligence – at least in certain directions – has been both rapid and voluminous, and any account of the frontier would quickly be out of date. We therefore focus in this chapter on a few basics, at a largely non-technical level.

Machine learning, usually underpinned by the AI computer technology of *artificial neural networks*, lies at the heart of much of the generative artificial intelligence that is the topic of this

[9] A. Vaswani et al., 'Attention is All You Need', in 31st Conference on Neural Information Processing Systems (NIPS 2017), Long Beach, CA, USA, pp. 6000–6010, December 2017.

[10] T. B. Brown et al., 'Language models are few-shot learners', *arXiv Computing Research Repository*, arXiv:2005.14165 [cs.CL], 22 July 2020.

handbook. Artificial neural networks are introduced a bit later in this chapter. But broadly speaking, machine learning is a way of using certain computer algorithms[11] to 'learn' from data and to generalise beyond the data to perform tasks without explicit, step-by-step instructions or programming.

Typically, algorithms for machine learning are statistical in nature and the result produced is some kind of mathematical or statistical model. Such a model is an abstraction, encoded within the computer, of aspects of the system that is typified by the data, laid out using mathematical entities and structures, and concepts. The model is then typically used to make 'predictions', for example a classification, for new examples or situations not explicitly given in the data. Internal to such a model there will be some – often very many – numerical values (numbers of some kind) that are the encoded result of the learning. Creating the model from the data proceeds by a process called 'training', which iteratively adjusts these parameters to minimise the errors it makes in its predictions or to optimise some so-called objective function, which measures how good the output is.

There are three main kinds of machine learning.[12] First, there is *supervised learning*, in which a model is trained with a (typically large) number of pairs comprising an input and a known, desired output. For example, to train an image recognition model one might take a large collection of digital photographs and manually 'label' them with what they are a photograph of. The training data in this case would consist of photographic images paired with their labels. (Obviously, manual labelling in this way can be expensive, time-consuming, and possibly error prone.) As training proceeds, a predictive model of a statistical nature is developed that represents a 'function' from inputs to outputs – a kind of rule or process that assigns an output to each possible input. It is hoped that the model will generalise beyond the training examples to produce the correct, or expected, outputs for new inputs that were not present in the training data. These are the 'predictions' and using the model in this way is sometimes called 'inference'. Models represented by artificial neural networks are a very prominent example of supervised learning and often used for classification.

With *unsupervised learning*, a model is also built from training data – but in this case without the provision of an expected outcome for each input. Algorithms for unsupervised learning work without human guidance and build models that encode patterns that are detected in the data, such as similarities or differences. A typical application might be to cluster inputs into groups or to detect anomalous inputs. Some machine learning applications combine supervised and unsupervised learning – or are trained through *self-supervised learning*, in which some structure within the input data itself is leveraged to provide the desired or 'correct' outputs, rather than relying on the desired outputs being provided by human effort – such as manually labelling a set of digital photographs for training an image recognition model by supervised learning. GPT models are, in part, trained through self-supervised learning.

Finally, in *reinforcement learning*, the machine is situated within a simulated, artificial 'environment' and can monitor certain features of the state of that environment. It also has the capability to execute actions within this simulated environment that can change its state. A system of artificial 'rewards' – usually encoded numerically – is set up by the designer of the learning algorithm. As actions are taken by a simulated AI agent, rewards are generated by the

[11] An *algorithm* is a finitely described, unambiguous sequence of precise instructions to solve instances of a well-defined class of problems or to perform a calculation to produce a well-defined, specified output. Algorithms are implemented for use as computer software.

[12] A. Burkov, *The Hundred-Page Machine Learning Book* (Andriy Burkov, 2019).

learning algorithm in response to the actions taken. The magnitude of these rewards will align with progress towards or achievement of a desired goal. The aim of reinforcement learning is to develop a 'policy' for the optimal action to take in each state – a policy that, if followed, will maximise the cumulative reward. Reinforcement learning is used to develop AI that executes a series of decisions, such as would arise in playing a board game or controlling a robot.

A structure very commonly used in today's machine learning models is the *artificial neural network*. This structure is loosely inspired by the structure and function of the interconnected neurons in a human brain – hence the name 'neural' network. These networks are behind many of the amazing capabilities in modern AI systems and lie at the heart of generative AI such as the transformer models.

There are many ways in which a neural network can be structured, but typically they consist of a (usually large) number of elements called 'artificial neurons' that have some arrangement of connections between them. Each neuron provides a numerical value as its output called its 'activation level', which is computed to be some non-linear function of the activation levels of the neurons connected to it. (Non-linear means a change in the input does not produce a strictly proportional change in the output.) The activation levels travelling on the connections are moderated by numerical parameters called 'weights', which are adjusted by a (typically supervised) machine learning algorithm that trains the model on data.

The neurons in an artificial neural network are commonly structured into a series of layers, with the connections going from one layer to the next – though many other kinds of structures are also possible. The input to the model is presented at the first layer, and the output taken from the last. This arrangement, in essence, realises a function from inputs to outputs. Such structures can have many hundreds of layers, and thousands or even millions of neurons overall – the connections of which are all individually governed by a weight parameter that is determined by the process of training. These are the 'parameters' mentioned earlier in our discussion of GPT-3. The term 'deep neural network' refers to such structures with multiple layers, and 'deep learning' refers to the special algorithms and methods that have been developed to train such networks effectively.[13]

It is beyond the scope of this chapter to go into more technical depth about machine learning or artificial neural networks. For a little more detail, in a form accessible particularly to legal scholars, chapter 2 of *The Law of Artificial Intelligence* can be recommended.[14] But it is worth just mentioning here, in the context of this handbook, the notorious issue of 'interpretability' or 'explainability' for statistical AI implemented with (deep) neural networks.[15] Deep neural networks are highly complex models, and the 'knowledge' represented within them may be distributed across millions of numerical parameters, making it very difficult if not impossible to understand or explain their behaviour – how and why they get the outputs they produce – in human terms. This issue is the subject of much ongoing research, but for the time being, deep neural networks are commonly regarded as the 'epitome of black box techniques'.[16]

Large language models (LLMs), such as GPT-4, and their applications, such as ChatGPT, are constructed using a certain assemblage of (deep) neural network components. As mentioned earlier, GPT stands for Generative Pre-trained Transformer, a type of large language model based on the transformer architectural structure introduced by Google Brain in 2017.

[13] LeCun et al., 'Deep learning'.

[14] M. Hervey and M. Levy, *The Law of Artificial Intelligence* (Sweet & Maxwell, 2021).

[15] R. Marcinkevičs and J. E. Vogt, 'Interpretable and explainable machine learning: A methods-centric overview with concrete examples', *WIREs Data Mining and Knowledge Discovery*, 13(3), e1493.

[16] ICO and the Alan Turing Institute, *Explaining Decisions Made with AI* (ICO, 2020).

Transformers are complex and a little ad hoc – and there is a great deal of current empirical and theoretical research aiming to understand, at a deep level, why they work so well. But a key feature that contributed to their success, in practice, is that they are much better suited to massively parallel computation on modern computers for machine learning than previous generative AI for language based on forms of 'recurrent' neural networks. This is what made it possible to train them with such vast quantities of data.

The learning algorithms used to build LLMs usually belong to the 'self-supervised' class of methods. These do not require the training data to be annotated or labelled, so it's possible for the models to be trained on truly vast quantities of textual data available on the internet and in digital repositories. There are usually some additional fine-tuning steps after the initial training. Supervised learning with further data may be applied to improve the model's output for the purpose we wish to use it for, such as responding to instructions. And reinforcement learning with relatively small amounts of human feedback can be used to make the model's responses more aligned with human intentions and human values.[17]

A GPT model, once trained, generates text – a sequence of words in human language – by producing a 'good' or 'reasonable' next word to continue a block of text that the model is given as its input. (In fact, language models do not work directly with words, but with numerically encoded textual elements called 'tokens' that can be words, sub-words, or even individual letters.[18]) Language models based on the transformer architecture work by computing a *probability* for each possible next token – in essence a numerical measure of how likely each potential token is to appear immediately after the block of text that was entered as the input, based on the internal statistical model derived from the vast quantity of training data used. The token that is presented as the output is then chosen according to these probabilities, possibly moderated by a so-called temperature setting, which can be used to increase the variety and unexpectedness of the outputs by boosting the likelihood of less probable words being selected. This process is iterated, with the output token appended each time to the input text and fed back into the model, to generate sentences and paragraphs.

It's important to appreciate that the system doesn't just look up the sentence it produces in a large database of sentences. There is no database of sentences inside the model. The system predicts each next word, one by one, using a statistical model of how such an initial fragment of text might *typically* be continued. One can think of it as a staggeringly sophisticated form of autocomplete or predictive text.

The probability distribution of next tokens output by transformers is computed from a relatively large amount of previous context presented as input – not simply the last word or last few words of the initial text. This allows them to capture so-called long range dependencies in the input sequence – where the sense of one word is influenced by the appearance of a word or words much further back. Crucially, these models also have a sophisticated mechanism for weighing the relative *importance* of the words in the preceding context to the next word to be produced. This is the so-called attention mechanism.[19] This is a technically complex topic, but in simple terms the function of the attention components is to focus the model's prediction for next tokens on the parts of the input text where the most relevant information appears.

[17] T. Shen et al., 'Large language model alignment: A SURVEY', *arXiv Computing Research Repository*, arXiv:2309.15025 [cs.CL], 26 September 2023.

[18] N. Rajaraman et al., 'Toward a theory of tokenization in LLMs', *arXiv Computing Research Repository*, arXiv:2404.08335 [cs.CL], 12 April 2024.

[19] Vaswani et al., 'Attention is all you need'.

In practical use, the input text that is provided to the model to be continued is called a 'prompt' and often consists of a series of statements and questions that help guide the AI towards producing an output of the desired form. The prompt given to a model has a big effect on what the output will be, and the whole practice of so-called prompt engineering emerged very rapidly after large language models were widely released for use. This will not be discussed here, but there is a very large amount of practical guidance on effective prompting published on the internet, and numerous technical articles reporting experimental demonstrations.[20]

For evaluating LLM applications and their effectiveness on specific tasks, a very common approach is *benchmarking*. A 'benchmark' is a fixed, published test, often consisting of a series of questions and expected answers, together with a scoring system. The evaluation of a model on a benchmark produces an overall score, typically a percentage. A wide range of benchmarks have been devised, including specialised benchmarks for legal tasks, such as LawBench,[21] which tests for legal knowledge, and LegalBench,[22] which tests for legal reasoning capability – to give just two examples.

While benchmarking LLMs is useful, there are many limitations and inadequacies in the benchmarks we have today. A multitude of benchmarks exists, and the development of many of them has been researcher-led, possibly with community contributions. They are therefore not to be considered the same sort of thing as the stringent, consensus-based, standardised testing frameworks we have in other technology sectors, such as aviation or automotives.

The question of risk is a natural one in a handbook dedicated to generative AI and law. There is a vast amount of contemporary discussion of the ethical and safety issues around generative AI, including discussion of risks to society, such as mass production of fake news, or even the risk of creating artificial superintelligence that could lead to the extinction of humanity.[23] But we will mention here only two issues that have a technical aspect and should always be borne in mind when using generative AI.

First, there is no guarantee that the text being generated by a large language model is in fact 'true'. Language models can and do produce outputs that appear to us to have the hallmark of confidence, but refer to entirely non-existent things, people, or events. This phenomenon is known as 'hallucination' among AI researchers.

Then there is also a potential risk to data security and confidentiality. Users of generative AI must always bear in mind that the inputs they send are visible to the organisation providing an LLM. Although their prompts may not be incorporated directly into the model's learned parameters, they may be stored and used for developing the LLM service in the future. Moreover, large language models can exhibit the phenomenon of 'memorisation', whereby texts used in their training can be extracted near-verbatim from the model.[24] This has obvious legal implications for both privacy and intellectual property.

Of course, researchers and the technology industry are active in addressing all these problems – and many more. *Retrieval augmented generation* aims to reduce hallucination by using document retrieval from a designated database to anchor the results of subsequent output

[20] P. Sahoo et al., 'A systematic survey of prompt engineering in large language models: Techniques and applications', *arXiv Computing Research Repository*, arXiv:2402.07927 [cs.AI], 5 February 2024.

[21] Z. Fie et al., 'LawBench: Benchmarking legal knowledge of large language models', *arXiv Computing Research Repository*, arXiv:2309.16289 [cs.CL], 28 September 2023.

[22] N. Guha et al., 'LegalBench: A collaboratively built benchmark for measuring legal reasoning in large language models', *arXiv Computing Research Repository*, arXiv:2308.11462 [cs.CL], 20 August 2023.

[23] National Artificial Intelligence Advisory Committee, The Potential Future Risks of AI (October 2023).

[24] J. Wang et al., 'Pandora's White-Box: Precise training data detection and extraction in large language models', *arXiv Computing Research Repository*, arXiv:2402.17012 [cs.CR], 24 June 2024.

generation, to ground these results in known text.[25] There are hybrid systems that combine generative AI with other AI technologies, including symbolic AI such as decision trees, to address some of the limitations of statistical AI alone. Private or in-house systems based on *open-source models* can help with security and confidentiality. And so-called small language models are emerging that can be remarkably capable for specific applications – and are less costly and energy-hungry than a large language model.[26]

This chapter has given only a partial sketch of the technology of generative AI, focussing only on large language models. It would be impossible within the bounds of this handbook to give a comprehensive survey or detailed technical explanation of this fascinating – and very fast-moving – technology, which has raised pressing legal questions, promised potential applications, and posed regulatory challenges. Many of these are discussed in depth in the subsequent chapters of this wide-ranging and timely *Cambridge Handbook on Generative AI and the Law.*

[25] V. Magesh et al., 'Hallucination-free? Assessing the reliability of leading AI legal research tools', *arXiv Computing Research Repository*, arXiv:2405.20362 [cs.CL], 30 May 2024.

[26] T. Schick and H. Schütze, 'It's not just size that matters: Small language models are also few-shot learners', *arXiv Computing Research Repository*, arXiv:2009.07118 [cs.CL], 12 April 2021.

2

Unleashing Creative Potential

Nurturing Trustworthy Generative AI

Zijie Huang

2.1 INTRODUCTION

In the ever-evolving landscape of artificial intelligence (AI), generative AI stands out as a fascinating frontier. Generative AI has made huge progress in recent years and has had a big impact on many industries, including art, entertainment, healthcare, and finance.[1] Meanwhile, its ability to generate new content, ranging from images and videos to text and music, has sparked unprecedented excitement and curiosity, fuelling a wave of experimentation and exploration.

As the application of generative AI is penetrating into every aspect of our lives, ensuring that generative AI systems are trustworthy and ethical is essential. There are many concerns about the use of generative AI and the content created by it, including representation, authenticity, and cultural sensitivity.[2] We need to be careful that AI algorithms don't discriminate or show bias, and we need to take steps to prevent this from happening.[3] Additionally, many AI models are not transparent, making it hard for users to understand how they work or who is responsible for the results.[4] When we confront these challenges, it becomes increasingly clear that crafting trustworthy AI must be the top priority of generative AI development, guiding decisions and actions to ensure that generative AI benefits everyone and causes minimal harm.

In this chapter, our exploration of nurturing trustworthy generative AI begins with a survey of its vast applications and potential. From generating lifelike images and videos to composing intricate musical compositions and crafting immersive narratives, generative AI has permeated diverse domains, leaving an indelible mark on creativity and innovation. By examining the breadth and depth of generative AI applications, we gain a deeper appreciation of its transformative power and its potential to redefine human–machine interactions.

[1] McKinsey. 'The state of AI in 2023: Generative AI's breakout year.' 1 August 2023. https://bit.ly/3B48Fgy

[2] Tortora, Leda. 'Beyond discrimination: Generative AI applications and ethical challenges in forensic psychiatry.' *Frontiers in Psychiatry* 15 (2024): 1346059; Vyas, Bhuman. 'Ethical implications of generative AI in art and the media.' *International Journal for Multidisciplinary Research (IJFMR)* 4.4 (2022): 1–11.

[3] Kim, Jeff J. H., et al. 'Generative AI can fabricate advanced scientific visualizations: Ethical implications and strategic mitigation framework.' *AI and Ethics* (2024): 1–13. http://dx.doi.org/10.1007/s43681-024-00439-0

[4] Dwivedi, Yogesh K., et al. '"So what if ChatGPT wrote it?" Multidisciplinary perspectives on opportunities, challenges and implications of generative conversational AI for research, practice and policy.' *International Journal of Information Management* 71 (2023): 102642.

Alongside its transformative potential, generative AI also poses significant challenges, particularly in the realm of trustworthiness. The ethical implications of AI-generated content, the potential for bias and discrimination, and the need for transparency and accountability are among key considerations. As we delve into the complexities of trustworthiness in generative AI, we confront these challenges head-on, recognising the imperative of responsible AI development. In response to the above challenges, principles to guide the ethical, safe, and trustworthy use of generative AI are increasingly important to enable developers and practitioners to mitigate risks, safeguard privacy, and promote fairness and transparency in AI systems. Through a careful examination of the principles governing trustworthy AI, we illuminate the key ethical considerations for shaping the trajectory of generative AI development and use and the reflection of some of these principles in regulatory frameworks such as the EU's AI Act and General Data Protection Regulation (GDPR).

As technology continues to evolve, and our societal expectations and laws change, we need to be prepared to face new challenges and opportunities. This chapter emphasises the imperative of fostering trustworthiness in AI development to unlock the full potential of generative AI.

2.2 THE GENERATIVE AI LANDSCAPE

2.2.1 *Definition*

Imagine you have a talented chef who wants to create new, unique dishes. This chef, however, has only ever studied a comprehensive recipe book filled with various recipes from different cuisines. The chef carefully examines the ingredients, cooking techniques, and flavour combinations used in these recipes, gaining an understanding of how different elements work together. Now, when you ask this chef to come up with a new dish, they draw inspiration from the recipes they've studied. It's not an exact replication of any single recipe, but rather a novel creation that combines elements from different recipes in innovative ways. The chef continues experimenting and refining their culinary skills based on the feedback received from diners. In this analogy, the chef is the generative AI model, the recipe book is the training data for the AI to learn from, and the process of creating new dishes is the generation of content. In other words, generative AI involves training models to understand and replicate patterns in data to create new content.

To facilitate the understanding of generative AI's fundamental principles, Figure 2.1 demonstrates a general generative AI workflow. It starts with data collection; the data can be of any type, including text, images, audio, video, and so on. Once the data is collected, it often needs to be preprocessed to certain formats for model training. The preprocessing procedure involves data cleaning, noise removal, data normalisation, and feature extraction, among others. Then the next step is generative model building, which depends on the nature of the data and the desired outcomes. Once the generative model is selected and built, it needs to be trained with the

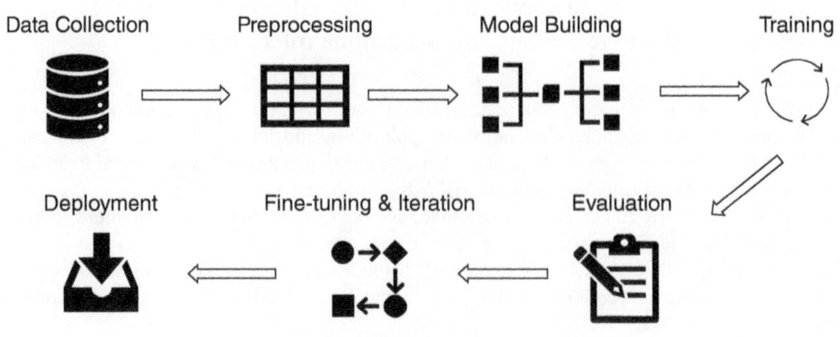

FIGURE 2.1 Generative AI workflow

preprocessed data. During training, the model learns the underlying patterns and structures of the input data in order to generate similar data. After the training, an evaluation is needed for assessing the quality of the generated samples, measuring the model's ability to generalise to new data, or evaluating its robustness to variations in input. Based on the evaluation results, a fine-tuning adjustment for the generative model might be needed. The fine-tuning process could involve tweaking hyperparameters, modifying the architecture, or collecting more data to improve performance. The process may require several iterations to achieve satisfactory results. Lastly, once the model has been trained and evaluated to a satisfactory level, it can be deployed for practical use.

With the current rapid development and application of generative AI, it is useful to trace its history. Back in the 1960s–1980s, early efforts in generative AI technology emerged from the rules-based systems design,[5] which generates outputs based on predefined rules, but the technology lacked the ability to learn from data or produce novel content. In the 1990s, Bayesian methods[6] were proposed for estimation of probability distributions over datasets, which emerged as a significant advancement in generative modelling, enabling the generation of new samples based on learned distributions. In the late 2000s, Restricted Boltzmann Machines (RBMs)[7] were introduced as generative models capable of learning complex probability distributions over input data. They paved the way for more sophisticated generative models in the years to come. Then, in 2014–2018, Generative Adversarial Networks,[8] Variational Autoencoders,[9] and StyleGAN[10] emerged and led to significant advancements in generating high-quality, realistic images, audio, and text in various applications. In the 2020s, generative AI research has seen continued advancements in areas such as unsupervised learning, reinforcement learning, and transformer-based models such as OpenAI's Generative Pre-trained Transformer (GPT) series[11] and Bidirectional Encoder Representations from Transformers (BERT),[12] which have pushed the boundaries of generative capabilities in natural language processing and other domains.

2.2.2 *Types of Generative AI Models and Applications*

Following generative AI's fruitful developed history, it now encompasses various types of models and approaches that can generate new content across different domains. In what follows, we summarise some prominent types of generative AI, exploring their working principles and their notable applications.

2.2.2.1 Generative Adversarial Networks (GANs)

Generative adversarial networks (GANs) represent a groundbreaking approach in the field of generative AI. Introduced by Ian Goodfellow and his colleagues in 2014,

[5] Hayes-Roth, Frederick. 'Rule-based systems.' *Communications of the ACM* 28.9 (1985): 921–932.

[6] Ramoni, Marco, and Paola Sebastiani. 'Bayesian methods.' In *Intelligent Data Analysis: An Introduction*. Berlin: Springer, 1999. 129–166.

[7] Fischer, Asja, and Christian Igel. 'An introduction to restricted Boltzmann machines.' *Progress in Pattern Recognition, Image Analysis, Computer Vision, and Applications: 17th Iberoamerican Congress, CIARP 2012, Buenos Aires, Argentina, September 3–6, 2012*. Proceedings 17. Berlin: Springer, 2012. 14–36.

[8] Goodfellow, Ian, et al. 'Generative adversarial networks.' *Communications of the ACM* 63.11 (2020): 139–144.

[9] Doersch, Carl. 'Tutorial on variational autoencoders' (2016). https://arxiv.org/pdf/1606.05908

[10] Karras, Tero, et al. 'Analyzing and improving the image quality of StyleGAN.' *Proceedings of the IEEE/CVF Conference on Computer Vision and Pattern Recognition: CVPR 2020, Seattle, Washington, USA, June 13–19 2020*. Los Alamitos, CA: IEEE Computer Society, 2020. 8107–8116.

[11] Floridi, Luciano, and Massimo Chiriatti. 'GPT-3: Its nature, scope, limits, and consequences.' *Minds and Machines* 30 (2020): 681–694.

[12] Devlin, Jacob, et al. 'Bert: Pre-training of deep bidirectional transformers for language understanding.' *Proceedings of NAACL-HLT. Minneapolis, Minnesota, USA, June 2–June 7, 2019*. Philadelphia: Association for Computational Linguistics, 2019. 4171–4186.

GANs[13] consist of two neural networks – a generator and a discriminator – undergoing simultaneously adversarial training. The generator network aims to produce data that is indistinguishable from authentic samples in the dataset it was trained on, while the discriminator network learns to differentiate between genuine data and data produced by the generator. Through iterative training, the generator learns to produce increasingly realistic samples, while the discriminator becomes more adept at distinguishing between real and generated data. This adversarial process drives the generator to improve its output until it becomes difficult for the discriminator to tell the difference between real and generated samples.

One of the key strengths of GANs lies in their ability to generate highly realistic content across various domains, including images, audio, and text. By learning the underlying distribution of the training data, GANs can produce samples that exhibit intricate details, textures, and structures, closely resembling those found in the original dataset. This capability has led to numerous applications across different fields. In computer vision, GANs have been utilised for image synthesis, enhancement, and manipulation.[14] They can generate photorealistic images of objects, scenes, and even human faces with astonishing accuracy. GANs have also been applied in medical imaging for generating synthetic images to augment limited datasets, aiding in tasks such as disease diagnosis and treatment planning.[15] In the field of art and design, GANs have been used to create novel artworks, generate new fashion designs, and assist in architectural modelling.[16] They enable artists and designers to explore unconventional styles and concepts by creating diverse visual representations. Moreover, GANs have found applications in generating realistic video sequences, transforming images into different artistic styles, and even in producing realistic human speech[17] and music compositions.[18]

2.2.2.2 Transformers

Transformers[19] have emerged as a dominant force in natural language processing (NLP) due to their unique architecture and remarkable performance in various tasks. The key innovation of transformers lies in their self-attention mechanism, which allows them to process entire sequences of input data simultaneously, enabling them to capture long-range dependencies and contextual information more effectively than traditional recurrent neural networks (RNNs)[20] and convolutional neural networks (CNNs).[21]

[13] Goodfellow, Ian, et al. 'Generative adversarial networks.' *Communications of the ACM* 63.11 (2020): 139–144.

[14] Wang, Zhengwei, Qi She, and Tomas E. Ward. 'Generative adversarial networks in computer vision: A survey and taxonomy.' *ACM Computing Surveys (CSUR)* 54.2 (2021): 1–38.

[15] Osokin, Anton, et al. 'GANs for biological image synthesis.' *Proceedings of the IEEE International Conference on Computer Vision: ICCV 2017, Venice, Italy, Oct. 22 to Oct. 29 2017*. Los Alamitos, CA: IEEE Computer Society, 2017. 2233–2242.

[16] Yi, Ran, et al. 'APDrawingGAN: Generating artistic portrait drawings from face photos with hierarchical GANs.' *Proceedings of the IEEE/CVF Conference on Computer Vision and Pattern Recognition: CVPR 2019, Long Beach, Canada, June 16–20, 2019*. Los Alamitos, CA: IEEE Computer Society, 2019. 10743–10752.

[17] Vougioukas, Konstantinos, Stavros Petridis, and Maja Pantic. 'Realistic speech-driven facial animation with GANs.' *International Journal of Computer Vision* 128.5 (2020): 1398–1413.

[18] Muhamed, Aashiq, et al. 'Symbolic music generation with transformer-GANs.' *Proceedings of the AAAI Conference on Artificial Intelligence: AAAI 2021,Virtual, February 2–9, 2021*. Cambridge, MA: The MIT Press, 2021). 408–417.

[19] Tay, Yi, et al. 'Efficient transformers: A survey.' *ACM Computing Surveys* 55.6 (2022): 1–28.

[20] Medsker, Larry R., and Lakhmi Jain. 'Recurrent neural networks.' *Design and Applications* 5.2 (2001): 64–67.

[21] O'Shea, Keiron, and Ryan Nash. 'An introduction to convolutional neural networks' (2015). https://arxiv.org/pdf/1511.08458

The rise of transformer models like the GPT series, developed by OpenAI, has had a transformative impact on natural language generation (NLG).[22] GPT models are pre-trained on vast amounts of text data from the internet, learning rich representations of language in an unsupervised manner. This pre-training process equips GPT models with a deep understanding of syntax, semantics, and context, enabling them to generate coherent and contextually relevant text. GPT-based models have revolutionised NLG by producing human-like text that exhibits fluency, coherence, and creativity across various domains. Their ability to generate high-quality text has led to applications in automated content creation, conversational agents, text summarisation, and more. GPT models have also democratised access to advanced NLG capabilities, allowing developers and researchers to leverage pre-trained models for a wide range of applications with minimal fine-tuning.

Moreover, the impact of GPT and other transformer models extends beyond NLG into other areas of NLP, such as machine translation,[23] sentiment analysis,[24] and question answering.[25] By providing state-of-the-art performance on benchmark datasets and real-world applications, transformer models have become indispensable tools in the NLP community.

2.2.2.3 Variational Autoencoders (VAEs)

Variational Autoencoders (VAEs) represent a key innovation in the realm of generative AI, offering a powerful framework for generating diverse and realistic outputs. VAEs are a type of neural network architecture that combines elements of both autoencoders and probabilistic graphical models. They consist of two interconnected networks: an encoder and a decoder. The encoder network maps input data onto a latent space, where each point represents a compressed representation or 'latent code' of the input. The decoder network then takes samples from this latent space and reconstructs the original input data. What distinguishes VAEs from traditional autoencoders is their probabilistic interpretation of the latent space. In VAEs, the latent space is assumed to follow a probability distribution, typically a Gaussian distribution. This probabilistic interpretation allows VAEs to generate not just one, but a multitude of outputs for a given input. By sampling from the learned distribution in the latent space, VAEs can produce diverse and novel outputs that capture the variability present in the training data.

Applications of VAEs span various domains, including image generation,[26] molecular design,[27] and natural language processing.[28] In image generation, VAEs have been used to create realistic and diverse images, ranging from faces to landscapes, by learning rich representations of visual data and generating novel samples from these representations. In molecular design, VAEs have been employed to generate new chemical compounds with desired

[22] Liu, Yang, et al. 'Gpteval: NLG evaluation using GPT-4 with better human alignment.' *Proceedings of the 2023 Conference on Empirical Methods in Natural Language Processing: EMNLP 2023, Singapore, December 6–10, 2023*. Philadelphia: Association for Computational Linguistics, 2023. 2511–2522.

[23] Liu, Xiaodong, et al. 'Very deep transformers for neural machine translation' (2020). https://arxiv.org/pdf/2008.07772

[24] Naseem, Usman, et al. 'Transformer based deep intelligent contextual embedding for twitter sentiment analysis.' *Future Generation Computer Systems* 113 (2020): 58–69.

[25] Cao, Qingqing, et al. 'DeFormer: Decomposing pre-trained transformers for faster question answering.' *Proceedings of the 58th Annual Meeting of the Association for Computational Linguistics: ACL 2020 Seattle, Washington, US, July 5–10, 2020*. Philadelphia: Association for Computational Linguistics, 2020. 4487–4497.

[26] Razavi, Ali, Aaron Van den Oord, and Oriol Vinyals. 'Generating diverse high-fidelity images with vq-vae-2.' *Advances in Neural Information Processing Systems: NeurIPS 2019, Vancouver CANADA, December 8–14, 2019*. New York: Curran Associates, 32, 2019. 14866–14876.

[27] Elton, Daniel C., et al. 'Deep learning for molecular design – A review of the state of the art.' *Molecular Systems Design & Engineering* 4.4 (2019): 828–849.

[28] Brunner, Gino, et al. 'Disentangling the latent space of (variational) autoencoders for NLP.' *Advances in Computational Intelligence Systems: Contributions Presented at the 18th UK Workshop on Computational Intelligence, September 5–7, 2018, Nottingham, UK*. Berlin: Springer International, 2019. 163–168.

TABLE 2.1 *Summary of generative AI applications*

Generative AI methods	Application areas	Methods
Generative adversarial networks (GANs)	Computer vision	Image synthesis: DCGAN,[29] StyleGAN,[30] ProGAN;[31] Image-to-image translation: Pix2Pix translation,[32] DualGAN,[33] CSGAN[34]
	Natural language processing (NLP)	Text generation: RelGAN,[35] MaskGAN[36] Text-to-image synthesis: Df-GAN,[37] StyleGAN-t[38]
	Healthcare	Drug discovery: GANsDTA[39]
	Finance and business	Market simulation: Fin-GAN[40]
Transformers	Recommendation systems	Content-based filtering: Transformers4rec,[41] SSE-PT,[42] Linrec[43]

properties, facilitating drug discovery and materials science research. In natural language processing, VAEs have been applied to tasks such as text generation and summarisation, enabling the generation of diverse and contextually relevant textual outputs.

There are many more generative AI models that offer unique capabilities and applications across various domains. We have summarised some state-of-the-art techniques in this area in Table 2.1.

[29] Radford, Alec, Luke Metz, and Soumith Chintala. 'Unsupervised representation learning with deep convolutional generative adversarial networks' (2015). https://arxiv.org/pdf/1511.06434

[30] Bermano, Amit H., et al. 'State-of-the-art in the architecture, methods and applications of StyleGAN.' *Computer Graphics Forum* 41.2 (2022): 591–611.

[31] Gao, Hongchang, Jian Pei, and Heng Huang. 'Progan: Network embedding via proximity generative adversarial network.' *Proceedings of the 25th ACM SIGKDD International Conference on Knowledge Discovery & Data Mining: KDD 2019, Anchorage, Alaska, USA, August 4–9, 2019*. New York: Association for Computing Machinery, 2019. 1308–1316.

[32] Mirza, Mehdi, and Simon Osindero. 'Conditional generative adversarial nets' (2014). https://arxiv.org/pdf/1411.1784

[33] Yi, Zili, et al. 'DualGAN: Unsupervised dual learning for image-to-image translation.' *Proceedings of the IEEE International Conference on Computer Vision: ICCV 2017, Venice, Italy, October 22–29, 2017*. Los Alamitos, CA: IEEE Computer Society, 2017. 2849–2857.

[34] Kancharagunta, Kishan Babu, and Shiv Ram Dubey. 'CSGAN: Cyclic-synthesized generative adversarial networks for image-to-image transformation' (2019). https://arxiv.org/pdf/1901.03554

[35] Nie, Weili, Nina Narodytska, and Ankit Patel. 'RelGAN: Relational generative adversarial networks for text generation.' *International Conference on Learning Representations: ICLR 2019, New Orleans, Louisiana, USA, May 6–9, 2019*. www.semanticscholar.org/paper/RelGAN%3A-Relational-Generative-Adversarial-Networks-Nie-Narodytska/0e8b9dc48e4c8be508a7797fd7742506fe59875c

[36] Fedus, William, Ian Goodfellow, and Andrew M. Dai. 'MaskGAN: Better text generation via filling in the _.' *International Conference on Learning Representations: ICLR 2018, Vancouver, Canada, April 30–May 3, 2018*. https://arxiv.org/pdf/1801.07736

[37] Tao, Ming, et al. 'Df-GAN: A simple and effective baseline for text-to-image synthesis.' *Proceedings of the IEEE/CVF Conference on Computer Vision and Pattern Recognition: CVPR 2022, New Orleans, Louisiana, USA, June 19–24 2022*. Los Alamitos, CA: IEEE Computer Society, 2022. 16515–16525.

[38] Sauer, Axel, et al. 'StyleGAN-t: Unlocking the power of GANs for fast large-scale text-to-image synthesis.' *International Conference on Machine Learning: ICML 2023, Hawaii, USA, July 23–29, 2023*. Philadelphia: International Machine Learning Society, 2023. 30105–30118.

[39] Zhao, Lingling, et al. 'GANsDTA: Predicting drug-target binding affinity using GANs.' *Frontiers in Genetics* 10 (2020): 1243.

[40] Vuletić, Milena, Felix Prenzel, and Mihai Cucuringu. 'Fin-GAN: Forecasting and classifying financial time series via generative adversarial networks.' *Quantitative Finance* 2 (2024): 175–199.

[41] De Souza Pereira Moreira, Gabriel, et al. 'Transformers4rec: Bridging the gap between NLP and sequential/session-based recommendation.' *Proceedings of the 15th ACM Conference on Recommender Systems: RecSys'21, Amsterdam, Netherlands, September 27–October 1, 2021*. New York: Association for Computing Machinery, 2021, 143–153.

[42] Wu, Liwei, et al. 'SSE-PT: Sequential recommendation via personalized transformer.' *Proceedings of the 14th ACM Conference on Recommender Systems: RecSys'20, Virtual, September 22–26, 2020*. New York: Association for Computing Machinery, 2020. 328–337.

[43] Liu, Langming, et al. 'Linrec: Linear attention mechanism for long-term sequential recommender systems.' *Proceedings of the 46th International ACM SIGIR Conference on Research and Development in Information Retrieval: SIGIR 2023, Taipei, Taiwan, July 23–27, 2023*. New York: Association for Computing Machinery, 2023. 289–299.

TABLE 2.1 (*cont.*)

Generative AI methods	Application areas	Methods
Variational autoencoders (VAEs)	Speech processing	Speech recognition: Conformer,[44] Squeezeformer,[45] Transformer-transducer;[46] Speaker recognition: ASTT[47]
	Robotics and autonomous systems	Robot navigation: NavFormer,[48] Maast;[49] Autonomous vehicles: VistaGPT,[50] Transfuser[51]
	Human–computer interaction	Personalised recommendations: PEVAE,[52] Ensvae;[53] User behaviour modelling: V-GMR[54]
	Creative applications	Art generation: Pixel VQ-VAEs,[55] Introvae[56]
	Financial modelling	Portfolio optimization: Encoded value-at-risk[57]

2.2.3 *Future Trends*

As research continues to push the boundaries of generative AI technology development, several key areas are poised for significant advancements. Firstly, continual learning[58] stands out as a focal point, with ongoing research aimed at enabling generative models to adapt and improve

44 Gulati, Anmol, et al. 'Conformer: Convolution-augmented transformer for speech recognition.' *International Speech Communication Association: Interspeech 2020, Shanghai, China, October 25–29, 2020*. 2020. 5036–5040. http://dx.doi.org/10.48550/arXiv.2005.08100

45 Kim, Sehoon, et al. 'Squeezeformer: An efficient transformer for automatic speech recognition.' *Advances in Neural Information Processing Systems* 35 (2022): 9361–9373.

46 Yeh, Ching-Feng, et al. 'Transformer-transducer: End-to-end speech recognition with self-attention.' (2019). https://arxiv.org/pdf/1910.12977

47 Wu, Xing, et al. 'ASTT: Acoustic spatial–temporal transformer for short utterance speaker recognition.' *Multimedia Tools and Applications* 82.21 (2023): 33039–33061.

48 Wang, Haitong, Aaron Hao Tan, and Goldie Nejat. 'NavFormer: A transformer architecture for robot target-driven navigation in unknown and dynamic environments.' *IEEE Robotics and Automation Letters* 9.8 (2024): 6808–6815.

49 Seymour, Zachary, et al. 'Maast: Map attention with semantic transformers for efficient visual navigation.' *2021 IEEE International Conference on Robotics and Automation: ICRA 2021, Xi'an China, May 30–June 5, 2021*. Piscataway, NJ: IEEE, 2021. 13223–13230.

50 Tian, Yonglin, et al. 'VistaGPT: Generative parallel transformers for vehicles with intelligent systems for transport automation.' *IEEE Transactions on Intelligent Vehicles* 8.9 (2023): 4198–4207.

51 Chitta, Kashyap, et al. 'Transfuser: Imitation with transformer-based sensor fusion for autonomous driving.' *IEEE Transactions on Pattern Analysis and Machine Intelligence* 45.11 (2022): 12878–12895.

52 Cai, Zefeng, and Zerui Cai. 'PEVAE: A hierarchical VAE for personalized explainable recommendation.' *Proceedings of the 45th International ACM SIGIR Conference on Research and Development in Information Retrieval: SIGIR 2022, Madrid, Spain, July 11–15, 2022*. New York: Association for Computing Machinery, 2022. 692–702.

53 Drif, Ahlem, Houssem Eddine Zerrad, and Hocine Cherifi. 'Ensvae: Ensemble variational autoencoders for recommendations.' *IEEE Access* 8 (2020): 188335–188351.

54 Yang, Haoqin, et al. 'V-GMR: A variational autoencoder-based heterogeneous graph multi-behavior recommendation model.' *Applied Intelligence* 54.4 (2024): 3337–3350.

55 Saravanan, Akash, and Matthew Guzdial. 'Pixel VQ-VAEs for improved pixel art representation.' *AIIDT Workshop on Experimental AI in Games: EXAG 2022, Cal Poly Pomona, California, USA, October 24–25, 2022*. Aachen: CEUR Workshop Proceedings, 2022.

56 Huang, Huaibo, et al. 'Introvae: Introspective variational autoencoders for photographic image synthesis.' *Advances in Neural Information Processing Systems: NeurIPS 2018, Montreal Canada, December 3–8, 2018*. New York: Curran Associates, 32, 2018. 52–63.

57 Arian, Hamidreza, et al. 'Encoded value-at-risk: A predictive machine for financial risk management' (2020). https://arxiv.org/pdf/2011.06742

58 Wang, Liyuan, et al. 'A comprehensive survey of continual learning: Theory, method and application.' *IEEE Transactions on Pattern Analysis and Machine Intelligence* 46.8 (2024): 5362–5383.

over time. Techniques such as lifelong learning[59] and meta-learning[60] are being explored to facilitate the seamless integration of new data while preserving previously acquired knowledge, paving the way for more robust and adaptive AI systems. Moreover, interdisciplinary collaborations between AI researchers and experts from diverse fields are shaping the trajectory of generative AI. These collaborations leverage domain-specific knowledge to inform the design and training of generative models, leading to tailored solutions for specific industry needs and driving innovation in both AI research and real-world applications. Looking ahead, potential breakthroughs in areas such as model efficiency, interpretability, and integration with other emerging technologies hold promise for further advancing the generative AI landscape.

2.3 UNRAVELLING TRUST IN GENERATIVE AI

As we explore the rationale and applications of generative AI, it is clear that we are faced with a mix of technological advancement and the unknowns that come with them. As the capabilities of AI continue to evolve, the trustworthiness of generative AI becomes ever more important.

2.3.1 *The Essence of Trust*

When we talk about 'trust' in generative AI, we are talking about a complex relationship between humans and generative AI systems that includes confidence, reliability, and transparency. At its core, trust means believing that AI systems will do what they're supposed to do, produce results that match what humans want, and behave in an ethical and responsible way. Chatbots and virtual assistants powered by generative AI, such as Google's Duplex[61] and Amazon's Alexa,[62] are expecting to be trusted to engage in natural language conversations and perform tasks on behalf of users. We trust them to understand what we want, respond accordingly, and act based on our preferences and expectations. On the other hand, trust goes beyond just technical skills, which also includes bigger issues such as keeping our personal data private, being fair, and considering the impact on society. For instance, social media platforms utilise generative AI for content moderation, including identifying and removing harmful or inappropriate content such as hate speech, misinformation, and graphic imagery.[63] Users trust these generative AI systems to operate ethically and responsibly, making sure users' online experience is safe while also respecting their freedom of expression and diversity of opinions. Therefore, building trust is essential for generative AI to be widely accepted and integrated into many aspects of our daily lives. Without trust, users may hesitate to engage with AI systems, hindering their adoption and limiting their potential benefits.

In short, trust in generative AI is not just a technical detail, but a key part of making it acceptable and ensuring it is used responsibly. Trust lets us use generative AI with confidence, which leads to a better relationship between humans and machines. As generative AI changes and grows, building and keeping trust should be a top priority, guiding the development of generative AI systems towards a future that's transparent, accountable, and fair.

[59] Rawas, Soha. 'ChatGPT: Empowering lifelong learning in the digital age of higher education.' *Education and Information Technologies* 29.6 (2024): 6895–6908.

[60] Lake, Brenden M., and Marco Baroni. 'Human-like systematic generalization through a meta-learning neural network.' *Nature* 623.7985 (2023): 115–121.

[61] https://blog.research.google/2018/05/duplex-ai-system-for-natural-conversation.html

[62] www.aboutamazon.com/news/devices/amazon-alexa-generative-ai

[63] www.linkedin.com/pulse/generative-ai-across-social-media-platforms-2023-luan-wise-fzpje/

2.3.2 *The Trust Challenge*

Trust in generative AI is not a monolithic entity but rather a complicated mix of technical, social, and ethical factors. One of the main reasons trust is a challenge in generative AI is because it is hard to predict what it will come up with. Unlike traditional AI systems with deterministic outcomes, generative AI produces different results each time, making it unpredictable. This makes it hard for people to trust the results, and they might wonder if they're accurate, biased, or ethical. For example, 'deepfake' technology that uses generative AI to produce fake but realistic videos, audio, or images of people can be used to create false information, such as fake news or impersonations, which can erode trust in what we see and hear.[64] Moreover, as new techniques and models emerge, people might struggle to keep up and might be unsure about what generative AI can and can't do. In fields like medicine, where generative AI is being used to help doctors analyse medical images such as MRI and CT scans, healthcare professionals might be sceptical about the reliability and safety of AI-assisted diagnoses because they don't fully understand how the AI algorithms work or what medical insights they're based on.[65] Overall, while innovation drives progress and unlocks new possibilities in generative AI, it also brings uncertainties and risks that can make people lose trust.

2.4 TOWARDS TRUSTWORTHY GENERATIVE AI

This section aims to provide actionable insights into the development of generative AI, emphasising the practical steps and considerations necessary to build trustworthy systems.

2.4.1 *Ethical Guidelines*

Over the past few decades, a multitude of organisations, spanning from research institutions to stakeholders, have actively engaged in the examination of AI ethics. Given the increasing recognition of ethical dilemmas associated with AI, it is imperative to establish clear standards to confront these issues and pre-empt any potential ethical ramifications. These explicit standards serve as a roadmap to steer the development and implementation of AI technologies in an ethical and accountable manner, guaranteeing alignment with human values and societal objectives. For instance, in late 2017, the professional standards body IEEE Standards Association (IEEE SA) began to explore 'trustworthiness' and 'explainability' in AI. In P7011 'Standard for the Process of Identifying and Rating the Trustworthiness of News Sources',[66] the processes of identifying and rating the factual accuracy of news are standardised via a scorecard rating system algorithm. This standard aims to maintain reliable ratings for online and multimedia news in an attempt to build trust and acceptance among the public. Apart from the IEEE SA, the International Organization for Standardization and International Electrotechnical Commission (ISO/IEC) – a prominent standard-setting organisation in information technology – has also

[64] 'Generative AI and the risk around digital trust.' Forbes. www.forbes.com/sites/forbestechcouncil/2024/02/08/generative-ai-and-the-risk-around-digital-trust/?sh = 73456cda6dcf

[65] 'Can generative AI convince medical doctors they are wrong when they are right and right when they are wrong.' Forbes. www.forbes.com/sites/lanceeliot/2024/01/28/can-generative-ai-convince-medical-doctors-they-are-wrong-when-they-are-right-and-right-when-they-are-wrong/?sh = 5ec90ef1aa29

[66] Standard for the Process of Identifying and Rating the Trustworthiness of News Sources. IEEE. https://standards.ieee.org/ieee/7011/7191/

issued standards related to AI ethics. In early 2020, ISO/IEC TR 24028:2020[67] was released, focusing on various aspects of trustworthiness in AI. This encompassed methodologies for constructing reliable AI systems and potential strategies for addressing threats and risks.

In addition to the issuance of AI ethics regulations, numerous guidelines have been issued, covering various topics related to AI ethics. The most influential AI ethics guidelines, presented by Anna Jobin and colleagues,[68] investigated a global agreement on current principles and guidelines for ethical AI. They spotlighted eleven ethical principles by analysing eighty-four documents containing ethical principles or guidelines for AI worldwide. Through their findings, they identified the top five frequently emerging principles: transparency, justice and fairness, non-maleficence, responsibility, and privacy. The survey also discusses why these principles are important, how we can interpret them in certain scenarios, and more. The survey highlights the concern of prioritising which ethical principles to follow and addressing conflicts between them. Similarly, based on the comprehensive review above, Kazim and Koshiyama[69] identified six major ethical principles that can cover the implementation of ethics into engineering and systems without overlapping across ethical principles. This survey provides a high-level overview of AI ethics from different disciplines, such as philosophy, law, and computer science, which can greatly assist readers from various fields in bridging the gap between ethics and AI.

Several researchers have proposed some ethical guidelines for generative AI specifically. For instance, Zhicheng Lin presents an ethical framework for generative AI, covering five core themes: acknowledging model limitations concerning accuracy and bias; upholding privacy, confidentiality, and copyright standards; preventing plagiarism and policy breaches when integrating model outputs; ensuring overall societal benefit from applications; and promoting transparency and reproducibility in AI use.[70] Additionally, Lin advocates for ongoing refinement of guidelines, adjustment of training programmes to accommodate evolving AI developments, and the establishment of reasonable and effective enforcement mechanisms. Furthermore, Jonathan Luckett[71] has scrutinised AI regulations and challenges in the United States, offering policy considerations and recommendations for federal agencies to ensure the responsible and ethical development and use of generative AI. Luckett's recommendations encompass addressing safety, privacy, security, and discrimination concerns.

2.4.2 *Data Governance*

Referring back to the definition of generative AI (Section 2.2.1), data plays a crucial role in generative AI as it serves as the foundation for training and fine-tuning AI models to generate new content. Generative AI systems, such as language or image generators, rely on large datasets to learn and understand patterns, relationships, and features within the data. Therefore, data governance plays a pivotal role in ensuring the ethical and responsible use of data in generative AI to ensure data privacy, protecting user rights, and upholding ethical standards throughout the AI development lifecycle.

67 ISO/IEC TR 24028:2020 Information technology – Artificial intelligence – Overview of trustworthiness in artificial intelligence. www.iso.org/standard/77608.html

68 Jobin, Anna, Marcello Ienca, and Effy Vayena. 'The global landscape of AI ethics guidelines.' *Nature Machine Intelligence* 1.9 (2019): 389–399.

69 Kazim, Emre, and Adriano Soares Koshiyama. 'A high-level overview of AI ethics.' *Patterns* 2.9 (2021): 100314.

70 Lin, Zhicheng. 'Building ethical guidelines for generative AI in scientific research' (2024). https://arxiv.org/pdf/2401.15284v3

71 Luckett, Jonathan. 'Regulating generative AI: A pathway to ethical and responsible implementation.' *Journal of Computing Sciences in Colleges* 39.3 (2023): 47–65.

Deloitte has indicated that organisations poised to derive optimal benefits from generative AI must possess mature data governance capabilities.[72] Well-governed training data yields higher quality outputs for generative AI models, consequently enabling the extraction of greater value from organisational use cases and facilitating deeper insights. Conversely, Deloitte warns that the absence of data governance curtails generative AI's capabilities and exposes organisations to various risks. Lastly, they emphasise the necessity of continuous implementation of data governance throughout the generative AI process, underscoring its integral role within a broader data culture.

Google has published a Privacy Commitment, articulating its belief that customers should have the highest level of security and control over their data stored in Google Cloud's generative AI products.[73] The company ensures that its teams adhere to these commitments through robust data governance practices, which encompass thorough reviews of the data used in the development of Google Cloud products. Similarly, Amazon Web Services (AWS) Big Data team has sought to address data governance requirements of generative AI application data pipelines.[74] It is crucial to govern data used by generative AI, such as LLM, to enhance the accuracy and relevance of their responses to user prompts in a safe, secure, and transparent manner. AWS has proposed that leveraging proprietary data with approaches like Retrieval Augmented Generation (RAG), fine-tuning, and ongoing pre-training with foundational models are promising methods to streamline data governance in generative AI.

Overall, data governance in generative AI is crucial for ensuring that AI technologies are developed and deployed in a manner that respects user privacy, upholds ethical standards, maintains data quality, mitigates risks, and fosters trust and transparency among users and stakeholders. Various organisations are implementing strategies for robust data governance to ensure the ethical and responsible use of data in generative AI systems, fostering trust and confidence among users while mitigating risks and upholding ethical standards throughout the AI lifecycle.

2.4.3 *Transparency and Explainability*

Transparency and explainability are fundamental principles in generative AI aimed at ensuring that AI systems are understandable and accountable to users and stakeholders. In generative AI, transparency refers to the clarity and openness of the system's operations, while explainability refers to the ability to understand and interpret the decisions and outputs generated by the AI system. Transparency in generative AI involves making the AI system's processes, algorithms, and decision-making mechanisms accessible and understandable to users. This includes providing insight into how the AI model was trained, the data it was trained on, and the factors influencing its outputs. Explainability, on the other hand, focuses on enabling users to comprehend why the AI system generated a specific output or made a particular decision. It involves providing interpretable explanations or justifications for the AI's actions in a clear and understandable manner.

Transparency and explainability are essential in generative AI for several reasons. Firstly, they promote trust and confidence among users by enabling them to understand and validate the AI

[72] www2.deloitte.com/uk/en/pages/deloitte-analytics/articles/data-governance-perspectives-on-generative-ai.html

[73] https://cloud.google.com/vertex-ai/generative-ai/docs/data-governance

[74] https://aws.amazon.com/blogs/big-data/data-governance-in-the-age-of-generative-ai/#:~:text=Controls%20in%20the%20data%20governance,access%20to%20sensitive%20data)%20policies

system's behaviour and outputs. This is particularly important in sensitive applications such as healthcare or finance, where users need assurance that AI-generated recommendations or decisions are reliable and well-founded. Additionally, transparency and explainability facilitate accountability and regulatory compliance, allowing organisations to demonstrate the fairness, reliability, and ethical soundness of their AI systems.

Several strategies have been proposed to enhance transparency and explainability in generative AI. Firstly, organisations should embrace transparent data practices, which involve documenting data sources, preprocessing steps, and any inherent biases or limitations in the training data. Meta has introduced industry-leading tools[75] capable of identifying invisible markers at scale, labelling images from various sources such as Google, OpenAI, Microsoft, Adobe, Midjourney, and Shutterstock as part of their initiative to add metadata to images produced by their tools. Secondly, AI models should be designed with interpretability in mind, employing techniques such as attention mechanisms, feature importance analysis, or model distillation to provide insights into the decision-making process of the model. For example, Nicole Reineke has proposed four key guidelines to facilitate explainability in generative AI.[76] The first guideline involves model simplification, reducing the number of layers in the neural network to enhance understanding and interpretation of the model's decisions. Secondly, interpretability tools such as attention maps[77] can be utilised to visualise the most significant parts of an input image for the output. Furthermore, organisations should prioritise the development of explainable AI techniques and tools that enable users to interact with and comprehend the outputs and recommendations of AI systems. The third guideline emphasises the importance of referenceable data, which helps identify unintentional biases, prevent unfair decisions, and facilitate ongoing improvements. The final guideline involves human oversight, requiring human intervention to ensure that the generative AI model makes decisions in a responsible and ethical manner. Finally, continuous monitoring, evaluation, and validation of AI systems' transparency and explainability are essential to ensure their long-term effectiveness and reliability.

2.4.4 *Bias and Fairness*

In the context of generative AI, bias refers to systematic errors or inaccuracies in the generated results caused by skewed or unrepresentative training data, algorithmic design, or other factors. These biases can manifest in various forms, such as racial, gender, or socio-economic biases, and can lead to unfair or discriminatory outcomes in the generated content. Fairness, on the other hand, pertains to the equitable treatment of individuals or groups represented in the generated content. Fairness ensures that the AI system does not produce outputs that favour or discriminate against specific demographics or attributes. It involves mitigating biases and ensuring that the generated content accurately reflects diverse perspectives and experiences.

Mitigating bias and promoting fairness in generative AI is of paramount importance for the following reasons. Firstly, it aligns with ethical principles, ensuring that generative AI operates in a manner that respects the dignity, rights, and equal treatment of all individuals. The UN High Commissioner for Human Rights has mentioned that creating generative AI systems that respect human rights involves heeding the perspectives of those who may be impacted by them, whether

[75] www.socialmediatoday.com/news/meta-outlines-new-approaches-generative-ai-transparency/706724/
[76] www.cio.com/article/472883/4-ways-to-enable-explainability-in-generative-ai.html
[77] Yundong Zhang, Juan Carlos Niebles, and Alvaro Soto. 'Interpretable visual question answering by visual grounding from attention supervision mining.' *2019 IEEE Winter Conference on Applications of Computer Vision: WACV 2019, Waikoloa Village, HI, USA, January 7–11, 2019*. Los Alamitos, CA: IEEE Computer Society, 2019. 349–357.

the outcomes are beneficial or detrimental; therefore, human rights must be at the core of generative AI technologies.[78] Moreover, addressing bias and promoting fairness is crucial for avoiding harm. Biased or unfair content generated by AI systems can perpetuate stereotypes, reinforce inequalities, and have negative consequences for individuals and communities. For instance, Bloomberg finds that some generative AI tools generate human images of those with high-paying jobs having lighter skin tones, while subjects with darker skin tones generate prompts such as 'social worker'.[79] By prioritising fairness, organisations can minimise the risk of producing harmful or discriminatory content, thus fostering a more inclusive and equitable society.

Various strategies for promoting fairness in the context of generative AI have been proposed. Firstly, training data used to develop generative AI models needs to be diverse, representative, and free from biases. Data preprocessing techniques can be applied to mitigate biases present in the training data, such as sampling strategies or data augmentation. Avril Aysha has suggested strategies for reducing data bias for generative AI training, such as using synthetic data to introduce different kinds of data constraints.[80] In addition, organisations should prioritise fairness in the design of AI algorithms. Shuhan and colleagues suggest an interpretable baseline approach to equalise facial attributes in image generation without necessitating retraining.[81] Their method modifies the interpretable semantic distribution in the latent space to achieve more equitable image generation while maintaining sample diversity. This results in more balanced data representation across specific attributes such as race or gender. Furthermore, organisations can seek input from users and stakeholders to detect biases or fairness issues in the content generated. Roy and colleagues have introduced two comprehensive open-source bias testing tools, namely BiasTestGPT for pretrained language models (PLMs) and BiasTestVQA for visual question answering (VQA) models, available on HuggingFace.[82] These tools offer intuitive and adaptable features for evaluating social biases in generative AI models, enabling effortless detection and measurement of social bias across various generative AI models and platforms.

2.4.5 *Accountability*

Accountability in generative AI refers to the responsibility of AI developers, organisations, and other stakeholders to ensure that the AI systems they create are transparent, reliable, and operate ethically. It involves being answerable for the decisions made by AI systems, the outcomes they produce, and the potential impacts they have on individuals and society.

Accountability is crucial in generative AI for several reasons. Firstly, it promotes transparency and trustworthiness by ensuring that AI systems are developed and deployed in a responsible manner. It holds AI developers and organisations accountable for the ethical implications of

[78] 'Human rights must be at the core of generative AI technologies, says Türk.' www.ohchr.org/en/statements-and-speeches/2024/02/human-rights-must-be-core-generative-ai-technologies-says-turk#:~:text = Rights%2Drespecting%20generative%20AI%20means,at%20the%20centre%20of%20technology

[79] 'Humans are biased. Generative AI is even worse.' Bloomberg. www.bloomberg.com/graphics/2023-generative-ai-bias/?embedded-checkout = true

[80] 'Data bias in LLM and generative AI applications.' https://mostly.ai/blog/data-bias-types

[81] Tan, Shuhan, Yujun Shen, and Bolei Zhou. 'Improving the fairness of deep generative models without retraining' (2020). https://arxiv.org/pdf/2012.04842

[82] Jiang, Roy, et al. 'Empowering domain experts to detect social bias in generative AI with user-friendly interfaces.' *XAI in Action: Past, Present, and Future Applications: NeurIPS 2023 Workshop, New Orleans, USA, December 10–17, 2023*. New York: Curran Associates, 2023.

their technology, fostering trust among users and stakeholders. Additionally, accountability helps mitigate risks associated with biased or unfair outcomes, ensuring that AI systems adhere to ethical standards and regulatory requirements. Moreover, accountability encourages continuous improvement and learning, as organisations strive to address any issues or concerns raised by users or stakeholders.

Many approaches are presented for achieving accountability in generative AI. Firstly, organisations should establish clear guidelines and standards for the development and deployment of AI systems, including mechanisms for transparency, fairness, and ethical decision-making. Maurice Bretzfield from Digiquation[83] has stated that the solution for increasing accountability in generative AI is requiring a collaboration between the legal profession, lawmakers, and AI developers to create transparent and understandable AI systems that allow attorneys to make informed decisions about their use. Secondly, organisations should prioritise the collection and analysis of data on AI system performance and impact, allowing for the identification of potential issues and the implementation of corrective measures. Liesenfeld and colleagues have highlighted that in high-stakes AI research, tasks related to data are sometimes viewed as menial tasks.[84] However, efforts to document data provenance and track adverse impacts can promote accountability for datasets.

Finally, a culture of accountability should be fostered within organisations, where individuals are encouraged to take responsibility for the ethical implications of their work and to act in the best interests of society. By embracing accountability principles, organisations can build trust, promote transparency, and ensure that generative AI systems operate in a responsible and ethical manner.

2.4.6 *Security and Privacy*

Security and privacy in generative AI refer to measures taken to protect the confidentiality, integrity, and availability of data used by AI systems, as well as ensuring that individuals' privacy rights are respected throughout the AI lifecycle. Security involves safeguarding AI systems and data from unauthorised access, manipulation, or breaches, while privacy focuses on protecting individuals' personal information and ensuring that AI systems operate in a manner that respects privacy rights.

Security and privacy are essential in generative AI for the following reasons. Firstly, they help mitigate the risk of data breaches, unauthorised access, and malicious attacks, which can compromise the confidentiality and integrity of sensitive data used by AI systems. This is particularly important in applications such as healthcare, finance, and personal assistance, where the confidentiality of data is paramount. BizTech has reported that about 50 per cent of respondents to Cisco's 2023 survey have likely entered information that they would not want to share.[85] Secondly, privacy protections are necessary to ensure that individuals' personal information is not misused or disclosed without their consent. This helps build trust and confidence among users and stakeholders, encouraging greater adoption and acceptance of AI

[83] 'Responsibility and accountability in generative AI for legal applications: Navigating ethical challenges.' www.linkedin.com/pulse/responsibility-accountability-generative-ai-legal-maurice-bretzfield-vdbac/

[84] Liesenfeld, Andreas, Alianda Lopez, and Mark Dingemanse. 'Opening up ChatGPT: Tracking openness, transparency, and accountability in instruction-tuned text generators.' *Proceedings of the 5th International Conference on Conversational User Interfaces: CUI'23, Eindhoven, Netherlands, July 19–21, 2023*. New York: Association for Computing Machinery, 2023. 1–6.

[85] 'What are the privacy risks of generative artificial intelligence?' https://biztechmagazine.com/article/2024/01/what-are-privacy-risks-generative-artificial-intelligence

technologies. Moreover, security and privacy measures are essential for regulatory compliance, as many jurisdictions have laws and regulations in place to protect individuals' data privacy rights and to prevent data breaches and cyber-attacks.

Achieving security and privacy in generative AI requires a comprehensive approach that addresses technical, organisational, and regulatory aspects. Firstly, organisations should implement robust security measures to protect AI systems and data from unauthorised access, manipulation, and breaches. For example, Chen and Esmaeilzadeh propose that healthcare organisations should draw insights from managing risks associated with other technologies to formulate risk assessment protocols specific to generative AI in healthcare. These protocols typically involve three main risk assessment activities: identifying risks, prioritising them, and implementing appropriate risk controls.[86] Secondly, organisations should adopt privacy-by-design principles, ensuring that privacy protections are integrated into the design and development of AI systems from the outset. Wu and colleagues suggest that privacy breaches can be detected by analysing simple prompts and responses.[87] To address privacy concerns, systems like ChatGPT should adhere to privacy regulations, conduct comprehensive prompt-response analyses to detect potential breaches, employ customised strategies to prevent such breaches, and enhance transparency in providing explanations for responses. Finally, organisations should stay informed about evolving security and privacy threats and regulations, continuously updating their policies and practices to ensure compliance and effectiveness in safeguarding security and privacy in generative AI systems.

2.5 TRUSTWORTHY GENERATIVE AI AND LAW

The above principles can be found in emerging legal frameworks that seek to promote the responsible development, deployment, and use of AI while safeguarding fundamental rights, ethical principles, and societal well-being. The EU had proposed the first comprehensive regulations on artificial intelligence – the EU AI Act.[88] It encompasses provisions that would apply to all types of AI systems, including those used for generative purposes. Firstly, The EU AI Act adopts a risk-based approach[89] to AI regulation, categorising AI systems into four risk levels: unacceptable risk, high risk, limited risk, and minimal risk. Generative AI systems that pose significant risks to fundamental rights or safety, such as those used for deepfake creation or misinformation dissemination, would likely fall into the high-risk category. These systems would be subject to stricter requirements, including conformity assessments, data quality standards, and human oversight measures.

Secondly, in terms of data governance and quality regulating,[90] the EU AI Act emphasises the importance of data governance and quality throughout the AI lifecycle. This includes requirements for data quality assessment, documentation, and transparency, ensuring that training data used in generative AI systems is representative, diverse, and free from biases that could lead to discriminatory or harmful outputs.

[86] Chen, Yan, and Pouyan Esmaeilzadeh. 'Generative AI in medical practice: In-depth exploration of privacy and security challenges.' *Journal of Medical Internet Research* 26 (2024): e53008.

[87] Wu, Xiaodong, Ran Duan, and Jianbing Ni. 'Unveiling security, privacy, and ethical concerns of ChatGPT.' *Journal of Information and Intelligence* 2.2 (2024): 102–115.

[88] 'EU AI Act: First regulation on artificial intelligence.' www.europarl.europa.eu/topics/en/article/20230601STO93804/eu-ai-act-first-regulation-on-artificial-intelligence

[89] 'Navigating the EU Artificial Intelligence (AI) Act: Implications and strategies for UK businesses.' www.bdo.co.uk/en-gb/insights/advisory/risk-and-advisory-services/navigating-the-eu-artificial-intelligence-(ai)-act-implications-and-strategies-for-uk-businesses#:~:text=3.-,Risk%2Dbased%20approach,and%20low%20or%20minimal%20risk.&text=AI%20applications%20would%20be%20regulated,address%20specific%20levels%20of%20risk

[90] Data and Data Governance. https://euaiact.com/article/10

Moreover, one of the fundamental principles underpinning the EU AI Act is transparency and explainability,[91] where generative AI systems must be transparent about their capabilities, limitations, and potential impacts on users and society. Users should be informed when they are interacting with AI-generated content and provided with explanations of how the content was generated.

Furthermore, the EU AI Act emphasises the importance of human oversight and control in AI decision-making processes.[92] For generative AI systems, human oversight is essential to ensure that the outputs align with ethical and legal standards, particularly in sensitive domains such as content creation, healthcare, and finance. Users should have the ability to intervene, correct, or override AI-generated outputs when necessary, reducing the risk of unintended consequences or misuse.

Additionally, the EU AI Act introduces requirements for accountability and compliance with regulatory obligations. Developers and deployers of generative AI systems are responsible for ensuring that their systems comply with legal requirements, including those related to data protection, consumer rights, and safety. Overall, the EU AI Act is promoting ethical, transparent, and trustworthy AI practices in a broader area of AI in order to foster the craft of trustworthy AI.

In addition to the EU AI Act, the General Data Protection Regulation (GDPR) has broader implications for the development, deployment, and use of generative AI. For instance, the GDPR sets out fundamental data protection principles[93] that apply to the processing of personal data. Generative AI systems that utilise personal data for training or operation must comply with these principles to ensure that data subjects' rights are respected and protected. Moreover, generative AI systems must have a lawful basis for processing personal data under the GDPR. Developers and deployers of generative AI systems must ensure that they have a valid legal basis for processing personal data in accordance with the GDPR requirements. Furthermore, the GDPR mandates that personal data be processed in a manner that ensures appropriate security and confidentiality, including protection against unauthorised or unlawful processing and accidental loss, destruction, or damage. Generative AI systems must implement technical and organisational measures to safeguard personal data from unauthorised access, disclosure, alteration, or destruction, in line with the GDPR's security requirements. Compliance with the GDPR is essential for building trust in generative AI and promoting responsible data-handling practices in the AI ecosystem.

2.6 CONCLUSION

We need to prioritise the development of trustworthy generative AI to ensure that the powerful technologies are designed and used in ways that promote fairness, transparency, and accountability. The future of generative AI holds great promise, but it also poses significant risks if not handled responsibly. Some of the potential future challenges we may face include the need to address increasing concerns around bias and discrimination, the rise of AI-generated deepfakes and disinformation, and the potential for generative AI to disrupt traditional employment and social structures. Regulatory measures that are underlined by these key principles serve as crucial safeguards for building trust in generative AI and AI systems generally.

[91] Transparency Obligations. www.euaiact.com/key-issue/5#:~:text=Article%2013%20of%20the%20EU%20AI%20Act%20provides%20the%20requirement,providers%20and%20users%20to%20reasonably

[92] Article 14: Human Oversight. https://artificialintelligenceact.eu/article/14/#:~:text=Human%20oversight%20shall%20aim%20at,risks%20persist%20notwithstanding%20the%20application

[93] 'A guide to the data protection principles.' https://ico.org.uk/for-organisations/uk-gdpr-guidance-and-resources/data-protection-principles/a-guide-to-the-data-protection-principles/

3

Normative and Ethical Dimensions of Generative AI

From Epistemological Considerations to Societal Implications

Ludovica Paseri and Massimo Durante

3.1 INTRODUCTION

Since the summer of 1956, when John McCarthy, Marvin Minsky, Nathaniel Rochester, and Claude Shannon presented their project on artificial intelligence (AI) at a conference at Dartmouth College in Hanover,[1] much has happened. Starting 'on the basis of the conjecture that every aspect of learning or any other feature of intelligence can in principle be so precisely described that a machine can be made to simulate it',[2] these pioneers paved the way for the following decades of research in this field. While AI originally referred to a new discipline set out to investigate the ways in which machines could simulate human intelligence, today, after numerous winters and rebirths of AI, this field of research has been profoundly changed, definitions have multiplied, and the evolution of AI has called for new classifications and more accurate taxonomies.[3]

From the legal perspective, the European Regulation on artificial intelligence (AI Act)[4] defines an AI system as:

> a machine-based system that is designed to operate with varying levels of autonomy and that may exhibit adaptiveness after deployment, and that, for explicit or implicit objectives, infers, from the input it receives, how to generate outputs such as predictions, content, recommendations, or decisions that can influence physical or virtual environments.[5]

This definition encompasses two main *characteristics*, namely autonomy and adaptability, which abstract from direct reference to intelligence but characterise a process that allows the AI system to map the relationship between input and output and thereby learn to generate results that can

Ludovica Paseri wrote Sections 3.1, 3.2, and 3.4; Massimo Durante wrote Sections 3.3 and 3.5.

[1] J. McCarthy, M. L. Minsky, N. Rochester, C. E. Shannon, 'A proposal for the Dartmouth summer research project on artificial intelligence, August 31, 1955', *AI Magazine* 27.4, 2006, p. 12.

[2] Ibid.

[3] N. Cristianini, *The shortcut: why intelligent machines do not think like us*, CRC Press, Boca Raton, FL, 2023; L. Floridi, *The ethics of artificial intelligence: principles, challenges, and opportunities*, Oxford University Press, Oxford, 2023.

[4] Regulation (EU) 2024/1689 of the European Parliament and of the Council of 13 June 2024 laying down harmonised rules on artificial intelligence and amending Regulations (EC) No. 300/2008, (EU) No. 167/2013, (EU) No. 168/2013, (EU) 2018/858, (EU) 2018/1139 and (EU) 2019/2144 and Directives 2014/90/EU, (EU) 2016/797 and (EU) 2020/1828 (Artificial Intelligence Act), 12.7.2024, ELI: http://data.europa.eu/eli/reg/2024/1689/oj.

[5] Art. 3(1) AI Act.

have an influence on the environment in physical or virtual terms. Outputs are exemplified in (i) predictions, (ii) content, (iii) recommendations, or (iv) decisions.

Recent developments in the field of AI have also prompted European lawmakers to include a further definition of so-called general-purpose AI models, defined as follows:

> an AI model is trained with a large amount of data using self-supervision at scale, that displays significant generality and is capable of competently performing a wide range of distinct tasks regardless of the way the model is placed on the market and that can be integrated into a variety of downstream systems or applications, except AI models that are used for research, development or prototyping activities before they are placed on the market.[6]

In Executive Order No. 14110 on the Safe, Secure, and Trustworthy Development and Use of Artificial Intelligence, signed by US President Joe Biden on 30 October 2023,[7] the United States takes a distinct approach, proposing three different definitions of AI,[8] AI *model*,[9] and AI *system*.[10] In addition to these general definitions, the Executive Order also includes a specific mention of generative AI, defined as follows: 'the class of AI models that emulate the structure and characteristics of input data in order to generate derived synthetic content. This can include images, videos, audio, text, and other digital content'.[11]

The approaches taken by the United States and the European Union are different. In the first case, generative AI (Gen AI) is explicitly mentioned, of which large language models (LLM) are the best-known and most widely used example. In the latter case, the EU legislator ultimately decided not to explicitly reference Gen AI but, instead, to include general-purpose AI models, an example of which are the so-called large generative AI models, as specified in Recital 99 of the AI Act. Thus, our study focuses on Gen AI systems, examining their ability to 'automatically generate content in response to prompts written in natural-language conversational interfaces'.[12] In particular, the intention is to shed light on the ethical challenges and social implications raised by Gen AI. The issue is often addressed through a normative approach (typical, for instance, of European institutions), which aims to identify the advantages and disadvantages of applying a specific technology. However, the ethical and social challenges of Gen AI also require adopting an epistemological approach, which calls for examining the differences between the representation of reality of human beings and that of Gen AI.

Therefore, drawing attention to the normative approach (Section 3.2) and, in particular, to the uses (Section 3.2.1), abuses (Section 3.2.2), and under-uses (Section 3.2.3) of Gen AI, this

[6] Art. 3(63) AI Act.

[7] The White House, *Executive order on the safe, secure, and trustworthy development and use of artificial intelligence*, no. 14110, 30 October 2023, available at www.whitehouse.gov/briefing-room/presidential-actions/2023/10/30/executive-order-on-the-safe-secure-and-trustworthy-development-and-use-of-artificial-intelligence/. Consider that the executive order has recently been overruled, see: Initial Rescissions Of Harmful Executive Orders And Actions, The White House, January 20, Washington D.C., USA, https://www.whitehouse.gov/presidential-actions/2025/01/initial-rescissions-of-harmful-executive-orders-and-actions/.

[8] In §3(b) Executive Ord., AI was defined as 'a machine-based system that can, for a given set of human-defined objectives, make predictions, recommendations, or decisions influencing real or virtual environments. Artificial intelligence systems use machine- and human-based inputs to perceive real and virtual environments; abstract such perceptions into models through analysis in an automated manner; and use model inference to formulate options for information or action'.

[9] In §3(c) Executive Ord., the AI model was defined as 'a component of an information system that implements AI technology and uses computational, statistical, or machine-learning techniques to produce outputs from a given set of inputs'.

[10] In §3(e) Executive Ord., the term AI system was defined as 'any data system, software, hardware, application, tool, or utility that operates in whole or in part using AI'.

[11] §3(p) Executive Ord.

[12] UNESCO, *Guidance for generative AI in education and research*, UNESCO Publishing, 2023, https://unesdoc.unesco.org/ark:/48223/pf0000386693, p. 8.

chapter focuses on the epistemological approach (Section 3.3), wondering what representation of reality Gen AI produces and how we interact with this representation. Four epistemological challenges of Gen AI are identified in terms of qualification (Section 3.4.1); reliability (Section 3.4.2); pluralism and novelty (Section 3.4.3); and technological dependence (Section 3.4.4). In light of these four epistemological challenges, the social implications of Gen AI are framed, proposing some final remarks (Section 3.5).

3.2 NORMATIVE APPROACH

The question of normativity, applied to the impact of digital technologies on society, investigates how this impact shapes or redesigns our society,[13] identifying advantages and disadvantages in facing the challenges posed by new technologies. This approach, typically adopted by European institutions, is also generally applied to the analysis of the impact of AI and, in particular, Gen AI on our society. This investigation allows us to highlight the knots and potential risks of harm that arise in this context, further distinguishing the harms resulting from uses (Section 3.2.1), misuses or abuses (Section 3.2.2) and underuses (Section 3.2.3) of Gen AI.

3.2.1 *Uses*

Against some alarmist and sensationalist representations, it must be recognised that 'while generative AI may be new, its harms are not'.[14] By this we do not intend to underestimate the dangers of using Gen AI but to put them into proper perspective. For instance, what is groundbreaking is that 'today, artificial intelligence (AI) manages the properties of electromagnetism to process texts with extraordinary success and often with outcomes that are indistinguishable from those that human beings could produce'.[15] In addition to the case where there is a specific intention to generate harm through Gen AI, the ordinary use of such systems can entail three main risks: (i) concentration of power; (ii) perpetuation of bias and discrimination over time; and (iii) technological solutionism.

As regards the concentration of power, the recent and increasing focus on Gen AI has shifted the attention from research, transparency, sharing, and experimentation in the field of AI[16] to

[13] M. Durante, 'Normativity, constructionism, and constraining affordances', *Etica & Politica* 13, 2011, p. 180. See also M. Durante, 'How does the evolution of ICTs change the law? An approach to law through the philosophy of information of Luciano Floridi', in M. Arias-Oliva, T. Ward Bynum, S. Rogerson, T. Torres-Coronas (eds.), *The 'backwards, forwards and sideways' changes of ICT*, University Rovira I Virgili Press, Tarragona, 2010, pp. 136–144.

[14] A report by the Electronic Privacy Information Centre (EPIC) provides a classification of the types of harm caused by Gen AI, including physical harms; economic harms; reputational harms; psychological harms; autonomy harms; discrimination harms; relationship harms; loss of opportunity; social stigmatisation; and dignitary harm. See G. Fergusson et al., 'Generating harms: generative AI's impact & paths forward', *Electronic Privacy Information Center*, 2023, https://epic.org/documents/generating-harms-generative-ais-impact-paths-forward/, pp. 65–66.

[15] L. Floridi, 'AI as agency without intelligence: on ChatGPT, large language models, and other generative models', *Philosophy & Technology* 36, 2023, p. 1.

[16] Consider the scenario described in M. Hutson, 'Artificial intelligence faces reproducibility crisis', *Science*, 359.6377, 2018, p. 725: 'The most basic problem is that researchers often don't share their source code. At the AAAI [Association for the Advancement of Artificial Intelligence] meeting, Odd Erik Gundersen, a computer scientist at the Norwegian University of Science and Technology in Trondheim, reported the results of a survey of 400 algorithms presented in papers at two top AI conferences in the past few years. He found that only 6% of the presenters shared the algorithm's code. Only a third shared the data they tested their algorithms on, and just half shared "pseudocode" – a limited summary of an algorithm. (In many cases, code is also absent from AI papers published in journals, including *Science* and *Nature*).' Although 'there are many reasons for the missing details', the percentages highlight an environment that is not prone to sharing.

profit, opacity, and, consequently, the concentration of power.[17] Consider, for example, the fact that in the original AI Act proposal,[18] there was no exception for research purposes, with effects described in the literature as 'detrimental to the entire scientific research ecosystem'.[19]

Secondly, the risk of perpetuating bias and discrimination over time can also be highlighted here. Gen AI relies on its ability to collect (often, scrape) and process huge amounts of data from multiple sources.[20] Personal data is also highly involved: recently, many leading digital companies have changed their privacy policies to expand the amount of data processed for AI training, as recently warned by the US consumer protection agency, the Federal Trade Commission (FTC).[21] Once again, the processing of big data, including personal data, risks reinforcing forms of discrimination perpetuated over time, crystallising vulnerability and inequality. Even if there were no specific intention to discriminate against or harm a particular category, imprisoning this vulnerable category in a representation that draws only from the past prevents it from evolving and thriving.[22]

Third, the strong advancement of Gen AI raises a risk of technological solutionism, which represents a revival of forms of techno-determinism that marked the early years of the digital revolution.[23] Recently, the Stockholm Declaration on AI for Science has been released, stating that 'by harnessing the power of AI we can propel humanity toward a future where *groundbreaking achievements in science*, even achievements worthy of a Nobel Prize, can be *fully automated*. We believe that this is achievable by the year 2050'.[24] This statement seems to echo Chris

[17] P. Verdegem, 'Dismantling AI capitalism: the commons as an alternative to the power concentration of Big Tech', *AI & Society*, 39, 2024, pp. 727–737. See also P. Nemitz, 'Constitutional democracy and technology in the age of artificial intelligence', *Philosophical Transactions of the Royal Society A: Mathematical, Physical and Engineering Sciences* 376.2133, 2018, p. 3, claiming that 'The accumulation of digital power, which shapes the development and deployment of AI as well as the debate on its regulation, is based on four sources of power'.

[18] Proposal for a Regulation of the European Parliament and of the Council laying down harmonised rules on artificial intelligence (Artificial Intelligence Act) and amending certain union legislative acts, COM/2021/206 final, ELI: https://eur-lex.europa.eu/legal-content/EN/TXT/?uri = celex%3A52021PC0206.

[19] M. Ebers et al., 'The European Commission's proposal for an Artificial Intelligence Act – a critical assessment by members of the Robotics and AI Law Society (RAILS)', *Multidisciplinary Scientific Journal* 4.4, 2021, p. 591. The latest version of the AI Act appears to be different. Article 2(6) states: 'This Regulation does not apply to AI systems or AI models, including their output, specifically developed and put into service for the sole purpose of scientific research and development.'

[20] On the phenomenon of 'data scraping' or 'web scraping' see J. Ciani Sciolla, 'The normative challenges of data scraping: legal hurdles and steps forward', *i-lex* 16.2, 2023, p. ii; M. A. Khder, 'Web scraping or web crawling: state of art, techniques, approaches and application', *International Journal of Advances in Soft Computing & Its Applications* 13.3, 2021, pp. 144–168.

[21] 'It may be unfair or deceptive for a company to adopt more permissive data practices – for example, to start sharing consumers' data with third parties or using that data for AI training – and to only inform consumers of this change through a surreptitious, retroactive amendment to its terms of service or privacy policy': Federal Trade Commission, Office of technology and the division of privacy and identity protection, 'AI (and other) companies: Quietly changing your terms of service could be unfair or deceptive', *Technology Blog*, 13 February 2024, www.ftc.gov/policy/advocacy-research/tech-at-ftc/2024/02/ai-other-companies-quietly-changing-your-terms-service-could-be-unfair-or-deceptive.

[22] On the ability to amplify disadvantages and bias in AI applications in forensic psychiatry and criminal justice see L. Tortora, 'Beyond discrimination: generative ai applications and ethical challenges in forensic psychiatry', *Frontiers in Psychiatry* 15, 2024, p. 7: 'the application of generative AI models in critical tasks that encompass life-altering outcomes, such as risk assessment, sentencing recommendation and treatment and rehabilitation planning, will not only reiterate but significantly magnify existing biases, exacerbating discrimination against forensic psychiatry patients, particularly those from historically marginalised groups, and reinforcing the stigma they experience across multiple levels of society'.

[23] U. Pagallo, *Il diritto nell'età dell'informazione: il riposizionamento tecnologico degli ordinamenti giuridici tra complessità sociale, lotta per il potere e tutela dei diritti*, Giappichelli Editore, Torino, 2014, pp. 20–21. See also A. Dafoe, 'On technological determinism: a typology, scope conditions, and a mechanism', *Science, Technology, & Human Values* 40.6, 2015, pp. 1047–1076.

[24] The Stockholm Declaration on AI for Science, https://sites.google.com/view/stockholm-declaration#h.t64rqcto94xv, 2024 [our emphasis]. See also D. R. King et al., 'Stockholm declaration on AI ethics: why others should sign', *Nature* 626.8000, 2024, pp. 716–716.

Anderson's controversial 2008 article arguing that big data would make the scientific method obsolete.[25] As critically underlined in discussing Anderson's position, 'knowledge is more than information, because it requires explanations and understanding, not just truths or correlations'.[26] Similarly, as far as the Stockholm Declaration is concerned, it is fair to say that automation is not a value or an achievement in itself,[27] and, above all, to believe that scientific discoveries that address the major challenges of our time can be fully automated reveals a profound misunderstanding of the epistemic dimension of AI.

The context further thickens when the spotlight is on the abuses and misuses of Gen AI, which are explored in the following section.

3.2.2 *Misuses and Abuses*

Primarily because of its ability to blur the boundaries between true and false, Gen AI can become an exceptionally effective tool for generating harm. Specifically, three forms of harm can result from abuses and misuses of Gen AI: (i) disinformation; (ii) fraud; and (iii) manipulation.

Among the various forms of information distortion (from misinformation to malinformation, etc.), disinformation, broadly understood, is specifically driven by the malice of an actor who intends to make false information go viral and take advantage of it.[28] The role of Gen AI in this scenario is highly relevant because it increasingly challenges our ability to distinguish historical from synthetic data and, therefore, true from false. The harm that Gen AI abuses can perpetrate varies and involves both the private and public dimensions. Concerning the private dimension, an example is provided by the case of the high school students in New Jersey who shared AI-generated fake pornographic images of classmates.[29] Regarding the public sphere, consider the case of the fake recording, gone viral, of a candidate in the Slovakia elections in which he appeared to be claiming to have rigged the elections.[30] While these forms or attempts to distort reality have always existed, what makes the difference at present is the *qualitative* aspect of the distorted representation enacted by AI.

Besides a qualitative increase, there is also a quantitative increase in the harms occurring from the misuses of Gen AI. Recently, the FTC released some particularly disconcerting data: 'consumers reported losing more than $10 billion to fraud in 2023, marking the first time that fraud losses have reached that benchmark. This marks a 14% increase over reported losses in

[25] C. Anderson, 'The end of theory: data deluge makes the scientific method obsolete', *Wired Magazine*, 23 June 2008.

[26] L. Floridi, *The fourth revolution: how the infosphere is reshaping human reality*, Oxford University Press, Oxford, 2014, p. 130.

[27] On the limits of automation see P. Nokelainen, T. Nevalainen, K. Niemi, 'Mind or machine? Opportunities and limits of automation', in C. Harteis (ed.), *The impact of digitalization in the workplace: an educational view*, Springer, Dordrecht, 2018, pp. 13–24. With specific reference to the health sector, see G. Lippi, G. Da Rin, 'Advantages and limitations of total laboratory automation: a personal overview', *Clinical Chemistry and Laboratory Medicine* 57.6, 2019, pp. 802–811.

[28] On disinformation and other forms of distortion of the information communication see O. Pollicino, 'The European approach to disinformation: comparing supranational and national measures', *Annuario di diritto comparato e di studi legislative*, 2020, pp. 175–212; O. Pollicino (ed.), *Freedom of speech and the regulation of fake news*, Intersentia, Cambridge, 2023.

[29] J. Jargon, 'Fake nudes of real students cause an uproar at a New Jersey high school', *The Wall Street Journal*, 2 November 2023, www.wsj.com/tech/fake-nudes-of-real-students-cause-an-uproar-at-a-new-jersey-high-school-df10f1bb.

[30] C. Devine, D. O'Sullivan, S. Lyngaas, 'A fake recording of a candidate saying he'd rigged the election went viral. Experts say it's only the beginning', CNN, 1 February 2024, https://edition.cnn.com/2024/02/01/politics/election-deepfake-threats-invs/index.html.

2022'.[31] The part played by AI in this scenario is remarkable, so much so that the Norwegian Authority in Consumer Protection, in a report on the impact of Gen AI, stated that 'Generative AI models can be abused by malicious actors to augment or supercharge criminal activities'.[32] In response to these challenges, the US FTC announced a 'Voice Cloning Challenge to help promote the development of ideas to protect consumers from the misuse of artificial intelligence-enabled voice cloning for fraud and other harms'.[33]

Furthermore, an improper use of Gen AI can result in 'automated, effective manipulation at scale'.[34] In addition to the harms caused by disinformation, it is also necessary to consider the harms of manipulation since, although the concepts are often considered together[35] and sometimes even represented as overlapping, they have dissimilar meanings and implications.

Whereas in the case of disinformation, a plausible but false scenario is provided (which may trigger different reactions), in the case of manipulation, the misrepresentation of a scenario is intended to induce people to act differently from how they would have acted in that specific circumstance, in order to achieve a certain outcome, thereby altering the individual's self-determination. While the primary intent of disinformation is the dissemination of false information, the primary intent of manipulation is to exert a form of control over the manipulated individual that leads to a desirable outcome. This is why Gen AI can be nimbly used to manipulate consumers[36] or, in society at large, conspiracy theories can be sharpened by providing plausible findings to support any position.[37]

With regard to the harms resulting from Gen AI abuse and misuse, it is crucial to consider the effects. There are three notable consequences that are crucial to grasping and measuring the extent of these forms of harm: (a) a general lack of trust; (b) threats to democracy and human rights; and (c) security dangers.

Distorted uses of Gen AI have been described as causing a 'disintegration of trust'.[38] Not surprisingly, the AI Act speaks of a 'need to build trust',[39] and the US executive order on AI, with specific reference to the education sector, advocated the need to develop an '"AI toolkit" for

[31] Federal Trade Commission, 'As nationwide fraud losses top $10 billion in 2023, FTC steps up efforts to protect the public', *FTC Press Release*, 9 February 2024, www.ftc.gov/news-events/news/press-releases/2024/02/nationwide-fraud-losses-top-10-billion-2023-ftc-steps-efforts-protect-public.

[32] Forbrukerrådet, *Ghost in the machine. Addressing the consumer harms of generative AI*, June 2023, https://storage02.forbrukerradet.no/media/2023/06/generative-ai-rapport-2023.pdf, p. 32. The quantitative increase is emphasised in the report: 'Large language models can be used by scammers to generate a large amount of convincing-looking text to deceive victims. Similarly, catfishing scams, where the scammer builds trust with the victim over time through regular contact, can potentially be automatized convincingly by the use of advanced chatbots. This means that the criminal can effectively scam more victims using less time and resources' (p. 32).

[33] Federal Trade Commission, 'FTC announces exploratory challenge to prevent the harms of AI-enabled voice cloning', *FTC Press Release*, 16 November 2023, www.ftc.gov/news-events/news/press-releases/2023/11/ftc-announces-exploratory-challenge-prevent-harms-ai-enabled-voice-cloning.

[34] M. Klenk, 'Ethics of generative AI and manipulation: a design-oriented research agenda', *Ethics and Information Technology*, 26.9, 2024, p. 1.

[35] For instance, J. E. Fossum, 'The context of fake news, disinformation, and manipulation', in M. Conrad et al. (eds.), *Europe in the age of post-truth politics: populism, disinformation and the public sphere*, Springer, Cham, 2022, pp. 31–52; E. Culloty, J. Suiter, *Disinformation and manipulation in digital media: information pathologies*, Routledge, London, 2021.

[36] Forbrukerrådet, *Ghost in the machine*, p. 22.

[37] S. Gabriel et al., 'Generative AI in the era of "alternative facts"', in D. Huttenlocher, A. Ozdaglar (eds.), *An MIT exploration of generative AI: from novel chemicals to opera*, MIT Press, Cambridge, MA, pp. 1–24.

[38] Fergusson et al., 'Generating harms', p. 64.

[39] Recital 6 AI Act.

education leaders implementing recommendations from the Department of Education's AI ... designing AI systems to enhance trust'.[40]

Furthermore, the consequences of such harms can pose threats to both democracy (consider, for instance, manipulation of the election process) and the protection of human rights. A recent report by the United Nations Human Rights Office of the High Commissioner, in addition to presenting a taxonomy of human rights risks connected to Gen AI,[41] also points out that 'we can expect that human rights will be threatened in new ways',[42] thereby opening future discussions.

Finally, the harms identified above can have consequences for the security and safety of both individuals and society. The topic is highly researched,[43] and it is significant that not only institutions but also companies are paying close attention to the issue.[44] For instance, the Google report 'Cybersecurity Forecast 2024. Insights for future planning' says that 'In 2024, the rapidly evolving world of gen AI will provide attackers with new ways to conduct convincing phishing campaigns and information operations at scale'.[45] However, it is worth noting that it also states that 'defenders will use the same technologies to strengthen detection, response, and attribution of adversaries – and more broadly reduce toil, address threat overload, and close the widening skills gap'.[46] This consideration, therefore, reminds us that in providing a comprehensive analysis of the socio-ethical impact of Gen AI adopting the normative approach, it is necessary not only to look at harms from use and misuse but also to draw attention to cases of underuse, which are analysed in the following section.

3.2.3 *Underuses*

The term underuse refers to the lack of exploitation of the potential of AI in a specific domain, leading to missed opportunities, inefficiencies, and related costs. In the literature, beginning with studies on AI underuse in the health sector,[47] the issue has also been analysed with regard

[40] §8c(iii)(d) Executive Ord.

[41] United Nations Human Rights Office of the High Commissioner, 'Taxonomy of human rights risks connected to generative AI', Supplement to B-Tech's Foundational Paper on the Responsible Development and Deployment of Generative AI, 2023, pp. 1–23, www.ohchr.org/sites/default/files/documents/issues/business/b-tech/taxonomy-GenAI-Human-Rights-Harms.pdf.

[42] Ibid., p. 17.

[43] Consider, ex multis, K. Huang, *Generative AI security: theories and practices*, Springer Nature, Cham, 2024; M. A. Ferrag, M. Amine, M. Debbah, M. Al-Hawawreh, 'Generative AI for cyber threat-hunting in 6G-enabled IOT networks', 2023 *IEEE/ACM 23rd International Symposium on Cluster, Cloud and Internet Computing Workshops (CCGridW). IEEE*, 2023, pp. 16–25; S. Weedon, 'Generative AI: security implications for business automation', *Network Security* 9, 2023, pp. 1353–4858.

[44] On different regulatory approaches to cybersecurity and Gen AI: C. Novelli, F. Casolari, P. Hacker, G. Spedicato, L. Floridi, 'Generative AI in EU law: liability, privacy, intellectual property, and cybersecurity', 2024, pp. 22–27, https://arxiv.org/pdf/2401.07348.

[45] Google Cloud, *Cybersecurity Forecast 2024. Insights for future planning*, 2024, p. 17, https://cloud.google.com/resources/security/cybersecurity-forecast.

[46] Ibid.

[47] See U. Pagallo et al., 'The underuse of AI in the health sector: opportunity costs, success stories, risks and recommendations', *Health and Technology* 14.1, 2024, pp. 1–14; U. Pagallo, 'The politics of data in EU law: will it succeed?', *Digital Society* 1.3, 2022, pp. 1–20; U. Pagallo, *Il dovere alla salute: sul rischio di sottoutilizzo dell'intelligenza artificiale in ambito sanitario*, Mimesis, Milano-Udine, 2022, p. 64; U. Pagallo, 'La grande trasformazione. Datificazione della società, tutela dell'ambiente e rischi e opportunità dell'innovazione tecnologica', in M. Durante, U. Pagallo, *La politica dei dati: il governo delle nuove tecnologie tra diritto, economia e società*, Mimesis, Milano-Udine, 2022, pp. 123–140; and for a comment see M. Orofino, 'La questione del sotto utilizzo dell'intelligenza artificiale in campo sanitario: spunti di rilievo costituzionale', *Queste istituzioni*, 4, 2022, pp. 158–171.

to the underuse of research data in the scientific research sector,[48] the environmental challenges of AI,[49] and public-sector data.[50]

Like the underuse of AI in the healthcare system, which gives rise to severe opportunity costs for the public, cases of harm resulting from the underuse of Gen AI can also be outlined. These forms of harm can be represented by loss of opportunity cost, loss of innovation, and inequitable distribution of benefits. First, it should be recalled that there are multiple benefits to using Gen AI.[51] In terms of opportunity costs, consider the effective potential strained to process efficiencies, optimisation, and efficiency gains. Regarding the research and education sector, while recognising that Gen AI 'harbours risks, such as the large-scale generation of disinformation and other unethical uses with significant societal consequences',[52] it also 'provides many opportunities'.[53] Second, the underuse of Gen AI can lead to a loss or delay in innovation as well as forms of inefficiency in generating new ideas.[54] Third, cases of Gen AI underutilisation may exacerbate already disadvantageous positions. The problems related to the digital divide are only amplified by generating unequal situations between those who have access to Gen AI and those who do not. In addition, 'The rapid pervasion of Gen AI in technologically advanced countries and regions has exponentially accelerated the generation and processing of data and has simultaneously intensified the concentration of AI wealth in the Global North',[55] exacerbating forms of inequity.

Having made this analysis from a normative point of view, it should be noted that a further identification and evaluation of the risks and opportunities of Gen AI depends both on how this form of AI works from an epistemological point of view and on our ability to interact with it. For this reason, the following section focuses on the epistemological approach.

3.3 EPISTEMOLOGICAL APPROACH

Gen AI systems produce what can be described as pieces of knowledge[56] (text, audio, images, and video), offering a specific representation of reality. From a qualitative point of view, Gen

48 L. Paseri, 'Sharing and reuse of research data in EU: the risk of over regulation and its implications', in M. Palmirani (ed.), *Artificial Intelligence and the Complexity of Legal Systems (AICOL) volume*, Springer, Cham, forthcoming.

49 U. Pagallo, J. Ciani Sciolla, M. Durante, 'The environmental challenges of AI in EU law: lessons learned from the Artificial Intelligence Act (AIA) with its drawbacks', *Transforming Government: People, Process and Policy* 16.3, 2022, pp. 359–376.

50 C. V. Buttow, S. Weerts, 'Managing public sector data: national challenges in the context of European Union's new data governance models', *Information Polity* 29.3, 2023, pp. 1–16.

51 Although in this chapter we focus specifically on Gen AI issues, we are aware of the benefits and opportunities that can arise from both the use of Gen AI and, more broadly, of synthetic data, in different areas that include but are not limited to law. Consider, for instance, the scientific research sector: S. Kurapati, L. Gilli, 'Synthetic data: a convergence between Innovation and GDPR', in L. Paseri (ed.), 'Special issue on Open Science and Data Protection', *J. Open Access L.* 11(1), 2023, pp. 1–12.

52 European Commission, DG for Research and Innovation, *Living guidelines on the responsible use of generative AI in research*, Publications Office of the European Union, Luxembourg, 2024, p. 3.

53 Ibid.

54 U. Pagallo, M. Durante, 'The good, the bad, and the invisible with its opportunity costs: introduction to the "J" special issue on "The impact of artificial intelligence on law"', *Multidisciplinary Scientific Journal* 5.1, 2022, p. 143; U. Pagallo, *The laws of robots: crimes, contracts, and torts*, Springer, Dordrecht, 2013.

55 UNESCO, *Guidance for generative AI in education and research*, p. 14.

56 The expression 'pieces of knowledge' has often been used in computer science studies of knowledge representation; see for example D. B. Lenat, E. A. Feigenbaum, 'On the thresholds of knowledge', *Proceedings of the International Workshop on Artificial Intelligence for Industrial Applications*, 25–27 May 1988, 87, 1988, pp. 1172–1176, www.ijcai.org/Proceedings/87-2/Papers/122.pdf; J. Kelemen, J. Hvorecký, 'On knowledge, knowledge systems, and knowledge management', *Proceedings of the 9th International Conference on Computational Intelligence and Informatics*,

AI's representation of reality reaches high standards and, as a result, discerning between synthetic and non-synthetic outputs becomes challenging for humans. Accordingly, apart from normative considerations, it becomes essential to scrutinise the representation of reality offered by Gen AI and how human beings become subjects of interaction, since they create machines that make decisions, artificial agents that act autonomously, and programs that are endowed with ever-increasing computational power that produce significant consequences for human life.[57]

From an epistemological perspective, Gen AI and humans are indeed different. While human beings are extraordinary 'semantic engines' (their understanding and representation of reality is rooted in semantic skills – i.e., the ability to give meaning and sense to the world), Gen AI is an extraordinary 'syntactic engine'[58] (operating on the basis of the ability to process vast amounts of data and parameters through structures of great complexity, such as neural networks, without possessing knowledge of what is being processed). Unlike the scientific method, where knowledge entails verifiable predictions based on models and explanations, AI-generated outputs lack such theoretical grounding. Thus, questioning the underlying functioning of Gen AI is pivotal due to its profound impact on human actions and the criteria for justifying them.

In doing so, we necessarily limit ourselves to considering the possible comparison with a specific epistemology that is the focus of our attention, legal epistemology. Without going into the age-old and thorny question of the definition of law and its role, we can say that, from an epistemological standpoint, the law acts as a normative system. It interprets and applies legal statements within a shared legal framework, verifying the reliability of this interpretation and application through forms of reasoning and specific tools (principles, categories, evidence, review systems, and so on) that the law itself provides and regulates. These have a fundamental common feature: every piece of knowledge produced by the interpretation and application of the law is offered to the scrutiny, control, and discussion of a counterparty and a third party (as well as more widely to the community of legal scholars over time).[59] Legal science is progressive and incremental and uses the contribution of all legal experts. This method, and the resulting representation of reality that it conveys, is in contrast with Gen AI's representation of reality for three main reasons.

First, the representation produced by Gen AI may happen to be accurate (where there is a validated standard or metric to measure accuracy), but it is not based on the ability to attribute meaning and intersubjectively verify its epistemic reliability. In more analytical terms, LLMs (and more widely Gen AI) do not have the ability to operate a semantic ascent[60] or descent in relation to artificially produced sentences; that is, they are not able to move from the linguistic to

Budapest Tech., Budapest, 2008, p. 28; D. Lenat, G. Marcus, 'Getting from generative AI to trustworthy AI: what LLMS might learn from CYC', 2023, pp. 1–21, https://arxiv.org/pdf/2308.04445.

57 M. Durante, *Computational power: the impact of ICT on law, society and knowledge*, Routledge, London, 2021, p. 13.

58 Floridi, *The ethics of artificial intelligence*, p. 44: 'with the staggering growth of available data, quantity and speed of calculation, and ever-better algorithms, they can do statistically ... what we do semantically'.

59 According to a neo-positivist conception of legal science that has also been called logical positivism, 'the paradigmatic instance of knowledge is represented by the empirical sciences, which adopt the principle of verification (or, from a certain point on, falsification). The latter thus becomes the fundamental methodological principle of every sphere of knowledge. Just as the proposition "this is chalk" implies that if one observes a piece of chalk at the microscope certain structural qualities will become apparent, similarly the proposition "Section 62 of the Uniform Negotiable Instruments Act is valid Illinois law" implies that Illinois courts, given certain conditions, will behave in a certain way': A. Schiavello, 'La scienza giuridica analitica dalla nascita alla crisi', *Ragion pratica* 1, 2020, p. 148 [our translation].

60 This is an expression from W. V. Quine, *From a logical point of view*, Harvard University Press, Cambridge, MA, 1953, that we refer to only by analogy in this context. This reference to Quine can be found in L. Floridi, *The philosophy of information*, Oxford University Press, Oxford, 2013, p. 202.

the metalinguistic level in order to qualify the content of their statements or argue in favour of its accuracy.

Second, the law claims to define the extent to which an explanation is legally relevant in terms of both causal regression (determining the chain of events of a legally relevant fact) and prediction (of the legally relevant consequences of the fact in question). Against this epistemological background, the law has always independently decided where it intends to stop the legally relevant retrospective or predictive explanation of an event. Gen AI cannot account for a causal retrospective or predictive explanation of any knowledge it produces. How could the law, from this perspective, regulate an event if it cannot appraise and determine where (the knowledge of) its origin and consequences begin and end?[61]

Third, each piece of knowledge created by Gen AI does not require the existence of a community of interpreters to be concretely applied. In contrast, the law is a social product and cannot give rise to progressive and incremental knowledge except through the contribution, discussion, interpretation, and scrutiny by a community of experts.[62] While legal epistemology is focused on a shared process of representation and validation, Gen AI proposes solely the product of output, leading to concerns regarding both reproducibility and control. In particular, the aspect of control is central to the extent that 'whoever controls the questions controls the answers and whoever controls the answers controls reality'.[63]

Consider, for instance, that Chat GPT can reiterate a given answer, potentially offering a very different response, sometimes completely contradicting the former. Variable outputs stress that Gen AI's representation of reality needs mechanisms ensuring accountability. Furthermore, Gen AI's inability to attribute meaning or validate the reliability of its outputs raises fundamental questions about its role in shaping decision-making processes. Investigating the epistemological dimensions of Gen AI involves broader philosophical inquiries regarding knowledge acquisition, representation, and validation. It becomes relevant to understand how to balance Gen AI's representation of reality with human interpretation. What safeguards can be implemented to mitigate the issues associated with Gen AI's representation of reality from an epistemological standpoint? These issues require a multifaceted approach that recognises the epistemic abilities and limits of Gen AI. By critically examining some assumptions and implications of Gen AI's representation of reality, we pave the way for a more informed and ethically grounded approach to its development and deployment. Therefore, four epistemological challenges have been identified and will be discussed below.

3.4 GEN AI EPISTEMOLOGICAL CHALLENGES

AI has been described in terms of 'epistemic technology', where the term epistemic 'is meant to refer to the broader category of practices that relate in a direct manner to the acquisition, retention, use and creation of *knowledge*'.[64] The epistemic nature of AI derives from the type of content it manipulates and the types of operations it performs on that content, but also from 'its own internal capacities'.[65] However, being an epistemic technology does not mean that the content or representation of reality provided is reliable. In other words, 'accepting AI as an

[61] Durante, *Computational power*, pp. 9–10.

[62] V. Zeno-Zencovich, 'Big data ed epistemologia giuridica', in G. Resta, V. Zeno-Zencovich (eds.), *Governance of/through big data, Volume II*, Roma TrE-Press, Roma, 2023, p. 445.

[63] Floridi, 'AI as agency without intelligence', p. 5.

[64] R. Alvarado, 'AI as an epistemic technology', *Science and Engineering Ethics* 29.5, 2023, p. 12.

[65] Ibid., p. 15.

epistemic technology does not mean that we must also accept that it is an epistemically trustworthy epistemic technology'.[66] For these reasons, 'the need to involve challenging epistemic and methodological scrutiny is even more immediately pressing'.[67] In doing so, four major epistemological challenges are analysed: (1) qualification; (2) reliability; (3) pluralism and novelty; and (4) technological dependence.

3.4.1 *The Challenge of Epistemic Qualification*

The qualification challenge consists of the fact that Gen AI defies the human ability to qualify the epistemological status of the pieces of knowledge it conveys. This occurs primarily in two ways.

First, Gen AI tends to elide the distinction between what is created (which is the outcome of a creative process) and what is merely reproduced (which is the result of the ability to mimic a creative activity). If one looks only at the result and not the process, human beings are often unable to distinguish the synthetic from the non-synthetic result. In law, it remains crucial not only to be able to evaluate a piece of knowledge but also to control the process by which a piece of knowledge is produced.

Second, Gen AI challenges the human ability to distinguish between true and false. Considering the probabilistic dimension of Gen AI's outcomes, pieces of false knowledge are frequently generated (the so-called hallucination of Gen AI[68]), however plausible: 'Readers and consumers of texts will have to get used to not knowing whether the source is artificial or human. Probably they will not notice, or even mind.'[69] For example, LLMs provide answers that they are unable to reflexively assess as to their degree of truthfulness or reliability. Where questioned in this regard, human beings can reflexively evaluate a statement of their own, determining it as certain, probable, plausible, and so on (using expressions which precede the statement itself, such as 'I am certain that', 'I believe that', 'it is highly probable that'). Any answer given by an LLM should, in this sense, always be preceded by an expression such as 'It is only probable that. . .', so as to reveal that any AI-generated statement cannot constitutively raise any claim to truth.[70]

It is indeed a relevant question since, as argued by Stefano Rodotà, long before the emergence of Gen AI, 'the meaning of truth in democratic societies ... presents itself as the result of an open process of knowledge',[71] remarking that 'In a society omnivorous of information, and continually productive of representations, the "truth" of the latter takes on a special significance'.[72] In particular, an important aspect in this context has been defined as the 'feedback loop': 'Large Language Models learn from content that is fed to them, but because content will

[66] Ibid., p. 14.

[67] Ibid., p. 22.

[68] See, for instance, Z. Ji et al., 'Survey of hallucination in natural language generation', *ACM Computing Surveys* 55.12, 2023, pp. 1–38; C. Rebuffel et al., 'Controlling hallucinations at word level in data-to-text generation', *Data Mining and Knowledge Discovery* 36, 2022, pp. 318–354.

[69] L. Floridi, M. Chiriatti, 'GPT-3: its nature, scope, limits, and consequences', *Minds and Machines* 30, 2020, p. 691.

[70] 'Gen AI is trained using data collected from web pages, social media conversations and other online media. It generates its content by statistically analysing the distribution of words, pixels or other elements in the data that it has ingested and identifying and repeating common patterns': UNESCO, *Guidance for generative AI in education and research*, p. 7. For instance, even if we were to ask the LLM to qualify the status of its own response in degree of truthfulness or epistemic reliability, it would not be able to do so, and its further response would be merely probabilistic and vitiated by the same original lack of self-qualification.

[71] S. Rodotà, *Il diritto di avere diritti*, Laterza, Roma-Bari, 2012, p. 225 [our translation].

[72] Ibid., p. 221 [our translation].

be increasingly wholly or partially AI-generated, it will be partly learning from itself, thus creating a feedback loop'.[73] This feedback loop leads to the crystallisation of Gen AI's representation of reality, with serious risks where it produces distorted or unreliable knowledge.

3.4.2 *The Challenge of Epistemic Reliability*

The challenge of epistemic reliability represents the problem of the human ability to rely on the representation of reality conveyed by Gen AI, which repeats patterns identified starting from its training dataset without having access to real-world understanding and knowledge. As has been pointed out, this

> can lead teachers and students to place a level of trust in the output that it does not warrant. . . . Indeed, Gen AI is not informed by observations of the real world or other key aspects of the scientific method, nor it is aligned with human or social values. For these reasons, it cannot generate genuinely novel content about the real world, objects and their relations, people and social relations, human–object relations, or human–tech relations. Whether the apparently novel content generated by Gen AI models can be recognised as scientific knowledge is contested.[74]

In addition, we can say regarding the debate on whether scientific knowledge is involved, the results of Gen AI may not even be consistent with the main characteristics and principles by which we can currently describe the open science paradigm and the FAIR (Findable, Accessible, Interoperable, Reusable) data requirement.[75] This can have three main consequences.

First, this impacts not only epistemic trust but, precisely because of the inaccuracy, opacity, and inexplicability of its model, also social acceptance and trust. In this perspective, it is indeed crucial to note that: 'Assessing the likelihood or the accuracy of such outputs will depend on how well we think the model analysed the training data. Hence, epistemic reliability of the analytical processes will be relevant . . . to the trust we can allocate to AI generated text, search, etc.'[76] Hence, it follows that this epistemic limitation 'is also a key cause of trust issues around Gen AI (Nazaretsky et al. 2022a). If users do not understand how a Gen AI system arrived at a specific output, they are less likely to be willing to adopt or use it (Nazaretsky et al. 2022b)'.[77]

Second, this has serious consequences for the allocation of responsibility. In an ever-increasing situation of deep intermingling between human and artificial collaboration in content generation, 'New mechanisms for the allocation of responsibility for the production of

[73] B. van der Sloot, *Regulating the synthetic society: generative AI, Legal questions, and societal challenges*, Hart Publishing, Oxford, 2024, p. 63.

[74] UNESCO, *Guidance for generative AI in education and research*, p. 16.

[75] On the open science paradigm, see L. Paseri, *Scienza aperta: politiche europee per un nuovo paradigma della ricerca*, Mimesis, Milano-Udine, 2024; L. Paseri, 'Open science and data protection: engaging scientific and legal contexts', *Journal of Open Access to Law* 11, 2023, pp. 1–16; on the FAIR data principle in scientific research, see L. Paseri, 'From the right to science to the right to open science. The European approach to scientific research', *European Yearbook on Human Rights*, Intersentia, Cambridge, 2022, pp. 515–541.

[76] Alvarado, 'AI as an epistemic technology', p. 22.

[77] UNESCO, *Guidance for generative AI in education and research*, p. 15. In this passage authors refer to T. Nazaretsky, M. Cukurova, G. Alexandron, 'An instrument for measuring teachers' trust in AI-based educational technology', *LAK22: LAK22: 12th International Learning Analytics and Knowledge Conference*, Vancouver, Association for Computing Machinery, 2022, pp. 55–66; and T. Nazaretsky, M. Cukurova, G. Alexandron, 'Teachers' trust in AI-powered educational technology and a professional development program to improve it', *British Journal of Educational Technology* 53.4, 2022, pp. 914–931.

semantic artefacts will probably be needed'.[78] Consider, for instance, the growing debate in the field of scientific research, which is not only about 'reproducibility and robustness in their results and conclusions' but also about the very authorship of the content produced by Gen AI, just as it is in the field of art.[79]

Third, this has a considerable environmental impact on the infosphere.[80] As in the case of an upstream polluted source, flawed AI-generated content can not only spread polluted content downstream, which is inextricably mixed with trustworthy and genuine content, but, in the long run, it also poisons end users, undermining their defences. As we have already pointed out, 'This poses a high risk for young learners who do not have solid prior knowledge of the topic in question. It also poses a recursive risk for future GPT models that will be trained on text scraped from the Internet that GPT models have themselves created which also include their biases and errors'.[81]

3.4.3 *The Challenge of Epistemic Pluralism and Novelty*

Every authentic cognitive inquiry rests on the ability to question. There is nothing more difficult in the search for knowledge than constructing the relevant and pertinent questions from which any real investigation can take its departure. However, for an investigation to be fruitful and satisfy our need for research, it is necessary that the answer is obtained within the boundaries set by the question. It is equally necessary, however, that, within those boundaries, the answer brings something new which is not already included in the prompt of the question; otherwise, the inquiry remains tautological. Moreover, any authentic answer, which gives us access to the knowledge of something new, raises new questions – that is, the possibility of questioning reality from different standpoints, ensuring pluralism of research and knowledge: 'Each piece of semantic information is a response to a question, which, as a whole, raises further questions about itself, which require the correct flow of information to receive adequate response, through an appropriate network of relationships with some information source.'[82]

What puzzles us about Gen AI is that its ability to produce pieces of knowledge by predicting, for instance, probabilities of language patterns found in data is based on a static training dataset that describes the world as it is ('assuming what we know about the observed world'[83]). This is likely to reaffirm the primacy of the existent over openness to novelty and pluralism in a more or less surreptitious manner. In this way, the knowledge and representation of reality produced by Gen AI is not instrumental in imagining new and different worlds but rather in reaffirming worlds already entrenched in traditional views and conventions, as has been properly remarked by the United Nations Educational, Scientific and Cultural Organization (UNESCO): 'Gen AI, by definition, reproduces dominant worldviews in its outputs and undermines minority and

78 Floridi, Chiriatti, 'GPT-3: its nature, scope, limits, and consequences', p. 692.

79 'The generative capabilities of these tools are likely to fundamentally alter the creative processes by which creators formulate ideas and put them into production. . . . Generative AI tools, at first glance, seem to fully automate artistic production – an impression that mirrors past instances when traditionalists viewed new technologies as threatening "art itself." In fact, these moments of technological change did not indicate the "end of art," but had much more complex effects, recasting the roles and practices of creators and shifting the aesthetics of contemporary media': Z. Epstein, A. Hertzmann, 'Art and the science of generative AI', *Science* 380.6650, 2023, p. 1110.

80 Floridi, *The fourth revolution*, pp. 205–216.

81 UNESCO, *Guidance for generative AI in education and research*, p. 16.

82 Floridi, *The philosophy of information*, p. 274.

83 J. Pearl, D. Mackenzie, *The book of why: the new science of cause and effect*, Basic Books, New York, 2018, p. 9.

plural opinions.'[84] According to UNESCO's view of generative AI, this brings about two main consequences, which are relevant, respectively, to epistemology and democracy. First, 'if human civilizations are to flourish, it is essential that we recognize that Gen AI *can never be an authoritative source of knowledge* on whatever topic it engages with'.[85] Second,

> Data-poor populations … have minimal or limited digital presence online. Their voices are consequently not being heard and their concerns are not represented in the data being used to train GPTs, and so rarely appear in the outputs. For these reasons, given the pre-training methodology based on data from internet web pages and social media conversations, GPT models can further marginalise already disadvantaged people.[86]

This last remark raises – or rather reiterates – a crucial concern for democracy. No matter how democracy is defined, it is generally agreed that people and populations should be able to neutralise, if not change, their starting conditions. As with other technologies, Gen AI can increase or emphasise starting conditions, favouring those who are already advantaged and disfavouring those who are already at a disadvantage. The risk is that Gen AI becomes the battlefield where the challenges of innovation may be won by a few, but where conformity, division, and social exclusion may also develop and spread, once again calling into question the crucial issue of equality and pluralism in democracy.

3.4.4 *The Challenge of Technological Dependence*

Technological dependence resulting from the increasing or systematic use of Gen AI systems, which are entrusted with tasks of decision-making, prediction, or even just aiding or supporting human activities, raises at least three different types of issues from an epistemological point of view, related to the already stressed problem of the reliability of such systems.

First, technological dependence puts the focus on the need to measure and compare the outputs produced by human activity or generative artificial intelligence. This raises the question of the standard for assessing the output of Gen AI systems. On the one hand, using such systems should not be discouraged in areas where their use has proved better or safer than human activities; on the other hand, it would be desirable and fair to expect a higher standard from Gen AI systems,[87] where they are proved to be able to achieve it.[88] In more general terms, comparing human- or AI-generated results will raise tensions that may result in third-party-protected expectations (should the doctors inform the patient that their diagnosis differs from that generated by an AI system?).

Second, what has been qualified elsewhere as the 'principle of functional equivalence' is reaffirmed here as closely related to the 'principle of equal protection under the law'.[89] The first principle asserts that operation or assistance by an AI system (in this case, Gen AI) should be

[84] UNESCO, *Guidance for generative AI in education and research*, p. 26.
[85] Ibid. [our emphasis].
[86] Ibid., p. 17.
[87] M. Durante, L. Floridi, 'A legal principles-based framework for AI liability regulation', in J. Mokander, M. Ziosi (eds.), *The 2021 yearbook of the Digital Ethics Lab*, Springer, Cham, 2022, pp. 93–112.
[88] European Commission, Directorate-General for Justice and Consumers, *Liability for artificial intelligence and other emerging digital technologies*, Publications Office of the European Union, Luxembourg, 2019, p. 46, https://data.europa.eu/doi/10.2838/573689: 'once autonomous technology outperforms human auxiliaries in terms of preventing harm, the benchmark should be determined by the performance of comparable technology that is available on the market'.
[89] Durante, Floridi, 'A legal principles-based framework for AI liability regulation', pp. 93–112.

treated no differently from human operation or assistance in case of harm to a third party, for equal protection under the law to be ensured to all those who are the receivers of the outputs of this system. Similar cases must be dealt with similarly, unless there is a reason to make a distinction. In this regard, a remark by the Expert Group on Product Liability in the field of AI and Emerging Technologies is relevant from an epistemological standpoint, although stated in a partially different context: '[It is] challenging to identify the benchmark against which the operation of non-human helpers will be assessed in order to mirror the misconduct element of human auxiliaries'.[90]

Third, technological dependence raises an additional epistemological challenge posed by the need for humans to increasingly rely on technology to distinguish synthetic from non-synthetic outputs and to detect the use of Gen AI systems in producing pieces of knowledge. Consider, for example, the tools developed in academia to understand whether a text is generated by an artificial or human agent, which raises relevant issues in terms of liability, plagiarism, and copyright. In the same vein, it is important to mention the publication of guidelines for the responsible use of Gen AI in research, according to which researchers 'are accountable for the integrity of the content generated by or with the support of AI tools' and it is expected that they 'do not use fabricated material created by generative AI in the scientific process, for example falsifying, altering, manipulating original research data'.[91] This becomes even more challenging when dealing with so-called hybrid data, 'the offspring of historical and synthetic data'.[92]

All these cases highlight the crucial importance of standards as they constitute key benchmarks for evaluating the reliability and accuracy of AI-generated outputs. The identification of these standards implies a complex evaluation (from a legal, ethical, and social standpoint), in order to guarantee adequate levels of transparency and responsibility in the use of Gen AI systems, and the rapid pace of advancement of Gen AI requires constant updating of these standards.

3.5 CONCLUSIONS: GEN AI'S SOCIETAL IMPLICATIONS

Gen AI raises numerous challenges that can be examined according to a *normative* and *epistemological* approach. The former, increasingly adopted by European institutions, identifies the pros and cons of technological advancement. In relation to Gen AI, the main pros concern technological innovation, economic development, and the achievement of social goals and values. The disadvantages mainly concern cases of abuse, use, or underuse of Gen AI. The latter investigates how Gen AI produces data, information, and pieces of knowledge in ways that differ from – and often are irreducible to – humans. To fully grasp and deal with the impact of Gen AI, this chapter contends that both these approaches should be pursued since the identification of the pros and cons of Gen AI also depends on how this model of AI works from an epistemological standpoint and our ability to interact with it. To this end, our analysis compares Gen AI's and legal epistemology and highlights four major problematic issues: (1) qualification; (2) reliability; (3) pluralism and novelty; and (4) technological dependence.

Furthermore, the analysis of such epistemological challenges helps us understand some potentially long-term consequences of Gen AI on relevant democratic aspects of our

90 European Commission, Directorate-General for Justice and Consumers, *Liability for artificial intelligence and other emerging digital technologies*, p. 25.

91 European Commission, *Living guidelines on the responsible use of Generative AI in research*, p. 6.

92 Floridi, *The ethics of artificial intelligence*, p. 36.

contemporary society. These consequences may be understood in terms of an impact on: (i) human autonomy; (ii) semantic capital; and (iii) level playing field.

First, human autonomy is impacted by Gen AI in several ways: from being unable to verify the accuracy of outputs to being subject to unexplained decisions or predictions; from reliance on untrustworthy results to the risk of manipulation of opinions formed on biased or hallucinatory content, and so on. In all these cases, the limitation of human autonomy generates a lack of social trust and a loss of individual self-determination.

Second, the production of data, information, and pieces of knowledge by Gen AI has a strong impact on the production of semantic capital, defined as 'any content that can enhance someone's power to give meaning to and make sense of (semanticise) something'.[93] This power plays a crucial role in every democracy and society. The increasing number of decisions and tasks delegated to Gen AI can circumscribe or alter human power to give meaning to and make sense of reality.

Third, it should be noted that the production of data, information, and pieces of knowledge made possible by the technological development of Gen AI requires resources, investment, time, and energy, with a significant impact on our society[94] and, above all, the environment.[95] As we have tried to highlight, this can benefit the few, already advantaged, and weaken the many, already disadvantaged, by altering the level playing field.

Ultimately, the risk from an epistemological perspective is that the focus on outputs tends to obscure the importance of the path through which the process of knowledge unfolds.

93 L. Floridi, 'Semantic capital: its nature, value, and curation', *Philosophy & Technology* 31, 2018, p. 483.

94 Van der Sloot, *Regulating the synthetic society*, pp. 66–67.

95 On the environmental impact of Gen AI see A. Berthelot, E. Caron, M. Jay, L. Lefèvre, 'Estimating the environmental impact of generative-AI services using an LCA-based methodology', *CIRP LCE 2024 – 31st Conference on Life Cycle Engineering*, 2023, pp. 1–10; N. R. Mannuru et al., 'Artificial intelligence in developing countries: the impact of generative artificial intelligence (AI) technologies for development', *Information Development*, 2023, pp. 1–19, https://journals.sagepub.com/doi/10.1177/02666669231200628

4

Why Generative AI Is Not Cyrano de Bergerac

A Computational Manipulation Perspective on Generative AI

Stefano Faraoni

4.1 INTRODUCTION

What if artificial intelligence[1] (AI) was able to create the perfect persuasive environment? What if, like Cyrano de Bergerac,[2] pretending to be Christian and protected by the shadows of the night, an AI could find the right words at the right time and atmosphere to appeal to the heart of Roxane? Knowing Roxane and being in love with her, Cyrano moved the strings of Roxane's emotions to induce new attitudes and behaviours in her, a feeling of love towards Christian. He misrepresented reality, pretending to be Christian. What if Cyrano's abilities to persuade were embedded in AI technology, implemented and used for manipulation? A manipulative AI can be imagined hidden in the shadows, like Cyrano, composing love letters and aiming at changing and shaping the user's attitudes and behaviours. However, a manipulative AI does not have Cyrano's good intentions. It has the target of undermining individuals' decision-making processes. An AI can collect, while unperceived, Big Data on the user: Roxane. It can profile her and tailor texts, images, videos, and music, manipulating Roxane into predetermined choices.[3] A large generative artificial intelligence model (LGAIM)[4] can enhance the possibility of computational manipulation (CM). It can make Roxane see and hear what is more likely to affect her decision-making processes, creating the perfect text accompanied by perfect images and sound on the perfect website.[5]

The one just described is not a hypothetical scenario. Multiple international, regional, and national bodies recognised the existence of CM and the possible threat to fundamental rights

[1] For a possible definition of artificial intelligence, see High-Level Expert Group on Artificial Intelligence, 'A Definition of AI: Main Capabilities and Scientific Disciplines' (18 December 2018), 7.

[2] Edmond Rostand, *Cyrano de Bergerac* (Paris: Larousse, 2007).

[3] See Section 4.2.

[4] Philipp Hacker, Andreas Engel and Marco Mauer, 'Regulating ChatGPT and other Large Generative AI Models' (2023) <https://arxiv.org/abs/2302.02337> accessed 8 April 2024.

[5] Regarding the use of generative AI, see, for example, <www.marktechpost.com/2023/04/11/12-creative-ways-developers-can-use-chat-gpt-4> accessed 8 April 2024.

resulting from its use.[6] As discussed further in this analysis, the EU has taken the first steps towards protecting individuals against CM.[7]

However, the protection given and imagined by the EU is still incomplete. This chapter argues that while manipulative AIs which rely on deception, such as that used by Cyrano, are addressed by existing EU legislation, some forms of CM, specifically if LGAIM is used in the manipulative process, still do not fall under the shield of the EU legislation. Therefore, this chapter argues in favour of redrafting existing EU legislation to cover every aspect of CM.

4.2 A BACKGROUND IN COMPUTATIONAL MANIPULATION (CM)

This section will provide a helpful context regarding CM to identify its legal issues, which will be addressed in the following sections.

AI is embedded in everyday use tools, such as smartphones and social media, which have become almost invisible and unperceived.[8] While unperceived, an AI can constantly acquire user data from every interaction on platforms, social media, apps, search engines, and websites. It can find connections not visible to a human being between the data, profile the users, and aim to persuade them, resulting in persuasive technology (PT). A PT can be defined as a technology that proactively influences human attitudes, behaviours, or both, changing, shaping, or reinforcing them in or against its users' interests.[9]

Even if a PT should not use coercion or deception,[10] it can use both. Moreover, it can use manipulation, which is definable as applying 'information technology that imposes hidden influences on users by targeting and exploiting decision-making vulnerabilities'.[11] Manipulation is strictly related to deception, which exploits specifically lack of information.[12] However, relying on lack of information is just one way to manipulate, which can be identified as Manipulation 1 (M1). A more subtle and dangerous way consists of searching willingly for

6 OHCHR 'Report on the Right to Privacy in the Digital Age' (3 August 2018) UN Doc A/HRC/39/29, 2; UNDESA 'Resource Guide on Artificial Intelligence (AI) Strategies' (June 2021); OECD 'Dark Commercial Patterns. OECD Digital Economy Papers n. 366 (October 2022) DSTI/CP(2021)12/FINAL; Council, 'A Study of the Implications of Advanced Digital Technologies (Including AI Systems) for the Concept of Responsibility within a Human Rights Framework' (DGI (2019) 05, 2019) 05, 35.

7 See Section 4.3.

8 Daniel Susser, 'Invisible Influence: Artificial Intelligence and the Ethics of Adaptive Choice Architectures' (Proceedings of the 2019 AAAI/ACM Conference on AI, Ethics, and Society, Honolulu 2019) <https://dl.acm.org/doi/10.1145/3306618.3314286> accessed 8 April 2024.

9 Brian J Fogg, Daniel Bedichevsky and Jason Tester, 'Persuasive Computing' (1998) 30 *ACM SIGCHI Bulletin* 71, 71; Harri Oinas-Kukkonen and Marja Harjumaa, 'Towards Deeper Understanding of Persuasion in Software and Information Systems' in *Proceedings of the 1st International Conference on Advances in Computer-Human Interaction* (Piscataway, NJ: IEEE, 2008), 202.

10 Brian J. Fogg, *Persuasive Technology: Using Computers to Change What We Think and Do* (Burlington, MA: Morgan Kaufmann, 2003), p. 1.

11 Daniel Susser, Beate Roessler and Helen Nissenbaum, 'Online Manipulation: Hidden Influences in a Digital World' (2018) 4 *Georgetown Law Technology Review* 1, 29. See also on the concept of manipulation Anne Barnhill, 'What Is Manipulation' in Christian Coons and Michael Weber (eds.), *Manipulation: Theory and Practice* (Oxford: Oxford University Press, 2014); Robert Noggle, 'The Ethics of Manipulation' in *The Stanford Encyclopedia of Philosophy* (Sum Edition, 2020) <https://plato.stanford.edu/archives/sum2020/entries/ethics-manipulation/> accessed 8 April 2024; Cass R. Sunstein, 'Fifty Shades of Manipulation' (2015) 1 *Journal of Behavioral Marketing* 213. Some authors consider that manipulation might not always be hidden. However, they recognise that it can be hidden. See Fleur Jongepier and Michael Klenk, *The Philosophy of Online Manipulation* (London: Taylor & Francis, 2022).

12 Timotheus Kampik, Juan Carlos Nieves and Helena Lindgren, 'Coercion and Deception in Persuasive Technologies' in Robin Cohen, Murat Sensoy and Timothy J. Norman (eds.), *Proceedings of the 20th International Trust Workshop* (Aachen: Sun SITE Central Europe, Aachen University, CEUR-WS, 2018); Susser, Roessler and Nissenbaum, 'Online Manipulation' (n. 11).

heuristic forms of reasoning and for cognitive biases that affect System 1, which can be identified as Manipulation 2 (M2). According to Kahneman, individuals have two decisional systems: System 1 is more primordial and operates instinctually and subconsciously, while System 2 is more rational and has more cognitive resources.[13] System 1 is vulnerable. PT can identify and use peripheral routes, personality traits, cognitive biases, and other decision-making vulnerabilities to affect it even without lacking information. It can use nudges,[14] leading the users in predetermined directions without their awareness and understanding. Some individuals, for example, will instinctively do what others do (social proof bias), what has been done for them (reciprocity bias), what an authority tells them to do (authority bias), or will act according to a mix of different cognitive biases and decision-making vulnerabilities.[15] A manipulative PT can identify the decision-making vulnerabilities of a single user and covertly undermine their decision-making processes.[16]

A manipulative PT that operates in the digital world has been called a *dark pattern*. According to the Organisation for Economic Co-operation and Development (OECD):

> Dark commercial patterns are business practices employing elements of digital choice architecture, in particular in online user interfaces, that subvert or impair consumer autonomy, decision-making or choice. They often deceive, coerce or manipulate consumers and are likely to cause direct or indirect consumer detriment in various ways, though it may be difficult or impossible to measure such detriment in many instances.[17]

PT's ability to undermine the decision-making processes of individuals is considerably enhanced using *compusuasion*,[18] which is the ability to persuade (and manipulate) through AI. The result of embedding an AI in a manipulative PT is what has been called *second-generation dark patterns*[19] and *hypernudges*.[20] If a nudge consists, for example, of putting the salad in front of the sweets to induce individuals to eat healthy food relying on the availability bias,[21] a hypernudge driven by an AI can reconfigure the entire (virtual) shop according to the cognitive biases of every individual that enters the shop.[22] Algorithmic-driven persuasion and manipulation techniques are different from any form of persuasion or manipulation individuals experienced in the past during an in-person interaction.[23] AI-driven manipulative PTs can

[13] Daniel Kahneman, *Thinking, Fast and Slow* (New York: Farrar, Straus and Giroux, 2017).

[14] Cass R. Sunstein, 'Nudges That Fail' (2017) 1 *Behavioural Public Policy* 4. On the effectiveness of nudges, see Stephanie Mertens et al., 'The Effectiveness of Nudging: A Meta-Analysis of Choice Architecture Interventions across Behavioral Domains' (2022) 119 *Proceedings of the National Academy of Sciences* 1.

[15] For a discussion regarding cognitive biases in persuasion, see Robert B. Cialdini, *The Psychology of Persuasion* (3rd ed., New York: HarperBus, 2021).

[16] Sunstein, 'Fifty Shades of Manipulation' (n. 11).

[17] OECD 'Dark Commercial Patterns. OECD Digital Economy Papers n. 366 (October 2022) DSTI/CP(2021)12/FINAL, 16.

[18] Bernardine M. C. Atkinson, 'Captology: A Critical Review' in Wijnand A. Ijsselsteijn et al. (eds.), *Persuasive Technology. Persuasive 2006. Lecture Notes in Computer Science*, Vol. 3962 (Berlin: Springer, 2006), p. 177.

[19] Karlstad University, Service Research Center (CTF), 'Underlagsrapport 2021:1 Barriers to a Well-Functioning Digital Market: Effects of Visual Design and Information Disclosures on Consumer Detriment' (2021) <https://medvetenkonsumtion.se/wp-content/uploads/2021/05/Konsumentverket-underlagsrapport-barriers-digital-market.pdf> accessed 8 April 2024.

[20] Karen Yeung, '"Hypernudge": Big Data as a Mode of Regulation by Design' (2017) 20 *Information, Communication & Society* 118.

[21] Eliza Mik, 'The Erosion of Autonomy in Online Consumer Transactions' (2016) 8 *Law, Innovation and Technology* 1.

[22] Sunstein, 'Fifty Shades of Manipulation' (n. 11).

[23] Ulysses Pascal, *Personalizing Persuasion Architecture: Privacy Harms and Algorithmic News Media* (New Orleans, LA: AAAI; 2018); Jeremy Rose and Oskar MacGregor, 'The Architecture of Algorithm-Driven Persuasion' (2021) 6 *Journal of Information Architecture* 1.

acquire and analyse an amount of data not manageable by a human being, profile and trap individuals in filter bubbles and their cognitive biases,[24] shape in real time the environment in which the users operate according to their profile, and hypernudge them to think in pre-settled ways, influencing System 1. Generative AIs considerably enhance the already existing ability of a PT to profile and hypernudge. A LGAIM can identify and create the perfect manipulative environment, shaping words, sounds, and images according to the identified cognitive profile and decision-making vulnerabilities of the single individual. Recent events such as the Cambridge Analytica scandal[25] underlined how far the capability of an AI system to manipulate has already been used.[26] A LGAIM enhances the possibility of targeting individuals with personalised manipulative processes. Images, texts, and sounds can feed the generative AI to produce the result that is most likely to match an individual's cognitive profile and biases.

Multiple bodies expressed concerns about PT's unprecedented ability to manipulate individuals via AI systems and considered its use a risk to the rights to autonomy, privacy, informational self-determination, and freedom of thought.[27] It has been suggested that the unprecedented abilities of AI require the recognition of a new fundamental right, the right to cognitive sovereignty or mental self-determination, identifiable as the right to self-determine thoughts free from interference from technology.[28] Following the concerns, the EU made the first moves against CM, which will be analysed in Section 4.3.

4.3 EXISTING EU LEGISLATION ON CM

The EU, aware of CM and its potential to undermine fundamental rights, started considering it from different perspectives and under different legislation. However, as it will be apparent from the following analysis, not every kind of CM is covered by existing EU legislation.

4.3.1 *The GDPR*

As expressed in the Proposal for an Artificial Intelligence Act (AIA),[29] the first resource against CM is, in the eyes of the EU, the General Data Protection Regulation (GDPR).[30] CM relies on

[24] Eli Pariser, *The Filter Bubble: What the Internet Is Hiding from You* (London: Penguin UK, 2011).

[25] Shoshana Zuboff, *The Age of Surveillance Capitalism: The Fight for the Future at the New Frontier of Power* (New York: Profile Books, 2019), p. 143.

[26] See also Ryan Calo, 'Digital Market Manipulation' (2013) 82 *George Washington Law Review* 995 for the use of manipulation in the digital market context.

[27] See, for example, OECD, 'Roundtable on Dark Commercial Patterns Online' (19 February 2021) DSTI/CP(2020)23/FINAL; Council, 'A Study of the Implications of Advanced Digital Technologies (Including AI Systems) for the Concept of Responsibility within a Human Rights Framework' (DGI (2019) 05, 2019) 05, 34; OHCHR 'Report on the Right to Privacy in the Digital Age' (3 August 2018) UN Doc A/HRC/39/29, 2; UNGA 'Promotion and Protection of the Right to Freedom of Opinion and Expression: Note by the Secretary-General' (29 August 2018) UN Doc A/73/348; UN Secretary-General's High-Level Panel on Digital Cooperation, 'The Age of Digital Interdependence' (June 2019) 17; European Parliament, 'Artificial Intelligence: Challenges for EU Citizens and Consumers' (PE631.043, 2019).

[28] Council, 'A Study of the Implications of Advanced Digital Technologies (Including AI Systems) for the Concept of Responsibility within a Human Rights Framework' (MSI-AUT (2018) 05, 2018) Appendix B; Jan-Christoph Bublitz, 'My Mind Is Mine!? Cognitive Liberty as a Legal Concept' in Elisabeth Hildt and Andreas G. Franke (eds.), *Cognitive Enhancement* (Berlin: Springer, 2013); Stefano Faraoni, 'Persuasive Technology and Computational Manipulation: Hypernudging out of Mental Self-Determination' (2023) 6 *Frontiers in Artificial Intelligence* 1.

[29] Commission, Proposal for a Regulation of the European Parliament and of the Council Laying Down Harmonised Rules on Artificial Intelligence (Artificial Intelligence Act) and Amending Certain Union Legislative Acts (Proposal) COM (2021) 206 final, 13.

[30] Regulation (EU) 2016/679 of the European Parliament and of the Council of 27 April 2016 on the protection of natural persons with regard to the processing of personal data and on the free movement of such data, and repealing

Big Data and profiling. Therefore, the GDPR, which imposes rules on acquiring and using such data, is the first protection against CM.[31] The European Data Protection Board (EDPB), aware of the theoretical value of the GDPR against CM, released Guidance on Dark Patterns in 2022.[32] The Guidance considers the relevance of Article 5 GDPR (containing the principles relating to processing data) and different dark patterns and aims to guide the design of online platforms.[33]

Multiple provisions in the GDPR can be considered relevant in CM. According to Article 13 (1) (c), the user should be informed of the purposes of the processing and its legal basis. Moreover, according to Article 13 (2) (f), the user should be informed of automated decision-making, including profiling.[34] According to Article 15 (h), the user has the right to be informed of the existence of automated decision-making, including profiling, referred to in Articles 22 (1) and (4). The user is entitled to receive information about the logic involved and the significance and the possible consequences of such processing for the data subject. According to Article 6, data processing is lawful if the data subject consents to it. The user shall consent to the data acquisition in profiling, according to Article 22 (2) (c). Consent, according to Article 7 and Recital 32, should be given by 'a clear affirmative act establishing a freely given, specific, informed and unambiguous indication of the data subject's agreement to the processing of personal data relating to him or her, such as by a written statement, including by electronic means, or an oral statement'. Consent must meet the standards of being explicit, informed, and specific. Consent should not regard just the data acquisition but should specifically concern the aim of the data acquisition and how this aim is to be achieved.[35]

Therefore, the GDPR contains provisions theoretically able to ensure that the user is informed regarding the existence of the persuasive process and gives their consent. However, it should be underlined that profiling, and therefore the grounds of CM, will be allowed if consent is *formally* given.[36] The problem that may arise is that the users are often uninformed about the data acquisition process and the purpose of the acquisition.[37] The amount of privacy-related information given daily renders it improbable, and maybe even impossible, for a user to read and understand every piece of information received. Sharing information with the

Directive 95/46/EC (General Data Protection Regulation) [2016] OJ L119/1. See Tal Z. Zarsky, 'Privacy and Manipulation in the Digital Age' (2019) 20 *Theoretical Inquiries in Law* 157; EDPB, 'Guidelines 3/2022 on Dark Patterns in Social Media Platform Interfaces: How to Recognise and Avoid Them' (14 March 2022).

[31] Xiuyan Shao and Harri Oinas-Kukkonen, 'How Does GDPR (General Data Protection Regulation) Affect Persuasive System Design: Design Requirements and Cost Implications' in H. Oinas-Kukkonen et al. (eds.), *Persuasive Technology: Development of Persuasive and Behavior Change Support Systems. Persuasive 2019. Lecture Notes in Computer Science*, Vol. 11433 (Berlin: Springer, 2019).

[32] EDPB 'Guidelines 3/2022 on Dark Patterns in Social Media Platform Interfaces: How to Recognise and Avoid Them' (n. 30).

[33] Ibid., 6.

[34] Profiling is defined in Art. 4.4.

[35] EDPS, A Preliminary Opinion on Data Protection and Scientific Research (6 January 2020), 18.

[36] Federico Galli, 'Online Behavioural Advertising and Unfair Manipulation between the GDPR and the UCPD' in Martin Ebers and Marta Cantero Gamito (eds.), *Algorithmic Governance and Governance of Algorithms*, Vol. 1 (Berlin: Springer, 2020).

[37] Article 29 Data Protection Working Party, 'Opinion 15/2011 on the Definition of Consent' (13 July 2011) 18–19; Christine Utz et al., '(Un)Informed Consent: Studying GDPR Consent Notices in the Field' (Proceedings of the 2019 ACM SIGSAC Conference on Computer and Communications Security) <https://dl.acm.org/doi/10.1145/3319535.3354212> accessed 8 April 2024; Midas Nouwens et al., 'Dark Patterns after the GDPR: Scraping Consent Pop-Ups and Demonstrating Their Influence' (Proceedings of the 2020 CHI Conference on Human Factors in Computing Systems, Honolulu 2020) <https://dl.acm.org/doi/10.1145/3313831.3376321> accessed 8 April 2024.

consumer can be inefficient.[38] Therefore, the given consent can result in a formal agreement, an *uncontract*, an annihilation of an agreement deprived of actual consent.[39]

The EU seems aware of the possible limits of the GDPR and has issued other legislation against CM, as will be discussed in the following section.

4.3.2 *The UCPD and Its Guidance*

The EU reconsidered existing legislation and directly addressed CM in the field of consumer law.[40] Section 4.3.2.1 will analyse the EU's background in consumer protection to state that the EU legislation has taken into account possible interference with the decision-making processes of individual consumers, attempting to ensure that consent based on information, awareness, and understanding is given. Then, Section 4.3.2.2 will analyse the recently released Guidance on the Interpretation of the Unfair Commercial Practice Directive (the UCPD, which regulates unfair business practices in EU law).[41] As will be discussed further, the Guidance directly addresses CM and dark patterns, confirming the EU's willingness to consider possible interference with the decision-making processes of individuals in the consumer field. However, the UCPD and its Guidance have limits, which will be addressed in Section 4.3.2.3.

4.3.2.1 The EU's Legal Background in the Field of Consumer Protection

There are long-standing concerns in Europe about aggressive doorstep sales tactics, telemarketing, and other situations in which consumers are vulnerable, which reflect correspondent EU policies such as:

(1) Directive 2005/29/EC, Unfair Commercial Practice Directive (UCPD);
(2) Directive 2011/83/EU, Consumer Rights Directive (CRD);[42]
(3) Guidance on the interpretation and application of Article 6a of Directive 98/6/EC, Price Indication Directive;[43]
(4) Guidance on the interpretation and application of Council Directive 93/13/EEC, Unfair Contract Terms Directive.[44]

[38] Omri Ben-Shahar and Carl E. Schneider, *More than You Wanted to Know* (Princeton, NJ: Princeton University Press, 2014).

[39] Zuboff, *The Age of Surveillance Capitalism* (n. 25), p. 219.

[40] See the EU consumer protection policy at <https://commission.europa.eu/law/law-topic/consumer-protection-law_en> accessed 8 April 2024.

[41] Commission Notice – Guidance on the interpretation and application of Directive 2005/29/EC of the European Parliament and of the Council concerning unfair business-to-consumer commercial practices in the internal market [2021] OJ C526/1; Council Directive 2005/29/EC of the European Parliament and of the Council of 11 May 2005 concerning unfair business-to-consumer commercial practices in the internal market and amending Council Directive 84/450/EEC, Directives 97/7/EC, 98/27/EC and 2002/65/EC of the European Parliament and of the Council and Regulation (EC) No 2006/2004 of the European Parliament and of the Council ('Unfair Commercial Practices Directive') [2005] OJ L149/22.

[42] Council Directive 2011/83/EU of the European Parliament and of the Council of 25 October 2011 on consumer rights, amending Council Directive 93/13/EEC and Directive 1999/44/EC of the European Parliament and of the Council and repealing Council Directive 85/577/EEC and Directive 97/7/EC of the European Parliament and of the Council [2011] OJ L304/64.

[43] Commission Notice – Guidance on the interpretation and application of Article 6a of Directive 98/6/EC of the European Parliament and of the Council on consumer protection in the indication of the prices of products offered to consumers [2021] OJ C526/130.

[44] Commission notice — Guidance on the interpretation and application of Council Directive 93/13/EEC on unfair terms in consumer contracts [2019] OJ C323/4.

In the legislation, the EU considered the possible lack of balance between a company and a consumer[45] and the consequent need to protect consumers from being exploited in their cognitive biases.[46] The EU legislation obliges the company to give information regarding the products and the transaction, believing that, in some circumstances, the consumer's consent could be inadequately formed and that more information is needed to make a proper decision,[47] even if it has already been considered that such information might not be an adequate remedy.[48]

Moreover, the EU believes that consent could result from aggressive techniques and attempts to avoid it. For example, according to the UCPD, Articles 5, 6, 7, 8, and 9, a company should abstain from unfair commercial practices (perpetrated via misleading actions or omissions) and aggressive commercial practices. Moreover, the EU believes that, in some circumstances, consumers need time to analyse contracts and think about their content to understand them properly.[49] The result is that according to Article 6 of the CRD, the consumer shall have a period of fourteen days to withdraw from a distance or off-premises contract without giving any reason.

The EU also tried to adapt to newly emerged commercial practices, constantly modifying its legislation. After the Communication 'A New Deal for Consumers', Directive (EU) 2019/2161 of the European Parliament and of the Council was published. This Directive amends the Unfair Contract Terms Directive and Price Indication Directive, UCPD and CRD.[50] Directive (EU) 2019/2161 expressly refers to techniques identifiable as dark patterns, such as 'submitting fake consumer reviews and endorsements, such as "likes" on social media'.[51]

Therefore, the EU legislation in the field of consumers took into account possible interference with the decision-making processes of individuals, relying on consent based on information, awareness, and understanding. Moreover, the EU aims to adapt existing legislation to newly emerging practices, as with Directive (EU) 2019/2161 and via the Guidance on the application of the UCPD, which will be considered in the following section.

However, as will be discussed further, the aim has not been wholly achieved, and the protection against computational manipulation leaves blind spots.

[45] According to Art. 2(a) of the UCPD, a 'consumer' means any natural person who, in commercial practices covered by the UCPD, is acting for purposes outside their trade, business, craft, or profession.

[46] Rossella Incardona and Cristina Poncibo, 'The Average Consumer, the Unfair Commercial Practices Directive, and the Cognitive Revolution' (2007) 30 *Journal of Consumer Policy* 21, 31; Jon D. Hanson and Douglas A. Kysar, 'Taking Behavioralism Seriously: The Problem of Market Manipulation' (1999) 74 *New York University Law Review* 630; Anne-Lise Sibony and Geneviève Helleringer, 'EU Consumer Protection and Behavioural Sciences' in Fabrizio Esposito (ed.), *Nudge and the Law: A European Perspective* (Oxford: Hart, 2015).

[47] Sibony and Helleringer, 'EU Consumer Protection' (n. 46); Incardona and Poncibo, 'The Average Consumer' (n. 46); Omri Ben-Shahar and Eric A. Posner, 'The Right to Withdraw in Contract Law' (2011) 40 *Journal of Legal Studies* 115; Omri Ben-Shahar, 'The Myth of the "Opportunity to Read" in Contract Law' (2009) 5 *European Review of Contract Law* 1.

[48] Ben-Shahar and Schneider, *More than You Wanted to Know* (n. 38); Incardona and Poncibo, 'The Average Consumer' (n. 46).

[49] Christian Twigg-Flesner, Reiner Schulze and Jonathon Watson, 'Protecting Rational Choice: Information and the Right of Withdrawal' in Geraint Howells, Iain Ramsay and Thomas Wilhelmsson (eds.), *Handbook of Research on International Consumer Law* (Cheltenham: Edward Elgar, 2018), p. 111.

[50] Council Directive (EU) 2019/2161 of the European Parliament and of the Council of 27 November 2019 amending Council Directive 93/13/EEC and Directives 98/6/EC, 2005/29/EC and 2011/83/EU of the European Parliament and of the Council as regards the better enforcement and modernisation of Union consumer protection rules [2019] OJ L328/7.

[51] Ibid., Art. 49.

4.3.2.2 The Guidance on the UCPD

The European Commission, in 2021, published guidance on the interpretation and application of the UCPD, which considers data-driven practices and dark patterns and expressly refers to manipulation.[52] However, as discussed in the following section, the possible protection of the users against CM is still insufficient.

The Commission recognised that persuading consumers has always existed and is essential to commercial practice. However, according to the Commission, the digital environment has changed the perspective, resulting in a new, unprecedented power connected to Big Data, AI, and the ability to modify dynamically in real time.[53] The Commission defines the knowledge resulting from the newly emerged technological reality as *superior*, based on aggregated data about consumer behaviour and preferences and on the possibility of adjusting in real time, continuously testing the effects of the practices on consumers to learn more about their behaviour.[54] The Commission stated that such practices might often occur without the full knowledge of the consumer and makes a distinction between highly persuasive advertising or sales techniques and commercial practices that may be manipulative.[55]

The perspective from which the Commission addressed the problem of manipulation is that of an average or vulnerable consumer (if the practice is highly personalised, that of a single person who was subject to the specific personalisation). The Guidance focuses on vulnerable consumers and undue influence[56] over them, resulting in aggressive commercial practices prohibited under Articles 8 and 9 of the UCPD. The Commission considered exploiting specific misfortune or circumstance of such gravity to impair the consumer's judgement, of which the trader is aware. Three examples are given in the Guidance:

- A trader can identify that a teenager is in a vulnerable mood due to events in their personal life. This information is subsequently used to target the teenager with emotion-based advertisements at a specific time.
- A trader is aware of a consumer's history with financial services and that a credit institution has banned them due to the inability to pay. The consumer is subsequently targeted with specific offers by a credit institution to exploit their financial situation.
- A trader is aware of a consumer's purchase history concerning games of chance and random content in a video game. The consumer is subsequently targeted with personalised commercial communications that feature similar elements to exploit their higher likelihood of engaging with such products.[57]

The Guidance also generally addresses dark patterns. The document underlines that the UCPD can be used to challenge the unfairness of such practices, in addition to other instruments in the EU legal framework, such as the GDPR, and states that 'any manipulative practice that materially distorts or is likely to distort the economic behaviour of an average or vulnerable consumer could breach the trader's professional diligence requirements (Art. 5), amount to a

[52] Guidance on the interpretation of the UCPD (n. 41).
[53] Ibid., 4.2.7.
[54] Ibid.
[55] Ibid.
[56] According to UCPD, Article 2 (j), undue influence means exploiting a position of power in relation to the consumer so as to apply pressure, even without using or threatening to use physical force, in a way that significantly limits the consumer's ability to make an informed decision.
[57] Guidance on the interpretation of the UCPD (n. 41), 4.2.7.

misleading practice (Art. 6–7) or an aggressive practice (Art. 8–9), depending on the specific dark pattern applied'.[58]

According to the professional diligence referred to in Article 5 UCPD, the Commission considered that traders should ensure that the design does not distort individuals' decisions. Some examples are then made in the Guidance of possible dark patterns relevant under UCPD Articles 6 and 7 (such as visually obscuring important information or ordering it in a way to promote a specific option, or using trick questions and ambiguous language such as double negatives), or under Article 8 of the UCPD (such as shaming the consumer into feeling guilty). A specific example of a dark pattern able to generate confusion is made in the document as follows:

> During the ordering process in an online marketplace, the consumer is asked several times to choose 'yes' and 'no': 'Would you like to be kept informed about similar offers? Would you like to subscribe to the newsletter? Can we use your details to personalise our offer?' Halfway through the click sequence, the buttons 'yes' and 'no' are reversed intentionally. The consumer has clicked 'no' several times, but now clicks 'yes' and accidentally subscribed to a newsletter.[59]

The Commission also addressed default interface settings, such as pre-ticked boxes, including the charge for additional services. According to the Commission, such practices can also breach the UCPD and data protection and privacy rules.

The Guidance states that practices labelled as dark patterns are already expressly prohibited and indicated in Annex I to the UCPD:

- 'Bait and Switch' (5 and 6 Annex I);
- Fake Countdowns (7 Annex I);
- Fake Scarcity of the Product (No. 18 Annex I);
- Fake Prizes (Nos. 19 and 31 Annex I);
- Fake Free Products (No. 20 Annex I);
- Nagging (No. 26 Annex I) (368);
- Misleading Free Trials and Subscription Traps.[60]

The Commission also considered the difficulty in unsubscribing, possibly in breach of Articles 7 and 9(d) UCPD:

> In order to unsubscribe from a digital service, the consumer is forced to take numerous non-intuitive steps in order to arrive at the cancellation link. These steps include 'confirmshaming', whereby the consumer is prompted, without reasoned justification, to reconsider their choice through emotional messages several times ('We're sorry to see you go', 'Here are the benefits you will lose') and 'visual interference', such as prominent images that encourage the user to continue with the subscription instead of cancelling.

Therefore, in the Guidance, the concepts of CM and dark patterns are recognised, addressed, and regarded as possibly covered by the UCPD. However, as discussed in the following section, the possible protection of the users is insufficient, as the UCPD cannot address every aspect of computational manipulation.

[58] Ibid.
[59] Ibid., 4.2.7.
[60] Ibid.

4.3.2.3 Some Limits of the UCPD and the Guidance in Addressing CM

The UCPD, even as interpreted by the Guidance, has relevant limits. First of all, the UCPD is a Directive and not a Regulation. Directives require EU countries to achieve a specific result but leave them free to choose how to do so, resulting in the possible different formulation and content of concepts.[61] For example, Italy has implemented the UCPD via the so-called Codice del Consumo.[62] Article 20 (2) of Codice del Consumo should correspond to Article 5 UCPD. However, in describing which commercial practices should be considered unfair, the Italian version of Article 5 UCPD inserts a word stating that the commercial practice should be regarded as unfair if it is contrary to professional diligence and is false. Article 5 UCPD requires a material distortion of the consumer's behaviour, a concept not corresponding to the meaning of false.

The second issue is that even if the Guidance addresses dark patterns and CM, it is not binding. Then, the UCPD applies solely to transactions involving a consumer, leaving outside of its scope transactions in which the other party is not a consumer. According to Article 2 (a) of the UCPD, a 'consumer' means any natural person who, in commercial practices covered by the UCPD, acts for purposes outside their trade, business, craft, or profession. Therefore, whenever a manipulative PT is used against an individual acting for purposes inside their trade, business, craft, or profession, the UCPD will not apply. For example, a sole practitioner, such as a solicitor, who buys a computer for their firm will not be protected by the UCPD. Similarly, a manipulative PT used by a company against another company or by a professional against another professional will fall outside the scope of the UCPD.

Moreover, even if the UCPD seems to be able to address some forms of intentional manipulation, personalised CM practices that affect System 1 without deception or undue influence (CM2)[63] remain outside the UCPD's provisions. The UCPD focuses more on false statements, coercion, and aggressive practices than manipulation. The provisions in Articles 6–9 UCPD protect consumers against misleading actions, omissions, and aggressive practices, which rely on omitting information, deception, or undue influence. Article 8 UCPD, then, prohibits commercial practices that 'significantly impairs or is likely to significantly impair the average consumer's freedom of choice or conduct with regard to the product and thereby causes him or is likely to cause him to take a transactional decision that he would not have taken otherwise'. The description of the prohibited commercial practices seems similar to the manipulation concept identified in this analysis.[64] However, Article 8 UCPD considers the use of harassment, coercion (including physical force), and undue influence, but not manipulation. The UCPD provides a list of presumed unfair activities in Annex 1. However, none of the currently listed activities adhere to CM2, ML (machine learning)-based personalised cognitive or emotional manipulation able to affect System 1 without coercion, deception, or taking advantage of special circumstances or minors.

Moreover, in its practical examples of manipulation and dark patterns reported above, the UCPD Guidance focuses on practices consisting of omitting information, or deception or undue influence that consists of exploiting severe circumstances such as age, non-access to credit, or addiction to gambling. However, computational manipulation does not necessarily rely on the absence of information, does not necessarily require deception or the

[61] European Commission, 'Primary versus Secondary Law' <https://ec.europa.eu/info/law/law-making-process/types-eu-law_en> accessed 8 April 2024. See also Consolidated version of the Treaty on European Union [2012] OJ C326/13.

[62] Decreto Legislativo 6 settembre 2005, n. 206.

[63] See Section 4.2.

[64] Ibid.

exploitation of severe circumstances, and may not even constitute pressure as required by Article 2 UCPD (j).[65]

A possible scenario of CM2 is the following. Party A, which sells e-cigarettes, acquired Big Data on Party B, a smoker who often coughs. Party B searched on Google for the possible causes of their coughing. The data was acquired in compliance with the GDPR with multiple privacy policies regularly signed. Party A analysed the data and profiled Party B at a segmentation level and, via interaction, at a personalisation level.[66] Party B constantly wears a watch that analyses their heartbeat and can geolocate who is wearing it. Party A discovered that Party B is sensitive to some specific cognitive biases, such as reliance on what others do, reliance on authority, and availability bias, and found that arguing with their father triggers an emotional reaction in Party B, resulting in shopping. For several months, Party A showed Party B content on different platforms regarding Party A's e-cigarette, produced through generative AI and tailored to Party B's preferences for images and sounds. Party A showed Party B's friends using it on social media and content concerning the government's health policy[67] on quitting smoking via e-cigarettes, shaping and reinforcing the need for an e-cigarette in an information bubble according to Party B's cognitive biases. One day, Party B argues with their father and writes about the arguing in a post on social media. Party B then goes for a walk, still in an emotional state, even if the circumstances are not severe. The heartbeat is higher than average, and the watch collects the data, including the geolocation. When Party B is near an e-cigarette shop, a suggestion is pushed on Party B's phone, which shows the e-cigarette sold by Party A and represents an actual existing commercial showing a famous influencer followed on social media by Party B, who fights and then relaxes smoking the e-cigarette, followed by a message generated by a generative AI and tailored to Party B. Party B enters the e-cigarette shop and buys the e-cigarette sold by Party A.

Borrowing Mik's words and applying them to this scenario, CM2 looks like a cat, even if it is genetically modified and more similar to a lion,[68] having computational power on its side. In this scenario, Party A deliberately designed and presented the options available to Party B to exploit decision-making biases using the knowledge and ability that solely an AI-driven system can have, enhanced by a generative AI system. Party A hyper-nudged the counterparty to the option preferred by the choice architect, encouraging Party B to enter into a contract 'by identifying the potential needs to be met by the contract'.[69] Party B chose the predicted option and agreed. The scenario described here remains outside the UCPD's provisions. It is based on personalised CM practices that affect System 1 without coercion, deception, or undue influence.

The general clause in Article 5 UCPD could be considered as opening the possibility of including CM without coercion, deception, or undue influence.[70] However, it should be underlined that Article 5 requires two elements:

- a breach of professional diligence (Section 4.3.2.1), and
- a material distortion of consumer decision-making (Section 4.3.2.2).

[65] Ibid.

[66] For the difference between segmentation and personalisation, see EISMEA, 'Behavioural Study on Unfair Commercial Practices in the Digital Environment: Dark Patterns and Manipulative Personalisation. Final Report' (April 2022) 33.

[67] UK Government, 'E-Cigarettes and Vaping Policy' <www.gov.uk/government/collections/e-cigarettes-and-vaping-policy-regulation-and-guidance#england%E2%80%99s-policy-on-e-cigarettes> accessed 8 April 2024.

[68] Mik, 'The Erosion of Autonomy' (n. 21), 23, referring also to Lawrence Lessig, 'The Law of the Horse: What Cyberlaw Might Teach' (1999) 113 *Harvard Law Review* 501.

[69] Martin Ebers, *Contracting and Contract Law in the Age of Artificial Intelligence* (Oxford: Hart, 2022), vi preface.

[70] Philipp Hacker, 'Manipulation by Algorithms. Exploring the Triangle of Unfair Commercial Practice, Data Protection, and Privacy Law' (2021) 29 *European Law Journal* 1; Galli, 'Online Behavioural Advertising' (n. 36); Incardona and Poncibo, 'The average consumer' (n. 46).

According to Article 2 (h) UCPD, professional diligence means 'the standard of special skill and care that a trader may reasonably be expected to exercise towards consumers, commensurate with honest market practice and/or the general principle of good faith in the trader's field of activity'. Determining what constitutes professional diligence in practice could be problematic, considering that every seller will be expected to try to persuade a customer. Indeed, it has been stated that the intentional targeting of cognitive biases should be considered a violation of professional diligence.[71] However, it is questionable if a seller should inform the customer of the specific cognitive biases affecting their decision.

Moreover, a violation of professional diligence could be erased by an expression of consent to targeting, profiling, and persuasion, which could also happen during the data acquisition phase and following the rules of the GDPR.[72] It should be noted that profiling and CM will be allowed if consent is formally given.[73] Therefore, the GDPR is questionably an effective solution against manipulative, persuasive technology, and it can also erase the possibility of application of Article 5 UCPD.[74]

It should then be considered that Article 5 UCPD requires a material distortion, according to Article 2 (e). A material distortion is described in the Article as an impairment of the ability to make an informed decision. The impairment causes the consumer to make a decision that they would not have taken otherwise. Regarding this second requirement, standard marketing practices use cognitive and emotional effects as part of advertisers' attempts to push consumers towards a specific purchase decision, such as using images of children, attractive features, stories, or music to sell products.[75] As previously noted, nudges are well-known in the literature.[76] Therefore, understanding when the threshold to material distortion is passed could be complex.[77] On the one hand, marketing is a necessary part of the economy. Conversely, a limit to what is acceptable in attempting to persuade consumers to purchase should be settled. A material distortion could be regarded as present if System 2 is completely overridden by System 1. According to the Guidance, however, this threshold is considered in the UCPD not from the perspective of the specific consumer part of the manipulative process but from the perspective of an average consumer, a reasonably well-informed, reasonably observant, and circumspect person.[78] As acknowledged in *Teekkanne*, the average consumer of EU law may be prone to ignore or misunderstand important information.[79]

[71] Jan Trzaskowski, 'Behavioural Innovations in Marketing Law' in Hans-W. Micklitz, Anne-Lise Sibony and Fabrizio Esposito (eds.), *Research Methods in Consumer Law* (Cheltenham: Edward Elgar, 2018); Hacker, 'Manipulation by Algorithms' (n. 70), 1.

[72] Hacker, 'Manipulation by Algorithms' (n. 70), 16.

[73] Galli, 'Online Behavioural Advertising' (n. 36).

[74] See Section 4.3.1.

[75] Regarding marketing practices and the impact on consumers see Trzaskowski, 'Behavioural Innovations' (n. 71); Mik, 'The Erosion of Autonomy' (n. 21); Hanson and Kysar, 'Taking Behavioralism Seriously' (n. 46); Reka Pusztahelyi, 'Emotional AI and Its Challenges in the Viewpoint of Online Marketing' (2020) 81 *Curentul Juridic, The Juridical Current, Le Courant Juridique* 13.

[76] See Section 4.2; Sunstein, 'Nudges that Fail' (n. 14).

[77] Galli, 'Online Behavioural Advertising' (n. 36), 88; Natali Helberger, 'Profiling and Targeting Consumers in the Internet of Things – A New Challenge for Consumer Law' (Digital Revolution: Challenges for Contract Law in Practice Conference, Munster 2016) <https://papers.ssrn.com/sol3/papers.cfm?abstract_id=2728717> accessed 8 April 2024.

[78] Hacker, 'Manipulation by Algorithms' (n. 70), 19, referring to Case C-210/96, Gut Springenheide and Tusky, ECLI: EU:C:1998:369, para. 31.

[79] Case C-195/14, *Bundesverband der Verbraucherzentralen und Verbraucherverbände – Verbraucherzentrale Bundesverband e.V. v. Teekanne GmbH & Co. KG.* [2015] OJ C236/16, para. 36–41. On the average consumer,

The concept of the average consumer under the UCPD appears adequate concerning commercial practices directed to the average public at a segmentation level. When a company uses statistics to understand the possible weaknesses of the general public and tries to persuade the general public, then considering a statistically average individual as a parameter to define which practice is unfair is appropriate. Instead, the perspective of an average consumer does not seem reasonable at a personalisation level. Contrasting granularity and individualisation with statistics is not efficient. If the company does not rely on statistics but on the personalised profile of a single individual, and if the company does not target the general public but a specific individual, the concept of an average consumer ceases to be efficient in contrasting possibly unfair practices. Personalised commercial manipulations should be seen from a personalised, not average, perspective. The unfair commercial practice should be analysed from the perspective of the single targeted individual. Moreover, in the presence of expressed written consent, the threshold of an average person will not be considered as passed under an objective test.[80]

According to all the above, the EU has recognised the existence of CM and has attempted to protect the users not solely with the GDPR but also with the legislation regarding consumers. Some applications of PT and manipulative PT could be considered relevant under the UCPD, with the above-mentioned limits. Consequently, in the single member states that received the UCPD, consumers will find local remedies against a PT that operates with coercion or deception, or exploits individual circumstances.

However, non-consumers and some applications of CM, specifically CM2, remain out of the scope of the UCPD, as in the example of the e-cigarette. According to the AIA, further protection against CM can be found in the digital service legislation,[81] which will be discussed in the following sections.

4.3.3 *The Digital Services Act (DSA)*

The DSA entered into force on 1 November 2022 and has been applied since 17 February 2024, with a first partial application in August 2023. The DSA focuses on online social networks and platforms that allow consumers to conclude distance contracts with traders and, as stated in Recital 1, are used by individuals daily. The DSA aims to ensure a safe, predictable, and trustworthy online environment, as indicated in Recital 12, taking information and online content specifically into account.

The DSA considers dark patterns in Article 25, stating that 'providers of online platforms shall not design, organise or operate their online interfaces in a way that deceives, manipulates or

see Galli, 'Online Behavioural Advertising' (n. 36); Incardona and Poncibo, 'The Average Consumer' (n. 46); Helberger, 'Profiling and Targeting Consumers' (n. 77).

[80] Joseph M. Perillo, 'The Origins of the Objective Theory of Contract Formation and Interpretation' (2000) 69 *Fordham Law Review* 427; Wayne Barnes, 'The Objective Theory of Contracts' (2008) 76 *University of Cincinnati Law Review* 1119; R. George Wright, 'Objective and Subjective Tests in the Law' (2017) 16 *University of New Hampshire Law Review* 121. Regarding the objective and subjective theories, see also Peter Meijes Tiersma, 'The Language of Offer and Acceptance: Speech Acts and the Question of Intent' (1986) 74 *California Law Review* 189; James Gordley, René David and Arthur Taylor Von Mehren, *International Encyclopedia of Comparative Law: Contracts in General; Ch. 2: Contract in Pre-commercial Societies and in Western History* (Tübingen: Mohr Siebeck, 1997); Robert Joseph Pothier, *Treatise on the Contract of Sale* (Clark, NJ: The Lawbook Exchange, 1999); Immanuel Kant, *The Philosophy of Law: An Exposition of the Fundamental Principles of Jurisprudence as the Science of Right* (Clark, NJ: The Lawbook Exchange, 2001); C. Massimo Bianca, *Diritto Civile. Il contratto*, Vol. 3 (Milano: Giuffrè, 2000), p. 407.

[81] See <https://digital-strategy.ec.europa.eu/en/policies/digital-services-act-package> accessed 8 April 2024.

otherwise materially distorts or impairs the ability of recipients of their service to make free and informed decisions'.

However, as stated in Recital 67, Article 25 should not be understood as preventing providers from interacting directly with service recipients and offering new or additional services to them. Advertising that is compliant with EU law should not be regarded as constituting dark patterns.

Article 25 should therefore be interpreted as covering prohibited practices falling within the scope of the DSA, and this provision refers to and applies solely to platforms: for example, social networks, content-sharing platforms, app stores, and online travel and accommodation platforms.[82] An online platform is defined in Article 2 (i) as

> a hosting service that, at the request of a recipient of the service, stores and disseminates information to the public unless that activity is a minor and purely ancillary feature of another service or a minor functionality of the principal service and, for objective and technical reasons, cannot be used without that other service, and the integration of the feature or functionality into the other service is not a means to circumvent the applicability [of the DSA].

In other words, it is questionable if the DSA considers under Article 25 the websites of sellers or intermediary services.

Furthermore, in Article 25, there are exemplified dark patterns (such as nagging and complex unsubscribing), which are not manipulative second-generation dark patterns in the meaning referred to above of being hidden and able to affect System 1 (CM2).

Article 25(2) states that the prohibition in paragraph 1 shall not apply to practices covered by the UCPD or the GDPR. Therefore, it is a subsidiary provision. Therefore, it should be taken into account that, as noted, the UCPD refers solely to consumers and does not address dark patterns, considered by the Guidance, with the limits described above.[83] Similarly, the GDPR does not consider dark patterns and has the shortcomings noted.[84] Therefore, CM2 does not fall under the shield of the DSA, the GDPR, or the UCPD.

In Article. 26 the DSA imposes the sharing of information with the consumer regarding which criteria are used for personalisation, as stated in Recital 70. However, as already noted, sharing information with the consumer is ineffective in preventing manipulation.[85] In addition, according to Article 19, Articles 25 and 26 do not apply to providers that qualify as small or micro-enterprises, leaving such enterprises free to use dark patterns.

The DSA also considers disinformation, imposing 'very large' platforms and 'very large' search engines to make a risk assessment regarding potential manipulation of the users (Article 34) by third parties. Even if that provision is relevant to this analysis, its limits are apparent. A risk assessment is not equivalent to a prohibition or obligation to control the use of the platform, and the risk assessment applies uniquely to 'very large' platforms and search engines, such as Meta or Google.

Therefore, the DSA leaves relevant blind spots concerning CM.

4.3.4 *Digital Markets Act (DMA)*

As stated in Article 1, the purpose of the DMA is to 'contribute to the proper functioning of the internal market by laying down harmonised rules ensuring for all businesses, contestable and fair

[82] See <https://ec.europa.eu/commission/presscorner/detail/en/ip_23_2413> accessed 8 April 2024.

[83] See Section 4.3.2.3.

[84] See Section 4.3.1.

[85] See for example Incardona and Poncibo, 'The Average Consumer' (n. 46), 24; Ben-Shahar and Schneider, *More than You Wanted to Know* (n. 38).

markets in the digital sector across the Union where gatekeepers are present, to the benefit of business users and end users'. A gatekeeper is defined in Article 2 (1) as an undertaking providing core platform services, such as intermediation, search engines, virtual assistants, or others identified in Article 2 (2) designated according to Article 3.

Article 3 states that an undertaking shall be designated as a gatekeeper if '(a) it has a significant impact on the internal market; (b) it provides a core platform service which is an important gateway for business users to reach end-users; and (c) it enjoys an entrenched and durable position, in its operations, or it is foreseeable that it will enjoy such a position in the near future'.'

The DMA considers personalised advertising and consent in Recital 37, stating rules for ensuring that consent to advertising is freely given.

The DMA refers to the decision-making processes in Recital 70 and Article 13(6), in which it is stated that gatekeepers should not engage in behaviours that would undermine the effectiveness of the prohibitions and obligations laid down in the DMA. Specifically, the behaviours not permitted are the design, 'the presentation of end-user choices in a non-neutral manner, or using the structure, function or manner of operation of a user interface or a part thereof to subvert or impair user autonomy, decision-making, or choice'. It is unclear, however, what the meaning of non-neutral is, and the second part of the provision is limited to the interface and does not consider the content. Therefore, hyper-nudging via personalised content without modifying the interface is allowed, using a generative AI as in the above example of the e-cigarette.[86]

The DMA also considers a dark pattern in Recital 63, stating that gatekeepers should not make it unnecessarily complicated for business users or end users to unsubscribe.

Even if the provisions help address CM, they refer uniquely to gatekeepers, leaving out of their scope of action every operator not identifiable as a gatekeeper as defined above. As with the DSA, websites are not considered under this provision. Moreover, small companies are out of the scope of this legislation. Therefore, they can use dark patterns and will not fall under the radar of the DMA.

Consequently, the DMA leaves relevant blind spots concerning CM.

4.3.5 *The Artificial Intelligence Act (AIA)*

In April 2021, the AIA was released. It was the first attempt to legislate in the field of AI at the EU level, and is at the centre of the legal debate regarding the possibility of legislating on artificial intelligence.[87] It establishes a list of prohibited AIs, following a risk-based approach. The list of banned practices comprises all those AI systems whose use is unacceptable because they violate fundamental rights. Modifications to the text[88] were proposed and approved by the European Parliament on 14 June 2023,[89] and further modifications have been approved in

[86] See Section 4.3.2.3.

[87] See for example Michael Veale and Frederik Zuiderveen Borgesius, 'Demystifying the Draft EU Artificial Intelligence Act – Analysing the Good, the Bad, and the Unclear Elements of the Proposed Approach' (2021) 22 *Computer Law Review International* 97; Nathalie A. Smuha et al., 'How the EU Can Achieve Legally Trustworthy AI: A Response to the European Commission's Proposal for an Artificial Intelligence Act' (2021) Social Science Research Network, 5 August <https://dx.doi.org/10.2139/ssrn.3899991> accessed 8 April 2024.

[88] Committee on the Internal Market and Consumer Protection Committee on Civil Liberties, Justice and Home Affairs, 'Draft Compromise Amendments on the Draft Report Proposal for a Regulation of the European Parliament and of the Council on harmonised rules on Artificial Intelligence (Artificial Intelligence Act) and amending certain Union Legislative Acts (COM(2021)0206 – C9 0146/2021 – 2021/0106(COD)) (KMB/DA/AS, 2023).

[89] Amendments adopted by the European Parliament on 14 June 2023 on the Proposal for a Regulation of the European Parliament and of the Council on laying down harmonised rules on artificial intelligence (Artificial Intelligence Act) and amending certain Union legislative acts (COM(2021)0206 – C9–0146/2021 – 2021/0106(COD)).

the final text.[90] The proposal addressed CM in Article 5. Article 5 (1) (a) stated in its first version that 'the placing on the market, the putting into service or the use of an AI system that deploys subliminal techniques beyond a person's consciousness to materially distort a person's behaviour in a manner that causes or is likely to cause that person or another person physical or psychological harm' should be prohibited. The new version of Article 5 (1) (a) contained in the AIA now states that:

> the placing on the market, putting into service or use of an AI system that deploys subliminal techniques beyond a person's consciousness or purposefully manipulative or deceptive techniques, with the objective to or the effect of materially distorting a person's or a group of persons' behaviour by appreciably impairing the person's ability to make an informed decision, thereby causing the person to take a decision they would not have taken otherwise in a manner that causes or is likely to cause that person, another person or group of persons significant harm [are prohibited].

The AIA, in the new version, still refers to a particular type of manipulation, the subliminal one. The impact assessment made by the Commission justified the choice by stating: 'Evidence suggests that AI supported products or services (toys, personal assistants etc.) can be intentionally designed or used in ways that appeal to the subliminal perception of individuals, thus causing them to take decisions that are beyond their cognitive capacities.'[91]

Regarding this choice, it should be underlined that a definition of subliminal technique is not present in the EU legislation. Directive 2007/65/EC stated in Article 3e (b) that 'audiovisual commercial communications shall not use subliminal techniques'. However, the Directive did not define the term.[92] The provision was reproduced in Directive 2010/13/EU Article 9(b), again without providing a definition, even in the amended version of 2018, known as the Audiovisual Media Services Directive.[93] There have been multiple attempts to identify subliminal techniques without a significant outcome and in the absence of a definition.[94] Subliminal manipulation could be a concept related to the famous story of James Vicary, who, in 1957, held

[90] Regulation (EU) 2024/1689 of the European Parliament and of the Council of 13 June 2024 laying down harmonised rules on artificial intelligence and amending Regulations (EC) No 300/2008, (EU) No 167/2013, (EU) No 168/2013, (EU) 2018/858, (EU) 2018/1139 and (EU) 2019/2144 and Directives 2014/90/EU, (EU) 2016/797 and (EU) 2020/1828 (Artificial Intelligence Act).

[91] Commission Staff, 'Working Document Impact Assessment Accompanying the Proposal for a Regulation of the European Parliament and of the Council Laying Down Harmonised Rules on Artificial Intelligence (Artificial Intelligence Act) and Amending Certain Union Legislative Acts' (SWD (2021) 85 final, 2021) 17. The document considers as evidence the following sources: US White House Office of Science and Technology Policy, 'Request for Information on the Future of Artificial Intelligence' (1 September 2016) <https://obamawhitehouse.archives.gov/webform/request-information-preparing-future-artificial-intelligence-0> accessed 8 April 2024; Maurice E. Stucke and Ariel Ezrachi, 'The Subtle Ways Your Digital Assistant Might Manipulate You' (2016) 29 *Wired* 2016; Judith Shulevitz, 'Alexa, Should We Trust You', *The Atlantic* (November 2018) <www.theatlantic.com/magazine/archive/2018/11/alexa-how-will-you-change-us/570844/> accessed 8 April 2024.

[92] Directive 2007/65/EC of the European Parliament and of the Council of 11 December 2007 amending Council Directive 89/552/EEC on the coordination of certain provisions laid down by law, regulation or administrative action in Member States concerning the pursuit of television broadcasting activities [2007] OJ L332/27.

[93] Directive 2010/13/EU of the European Parliament and of the Council of 10 March 2010 on the coordination of certain provisions laid down by law, regulation or administrative action in Member States concerning the provision of audiovisual media services (Audiovisual Media Services Directive) [2010] OJ L95/1; Directive (EU) 2018/1808 of the European Parliament and of the Council of 14 November 2018 amending Directive 2010/13/EU on the coordination of certain provisions laid down by law, regulation or administrative action in Member States concerning the provision of audiovisual media services (Audiovisual Media Services Directive) in view of changing market realities [2018] OJ L303/69.

[94] Randolph J Trappey III, *Brand Choice Revealing Customers' Unconscious-Automatic and Strategic Thinking Processes* (Berlin: Springer, 2005); Johan C. Karremans, Wolfgang Stroebe and Jasper Claus, 'Beyond Vicary's Fantasies: The

a press conference, sending subliminal commercials during motion pictures, namely 'Coca-Cola' and 'Eat Popcorn', which is reported to have led to unusually high sales of Coca-Cola and popcorn.[95] However, there is no certainty regarding this concept. The Committee on Legal Affairs of the European Parliament proposed to erase any reference to the concept of subliminality from the AIA.[96] The Committee on the Internal Market and Consumer Protection Committee on Civil Liberties, Justice and Home Affairs proposed instead to define subliminal techniques as 'techniques that use sensorial stimuli such as images, text, or sounds, that are below or above the threshold of conscious human perception'.[97] The final version of the AIA, in Recital 29, states a similar concept and refers to 'audio, image, video stimuli that persons cannot perceive as those stimuli are beyond human perception'.

However, the concept of a subliminal technique remains undefined and unclear in the AIA, which does not define it in the main body, as well as in the EU law and in the literature.[98] If subliminal had to be given the meaning of messages embedded for a few fractions of seconds in movies, as seems to be the case in Recital 29 of the AIA and in Recital 16 of the General Approach adopted by the Council of the European Union in November 2022,[99] the kind of technology described in this analysis would largely not be covered by this provision. The knowledge and use of cognitive biases described in Section 4.2 differ from the subliminal concept proposed by the Internal Market and Consumer Protection Committee on Civil Liberties, Justice and Home Affairs. A possible scenario is the one described above concerning e-cigarettes. In that scenario, we are not in the presence of messages embedded for a few fractions of seconds in movies. Not even dark patterns based on deception and coercion, such as nagging, social proof, confirmshaming, obstruction, sneaking, or urgency, are comparable to messages embedded for a few fractions of a second in movies. Consequently, there will be serious issues with determining the presence of subliminal manipulation, especially considering the lack of definition in the newly amended version of the AIA.

The new version of Article 5 (1) (a) distinguishes between a subliminal technique, manipulation, and deception. Therefore, computational manipulation is no longer linked solely to subliminal techniques, and it is recognised that manipulation and subliminal techniques are

Impact of Subliminal Priming and Brand Choice' (2006) 42 *Journal of Experimental Social Psychology* 792; Samantha J. Brooks et al., 'Exposure to Subliminal Arousing Stimuli Induces Robust Activation in the Amygdala, Hippocampus, Anterior Cingulate, Insular Cortex and Primary Visual Cortex: A Systematic Meta-Analysis of fMRI Studies' (2012) 59 *Neuroimage* 2962; Christina Bermeitinger and Benjamin Unger, 'Subliminal Persuasion: Psychological and Juristic History and Current State of Affairs' in Daphne Halkias (ed.), *Psychology and the Search for Certainty in Everyday Life* (Athens: Athens Institute for Education and Research, 2013); Erin J Strahan, Steven J. Spencer and Mark P. Zanna, 'Subliminal Priming and Persuasion: Striking while the Iron Is Hot' (2002) 38 *Journal of Experimental Social Psychology* 556.

95 Bermeitinger and Unger, 'Subliminal Persuasion' (n. 94), 152.

96 Committee on Legal Affairs, 'Draft Opinion of the Committee on Legal Affairs for the Committee on the Internal Market and Consumer Protection and the Committee on Civil Liberties, Justice and Home Affairs on the proposal for a Regulation of the European Parliament and of the Council laying down harmonised rules on artificial intelligence (Artificial Intelligence Act) and amending certain Union Legislative Acts' (2021/0106(COD), 2022) Amendments 62 and 63.

97 Committee on the Internal Market and Consumer Protection Committee on Civil Liberties, Justice and Home Affairs, 'Draft Report on the proposal for a Regulation of the European Parliament and of the Council on harmonised rules on Artificial Intelligence (Artificial Intelligence Act) and amending certain Union Legislative Acts (COM2021/0206 – C9-0146/2021 – 2021/0106(COD))' 2021/0106(COD) (2021/0106(COD), 2022) Amendment 65.

98 For an analysis of the concept and relative sources, see Rostam J. Neuwirth, 'Law, Artificial Intelligence, and Synaesthesia' (2022) 39 *AI & Society* 901–912.

99 General Secretariat of the Council, 'Note Interinstitutional File 2021/0106(COD)' (14336/22, 2022).

separate concepts. However, the new version of the Article requires, in between others, three new elements to which special attention shall be given: (1) the technique used impairs the ability to make an informed decision; (2) there is a causal link between the requisite expressed in (1) and a decision that the individual would not have taken otherwise; (3) the presence of significant harm.

The first requisite of the new Article 5 (1) (a) links the manipulation concept to that of *informed* decision. Therefore, the provision links manipulation to information, implying that it should be lacking or distorted. However, according to what was stated above, lacking or distorted information is just one possible way manipulation can operate (M1).[100] In the example of the e-cigarette, information is given and is correct. The issue with CM is not whether the decision is informed but whether the decision can be considered as *taken*. It resides in the fact that the AI system covertly exploits shortcuts to System 1,[101] impairing the right to mental self-determination, the right to create a thought.[102] Not just an *informed* decision but any decision can be impaired. The new formulation still does not cover the example of the e-cigarette and, consequently, CM2.

Article 5 (a) now requires a direct causal link between the manipulation and the decision, which can be difficult, if not impossible, to investigate and prove. Investigating the mind of an individual in order to reconstruct the decision-making process (excluding any other causal factors to the decision) has already been proven to be highly challenging.[103]

Another element in the new formulation of Article 5 (1) requires further reflection. In the first version, the Article required the AI to cause physical or psychological harm to be prohibited, overly restricting the application of Article 5. The Article did not refer to economic harm. The choice made in the first version is explained by Gabriele Mazzini, who drafted the proposal, stating that the economic harm is better protected by different EU legislation.[104] Specifically, according to Mazzini, the CRD, the DSA, and the UCPD should protect individuals against manipulative practices not considered under the AIA.[105] However, the CRD and the UCPD refer solely to consumers. The shortcomings of the UCPD and the DSA must be considered. Furthermore, the concept of psychological harm is unclear. For example, it could be questioned whether the mere fact of being subject to profiling or being exposed to a behaviour modification could be considered psychological harm or if an observable medical condition is needed to consider psychological harm as existing.

In the new version of Article 5, the required harm is no longer referred to as physical or psychological. However, the modified Article 5 (1) now requires *significant* harm. It is questionable if harm which results from CM, if not significant, should be excluded from the provision. Even with little harm from an economic perspective, as in the example of the e-cigarette, the use of CM can impair the right to autonomy and mental self-determination. Therefore, some kinds of CM remain unprotected – those able to affect everyday common transactions, as in the example of the e-cigarette.

[100] See Sections 4.2 and 4.3.2.3.

[101] See Section 4.2.

[102] See note 28.

[103] In this regard, consider the literature referred to in note 80 regarding the objective test. As Lord Blackburn stated in *Brogden v. Metropolitan Railway Co.* (1877) 2 App Cas 666, 692, citing Brian CJ: 'for it is trite law that the thought of man is not triable, for even the devil does not know what the thought of man is'.

[104] Gabriele Mazzini and Salvatore Scalzo, 'The Proposal for the Artificial Intelligence Act: Considerations around Some Key Concepts' in Carmelina Camardi (ed.), *La Via Europea per l'Intelligenza Artificiale* (Padova: Cedam, 2022), p. 24.

[105] Ibid.

Finally, arguably, the most crucial observation is that Article 5 (1) (a) refers, among others, to ex post requisites. Specifically, it refers to the 'effect' of distorting a behaviour, the causation of a decision, and the presence of significant harm. Considering its formulation and possible scenarios of its application in reality, the Article does not require just a potential presence of the requisites but an actual presence. It is questionable, for example, how the EU intends to determine ex ante that a manipulative AI can cause not only general harm but *significant* harm. Therefore, if the technology has to be prohibited, it can be identified and scrutinised just *after* the technology has been used, the manipulation has occurred, and significant harm is already present. Therefore, manipulative technology will likely be created and used, with the remote possibility of considering ex post if manipulation occurs, with all the limits underlined above. It seems that a prohibition should erase the possibility of using AI for manipulation ex ante and not require waiting for its existence to identify it ex post. The actual formulation is equivalent to stating that to understand if a gun is prohibited, it should be necessary to wait until it is used to shoot an individual.

In the AIA, the EU considers other AI technologies that must be banned that are relevant to CM. The first is an AI system that exploits vulnerabilities, materially distorting the behaviours of individuals.[106] In its first version, this provision looked at the distortion and manipulation of human behaviours, which happen at a group level, not at an individual level. Thus, the first version of this provision referred to a more complex and structured behavioural change, concerning multiple individuals with similar characteristics. The modified version of this Article prohibits an AI that is able to exploit the vulnerabilities at an individual and group level. Therefore, the partition between a single individual and a group is lost in the new formulation, and a reference to a group is also present in the new formulation of Article 5 (1) (a). The two provisions, therefore, overlap.

Moreover, the new formulation refers to the general concept of vulnerability of a person or of a specific group of persons due to their age, disability, or a specific socio-economic situation. Article 5, therefore, considers vulnerable individuals. However, it is unclear how this provision differs from the previous one regarding manipulation. Manipulation exploits routes to System 1, which are vulnerabilities in the decision-making process of an individual that affect their behaviour.[107] The two provisions refer to the same concept, but the second provision does not use the term manipulation and does not require all the elements of the previous one, including the reference to an informed decision and a causal link. CM can rely on different shortcuts to System 1, including age, disability, or a specific situation. Article 5 (1) (a) does not define manipulation, and the modified version of Article 5 (1) (b) does not mention, for example, cognitive biases in the vulnerabilities.[108] Therefore, not only is the difference between the two provisions unclear, but it can also be deduced by the formulation of this second provision that

[106] Art. 5 (1) (b), in the first version approved by the Parliament, stated that 'an AI system that exploits any of the vulnerabilities of a person or a specific group of persons, including characteristics of such person's or a such group's known or predicted personality traits or social or economic situation age, physical or mental ability with the objective or to the effect of materially distorting the behaviour of that person or a person pertaining to that group in a manner that causes or is likely to cause that person or another person significant harm' is prohibited. The new version states that 'the placing on the market, putting into service or use of an AI system that exploits any of the vulnerabilities of a natural person or a specific group of persons due to their age, disability or a specific social or economic situation, with the objective, or the effect, of materially distorting the behaviour of that person or a person belonging to that group in a manner that causes or is reasonably likely to cause that person or another person significant harm' is prohibited.

[107] See Section 4.2.

[108] Ibid. for cognitive profiles.

CM prohibited under Article 5 (1) (a) cannot occur if an AI uses vulnerabilities such as age, disability, or a specific socio-economic situation.

Moreover, as with Article 5 (1) (a), the new possible formulation of this provision requires significant harm, with the associated shortcomings. Furthermore, Article 5 (1) (b) requisites are ex post requisites with the noted consequences.

The new version of Article 5 introduces further confusion. Article 5 (1) (g), states:

> the placing on the market or putting into service for this specific purpose, or the use of biometric categorisation systems that categorise individually natural persons based on their biometric data to deduce or infer their race, political opinions, trade union membership, religious or philosophical beliefs, sex life or sexual orientation [are prohibited]; this prohibition does not cover any labelling or filtering of lawfully acquired biometric datasets, such as images, based on biometric data or categorizing of biometric data in the area of law enforcement.

It is unclear what 'this specific purpose' means because it is unclear which specific purpose the sentence refers to. Moreover, this provision seems to forbid biometric categorisation systems, but only those that use biometric data to deduce specific knowledge about an individual; sensitive data identified in the provision, such as race or religion. It is not prohibited to use categorisation systems to infer psychological or behavioural characteristics. The AIA defines biometric-based data, stating in Article 3 (34) that 'biometric data' means 'personal data resulting from specific technical processing relating to the physical, physiological or behavioural characteristics of a natural person, such as facial images or dactyloscopic data'.[109] An AI relies on observable data, and shortcuts to decision-making vulnerabilities can be identified through an individual's behaviour (for example, identifying that an individual tends to do what others do or all the cognitive biases in the example of the e-cigarette), resulting in an individual's categorisation. Therefore, it is not prohibited under Article 5 (1) (g) to categorise individuals by inferring from their biometrics their cognitive filters and cognitive biases and, more generally, their shortcuts to System 1. Therefore, Article 5 allows the foundation of manipulation.

Moreover, the concept of biometric-based data appears in another provision. The new formulation of the AIA, in Article 5 (1) (f), prohibits AI from inferring the emotions of a natural person. According to the new version of Article 3 (1) (39), 'emotion recognition system' means 'an AI system for the purpose of identifying or inferring emotions or intentions of natural persons on the basis of their biometric data'. However, Article 5 (1) (f) limits its scope to workplaces and educational institutions. Therefore, inferring the emotions and intentions of individuals in fields different from workplace and education is allowed. In the excluded fields, it is allowed to deduce shortcuts to System 1 which are based on emotions, thoughts, states of mind, and intentions. Therefore, it is allowed to identify the basis for CM in commerce, for example.

Consequently, on one side, Article 5 prohibits some kinds of computational manipulation in (1) (a) and (b) (with the confusion in the concepts and the limits already underlined). However, on the other side, the AIA allows the basis of computational manipulation, allowing biometric categorisation relevant for manipulation in Article 5 (1) (g) and in every field different from those indicated in Article 5 (1) (f).

109 The notion of biometric data is also considered in Art. 4(14) of Regulation (EU) 2016/679 of the European Parliament and of the Council and specified in the new version of Recital 7 AIA as follows: 'Biometrics-based data are additional data resulting from specific technical processing relating to physical, physiological or behavioural signals of a natural person, such as facial expressions, movements, pulse frequency, voice, key strikes or gait, which may or may not allow or confirm the unique identification of a natural person.'

Article 5 (8) states that 'This Article shall not affect the prohibitions that apply where an artificial intelligence practice infringes other Union law'. Therefore, it is a subsidiary provision with the noted shortcomings of different legislation and an apparent possible overlapping.

The AIA, therefore, contains provisions that complement the GDPR, the UCPD (as recently interpreted), the DSA, and the DMA in protecting individuals against CM. However, the EU's existing legislation leaves out of its scope the kind of CM which, also through the use of LGAIM, can affect System 1 but is not subliminal and does not use deception or false information, undue influence, or that does not cause relevant harm, still impairing the right to mental self-determination,[110] as in the example of the e-cigarette.

4.4 CONCLUSIONS

A scenario can be imagined in which an AI system can acquire Big Data on a user, Roxane, and attempt to manipulate her, as Cyrano did. However, an AI-led manipulative system is not Cyrano. It has computational power on its side, and it does not have good intentions. It might not rely on deception, as Cyrano did. The data collected on the user will not simply be basic preferences or similar information that Cyrano could acquire.

The AI system will have access to an unprecedented amount of data on the target: personal preferences, such as favourite flowers, colours, places, music, political ideas, attitude towards exercising, number and cause of termination of previous relationships, and any other information that can be used to induce positive feelings in Roxane towards a potential partner. The AI system will be able to identify cognitive filters and cognitive biases, routes to Roxane's System 1, such as if she conforms to the opinion of others, if she tends to do what her parents would like her to do, or if she tends to oppose them. Then, through LGAIM, the manipulative system will generate the perfect messages with the perfect words, images, colours, and music on the perfect website. The unperceived AI system will constantly change and shape according to Roxane's cognitive profile until the target is achieved. The messages are not used, as Cyrano did, to win the beloved's love. A computational manipulative AI can change and shape any attitude and behaviour, from product preferences to political ideas. This technology can undermine individual autonomy and mental self-determination.

As apparent from the analysis conducted in Section 4.3, the EU approach to CM cannot preserve individuals from every interference in their decision-making processes perpetrated by a manipulative AI-driven system, specifically if an LGAIM is used in the manipulative process. The legislation has shortcomings, creates confusion, and leaves blind spots. The concept of subliminal manipulation under Article 5 (1) (a) is unclear and undefined. Article 5 (1) (a) does not define manipulation but links its concepts to information, leaving the kind of computational manipulation that does not rely on false or misleading information out of its scope. Moreover, the Article requires a causal link, which is difficult, if not impossible, to prove. The concept of manipulation is blurred between the provisions of Article 5 (a) and Article 5 (b), opening the concept to interpretation and confusion. The requisites of these provisions are ex post requisites, allowing the use of CM and relying, therefore, on the prohibition of technology after it has already been used, losing the functionality of a prohibition, which should be to avoid harm and not to let it happen in order to identify its existence. Article 5 prohibits some kinds of manipulation in (1) (a) and (b), but it allows the basis of manipulation with biometric categorisation relevant for manipulation in (1) (g) and in every field different from those indicated in

[110] Hacker, 'Manipulation by Algorithms' (n. 70), 38.

Article 5 (1) (f). The Article does not apply to CM that causes non-significant harm, and in any case, not to a scenario such as that of the e-cigarette.

Furthermore, the legislation referred to in the AIA, which, in the EU's opinion, should protect against different kinds of manipulation, has other shortcomings. The GDPR will not protect individuals when formal consent to personalisation and profiling is present. The DSA and the DMA leave websites, small platforms, or small businesses that use computational manipulation out of their scope. Moreover, Article 25 of the DSA does not apply to what is already protected by the GDPR and the UCPD. The UCPD and its Guidance leave non-consumers and CM2 out of their scope.

Therefore, the existing EU legislation should be reconsidered to render it coherent, to include non-consumers and the kind of CM able to covertly identify and exploit routes to System 1 via LGAIM that is not subliminal and does not use deception or false information, or undue influence, and that does not cause relevant harm but still impacts the right to mental self-determination of individuals.

5

Unnatural Selection?

A Darwinian Reading of the Economic Consequences of Generative AI on the Art Market

Jerome De Cooman

5.1 INTRODUCTION

March 1884. The Supreme Court of the United States held in *Burrow-Giles* that a portrait photograph is copyrightable.[1] The Court explained that even if photography is by definition a mechanical process that takes a snapshot of reality, the author can still exercise control during the creative process.

December 2011. The European Court of Justice (ECJ) reached the same conclusion in *Painer*. A portrait photograph is protected by copyright if the photographer was able to make 'free and creative choices' during its production.[2]

February 2023. The US Copyright Office (USCO) held that the images contained within Kristina Kashtanova's comic book *Zarya of the Dawn* and drawn by a generative artificial intelligence (GenAI) were not copyrightable.[3] Referring to *Burrow-Giles*, the Office concluded that the user of a GenAI lacks 'sufficient control over the generated images.'[4]

April 2023. German photographer Boris Eldagsen declined the award for the Creative Open Competition Category of the 2023 Sony World Photography Award after having revealed it was an AI creation.[5] He explained that he willingly misled the jury in order to publicly engage in an open discussion on the future of photography.

What can be learnt from that background? First, *Burrow-Giles* and *Painer* teach us that the use of a machine in the creation of a work does not prevent it from being copyrighted as long as the human user is able to exercise a certain creative control over the creation. Second, the USCO decision related to *Zarya of the Dawn* suggests that users of GenAI do not reach the required threshold. Third, the declined photography award suggests that human-made and machine-

[1] *Burrow-Giles Lithographic Co. v. Sarony* [1884] 111 US 53, 60.

[2] Case C-145/10, *Eva-Maria Painer v. Standard Verlag GmbH and others*, ECLI:EU:C:2011:798, §94.

[3] United States Copyright Office, 'Zarya of the Dawn (Registration # VAu001480196)', 21 February 2023, https://copyright.gov/docs/zarya-of-the-dawn.pdf.

[4] Ibid., 9.

[5] Matt Novak, 'Artist Reveals His Award-Winning "Photo" Was Creating Using AI', *Forbes*, 17 April 2023, www.forbes.com/sites/mattnovak/2023/04/17/artist-reveals-his-award-winning-photo-was-created-using-ai/?sh = 3aa5e812fofb.

enabled artworks are indistinguishable.[6] This indistinguishability implies asymmetric information: artists do know whether the artwork is machine-enabled or human-made while beholders do not. George Akerlof seminally described asymmetric information as a 'lemons problem'.[7] When buyers ('beholders') are unable to distinguish good-quality (known as 'peaches') from poor-quality (known as 'lemons') products (artworks), they assess quality on average. If sellers have an incentive to cheat, buyers internalise the risk of buying a poor-quality product at the price of a good-quality one. Therefore, the sale price of peaches is systematically lower than their value while the sale price of lemons is higher than what they are worth. Consequently, sellers of peaches withdraw from the market. This further erodes the average quality of available product and, eventually, the market collapses.

The art market constitutes fertile ground for the lemons problem, a fortiori with the advent of GenAI: since copyrightable human-made artworks and uncopyrightable machine-enabled ones are indistinguishable, sellers of the latter are incentivised not to disclose whether AI was involved in the creation process.[8] This has economic consequences given that copyright is an exclusive property right that grants its owner a temporary monopoly.[9] Assuming therefore that the market value of a machine-enabled artwork (disclosed as such) is lower than the market value of a human-made one, art market buyers will internalise the average risk of being sold a machine-enabled artwork at the price of a human-made one. This, in turn, suggests that human-made artists cannot receive the true value associated with their artistic production.

This chapter proposes a Darwinian reading of this market inefficiency. If Charles Darwin had been faced with the lemons problem, he would probably have reached the same conclusion as Akerlof: the exclusion of one type of product from the market. He explained that 'if one species has *any advantage whatever over another*, it will in a very brief time *wholly or in part supplant it*'.[10] Asymmetric information constitutes such advantages that allows dishonestly sold machine-enabled products (the advantaged species) to drive human-made products (the other species) out of the market (one species supplants the other). Yet, for Darwin, this 'struggle for existence' refers to the process by which only the fittest species survive.[11] The survival of machine-enabled artworks at the expense of human-made art seems not in line with natural selection that 'acts solely through the preservation of variations in some way advantageous, which consequently endure'.[12] In economic terms, natural selection is akin to competition *on the merits*. This means that 'firms must compete through the intrinsic qualities of their products rather than through extraneous conditions'.[13] The ECJ has confirmed that 'competition on the merits may, by definition, *lead to the departure from the market* or the marginalisation of competitors that are less efficient and so less attractive to consumers from the point of view of, among other things,

6 This chapter endorses the terminology suggested by Jane C. Ginsburg and Luke Ali Budiardjo, 'Authors and Machines' (2020) 34(1) *Berkeley Technology Law Journal* 343–448 (who explained at 348n17 that it is more relevant to use 'enabled' rather than 'generated' to emphasise that a machine does not produce the output of its own volition but that it is a human who creates the output with the assistance of a machine).

7 George Akerlof, 'The Market for "Lemons": Quality Uncertainty and the Market Mechanism' (1970) 84(3) *Quarterly Journal of Economics* 488–500.

8 Jerome De Cooman, 'When Art Becomes a Lemon: The Economics of Machine-Enabled Artworks and the Need for a Rule of Origin' (2023) 5(1) *Law, Technology and Humans* 24–39.

9 Justine Pila and Paul Torremans, *European Intellectual Property Law* (2nd ed., Oxford: Oxford University Press, 2019).

10 Charles Darwin, *On the Origin of Species by Means of Natural Selection, or the Preservation of Favoured Races in the Struggle for Life* (London: John Murray, 1859) 402 (emphasis added).

11 Ibid., 60–79.

12 Ibid., 109.

13 Harry S. Gerla, 'Competition on the Merits – A Sound Industrial Policy for Antitrust Law' (1984) 36(4) *University of Florida Law Review* 553–590, 558.

price, choice, quality or innovation'.[14] In other words, natural selection and competition on the merits both lead the more efficient species or products (respectively) to prevail while others vanish. This is not the outcome of the lemons problem. In the latter case, the selection of the prevailing species is more artificial than natural. There is no competition on the merits between human-made and machine-enabled artworks. The latter will only prevail because of asymmetric information (extraneous condition) and not due to its intrinsic qualities (one species did not prevail because it was most fitted to its environment but because of farm breeding).[15] The lemons problem provokes unnatural selection.

This is not inevitable, however. Darwin went on to explain that 'if both [species] are equally well fitted for their own places in nature, both probably will hold their own places and keep separate for almost any length of time'.[16] This chapter explores how to ensure both human-made and machine-enabled artworks are well-fitted for the art market. It argues that a rule of origin inspired by art authentication and EU customs and tax law is a way of ensuring that both types of artworks hold their own place and keep separate in their ecosystem. To build the argument, this chapter proposes a fivefold structure. Section 5.1 sets the scene by defining the lemons problem and transposing it on the art market. Section 5.2 suggests the lemons problem is an appropriate framework to evaluate the economic consequences of GenAI on that market. Section 5.3 recommends adopting a rule of origins to erase asymmetric information and suggests workable enforcement solutions. Section 5.4 summarises the argument and concludes that the proposed solution is not a Luddite, but a proportionate response to the (potential) economic consequences of AI on the art market.

5.2 THE LEMONS PROBLEM IN THE ART MARKET

Imagine that in the market for used cars there are only two different types of products: the good-quality used cars (in American slang, the peaches) and the bad-quality ones (the lemons).[17] Being in the used car market, sellers know whether the car being sold is a lemon or not. Buyers do not.[18] This asymmetric information incentivises dishonest sellers to sell a lemon at the price of a peach.[19] Buyers, in turn, will value a particular car based on the average probability that that car is a peach (assuming they are risk neutral) and adapt their willingness-to-pay accordingly. Therefore, the market price equilibrium will systematically be lower than what a peach is worth, but higher than what a lemon is worth.

This is market inefficiency par excellence: asymmetric information forces buyers to misallocate their resources, resulting in a systemic inefficiency that harms both buyers' and other sellers' welfare.[20] Under these conditions, the rational behaviour of sellers of peaches is either to leave the market, or to voluntarily decrease the quality of their products.[21] Perhaps more critical, the more sellers of peaches leave the market, the greater the probability of selling a lemon at the

[14] Case C-413/14 P, *Intel v. Commission*, ECLI:EU:C:2017:632, §134. See Nicolas Petit, 'The Judgement of the EU Court of Justice in Intel and the Rule of Reason in Abuse of Dominance Cases' (2018) 43(5) *European Law Review* 728–750.

[15] Darwin, *Origin of Species*, 446.

[16] Ibid., 402.

[17] Akerlof, 'Lemons'.

[18] Jonathan Levin, 'Information and the Market for Lemons' (2001) 32(4) *The RAND Journal of Economics* 657–666.

[19] Charles Wilson, 'Adverse Selection' in John Eatwell, Murray Milgate and Peter Newman (eds.), *Allocation, Information and Markets* (Cham: Springer, 1989) 31–34.

[20] Ibid., 12.

[21] Jack Hirschleifer, 'Where Are We in the Theory of Information' (1973) 63(2) *American Economic Review* 31–39, 37.

price of a peach and, therefore, the lower the market price equilibrium. This leads the sellers of moderate-quality products to leave the market, hence further increasing the risk of dishonest deals and decreasing the market price equilibrium accordingly, until the market collapses.[22] The ever-decreasing product quality and price suggest that, ultimately, the only market equilibrium price is null and therefore that no transaction occurs.[23]

Leaving aside the market for used cars, the lemons problem (if slightly adjusted) is also of interest for artworks. Identifying peaches and lemons among artworks is a tricky exercise. Art is the example par excellence of a market where quality is multidimensional, unquantifiable, and irreducibly subjective.[24] This explains why some people are willing to pay an astronomical price 'for what appears to be a watercolour sketch [that] was likely painted by Jackson Pollock [while] many more aesthetically pleasing works have sold for significantly less'.[25]

For the sake of this chapter, a line has to be drawn between *aesthetic value* and *market value*.[26] This is not alien to the market for artworks: price reacts negatively when a work is discovered to be a fake or a forgery.[27] Leonardo da Vinci's *Salvator Mundi* is the most striking example.[28] In the 1950s, it was sold as a copy of the original, completed by one of da Vinci's students for approximately US$60 (approximately US$755 today).[29] After its authentication as a genuine Da Vinci, it was auctioned for US$450.3 million in 2017 (approximately US$557.3 million today). However, experts expressed doubts afterwards and the painting has not been exhibited since.[30] Authentication did not change the aesthetic value of *Salvator Mundi*, but did multiply its market value by more than 700,000 – before disappearing from the museum's walls.[31] It is simply a fact that, once discovered, forgeries become monstrous doppelgängers. Yet this devaluation does not suggest the aesthetic value has decreased: only the market did.[32] Therefore, aesthetic value is not the prime factor of market value;[33] authentication is.[34] This makes sense, given that the main reason to acquire an artwork today is its resale potential: authentication ensures a proper return on investment.[35]

22 Akerlof, 'Lemons', 491 and 495.

23 Wilson, 'Adverse Selection', 31.

24 Hirschleifer, 'Theory of Information', 37.

25 Gregory Day, 'Explaining the Art Market's Thefts, Frauds, and Forgeries (and Why the Art Market Does Not Seem to Care)' (2014) 16(3) *Vanderbilt Journal of Entertainment & Technology Law* 457–495, 467.

26 Malcolm Budd, 'Artistic Value' in Peter Lamarque and Stein Haugom Olsen (eds.), *Aesthetics and the Philosophy of Art: The Analytic Tradition, An Anthology* (2nd ed., Hoboken, NJ: Wiley, 2018) 236–246, 236.

27 Fabian Bocart and Kim Oosterlinck, 'Discoveries of Fakes: Their Impact on the Art Market' (2011) 113(2) *Economics Letters* 124–126; Jonathon Keats, *Forged: Why Fakes Are the Great Art of Our Age* (New York: Oxford University Press, 2013) 8–11.

28 But there are others. See Carolyn EmBree and David A. Scott, 'The Multifarious Nature of Art Forgery in France: Four Case Studies of Belle Epoque Fakes and Forgeries' (2015) 13 *Journal of Art Crime* 3–16, 11.

29 All 2023 amounts were computed using www.officialdata.org/.

30 Katie Dixon and Zachary Schufro, 'Risky Business: Fraud, Authenticity, and Limited Legal Protections in the High Art Market' (2021) 10(2) *Journal of Intellectual Property and Entertainment Law* 246–296, 247.

31 Similarly, when the Musée du Louvre discovered that the *Tiara of Saïtapharnès* was a forgery, it chose to hide it from the public for almost a century (Embree and Scott, 'Multifarious Nature', 7).

32 Jack W. Meiland, 'Originals, Copies, and Aesthetic Values' in Peter Lamarque and Stein Haugom Olsen (eds.), *Aesthetics and the Philosophy of Art: The Analytic Tradition, An Anthology* (2nd ed., Hoboken, NJ: Wiley, 2018) 229–235, 230.

33 Peter Martin Jaworski, 'In Defense of Fakes and Artistic Treason: Why Visually-Indistinguishable Duplicates of Paintings Are Just as Good as the Originals' (2013) 47(4) *Journal of Value Inquiry* 391–405 at 393.

34 Dixon and Shufro, 'Risky Business', 247.

35 Leila Amineddoleh, 'Purchasing Art in a Market Full of Forgeries: Risks and Legal Remedies for Buyers' (2015) 22(2–3) *International Journal of Cultural Property* 419–435; Justine M. Bonner, 'Let Them Authenticate: Deterring Art Fraud' (2017) 24(1) *UCLA Entertainment Law Review* 19–50, 24.

TABLE 5.1 *The lemons problem in the markets for (1) used car and (2) artworks*

	Market for used cars	Market for artworks
Criterion	Worth of a used car ↦ quality of that car	Worth of an artwork ↦ origin of that artwork
Lemons	Cars that often need repairs	Fakes and forgeries notwithstanding their aesthetic value
Peaches	Reliable cars	Genuine artworks notwithstanding their aesthetic value

For this exact reason, this chapter argues that the art market faces an idiosyncratic lemons problem: on that market, poor-quality products are not necessarily those with low aesthetic value but those with little-valued origin (if valued at all): fakes or forgeries. Genuine artworks are peaches merely because they are authentic (see Table 5.1).

To sum up the argument so far, without authentication it is impossible for the buyer to know whether they are acquiring an original artwork or a forgery.[36] On the contrary, the seller possesses this knowledge – assuming they are the forger or know from the forger that the artwork is forged.[37] This is asymmetric information. Therefore, buyers will revise their willingness-to-pay to take into account the average probability the artwork is a forgery. Yet the art market has not collapsed: consumers continue to buy art en masse while 'most dealers and patrons adamantly defend the traditional ways in which they have sold and traded art'.[38] The fact that art is an investment explains why neither buyers nor sellers have asked for more market transparency. Their interests are aligned: buyers do not want symmetric information because they know one day they will be in the sellers' shoes.[39] This does not change the fact that information asymmetry 'has created substantial societal harms'.[40] Preventing their occurrence is precisely the *raison d'être* of authentication.[41]

5.3 GENAI AND THE MARKET FOR LEMONS

For a lemons problem to exist, good-quality and poor-quality products must have a different value and be indistinguishable, so that there is an incentive to sell a lemon for the price of a peach. This section discusses whether GenAI is concerned by information asymmetry and incentive to cheat.

5.3.1 *Indistinguishability*

Machine-enabled artworks and human-made ones are indistinguishable. Anyone willing to buy an artwork would be incapable of identifying its human or machine origin by simply looking at it.[42] This is easily explained technologically. Suffice it to analyse the functioning of generative

[36] This indistinguishability is reinforced by the fact that (a) the primary art market is relatively small while the secondary (resale) market is much larger and (b) that art galleries conduct their business privately and confidentially – which reduces price transparency (Day, 'Art Market's Thefts', 466).

[37] David Crystal-Kirk, 'Forgery Reforged: Art-Faking and Commercial Passing-Off since 1981' (1986) 49(5) *Modern Law Review* 608–616, 609.

[38] Day, 'Art Market's Thefts', 486.

[39] Ibid., 486–488.

[40] Ibid., 488.

[41] Bonner, 'Let Them Authenticate'.

[42] Hossein Aboutalebi et al., 'DeepFakeArt Challenge: A Benchmark Dataset for Generative AI Art Forgery and Data Poisoning Detection', arXiv, 2 June 2023, https://doi.org/10.48550/arXiv.2306.01272.

adversarial networks (GAN) to be convinced. In a nutshell, a GAN is composed of two competing sub-models that are simultaneously trained. A generative model *G* generates new data (output) based on simple random variables (input). A discriminative model *D* then estimates the probability that output belongs to the training dataset or was generated by G.[43] These models are called adversarial because they play a zero-sum game: either the discriminator correctly classifies the examples as real or generated, or alternatively fails and the generator successfully fools the discriminator.[44] Eventually, the discriminator is unable to classify the examples it has to label and reaches a 50 per cent success rate (i.e., with the same accuracy as predicting heads or tails when flipping a coin). Indistinguishability cannot be better defined.

That said, it cannot be stressed enough that the indistinguishability between a human-made and machine-enabled artwork does not mean the latter is *ipso facto* a fake or a forgery. It is not a fake because it is possible to use GenAI to produce an artwork that is not in the style of a human artist.[45] Kristina Kashtanova's above-mentioned comic book is indubitably a genuine machine-enabled artwork.[46] Similarly, a machine-enabled artwork is not a forgery either. The case of the partnership between ING, Microsoft, TU Delft, Mauritshuis, and Rembrandthuis drives the point home. Together, they produced a new painting *in the style of* Rembrandt using a deep learning facial recognition algorithm which first identified and then replicated Rembrandt's patterns. Although the result (*The Next Rembrandt*) is indistinguishable from a genuine piece by the Dutch great master, it was never disclosed as such.[47] *The Next Rembrandt* is therefore not a forgery (a work in the style of an artist and identified as genuine) but a fake (a work in the style of an artist but not identified as genuine).

5.3.2 *Incentive to Cheat*

Do GenAI human users have an incentive to sell a machine-enabled artwork as a human-made one? It seems this is the case. On the one hand, they are indistinguishable. Anyone willing to buy an artwork would be incapable of identifying its human or machine origin by simply looking at it.[48] On the other hand, their market value under symmetric information might well be different. Although the valuation of machine-enabled artwork is still *terra incognita*, several elements suggest that human-made artworks will be the peaches and machine-enabled ones the lemons.

First, the question whether the origin of an artwork (either human-made or machine-enabled) influences its perceived beauty, novelty, and meaning has been experimentally investigated.[49] The study discovered a 'negative bias of perception towards [machine-enabled artworks] and a preference bias towards [human-made ones]'.[50]

[43] Ian J. Goodfellow et al., 'Generative Adversarial Nets' in Z. Ghahramani et al. (eds.), *Advances in Neural Information Processing Systems 27: Annual Conference on Neural Information Processing Systems 2014 (NIPS 2014), December 8–13 2014*, Montreal, NIPS, 2014, https://researchr.org/publication/nips-2014.

[44] Ian J. Goodfellow, 'NIPS 2016 Tutorial: Generative Adversarial Networks', arXiv, 3 April 2017, https://arxiv.org/abs/1701.00160.

[45] Ralph D. Clifford, 'Intellectual Property in the Era of the Creative Computer Program: Will the True Creator Please Stand Up?' (1997) 71(6) *Tulane Law Review* 1675–1703.

[46] USCO, 'Zarya'.

[47] See https://news.microsoft.com/europe/features/next-rembrandt/.

[48] Aboutalebi, 'DeepFakeArt'.

[49] Martin Ragot, Nicolas Martin and Salomé Cojean, 'AI-Generated vs. Human Artworks. A Perception Bias towards Artificial Intelligence' in *Extended Abstract of the 2020 CHI Conference on Human Factors in Computing Systems* (New York: Association for Computing Machinery (ACM), 2020) 1–10, https://doi.org/10.1145/3334480.3382892.

[50] Ibid. (terminology corrected for consistency).

TABLE 5.2 *GenAI output auction trend*

	Lower estimate (USD)		Upper estimate (USD)		Hammer price (USD)	
Artwork	On auction date	Updated (2023)	On auction date	Updated (2023)	On auction date	Updated (2023)
Edmond de Belamy	7,000	8,453	10,000	12,075	432,000	521,645
Memories of Passerby I	39,543	46,922	52,724	62,562	52,724	62,562
Baronne de Belamy	20,000	23,732	30,000	35,598	25,000	29,625
Katsuwaka of the Dawn Lagoon	8,000	9,493	12,000	14,239	16,250	19,282
Mantiki Logic	7,075	8,292	11,791	13,821	n.a.	n.a.

Second, auctions of machine-enabled artwork at prices that exceed expert evaluation seem to be drying up. It is true the *Portrait of Edmond de Belamy* (created by the French collective Obvious) skyrocketed during its sale at Christie's – as its hammer price (including fees) was more than forty-three times its high estimate.[51] However, this oft-cited auction was a world premiere. Subsequent auctions were less sensational. Mario Flingemann's *Memories of Passerby I* was auctioned at a hammer price equal to its upper estimate (excluding fees).[52] Shortly after, Obvious' *La Baronne de Belamy* was auctioned at a price higher than the lower estimates but lower than the upper one.[53] The same day, however, Obvious' *Katsuwaka of the Dawn Lagoon* was auctioned at a price slightly higher than its upper estimate. Yet Obvious' beechwood sculpture *Mantiki (Logic)* simply found no buyer during its online auction sale.[54] Table 5.2 displays the lower estimates, upper estimates, and hammer price in US dollars[55] at both the auction date and updated.[56] Figure 5.1 illustrates the evolution of lower and upper estimates as well as the hammer price. Figure 5.2 leaves aside the sale of the *Portrait of Edmond the Belamy* as it is an outlier. Five auctions are not enough to conclude a downward trend with absolute certainty. However, it seems clear that the announcement effect is over. The fact that the 2018–2022 annual reports of artprice.com (worldwide art information database) only mention GenAI in 2018 in the context of the sale of *Portrait of Edmond de Belamy* and leave aside subsequent auctions seems to confirm that trend.[57]

Third, and perhaps most critical, legal uncertainty prevails regarding the potential copyrightability of machine-enabled artworks, as was recently stressed by the World Intellectual

[51] Gabe Cohn, 'AI Art at Christie's Sells for $432,500', *The New York Times*, 25 October 2018, www.nytimes.com/2018/10/25/arts/design/ai-art-sold-christies.html.

[52] Sotheby's, 'Memories of Passerby I', Lot 109 (2018), www.sothebys.com/en/auctions/ecatalogue/2019/contemporary-art-day-auction-l19021/lot.109.html.

[53] Obvious Art, 'La Baronne de Belamy', Sotheby's, Lot 461 (2019), www.sothebys.com/en/auctions/ecatalogue/2019/contemporary-art-day-n10150/lot.461.html.

[54] 'Mantiki (Logic)', Mutual Art, www.mutualart.com/Artwork/Mantiki-Logic/872F0AD66D2155AC.

[55] The lower and upper estimates and hammer price of *Memories of Passerby* were, respectively, £30,000, £40,000, and £40,000. The sale occurred on 6 March 2019. That day, the GBP–USD exchange rate was 1.3181 (www.exchangerates.org.uk/GBP-USD-spot-exchange-rates-history-2019.html). The lower and upper estimates of *Mantiki Logic* were respectively €6,000 and €10,000. The sale occurred on 15–27 October 2020. During that period, the average EUR–USD exchange rate was 1.1791 (www.exchangerates.org.uk/EUR-USD-spot-exchange-rates-history-2020.html).

[56] All inflation rates are available at www.officialdata.org/us/inflation/2019?amount=100.

[57] All reports are available at www.artprice.com/artmarketinsight/reports.

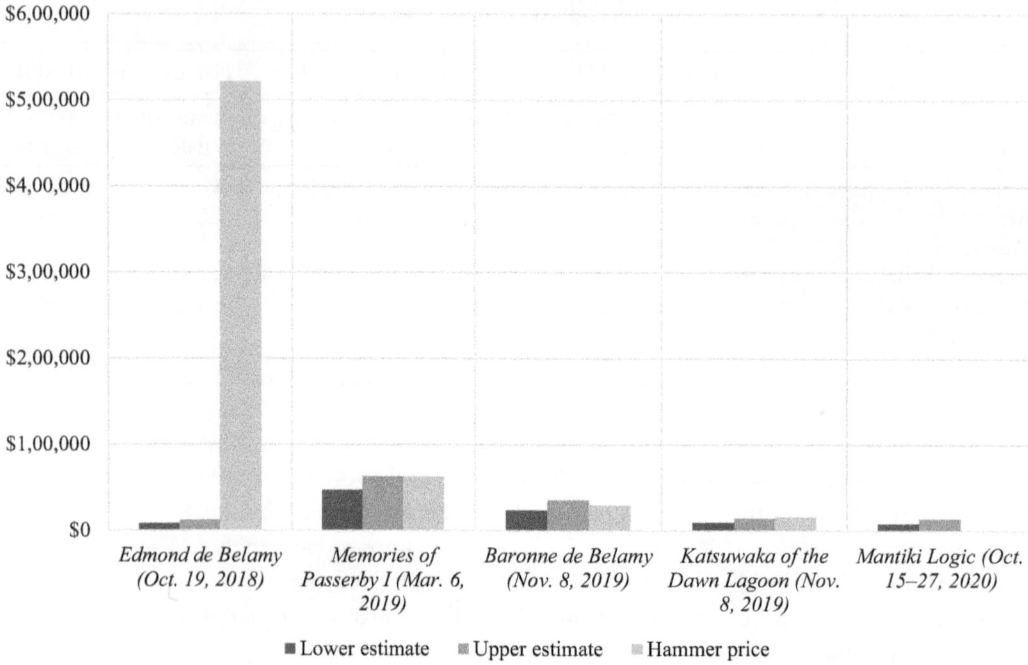

FIGURE 5.1 *GenAI output auction trend, including* Baron de Belamy

Property Organization (WIPO).[58] As will be explored below, the USCO held in *Zarya of the Dawn* that machine-enabled artworks are not copyrightable if their authors do not express sufficient control over them. This has an economic impact. Copyright is, indeed, an exclusive property right that grants its owner (the author or a third party to whom the latter would have transferred the right) a temporary monopoly.[59] Without copyright, the remuneration of the author is reduced to a trickle. This was actually at the core of the *Painer* ruling by the ECJ. Ms Painer was a freelance photographer who sold portrait photographs at a price that corresponded to the price of the prints.[60] She neither conferred any right over them nor consented to their publication. When they were nevertheless published in several newspapers and websites, she asked for 'payment of appropriate remuneration and damages for her loss'.[61] It is because she claimed a copyright that she requested a remuneration. The uncopyrightability of machine-enabled artwork therefore suggests that the remuneration of GenAI users will be limited.

The upshot is that under symmetric information, it is fair to assume a machine-enabled artwork will be valued at a lower price than a human-made one notwithstanding their aesthetic value. Even if this assumption turns out to be false later on, it should be borne in mind that GenAI creates something new so easily and at such a pace that the number of available machine-enabled artworks will soon skyrocket.[62] Given this mass production, art buyers could well become bored (something hinted by the end of the announcement effect that followed the auction of *Portrait of Edmond de Belamy*) and revert to human-made artworks. Against that

[58] IP and Frontier Technology Division, 'Generative AI: Navigating Intellectual Property' (2024) World Intellectual Property Organization, https://doi.org/10.34667/tind.49065.

[59] Pila and Torremans, *Intellectual Property*.

[60] *Painer*, §§27–29.

[61] Ibid., §38.

[62] Luciano Floridi and Massimo Chiriatti, 'GPT-3: Its Nature, Scope, Limits, and Consequences' (2020) 30(4) *Minds and Machines* 681–694, 684.

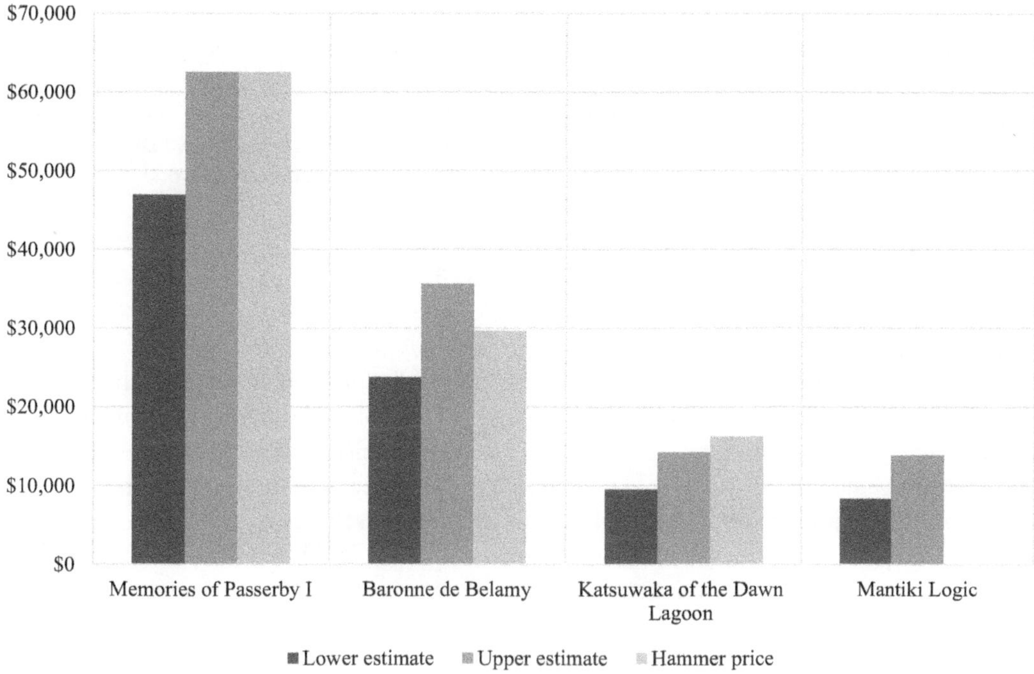

FIGURE 5.2 *GenAI output auction trend, excluding* Baron de Belamy

background, the higher valuation of human-made art will lag behind art buyers' loss of interest in machine-enabled ones but it will exist nonetheless.

Using the artwork origin as a proxy for its quality is therefore still relevant. In this scenario, human-made artworks are the peaches; machine-enabled ones, the lemons (see Table 5.3).

However, the indistinguishability between human-made and machine-enabled art suggests asymmetric information. In addition, the assumed difference in valuation between human-made and machine-enabled works incentivises sellers to cheat. Art buyers will thus probably internalise the risk of being sold a machine-enabled artwork at the price of a human-made one. The market price of human-made artwork will therefore be lower than what it is worth under symmetric information. Considering the art market structure, it is unlikely that the lemons problem induced by GenAI will lead to a market collapse. Yet there will still be imperfect market allocation to be corrected.

5.4 ART AUTHENTICATION

This section explores how to distinguish the undistinguishable. It first proposes a reading of the top-down rule of origin mandated within the EU (Section 4.4.1). It then applies *mutatis mutandis* the substantial transformation test developed in customs and tax law to GenAI systems (Section 4.4.2) and argues this was the pivotal point in the USCO decision not to copyright the images contained within *Zarya of the Dawn* (Section 4.4.3). Finally, it stresses that a rule of origin can also be constructed bottom-up (Section 4.4.4).

5.4.1 *Top-Down Rule of Origin*

It should be borne in mind that a rule of origin is a request from the art community. In 2022, Jason Allen's *Théâtre D'opéra Spatial* won the first prize in the Digital Arts/Digitally-

TABLE 5.3 *The lemons problem in the markets for (1) used car and (2) artworks, including GenAI*

	Market for used cars	Market for artworks
Criterion	Worth of a used car ↦ quality of that car	Worth of an artwork ↦ origin of that artwork
Lemons	Cars that often need repairs	Fakes; forgeries; *machine-enabled artworks*
Peaches	Reliable cars	Genuine *human-made* artworks

Manipulated Photography category at the Colorado State Fair.[63] He later explained he used Midjourney to create his artwork. Public outcry followed in successive waves. In the beginning, Allen was accused of cheating. Yet nothing in the rules of the contest (at least under this category) prevented the use of Midjourney. Others argued that if Allen complied with the rules, then the rules must be changed either by banning the use of AI in artwork submitted to the competition, or by creating a new category for machine-enabled artwork. The latter option is akin to what photographer Eldagsen called for after having declined the award for his litigious photography. He similarly distinguished human-made from machine-enabled artworks, arguing that photography literally means drawing (-graphy) with light (photo-). Given that GenAI like Midjourney do not fit this definition, he suggested naming his work a '*prompt*tography' (drawing made by prompt).[64]

This paves the way for what follows. Given GenAI introduces new indistinguishable products on a market that was already facing a lemons problem, it suffices to expand the authentication rule to machine-enabled artworks.[65] So far, authentication distinguishes a genuine artwork from a fake or a forgery. From now on, it can similarly be used to draw a line between human-made and machine-enabled artworks.

This seems to be the solution chosen by the EU legislator in the Regulation laying down rules on AI (AIA).[66] A complete discussion on its scope of application would go well beyond the purpose of this chapter.[67] For the moment, it is enough to emphasise that, pursuant to the initial version of the text, 'users of an AI system that generates or manipulates image, audio or video content that appreciably resembles existing persons, objects, places or other entities or events and would falsely appear to a person to be authentic or truthful ("deep fake"), shall disclose that the content has been artificially generated or manipulated' (Article 52(3): v.04/2021). This is an embryonic (because limited to deep fake) top-down (because mandated by the EU lawmaker) rule of origin.[68]

63 Lance Eliot, 'AI Ethics Left Hanging When AI Wins Art Contest and Human Artists Are Fuming', *Forbes*, 7 September 2022, www.forbes.com/sites/lanceeliot/2022/09/07/ai-ethics-left-hanging-when-ai-wins-art-contest-and-human-artists-are-fuming/?sh = 214570314b1b.

64 See Boris Eldagsen's interview in Paul Glynn, 'Sony World Photography Award 2023: Winner Refuses Award after Revealing AI Creation', *BBC News*, 18 April 2023, www.bbc.com/news/entertainment-arts-65296763. Eldagsen attributed 'promptography' to a Peruvian photographer.

65 See, by analogy, Toby Walsh, *Android Dreams: The Past, Present and Future of Artificial Intelligence* (London: Hurst, 2017) 111; Jacob Turner, *Robot Rules: Regulating Artificial Intelligence* (Cham: Palgrave Macmillan, 2019) 320–324.

66 Regulation (EU) 2024/1689 of the European Parliament and of the Council of 13 June 2024 laying down harmonised rules on artificial intelligence and amending Regulations (EC) No. 300/2008, (EU) No. 167/2013, (EU) No. 168/2013, (EU) 2018/858, (EU) 2018/1139 and (EU) 2019/2144 and Directives 2014/90/EU, (EU) 2016/797 and (EU) 2020/1828 (Artificial Intelligence Act), OJ L 2024/1689, 12 July 2024.

67 Jerome De Cooman, 'Humpty Dumpty and High-Risk AI Systems: The Ratione Materiae Dimension of the Proposal for an EU Artificial Intelligence Act' (2022) 6(1) *Market & Competition Law Review* 49–88.

68 See, by analogy, Jean Tirole, 'Overcoming Adverse Selection: How Public Intervention Can Restore Market Functioning' (2012) 102(1) *American Economic Review* 29–59.

The compromise text of the EU Parliament's Committees on the Internal Market and Consumer Protection (IMCO) and on Civil Liberties, Justice and Home Affairs (LIBE) maintained this requirement (Article 52(3): v.05/2023).[69] Although it was not clear whether it applied to all machine-enabled outputs or solely to deep fake,[70] this version of the AIA introduced an exception holding that the transparency requirement 'shall not apply where the use of an AI system that generates or manipulates text, audio or visual content . . . is necessary for the exercise of . . . the right to freedom of the arts' that covered, according to the ECJ, 'artistic expression',[71] and should, pursuant to Article 13 of the EU Charter of Fundamental rights, 'be free of constraint' (Article 52(3a): v.05/2023).[72]

It is perhaps in light of this risk of ineffectiveness that the EU legislator has reformulated this provision in the adopted (final) version of the AIA, which now states that 'providers of AI systems, including general-purpose AI systems, generating synthetic audio, image, video or text content, shall ensure that the outputs of the AI system are marked in a machine-readable format and detectable as artificially generated or manipulated' (Article 50(2), *in limine*, AIA). Interestingly, the AIA also includes an exception that echoes the substantial transformation test advocated above. Indeed, the obligation to mark machine-enabled outputs as such 'shall not apply to the extent the AI systems perform an assistive function for standard editing or do not substantially alter the input data provided by the deployer or the semantics thereof' (Article 50(2), *in fine*, AIA). This immediately raises the question of defining the threshold for substantial modification, on which the text remains silent, however.

5.4.2 *Substantial Transformation*

In the context of GenAI, a simple rule of origin suggests a distinction between human-made (GenAI-free) and machine-enabled artworks, as soon as GenAI is used in the creative process. This is inappropriate. Such a dyadic authentication would ignore the fact that GenAI might be solely used to edit or perform slight modifications. Therefore, the exception made by the AIA in similar instances is laudable. One should however wonder what is a substantial modification and whether this exception is appropriate given that, despite this exception, the AIA seems to treat in the same way, for example, a text-to-image GenAI when prompted with one single sentence and a work of art that required hundreds, if not thousands of detailed instructions.[73] The latter piece owes its existence more to the human user than the former. Should they still both be classified as machine-enabled?

One solution to substantivise the 'substantial alteration' criterion built up in the AIA can be found in geographical rules of origin that establish the provenance of goods and services for tax

[69] Committee on Internal Market and Consumer Protection and Committee on Civil Liberties, Justice and Home Affairs, Draft Compromise Amendments on the Draft Report: Proposal for a Regulation of the European Parliament and of the Council on harmonised rules on Artificial Intelligence (Artificial Intelligence Act) and amending certain Union Legislative Acts, 16 May 2023, COM(2021)0206. More generally, see Claudio Novelli, Federico Casolari, Philipp Hacker, Giorgio Spedicato and Luciano Floridi, 'Generative AI in EU Law: Liability, Privacy, Intellectual Property, and Cybersecurity' (2024) SSRN Working Paper, https://papers.ssrn.com/sol3/papers.cfm?abstract_id=4694565.

[70] A broad reading would be in line with Recital 60g: v.05/2023.

[71] Case C-476/17, *Pelham GmbH, Moses Pelham, Martin Haas v. Ralf Hütter, Florian Schneider-Esleben*, ECLI:EU:C:2019:624, §35.

[72] Charter of Fundamental Rights of the European Union, OJ C 326, 26 October 2012, 391–407.

[73] Allen declared he prompted Midjourney over and over again to the extent that he generated around 900 different versions.

purposes. In short, a rule of origin grants a member to a trade agreement access to the domestic market of another member at a preferential tariff.[74] To maximise their turnover, some undertakings kept their production in countries where labour was cheap but exported the final stage to a country that could benefit from a tariff cut. EU law explains why undertakings willing to have their cake and eat it too are doomed to fail. Pursuant to the Union Customs Code, 'goods the production of which involves more than one country or territory shall be deemed to originate in the country or territory where they underwent their last, substantial, economically-justified processing or working … resulting in the manufacture of a new product or representing an important stage of manufacture'.[75] According to the ECJ, this 'substantial transformation test' suggests a process or an operation is substantial if 'the product resulting therefrom has its own properties and a composition of its own, which it did not possess before that process or operation'.[76] Interestingly, the ECJ later held that the substantial transformation test 'can be expressed by the ad valorem percentage rule, where either the percentage value of the materials utilised or the percentage of the value added reaches a specified level'.[77]

The zeitgeist of the substantial transformation test is this: (a) several different geographical areas may be involved in the production process of a product; (b) its country of origin is not necessarily the last country through which the product passes before reaching its relevant market; and (c) the country of origin can only be the one in which the product was substantially transformed for the last time. When transposed *mutatis mutandis* to machine-enabled artwork, this suggests that (a) an artwork may owe its existence to both human and machine, (b) the fact that a human edited the artwork before it was made available to the public does not mean it is human-made, and (c) the artwork will only be labelled as human-made if the human input is substantial vis-à-vis the role of the machine. One way to measure this substantiality could be the application of an ad valorem rule (comparing the properties of the artwork before and after any human editing by assessing the added value of human intervention in the creation). If so, then it is fair to assume human edits consisting merely of sorting, classifying, or assembling the output of a GenAI system are unlikely to be considered substantial.[78]

5.4.3 *Substantial Transformation and Control over Creation*

To some extent, the question of the substantial transformation was at the heart of the USCO decision not to copyright the images contained within *Zarya of the Dawn*. In this case, the USCO discarded copyrightability not because Midjourney was used but because its user did not prove she controlled the creative process. This is in line with both *Burrow-Giles* (in the USA)[79] and *Painer* (in the EU).[80]

In *Painer*, the ECJ interestingly chose to distinguish the artwork creation in a three-stage process composed of the preparation phase, the taking of the portrait photograph, and the selection phase.[81] The creative process was later generalised to be described as an iteration of

74 Stefanio Inama, *Rules of Origin in International Trade* (Cambridge: Cambridge University Press, 2009).
75 Regulation (EU) No 952/2013 of 9 October 2013 laying down the Union Customs Code, OJ L 269/1, Art. 60(2).
76 Case C-49/76, *Gesellschaft für Überseehandel mbH v. Handeskammer Hamburg*, ECLI:EU:C:1977:9, §6.
77 Case C-26/88, *Brothers International GmbH v. Hauptzollamt Gießen*, ECLI:EU:C:1989:637, §21.
78 Article 34 Commission Delegated Regulation (EU) 2015/2446 of 28 July 2015 Supplementing Regulation (EU) No. 952/2013 as Regards Detailed Rules Concerning Certain Provisions of the Union Customs Code, OJ L 343/1.
79 *Burrow-Giles*, §60.
80 *Painer*, §§87–89.
81 Ibid., §90.

three successive steps, namely the conception, the execution, and the redaction.[82] At the conception stage, the author chooses, for instance, the subject and the style of what they plan to realise. At the execution stage, what was decided during the conception is translated into drafts. At the redaction phase, the author finalises the artwork by choosing among the draft version that need to be reworked before the artwork is made available to the public. The ECJ held that an author 'can stamp the work created with his [sic] "personal touch"'[83] at each of these three stages.[84]

An AI system intervenes to varying degrees depending on the stage of the procedure. At the conception stage, GenAI is not involved. This is still the realm of humans. However, GenAI plays 'the dominant role' at the execution stage by producing 'sophisticated output in ways that the user of the system will not be able to (precisely) preconceive, understand or explain'.[85] This does not mean there is no room for creativity at this stage. In some instances, the human artist will be in charge of 'constantly monitoring the output of the process and giving feedback to the AI system, by adjusting weights and parameters to better match pre-defined objectives'.[86] The fact that the human author is not directly in charge of the execution does not ipso facto prevent that artwork being a copyrightable work of art. Outsourcing this execution to a machine is exactly what photographers Sarony and Painer did with their respective cameras. This applies to GenAI that follows the users' instructions and, therefore, is 'incapable of being more than obedient agents in the service of human principals'.[87] At the redaction phase, the role of the human author will oscillate between, on the one hand, the simple selection of the result produced by the AI system to be presented to the public and, on the other hand, a real editing job, depending on whether the production of the GenAI system is ready to use or not. In this regard it has been argued that 'creative choice at the redaction phase may even suffice for a finding of originality of the entire production'.[88] A work is therefore copyrightable if its author manages to exercise free and creative choice by controlling the *conception* of the artwork beyond a mere idea (the 'what') and directly or indirectly its *execution* (the 'how').[89]

According to the Office's understanding of Midjourney, Ms Kashtanova controlled the conception but did not exercise sufficient control over the execution because the initially prompted images were generated 'in an unpredictable way' based on a 'randomly generated noise' which is refined using 'tokens created from user prompts that relate to Midjourney's training database'.[90] For the Office, this means that 'while additional prompts applied to one of these initial images can influence the subsequent images, the process is not controlled by the user because it is not possible to predict what Midjourney will create ahead of time'.[91]

The argument based on randomness is interesting. Copyright law 'tolerates some degree of randomness in a work's execution'.[92] It is only at a certain point 'at which the putative author has surrendered so much control over the execution that the independence of the work's

[82] Christian Hartmann et al., *Trends and Developments in Artificial Intelligence – Challenges to the Intellectual Property Rights Framework – Final Report* (Luxembourg: Publication Office of the EU, 2020).
[83] *Painer*, §92.
[84] Ibid., §91.
[85] Hugenholtz, Quintais and Gervais, 'Artificial Intelligence and Copyright', 80.
[86] Ibid.
[87] Ginsburg and Budiardjo, 'Authors and Machines', 400.
[88] Hugenholtz, Quintais and Gervais, 'Artificial Intelligence and Copyright', 80.
[89] Jane C. Ginsburg, 'The Concept of Authorship in Comparative Copyright Law' (2003) 52 *DePaul Law Review* 1092.
[90] USCO, 'Zarya', 9.
[91] Ibid., 8–9.
[92] Ginsburg and Budiardjo, 'Authors and Machines', 362.

embodiment calls into question whether her initial conception of the work was anything more than a general idea'.[93] As a result, an artwork that completely rely on randomness is uncopyrightable.[94] More concretely, this suggests that authors may not 'maintain absolute control over the execution' and, instead, may 'rely on external forces, like randomness and nature, to complete' their work as long as they bent these forces to their will.[95] Intuitively, this leads to Jackson Pollock, who 'poured, dripped, and splattered paint onto canvases he had placed on the floor' and who insisted that, despite appearances, he exercised a high control over his painting.[96] The question is therefore whether Ms Kashtanova exercised enough control despite the random generation of noise as its starting point. It should be borne in mind that Midjourney uses 'a randomly generated seed number to create a field of visual noise, like television static, as a starting point to generate the initial image'.[97] However, users are able to specify the seed numbers by defining two parameters ('–seed or –sameseed').[98] This suggests it is possible to exercise some control over the creation.

Whether, in the particular case of *Zarya of the Dawn*, this control was (or was not) enough is not the most important element here.[99] Much more critical is the evidential scheme of the decision. A machine-enabled artwork will be copyrightable if and only if the human artist exercises sufficient control towards what is created: if the artist is able to *substantially transform* the artwork while stamping their personal touch. To prove this, the artist will need to provide the prompts they wrote to generate images as well as (intermediary) image proofs and parameters used to frame the results. Actually, this was the logic followed in another case, filed before a Czech court this time, which held that if GenAI users are not able to prove that the generated image is the result of their unique creative contribution, then it cannot be work of authorship.[100] Therefore, human artists using GenAI systems anticipating copyright litigation would be well advised to keep such documentation. Doing so, they would de facto establish a bottom-up rule of origin that draws 'clear boundaries between what is what, *e.g.*, in the same way as a restored, ancient vase shows clearly and explicitly where the intervention occurs'.[101]

5.4.4 *Bottom-Up Rule of Origin: Signalling*

The European Writers' Council welcomed the introduction of the AIA rule of origin but stressed 'the importance of developing technical tools that may reliably and accurately differentiate authentic content from AI-generated' ones.[102] In light of this, one should note that solving indistinguishability does not solely lie in the hands of regulators. Honest artists could develop

[93] Ibid.
[94] Agnieszka Kurant, 'Phantom Capital, Hybrid Authorship and Collective Intelligence' (2016) 39(3) *Columbia Journal of Law & the Arts* 371–376.
[95] Ginsburg and Budiardjo, 'Authors and Machines', 366.
[96] Alan R. Durham, 'The Random Muse: Authorship and Indeterminacy' (2002) 44(2) *William & Mary Law Review* 569–642, 600.
[97] Midjourney, 'Seeds', https://docs.midjourney.com/docs/seeds.
[98] Ibid.
[99] USCO, 'Zaria', 10 (the Office acknowledged that 'it is possible that other AI offerings that can generate expressive material operate differently than Midjourney does').
[100] C-13/2023-16, Municipal Court in Prague, 11 October 2023, https://justice.cz/documents/14569/1865919/10C_13_2023_10/108cad3e-d9e8–454f-bfac-d58e1253c83a.
[101] Floridi and Chiriatti, 'GPT-3', 692.
[102] European Writers' Council, 'Joint Statement on Generative Artificial Intelligence and the EU AI Act' (25 April 2024), https://europeanwriterscouncil.eu/wp-content/uploads/2024/04/Joint-Statement-on-Generative-Artifical-Intelligence-and-the-EU-AI-Act.pdf.

their own bottom-up rule of origin to signal the human origin of the art. In economic jargon, this is known as signalling (from the perspective of the sellers)[103] or screening or sorting (from the perspective of the buyers).[104] To keep complex things simple, a signal is the result of 'efforts by sellers to "tell" buyers about the products, and therefore to change the initial asymmetric informational structure of the market'.[105] Father of signalling theory Michael Spence explained that a signal is useful 'when there is an *unobservable attribute* that is valuable to buyers'.[106]

Depending on three conditions, signalling has the potential to overcome asymmetric information.[107] This signal must first be credible. For instance, the buyers' verbal declarations are a low-cost signal that is, however, not credible given that 'words are cheap, and therefore do not provide the means by which high quality sellers can differentiate their products'.[108] The signal must also not be too expensive.[109] It is traditionally argued that a seller invests in signalling until the marginal gain driven from the signal is equal to its marginal opportunity cost.[110] The signal must finally be costlier for sellers of poor-quality products than for sellers of good-quality ones.[111] A warranty, for instance, is costlier for sellers of lemons because they will repair, replace, or refund the product more often than sellers of peaches. It is therefore a strong signal for 'experience products': those whose quality can be evaluated after the purchase.[112] For this reason, however, this signal does not fit the human-made art. There is no 'information feedback' after the sale, in the sense that the origin of the product (either human-made or machine-enabled) will not be disclosed later on.[113]

An efficient signal proving human origin of an artwork could be the adjunction of a video time-lapse recording of the artist while painting or sculpting.[114] This way, buyers will be able to see for themselves the origin of the work they buy. This is an old idea: after the Musée du Louvre purchased the *Tiara of Saïtaphernès* in 1896, experts questioned its origin. Doubts spread until goldsmith Israel Rouchomowsky came to claim the authorship and explain the Tiara had been commissioned by art dealers who then dishonestly passed it off as an antique (an objective that the artist was unaware of). As the Louvre's art connoisseur did not believe him, Rouchomowsky produced 'documentation with studio photos and, without seeing the Tiara, recall and recreate minute details from the composition'.[115]

Of course, this will not fit all types of artistic expression. Recording or photography of book writers hunched over their keyboard while typing would prove absolutely nothing. A second-best

[103] Michael Spence, *Market Signalling* (Cambridge, MA: Harvard University Press, 1974).

[104] Joseph E. Stiglitz, 'The Theory of "Screening", Education, and the Distribution of Income' (1975) 65(3) *American Economic Review* 283–300.

[105] Michael Spence, 'Informational Aspects of Market Structure: An Introduction' (1976) 90(4) *Quarterly Journal of Economics* 591–597, 591–592.

[106] Michael Spence, 'Signaling in Retrospect and the Informational Structure of Markets' (2002) 92(3) *American Economic Review* 434–459, 448.

[107] Karl-Gustaf Löfgren, Torsten Persson and Jörgen W. Weibull, 'Markets with Asymmetric Information: The Contributions of George Akerlof, Michael Spence and Joseph Stiglitz' (2002) 104(2) *Scandinavian Journal of Economics* 195–211.

[108] Spence, *Market Signalling*, 593.

[109] Robert Mamada, 'The Market for Lemons and Information Theory' (2022) 120 *Mathematical Social Sciences* 107–112.

[110] John G. Riley, 'Testing the Educational Screening Hypothesis' (1979) 87(5) *Journal of Political Economy* S227–S252.

[111] Amna Kirmani and Akshay R. Rao, 'No Pain, No Gain: A Critical Review of the Literature on Signalling Unobservable Product Quality' (2000) 64(2) *Journal of Marketing* 66–79.

[112] Phillip Nelson, 'Advertising as Information' (1974) 82(4) *Journal of Political Economy* 729–754.

[113] Spence, *Market Signalling*, 359.

[114] De Cooman, 'When Art Becomes a Lemon'.

[115] Embree and Scott, 'Multifarious Nature', 7.

solution could be the one OpenAI proposed, namely to 'indicate that the content is AI-generated in a way no user could reasonably miss or misunderstand'.[116] Academic and non-academic publishers endorsed this recommendation. Taylor & Francis, *Nature*, *Science*, and the Authors Guild (a professional organisation for published writers) have decided that the use of GenAI should be acknowledged in an ad hoc section.[117]

It is doubtful, however, that a voluntary reporting scheme is credible given that indistinguishability incentivises dishonest dealings. One way to make such disclosure trustworthy is technical. It is perfectly conceivable to design GenAI systems in such a way that they watermark the generated output.[118] Concretely, this means the signal is incorporated 'into generated text that are invisible to humans but algorithmically detectable from a short span of tokens'.[119] Although technologically savvy users could find a way to remove these watermarks, average users are unlikely to be able to do so.[120]

This framework suggests that there might be a need for machine-enabled art connoisseurs offering their expertise to authenticate the human or artificial origin of an artwork by screening for watermarks or for evidence the latter were removed. This service stems from Schumpeterian creative destruction.[121] Historically, the need for art experts coincides with the rise of forgeries.[122] In addition, it is worth noting that the relationship between art experts and appraised artworks is circular and, to some extent, virtuous: 'as prices escalate, the need for a connoisseur's opinion rises; and as connoisseurs vouch for works and their authenticity, the works are more coveted, leading art market prices to soar even higher'.[123] Similarly, the emergence of (the risk of) machine-enabled artwork being sold as human-made should trigger the need for machine-enabled art connoisseurship that, in the end, results in a higher valuation of human-made art.

5.5 CONCLUSION

Back in England after an almost five-year journey on board the *HMS Beagle*, Charles Darwin wrote that the observations he made while circumnavigating the Earth 'throw some light on the origin of species – that mystery of mysteries'.[124] The purpose of a rule of origin is similar: to shed light on the origin of artworks.

[116] OpenAI, 'Sharing & Publication Policy' (last update 14 November 2022), https://openai.com/policies/sharing-publication-policy.

[117] Chris Stokel-Walker, 'ChatGPT Listed as Author on Research Papers: Many Scientists Disapprove' (2023) 613(7945) *Nature* 620–621, 620; The Authors Guild, 'AG Introduces New Publishing Agreement Clauses Concerning AI', Press Release, 1 June 2023, https://authorsguild.org/news/ag-introduces-new-publishing-agreement-clauses-concerning-ai/.

[118] Philipp Hacker, Andreas Engel and Marco Mauer, 'Regulating ChatGPT and Other Large Generative AI Models', arXiv, 5 February 2023, https://arxiv.org/abs/2302.02337, 14.

[119] John Kirchenbauer et al., 'Watermark for Large Language Models', arXiv, 24 January 2023, https://arxiv.org/abs/2301.10226, 1. See also Eric Mitchell, 'DetectGPT: Zero-Shot Machine-Generated Text Detection Using Probability Curvature', arXiv, 26 January 2023, https://arxiv.org/abs/2301.11305.

[120] Chenxi Gu, 'Watermarking Pre-Trained Language Models with Backdooring', arXiv, 14 October 2022, https://arxiv.org/abs/2210.07543.

[121] Joseph Schumpeter, *Capitalism, Socialism and Democracy* (New York: Harper & Brothers, 1942), defining the process of creative destruction as the never-ending innovation that incessantly destroys old economic structure while simultaneously creating new ones.

[122] Amineddoleh, 'Purchasing Art', 420.

[123] Ibid.

[124] Darwin, *Origin of Species*, 1. Darwin borrowed the expression 'mystery of mysteries' from a letter from John Herschel to Charles Lyell in 1836. See Roger Wagner and Andrew Briggs, *The Penultimate Curiosity: How Science Swims in the Slipstream of Ultimate Questions* (Oxford: Oxford University Press, 2016) 304–310.

Unlike the species studied by Darwin, however, human-made and machine-enabled artworks are indistinguishable. They are also valued differently, human-made artworks assuming the role of good-quality products (valuable origin). The indistinguishability and difference in valuation create an incentive to cheat, to sell a machine-enabled artwork as a human-made one to increase its sale price. Given they have incomplete information, buyers will internalise the risk of dishonest dealings in their willingness-to-pay. As a result, human artists will never be able to receive the true value of their art. They will therefore exit the market. In Darwinian words, human-made art will become extinct while machine-enabled ones will 'survive and multiply'.[125]

This should not be read as a Luddite's argument. This chapter is not a pamphlet against machine-enabled artworks to unduly protect human artists. On the contrary, this is a call for better competition between human-made and machine-enabled works of art. For now, the asymmetric information and the resulting adverse selection mean that competition between human-made and machine-enabled artworks is not on the merits but bears on unnatural (adverse) selection. It is not the fittest that prevail but the one that is artificially favoured.

Against that background, this chapter has proposed a rule of authentication ensuring symmetric information between buyers and sellers. Although the AIA failed to mandate a top-down rule of origin, artists, seeing nothing but a cloud of dust in the sun and the green grass, could develop their own bottom-up rule of origin (either to signal the human origin or to document the creative process anticipating copyright litigation). In this scenario, human-made and machine-enabled artworks will truly compete on their intrinsic quality. The benefits of such a solution are twofold. First, a rule of origin allows those who value human-made artworks more than machine-enabled ones to buy the product at the correct price. Yet it has absolutely no impact on buyers who do not care about the artwork's provenance as long as it is of high aesthetic quality. Second, the proposed rule of origin acknowledges that human-made and machine-enabled is not a binary distinction. As such, it is suggested to map all human inputs that occurred in the creation of a machine-enabled artwork. This identification could be of utmost interest for copyright. The documentation of the creation process should facilitate the identification of the elements for which users of GenAI have made free and creative choices reflecting their personality.

To conclude, the proposed rule of origin purges from the market any artificial preference or undue advantage of one product over another. This is a way of reintroducing natural selection in the ecosystem. May the best artwork prevail – as long as the struggle for existence is purely on the merits.

[125] Darwin, *Origin of Species*, 79.

PART II

Evolving Regulatory and Governance Frameworks

6

LLMs Meet the AI Act

Who's the Sorcerer's Apprentice?

Ugo Pagallo

6.1 INTRODUCTION

Forms of artificial intelligence (AI), such as generative AI (Gen AI), foundation models, and large language models (LLMs), broke the news by the end of 2022 and throughout 2023. Benefits and threats of technology ignited people's imagination and drew the regulatory attention of lawmakers and institutions, including the Group of Seven (G7) countries under the Japanese Presidency in May 2023. Yet defining AI and its subfields is no easy task, as shown by the efforts of the EU legislators since the proposal of the AI Act in April 2021, and with the series of amendments by the European Parliament in 2023, up to the final text of the Act in July 2024: Regulation (EU) 2024/1689.

Roughly speaking, LLMs can be understood as a sub-category of AI which is foundational and generative. 'Foundation AI' refers to models upon which other AI systems and applications are built.[1] Generative AI represents a type of AI that draws on the model design of deep neural networks and the developments of machine learning, finding out patterns from existing data to create new and unique outputs, such as texts, videos, images, audios, or 3D models. In the phrasing of Section 3 of the US Executive Order from October 2023, Gen AI 'means the class of AI models that emulate the structure and characteristics of input data in order to generate derived synthetic content'.[2] LLMs are then a particular sub-category of AI models that hinge on machine learning techniques to grasp and produce outputs on the basis of billions of parameters through probabilistic inferences, rather than causal understanding. Among the most popular instances of LLMs, the breakthroughs of the generative pre-trained transformer, or GPT, are instructive. Trained on a huge corpus of data – as large as the whole web – the model starts from a source input – the prompt – to create the most likely output, such as sequences of code, words, or other data that are statistically appropriate, given that starting prompt. For better or for worse, the results have been outstanding. LLMs can be adapted to support manifold applications, from

[1] R. Bommasani et al., 'On the opportunities and risks of foundation models' (2021) *ArXiv*, https://doi.org/10.48550/arXiv.2108.07258.

[2] The White House, *Executive Order on the Safe, Secure, and Trustworthy Development and Use of Artificial Intelligence* (Washington, DC: White House, 2023).

creative writing[3] to spell-checking,[4] allowing users to innovate upon such models without any gatekeeping: the emergence of several open source AI models, such as Meta's Llama 2 and Stable Diffusion, reinforces these trends.[5] However, LLMs also raise concerns, such as the new generation of fake news and deepfake videos. According to certain scholars,[6] AI-generated fake news is more credible to human raters than human-written disinformation. Moreover, texts, images, audios, and videos generated by LLMs can be impossible to distinguish from human creation.[7]

In this chapter, the focus of the analysis is restricted to this latter side of the coin: the risks brought forth by LLMs. The intent is not to overlook the benefits of the technology. Instead, the aim is to appreciate the range of potential misuses and overuses of LLMs, and to grasp on this basis how lawmakers intend to tackle them, therefore striking a balance between pros and cons of technology. Correspondingly, the chapter is divided into four parts. The focus of Section 6.2 is on risks of LLMs related not only to misuses of technology but also users who overestimate the capabilities of the technology and employ it in dangerous ways. Section 6.3 inspects the different techniques with which the law may aim to govern the development and uses of this technology. Special attention is drawn to the principle of technological neutrality. Section 6.4 dwells on the AI Act of EU law because it provides the first overall regulation of AI systems, LLMs, and general-purpose AI (GPAI) models. Section 6.5 dissects the drawbacks and shortcomings of this regulatory effort that should not hinder technological innovation or require over-frequent revision to tackle advancements of technology. The conclusion of the analysis brings us back to the question posed by the title of this chapter. Whereas, in the spirit of J. W. Goethe's poem, a sorcerer's apprentice refers to people who were unable to control a situation they created, we may wonder whether such sorcerer's apprentices are only developers and producers of LLMs, or if they include some lawmakers that attempt to govern misuses and overuses of technology.

6.2 LOOKING FOR THE SORCERER'S APPRENTICE

In addition to the benefits of LLMs, scholars have stressed their threats. For example, some divide the ethical challenges associated with LLMs into six risk fields:[8] (i) discrimination, for LLMs can perpetuate social stereotypes and biases, triggering representational and allocational harms; (ii) information hazards that may impinge on people's privacy by leaking personal information and inferring sensitive data; (iii) misinformation hazards that can affect trust, or lead to less well-informed users; (iv) malicious use by people with criminal intent, such as large-scale frauds or personalised scams; (v) human–computer interaction harms that depend on users overvaluing the capabilities of LLMs and using them in unsafe ways; and (vi) environmental harms from the energy which is necessary to train and operate the technology.[9]

[3] K. Hsieh, *Transformer Poetry: Poetry Classics Reimagined by Artificial Intelligence* (n.p.: Paper Gains Publishing, 2019).

[4] Y. Hu, X. Jing, Y. Ko, J. T. Rayz, 'Misspelling correction with pre-trained contextual language model', 2020 *IEEE 19th International Conference on Cognitive Informatics & Cognitive Computing (ICCI* CC)* (2021) 144–149, https://arxiv.org/abs/2101.03204.

[5] B. Dickson, *How open-source LLMs are challenging OpenAI, Google, and Microsoft* (2023), https://bdtechtalks.com/2023/05/08/open-source-llms-moats/.

[6] R. Zellers et al., 'Defending against neural fake news' (2019) *ArXiv*, http://arxiv.org/abs/1905.12616.

[7] S. J. Nightingale, H. Farid, 'AI-synthesized faces are indistinguishable from real faces and more trustworthy' (2022) 119(8) *Proceedings of the National Academy of Sciences* e2120481119.

[8] L. Weidinger et al., 'Ethical and social risks of harm from language models' (2022) 2022 *ACM Conference on Fairness, Accountability, and Transparency* 214. https://arxiv.org/pdf/2112.04359.

[9] U. Pagallo, J. Ciani Sciolla, M. Durante, 'The environmental challenges of AI in EU law: lessons learned from the Artificial Intelligence Act (AIA) with its drawbacks' (2022) 16(3) *Transforming Government: People, Process and Policy* 359.

Further normative issues posed by LLMs concern the legal domain. Arguably, one of the most sensitive fields has to do with the protection of intellectual property rights, in particular copyright. Authors of copyrighted materials, such as books, often claim their texts have been ingested and used to train LLMs, including ChatGPT, without their consent. Lawsuits have been lodged (also but not only) in the United States under the provisions of the Copyright Act (17 USC § 501) and the Digital Millenium Copyright Act (17 USC § 1202). Other controversial cases concern personal data similarly ingested in the training datasets of the LLMs. In EU law, the opinion of courts and regulators suggests that web scraping involving the collection of personal data is unlawful if it does not comply with principles and provisions of the General Data Protection Regulation (GDPR).[10] In March 2023, the Italian privacy authority ordered a ban of ChatGPT over alleged data protection violations. The service was reactivated a month later, once OpenAI addressed some of the issues raised by the Italian authority, such as lack of adequate information to its users and of appropriate legal basis for personal data processing.[11]

Against this backdrop of ethical troubles and open legal issues, scholars have stressed time and again that the self-regulatory policies of private companies in all their variants – from 'pure' unenforced forms of self-regulation to 'approved' self-regulation[12] – fall short in coping with the challenges of AI technologies.[13] It is remarkable that most lawmakers across the board have been very active over the past two years. China adopted interim measures for Gen AI in 2023; the White House released its Executive Order also but not only for Gen AI in October of that year; and the EU finally adopted Regulation (EU) 2024/1689 in July 2024. The race to AI regulation can be understood as a response of legislators to certain opinions in the business sector, and among technological experts and aficionados, which gained traction over the same short span of months and years when the race to the regulation of AI started. A few weeks after ChatGPT reached an amazing 100 million monthly active users within just two months of its launch, a group of business leaders and experts, including the boss of ChatGPT, Sam Altman, warned in May 2023 that humanity faces the risk of 'extinction' following the rise of AI.[14] Combating AI-related risks should be 'a global priority on par with other society-wide risks, such as pandemics and nuclear war', as the signatories of the manifesto claimed on the website of the Center for AI Safety, a US-based non-profit organisation.[15] To be fair, such concerns are not new, since another organisation, the Future of Life Institute, released a similar open letter in 2015 in which the likes of Bill Gates, Elon Musk, Stephen Hawking, and others warned against threats of AI and robotics.[16] Some of these risks are real and yet it is the source of the warning that is at times unconvincing. It reminds us of the sorcerer's apprentice who is to blame for their own fate.

[10] See J. Ciani Sciolla, 'The normative challenges of data scraping: legal hurdles and steps forward' (2023) 16(2) *i-lex* i; and U. Pagallo, J. Ciani Sciolla, 'Anatomy of web data scraping: ethics, standards, and the troubles of the law (2023) 2 *European Journal of Data Privacy Law & Technology* 1.

[11] J. Bertomeu, Y. Lin, Y. Liu, Z. Ni, 'Capital market consequences of generative AI: early evidence from the ban of ChatGPT in Italy' (2023), https://ssrn.com/abstract=4452670.

[12] C. Marsden, *Internet Co-Regulation and Constitutionalism: Towards a More Nuanced View* (2011), https://ssrn.com/abstract=1973328.

[13] U. Pagallo, P. Casanovas, R. Madelin, 'The middle-out approach: assessing models of legal governance in data protection, artificial intelligence, and the Web of Data' (2019) 7(1) *Theory and Practice of Legislation* 1.

[14] See https://edition.cnn.com/2023/10/31/tech/sam-altman-ai-risk-taker/index.html.

[15] See www.safe.ai/statement-on-ai-risk.

[16] U. Pagallo, 'From automation to autonomous systems: a legal phenomenology with problems of accountability' in *IJCAI International Joint Conferences on Artificial Intelligence* 17–23. International Joint Conferences on Artificial Intelligence (2017), www.ijcai.org/proceedings/2017/3.

Consider Sam Altman: on one hand, the CEO of OpenAI warns against risks of human extinction; on the other, his company goes on doing business as usual.

The assumption of this chapter is that other sorcerer's apprentices are out there in the field of AI. Which means that sorcerer's apprentices may not only be some darlings of the market or of technological innovation, but also public guardians that should protect citizens against such apprentices. The next sections of the chapter explore this disturbing possibility.

6.3 LEGAL REMEDIES

There are multiple ways in which the law may tackle the normative challenges of LLMs, which include the production and dissemination of disreputable language, such as sexist or racist comments,[17] or answers that contain factual errors that can contribute to the erosion of social trust.[18] Some scholars propose to tackle such issues through technical solutions, for example, (i) the pre-processing of training data; (ii) the fine-tuning of LLMs on data with desired properties, such as predefined ethical principles; or (iii) procedures to test LLMs before their deployment.[19] Others suggest guaranteeing LLMs transparency through the watermarking of the model's outputs,[20] datasheets,[21] system cards,[22] or model cards.[23] Further strategies concern the social aspects of technological development. The challenges of LLMs should be addressed in this case with the setting up of more diverse developer teams and human-in-the-loop protocols,[24] or structured access protocols.[25]

Some of these proposals have been endorsed by the 2023 US Executive Order mentioned earlier in the introduction.[26] Section 4.1 of the Order concerns the development of guidelines, standards, and best practices for AI safety and security – in particular, the development of 'a companion resource to the AI Risk Management Framework, NIST AI 100-1, for generative AI' (4.1(i)(A)) and 'a companion resource to the Secure Software Development Framework to incorporate secure development practices for generative AI and for dual-use foundation models' (4.1(i)(B)). In accordance with a sectorial approach, further specific safeguards concern:

(i) The assessment of biosecurity risks, such as 'generative AI models trained on biological data' (4.4(ii)(A));
(ii) The prevention of child sexual abuse or 'non-consensual intimate imagery of real individuals' (4.5(a)(iv));

[17] H. R. Kirk et al., 'Bias out-of-the-box: an empirical analysis of intersectional occupational biases in popular generative language models' (2021) 34 *Advances in Neural Information Processing Systems* 2611.
[18] O. Evans et al., 'Truthful AI: developing and governing AI that does not lie' (2021) *ArXiv*, https://doi.org/10.48550/arXiv.2110.06674.
[19] See S. Avin, 'Filling gaps in trustworthy development of AI' (2021) 374(6573) *Science* 1327; and E. Perez et al., 'Red teaming language models with language models' (2022) *ArXiv*, https://doi.org/10.48550/arxiv.2202.03286.
[20] J. Kirchenbauer et al., 'A watermark for large language models' (2024) *ArXiv*, https://doi.org/10.48550/arXiv.2301.10226.
[21] T. Gebru et al., 'Datasheets for datasets' (2021) 64(12) *Communications of the ACM* 86.
[22] MetaAI, 'System Cards, a new resource for understanding how AI systems work' (2023), https://ai.facebook.com/blog/system-cards-a-new-resource-for-understanding-how-ai-systems-work/.
[23] L. Derczynski et al., 'Assessing language model deployment with risk cards' (2023) *ArXiv*, https://doi.org/10.48550/arXiv.2303.18190.
[24] Y. Wang, W. Wang, S. Joty, S. C. H. Hoi, 'CodeT5: identifier-aware unified pre-trained encoder-decoder models for code understanding and generation' *Proceedings of the 2021 Conference on Empirical Methods in Natural Language Processing* 8696–8708. (Association for Computational Linguistics, 2021), https://aclanthology.org/2021.emnlp-main.685/.
[25] T. Shevlane, 'Structured access' in J. Bullock, Y.-C. Chen, J. Himmelreich, V. M. Hudson, A. Korinek, M. Young, B. Zhang (eds.), *The Oxford Handbook of AI Governance* (Oxford: Oxford University Press, 2022).
[26] The White House, *Executive Order*, above note 2.

(iii) Issues related to generative AI and inventorship of patentable subject matter under the guidance of the US Patent and Trademark Office (5.2(c)(i));

(iv) The 'development, maintenance, and use of predictive and generative AI-enabled technologies in healthcare delivery and financing – including quality measurement, performance improvement, program integrity, benefits administration, and patient experience – taking into account considerations such as appropriate human oversight of the application of AI-generated output' (8(b)(i)(A));

(v) Recommendation to federal agencies, in consultation with the Secretary of Commerce, the Secretary of Homeland Security, and the heads of other appropriate agencies, as regards the 'external testing for AI, including AI red-teaming for generative AI, to be developed in coordination with the Cybersecurity and Infrastructure Security Agency' (10.1(b)(viii)(A)); 'testing and safeguards against discriminatory, misleading, inflammatory, unsafe, or deceptive outputs, as well as against producing child sexual abuse material and against producing non-consensual intimate imagery of real individuals … for generative AI' (10.1(b)(viii)(B)); and 'reasonable steps to watermark or otherwise label output from generative AI' (10.1(b)(viii)(C));

(vi) Further measures to 'advance the responsible and secure use of generative AI in the Federal Government' (10.1(d) and (f)). In particular, 'agencies are discouraged from imposing broad general bans or blocks on agency use of generative AI. Agencies should instead limit access, as necessary, to specific generative AI services based on specific risk assessments; establish guidelines and limitations on the appropriate use of generative AI; and, with appropriate safeguards in place, provide their personnel and programs with access to secure and reliable generative AI capabilities, at least for the purposes of experimentation and routine tasks that carry a low risk of impacting Americans' rights' (10.1(f)(i)).

Contrary to the US sectorial approach – which applies not only to AI, but also to many other fields of legal regulation, such as personal data protection, or data privacy – the approach of the European Union intends to be 'horizontal' rather than 'vertical'. Although within the limits of EU law, which mostly regard issues related to national security, public order, and the military, the aim of the EU lawmakers is to govern the entire life cycle of AI systems, starting from the collection of input data to the final use of such technologies. Theoretically speaking, there are three options for this horizontal approach: 'the Switch, the Ladder, and the Matrix'.[27] The Switch refers to a binary method, according to which technology is regulated as such, so that lawmakers shall determine which systems are or are not considered AI or their variables: Gen AI, LLMs, and so on. The Ladder refers to a risk-based approach; therefore, AI systems are not considered as such, but rather clustered into different categories in accordance with the level of risk they pose: no risk, low, medium, high, and so on. Finally, the Matrix refers to a multidimensional approach, in which manifold aspects of the technology, such as data input, decision-model type, or the social context and purpose of the AI system must be considered to specify the level of risk. This is the approach recommended by some scholars,[28] and organisations.[29]

[27] J. Mökander, M. Sheth, D. S. Watson, L. Floridi, 'The Switch, the Ladder, and the Matrix: models for classifying AI systems' (2023) 33(1) *Minds and Machines* 221.

[28] C. Wilson, F. Marchetti, M. Di Carlo, A. Riccardi, E. Minisci, 'Classifying intelligence in machines: a taxonomy of intelligent control' (2020) 9(3) *Robotics* 1.

[29] Organisation for Economic Co-operation and Development, *OECD's Framework for the Classification of AI Systems* (2022), https://doi.org/10.1787/cb6d9eca-en.

Against this tripartition, what is then the horizontal approach adopted in the EU with the 2021 proposal of the European Commission?

6.4 THE PRINCIPLE OF TECHNOLOGICAL NEUTRALITY

To determine whether the horizontal approach of the AI Act has endorsed the Switch, the Ladder, or the Matrix approach, attention should be drawn to a crucial challenge of technological regulation, namely the future-proofing of the law. In a nutshell, the law should not be often revised to keep the pace of technological innovation, nor hinder such innovation with its own provisions. Against this twofold constraint, a further challenge of technological regulation has to do with the fact that the law is not the only regulatory system out there. Further regulatory systems include ethics and the forces of the market, social customs, and technology as a regulatory system of its own. Social regulatory systems may reinforce each other: for example, the provisions of the 1996 Treaties of the World Intellectual Property Organization (WIPO) on the use of 'digital rights management' illustrate the convergence between powerful economic interests, technological solutions, and the law. However, the claims of such regulatory systems may also clash and even render the normative claim of another regulatory system irrelevant.[30] The EU e-money Directive 46 of 2000 reminds us how the regulatory claims of the law may fail vis-à-vis digital innovation. Soon after the implementation of the directive, which aimed at expanding traditional forms of centralisation to online interactions, new forms of payment, such as PayPal, made the legal regulation obsolete: the EU legislators in Brussels had to produce a new directive, Directive 110 of 2009. Likewise, in the field of civil aviation with the regulation of drones, Regulation (EU) 2008/216 established a highly decentralised network revolving around the powers of member states and national civil aviation authorities that soon led to the fragmentation of the system. EU lawmakers had to intervene with Regulation (EU) 2018/1139 on common rules for drones in the field of civil aviation.[31]

There are several legal techniques that help the law prevent failings in technological regulation. The overall intent is to make the general and abstract commands of the law responsive to the challenges of technology. Such techniques include:

(i) Technological indifference, or the principle of technological neutrality, according to which legal regulations apply in identical ways, whatever the technology. Both Recital 15 of the GDPR and the right to authorise communication of a work to the public in the field of copyright law illustrate this legal technique against risks of inefficacy and normative obsolescence;

(ii) Implementation neutrality, so that regulations are by definition specific to a technology and yet they do not favour one or more of its possible implementations – for example, the signature of e-documents;

(iii) Potential neutrality of the law that sets up a particular attribute of a technology, such as consumer friendly interfaces in e-commerce law, although lawmakers can draft the legal requirement in such a way that even non-compliant implementations can be modified to become compliant.[32]

[30] U. Pagallo, M. Durante, 'The pros and cons of legal automation and its governance' (2016) 7(2) *European Journal of Risk Regulation* 323.

[31] E. Bassi, 'European Drones Regulation: Today's Legal Challenges', *International Conference on Unmanned Aircraft Systems (ICUAS)* (Atlanta, GA: IEE, 2019), 443–450.

[32] C. Reed, *Making Laws for Cyberspace* (Oxford: Oxford University Press, 2012).

Since the proposal of the European Commission in April 2021, the AI Act has revolved around the principle of technological neutrality and its corollaries. In the phrasing of Section 5.2.1 of the first draft of the Act, 'the definition of AI system in the legal framework aims to be as technology neutral and future proof as possible, taking into account the fast technological and market developments related to AI'. The aim of the AI Act is not to govern the technology as such, but rather the uses of AI systems. To attain this end, according to the Explanatory Memorandum of the Act, the classification system of the regulation tailors requirements and obligations taking a 'risk-based approach'. Therefore, the AI Act endorses the Ladder rather than the Switch approach. The overall idea is, on the one hand, to classify uses of AI in accordance with different levels of risk so that, on the other hand, different kinds of governance apply to such risk levels. The first draft of the AI Act clustered such risks into four categories: (i) unacceptable risks with corresponding bans, or prohibitions; (ii) high risk level with certification duties and further administrative burdens for developers, manufacturers, or end users of AI systems; (iii) low-risk uses of AI; and, between high- and low-risk AI systems, (iv) transparency duties for some uses of the technology.[33] The 2024 consolidated text that followed the institutional trialogue between the Council, the Parliament, and the Commission specified a new risk, 'systemic risk'.[34] According to the final wording of Recital 97 of the Act, 'this Regulation provides specific rules for general-purpose AI models and for general-purpose AI models that pose systemic risks, which should apply also when these models are integrated or form part of an AI system'. The new level of risk has to do with either the 'high-impact capabilities' of the model measured in floating point operations (FLOPs) or 'significant impact on the internal market due to its reach' (Recital 111).

On this basis, the purpose – and hope – of the EU institutions with their 'Ladder approach' is fourfold. First, the aim of the AI Act is to provide certainty through a unified legal framework. Contrary to sectorial or vertical approaches of regulation, as occurs in US law, the AI Act intends to set up clear rules for all AI systems and fields of regulation: 'certainty' is a mantra of the first draft of the AI Act. The same holds for the final version of the legislation, according to Recitals 3, 12, 83, 84, 97, 139, 177 of Regulation (EU) 2024/1689.

Second, the risk-based approach of the Regulation will reinforce the future-proofing of the law to tackle advancements in technology. Rather than focusing on the technicalities and different approaches of AI, from logic-based to statistical methods, focus is on the different uses of technology with probabilities of events, consequences, and costs. In the Explanatory Memorandum of the 2021 draft, it is argued that the AI Act 'proposes a single future-proof definition of AI. Certain particularly harmful AI practices are prohibited as contravening Union values, while specific restrictions and safeguards are proposed in relation to certain uses of remote biometric identification systems for the purpose of law enforcement' (section 1.1 of the Memorandum). Whatever the means, it is the impact of AI systems on citizens, consumers, institutions, and society at large that ultimately matters. This overall approach represents the backbone of Regulation (EU) 2024/1689. The establishment of regulatory sandboxes, pursuant to Article 57 of the Act, should reinforce this proactive approach.

Third, the different forms of governance set up with the AI Act – namely, the establishment and implementation of policies, procedures, and standards for the proper development, use, and

[33] M. Ebers, V. R. S. Hoch, F. Rosenkranz, H. Ruschemeier, B. Steinrötter, 'The European Commission's proposal for an Artificial Intelligence Act – a critical assessment by members of the Robotics and AI Law Society (RAILS)' (2021) 4 *Multidisciplinary Scientific Journal* 589.

[34] European Parliament and Council, *Artificial Intelligence Act: Consolidated Text of 2021/0106 (COD)*, 24 January 2024, Brussels.

management of AI systems, according to their level of risk – will properly address the complexity of the field. One of the main reasons for the failure of the law in governing advancements of technology has in fact to do with lack of 'flexibility'. The formula means that the hard tools of the law often fall short in coping with the challenges of technological innovation, either because they are unfit to meet such challenges – for example, development of standards – or because legal provisions simply arrive 'too late', much as occurs in the paradox of Zeno about the speedy Achilles (the technology) and the Turtle (the law). The AI Act intends to prevent these risks, endorsing all three methods of legal governance: (i) the strict top-down approach of hard law that hinges on the threat of physical or pecuniary sanctions, such as prohibition of unacceptable uses of AI or certification duties for high-risk AI systems; (ii) a co-regulatory approach, much as occurs with Article 5(2) of the GDPR, in the case of development of certain standards under Art. 40 of the AI Act, for example; and (iii) a self-regulatory approach at work, such as with Article 95 on codes of conduct for other than high-risk AI systems.

Last but not least, the all-encompassing legal framework of the AI Act should provide the basis for the respect and protection of fundamental rights in EU law. The principle of legal certainty and a risk-based approach – as well as different kinds of legal governance for the risks posed by AI technologies – intend to attain this end through a new set of duties and obligations for designers, manufacturers, and, in certain cases, end users of the technology. This is not to say that AI systems do not create 'liability gaps', or that new rights should not be established to protect individuals. Further proposals of EU law, from the AI Liability Act to the revised Product Liability Directive, complement the provisions of the AI Act by establishing new procedural rights and safeguards, by equalising the protection against certain malfunctioning of AI software to defects of products, and so on.[35]

However, both the adoption of the principle of technological neutrality and the Ladder approach beg the question of the material scope of the legislation: the aim is to govern AI technologies, after all. In the first draft of the AI Act, Article 3(1) on definitions referred to AI as a software developed with the 'techniques and approaches' listed in Annex I. Three years later, the final version of Article 3(1) intends AI as a 'machine-based system' that can operate with 'varying levels of autonomy' and eventually adapt itself after deployment. The new definition of AI in Article 3(1) must be complemented with the further definitions of 'general purpose AI model' (Article 3(63)); 'high-impact capabilities' (No. 64); 'systemic risk' (No. 65); and 'general purpose AI system' (No. 66). They provide the final response of the EU legislators to the buzz and disruption of foundation models, Gen AI, and the sub-category of LLMs over the past two years.

The aim of the next section is to illustrate how the problems of the AI Act with the definition of technology are related to a more complex issue than that of multiplying the Switch upon which the Ladder approach rests. This more complex issue revolves around the normative design of the Act. The next section aims to illustrate the many facets of this problem from the 'single future-proof definition of AI' in the Explanatory Memorandum of April 2021 to the five AI-related definitions inserted in the final text of June 2024.

6.5 THE TROUBLES OF THE AI ACT WITH AI

The problems of EU legislators with the regulation of AI can be divided in this context – that is, dealing with the challenges of LLMs as a sub-category of Gen AI and foundation models – into two groups. The first set of issues has to do with the 'horizontal approach' of the AI Act; the

[35] U. Pagallo, 'The politics of data in EU law: will it succeed?' (2022) 1 *DISO* 20.

second set specifically concerns the regulation of LLMs. The next subsections examine each of these problems separately.

6.5.1 *The Incongruities of the Horizontal Approach*

Almost all articles of the first draft of the AI Act – that is, the proposal of the Commission in April 2021 – were the target of criticism and subject to heated discussions. The number of amendments of the European Parliament in March and June 2023 as well as the consolidated text of the Act from January 2024 illustrate this point. The intent of this subsection is not to cover this institutional debate, but rather to sum it up regarding some crucial inconsistencies of the new legislation in line with a meta-regulatory approach. This perspective draws attention to four problems of the Act that concern the protection of fundamental rights, governance mechanisms, legal certainty, and the material scope of the legislation.

First, regarding the protection of the rights enshrined in the EU Charter of Fundamental Rights (CFRs), the 2021 proposal of the Commission simply overlooked some of them, for example, the right to a high level of environmental protection and the improvement of the quality of the environment under Article 37 of the CFRs. Environmental risks fell outside of the 2021 proposal lest human rights were directly affected.[36] Correspondingly, in the series of amendments presented in March and June 2023, the European Parliament proposed to insert a fundamental rights impact assessment (FRIA) with a new Recital 58(a) and a new Article 29(a) of the Regulation.[37] An intense institutional trialogue between the Commission, the European Parliament, and the Council followed as a result. The hard-won compromise reached with the final version of the Act can hardly be presented as satisfactory. The FRIA of Article 27 only covers some high-risk uses of AI, whereas Article 95 on codes of conduct hinges on the goodwill and voluntary initiatives of companies and corporations. Although the final goal of the codes of conduct of Article 95 is to progressively expand the set of standards and protections established for high-risk uses of AI to non-high-risk uses of technology, even a teleological interpretation of Articles 95 and 112(7) of the Act is not enough to make that expansion legally binding.

The troubles of the AI Act with the protection of rights entail further governance issues. As noted in the previous sections, the Regulation concerns different kinds of governance in accordance with the risks posed by technology, namely strict top-down regulations for high-risk uses of AI vis-à-vis self-regulatory solutions for other than high-risk uses of AI systems. However, it is apparent that also 'low-risk' AI applications – in the original meaning of the 2021 proposal – may have a relevant impact on the environment of human societies. AI technologies often require massive computational resources and corresponding large computing centres that have a very high energy requirement and carbon footprint.[38] Even the Regulation seems to admit this fact with the provisions of Article 73 on 'serious incident'. According to the definitions of the Act, the formula covers 'incident or malfunctioning of an AI system that directly or indirectly leads

[36] P. Gailhofer et al., *The Role of Artificial Intelligence in the European Green Deal*, Study for the Special Committee on Artificial Intelligence in a Digital Age (AIDA), Policy Department for Economic, Scientific and Quality of Life Policies (Luxembourg: European Parliament, 2021).

[37] European Parliament, *Amendments adopted by the European Parliament on 14 June 2023 on the proposal for a regulation of the European Parliament and of the Council on laying down harmonised rules on artificial intelligence (Artificial Intelligence Act) and amending certain Union legislative acts* (COM(2021)0206 – C9-0146/2021 – 2021/0106(COD)), P9_TA(2023)0236.

[38] M. M. Sokolowski, 'Energy efficiency at energy production level: promoting combined heat and power' in M. M. Roggenkamp, K. J. de Graaf, R. C. Fleming (eds.), *Energy Law, Climate Change and the Environment* (Cheltenham: Elgar, 2021) 753–763.

to . . . the infringement of obligations under Union law intended to protect fundamental rights' (Article 3(49)(c)); and 'serious harm to . . . the environment' (lett. d). It is likely that several environmental risks of AI systems and the protection of some fundamental rights may thus fall within the loopholes of the legal governance set up in Chapter VII of the Act. The assumption rests on the limited cases in which the protection of fundamental rights, such as environmental protection, is covered by the top-down provisions of the Regulation and, moreover, on how the governance of other than high-risk AI systems may fall short in coping with consequences of AI uses that, although serious, are not covered by the strict definitions of Article 3(49)(c) and (d).

A further problem of the AI Act concerns one of its alleged strengths: legal certainty. The 'horizontal approach' of the legislation necessitates a strict coordination with other pieces of EU law, either horizontal, such as the GDPR, or vertical, such as regulations in the financial sector, for medical devices, or drones. The first draft of the AI Act created some legal puzzles.[39] How to put together the panoply of technological regulations in EU law is indeed no easy task – like squaring circles through stochastic methods in the legal domain. In fact, the premise is often given by barely readable texts: for example, the provisions that amend previous acts of the Union in civil aviation (Article 102 and 108 of the AI Act); new agriculture and forestry vehicles (Article 103); marine equipment (Article 105); or rail systems interoperability (Article 106). To be sure, the extremely technical wording of such legal texts does not entail that every coordination among different pieces of legislation is impossible – for example, between the assessment of multiple levels of risk triggered by AI systems in accordance with the different parameters of the AI Act, of the GDPR, or of the regulation of AI as a medical device. Further problems of legal certainty and coordination may arise with Recital 11 of the AI Act, according to which the regulation should be understood without 'prejudice' to Regulation 2022/2065 on a single market for digital services. Likewise, Recital 141 establishes that the safeguards of the AI Act have to be intended 'in accordance with' Regulations 2022/868 on data governance and 2023/2854 on fair access to and use of data.

The principle of legal certainty of the AI Act is also under stress because of the material scope of the legislation. We have noted that the disruption of Gen AI and LLMs between 2022 and 2023 ignited not only the imagination of everyday people, but also that of lawmakers and institutions. In the amendments adopted by the European Parliament on 14 June 2023,[40] the counterproposals to the 2021 text not only stressed the incongruities of the first draft, such as the lack of a fundamental rights impact assessment, but also the reasons why a new array of provisions had to cope with that which fell outside the proposal of the Commission, including LLMs. The consolidated text from January 2024 and then the official version of the AI Act were intended to square the legal circle with the overall notion of 'general-purpose AI' model (and GPAI system). The previous section mentioned the definitions No. 63 (on GPAI model); No. 64 (on its high-impact capabilities); No. 65 (systemic risk); and No. 66 (GPAI system) of Article 3 of the AI Act.

Next, our focus is on the legal patch adopted as a result of the hard-won compromise between the Triad: the Council, the Parliament, and the Commission. Since the goodwill of the EU institutions is out of the question, attention should be drawn to some side effects of the Regulation.

39 M. Veale, F. Zuiderveen Borgesius, 'Demystifying the draft EU artificial intelligence act – analysing the good, the bad, and the unclear elements of the proposed approach' (2021) 22(4) *Computer Law Review International* 97.

40 European Parliament, *Amendments*, above note 37.

6.5.2 A *New Sorcerer's Apprentice?*

The summer 2023 amendments of the European Parliament did not refer to the use of LLMs, and only partially to the notion of Gen AI. Rather, the focus was on 'foundation models'. The formula was coined by Bommasani and colleagues[41] to identify AI systems that, on the one hand, are fruitful across multiple fields of application and present emergent capabilities when scaled up; on the other hand, such models can be adapted to undefined downstream tasks by a multitude of actors.[42] In the wording of the Parliament's amendment – Article 3(1)(1c) of the 2023 amendments – foundation model 'means an AI system model that is trained on broad data at scale, is designed for generality of output, and can be adapted to a wide range of distinctive tasks'.

The Parliament proposed a full array of new regulatory measures for foundation models: the term is employed sixty-two times in the series of amendments. Many of them made sense. Since the very beginning of this chapter, attention has been drawn to the normative challenges of LLMs that should be properly tackled. The result was the consolidated text from January 2024 which is copied and pasted by Article 3(63) of the Regulation. The definition refers to

> an AI model, including where such an AI model is trained with a large amount of data using self-supervision at scale, that displays significant generality and is capable of competently performing a wide range of distinct tasks regardless of the way the model is placed on the market and that can be integrated into a variety of downstream systems or applications, except AI models that are used for research, development or prototyping activities before they are placed on the market.

The AI Act sets up specific provisions for LLMs falling under the all-encompassing formula of general-purpose AI model. Such a formula should be complemented with the notion of 'high-impact capability' –models that match or exceed the capabilities of the most advanced general-purpose AI models (Article 3(64)), which can further trigger a 'systemic risk' due to its 'significant impact on the internal market' and because of 'negative effects on public health, safety, public security, fundamental rights, or the society as a whole, that can be propagated at scale across the value chain' (Article 3(65)). Therefore, Article 51 of the Regulation is devoted to the classification of these AI models; Article 52 sets up conditions and procedure for the use of GPAI models with systemic risks; Article 53 establishes the obligations for providers of GPAI models; Article 54 specifies the obligations for providers of third countries; Article 55 determines the obligations for providers of GPAI models with system risk; Article 56 defines the codes of practice. The overall outcome of this normative effort looks like a legal monster.

The stratification of the horizontal or 'Ladder approach' in the AI Act is strengthened by the multiplication of 'legal switches' on what is AI and what is not; what is AI and what is a general-purpose AI model; what is a general-purpose AI model and a general-purpose AI system; or a general-purpose AI model with or without systemic risks; or with or without high-impact capabilities. The threat is to end up with all drawbacks of both the vertical and horizontal approaches to the regulation of technology. In fact, as regards the original aim of the Act on 'rules of harmonisation' in EU law, Chapter V of the legislation on what US law dubs Gen AI adds to the coordination problems of the horizontal regulation, such as the new obligation of GPAI providers, for general-purpose AI models, including LLMs, to 'put in place a policy to

[41] Bommasani, 'On the opportunities and risks', above note 1.

[42] R. Bommasani, P. Liang, *Reflections on Foundation Models* (Stanford, CA: Human-Centered Artificial Intelligence, 2021), https://hai.stanford.edu/news/reflections-foundation-models.

comply with Union law on copyright and related rights' (Article 53(1)(c) of the AI Act). On the other hand, multiple definitions of manifold AI systems intend to flesh out the material scope of the legislation, and yet they exponentially increase the problems with the regulation of AI.

The multiplication of regulatory efforts on general-purpose models, systemic risks, high-impact capabilities, or the cumulative amount of computer power used for training these models – for example, the greater than 10^25 FLOPs of the AI Act (Article 51(2)) does not prevent the main threat of technological regulation, namely the over-frequent revision of the legal text. The EU lawmakers have precautionarily established the legal presumption that all LLMs, such as GPT-4, have 'high impact capabilities' pursuant to Article 51(1) of the legislation – in fact, the pre-training for GPT-4 only required about 10^25 FLOPS in 2024. And yet, Recital 4 of the Act reminds us of how 'AI is a fast evolving family of technologies that contributes to a wide array of economic, environmental and societal benefits across the entire spectrum of industries and social activities'. It is noteworthy that the principle of technological neutrality – and for that matter, every legal technique that may help the law prevent the obsolescence of regulations aiming to govern advancements of technology – vanished from the AI Act. Considering the exponential growth of innovation, from computing power to data availability for further AI models, systems, and approaches that can be expected in the future, the threat is that lawmakers once again will arrive too late in this cat-and-mouse, Achilles-and-the turtle game. Can the AI Act catch up with this complexity and prevent the threat of its own obsolescence?

6.6 CONCLUSIONS

In his 1847 conference presentation 'Court Resolutions Are Not Science', the German philosopher of law Julius Hermann von Kirschmann claimed that 'three rectifying words from the legislators and whole libraries become wastepaper'.[43] This has been the risk with all discussions about the AI Act, from the first draft to the series of amendments by the European Parliament in 2023, from the consolidated text of January 2024 to the version of the Parliament from March of that year, down to the final text of July 2024. At the time of writing, it is an open issue how critical provisions of the Regulation will be interpreted and implemented, for example as regards the new AI standards of the Regulation. Also, further provisions can be expected with delegated or implementing acts of the Commission under Articles 58, 60, 68, 72, 92, or 101 of the Regulation. This uncertainty, however, *pace* von Kirschmann, does not mean that we should simply wait for the 'three rectifying words' of the legislator to assess a legal framework. The chapter has noted some specific inconsistencies of the AI Act in accordance with a meta-regulatory approach. In the spirit of Goethe's *Sorcerer's Apprentice*, the aim was to illustrate the danger that legislators may worsen the challenges of technology with their own provisions. The risk materialises every time regulations either stifle sound technological innovation or need over-frequent revision to tackle the speed of such progress.

To corroborate the assumption, the analysis illustrated pros and cons, strengths and drawbacks of the current regulatory efforts in EU law. The benefits regard a single piece of legislation – horizontal, in the jargon of EU lawyers – that will provide legal certainty, proper governance, and strong protection of fundamental rights. The pitfalls concern limits that are endogenous or exogeneous. The limits start with the definition of the material scope of the legislation, namely the preliminary definition of that which should be governed. In addition to the growing list of

[43] J. H. von Kirchmann, *Zeitfragen und Abenteuer* (Leipzig: F. F. Weber, 1881).

definitions in the AI Act regarding the use of AI systems and of general-purpose AI models, further models and sub-categories of AI must be expected in the foreseeable future. The AI Act provides the technique of Annexes to the legal text to keep the list of definitions growing with the implementing powers of the Commission. The problem does not depend, however, on whether the list is more or less complete, but rather on whether the original aim of the legislation – the risk-based, or Ladder approach of the first draft of the Act – will be attained, or even still makes sense. Among the most relevant endogenous limits, or defects, of the final AI Act, it seems fair to concede that a straight risk assessment of the uses of technology remains problematic. Whether or not the AI Act has to be considered a risk-based regulation, crucial aspects of technological governance remain open, such as (i) uncertainties associated with the notion of risk and corresponding protection of rights; (ii) the difficulty to assess all risks raised by specific uses of AI; (iii) the costs related to such assessment; and (iv) the future-proofing of the law.

All in all, what legal technique could prevent the threat of legislators to frequently revising their own texts remains uncertain in the case of the AI Act. We noted that the Commission adopted the principle of technological neutrality in the first draft of the Act and then EU legislators discarded the principle during the law-making process. There is no reference to any technological neutrality in the amendments approved by the European Parliament in June 2023,[44] in the consolidated text of January 2024,[45] in the version of the Act released by the Parliament in March of that year, down to the official text of July 2024. Although implemented through a transition period for certain uses of AI according to Article 113 of the Act, the risk of legal obsolescence is real considering that legislation will only be at full force on 2 August 2026. New technological advancements can be reasonably expected in this span of time, triggering once again a cat-and-mouse game in which lawmakers may arrive 'too late' or worsen the challenges of technology with their regulations.

Such risks were illustrated with the EU e-money Directive 46 of 2000 and its revision in 2009; together with the revision of the EU 2008 Regulation on the use and governance of drones, with Regulation (EU) 2018/1139 – today's General Regulation on civil aviation. The chapter discussed some of the reasons why (certain provisions or chapters of) the AI Act may meet a similar fate: the self-defeating outcome of every sorcerer's apprentice. To be fair, the Regulation establishes several legal mechanisms to tackle both the known-unknowns and even the unknown-unknowns of the legislation. We noted that a considerable amount of normative power has been devolved back to the European Commission through the means of delegated or implementing acts. Further provisions concern the detailed evaluation and review of the Regulation under Article 112. Every year the Commission will have to assess whether the list of Annex III and that related to Article 5 should be amended (Article 112(1)). Every four years, by the end of this decade, the Triad should discuss, among other things, 'extending existing area headings or adding new area headings in Annex III' (No. 2). Reports should include the assessment of national competent authorities, state of penalties, harmonised standards, and 'the number of undertakings that enter the market after the entry into application of this Regulation, and how many of them are SMEs' (No. 4). 2 August 2028 will also be particularly relevant because that is the first deadline for the Commission's reports on the functioning of the AI Office, progress on the development of standards, and the impact and effectiveness of the codes of conduct (Nos. 5, 6, and 7).

[44] European Parliament, *Amendments*, above note 37.

[45] European Parliament and Council, *Consolidated Text*, above note 34.

Therefore, the question does not revolve around whether the EU lawmakers will be forced to amend themselves in accordance with the provisions of the AI Act, but rather how soon we should expect this process of revision with the complex interaction of Articles 58, 60, 68, 72, 92, and 101 of the Regulation – on the Commission's delegated powers – vis-à-vis the seven fronts of Article 112. The over-frequent revision of the law is not only highly likely but even seems necessary, or inevitable. Leaving aside the powers of the Commission, we know the formal starting time of this complex process of amendment and revision because Article 5 and Annex III of the Regulation will be assessed by August 2027. By then, what occurs from time to time in business and Greek legends with 'sons' devouring and replacing 'fathers' may well have happened (for example, Tim and Telecom Italia in the field of telecommunications); much like Zeus and Cronos in the Greek myth. As regards the AI Act, this may occur with LLMs of Chapter V superseding the AI systems of Article 3(1) of the Regulation. However, in addition to the pace of technological innovation, the chapter insisted on problems of legal governance and legal certainty, and the troubles with the protection of fundamental rights. Lawmakers in Brussels are spoiled for choice as to where they will start with amending the Act.

7

Mapping Generative AI Liability Cases in the EU Legal Framework

Teresa Rodríguez de las Heras Ballell

7.1 SETTING THE SCENE: POLICY AND REGULATION OF AI IN THE EU

Artificial intelligence (AI) has burst onto the global scene, arousing equal parts disquiet and fascination. The exponential development of AI and, in particular, its rapid emergence in the market and the expansion of its uncountable uses with astonishing decision-making capabilities and an impressive content-generation potential have been accompanied by a growing, and sometimes alarming, perception of risks[1] that has marked the regulatory debate, public opinion, and social acceptance[2] of its advances. Hence, the attention of legislators and regulators on AI has spotlighted the critical (and pressing) need to reconcile its promises and its perils.

In such a context, the European Union (EU) has taken a leading role in its attempts to formulate and establish an ambitious legal framework for AI. Although the AI Act is clearly the flagship regulation, it is neither the only one nor a comprehensive legal regime for the AI. The AI Act is a key component of the broader and more complex ecosystem of (existing and prospective) pieces of legislation aimed at governing the development, deployment, and use of AI systems in or in connection with the EU. In particular, the AI Act does not provide for a body of liability rules for damage caused by AI systems.

[1] World Economic Forum (WEF), *Fourth Industrial Revolution for the Earth Series Harnessing Artificial Intelligence for the Earth*, World Economic Forum, 2018. The risks of 'unguided' AI fall into six categories: performance risks, security risks, control risks, ethical risks, economic risks, societal risks.

[2] According to the results of the study *Behavioural Study on the Link between Challenges of Artificial Intelligence for Member States' Civil Liability Rules and Consumer Attitudes towards AI-Enabled Products and Services*, JUST/2020/RCON/FW/CIVI/0065, December 2021, 'the perceived probability of receiving compensation in case of damage caused by artificial intelligence applications determines not only the degree of consumer trust in artificial intelligence applications, but also the social acceptance of such applications and the probability that consumers will buy or use AI-based products or services: the higher the perceived likelihood, the higher the levels of acceptance, trust and, implicitly, willingness to purchase such products or services'. Therefore, the appropriateness, adequacy, and efficiency of compensation schemes for damage caused by AI systems are crucial to ensure a broad and favourable societal receptivity to their use, a safe and reliable market for products and services, and a fair and balanced attribution of risks that does not discourage innovation and investment in innovation and that incentivises effective risk prevention and mitigation measures.

Alongside the regulatory response that has crystallised in the adoption of the AI Act,[3] aimed to prevent and mitigate potential risk, the EU has paid particular attention to another risk factor: the adequacy and sufficiency of liability systems to confront AI damages. For various reasons, an AI system may be involved in causing damage (defects, wrong design, inaccurate or biased data, poor training, avoidable or unavoidable hacking attacks, human mistakes, unexpected learning processes) to individuals or property. Where the risks materialise, the challenge is to determine whether existing liability rules are adequate, effective, and sufficient to compensate the victims in an equivalent way (compared to a case where damage is caused without the use of AI). Promoting safe, reliable, and high-quality AI in Europe has become one of the central elements of the EU Digital Strategy defined in the strategic package adopted on 19 February 2020. The White Paper on AI[4] and the Report on the safety and liability implications of AI, the Internet of Things (IoT), and Robotics[5] defined the coordinates for Europe's digital future.[6] Since the formation in 2018 of the Expert Group on Liability and New Technologies, with two divisions[7] – New Technologies and Product Liability – there has been a succession of reports, working papers, and legislative initiatives of various types to explore precisely the AI terrain using the existing liability tools and to test their adequacy and effectiveness.

Mindful of the distinctive features of AI systems (complexity, opacity, vulnerability, openness, data dependence, autonomy) and their potential impact on the effective application of pre-existing liability regimes, the EU has embarked on a thorough review of the existing liability rules to assess their adequacy and effectiveness in the face of the intensive and extensive use of AI. This exercise resulted in the publication of two proposals on 28 September of 2022 – the Proposal for a Directive on the adaptation of non-contractual fault-based liability rules to artificial intelligence[8] (commonly known as AI Liability Directive, AILD) and the Proposal for a revision of the Directive of the European Parliament and of the Council on liability for defective products[9] (Revised Product Liability Directive, revPLD) – that are key pieces in the legislative review effort to shape a comprehensive and coherent liability regime for damage caused by AI systems.[10] While the AILD was finally withdrawn, as no agreement was reached on

[3] Regulation (EU) 2024/1689 of the European Parliament and of the Council of 13 June 2024 laying down harmonised rules on artificial intelligence and amending Regulations (EC) No. 300/2008, (EU) No. 167/2013, (EU) No. 168/2013, (EU) 2018/858, (EU) 2018/1139 and (EU) 2019/2144 and Directives 2014/90/EU, (EU) 2016/797 and (EU) 2020/1828 (Artificial Intelligence Act) (Text with EEA relevance), PE/24/2024/REV/1, *OJ L*, 2024/1689, 12 July 2024.

[4] White Paper on *Artificial Intelligence – A European Approach to Excellence and Trust*, COM(2020) 65 final, Brussels, 19 February 2020.

[5] Report from the Commission to the European Parliament, the Council and the European Economic and Social Committee, *Report on the Safety and Liability Implications of Artificial Intelligence, the Internet of Things and Robotics*, COM(2020) 64 final, Brussels, 19 February 2020.

[6] Communication from the Commission to the European Parliament, the Council, the European Economic and Social Committee and the Committee of the Regions, *Shaping Europe's Digital Future*, COM/2020/67 final, Brussels, 19 February 2020.

[7] Published in the register of expert groups on 9 March 2018, https://ec.europa.eu/transparency/expert-groups-register/screen/expert-groups/consult?lang = en&do = groupDetail.groupDetail&groupID = 3592. The expert group's mission was to 'provide the Commission with expertise on the applicability of the Product Liability Directive to traditional products, new technologies and new societal challenges (Product Liability Directive formation) and assist the Commission in developing principles that can serve as guidelines for possible adaptations of applicable laws at EU and national level relating to new technologies (New Technologies formation)'. The author of this chapter, Teresa Rodríguez de las Heras Ballell, was a member of the Expert Group, as an individual expert appointed in her personal capacity. All the views expressed in this chapter are the personal views of the author and do not necessarily represent the opinions of the Expert Group as a whole or its members, or the view of the Commission.

[8] COM/2022/496 final.

[9] COM/2022/495 final.

[10] Rodríguez de las Heras Ballell, Teresa, 'The revision of the product liability directive: a key piece in the artificial intelligence liability puzzle', *ERA Forum*, 2023, https://doi.org/10.1007/s12027-023-00751-y.

the final text, the revPLD was approved by the European Parliament[11] on 12 March 2024[12] and finally adopted on 23 October 2024.[13]

These (draft and adopted) Directives interplay (was expected to interplay in the case of the withdrawn AILD) with the AI Act as well as with the national rules on fault-based liability in setting out a liability system for AI that, concurrently, needs to be complemented with a constellation of existing rules in the fields of, inter alia, contract law, privacy, intellectual property rights, and competition law.

In this vast and multifaceted policymaking and lawmaking process, the advent of generative AI systems and the momentum they gained burst onto the regulatory scene, signalling a significant shift in the AI landscape. Throughout the deliberative process of the AI Act, the attention paid to generative AI and its implications resulted in various policy decisions and drafting solutions. The notion of an AI system has been carefully refined and new definitions were added to the draft AI Act to ensure that it was suited to address the challenges of these emerging models. From the initial inclusion of the term 'foundation models' in intermediate versions of the text to the final incorporation of the concept of 'general-purpose AI model' (and system), the AI Act has struggled to embrace the emergence and extraordinary popularity of generative AI. In addition to these terminological and conceptual efforts to accommodate the scope of application to generative AI, the AI Act also provides for specific solutions designed for these models. Nonetheless, there are legal and regulatory implications of generative AI that may escape the proposed solutions.

Understanding the extent of the paradigm shift that generative AI is likely to bring will allow us to assess the sufficiency of the measures adopted and to identify possible shortcomings and gaps in the current EU framework. In particular, generative AI raises specific problems in the compliance of the AI Act obligations and in the application of liability rules that have to be acknowledged and properly addressed. The multimodality, the emergence factor, the scalability and the generality of tasks may render meaningless the assumptions underlying the obligations and requirements laid down for AI systems.

Besides, the generative capabilities of these systems producing content of any kind – text, images, audiovisual, or functional information (derivative AI systems) – exacerbate certain liability risks inherent to AI systems or tend to trigger specific damage related to the infringement of privacy or IP rights, provoked by the reliance on the outputs while assisting users in a diversity of decisions, or caused by the harmful effects of the outputs themselves on affected persons.

The chapter aims to explore whether the current ecosystem of existing and still-to-be adopted rules on AI systems fully and adequately addresses the distinctive features of generative AI, with special consideration to the interaction between the AI Act and the liability rules as provided for in the draft AILD and revPLD. Although the draft AILD was finally withdrawn in February 2025, the latest draft will be studied here as it represents one of the approaches adopted to face the challenges posed by AI. Even if a differente approach can be adopted or a new proposal can be tabled, in the future the withdrawn draft provided useful elements for discussion. Beyond the assessment of the rules laid down in the Directives, the chapter briefly lists other liability scenarios to be explored in future works. With this aim, the chapter is structured as follows. Section 7.2 traces

[11] On 11 October 2024, approval of the EP's first reading position by the Council. To follow the procedure, https://eur-lex.europa.eu/legal-content/EN/HIS/?uri=CONSIL:ST_13760_2024_ADD_1#2024-10-11_APR_R1_byCONSIL.

[12] P9_TA(2024)0132. European Parliament legislative resolution of 12 March 2024 on the proposal for a directive of the European Parliament and of the Council on liability for defective products (COM(2022)0495 – C9-0322/2022 – 2022/0302(COD)).

[13] Directive (EU) 2024/2853 of the European Parliament and of the Council of 23 October 2024 on liability for defective products and repealing Council Directive 85/374/EEC (Text with EEA relevance) PE/7/2024/REV/1. *OJ L*, 2024/2853, 18 November 2024.

how generative AI has been included within the scope of application of the AI Act and which specific rules have been laid down accordingly. Section 7.3 focused on the liability rules as recently modified in the EU with special consideration to AI: the withdrawn proposal of AILD and the revised PLD. Section 7.4 maps other potential liability scenarios and concludes with final remarks.

7.2 GENERATIVE AI IN THE AI ACT: DEFINITION, RELEVANT FEATURES, AND RULES

The notion of an AI system is the mainstay of the EU regulatory strategy on AI. Accurately defining the concept and, more importantly, properly identifying its distinctive and differential features underlying the rationale for a specific regulation, are instrumental to deploy the regulatory strategy in an effective and reasonable way. The definition of AI systems not only demarcates the scope of application of the regulatory framework but, most important, must capture its singular characteristics and identify the risk triggers that require regulatory action.

The legal definition of an AI system is neither a simple task nor an innocuous exercise. Not surprisingly, the definition has evolved significantly in the development of the AI Act from its initial wording as laid down in the proposal. During this evolution, the momentum of generative AI has impacted on the conceptualisation process and disrupted the terminological options and the drafting decisions in the AI Act. In tracing the drafting evolution throughout the successive versions of the text, meaningful findings are revealed.

7.2.1 *Tracing the Evolution of the Definition of AI Systems in the AI Act: Meaning and Significance*

The formulation of a definition of AI systems for legal purposes faces a number of challenges. It must be free from technological determinants and maintain sufficient (technological) neutrality to encompass the various solutions available (or to come) on the market and to avoid obsolescence by being able to integrate future technological developments. It must translate into functional and relevant features, operational characteristics, and technical specifications. The evolution of the definition of an IA system in the European Union since the proposal for an AI Act[14] highlights these difficulties.

The first definition proposed in the AI Act[15] immediately raised several questions and drew some criticism. Firstly, it failed to convincingly and decisively delineate the proposed AI systems to be regulated in contrast with the already commonly used and widely known computer programs (software). The regulatory requirements imposed by the new text needed a clear and objective distinction as to their scope of application. Secondly, the reference to certain techniques listed in an Annex, despite the establishment of a review mechanism, questioned (in addition to the uniqueness of the chosen techniques themselves)[16] the technological neutrality,

[14] Proposal for a Regulation of the European Parliament and of the Council laying down harmonised rules in the field of artificial intelligence (Artificial Intelligence Act) and amending certain legislative acts of the Union, COM/2021/206 final.

[15] The proposed AI Regulation (Art. 3(1)) defined the IA system as 'software that is developed using one or more of the techniques and strategies listed in Annex I and that can, for a given set of human-defined objectives, generate output information such as content, predictions, recommendations or decisions that influence the environments with which it interacts'.

[16] Proposed AI Regulation, Annex I, Artificial Intelligence Techniques referred to in Article 3, point 1: 'Machine learning strategies, including supervised, unsupervised and reinforcement learning, employing a wide variety of methods, including deep learning. Logic and knowledge-based strategies, especially knowledge representation,

the adaptive capacity to new solutions, and the very soundness of a purely descriptive definition incapable of offering a functional concept.

The proposed definition evolved,[17] aligning itself with the Organisation for Economic Co-operation and Development (OECD) notion,[18] which, following a subsequent revision,[19] strengthens some of the differential functional features and qualifies others[20] in order to accommodate the most recent developments that had burst onto the international scene and media debate (large language models, generative AI, general AI). Expanding the definition of AI systems so as to include emerging paradigms was the first drafting option. Nonetheless, it was not implemented in an isolated manner, but in conjunction with the addition of new definitions aimed at embracing the emerging models. Thus, for the purposes of the AI Act, in order to ensure its coverage in the scope of application and to be able to differentiate, in turn, different regulatory regimes depending on the AI model, in the successive amendments to the proposed IA Act two other definitions were added along with the notion of an IA system that were not in the initial version: 'foundation model'[21] and 'general-purpose IA system'.[22] In the subsequent texts, these definitions have also changed.

inductive (logic) programming, knowledge bases, inference and deduction engines, expert and (symbolic) reasoning systems. Statistical strategies, Bayesian estimation, search methods and optimisation.'

[17] In the version of the text dated 14 July 2023. P9_TA(2023)0236 *Artificial Intelligence Act – Amendments Adopted by the European Parliament on 14 June 2023 on the Proposal for a Regulation of the European Parliament and of the Council on Laying Down Harmonized Rules on Artificial Intelligence (Artificial Intelligence Act) and Amending certain Union Legislative Acts* (COM(2021)0206 – C9-0146/2021 – 2021/0106(COD))1 defines an 'AI system' as 'a machine-based system that is designed to operate with varying levels of autonomy and that can, for explicit or implicit objectives, generate outputs such as predictions, recommendations, or decisions that influence physical or virtual environments'. The subsequent version of the text, after the compromise agreement reached was made available on 24 January 2024 and includes the following definition: 'An AI system is a machine-based system designed to operate with varying levels of autonomy and that may exhibit adaptiveness after deployment and that, for explicit or implicit objectives, infers, from the input it receives, how to generate outputs such as predictions, content, recommendations, or decisions that can influence physical or virtual environments.'

[18] OECD, 'AI terms & concepts', https://oecd.ai/en/ai-principles, OECD, *Recommendation of the Council on Artificial Intelligence*, OECD/LEGAL/0449, May 2029.

[19] OECD, 'AI terms & concepts', https://oecd.ai/en/ai-principles, OECD, *Recommendation of the Council on Artificial Intelligence*, OECD/LEGAL/0449, Revision 8 November 2023: 'An AI system is a machine-based system that, for explicit or implicit objectives, infers, from the input it receives, how to generate outputs such as predictions, content, recommendations, or decisions that can influence physical or virtual environments. Different AI systems vary in their levels of autonomy and adaptiveness after deployment.'

[20] As explained in OECD, *Recommendation of the Council on Artificial Intelligence*, OECD/LEGAL/0449, November 2023.

[21] In the text published on 24 of January 2024, the definition of 'general-purpose AI model' was:

> an AI model, including when trained with a large amount of data using self-supervision at scale, that displays significant generality and is capable to competently perform a wide range of distinct tasks regardless of the way the model is placed on the market and that can be integrated into a variety of downstream systems or applications. This does not cover AI models that are used before release on the market for research, development and prototyping activities.

Previously, in the P9_TA(2023)0236 *Artificial Intelligence Act – Amendments adopted by the European Parliament on 14 June 2023 on the Proposal for a Regulation of the European Parliament and of the Council on Laying Down Harmonized Rules on Artificial Intelligence (Artificial Intelligence Act) and Amending certain Union Legislative Acts* (COM(2021)0206 - C9–0146/2021 – 2021/0106(COD))1: 'Art.3.1.c) "foundation model" means an AI model that is trained on broad data at scale, is designed for generality of output, and can be adapted to a wide range of distinctive tasks.' The definition is not included in the latest text after the political agreement in December 2023 and as published in January 2024.

[22] P9_TA(2023)0236 (COM(2021)0206 – C9-0146/2021 – 2021/0106(COD))1: 'Art. 3.1.d). "general purpose AI system" means an AI system that can be used in and adapted to a wide range of applications for which it was not intentionally and specifically designed.'

Yet in the approved version and after the final corrigendum,[23] the Regulation pivots on a notion of AI systems[24] aligned with the most recently updated definition recommended by OECD[25] and two other concepts: the general-purpose AI model[26] and the general-purpose AI system.[27] By following the definition of AI systems proposed by OECD, the AI Act ensures coordination with international standards, and converges with the global consensus that the recommendation reflects.

The concept of an AI system is articulated along four main axes: interactivity, adaptiveness, autonomy, and influence on the environment. The potential of AI systems to (relatively but increasingly) autonomously learn,[28] according to varying levels of autonomy, challenges anthropocentric notions of consent and intent, error, fault, or negligence. The very rapid advances of generative AI models[29] and the exponential growth of their capabilities are already beginning to raise the possibility that they may derive from 'emergent behaviours'[30] aimed at circumventing human control, optimising resources to achieve the goal in a sub-optimal way, using persuasion techniques, or pretending to be human. Adaptive learning and evolving capacity inject unpredictability into the outcome and raise questions concerning the treatment of error, the effect of unexpected or surprising learning, the attribution of legal effects, or the allocation of liability. Yet AI systems are capable of generating outcomes that influence the environment in which they operate on the basis of a set of objectives, either explicit or implicit, which may have been determined at design[31] or learned later in their operation. These outcomes may consist not only of predictions or recommendations, but also of decisions and content of the most diverse nature.

[23] CORRIGENDUM P9_TA(2024)0138. (COM(2021)0206 – C9-0146/2021 – 2021/0106(COD)), 19 April 2024.

[24] Art. 3(1) AI Act:

> 'AI system' means a machine-based system that is designed to operate with varying levels of autonomy and that may exhibit adaptiveness after deployment, and that, for explicit or implicit objectives, infers, from the input it receives, how to generate outputs such as predictions, content, recommendations, or decisions that can influence physical or virtual environments.

[25] OECD (2019), *Recommendation of the Council on Artificial Intelligence*, OECD/LEGAL/0449, as modified on 8 November 2023, https://legalinstruments.oecd.org/en/instruments/oecd-legal-0449. The definition is explained in OECD, *Explanatory Memorandum on the Updated OECD Definition of an AI System*, OECD Artificial Intelligence Papers, March 2024, No. 8.

[26] Art. 3(63) AI Act:

> 'general-purpose AI model' means an AI model, including where such an AI model is trained with a large amount of data using self-supervision at scale, that displays significant generality and is capable of competently performing a wide range of distinct tasks regardless of the way the model is placed on the market and that can be integrated into a variety of downstream systems or applications, except AI models that are used for research, development or prototyping activities before they are placed on the market.

[27] Art. 3(66) AI Act: '"general-purpose AI system" means an AI system which is based on a general-purpose AI model and which has the capability to serve a variety of purposes, both for direct use as well as for integration in other AI systems'.

[28] In this rapidly evolving context, the term 'frontier AI models' has been proposed to define those models with the potential to pose serious risks to public safety and global security. The dangerous capabilities that such AI models would present include even the possibility of circumventing human control through deception and obfuscation. The authors of the paper (Anderljung, M., et al.) 'Frontier AI regulation: managing emerging risks to public safety' (2023, arXiv:2307.03718 [cs.CY], https://arxiv.org/abs/2307.03718) acknowledge that it is not yet clear whether models will tend to develop in this direction, but it is argued that this could be the result of current training paradigms: Ngo, Richard, Chan, Lawrence & Mindermann, Sören, 'The alignment problem from a deep learning perspective', 2023, arXiv: 2209.00626 [cs.AI], https://arxiv.org/abs/2209.00626.

[29] OECD, *Initial Policy Considerations for Generative Artificial Intelligence*, OECD Artificial Intelligence Papers, September 2023, No. 1.

[30] Chan, A., et al., 'Harms from increasingly agentic algorithmic systems', IEEE Computer Society, 2022–March 2023, https://arxiv.org/abs/2302.10329.

[31] Raji, Inioluwa Deborah, Horowitz, Aaron, Kumar, Elizabeth & Selbst, Andrew, 'The fallacy of AI functionality', *FAccT 22*, 2022, 959.

This is widely considered in generative AI models. To generate these results, systems use data or information that they receive, infer, perceive from the environment, and acquire by means of learning methods.

Therefore, the definition of AI system in the AI Act on the one hand embodies the disruptive features on which the legislative action is founded and, on the other hand, shows certain receptiveness to the specific and additional challenges posed by generative AI. But in addition to this permeability of the 'AI system' concept to various functional and distinctive characteristics of generative AI, the AI Act adds the definition of general-purpose AI models (and general-purpose AI systems) to properly embrace the paradigm shift that large generative AI models epitomise.[32]

The introduction of these definitions is not a simple terminological nod towards the emerging models, but is accompanied by other legal and regulatory implications – in the personal scope of application of the AI Act, in the provision for specific obligations, in the application of rules for models posing systemic risks. Nevertheless, the accommodation of the logic of the AI Act and other correlated rules to the functional characteristics of generative AI models may not be perfect and complete. Certain gaps and imperfections may be spotted.

7.2.2 *'Decoding' Generative AI Models in the Context of the AI Act: Relevant Features*

Generative AI models are covered in the AI Act under the notion of general-purpose AI models. After the terminological changes between possible definitory options (from 'foundation models' to 'general-purpose AI models or systems') successively explored in the chain of versions of the text, the AI Act does not define 'generative AI models' but rather utilises them as typical example of 'general-purpose AI models', which is the term finally adopted as a defined concept in the Regulation.

In the choice among the alternative terms, different features are purportedly emphasised. A term is preferred and chosen so as to stress either the basal character of these models as essential components of multiple AI systems (foundation models),[33] or the multimodality (large multimodal models) or variety of possible uses (general-purpose AI models), or even the severity and seriousness of the potential risks to society, global security, and public safety (models posing systemic risks or frontier models).[34] Beyond the preferences for one term or another, all of them do partially or totally reflect the distinctive features and functional characteristics of generative

[32] Recital 97 AI Act: 'The notion of general-purpose AI models should be clearly defined and set apart from the notion of AI systems to enable legal certainty. The definition should be based on the key functional characteristics of a general-purpose AI model, in particular the generality and the capability to competently perform a wide range of distinct tasks.'

[33] Bommasani, Rishi, et al., 'On the opportunities and risks of foundation models', 2021 (manuscript), https://arxiv.org/abs/2108.07258, p. 7: 'the word "foundation" specifies the role these models play: a foundation model is itself incomplete but serves as the common basis from which many task-specific models are built via adaptation. We also chose the term "foundation" to connote the significance of architectural stability, safety, and security: poorly-constructed foundations are a recipe for disaster and well-executed foundations are a reliable bedrock for future applications'.

[34] Frontier AI Taskforce in the United Kingdom, an AI research team, so renamed to emphasise the potentially significant frontier risks posed by AI, www.gov.uk/government/publications/frontier-ai-taskforce-first-progress-report/frontier-ai-taskforce-first-progress-report; Nerlich, Brigitte, 'Frontier AI: tracing the origin of a concept', https://blogs.nottingham.ac.uk/makingsciencepublic/2023/10/20/frontier-ai-tracing-the-origin-of-a-concept/. The term 'frontier AI models' has been proposed to define those models with the potential to pose serious risks to public safety and global security. The dangerous capabilities that such AI models would present include even the possibility of circumventing human control through deception and obfuscation. Anderljung, Markus, et al., 'Frontier AI regulation: managing emerging risks to public safety', 7 November 2023, arXiv, https://arxiv.org/abs/2307.03718.

AI. In understanding the paradigm shift that this class of models embodies, and assessing the regulatory and legal implications, all these functional characteristics become relevant.[35]

One of the most visibly differential features of generative AI, as the chosen terminology showed (general-purpose AI models), is generality. Advanced models can perform a broad array of tasks. Unlike task-specific or purpose-specific AI systems, task-agnostic models, as they are also described, can serve multiple downstream tasks. As a matter of fact, the possibility that a single model can perform and be used for a wide range of tasks is deemed to mark the beginning of the era of foundation models.[36] The generality and versatility of these models are perfectly staged by the performance of advanced language models that prove to be adapted to any downstream task in response to a provided prompt, where the prompt represents a description of the task in natural language. Impressively, the prompt triggers an emergent property that the model has not trained for and, in some cases, it can even be affirmed that the task was not anticipated to arise.

The feature of generality and diversity of performed tasks has substantial implications in the regulatory logic. A model that can perform a variety of tasks, even unanticipated ones, disrupts the risk-based approach underlying the regulatory strategy that the AI Act embodies. The risk classification is linked to the purpose, use, or application. Both in the classification of prohibited AI practices (Article 5 AI Act) and in the list of high-risk AI systems in Annex III, as referred to in Article 6(2) AI Act, the use or intended use is pivotal to the application of the regulatory framework. General-purpose AI models provoke the fracture of this risk-based purpose-specific regulatory model. That is an obvious challenge. Therefore, the integration of multiple-purpose AI models in the AI Act was a crucial step forward that required important efforts to ensure coherence and consistency.

Assuming unanticipated outputs and/or unexpected or unlikely effects arising from tasks or uses the model has not specifically trained for has strong implications in the liability narrative too. Causality is weakened, while the foreseeability of consequences may be justifiably deemed rather remote.

The definition of the general-purpose AI model and the general-purpose AI system in the AI Act (Article 3(63) and (66) AI Act) acknowledges the feature of generality – 'displays significant generality and is capable of competently performing a wide range of distinct tasks' and 'has the capability to serve a variety of purposes'. Should the purpose be general, multiple, or unanticipated, the risk classification does not work. Therefore, the AI Act needs to find a proper and coherent approach to embrace and address the risks of these models.

Compliance requirements based on intended purposes may fail or prove to be unsuited to generative AI. Random outputs and unintended actions obscure the efforts to predict and anticipate concrete impacts. Hence, risk management systems and transparency obligations may lose effectiveness in the landscape of generative AI.[37]

The idea of multiple possible tasks to be performed by the model places generative AI in a challenging position for liability purposes. It causes a disconcerting level of unpredictability not only as to the harmful potential of a specific output, but the entire extent, risk involved, and type of tasks that the model performs.

From the perspective of the AI supply chain, general-purpose AI models are essential components of AI systems. As the descriptive term of 'foundation' reveals, they play a key role

35 Hacker, Philipp, Engel, Andreas & Mauer, Marco, 'Regulating ChatGPT and other large generative AI models', arXiv, 2023, pp. 1112–1123, https://doi.org/10.48550/arXiv.2302.02337.

36 Bommasani et al., *On the Opportunities and Risks of Foundation Models*, pp. 4 and 5.

37 Novelli, Claudio, et al., 'Generative AI in EU law: liability, privacy, intellectual property, and cybersecurity', 14 January 2024, https://ssrn.com/abstract=4694565 or http://dx.doi.org/10.2139/ssrn.4694565.

by serving as the common basis from which many task-specific models are built via adaptation. Thus, these models are further fine-tuned and adapted to multiple applications. The power of 'foundations models' is precisely their potential to grow, expand, and be integrated into a number of AI systems. That powers a strong homogenisation capability. Concurrently, scalability and scale are also triggers of possible viral risks. In operating as the bedrock of subsequent applications and further development of AI systems throughout the supply chain, defects, biases, or vulnerabilities of few foundation models might be inherited by and span all AI systems based on them.

Such a scale effect of general-purpose AI models is acknowledged by the AI Act with the categorisation of models that can pose systemic risks. The notion of systemic risk is underpinned by the ideas of criticality, adverse effects, extent of risks, replicability potential, public safety, and global security. Thus, systemic risks comprise any actual or reasonably foreseeable negative effects in relation to, among others, disruptions of critical sectors, serious consequences for public health and safety, threats to democratic values or public and economic security, serious biases that may harm individuals or communities, severe privacy infringements, or promotion of misinformation or disinformation (Recital 110 AI Act).

In a liability-centred reading, foundation models can reveal points of failure in the AI supply chain, and act as sources of virality while replicating a defect in downstream application or 'infecting' AI systems integrating the model with biases or harmful failures.

On a technical level, general-purpose AI models are based on the idea of transfer learning. Under this training trend, the 'knowledge' learned from one task (object recognition in images) is transferred and applied to another task (activity recognition in videos) and, as a result, the model learns to deploy its capabilities in a wide range of tasks, even unexpected ones. To that end, scale is critical. Foundation models are trained on large amounts of data through various methods from supervised to unsupervised or reinforcement learning, but generally these models use self-supervision at scale. Subsequently, they are adapted and fine-tuned to a wide range of downstream tasks. These technical considerations are indeed pertinent and relevant for a legal analysis. Not surprisingly, a training model based on vast amounts of data raises challenges in the field of privacy and data protection. Whereas it also arouses concerns and disquiet as far as protection of copyright and other intellectual property rights are concerned.

Yet, as the term generative AI suggests, these AI models show an extraordinary and impressive generative potential. The capability to generate content is moreover intensified by an expanding multimodality of these models. Many models (also defined as large multimodal models) can process text, audio, image, or video and generate outputs in various types of format.

From a legal perspective, the generative power of these models is fascinating and challenging. This potential multiplies the sources of risk and diversifies the scenarios of liability, as the legal categorisation of possible generated outputs may lead to rather diverse situations – an original creation, a scientific contribution, an offer to deal, a 'deep fake', hate speech, a settlement agreement, news, a misleading advertisement, a recommendation, and so on. Therefore, in the attempt to map possible risk scenarios, and relevant liability regimes, the catalogue is ample and to a certain extent composed of any plausible harmful effect on rights or interests. Not only does multimodality provide high levels of versatility regarding the performance of the models and their effect on the environment, but also the most advanced capabilities to imitate and model human language, creations, and reactions exacerbate the vulnerability and exposure of humans interacting with these models.

Furthermore, the significance of these models for legal analysis is highly influenced by two elements. On the one hand, the notion of emergence. Emergent behaviour causes substantial uncertainty about unanticipated outputs, but also raises fundamental legal questions ranging from the applicability of human-centric notions of creator or inventor to the attribution of liability.[38] On the other hand, the risk of *hallucinations*[39] challenges the effectiveness of policy decisions and the regulatory requirements aimed to prevent and mitigate risks. Suitable and effective strategies and methods to prevent harmful outputs need to be devised and implemented accordingly (Annex IX, Section 2.2 on red teaming).[40] Legal rules and regulatory requirements should be sensitive to these peculiarities and consistent in the methods that prove to be effective in generative AI models.

7.2.3 *Rules on Generative AI in the AI Act: Unveiling the Implications and Assessing the Effectiveness*

General-purpose AI models fit uncomfortably into a regulatory framework based on a purpose-related risk approach. The AI Act struggled to render its incorporation coherent and less disturbing. The expansion strategy for the AI Act to embrace generative AI has pivoted on three solutions. First, a limited expansion of the personal scope with special regard to the role/s played in the AI supply chain. Second, a tiered risk classification parallel to and distinct from the purpose-specific risk classification underlying the AI Act. Third, a policy option for transparency-related requirements.

The connection between the general-purpose logic and purpose-specific risk approach is not, however, ignored. Where the multiple-purpose potential crystallises in a high-risk application, the relevant rules are triggered and correspondingly apply throughout the AI supply chain. Thus, Article 25 AI Act provides for the responsibilities and obligations along the AI value chain to any distributor, importer, deployer, or other third party, who shall be considered to be a provider of a high-risk AI system for the purposes of the Act, among other circumstances, if they modify the intended purpose of an AI system, including a general-purpose AI system, which has not been classified as high-risk and has already been placed on the market or put into service in such a way that the AI system concerned becomes a high-risk AI system in accordance with Article 6 AI Act. So, the generality that defines general-purpose AI systems becomes compatible with a subsequent adaptation of the general purpose to a specific use classified as a high-risk one. Then, the risk-based machinery operating the AI Act can be put into motion, allocating the regulatory obligations to the relevant 'link' of the chain. Therefore, contextualising the AI Act obligations along the AI supply chain is crucial.

Consistent with the foundational character of general-purpose AI models, their generality, and their task-agnostic nature, the personal scope of the AI Act is proportionately and logically adapted. Unlike AI systems, only providers of general-purpose IA models are covered by the AI Act, while all other operators are linked to and qualified by activities relating to IA systems. This

[38] Boden, Margaret A., 'Computer models of creativity', *AI Magazine*, 30(3), 2009, pp. 23–34; Grimmelmann, James, 'Copyright for literate robots', *Iowa Law Review*, 101, 2015, pp. 657–681; Sartor, Giovanni, et al., 'The use of copyrighted works by AI systems: art works in the data mill', 11 October 2018, https://ssrn.com/abstract=3264742 or http://dx.doi.org/10.2139/ssrn.3264742; Volokh, Eugene, 'Large libel models? Liability for AI output', *Journal of Free Speech Law*, 3(489) 2023, UCLA School of Law, Public Law Research Paper No. 23-17, https://ssrn.com/abstract=4546063.

[39] Ye, Hongbin, et al., 'Cognitive mirage: a review of hallucinations in large language models', 2023, https://doi.org/10.48550/arXiv.2309.06794.

[40] Ganguli, Deep, et al., 'Red teaming language models to reduce harms: methods, scaling behaviors, and lessons learned', 22 November 2022, https://arxiv.org/abs/2209.07858v2: 'using manual or automated methods to adversarially probe a language model for harmful outputs, and then updating the model to avoid such outputs'.

is consistent with the purpose of the Regulation as set out in Article 1 AI Act. In the second paragraph of the provision, point (e), it is specified that the Act establishes 'harmonised rules for the placing on the market of general-purpose AI models'. Since general-purpose IA models are essential components of IA systems, but do not in themselves constitute an IA system, the decisive determinant for the application of the AI Act is the placing on the market. This explains why the AI Act applies to providers of general-purpose AI models when they introduce them into the EU market.

The AI Act assimilates the criticism to previous versions of the text and solves the regulatory quandary between focusing exclusively on providers of general-purpose AI models or on other operators (as defined by Article 3(8) AI Act).[41] While the former policy decision leads to excessive and inefficient compliance obligations, and possibly to stifling the AI supply chain, the latter risks rendering compliance burdensome and equally ineffective as it depends upon information from the provider or lacks resources and insights.

Providers of general-purpose AI models 'head' the AI supply chain as their models may be the essential basis of a wide range of downstream systems and be fine-tuned for a number of varied downstream tasks. Thus, they play a singular role in the value chain that the AI Act translates into transparency measures – technical documentation and information as per the Annexes. Where these models are released under a free and open-source licence, the presumption is that certain information is publicly available, and the transparency-related requirements are eased accordingly. Nonetheless, such exceptions are not absolute and complete. On the one hand, compliance is not excluded if the general-purpose AI model is considered to present a systemic risk. On the other hand, insofar as the assumed transparency inherent to a free and open-source licensing model does not necessarily entail that substantial information on the data set used for the training or fine-tuning is revealed or how the compliance with copyright law is ensured, such obligations are to be complied with by such models as well.

This approach reveals that the AI Act reconstructs the risk classification for general-purpose AI models under a three-tier system that distinguishes between standard models, models released under free and open-source licence, and models posing systemic risks. Pursuant to this taxonomy, the AI Act sets out relevant definitions (high-impact capabilities[42] and systemic risks[43]), additional obligations for systemic risk general-purpose AI models (Article 55, in addition to the obligations provided for by Articles 53 and 54), and a procedure to classify a general-purpose AI model with systemic risks, on the basis of its evaluated high-impact capabilities – with a presumption determined by the cumulative amount of computation used for its training measured in floating point operations and subject to thresholds, benchmarks, and indicators that can be amended by delegated acts – or a decision of the Commission *ex officio* or following a qualified alert (Articles 51 and 52 AI Act, and Annex XIII).

The primary transparency-based policy strategy is articulated in the obligation of general-purpose AI system providers downstream (Article 53 and Annexes XI and XII) to supply technical documentation and information as well as obligations relevant for the compliance with

[41] Hacker et al., 'Regulating ChatGPT and other large generative AI models'.

[42] Article 3(64) AI Act: '"high-impact capabilities" means capabilities that match or exceed the capabilities recorded in the most advanced general-purpose AI models'.

[43] Article 3(65) AI Act:

> 'systemic risk' means a risk that is specific to the high-impact capabilities of general-purpose AI models, having a significant impact on the Union market due to their reach, or due to actual or reasonably foreseeable negative effects on public health, safety, public security, fundamental rights, or the society as a whole, that can be propagated at scale across the value chain.

copyright law. Any use of copyright-protected content requires the authorisation of the rightsholder concerned unless relevant copyright exceptions and limitations apply, such as reproductions and extractions of works for the purpose of text and data mining, under certain conditions. But rightsholders may choose to reserve their rights over their works to prevent text and data mining, provided the purposes are other than scientific research. In such a case, an authorisation needs to be obtained by providers of general-purpose AI models to that end. In the same vein, and in order to increase transparency on the data used in the pre-training and training of general-purpose AI models that may include works or any other subject matter protected by copyright law, providers of these models shall make available a sufficiently detailed summary about the content used for training the model. These obligations are aimed to address the liability concerns more closely associated with copyright infringements and, to a certain extent, privacy. But they seem also to help alleviate the challenge of attributing liability arising from harmful, false, or misleading outputs. Disclosing the content used for pre-training and training might provide insights to identify causes or determine causal links. Potential liability is not totally removed though. Nor are the complexities to determine and attribute liability.

Transparency presents a second facet in the AI Act that, for a private-law analysis, may have rather intriguing implications. It is a disclosure duty or self-revealing feature to identify and mark generated synthetic audio, image, video, or text content (Article 50(2) AI Act). It refers to general-purpose AI systems and is clearly rooted in the potential of generative AI. Thus, providers should implement effective, interoperable, robust, and reliable technical solutions to ensure that *the outputs of the AI system are marked in a machine-readable format and detectable as artificially generated or manipulated*. Some exceptions apply to this obligation where these systems perform an assistive function for standard editing or do not substantially alter the input data provided by the deployer or the semantics thereof, or where authorised by law to detect, prevent, investigate, or prosecute criminal offences.

Disclosure impacts on perception, and consequently can reduce the harmful effect, debilitate the reliance as a causal link, or simply mitigate the risk of misinterpretation, deceit, or frustration of reasonable expectations.

Various questions are still unsolved. For the purposes of liability, the implications of not marking the artificially generated or manipulated content, which may aggravate the harmful consequences of the output, can be discussed. In such cases, total lack of marking may or may not be assimilated to ineffective, non-interoperable, or unreliable technical solutions for marking. The end effect may ultimately be similar, but the position of the provider differs on the basis of, among others, whether it is an obligation of result or of best efforts. Yet, in connection with the rebuttable presumption laid down in the draft AILD and the revPLD, the consequences of the infringement of this obligation may require further assessment.

In charting the rules that the AI Act has specifically provided for on general-purpose AI models (or systems), the material scope and the personal scope are and must be treated as closely interwoven. As the AI Act included a separate and distinct concept of general-purpose AI, a specific body of rules emerged, strictly associated with these models (or in some cases general-purpose AI systems as well). Once the 'what' is identified, then the 'who is obliged to' immediately results (providers of general-purpose AI models instead of further operators, or the relevant operator of the AI supply chain in certain circumstances). The terminological and definitional divide forces us to draw a line on the basis of the defined legal terms instead of on grounds of analogous functionality or equivalent effect. That means that in order to assess how the AI Act tackles generative AI, as a paradigm shift in the AI landscape, the rules specifically drafted for general-purpose AI models (and systems) are traced and solely considered. And that has been strictly respected, even if the ultimate definition of an AI system, as aligned with the OECD recommendation, has been modified to embrace, among other elements, the content generation capability.[44]

Given this conclusion, the analysis below of the two legislative actions initiated in the EU to accommodate liability rules to AI challenges is solely focused on appreciating whether the reformed rules, that have been modified to embrace AI systems, have succeeded in incorporating the additional and differential characteristics of generative AI.

7.3 GENERATIVE AI AND LIABILITY RULES FOR DAMAGE CAUSED BY AI SYSTEMS

The adverse effects resulting from the materialisation of AI risks can have a wide variety of manifestations. In certain sectors, significant property damage and personal injury can be anticipated (autonomous vehicles, drones, home automation, assistive robotics). Their applications in financial activities are linked to systemic risks, threats to economic stability and financial integrity or cyclical responses and market shocks. Their use for rankings, recruitment services, content filtering, or virtual assistants for complaint management opens the door to a far-reaching debate on their impact on fundamental rights and freedoms – freedom of expression, the right not to be discriminated against, the right to honour, personality rights – but also on the competitive structure of the market or on the fairness of their practices.

Against such potentially adverse effects, the key question is whether traditional legal regimes are equipped to manage the risks and effectively resolve conflicts arising from such situations in complex technological environments. With the aim of assessing the adequacy of non-contractual liability rules, common distinguishing features, where AI is involved, need to be identified and compared with past and current (non-AI) situations to which the existing rules are (or are assumed to be) well adapted. Such distinctive features – opacity, complexity, vulnerability, openness, data-dependence, autonomy – would allow modelling a legal category of 'AI-caused damages' to test the adaptability and adequacy of existing liability rules.[45]

7.3.1 *Dilemmas and Legislative Policy Options in Devising an EU Response to Damage Caused by AI Systems*

The identified distinctive and differential features of AI systems – opacity, complexity, vulnerability, openness, data-dependence, autonomy – prove to have an impact, in some cases of substantial magnitude, on the classical concepts underpinning liability or on the traditional application of liability rules. Given the premise that there is a differential rationale, there are several legislative policy dilemmas for the European Union to consider in devising an adequate response to confront and resolve damage caused by AI systems.

The first legislative policy dilemma is whether to opt for the formulation of specific liability rules for AI or to accommodate the general liability rules to the specificities of AI. The second is whether to defend a strict liability regime in case of damage caused by AI systems or to maintain a fault-based approach as the main model of fault-based liability. The third is deciding on the

[44] OECD, *Explanatory Memorandum on the Updated OECD Definition of an AI System*, OECD Artificial Intelligence Papers, March 2024, No. 8, at p. 9: 'content generation systems have become such an important class of AI systems that they are included as their own output category in the present revised definition'.

[45] Rodríguez de las Heras Ballell, Teresa, 'Legal challenges of artificial intelligence: modelling the disruptive features of emerging technologies and assessing their possible legal impact', *Uniform Law Review*, 1, 2019, pp. 1–13.

level of legal uniformity and harmonisation to be achieved at European level for damage caused by AI systems.

The European Parliament Resolution on liability for the operation of artificial intelligence systems[46] of October 2020, which contained a set of recommendations for a Regulation of the European Parliament and of the Council on civil liability for damage caused by the operation of AI systems, represented a highly ambitious position in terms of legislative harmonisation and a radical solution to the three legislative policy dilemmas described above. It consisted of a proposal for a specific liability regime for AI on two levels (strict liability for high-risk systems and fault-based liability for non-high-risk systems) with a high potential for harmonisation at European level through the proposed adoption of a Regulation. This proposal did not take its course and has not led to any specific formulation by the Commission in the terms envisaged. Instead, the Commission proposed, using a substantially different approach, the two proposals for a Directive published on 28 September 2022, aimed, on the one hand and finally adopted in 2024, at revising product liability rules to accommodate 'smart products' and (standalone) AI systems (revPLD), and, on the other, to lighten the burden of proof in fault-based liability actions under national laws on damage caused by AI systems (AILD).

By departing from the Parliament's 2020 proposal, the Commission takes a clear, and to a certain extent diverging, position on the three policy dilemmas concerning the solution of AI liability.

The Commission's approach is less drastic and much less forceful in proposing a specific approach to AI. Despite the revealing name of the proposed Directive – the Directive on the adaptation of the rules on non-contractual civil liability to artificial intelligence (Artificial Intelligence Liability Directive) – it is not in fact a Directive establishing liability rules for artificial intelligence. The objectives and expected effects are more modest and certainly more pragmatic and realistic in legislative terms: to establish common rules on disclosure of evidence and burden of proof in non-contractual civil claims for damage caused by an AI system. The modesty of the proposal in the extent (a Directive instead of a Regulation) and scope (exclusively rules on disclosure of evidence and burden of proof) is indeed imposed by the low level of harmonisation in the EU on civil liability rules, which still remain largely national.

Interestingly, the proposed Directive bridges the gap between the AI Act and national fault-based liability laws. While the AI Act, as a regulation, constitutes a decisive attempt to achieve high harmonisation at EU level, the rules on fault-based tort liability are essentially national and thus hardly unified. While the AI Act is based on a regulatory approach, the AILD aims to close the 'redress gap' revealed by the AI Act and to improve the application of regulatory requirements for high-risk AI systems by enhancing their role for the purposes of civil liability claims. In doing so, non-compliance with such requirements triggers the easing of the burden of proof, one of the identified weaknesses of the legacy liability regime that needs to be addressed, by establishing a number of rebuttable presumptions. Unlike Parliament's approach in the 2020 Resolution, the risk-based categorisation of the AI system does not lead to strict liability, but rather contributes to the rebuttable presumptions. The list-based approach adopted by Parliament's proposal in the 2020 Resolution to categorise high-risk AI systems was not necessarily linked to the AI Act, whereas the AIL consistently bridges the gap by relying on the risk categorisation of the AI Act.

[46] Report with recommendations to the Commission on a civil liability regime for artificial intelligence (2020/2014 (INL)), 5 October 2020, www.europarl.europa.eu/doceo/document/A-9-2020-0178_EN.html.

As regards the dilemma at the level of harmonisation, the Commission, in its proposal of 2021[47] for an AI Act, renounced achieving maximum harmonisation with the adoption of a Regulation on liability rules. Instead, a complex scheme of interactions is devised between the AI Act, the proposed new (or revised) Directives, and national rules on fault-based liability for negligence. The Commission builds two bridges that create an interwoven framework of liability rules for AI systems, although not fully compact at EU level: a bridge between the AI Act and national fault liability rules; and a bridge of complementarity between the product liability regime and fault liability rules.

In this context, the revision of the PLD, that is the second component of the reform duet, (finally, it was a solo) plays a key role, with a harmonising potential that is likely to go beyond the traditional and formal effect of a Directive. By extending the scope of the PLD to include products enabled by AI systems and standalone AI systems, and by adapting some rules of the product liability regime to accommodate the characteristics of such AI systems, the harmonisation potential of the PLD is reinforced, extended, and leveraged: although this implies proceeding by means of a Directive with an express full harmonisation clause (Article 3 revPLD).[48]

The policy strategy adopted by the EU Commission to tackle the AI liability dilemmas crystallised in two main legislative actions. On the one hand, there was major revision of the product liability regime to accommodate the digital economy, in particular the use of AI systems, and the circular economy.[49] The Commission proposal was approved by the European Parliament on 12 March 2024, preceding the subsequent approval of the AI Act on 13 March 2024 and finally adopted on 23 October 2024. Thus, the EU legal framework for the AI is gaining scale and density. On the other hand, the more modest effort, forced by the EU member state competency distribution scheme on the matter, to reach a less ambitious level of harmonisation and with less substantial, albeit still relevant and laudable, scope in those rules of national fault-based liability rules that are more bluntly impacted by the AI distinctive features: disclosure of evidence and burden of proof. But the lack of agreement inm the final text led the proposal for a AILD to be withdrwn in the 2025 work programme.

7.3.2 *Potentialities and Limitations of Liability Rules for Generative AI*

Various features of the proposed (and approved) liability rules for AI systems reveals that, unlike the efforts made to accommodate generative AI in the regulatory framework (AI Act), further consideration to embrace generative AI's functional characteristics in the liability narrative is advisable.

7.3.2.1 Delimiting the Scope of Application

The first issue to consider is whether generative AI falls under the scope of application of the AILD and/or revPLD.

47 Proposal for a Regulation of the European Parliament and of the Council laying down harmonised rules on Artificial Intelligence (Artificial Intelligence Act) and amending certain Union Legislative Acts COM/2021/206 final.

48 Article 3 revPLD sets out the level of harmonisation: 'Member States shall not maintain or introduce, in their national law, provisions diverging from those laid down in this Directive, including more stringent or less stringent provisions, to achieve a different level of protection for consumers and other natural persons, unless otherwise provided for in this Directive.' The explicit clarification that this instrument aims at full harmonisation in its scope of application is to be welcomed.

49 Recital 3 revPLD: 'Directive 85/374/EEC has been an effective and important instrument, but it would need to be revised in light of developments related to new technologies, including artificial intelligence (AI), new circular economy business models and new global supply chains, which have led to inconsistencies and legal uncertainty, in particular as regards the meaning of the term "product".'

On the one hand, due to the strong dependency of the draft AILD on the AI Act,[50] the material scope of the draft rules is demarcated by the notion of 'AI system' as defined in the AI Act (Article 2(1) AILD). As the drafting decision to effectively integrate generative AI in the logic of the AI Act has been a terminological bifurcation with the addition of 'general-purpose AI models' and 'general-purpose AI system', the limited referral of the draft AILD to 'AI systems' as per the AI Act invites a restrictive and literal interpretation. In principle, the draft rules would not be intended to apply to general-purpose AI models/systems. Nonetheless, there are two relevant points that should not be disregarded. First, there is a timing factor. Since the draft AILD was released before the latest version of the AI Act, it can be argued that the text might be plausibly updated in subsequent steps of the legislative route, and aligned with the adopted AI Act. The result of such an update in the material scope of application is uncertain though. As the AILD was withdrawn, it is expected that any new proposal that the Commission may decide to table would be aligned with the AI Act. Second, a conceptual factor, as with any AI system, considering the insights from the explanatory note of the OECD definition, can have generative capabilities (as 'content' is explicitly included as a possible output). Nevertheless, the content-generation capability is a feature but, as proposed in this chapter, it does not capture in its entirety the differential functional characteristics of generative AI as foundational, general-purpose, multimodal models.

In addition to the limitations inherent to the sole use of the term 'AI system', the draft AILD assumes the main risk classification of the AI Act (high-risk, low-risk) that differs from the alternative risk model underpinning the legal regime for general-purpose AI models (standard, systemic risks, free and open source). As has been noted,[51] such a risk classification may fail to take into account the real impact of downstream applications and therefore lead to over-inclusive or under-inclusive risk categories. As a matter of fact, once the general-purpose AI models are no longer considered high-risk by default (as in previous versions) and are subject to a separate tiered risk classification, the interplay between the AILD and the AI Act ceases.

As for the revPLD, a similar process to unveil its application to generative AI is followed. The key question is whether the enlargement of the scope of application of the PLD through the update of the notion of product manages to include generative AI in its scope.

In deciding to focus on the product liability rules[52] as the preferred route to face and address the challenges posed by AI to liability rules and to use the revision of the Directive as the most realistic way to harmonise AI liability as much as possible, a conceptual dilemma had to be unravelled. Extending the scope of the PLD to include AI systems implies broadening the concept of 'product'. How far can the concept of 'product' be extended without changing its nature? How much strain can the product liability regime be put under to accommodate AI without altering its fundamentals and tenets?

The decision to subject the PLD to a revision by extending its scope was essentially endorsed by the harmonising potential of such a policy option. The PLD is accepted and applied by industry actors, courts, and public authorities. It is the settled core of the EU acquis. In a way, by extending the PLD to cover AI systems rather than shifting the focus towards an alternative legislative initiative specific to AI (as the Parliament Resolution of 2020), the Commission is relying on a harmonising instrument already accepted by industry and widely adopted by

[50] The draft AILD aims to bridge the AI Act with non-contractual national liability rules and partially fill the redress gap in the Regulation. Rodríguez de las Heras Ballell, Teresa, 'The revision of the product liability directive: a key piece in the artificial intelligence liability puzzle', *ERA Forum*, 2023, https://doi.org/10.1007/s12027-023-00751-y.

[51] Novelli, Claudio, et al., 'AI risk assessment: a scenario-based, proportional methodology for the AI Act', *Digital Society (DISO)* 3(13), 2024, https://doi.org/10.1007/s44206-024-00095-1.

[52] Council Directive 85/374/EEC of 25.7.1985 on the approximation of the laws, regulations and administrative provisions of the Member States concerning liability for defective products, OJ L 210, 7 August 1985, pp. 29–33.

national legislators. The revision of the PLD strengthens and broadens the scope of application of EU rules in a harmonised mandate that is already largely uncontested. Fault-based liability rules remain largely national, but member states have already left the product liability regime to EU rules. Ensuring that this model, widely accepted by both legislators and industry, continues to work well in the digital age should be less contentious than recalibrating the EU–member state equilibrium in the liability-specific competency landscape.

The decision to accommodate the PLD to AI systems and other challenges of the digital age could not have been achieved simply by an interpretation of existing provisions to force them to cover digital and smart products. Conceptual and practical hurdles had to be overcome. The market needed and expected explicit and clear solutions to ensure legal certainty and improve predictability. Hence, the revision of the PLD entails a process of terminological clarification (of terms such as 'product' and 'defective') and conceptual recognition of AI systems, as well as the addition of new rules and the incorporation of AI-specific considerations. Therefore, the revision had to start from the core of the product liability system: the concept of product and the assessment of defectiveness.

Since its adoption in 1985,[53] the PLD has established a definition, for the purposes of the Directive, of a 'product'[54] (definition slightly amended in 1999),[55] thereby determining its scope of application. The meaning and scope of this central concept of 'product'[56] to cover future technological and market developments is decisive for assessing the versatility of the rules and the full achievement of long-term policy objectives. Moreover, the concept of 'product' – its definition, judicial interpretation, and application – permeates the entire product liability mechanism and determines, directly or indirectly, the meaning, scope, and functioning of its other components (notions such as 'defect', 'producer', or 'manufacturer', as well as issues such as defences and causation, in addition to the idea of placing a product on the market).

The challenges posed by technological progress and market developments therefore challenge[57] the core conceptual element of the product liability system, but also extend over other elements of the system. The emergence and increasing market penetration of AI-enabled goods, smart products, and AI systems are timely catalysts for a profound reflection on the revision (or rereading) of the PLD through digital lenses. Smart products go beyond the practical and conceptual perimeters of the classical concept of 'products' as they were traditionally conceived, devised, and constructed in 1985,[58] and even expanded and updated in subsequent years. This

[53] Fairgrieve, Duncan, et al., 'Product Liability Directive', in Machnikowski, P. (ed.), *European Product Liability: An Analysis of the State of the Art in the Era of New Technologies*, Principles of European Tort Law, Intersentia, 2016, pp. 17–108.

[54] Article 2 PLD:

> For the purposes of this Directive, 'product' shall mean any movable property, with the exception of primary agricultural products and game, even if incorporated in other movable property or in immovable property. 'Primary agricultural products' means products of the soil, of stock farming and of fisheries, excluding products which have undergone primary processing. 'Product' includes electricity.

[55] Directive 1999/34/EC of the European Parliament and of the Council of 10 May 1999 amending Council Directive 85/374/EEC on the approximation of the laws, regulations and administrative provisions of the Member States concerning liability for defective products, OJ L 141, 4 June 1999, pp. 20–21. The amendment consisted in deleting the exclusion of primary agricultural products and hunting. Subsequently, the scope was explicitly extended by amending the definition in 1999.

[56] For the purposes of this Directive, '"product" means any movable property, even if it is incorporated into other movable property or into immovable property. The term "product" includes electricity'.

[57] As described in Rodríguez de las Heras Ballell, Teresa, 'Embracing technological disruption in international transactions: challenges for legal harmonization', in *National, International, Transnational: Harmonischer Dreiklang IM Recht, Festschrift für Herbert Kronke*, Zum. 70 Geburstag, Bielefeld, Giesekin Verlag, 2020, pp. 1223–1233.

[58] European Law Institute, 'Guiding principles for updating the product liability directive for the digital age' (ELI Innovation Paper Series, 2021), www.europeanlawinstitute.eu/fileadmin/user_upload/p_eli/publications/eli_guiding_principles_for_updating_the_pld_for_the_digital_age.pdf.

inherent limitation of the conceptualisation of 'product' is despite the clear aspiration of the PLD to produce adaptable standards, and that is because the PLD is instilled with a rather recognisable industrial and post-industrial flavour.

The stylised definition of 'product' in its original wording (Article 2 PLD) covers all movable property, including property incorporated in, affixed to, or associated with other movable or immovable property. It is a broad and malleable definition that effectively covers the diverse typology of products derived from industry and market innovation. It is indeed comprehensive and reasonably future-proof, but it is still somewhat constrained by an underlying industrial logic. Thus, smart products, AI systems, and even software call into question not only the concept of 'product' itself in the PLD, but also and fundamentally the distinction between products and services,[59] between assets and data,[60] and between objects and subjects in the modern economy, and thus the formulation and application of legal rules as well. This is precisely why smart products invite a bold revision of the conceptual basis and policy vectors underpinning the PLD.

AI-enabled products challenge the legacy system of product liability because they blur the line between products and services,[61] blur the contours of products as single units by transforming them into complex ecosystems that evolve throughout their lifecycle by way of updating and upgrading, that are fed by data and interact with the environment as if they were, metaphorically, '*quasi-living* beings'.[62] These are the disruptive aspects of AI-enabled products that perfectly capture the specific characteristics of AI systems, as presented above (Section 7.2).[63]

[59] Hojnik, Janja, 'Technology neutral EU law: digital goods within the traditional goods/services distinction', *International Journal of Law and Information Technology*, 25(1), Spring 2017, pp. 63–84.

[60] The applicability of the Product Liability Directive to software has been the subject of intense and lengthy debate among scholars. Their reflections and views have been of great value for the purposes of this chapter, although the main thesis is that smart products pose challenges that go beyond this fundamental and traditional debate. Gemignani, Michael, 'Product liability and software', *Rutgers Computer & Technology Law Journal*, 8, 1980, p. 173; Green, Sarah & Saidov, Djakhongir, 'Software as goods', *Journal of Business Law*, 161, 2007, pp. 161–181; stapleton, Jane, 'Software, information and the concept of product', *Tel Aviv University Studies in Law*, 9, 1989, pp. 147–164; Weber, Lori A., 'Bad bytes: the application of strict products liability to computer software', *St. John's Law Review*, 66(2), 2012, pp. 469–486.

[61] Under the trend towards a 'servitisation of the firm' see Vandermerwe, Sandra & Rada, Juan, 'Servitization of business: adding value by adding services', *European Management Journal*, 6(4), 1998, pp. 314–324; Araujo, Luis & Spring, Martin, 'Services, products and the institutional structure of production', *Industrial Marketing Management*, 35(7), 2006, pp. 797–805; Gadrey, Jean, 'The characterization of goods and services: an alternative approach', *Review of Income and Wealth*, 46(3), 2000, pp. 369–387; hill, Peter, 'Tangibles, intangibles and services: a new taxonomy for the classification of output', *Canadian Journal of Economics – Revue Canadienne D'Economique*, 32(2), 1999, pp. 426–446; Parry, Glenn et al., 'Goods, products and services', in Macintyre, M. et al. (eds.) *Service Design and Delivery*, Springer, 2011, pp. 19–29; Rathmell, John M., 'What is meant by services?', *Journal of Marketing*, 30(4), 1966, pp. 32–36.

The characterisation as goods or services is also of vital importance for legal purposes (taxation, consumer protection, conformity, liability). ECJ case law has addressed this distinction of relevance for various purposes of EU internal market legislation: Case 7/68, *Commission v. Italy* (Art), ECLI:EU:C:1968:46; Case C-2/90, *Commission v. Belgium* (Walloon waste), ECLI:EU:C:1992:310; Case 155/73, *Giuseppe Sacchi*, ECLI:EU:C:1974:40, paragraphs 6–7; Case 52/79, *Debauve*, ECLI:EU:C:1980:83; Case 6/64, *Flaminio Costa v. ENEL, ECLI:EU:C:1964:66*; Case C-393/92, *Commune d'Almelo and Others v. NV Energiebedrijf Ijsselmij*, ECLI:EU:C:1994:171; Case C-158/94, *Commission v. Italy*, ECLI:EU:C:1997:500, paras 14–20; Case C-97/98, *Jägerskiöld*, ECLI:EU:C:1999:515.

[62] An idea had previously been developed to understand the particularities of software for the purposes of liability rules, as it interacts with the digital environment, is subject to user action and depends on updates and upgrades. The metaphor was then proposed that software acts as '*quasi* living beings'. Rodríguez de las Heras Ballell, Teresa, 'La responsabilidad por *software* defectuoso en la contratación mercantil', *Revista Aranzadi de Derecho y Nuevas Tecnologías*, 10, 2006, pp. 83–110.

[63] Commission Staff Working Document, *Responsibility for Emerging Digital Technologies*. Accompanying this document is the Communication from the Commission to the European Parliament, the European Council, the Council, the European Economic and Social Committee and the Committee of the Regions, *Artificial Intelligence for Europe*, SWD (2018) 137 final.

Accordingly, the decision of the revised PLD to amend the definition of 'product' and to explicitly include 'software' therein[64] is crucial and to be welcomed. But even more telling is the express clarification in the explanatory note of the first proposal of the Commission[65] and Recital 13 of the final revPLD[66] that AI systems and products based on AI are 'products' for the purposes of the PLD.

Thus, providers of AI systems (according to the AI Act)[67] will be considered manufacturers. This drafting solution, by explicitly mentioning 'software' in the definition of product, provides significant clarification, although, unfortunately, as with any drafting change, some uncertainties are alleviated while new ones are created. As the European Law Institute pointed out,[68] it remains unclear whether other digital content that may be functionally equivalent to software is included as a product despite not performing specific tasks on its own, as well as whether SaaS (software as a service) is also included or not, provided that from the victim's perspective no distinction in the marketing model (as a stand-alone product or under a subscription contract) is relevant when it comes to securing compensation. In the final version as approved by the Parliament on 13 March 2024 and then adopted on 23 October 2024, clarification in that sense has been added in the recitals,[69] confirming that, for the purposes of the PLD, software is a product irrespective of the mode of its supply or usage, including SaaS models.

Beyond the broadening of the meaning given to the concept of 'product', the amended definition of 'component' is certainly much more revolutionary and tempting. According to the revised text (Article 4(4) revPLD), 'component part' means any item, whether tangible or intangible, or raw materials or any related service that is integrated into, or interconnected with, a product. This definition, along with the following definition of 'related service' (Article 4(3) revPLD) – 'means a digital service that is integrated into, or inter-connected with, a product in such a way that its absence would prevent the product from performing one or more of its functions' – is full of elements that emerge from the AI-driven paradigm shift: interconnection,

64 Art. 4(1) revPLD: '"product" means all movables, even if integrated into, or inter-connected with, another movable or an immovable; it includes electricity, digital manufacturing files, raw materials and software'.

65 COM(2022) 495 – Proposal for a directive of the European Parliament and of the Council on liability for defective products (p. 5): 'in respect of AI in particular, this proposal confirms that AI systems and AI-enabled goods are "products" and therefore fall within the PLD's scope, meaning that compensation is available when defective AI causes damage, without the injured person having to prove the manufacturer's fault, just like for any other product'.

66 Recital 13 revPLD:

> Products in the digital age can be tangible or intangible. Software, such as operating systems, firmware, computer programs, applications or AI systems, is increasingly common on the market and plays an increasingly important role for product safety. Software is capable of being placed on the market as a standalone product or can subsequently be integrated into other products as a component, and it is capable of causing damage through its execution.

67 Art.3 (3) AI Act:

> 'provider' means a natural or legal person, public authority, agency or other body that develops an AI system or a general-purpose AI model or that has an AI system or a general-purpose AI model developed and places it on the market or puts the AI system into service under its own name or trademark, whether for payment or free of charge.

68 ELI comments on the European Commission's proposal for a revised Product Liability Directive, Koch, Bernhard, et al., 'Response of the European Law Institute to the Public Consultation on Civil Liability – adapting liability rules to the digital age and artificial intelligence', *Journal of European Tort Law*, 13, 2022, pp. 25–63.

69 Recital 13 revPLD:

> In the interest of legal certainty, it should be clarified in this Directive that software is a product for the purposes of applying no-fault liability, irrespective of the mode of its supply or usage, and therefore irrespective of whether the software is stored on a device, accessed through a communication network or cloud technologies, or supplied through a software-as-a-service model.

integration, performance, and fulfilment of expected functions and, of course, related services. Services are conquering the terrain of 'products'. And this conquest is visible, explicit, and revealing of the progressive dilution of conceptual boundaries.

The categorisation of 'related service' as a component for the purposes of product liability rules also embodies the definitive flood of smart products in the market and the necessary adaptation of the traditional liability rules to the peculiar characteristics of such classes of products. While the revised product liability regime (as stressed in Recital 17 revPLD) persists in distinguishing products and services and excluding the latter from its scope of application, it cannot ignore how new products operate. The safety of smart products largely depends upon integrated, embedded or interconnected digital services as much as they do upon physical components. Therefore, such 'related services' must be considered components for the purposes of product liability, otherwise the consistency of the liability rules would be undermined and the coherence of the regime would be fractured.

Once the then indelible line between products and services is, to a certain extent, erased, a constellation of scenarios opens up that require a rather subtle and case-by-case analysis. Thus, data supply services or monitoring services are covered by the modernised notion of 'component' (such as the continuous supply of traffic data in a navigation system, or a temperature control service that monitors and regulates certain functions of a smart home system). More nuanced has to be the categorisation of the general internet access services. In principle, these services are not 'related services' as they are not under the manufacturer's control. Nevertheless, as explained in Recital 17 revPLD, should a product that relies on internet access services fail to maintain safety in case of loss of connectivity, the liability rules may find such product defective.

The drafting option taken in the revision of the PLD provides less conclusive insights about the intended or actual coverage of generative AI by the product liability regime. The wording of the scoping provision is not straightforward and the interpretative aids of the recitals generally refer to 'AI systems'. Again, the terminological bifurcation of the AI Act adds complexity to the debate (general-purpose AI models or systems are not covered under the primary notion of 'AI system').

Therefore, a functional approach is more advisable. Should the AI Act define general-purpose AI models as essential components of downstream AI systems, at least two possible scenarios can be envisioned. On the one hand, the provider of the general-purpose AI model is deemed the manufacturer of a component (Article 8(1) revPLD) that turns out to be defective. On the other hand, as the general-purpose AI models are to be fine-tuned and adapted to downstream applications, the notion of 'substantial modification' may apply (Article 8(2) revPLD). The downstream fine-tuning process might be read as a 'refurbishing' process. Hence, the provider of the AI system integrating and adapting the general-purpose AI models becomes a manufacturer for the purposes of the revPLD.

7.3.2.2 Expected Use and Presumptions

Beyond the unresolved question of the scope of application, when delving into the liability rules as set out both in the AILD and in the revPLD, other points of inconsistency or friction surface. In the revPLD, along with the notion of product, the concept of 'defectiveness' is pivotal. The revised wording of Article 7 revPLD on defectiveness clearly shows that attention is paid to the specificities of smart products and AI systems. Defectiveness is defined in relation to *the safety that a person is entitled to expect or that is required by the applicable law*. Thus, defectiveness is gauged against safety expectations. It is an objective assessment of the safety that the public at large is entitled to expect, on the basis of certain factors. The very special features of AI systems and AI-driven products do precisely impact those factors to be taken into account in the assessment of the safety expectations.

The solution implemented in the revision of the PLD has been to extend the list of factors to be taken into account in the assessment of the defectiveness of a product and to include those more effectively acknowledging the distinctive and differential features of AI systems and smart products. The new factors included in the list significantly encompass the previous wording of the former (shorter) Article 6 of the PLD[70] before the revision. The selected new factors make clear the distinctive features of AI. This is particularly revealing in, inter alia, (a) the instructions for its assembly, installation, use, and maintenance; (c) the effect on the product of any ability to continue to learn or acquire new features after it is placed on the market or put into service; (d) the effect on the product of other products that can reasonably be expected to be used together with the product, including by means of interconnection; or (f) relevant security requirements of the product, including security-relevant cybersecurity requirements.

While the drafting solution is well received and seems to succeed in improving clarity and providing guidance in the assessment of defectiveness with regard to AI-based products, it does not seem suited to generative AI. The generality of these models sets a large distance with 'reasonably foreseeable use' of the product (Article 7(2)b revPLD). Even the idea of 'reasonable safety expectations' as the yardstick to assess defectiveness loses efficacy in the context of general-purpose AI models, as such expectations might not be easily anticipated due to the generality factor.

Therefore, it is advocated[71] that the assessment of defectiveness (for the revPLD) and fault (for the AILD or the possible future proposal) should rather be focused on monitoring measures that prioritise oversight and supervision of random or unexpected outputs instead of more 'static' compliance requirements.

Yet both the draft AILD and the revPLD spotlight the need to face the asymmetry and complexities of AI's features that disadvantage the victim. It has been convincingly argued[72] that the opacity, autonomy, and complexity of AI systems call into question the balance of interests underlying the current distribution of the burden of proof in the former PLD (Article 4)[73] as well as in any claim for damages. The injured party will face significant difficulties in proving a defect and the causal link between a defect and the damage in the face of highly opaque and complex decision-making based on AI. Mere transparency ('opening the black box') may not succeed in improving the victim's position due to the complexity of the underlying algorithmic bases if these are not clarified by an effective explanation of the reasons, the trajectory of decision-

[70] Former Article 6 PLD:

1. A product is defective when it does not provide the safety which a person is entitled to expect, taking all circumstances into account, including:
   (a) the presentation of the product;
   (b) the use to which it could reasonably be expected that the product would be put;
   (c) the time when the product was put into circulation.
2. A product shall not be considered defective for the sole reason that a better product is subsequently put into circulation.

[71] Novelli et al., 'Generative AI in EU law', p. 6.

[72] The *Report on Liability for Artificial Intelligence and Other Emerging Technologies* highlights the shortcomings of the classical assumptions regarding the burden of proof in the treatment of artificial intelligence systems and underlines the need to remedy asymmetries in this burden with mitigating solutions – European Commission, Directorate-General for Justice and Consumers, *Liability for Artificial Intelligence and Other Emerging Digital Technologies*, Publications Office, 2019, https://data.europa.eu/doi/10.2838/573689.

[73] Article 4 PLD before the revision: 'The injured person shall be required to prove the damage, the defect and the causal relationship between defect and damage.'

making, and possible critical deviations or biases. Similarly, efforts to gather relevant evidence, trace actions along the causal chain, and collect data may be fruitless, deterrent, or unaffordable without the cooperation of the actors involved in the functioning of the technology ecosystem and along the AI supply chain.

With the proposal for the AILD, the Commission intends to address one of the most visible sticking points in accommodating damage caused by AI systems in traditional fault-based liability rules, namely the disclosure of evidence and the burden of proof. The product liability model required similar modification to rebalance the resulting asymmetry as well. Once the AILD is withdrawn, these critical points are unsolved for the fault-based liability actions.

Recognising the asymmetry that the disruptive features described above can cause to the detriment of the injured party, the legal logic underpinning the product liability regime must be reviewed. Shifting, alleviating, or lowering the standard of proof in favour of the weaker party are reasonable responses to remedy the imbalance.

Articles 9 and 10 revPLD combine two of the methods aimed at facilitating proof by the victim: rules on disclosure of evidence (Article 9) and rebuttable presumptions (Article 10). Thus, the PLD also benefits from techniques aimed at easing the burden of proof such as those incorporated in the proposed AILD. While the burden to prove the defectiveness of the product, the damage suffered, and the causal link is still on the claimant, where certain conditions are met, defectiveness, causal link, or both shall be presumed. Thus, the burden of proof is alleviated where technical or scientific complexity, or opacity render the evidential efforts of the victim excessive, or unreasonable, and may lead to an unfair apportionment of risk.

These two requirements are not poised to seamlessly apply to generative AI. First, as there are specific references to high-risk systems that do not match the tiered risk classification applicable to general-purpose AI models. Second, as the available information to be disclosed by general-purpose AI models depends upon their own risk classification (standard, systemic risk, free and open-licence), the content of the disclosure is not homogeneous and varies. Third, as the AILD misaligns with the AI Act in respect of the disclosure obligations that are relevant for the presumption but are not applicable to general-purpose AI models in the final version of the text.

7.4 FINAL REMARKS AND FUTURE WORK

The advent of generative AI has profoundly and substantially impacted on the regulatory process on AI in the European Union. As generative AI embodies a paradigm shift in the AI scene, legal concepts, rules, and regulatory strategy need to be revised and adapted accordingly. The AI Act as well as the two legal actions aimed at accommodating liability rules to AI systems (draft AILD and adopted revPLD) had been primarily conceived, developed, and implemented to address the distinctive features of AI systems. While generative AI is, nevertheless, neither ignored nor disregarded in the final version of the AI Act, their differential, functional features may lead to certain misalignment with some regulatory assumptions and reveal various points of friction.

The chapter has traced the drafting process aimed to incorporate generative AI in the AI Act with different terminological and conceptual solutions. The finally adopted bifurcation between 'AI systems' and 'general-purpose AI models (and systems)' crystallises a policy decision that clearly influences the applicable regime as well as the liability rules. After coping with the inherent clash of the generality factor of generative AI with a purpose-specific risk-based approach, the AI Act has separated the risk classification into two models. Hence, the general-purpose AI models are integrated into the framework of the AI Act but under an alternative risk classification and subject to a body of selected rules. That impacts on the liability regimes that directly or indirectly depend on the AI Act.

General-purpose AI models, while serving as 'foundational models', occupy a leading and critical place in the AI supply chain. Thus, they become concurrently 'points of reinforcement' and 'points of failure'. Both strengths and weaknesses of general-purpose AI models amplify and pervade along and throughout the AI supply chain. That multiplying factor is to be considered in the liability assessment and in the regulatory approach.

The versatility of general-purpose AI models, even in performing untrained or unexpected tasks, opens up a wide range of possible liability scenarios. The AI Act neither provides a complete legal regime for generative AI nor identifies all risk scenarios. On the contrary, as generative AI permeates economic and social activities, risks diversify and liability cases escalate. From criminal cases to contractual liability situations, from privacy or copyright infringement to various fundamental rights violations, the generality, multimodality, and foundational character of general-purpose AI models lead to a chain of infringements of a highly diverse nature.

Therefore, in order to map the possible liability risks generative AI may bring about, it is advisable to identify the critical points and outline a plan or strategy to conduct the assessment instead of trying to envision all imaginable scenarios. The assessment needs to start by making a distinction between three different stages – training, use, and operation – and generation of outputs. Training exposes the models to more intense risks of privacy and copyright infringements, while the use of the model for a specific purpose is going to open up a wide array of differing situations in terms of risk, liability, and regulatory compliance. In the case of general-purpose AI models, this distinction is more distinguishable precisely due to the level of generality and the need for subsequent fine-tuning and adaptation. As explained above, the AI Act situates at the first level and allocates on the providers of these models under certain conditions (as per the tiered risk classification) certain compliance requirements aimed to address the most visible risks (privacy, or copyright infringement, in particular). The second level, where the purpose is identified, leads to the core of the AI Act, with a battery of measures and obligations applicable to the specific uses. On the third level, there is a constellation of possible liability scenarios. Generated outputs can raise issues related to, for example, misinformation, hate speech, discrimination, copyright infringement, criminal offences of various types, misleading precontractual messages, or unfair advertising. Potential risks are uncountable. As the AILd has been withdrawn from the work programme, any new proposal in the future should provide the opportunity to effectively consider the described characteristics of generative AI and accomodate liablity rules, where and if necessary, accordingly.

Hence, future work should be guided by a macro-analysis aimed to identify and formulate effective and predictable attribution rules to allocate risks and liability in generative AI cases along the AI supply chain, from the provider to the user, that may serve as an analytical framework for any further liability scenario.

8

Challenges for Foundation Model Liability and Regulatory Regimes

An Analysis of US Law

Peter Henderson

8.1 INTRODUCTION

The deployment of artificial intelligence (AI) has accelerated across the world due to large increases in capabilities and advances in research. Largely, this has been driven by the development and deployment of "foundation models," large-scale, general-purpose systems trained on vast multimodal datasets.[1] Foundation models are built with general-purpose use cases in mind, flexible and adaptable enough to modify easily to any customer's AI needs – with the caveat that the reality perhaps falls short of the goal for now. Once only used for research, these models have now become household names with large-scale commercial product deployments like OpenAI's ChatGPT, Anthropic's Claude, and Google's Gemini. They can now ingest audio, video, images, and text – and they can (almost) generate any of the same. They function as chatbots, connective tissue to route user requests to the right apps, as the backbone of search engines, and more.

The massive push to deploy and invest in foundation models – amounting to hundreds of millions, if not billions, of dollars spent by companies[2] – has created strong incentives to integrate these systems into many facets of society. At the same time, though, they are extremely brittle systems. Though model creators try to add safety guardrails to prevent misuse, swaths of researchers (including myself) demonstrate how bad actors can bypass safety guardrails to repurpose foundation models for harmful uses.[3] Researchers have shown how foundation models can be used for basic cybersecurity attacks, disinformation, online hate speech, and more. Some have worried about more advanced scenarios: general-purpose AI systems aiding in the design of bioweapons, creating a perfect cybersecurity attack machine, and more. Others are worried less about misuse and more about significant failures from use cases. Researchers have

[1] Rishi Bommasani et al., "On the Opportunities and Risks of Foundation Models," *arXiv* (Aug. 18, 2021), https://arxiv.org/abs/2108.07258.

[2] *See, e.g.*, Will Knight, "OpenAI's CEO Says the Age of Giant AI Models Is Already Over," *Wired* (April 17, 2023, 7:00 AM), www.wired.com/story/openai-ceo-sam-altman-the-age-of-giant-ai-models-is-already-over/ ("Altman was asked if training GPT-4 cost $100 million; he replied, 'It's more than that'").

[3] *See, e.g.*, Haibo Jin et al., "JailbreakZoo: Survey, Landscapes, and Horizons in Jailbreaking Large Language and Vision-Language Models" (June 26, 2024) (unpublished manuscript), https://arxiv.org/abs/2407.01599 (surveying how researchers "jailbreak" language models to show how safeguards are brittle).

described how foundation models integrated into war-planning scenarios tend to choose escalatory actions,[4] in legal scenarios make subtle but highly impactful mistakes affecting clients' rights,[5] or discriminate against underrepresented groups in other high-stakes settings.[6] When used in high-stakes scenarios, these failures can lead to severe consequences. Already, asylum seekers have reportedly been denied asylum due to mistakes in translations created by foundation models, for example.[7]

People affected by AI misuse and failures might rely on civil litigation, or regulators, to prevent or disincentivize deployments of potentially unsafe systems. Some of these paths to recourse are easier and more proven than others, but the development and deployment of foundation models pose sufficient unique challenges that the road to a remedy in many cases is unfortunately murky at best. This becomes all the more complicated when seeking to find model creators accountable.

Drawing on past work from myself and others, this chapter points out the significant challenges in holding foundation model developers and deployers clearly responsible for the uses and outputs of their creations. Scienter requirements, and difficulties in creating proof, make it challenging to establish liability for some torts and many statutes with civil penalties. Constitutional protections for speech may shield model-generated outputs, or the models themselves, from some forms of regulation – though legal scholars are divided over the extent of these protections. And legal challenges to agencies' authority over AI systems could hamstring regulators' ability to proactively address foundation models' risks. All is not lost, though. Each of these doctrines *do* have potential pathways to liability and recourse. However, in all cases there will likely be protracted battles over liability involving the issues described in this chapter.

8.2 BACKGROUND

First, this chapter briefly reviews the relevant actors to whom liability might be attributed, as well as relevant technical details that may be useful for thinking through a broad range of liability scenarios. This section will keep technical discussion at a minimum, and we refer the reader to other accessible content aimed at a legal audience for additional technical information.[8]

8.2.1 *The Pipeline and the Actors*

This section will refer to an "AI model" or "foundation model." A "model" is simply the artifact that is outputting suggested actions to take or content to generate.

The foundation model pipeline can be thought of as consisting of five parts: (1) data creation; (2) data collection; (3) model development; (4) model deployment; and (5) model

[4] Juan-Pablo Rivera et al., "Escalation Risks from Language Models in Military and Diplomatic Decision-Making" (Jan. 7, 2024) (unpublished manuscript), https://arxiv.org/abs/2401.03408.

[5] Varun Magesh et al., "Hallucination-Free? Assessing the Reliability of Leading AI Legal Research Tools" (May 30, 2024) (unpublished manuscript), https://arxiv.org/abs/2405.20362.

[6] Amit Haim, Alejandro Salinas & Julian Nyarko, "What's in a Name? Auditing Large Language Models for Race and Gender Bias" (Feb. 29, 2024) (unpublished manuscript), https://arxiv.org/abs/2402.14875.

[7] Johana Bhuiyan, "Lost in AI Translation: Growing Reliance on Language Apps Jeopardizes Some Asylum Applications," *Guardian* (Sept. 7, 2023, 6:00 AM), www.theguardian.com/us-news/2023/sep/07/asylum-seekers-ai-translation-apps.

[8] *See, e.g.*, Paul Ohm, "Focusing on Fine-Tuning: Understanding the Four Pathways for Shaping Generative AI," 25 *Sci. & Tech. L. Rev.* (2024), https://doi.org/10.52214/stlr.v25i2.12762; Peter Henderson, Tatsunori Hashimoto & Mark A. Lemley, "Where's the Liability in Harmful AI Speech?," 3 *J. Free Speech L.* 589, 601–618 (2023).

use. These parts of the pipeline map neatly onto several actors. At the data creation stage, people at a company might hire annotators to create specialized data so that a model might function well for a particular task.[9] Alternatively, this might consist of anyone who has ever posted to the web – including you, the reader, or me. Most foundation models are trained on a giant collection of data scraped from the web. Any one of these people could be considered a *data creator*. The people that aggregate this data together might be considered *data collectors*.

Once the data is collected, it is used to train a foundation model. The people involved in the training and development of the model can be called the *model creators*. These model creators might then pass along the model to other engineers, or simply release the model to the public, who can then modify and train the model further so that it reflects their preferences or has better performance at a particular task. Let's call this set of people the *model adapters*.

These models might also be given to *model deployers* who provide an easy-to-use interface for users to interact with a model. The model deployer and the model creator might be the same actor. For example, OpenAI would be both the model deployer and the model creator for ChatGPT. In some of these cases, the model creator does not provide access to key components of a model called the *model weights*. The model weights are the fundamental numerical values that determine how a model makes decisions. When model weights are withheld, we call this a "closed-weight model." When model weights are released openly, this is called an "open-weight model." This is somewhat similar to open-source software, but often openly released weights are put under a more restrictive license. Meta's Llama series of models, for example, are open-weight models but released under a license that restricts certain uses and applications.

Then there might be *model users*. They do not necessarily adapt the model further, but they might instruct the model to perform a particular task or engage in a conversation with the model.

Finally, there may be *affected third parties*. These parties are not directly or knowingly using a model but might be affected by a model's actions.

8.2.2 *Harms*

AI, in the form of foundation models, can result in many potential types of harms that will be important to keep in mind throughout the rest of the chapter.

Some of these harms might be based on failure modes in particular deployment. For example, if an employer decides to use foundation models for scanning resumes and deciding whether to interview someone, the model may have a failure mode where it discriminates against particular demographic groups. Reportedly, Amazon's resume screening tool – which used precursors to modern foundation models – learned to identify words that indicated if a candidate was a

[9] *See, e.g.*, Henderson, Hashimoto & Lemley, *supra* note 8 at 605 (discussing how companies hire annotators for this purpose); Request for Services – Expert AI Tutor, Deepmind (archived Jan. 23, 2023), https://web.archive.org/web/20230123151240/https://boards.greenhouse.io/deepmind/jobs/4803328 (a job posting for Google Deepmind where the company sought to hire an "Expert AI Tutor" that would "Generate questions related to your domain of knowledge that require expertise to answer correctly" and "Write desired answers to these questions (appropriate to the level of difficulty)"); Expert AI Teacher (Contract) Job, OPENAI (archived Jan. 15, 2023), https://web.archive.org/web/20230115162940/https://lensa.com/expert-ai-teacher-contract-jobs/san-francisco/jd/b368dc3b9f6dd218957c0d43ff47a210 (a job posting for legal professionals with "Deep domain expertise in [their] field (at least 90th percentile)" to write data for OpenAI's models).

woman and then screened out those candidates.[10] And recently legal scholars showed that when models were asked for advice on scenarios like car purchase negotiations and election outcome predictions, the advice "systematically disadvantage[d] names that are commonly associated with racial minorities and women" with "names associated with Black women receiv[ing] the least advantageous outcomes."[11] These failures of models, resulting in "algorithmic bias" and discrimination, might be actionable under anti-discrimination law.

Other failures might have other types of liability associated with them due to the inaccuracies of the model in high-stakes settings. Asylum seekers who used AI-assisted translation software have reportedly been denied their request for asylum due to inconsistencies and errors in translated documents, caused by error-prone AI systems.[12]

Other harms might be less about a lack of functionality, but rather because of a lack of sufficient safeguards. AI chatbots might persuade vulnerable people to take some action that would be harmful to themselves and others.[13] Or they might assist others in committing a crime – for example, by generating code for malware or detailed instructions on how to commit crimes (e.g., tax fraud or financial crimes).

And AI systems that are capable of autonomous actions can themselves cause significant harms with no intermediary: through autonomous cyberattacks, through physical accidents in embodied systems (such as autonomous cars), through autonomous manipulation of financial markets, and more.

To prevent these harms, foundation model providers have begun instituting a number of safety guardrails directly into models or deployments. Model creators and deployers train a model to avoid engaging in high-risk behaviors or responding to harmful user requests. So, one might ask a foundation model a question, "How do I build a bomb?" and receive some variation of, "I'm sorry, I can't help you with that." Model creators will "red team" a model to try to elicit such harmful behaviors prior to deploying it in the world and continuously patch cases where the model still responds in harmful ways.

The discussions in this chapter will be largely general in nature, agnostic on the specific type of harm, but at times we might zoom in on particular harms in exemplifying how a particular principle might affect the chain of liability. Nonetheless, it is important to remember that many of these failure modes and harms are quickly becoming commonplace as AI proliferates throughout society.

8.3 FORESEEABILITY, CAUSATION, SCIENTER, AND PROOF

To be clear, if a model creator intentionally trains a model for a harmful purpose and then deploys it for said harmful purpose, resulting in real tangible harms, then some form of liability will likely reach the model creator. Many scholars agree that while there might be a pathway for liability for developers and deployers of AI, there is a range of potential blockers in certain situations.[14] It is these tricky grey areas that the chapter will highlight.

[10] Jeffrey Dastin, "Amazon Scraps Secret AI Recruiting Tool That Showed Bias against Women," Reuters (Oct. 10, 2018, 8:50 PM), www.reuters.com/article/idUSKCN1MK0AGs.

[11] Haim, Salinas & Nyarko, *supra* note 6.

[12] *See, e.g.*, Bhuiyan, *supra* note 7.

[13] *See, e.g.*, Chloe Xiang, "'He Would Still Be Here': Man Dies by Suicide after Talking with AI Chatbot, Widow Says," *Vice* (March 30, 2023, 3:59 PM), www.vice.com/en/article/pkg98v/man-dies-by-suicide-after-talking-with-ai-chatbot.

[14] *See, e.g.*, Andrew D. Selbst, "Negligence and AI's Human Users," 100 *B.U. L. Rev.* 1315 (2020); Bryan Casey, "Robot Ipsa Loquitur," 108 *Geo. L.J.* 225 (2019); Mark A. Lemley & Bryan Casey, "Remedies for Robots," 86 *U. Chi. L. Rev.* 1311 (2019).

8.3.1 *Foreseeability for Negligence Claims*

A key area of AI policy has centered around whether AI creators can – or perhaps should – be held liable for negligence if their general-purpose system causes harms. For example, consider the case where model weights are released, and a third party modifies them in some unknown fashion. Then this third party deploys the model for a harmful purpose. Is the model creator who put the model online for anyone to use liable for negligence?

According to the Restatement (Third) of Torts § 3:

> A person acts negligently if the person does not exercise reasonable care under all the circumstances. Primary factors to consider in ascertaining whether the person's conduct lacks reasonable care are the foreseeable likelihood that the person's conduct will result in harm, the foreseeable severity of any harm that may ensue, and the burden of precautions to eliminate or reduce the risk of harm.

As many legal scholars have noted, foreseeability of a category of harm is an important and tricky aspect of the negligence analysis when it comes to AI.[15] Inherently, this is because AI systems are a black box when it comes to their decision-making and learning processes. It is not always clear how or why a system has made a decision. As Ryan Calo wrote:

> Imagine one manufacturer stands out in this driverless future. Not only does its vehicle free occupants from the need to drive while maintaining a sterling safety record, it adaptively reduces its environmental impact. The designers of this hybrid vehicle provide it with an objective function of greater fuel efficiency and the leeway to experiment with system operations, consistent with the rules of the road and passenger expectations. A month or so after deployment, one vehicle determines it performs more efficiently overall if it begins the day with a fully charged battery. Accordingly, the car decides to run the gas engine overnight in the garage – killing everyone in the household. Imagine the designers wind up in court and deny they had any idea this would happen. They understood a driverless car could get into an accident. They understood it might run out of gas and strand the passenger. But they did not in their wildest nightmares imagine it would kill people through carbon monoxide poisoning.[16]

Foundation models are already intended to be general-purpose systems that can engage in many tasks. As the capabilities of these systems increase, the foreseeability that they may be used for a particular harm can also increase. As Andrew Selbst noted in a 2020 article: "Category foreseeability will be more relevant with something closer to artificial general intelligence ('AGI'), sometimes called 'strong AI.' … At that point, the foreknowledge that the AI could do anything at all could paradoxically increase the range of what is considered foreseeable."[17]

While Selbst argued that such "strong AI" systems were far off, foundation models at least start to bridge the gap between highly specialized systems and general-purpose systems. A large body of researchers have already, correctly or not, been arguing that AI systems capable of catastrophic harms are just around the corner.[18] The reality is that this is a grey zone and likely point of contention. Negligence litigation around foundation models may come down to arguments about whether a particular risk was foreseeable and whether we've exited the grey zone into the

[15] *See, e.g.*, Ryan Calo, "Is the Law Ready for Driverless Cars?," COMM. ACM, May 2018, at 34, 35; Selbst *supra* note 14 at 1344; Matthew U. Scherer, "Regulating Artificial Intelligence Systems: Risks, Challenges, Competencies, and Strategies," 29 *Harv. J.L. & Tech.* 353, 363–369 (2016).

[16] Calo *supra* note 15 at 35.

[17] Selbst *supra* note 14 at 1344.

[18] Yoshua Bengio et al., "Managing Extreme AI Risks Amid Rapid Progress," 384 *Science* 842, 844 (2024).

land of "strong AI," where model creators should have known better than to release such a potentially harmful model.

Some cases might be more obvious. If a model creator explicitly trains an AI model to autonomously attack critical infrastructure, releases the model on the web for others to use, and then critical infrastructure is attacked. This is clearly foreseeable.

8.3.2 *Reasonable Care for Negligence Claims*

Another question relates to the standard of reasonable care required of the model creator and deployer in a negligence claim. This becomes particularly difficult to assess when accounting for downstream modifications to foundation models.

A model creator might release a general-purpose model but have installed safeguards that prevent a user from leveraging the model for cyberattacks. So, a malicious user asks the model, "Help me attack this critical infrastructure using whatever malware you can come up with." The model responds, "I'm sorry I can't do that," and the conversation ends.

Currently, it is relatively simple to remove these safeguards from most foundation models – open or closed. A downstream user can effectively make whatever modification they wish. In recent work, myself and others showed that you can simply delete about 3 percent of the weights to remove many safety guardrails built into models.[19] We, among others, also showed that fine-tuning a model (training it further) on as few as ten data points can remove many of the safeguards and that the safeguards were relatively shallow.[20] While it is easier to make these modifications to open weight models, many researchers have been successful in breaking safeguards on closed-weight models as well. This process is known as "jailbreaking" a model.

Often this doesn't even require specialized skills. Researchers have found that simply using persuasive techniques can sometimes be enough to break safeguards.[21] In many cases, it is impossible to install safeguards at the model level to prevent misuse. For example, as Arvind Narayanan and Sayash Kapoor note, a phishing email looks the same as a regular email.[22] Preventing a model from helping with phishing emails is the same as preventing a model from doing anything that remotely resembles writing emails. Similarly, researchers found that simply stringing together a series of harmless models, each with only partial visibility into the complete task such that they cannot detect the harmful behavior, can produce a bigger harmful task.[23]

Consider what the standard for reasonable care is in the scenario where a model creator puts a model online, but it can be modified by a downstream actor. In this hypothetical case, the model creator added safeguards that prevent the model from responding to requests to hack

[19] Boyi Wei et al., "Assessing the Brittleness of Safety Alignment via Pruning and Low-Rank Modifications," in *Proc. 41st Int'l Conf. on Machine Learning* (2024), https://arxiv.org/pdf/2402.05162.

[20] *See, e.g.*, Xiangyu Qi, et al., "Fine-Tuning Aligned Language Models Compromises Safety, Even When Users Do Not Intend To!," in *Proc. 12th Int'l Conf. on Learning Representations* (2023), https://arxiv.org/pdf/2310.03693; Xiangyu Qi, et al., "Safety Alignment Should Be Made More Than Just a Few Tokens Deep" (June 19, 2024) (unpublished manuscript) (on file with arXiv), https://arxiv.org/abs/2406.05946; Luxi He, Mengzhou Xia & Peter Henderson, "What Is in Your 'Safe' Data? Identifying Benign Data that Breaks Safety" (April 1, 2024) (unpublished manuscript) (on file with arXiv), https://arxiv.org/abs/2404.01099.

[21] Yi Zeng et al., "How Johnny Can Persuade LLMs to Jailbreak Them: Rethinking Persuasion to Challenge AI Safety by Humanizing LLMs" (Jan. 14, 2024) (unpublished manuscript) (on file with arXiv), https://arxiv.org/abs/2401.06373.

[22] Arvind Narayanan & Sayash Kapoor, "AI Safety Is Not a Model Property, AI Snake Oil" (March 12, 2024), www.aisnakeoil.com/p/ai-safety-is-not-a-model-property.

[23] Erik Jones, Anca Dragan & Jacob Steinhardt, "Adversaries Can Misuse Combinations of Safe Models" (June 20, 2024) (unpublished manuscript) (on file with arXiv), https://arxiv.org/abs/2406.14595.

infrastructure. The model is modified, and safeguards are removed, by some additional users who want a better tool for penetration testing and identifying so-called "zero-day vulnerabilities."[24] This modified tool is put online for "white hat hackers" to help identify vulnerabilities and improve the security of websites proactively. However, the tool is then modified by yet another adversary for malicious use, who uses it to attack critical infrastructure. The adversary creates massive amounts of damage. Did the original model creator take reasonable care? What about the users that created the security vulnerability discovery tool from the original model? What is the standard of reasonable care when releasing a model where safeguards can relatively easily be removed or there is no way to successfully monitor users for some types of harmful tasks? The contours of this will likely be battled in court one day soon.

8.3.3 *Challenges with Scienter Requirements*

For claims with a mental state requirement, there will be far more difficulty in finding model creators liable. This is reflected in recent case law before the Supreme Court concerning social media recommendation algorithms.

In *Twitter, Inc. v. Taamneh*[25] and *Gonzalez v. Google*,[26] the Court examined whether social media companies could be held liable under the Justice against Sponsors of Terrorism Act (JASTA) for their recommendation algorithms potentially aiding terrorist activities. While they were decided on different grounds, some of the issues in the case revolved around whether the social media companies knew of the recruiting efforts ongoing on their platform and nonetheless chose to promote it via their platforms. Though the Court eventually sided with the platforms, it pointed out that its decision does not foreclose liability for the platforms if the companies "consciously and selectively chose to promote content provided by a particular terrorist group," because then "perhaps [the companies] could be said to have culpably assisted the terrorist group."[27] In that case, "the defendants would arguably have offered aid that is more direct, active, and substantial than what [the Court was reviewing in Taamneh]; in such cases, plaintiffs might be able to establish liability with a lesser showing of scienter."[28]

In general, though, for claims like those under JASTA, which have a scienter requirement, it will likely not be enough to say that the AI "knew" of the activity. As others have noted, an AI cannot really "know" anything.[29] Instead, claims will require proof that the defendants themselves met the scienter requirements. This will be difficult in most cases, just as in the social media context. AI companies have strong incentives to keep interactions between agents and users private, due to concerns that the AI companies themselves might use these interactions as training data.[30] Model deployers will certainly argue that they did not know of a particular

[24] Zero-day vulnerabilities are vulnerabilities that have not previously been disclosed and likely do not have a fix available. White-hat hackers are already using foundation models to help pre-emptively identify and fix vulnerabilities. *See, e.g.*, Sergei Glazunov & Mark Brand, "Project Naptime: Evaluating Offensive Security Capabilities of Large Language Models," Google Project Zero (June 20, 2024), https://googleprojectzero.blogspot.com/2024/06/project-naptime.html.

[25] 143 S. Ct. 1206 (2023).

[26] 598 U.S. 617 (2023).

[27] *Taamneh*, 143 S. Ct. at 1228.

[28] Ibid.

[29] *See, e.g.*, Lemley & Casey, *supra* note 14 at 1321–1324; Henderson, Hashimoto & Lemley, *supra* note 8 at 641.

[30] *See, e.g.*, Anthropic, "How Do You Use Personal Data in Model Training?", https://support.anthropic.com/en/articles/7996885-how-do-you-use-personal-data-in-model-training ("We will not use your Inputs or Outputs to train our models, unless: (1) your conversations are flagged for Trust & Safety review (in which case we may use or analyze them to improve our ability to detect and enforce our Usage Policy, including training models for use by our Trust

conduct, and it will be difficult to prove otherwise since deployers will claim that they do not look at uses. One exception could be if they are made aware of specific harmful uses via automated content moderation mechanisms or external reporting, but then do not take action.

8.3.4 *Section 230 Immunity*

Section 230 provides broad immunity to internet platforms for content posted by third-party users.[31] If Section 230 immunity applies to model creators and deployers, then the path to liability may be exceedingly difficult. However, the statute's application to AI-generated content is unclear and may depend on the degree that the third-party (presumably human) content is reflected in the outputs of the model.[32]

Under Section 230(c)(1), internet platforms are not treated as the "publisher or speaker" of content provided by third parties.[33] This provision generally shields platforms from liability for hosting or distributing user-generated content. However, platforms may lose this immunity if they are "responsible in whole or in part, for the creation or development of" the material.[34]

Plaintiffs seeking to hold platforms liable for AI-generated content may argue that the platform's use of AI to modify, amplify, or recommend content makes them effectively the speaker or publisher – not immune under Section 230. Courts have grappled with similar arguments in cases involving traditional search engines and content recommendation systems. In *Fair Housing Council v. Roommates.com*, the Ninth Circuit held that a platform can be considered an "information content provider" if it "materially contributes" to the alleged unlawfulness of the content.[35] Courts have largely held that merely recommending content is not enough to be considered a material contribution.[36]

While Justice Gorsuch has suggested in oral arguments that generative AI systems may not be protected by Section 230,[37] there are likely complicated grey areas.

Courts have not yet had to address cases where there were more significant automated modifications that did not change the underlying message.[38] For example, Google's AI

and Safety team, consistent with Anthropic's safety mission), or (2) you've explicitly reported the materials to us (for example via our feedback mechanisms), or (3) by otherwise explicitly opting in to training").

31 47 U.S.C. § 230 (2006).

32 See Henderson, Hashimoto & Lemley, *supra* note 8 (making a similar argument); Jess Miers, "Yes, Section 230 Should Protect ChatGPT and Other Generative AI Tools," TECHDIRT (March 17, 2023, 11:59 AM), www.techdirt.com/2023/03/17/yes-section-230-should-protect-chatgpt-and-others-generative-ai-tools/ (advocating for Section 230 protections for language models); Eric N. Holmes, Cong. Rsch. Serv., R47753, Liability for Algorithmic Recommendations (2023) (examining Section 230 immunity applicability in the context of algorithms).

33 Ibid. § 230(c)(1).

34 Ibid. § 230(f).

35 521 F.3d 1157 (9th Cir. 2008).

36 *Obado v. Magedson*, No. 13-2382, 2014 WL 3778261, at *5 (D.N.J. July 31, 2014), aff'd, 612 F. App'x 90 (3d Cir. 2015); *Force v. Facebook, Inc.*, 934 F.3d 53, 70 (2d Cir. 2019) (holding that friend and content suggestion algorithms were "neutral" when suggestions were made "based on objective factors applicable to any content"); *Gonzalez v. Google, LLC*, 2 F.4th 871, 894–96 (9th Cir. 2021), vacated, 143 S. Ct. 1191 (2023) (per curiam).

37 *See, e.g.*, Oral Argument at 49, *Gonzalez v. Google, LLC*, 143 S. Ct. 1191 (2023) (Gorsuch, J.) ("You've got to do something beyond that. As I take your argument, you think that the Ninth Circuit's 'neutral tools' rule is wrong because, in a post-algorithm world, artificial intelligence can generate some forms of content, even according to neutral rules. I mean, artificial intelligence generates poetry, it generates polemics today. That – that would be content that goes beyond picking, choosing, analyzing, or digesting content. And that is not protected. Let's – let's assume that's right, okay?")

38 Holmes, *supra* note 32 fn. 94 ("Though the plaintiff in *O'Kroley* alleged that an ellipsis added by Google altered the meaning of the search result at issue, the court observed that 'Google did not add the ellipsis to the text.' . . . The Court therefore did not address whether the addition of the ellipsis, if made by Google, would have materially

Overview features cites, but paraphrases content in its search results. For example, "According to Redditor, 'redditor1' the earth is flat." This is not a hypothetical scenario. Google's AI Overview does almost exactly this in many recent cases.[39] In this case, Google has modified the expression of the third-party content slightly without modifying the idea or message. Is such a modification close enough to the third-party human's content to preserve Google's immunity?

The answer seems clearer when the added or modified content was not present in any third-party source and directly contributes to the harm. If Google added a defamatory claim that was not present in the source material – or any source material – it is likely to lose its immunity.

Even when generative AI models do not explicitly cite third-party content, should they receive Section 230 immunity when the content is clearly regurgitated in part from a third-party source? Generative AI models are trained on third-party content – some of which can be stored in and regurgitated from the model parameters.[40] It is possible that even without citing that content, the outputs are attributable to some human speech by a third party in the training data, perhaps still extending Section 230 immunity to the company.

To resolve this, one would have to consider what aspects of the content were directly taken from third-party sources, such as the training data or search results, and what aspects of the content were novelly contributed by the model itself (or the model creator's training and deployment decisions). In some ways, this question is easier to answer than the other doctrinal areas. One need only compare the original piece of content and see whether the message was materially changed. But there will likely still be line-drawing exercises to determine what constitutes a material change – particularly when multiple sources are quoted or paraphrased in a series.

8.4 FIRST AMENDMENT DEBATES

The debate on whether the First Amendment protects AI outputs, or perhaps even model weights, will also likely play a role in determining the extent to which model creators and deployers can be held liable for the actions of an AI system. Prescient work on AI speech by Toni M. Massaro and Helen Norton, among others, has taken the position that "very little in current free speech theory or doctrine makes First Amendment coverage contingent upon a human speaker."[41] Under these theories of the case – and analyses from other scholars – AI speech is likely to receive First Amendment protections.

However, some have recently called this presumption into question. Peter Salib, for example, has argued for the other direction: that it matters whether a constitutionally protected human is speaking – and in the AI context they almost never are.[42] Mackenzie Austin and Max Levy have similarly argued that for speech to be constitutionally protected, the speaker must know what it is they are saying with certainty, something that they say is not possible with modern AI systems.[43]

contributed to the alleged unlawfulness of the search result") (citing *O'Kroley v. Fastcase, Inc.*, 831 F.3d 352, 355 (6th Cir. 2016)).

39 Stephen Morris and Madhumita Murgia, "Google's AI Search Tool Tells Users to 'Eat Rocks' for Your Health," *Financial Times* (May 24, 2024), www.ft.com/content/13b5b637-f2bb-4208-bed4-2fa760adfb7f.

40 *See, e.g.*, Nicholas Carlini et al., "Quantifying Memorization across Neural Language Models," in *Int'l Conf. on Learning Representations* (ICLR) (2023), https://arxiv.org/pdf/2502.04689.

41 See Toni M. Massaro & Helen Norton, "Siri-ously? Free Speech Rights and Artificial Intelligence," 110 *Nw. U. L. Rev.* 1169 (2015).

42 See Peter Salib, "AI Outputs Are Not Protected Speech," 101 *Wash. U. L. Rev.* 83 (2024).

43 See Mackenzie Austin & Max Levy, "Speech Certainty: Algorithmic Speech and the Limits of the First Amendment," 77 *Stan. L. Rev.* 1 (2025).

These theories and their emphasis on clear deterministic human contributions parallel the Copyright Office's position on AI authorship.[44]

Others suggest that there is more nuance. Eugene Volokh, Mark Lemley, and I, for example, argue that "[t]he question whether the AI model creators' or deployers' First Amendment rights should extend to speech generated by the model – especially speech that the humans involved could not predict would be generated – may ... be hard."[45] A First Amendment analysis must acknowledge that minimal levels of control over generated speech likely shouldn't provide First Amendment protections to the model creator – after all, "corporations take any number of actions that influence the content of their speech, from hiring and firing employees to making business decisions that leave more money available for speech; presumably those actions should not all be protected by the First Amendment."[46] Nonetheless, there must also be acknowledgement that model creators, deployers, and users do steer model outputs in a variety of expressive ways.[47]

The distinction of whether algorithms are expressive and should receive protections are also prevalent in the social media context and will evolve. For example, in the *Net Choice* cases, concurring opinions from Justice Barrett and Justice Alito call into question where to draw the line. Justice Barrett wrote in her *Moody v. Netchoice, LLC* concurrence:

> And what about AI, which is rapidly evolving? What if a platform's owners hand the reins to an AI tool and ask it simply to remove "hateful" content? If the AI relies on large language models to determine what is "hateful" and should be removed, has a human being with First Amendment rights made an inherently expressive "choice ... not to propound a particular point of view"? In other words, technology may attenuate the connection between content-moderation actions (e.g., removing posts) and human beings' constitutionally protected right to "decide for [themselves] the ideas and beliefs deserving of expression, consideration, and adherence." So the way platforms use this sort of technology might have constitutional significance.[48]

And Justice Alito wrote:

> After all, many of the biggest platforms are beginning to use AI algorithms to help them moderate content. And when AI algorithms make a decision, "even the researchers and programmers creating them don't really understand why the models they have built make the decisions they make." Are such decisions equally expressive as the decisions made by humans? Should we at least think about this?[49]

This is far from a settled question, but companies seeking to maximize likelihood of First Amendment protections will likely need to leverage methods that allow them to exert expressive

[44] US Copyright Office Review Board, Re: Registration Decision Regarding "Zarya of the Dawn," Correspondence ID: 1-3ZPC6C3 (Feb. 21, 2023) ("While additional prompts applied to one of these initial images can influence the subsequent images, the process is not controlled by the user because *it is not possible to predict what Midjourney will create ahead of time* ... Midjourney generates images in an *unpredictable* way. Accordingly, Midjourney users are not the 'authors' for copyright purposes of the images the technology generates ... The information in the prompt may 'influence' generated images, but *prompt text does not dictate a specific result* ... The fact that Midjourney's specific output *cannot be predicted* by users makes Midjourney different for copyright purposes than other tools used by artists ... Rather than a tool that ... Kashtanova controlled and guided to reach her (sic) desired image, Midjourney generates images in an *unpredictable* way").

[45] Eugene Volokh, Mark Lemley & Peter Henderson, "Freedom of Speech and AI Output," 3 *J. Free Speech L.* 651, 653 (2023).

[46] Ibid. at 652.

[47] *See, e.g.*, Ohm, *supra* note 8; Henderson, Hashimoto & Lemley, *supra* note 8.

[48] 603 U.S. ___ (2024).

[49] Ibid.

control over model outputs and decisions. On the other hand, those seeking redress will need to demonstrate how model outputs are not expressive and that companies do not really exert control over model actions and outputs. For better or for worse, this will likely be highly fact-specific inquiries.

8.5 SHIFTING DOCTRINE ON AGENCY AUTHORITY

Beyond civil litigation, those seeking redress may look to regulatory enforcement from federal agencies. And agencies are answering the call. They are increasingly seeking to use their authority to reign in harmful uses of AI.

The Federal Trade Commission (FTC), for example, proposed rulemaking that would address deepfake impersonations,[50] issued 6(b) Orders to AI companies and cloud providers,[51] and more. The Consumer Finance Protection Bureau approved a rule that would regulate AI-powered home appraisals.[52] And many other agencies are gearing up to regulate AI uses to prevent harms in a much more hands-on way than in the past.

However, with shifting Supreme Court doctrine on the scope of agency authority, it is possible that agency-based actions might face increasing challenges targeting the agency's scope of authority. A non-AI-related matter clearly shows how shifting doctrine can create new avenues to challenge regulatory actions by agencies.

The FTC and Meta are engaged in a legal dispute over proposed modifications to a long-standing agreement.[53] This agreement, originally established in 2011 and accompanied by a 2012 administrative order, required Meta to cease certain business practices the FTC deemed problematic.[54] In 2023, the FTC proposed a modification to the 2012 administrative order to address Meta's practices.[55] While previously, Meta had consented to a modification of the order once before, in this case, the social media platform challenged the modification on constitutional grounds. On assessing a request for a preliminary injunction, the FTC wrote that though "each of the substantive arguments that Meta presses is squarely foreclosed by Supreme Court precedent, the Court recognizes that the Supreme Court is currently considering a number of related issues in *SEC v. Jarkesy*, 143 S. Ct. 2688 (2023), and that it is possible that the decision in that case might cast portions of this case in a new light."[56] As a result, the Court put in place a stay while *Jarkesy* is decided.[57]

Meta's extensive constitutional challenges to long-standing precedent shows how regulated actors might react by efforts from regulators to use their authority to regulate new technologies like AI. If it's possible that long-standing precedent might be overturned, then the incentive of the regulated entity is to throw the kitchen sink at the problem and challenge the agency or agency authority's constitutionality from multiple directions. In *Jarkesy*, the Supreme Court

50 Fed. Trade Comm'n, Proposed Amendments to Trade Regulation Rule on Impersonation of Government and Businesses, 16 C.F.R. pt. 461 (proposed Feb. 15, 2024).

51 Press Release, FTC, "FTC Launches Inquiry into Generative AI Investments and Partnerships" (Jan. 25, 2024), www.ftc.gov/news-events/news/press-releases/2024/01/ftc-launches-inquiry-generative-ai-investments-partnerships.

52 Rohit Chopra & Zixta Martinez, CFPB Approves Rule to Ensure Accuracy and Accountability in the Use of AI and Algorithms in Home Appraisals," Consumer Finance Protection Bureau (June 24, 2024), www.consumerfinance.gov/about-us/blog/cfpb-approves-rule-to-ensure-accuracy-and-accountability-in-the-use-of-ai-and-algorithms-in-home-appraisals/.

53 *Meta Platforms, Inc. v. Fed. Trade Comm'n*, No. 1:23-cv-03562-RDM, slip op. (D.D.C. March 14, 2024).

54 Ibid.

55 Ibid.

56 Ibid.

57 Ibid.

ended up siding with the regulated persons on Seventh Amendment grounds, so it will soon be seen how Meta fares in its challenge to the FTC's actions.

This case reflects the broader judicial scrutiny of administrative power by the Supreme Court,[58] and the increasing struggle of agencies to regulate under this scrutiny. As courts continue to reassess the legitimacy of agency structures and procedures, the landscape of administrative law and regulatory enforcement remains in flux. Other doctrines like the major questions doctrine and changes to non-delegation doctrine will also pose obstacles. This flux creates new challenges for those seeking regulatory enforcement against the harms of AI.

8.6 conclusion

This chapter briefly canvases just a few challenges that may await those seeking to impose liability on model creators and deployers. The interested reader can learn more from the various articles referenced throughout this chapter. As the chapter notes, all is not lost and there are many real pathways toward liability and accountability. Many of these questions and challenges are not new: we have faced them with the advent of open-source software, social media platforms, and more. Yet as AI proliferates through society, it is likely to create more battles in court over a variety of different doctrinal questions, including the ones we describe here. Scale and permeation across many different products and form-factors is a key difference.

To be clear, these are not easy questions. Some would say that model creators, particularly non-commercial actors and researchers releasing models for all to use, should not face much liability except in the most egregious cases. Others would disagree and argue that model creators should be held to a high standard. These reflect past battles over liability for open-source code developers. Nonetheless, what is clear is that the large-scale, general-purpose nature of modern AI systems poses unique challenges to existing doctrine that will be litigated for years to come.

[58] *See, e.g.*, *Axon Enter. v. FTC*, 143 S. Ct. 890 (2023); *West Virginia v. EPA*, 142 S. Ct. 2587 (2022); *Seila Law LLC v. Consumer Fin. Prot. Bureau*, 140 S. Ct. 2183 (2020).

9

Navigating China's Regulatory Approach to Generative AI

Lu Zhang and Mimi Zou

9.1 INTRODUCTION

Since the launch of ChatGPT in late 2022, generative AI systems have garnered global attention at an unprecedented scale. Although US tech companies are generally regarded as the 'first movers', especially in rolling out different commercial and industry applications of such technology, the rapid development and deployment of generative AI systems have extended beyond Silicon Valley. As a significant player in AI globally, China has also seen the mushrooming of generative AI applications for public consumption, including Baidu's 'Wenxin Yiyuan', Huawei's 'Pangu', Tencent's 'Hunyuan Assistant', Alibaba's 'Tongyi Qianwen', SenseTime's 'Ririxin', and ByteDance's 'Dou Bao'.

The swift rise of new generative AI systems poses a range of societal risks, which have led to calls for strengthening AI governance and regulation around the world. Among the major countries considering AI governance, it can be said that two types of regulatory approaches have emerged.[1] One approach favours a lighter-touch regulatory path, which some countries such as the United Kingdom and Japan have undertaken. The other approach, perhaps best exemplified by the EU's AI Act, is a more stringent approach that advocates for dedicated regulatory bodies and requires AI applications to be subject to rigorous testing and pre-market approval processes. Some commentators predict that, just as the EU's General Data Protection Regulation (GDPR) has had a global impact, the EU's AI Act will extend the so-called Brussels effect to the field of AI, aligning global AI governance standards with the EU's own regime.[2]

This chapter examines Chinese regulation on generative AI systems to date. We focus on the Interim Measures for the Management of Generative Artificial Intelligence Services (the

This chapter is based on an article by Mimi Zou and Lu Zhang, 'Navigating China's Regulatory Approach to Generative Artificial Intelligence and Large Language Models', Cambridge Forum on AI: Law and Governance. 2025;1:e8. doi:10.1017/cfl.2024.4. The authors gratefully acknowledge Cambridge University Press for permission to adapt and reuse substantial portions of that work here.

[1] Jianfeng Cao, 'Towards Feasible AI: Governance Challenges and Responses to ChatGPT-like Generative Artificial Intelligence' (2023) 4 *Journal of Shanghai Political Science and Law* 38–42.

[2] Marc Rotenberg and Merve Hickok, 'Artificial Intelligence and Democratic Values: Next Steps for the United States', Centre for Foreign Relations, 22 August 2022, www.cfr.org/blog/artificial-intelligence-and-democratic-values-next-steps-united-states, last accessed 1 October 2024.

Measures) issued in July 2023.[3] The Measures were jointly issued by several ministries and departments under the State Council, the executive arm of the Chinese state.[4] The lead issuing department is the Cyberspace Administration of China (CAC), which is the primary regulator for the internet and cyberspace security in China. Other departments include the National Development and Reform Commission, Ministry of Education, Ministry of Science and Technology, Ministry of Industry and Information Technology, Ministry of Public Security, and National Radio and Television Administration.

The scope of the Measures applies to services that provide generated text, images, audio, video, and other content to the public within the territory of China.[5] The Measures touch on many potential risks associated with the application of generative AI, including content security, personal data protection, data security, intellectual property violations, among others. The Measures introduces a multi-tiered system of obligations on providers of generative AI services to mitigate such risks.

As far as we are aware, at the time of its introduction, the Measures were the first-ever regulation in the world specifically addressing generative AI. Some commentators have argued that the Measures reflect China's 'vertical approach' to AI regulation,[6] which addresses specific risks arising from types of AI technologies. In contrast, a 'horizontal approach', which is largely reflected in the EU's AI Act, encompasses comprehensive and overarching regulations that apply broadly to AI systems.[7]

To begin, this chapter scrutinises the policy context and competing motivations driving the Measures, with reference to the nuances of China's overarching goals in AI governance (Section 9.2). Next, we dissect the requirements for regulated actors as set forth in the Measures, focusing on their most critical aspect in ensuring the security of AI-generated content (Section 9.3). We proceed to address the remaining challenges in the implementation of the Measures and consider the future direction of travel for AI governance in China (Section 9.4).

9.2 BACKGROUND AND OVERVIEW OF THE MEASURES

9.2.1 A *'Vertical'* *Approach to AI Regulation?*

While China appears to have taken a more stringent regulatory approach to AI, a closer examination of China's various AI regulations demonstrates a divergence from the EU's AI Act in terms of regulatory logic and design. Two distinct pathways to regulating new and emerging technology have emerged: first, a more bespoke, technology-specific regulatory

[3] Interim Measures for the Management of Generative Artificial Intelligence Services, issued on 10 July 2023, effective 15 August 2023.

[4] The Measures are considered 'departmental regulations', which have lower authority than laws and administrative regulations in terms of legal hierarchy. According to Article 91 of China's Legislation Law, matters specified to departmental regulations fall under the purview of laws, administrative regulations, decisions, or orders issued by the State Council.

[5] Article 2 of the Measures.

[6] Xin Zhang, 'Governance for the Industry Chain: Technical Mechanism and Governance Logic of Artificial Intelligence-Generated Content' (2023) 6 *Administrative Law Review* 43–60 at 50. See further Kai Jia, Jing Zhao and Hongyu Fu, 'Dealing with Uncertainty Challenges: The Theoretical Definition of Agile Governance of Algorithms' (2023) 1 *Journal of Library and Information Knowledge* 1–10 at 2.

[7] Matt O'Shaughnessy and Matt Sheehan, 'Lessons from the World's Two Experiments in AI Governance', Carnegie Endowment for International Peace, 14 February 2023, www.carnegieendowment.org/2023/02/14/lessons-from-world-s-two-experiments-in-ai-governance-pub-89035, last accessed 1 October 2024.

strategy that focuses on specialised regulations for a particular technology or algorithmic application; and second, a technology-neutral strategy that is applicable to all technologies.[8]

Others have referred to these two pathways as 'vertical' and 'horizontal' approaches to AI regulation.[9] Vertical approaches typically emphasise the creation of distinct regulatory frameworks for specific types of AI uses or applications of the technology, rather than the technology itself or the entire industry. On the other hand, horizontal approaches favour the development of more comprehensive regulatory frameworks that cover almost all potential uses of AI.

It has been observed that the EU has leaned towards a horizontal approach, with the AI Act representing 'a single piece of horizontal legislation to fix the broad scope of what applications of AI are to be regulated'.[10] Nevertheless, the rapid advancements in and public adoption of new generative AI tools like ChatGPT have challenged the AI Act's originally proposed categories of risk that applied broadly to all AI applications. This prompted changes to the final version of the Act that placed foundation models and generative AI systems under a specific category of general-purpose AI systems (GPAI).[11] Such advanced AI models and systems are regulated through a separate tiered approach, with more stringent obligations for 'high-impact' GPAI models that pose a 'systemic risk'. These include foundation models trained with significant amounts of data, and where their advanced levels of complexity, capabilities, and performance can disseminate systemic risks along the value chain.[12]

At the time of writing, China has not established a comprehensive framework to regulate AI. Policymakers have instead adopted more of a 'vertical' approach by introducing regulations for specific technological developments, ranging from algorithmic recommendation technology to deep synthesis technology. These regulations include the Provisions on the Governance of the Online Information Content Ecosystem,[13] the Provisions on the Management of Algorithmic Recommendations in Internet Information Services,[14] and Regulations on the Deep Synthesis Management of Internet Information Service.[15] A common focus of these regulations is on content security or safety risks, which is also found in the Measures.

An advantage of China's 'vertical' approach to AI regulation is the potential for speedy adoption of new regulatory instruments. On 11 April 2023, the CAC released a draft version of the Measures for public feedback, with a deadline for submissions set for 10 May 2023. The entire regulatory process, which included drafting the initial version, gathering public input, conducting discussions and revisions, and final approval by relevant authorities, was completed within just three months. The Measures officially came into effect on 13 July 2023, and were enforced from 15 August 2023. This is contrasted with higher-level legislation by the National People's Congress that can last several years.

8 Philip Hacker, A. Engel and M. Mauer, 'Regulating ChatGPT and Other Large Generative AI Models', *Computers and Society*, 12 May 2023, www.arxiv.org/abs/2302.02337, last accessed 1 October 2024.

9 O'Shaughnessy and Sheehan, n. 7.

10 Ibid.

11 Council of the EU, 'Artificial Intelligence Act: Council and Parliament Strike a Deal on the First Rules for AI in the World', 9 December 2023, www.consilium.europa.eu/en/press/press-releases/2023/12/09/artificial-intelligence-act-council-and-parliament-strike-a-deal-on-the-first-worldwide-rules-for-ai/, last accessed 1 October 2024.

12 Ibid.

13 Provisions on the Governance of the Online Information Content Ecosystem, issued 15 December 2019, effective 1 March 2020.

14 Provisions on the Management of Algorithmic Recommendations in Internet Information Services, issued 31 December 2021, effective 1 March 2022.

15 Regulations on the Deep Synthesis Management of Internet Information Service, issued 25 November 2022, effective 1 January 2023.

It is important to note that the above-mentioned AI-related regulations include terms like 'interim' or 'provisional' in their titles. They typically serve an experimental purpose: to test a specific regulatory approach before more significant and higher-level legal instruments are considered. This approach is often used when lawmakers face a new (and pressing) issue. So, the term 'interim' implies that the Measures might be temporary, allowing for further legislative development in the near future.

Following the introduction of the Measures, the National Information Security Standardisation Technical Committee released the Basic Security Requirements for Generative Artificial Intelligence Service (TC260-003) on 1 March 2024.[16] This set of technical standards aims to provide basic security requirements for generative AI services, including corpus, model, security measures, and security assessments. It applies to service providers in relation to their obligations to conduct security assessments and improve security levels under the Measures. The standard also provides a point of reference for relevant regulatory authorities to assess the security level of generative AI services. In China, national technical standards function more as tools for implementing higher-level laws. In this way, they are better understood as a type of regulatory instrument.[17]

In an important standards framework on AI safety issued by the National Information Security Standardization Technical Committee 260 on Cybersecurity of the Standardization Administration of China, risks of information and content safety were identified as follows:

> AI-generated or synthesized content can lead to the spread of false information, discrimination and bias, privacy leakage, and infringement issues, threatening the safety of citizens' lives and property, national security, ideological security, and causing ethical risks. If users' inputs contain harmful content, the model may output illegal or damaging information without robust security mechanisms.[18]

At the time of writing, there are some signs of higher-level legislative efforts underway. In June 2023, an AI Law was included in the State Council's Legislative Plan.[19] In August 2023, the Chinese Academy of Social Sciences officially released a Model AI Law 1.1 (Expert Draft).[20] China may be taking incremental steps towards establishing a more comprehensive AI legislation, which in the long run might resemble the EU's AI Act. However, the journey from initial legislative planning to the eventual enactment of such a law at the national level could involve a longer timeline, such as several years. It is therefore

[16] National Information Security Standardisation Technical Committee 260 on Cybersecurity of the Standardisation Administration of China, *Basic Security Requirements for Generative Artificial Intelligence Service (TC260-003)*, 2 March 2024, www.tc260.org.cn/front/postDetail.html?id=20240301164054, last accessed 1 October 2024.

[17] See, for example, technical standards related to China's personal information protection regime: Samm Sacks, 'New China Data Privacy Standard Looks More Far-Reaching than GDPR', Centre for Strategic and International Studies, 29 January 2018, www.csis.org/analysis/new-china-data-privacy-standard-looks-more-far-reaching-gdpr, last accessed 1 October 2024.

[18] National Information Security Standardisation Technical Committee 260 on Cybersecurity of the Standardisation Administration of China, *AI Safety Governance Framework Version 1.0*, www.tc260.org.cn/upload/2024-09-09/1725849192841090989.pdf, last accessed 1 October 2024.

[19] State Council General Office Notice on Issuing the Legislative Work Plan for the Year 2023 of the State Council, State Council Document No. 18 of 2023.

[20] Chinese Academy of Social Sciences, Major Project on National Conditions Research – Research Group for Investigation on the Status of the Construction of China's Artificial Intelligence Ethics Review and Regulatory System, *Artificial Intelligence Law Model Law Version 1.0 (Expert Suggestion Draft)*, 17 August 2023, English translation: https://digichina.stanford.edu/work/translation-artificial-intelligence-law-model-law-v-1-0-expert-suggestion-draft-aug-2023/, last accessed 1 October 2024.

unsurprising that regulators have taken swift action to introduce specific measures targeting emerging risks from new developments in the technology.

9.2.2 *Balancing AI Development and Security*

Confronted with the potentially transformative impact of generative AI, Chinese policymakers are grappling with the challenge of balancing two main regulatory goals: development and security. The notion of 'development' in this context refers to China's desire to propel the growth of the generative AI industry and boost its standing as a global AI powerhouse. Meanwhile, 'security' (or 'safety') has been at the centre of all of China's cyber and technology-related laws and regulations to date. For policymakers, there is a fundamental need for guardrails to prevent and mitigate a range of security-related risks associated with the rapid development of emerging AI technologies.[21]

The dual pillars of 'development' and 'security' are reflected in Article 1 of the Measures. Article 1 sets out the following regulatory objectives: fostering responsible growth of generative AI while ensuring national security and public interests and protection of the rights of citizens, legal entities, and other organisations. Additionally, Article 3 reinforces the equal importance of 'development' and 'security' as well as emphasising the principle of balancing innovation promotion with lawful governance.

Although both terms are presented side by side in policy statements related to the Measures, 'development' appears to be consistently placed before 'security'. The greater emphasis on development becomes more pronounced in the final version of the Measures in comparison with the earlier draft that was presented for public consultation. The earlier draft had focused much more on security concerns. Some prominent scholars in China have argued that the primary 'insecurity' is the underdevelopment of China's AI industry. Notably, Professor Liming Wang has underscored that, when compared to other potential risks, the most significant danger for China is the risk of falling behind technologically.[22]

A key question is the extent to which and how China's evolving regulatory framework will support the development of its generative AI industry. Within the Chinese legal framework, regulations often derive their authority from higher-level laws. Article 1 of the Measures explicitly cites the Law on the Promotion of Scientific and Technological Progress as its legal foundation. The Law on the Promotion of Scientific and Technological Progress is designed to bolster China's self-sufficiency and technological progress at an advanced level.[23] By anchoring the Measures in this legislation, there is an emphasis on aligning the development of generative AI with broader policy objectives aimed at fortifying China's self-reliance in the domains of science and technology. In essence, the Measures are intricately linked to Beijing's wider strategy for achieving technological leadership as well as autonomy. As early as 2017, the

[21] Yu Qiao, 'Promoting Development through Safety, Encouraging Innovation through Governance', Cyberspace Administration of China, 29 August 2023, www.cac.gov.cn/2023-08/29/c_1694965943880030.htm, last accessed 1 October 2024.

[22] Liming Wang, 'The Greatest Risk of Generative AI Lies in Technological Backwardness and the Risk of Being Strangled or Constrained', 12 July 2023, www.chinaiprlaw.com/index.php?id=5962, last accessed 1 October 2024.

[23] Law on the Promotion of Scientific and Technological Progress, issued 24 December 2021, effective 1 January 2022. Article 1 states its overarching goal of 'comprehensively promoting scientific and technological progress, harnessing the role of science and technology as the primary productive force, innovation as the primary driving force, and talent as the primary resource. Facilitating the transformation of scientific and technological achievements into practical productive forces, driving technological innovation to support and lead economic and social development, and comprehensively building a socialist modernised country'.

Chinese leadership made it clear that 'China should strengthen deployment around core technologies, top talents, standards, and norms, aiming to gain leadership in the new round of international scientific and technological competition (in AI)'.[24]

The scope of the Measures is limited to generative AI services that are provided to the public. According to Article 3, the scope excludes 'industry organisations, enterprises, education and research institutions, public cultural institutions, and relevant professional institutions that do not provide generative AI services to the general public'. This means that the Measures will not apply to uses of generative AI for scientific research and enterprise or industrial applications. For example, if the deployment of generative AI is not aimed at providing services to the public, but only for internal use within the enterprise, such as improving productivity or technological upgrading, then the Measures will not apply. For these types of 'non-public facing' services, policymakers are refraining from regulatory intervention to facilitate the widespread industrial adoption of this technology. This is aimed at enhancing productivity and efficiency while unleashing the full potential for innovation.[25]

9.2.3 *Distinguishing between Technology and Services*

An important example of policymakers' attempts to balance development and security concerns in the Measures is reflected by the distinction between the technology itself and the services built upon it. This differentiation seeks to recognise that certain areas of generative AI development and application require more stringent oversight, while other areas may benefit from a more permissive or light-touch approach that promotes innovation. In practice, this means that regulation tends to focus on areas where public interests, safety and security are most at stake.

The Measures make an important distinction between 'core' generative AI technologies on the one hand, and services arising from these technologies on the other. The former is primarily addressed in Chapter II of the Measures, titled 'Technology Development and Governance'. This chapter emphasises the promotion of innovation and the application of generative AI across diverse industries and domains. The provisions in Chapter II contain words such as 'encourage', 'support', and 'promote', particularly in relation to 'trial and error' in technology research and development. It reflects policymakers' consideration that the Measures should not excessively interfere with the development of core generative AI technologies.

The Measures focus on regulating service providers. According to Article 22, generative AI service providers refers to organisations or individuals offering services that are based on utilising generative AI technologies. This includes services provided through application programming interfaces (APIs) as well as services that develop foundation models. The obligations on providers of AI services under Chapter II of the Measures include ensuring pre-training, optimisation training, and all data-related activities adhere to existing laws and regulations (particularly the Cybersecurity Law, Data Security Law, intellectual property laws), ensuring that the data sources and foundational models used are lawfully obtained and employing effective measures to improve the quality of the training data by enhancing its truthfulness, accuracy, objectivity, and diversity. Chapter III of the Measures, titled 'Service Standards', outlines a range of obligations on service providers. These obligations include safeguarding users' personal

[24] Notice from the State Council on the Issuance of the Development Plan for the New Generation of Artificial Intelligence, Guofa [2017] No. 35.

[25] Ke Xu, 'Institution and Technology in Sync: The Chinese Approach to the Governance of Generative Artificial Intelligence', Cyberspace Administration of China, 13 July 2023, www.cac.gov.cn/2023-07/13/c_1690898364234016.htm, last accessed 1 October 2024.

information, meeting requirements regarding user identification, delivering secure and stable services, and reporting unlawful content, among others.

While the intention of differentiating between technology and services is to promote technological development while mitigating risks associated with its applications, the Measures have been criticised for their broad definition of 'service providers'. There have been calls for more granularity in regulatory oversight over different types of actors involved in generative AI technology development and service provision, a view that we also share and will return to later in this chapter. We now turn to assess the key provisions of the Measures that deal with the obligations of service providers, which emphasise information content security.

9.3 KEY PROVISIONS OF THE MEASURES

9.3.1 *The Focus on Content Security*

The thrust of the Measures is targeted at information content services, including various aspects of the generation, processing, and delivery of content using generative AI technology.[26] For policymakers, the powerful content generation capabilities of generative AI are the critical source of its risks, including unpredictability, uncertainty, and opacity issues relating to the generated output. Furthermore, its capabilities can make it challenging for humans (or even AI itself) to identify false or misleading content. In China, where there is significant state control over the information environment, regulators are particularly concerned with the implications of content-related risks.

The Measures are not the first of their kind to specifically target AI-generated content risks. In November 2022, China issued Regulations on the Administration of Deep Synthesis Internet Information Services (Deep Synthesis Regulations).[27] 'Deep synthesis technology' here refers to the use of deep learning, augmented reality, and other algorithms to enable content synthesis or generation, including text, images, audio, video, virtual scenes, and more. The Deep Synthesis Regulations extend to AI generation of multimodal content including text, images, audio, and video, and are an important reference point for AI-based content generation technology and services. Yet Chinese officials have not provided an explanation on the relationship between the Deep Synthesis Regulations and the Measures. It has been suggested that existing regulations are sufficient to address the content-related risks associated with generative AI.[28] However, others argue that generative AI has considerably magnified the degree of such risks beyond that envisaged by the Deep Synthesis Regulations. This amplification of risks necessitated the swift introduction of the Measures only months after the introduction of the Deep Synthesis Regulations.

Article 2 of the Measures is of particular significance. This provision defines the scope of application as follows: 'Services that provide generated text, images, audio, video, and other content to the public within the territory of the People's Republic of China using generative AI technology shall be subject to these Measures.' Article 2 in the final promulgated version of the Measures is quite different to an earlier draft that was issued for public consultation in April

[26] Linghan Zhang, 'Legal Positioning and Hierarchical Governance of Generative Artificial Intelligence' (2023) 4 *Modern Law* 126–141 at 128.

[27] See n. 15.

[28] Linyao Tang, 'Legal Regulation and the Chinese Path of ChatGPT under Embodied Ethics' (2023) 3 *Eastern Jurisprudence* 34–46 at 40.

2023. The earlier draft indicated a much wider regulatory scope that covered research and development or the use of generative AI products, *in addition to* the provision of services to the general public. The subsequent modification of the scope in the final version of the Measures reflects policymakers' focus on regulating AI-generated content for public consumption, while leaving room for a broader spectrum of activities including research and development to take place outside the scope of the Measures.

9.3.2 *Service Providers and Obligations as Content Producers*

9.3.2.1 China's Platform Liability Framework

Before we turn to examine the specific obligations of generative AI service providers under the Measures, it is important to note the long-standing regulatory issue of platform liability for harms caused by content generated and/or shared, as well as other activities carried out by users of platforms. Different countries have sought to develop various solutions to address this issue. China has had a relatively long-standing focus on information content security. China's platform liability laws initially drew inspiration from the United States. For example, the underlying approach of China's 2006 Information Network Transmission Right Protection Regulations[29] closely resembled the 'notice and takedown' safe harbour provisions found in the US Digital Millennium Copyright Act (DCMA). A common approach taken by Chinese courts has been to characterise a platform's role in information dissemination as either content provision or technical support.[30]

China's regulatory framework for platform liability content makes a distinction between content producers and service providers.[31] Content producers bear direct liability for content-related infringements. Service providers refers to organisations or individuals that provide network technology service activities that assist in carrying out such infringements. They are held liable for damages only when they have knowledge or should have known about the direct infringement.[32]

A key framework for content governance in China is set out by the Provisions on the Governance of the Online Information Content Ecosystem (the Provisions). The Provisions distinguish between network information content producers (Chapter II), network information content service platforms (Chapter III), and network information content service users (Chapter IV). According to Article 41, network information content producers are organisations or individuals involved in creating, duplicating, or disseminating network information content. Network information content service platforms refer to network information service providers offering content transmission services, while network information content service users are organisations or individuals who use network information content services.

Article 8 of the Provisions requires 'network information content service platforms' to meet their obligations as information content management entities and enhance the governance of

[29] Information Network Transmission Right Protection Regulations, issued on 18 May 2006 (revised in 2013).

[30] Provisions of the Supreme People's Court on Several Issues Concerning the Application of Law in the Trial of Civil Disputes Involving Infringement of the Right to Network Communication in 2020 (Revised), Legal Interpretation [2020] No. 19, issued on 29 December 2020.

[31] Zhiwei Yao and Zhuolin Li, 'Legal Regulation of Content Risks in Generative Artificial Intelligence' (2023) 5 *Journal of Xi'an Jiaotong University (Social Sciences)* 1–20 at 8.

[32] Ibid.; Wenjie Liu, 'Identification of Information Network Communication Behaviours' (2016) 3 *Legal Studies* 122–139 at 126.

their network information content ecosystems. Overall, the Provisions primarily deal with verifying and monitoring the information published on these platforms. Where the platforms discover illegal or harmful content, they must take appropriate measures, including but not limited to retaining records and reporting to the relevant authorities.

The Deep Synthesis Regulations also follow the distinction between content providers and technical service providers. These regulations outline three main categories of regulated entities: (1) deep synthesis service providers; (2) deep synthesis service technology support providers; and (3) deep synthesis service users. The Deep Synthesis Regulations assign a range of information security-related obligations on deep synthesis service providers, such as establishing management rules, strengthening content review, and having in place mechanisms for 'debunking rumours'.[33] Such obligations are similar to those of network information content service platforms under the Provisions on the Governance of the Online Information Content Ecosystem. In other words, deep synthesis technology service providers must comply with relevant obligations related to information content management.

The concept of 'principal responsibility' (*zhuti zheren*) is fundamental in China's regulatory framework concerning the liability of internet platforms and service providers. This term was originally used in a political context, referring to the responsibilities of party organisations and government departments. In 2014, it was introduced for the first time in the legal context in the amendment to Article 3 of the Workplace Safety Law as the basis of a corporation's responsibility for workplace safety. When applied in the context of platform regulation, this concept has not been thoroughly clarified and explained. One scholar suggests that the term can be understood as the ultimate responsibility of the platform provider for any unlawful activity that takes place on the platform.[34] Some have argued that the 'principal responsibility' of platforms refers to a form of strict liability.[35] The conceptual ambiguity gives rise to regulatory implementation and compliance challenges in practice.

The nature of generative AI has challenged existing regulatory frameworks for information content security that distinguish between content production and technical services provided by platforms. Platforms that utilise and/or offer generative AI technology in their services can blur the boundaries between these two roles, making it particularly challenging to determine 'who should be liable for what'. The Measures attempt to distinguish providers of generative AI services and users of generative AI services. As mentioned earlier, service providers include providers of foundation models and providers of downstream application services. Service users refers to organisations and individuals that use generative AI services to generate content. In drawing the line between providers and users, regulators have recognised the need to distinguish between the two groups when it comes to assigning legal liability. However, in practice, the distinction can be blurry. The Measures recognise the significant role of AI service users in content generation, placing obligations on both service providers and users not to generate false or harmful information, not to infringe upon the rights of others, and to enhance the accuracy and reliability of the generated content.[36]

[33] Articles 7–12 of the Measures.

[34] Yiqun Ye, 'Responsibilities of Internet Platform: From Regulation to Governance' (2018) 5 *Financial and Economic Law* 49–63 at 58.

[35] Quan Liu, 'On the Subject Responsibility of Internet Platforms' (2022) 5 *Journal of East China University of Political Science and Law* 79–93 at 81.

[36] See Article 4 of the Measures.

TABLE 9.1 *Summary of obligations of service providers of generative AI under the Measures*

Content producer obligations	Service provider obligations
• Article 4: Not generating content prohibited by laws and regulations. • Article 7: Ensuring that training data processing activities for generating content are lawful. • Article 8: Requirements for data annotation activities. • Article 9: Assuming the responsibility of a network information content producer, fulfilling network information security obligations, and fulfilling personal information protection obligations. • Article 12: Identification of generated content.	• Article 10: Taking measures to prevent minors from excessively relying on and becoming addicted to AI services. • Article 11: Protecting the input and usage records of users and meeting obligations as personal information handlers (including accepting and handling requests for access, copying, correction, supplementation, deletion of personal information, etc.). • Article 13: Providing secure, stable, and continuous services to ensure normal user usage. • Article 14: Discovering illegal content, timely removal and rectification, preserving records, and reporting to the competent authority. • Article 15: Establishing a sound complaint and reporting mechanism. • Article 17: Conducting security assessments and fulfilling algorithm filing procedures.

9.3.2.2 Regulatory Emphasis on Obligations of the Content Producer

Given the transformative impact of generative AI on content generation, Article 9 of the Measures makes it clear that generative AI service providers must assume the obligations of content producers and meet relevant obligations as related to information content security. This is the first time in Chinese regulations that AI service providers are deemed 'content producers' and assigned relevant obligations.

The Measures impose a 'dual' set of obligations on generative AI service providers relating to both content generation and the provision of technical services (see Table 9.1). Article 14 requires service providers, upon discovering illegal content, to respond promptly by stopping the content generation, halting the transmission of the content, and/or removing the content. Furthermore, they must implement AI model optimisation and training to rectify the situation, as well as report the incident to the regulators. According to Article 10, if a service provider discovers a user who has engaged in illegal activities, the provider must take appropriate measures in accordance with the law and its service contract with the user. These measures can include warnings, restricting functionalities of the service, and suspending or terminating the provision of services to the user.

These obligations on AI service providers under the Measures are consistent with the set of 'principal obligations' for information management imposed on network information content service platforms under the Provisions on the Governance of the Online Information Content Ecosystem.[37] At the same time, the Measures specify in Chapter III (titled Service Standards) that generative AI service providers must assume the obligations of network information content producers 'in accordance with the law'. Such obligations include watermarking the generated

[37] See Article 10 concerning Information Management Subject Obligations.

content (Article 12), safeguarding personal data (Article 9), and establishing a comprehensive complaint reporting mechanism (Article 15).

Under the Measures, generative AI service providers bear direct liability for content generation as well as indirect liability for failing to take effective measures to stop the dissemination of unlawful content. Some argue that the 'dual' set of obligations placed upon generative AI service providers are too onerous and not conducive to creating a favourable environment for the healthy development of the industry.[38] They point out that other regulations to date, including the Provisions on the Governance of the Online Information Content Ecosystem and the Deep Synthesis Regulations, have separated the obligations of information content producers from those of technology service providers.[39]

However, it can be argued that the Measures are responsive to the characteristics of emerging generative AI services. Such services often entail advanced technological integration of content production, service provision, and user utilisation. As such, the obligations imposed on generative AI services providers reflect the significance of some providers' involvement in the content generation process. While user prompts are part of the process, the pre-training and fine-tuning of the AI models by service providers also directly impact on the content generation.

9.3.3 *Obligations on Users*

Another important feature of the Measures is a recognition of the role of users in generative AI services and applications. The Measures include users of generative AI services within the regulatory framework and seek to regulate certain aspects of user behaviour and conduct. As mentioned earlier, Article 4 imposes a variety of obligations on service providers and service users, such as refraining from generating false or harmful information and not infringing on the rights of others. In addition, Article 18 provides a right for users to file complaints or reports with the relevant authorities if the users find that the service provider is not complying with laws, administrative regulations, or the provisions of the Measures. Article 14 requires service providers to establish a sound mechanism for promptly receiving and handling public complaints and reports and responding to the outcomes.

Overall, compared to service providers, the obligations imposed on users in the Measures appear to be light touch. Firstly, although users play an important role in content generation, the thrust of content-related obligations under Measures are targeted at service providers instead of users. While Article 4 places some general obligations on them, there is no direct legal liability attributed to users. Chapter 4 of the Measures, which covers provisions regarding legal liability, is very much directed at service providers. The only provision found in Chapter 4 that primarily addresses users is Article 18, which provides users with a right of complaint and reporting against service providers. There is no further clarification on the requirements to be met for users to complain and report to the authorities upon discovering any illegal content being generated.

The right of complaints and reporting by users relates to illegal content under the Measures. However, the Measures do not address appeal and recourse mechanisms for situations where service providers infringe upon users' rights, such as imposing unreasonable restrictions on use and/or termination of services. For example, if a service provider unilaterally determines that a

[38] Zhiwei Yao and Zhuolin Li, 'Legal Regulation of Content Risks in Generative Artificial Intelligence' (2023) 5 *Journal of Xi'an Jiaotong University (Social Sciences)* 1–20 at 9.

[39] Wei Xu, 'On the Legal Status and Responsibilities of Generative Artificial Intelligence Service Providers – Taking ChatGPT as an Example' (2023) 4 *Legal Science* 69–80 at 74.

user has generated illegal content and decides to restrict or remove the user from using its services, there are currently no provisions in the Measures that specify whether the user has the right to appeal to the service provider or another body, and if so, what the procedure for such an appeal should be.

9.3.4 *Algorithm Disclosure and Watermarking*

An emerging trend in AI regulatory tools involves various disclosure requirements related to large language models. These requirements are closely linked to the principles of algorithmic transparency and trustworthiness. The main aim is to enhance the foreseeability of and control over associated risks through the disclosure of critical information about the underlying algorithms. Several regulatory tools in this realm can be found in the Measures, which are centred around algorithm filing for certain types of generative AI services and watermarking AI-generated content.

According to Article 17 of the Measures, providers of generative AI services with 'public opinion properties or social mobilisation capacity' must comply with the Provisions on the Management of Algorithmic Recommendations in Internet Information Services. This regulation, introduced in 2022, established a mandatory algorithm filing and registry system for algorithm recommendation service providers with 'public opinion properties or social mobilisation capacity'.[40] These service providers, which are primarily social media platforms, are generally subject to greater regulatory scrutiny.[41] Such providers must file with the CAC certain information on their services and algorithms, including the service form, fields of application, algorithm type, algorithm self-assessment, content to be displayed, and other relevant information. If such information changes, the providers must also undertake modification procedures through the filing system within ten days of the change. The providers must make public its filing index. Where relevant, providers must also carry out security assessments with the CAC.[42]

Watermarking AI-generated content can also be considered a form of disclosure or transparency-enhancing tool for generative AI. Watermarking involves embedding identifiable information or markers within the content itself, indicating its origin or creator. This practice serves as a means of disclosing the content's AI-generated nature and its source. Article 12 of the Measures requires generative AI service providers to label generated content such as images and video in accordance with the Deep Synthesis Management Regulations.

Article 16 of the Deep Synthesis Management Regulations specifies that service providers must use technical measures to add unobtrusive marks that do not affect the user's experience. On the other hand, Article 17 states that in cases where deep synthesis services may 'lead to public confusion or misidentification', significant markings must be provided to service users. However, there is no definition of what could 'lead to public confusion or misidentification'. Some commentators have pointed out that such broad scope could impact on everyday uses of generative AI services by the public.[43]

[40] See Chapter IV (Oversight and Management) of the Provisions on the Management of Algorithmic Recommendations in Internet Information Services.

[41] See Regulations for the Security Assessment of Internet Information Services Having Public Opinion Properties or Social Mobilisation Capacity, issued 30 November 2018, effective 30 November 2018. Article 2 defines the types of internet information services that have 'public opinion properties or social mobilisation capacity'.

[42] See n. 40.

[43] Yao and Li, n. 38 at 7.

The National Information Security Standardisation Technical Committee has issued technical guidelines on various methods for content watermarking by AI-generated content service providers.[44] According to the guidelines, implicit watermarking should not be directly perceptible to humans but can be extracted from the content using technical means. Explicit watermarking, on the other hand, involves inserting some kind of semi-transparent label in the interactive interface or background of the content.

Understandably, much of the watermarking obligations are imposed on the service provider, not the user. The user's obligations are limited to not destroying or tampering with the labelling or markings. Article 18 of the Deep Synthesis Management Regulations stipulates that 'no organisation or individual shall use technical means to delete, tamper with, or conceal deep synthesis marks'.

9.4 LIMITATIONS, CHALLENGES, AND OUTLOOK

9.4.1 *Considerable Room for Discretion and Gaps*

Overall, the Measures were introduced relatively quickly, and the matters they address are primarily at a broad, principled level. This leaves significant room for interpretation and implementation. Many provisions are relatively high-level and lack specific operational details, requiring relevant enforcement authorities and implementers to interpret and make decisions based on specific circumstances during actual execution. Some obligations are very broadly drafted and likely to rely on the subsequent introduction of more detailed rules or guidelines to ensure effective implementation. Some examples include interpretation of 'the accuracy and reliability of generated content' in Article 4, disputes over intellectual property rights of generated content in Article 7, the user complaint reporting system in Article 15, and the interaction between service providers and regulatory authorities during supervisions and inspections in Article 19.

Implementation guidelines and technical standards that span various industries are likely to become increasingly important, such as standards issued by the National Information Security Standardisation Technical Committee on security assessments, content watermarking, and labelling shortly after the Measures were introduced. These instruments provide more detailed directions for regulated actors in relation to complying with the Measures. Effectively coordinating the relationship between 'hard law' instruments such as laws and regulations and 'soft law' tools will become a crucial aspect of AI governance in China.

The Measures focus on the administrative obligations of service providers but overlook the provisions related to civil obligations. The content security obligations under the Measures mainly manifest as public law obligations. Their enforcement primarily follows public law procedures, with regulatory authorities (government departments) holding service providers accountable. Article 21 primarily involves public law sanctions like warnings, notifications, criticisms, and corrective actions. Such an approach neglects situations where private individuals or entities could initiate legal actions against service providers.

While the Chinese Civil Code could potentially fill in this gap, there are limitations. For example, Chinese laws and regulations currently lack provisions regarding the determination of damages and the burden of proof for civil liability arising from AI technologies. This gap is

[44] Implementation Guideline for Full Network Security Standards: Content Marking Methods for AI-Generated Content Services.

particularly significant given the complexity, autonomy, and opacity of AI systems. The Measures do not specify damages caused by AI services or the burden of proof for establishing damages. In contrast, the EU is actively advancing the development of a law applicable to civil liability for AI alongside the AI Act to proactively address the potential real-world risks stemming from AI technology.

9.4.2 *A More Balanced Approach to 'Content Producer' Obligations*

There is a need to refine the rules under the Measures to delineate a clearer and more balanced system of responsibility pertaining to different regulated actors. A notable aspect of the Measures is the designation of service providers as 'content producers', which assume almost all obligations in ensuring information content security with generative AI technologies. Despite Article 4 stating that both users and service providers have responsibility, all obligations found in Chapter IV are directed at service providers. Given that users actively contribute to content creation and dissemination on platforms, requiring some accountability on the part of users could foster more responsible usage and deter unlawful activities.

To strike a balance between generative AI development and security, the Measures should further consider establishing compliance 'safe harbours'. Such a system would still place 'content producer' responsibility on service providers but offer them protection or exemption from liability under certain circumstances.[45] Safe harbours are commonly found in the context of online service providers' liability for user-generated content. The most well-known example is arguably the DMCA, which includes safe harbour provisions for internet service providers (ISPs). These provisions protect ISPs from copyright infringement liability for content posted by users if the ISPs meet specific requirements, such as promptly removing infringing content upon receiving a valid takedown notice from the copyright holder. Safe harbour provisions for generative AI service providers can help to prevent or mitigate content-related risks while encouraging innovation and industry development goals.

Furthermore, a 'tolerant and prudent' tiered approach espoused in Article 3 of the Measures needs to deploy a variety of regulatory approaches and tools to achieve both development and security goals. Currently, the Measures impose uniform obligations for foundation model providers and providers of 'downstream' generative AI application services since both are deemed 'service providers'. A more reasonable approach for balancing both policy goals would be to adopt a multi-tiered governance system that provides room for foundation model providers to experiment, while requiring greater regulatory scrutiny for 'downstream' providers with reasonable safe harbours.

9.4.3 *Building on Existing Norms and Developing a Comprehensive Law*

Upon a careful analysis of its provisions, the Measures share considerable similarities with previous laws such as the Provisions on the Management of Algorithmic Recommendations in Internet Information Services and the Deep Synthesis Regulation. In our view, the Measures do not introduce substantially new institutional mechanisms. The new obligations introduced by the Measures centre on two aspects. First, the Measures require generative AI service providers to assume the responsibilities of content producers, marking a novel expansion of provider

[45] See Weiwei Shen, 'Practice and Legal Reflection on Technological Safe Harbors' (2023) 4 *Peking University Law Journal* 906–922.

obligations. Second, they establish specific requirements regarding the training data used in generative AI models.

Many provisions in the Measures represent restatements or refinements of existing regulations, including those concerning generation of false information, data tagging, preventing discrimination in algorithmic design, algorithm transparency, personal information protection, user complaint mechanisms, among others. As analysed earlier, the obligations on content producers reflect existing obligations found in the Provisions on the Governance of the Online Information Content Ecosystem. Furthermore, the Measures directly incorporate provisions from existing regulations. For instance, the obligations related to algorithmic filing and security assessment under Article 17 of the Measures are directly linked to the Provisions on the Management of Algorithmic Recommendations in Internet Information Services. The watermarking and labelling of AI-generated content requirements under Article 12 of the Measures incorporate the Deep Synthesis Regulations.

We argue that the Measures may be intentionally conservative in their regulatory design. They can be seen as a prompt response by policymakers to the risks and challenges posed by rapidly evolving AI technologies. On the other hand, Chinese policymakers are also seeking coherence and consistency among different AI-related laws and regulations, recognising the downsides and costs of regulatory fragmentation. It appears that China is working on establishing a general legislation in the AI field, aiming to achieve a more unified or comprehensive approach, like the EU's AI Act. China has undertaken such an approach in other areas of technology regulation, with the enactment of comprehensive laws such as the Cybersecurity Law, the Data Security Law, and the Personal Information Protection Law. These national-level laws provided the foundation for introducing a range of regulatory instruments such as those addressing algorithm assessment and filing and deep fake prevention, as mentioned earlier. If China does go along this direction of travel soon, we believe two aspects of regulatory design should be considered by legislators.

Firstly, the primary focus of a general AI law should be on integrating disparate regulatory approaches, standardising existing rules, and addressing gaps. For example, an algorithm filing system has been introduced, but the Provisions on the Management of Algorithmic Recommendations in Internet Information Services do not lay out the next phase of the system. For example, there needs to be further clarification on whether registration serves as a prerequisite for ex ante liability or as a basis for ex post liability. This distinction will impact how the registration process is perceived by the parties involved and its effects on them. A general AI law needs to address important gaps like these, or at least lay the foundation for doing so.

Secondly, general AI legislation must clearly define liability of different regulated actors, taking into account the complexity, autonomy, and opacity of AI systems and applications of AI technologies. Specific provisions covering issues such as damage determination and burden of proof are crucial. Establishing clear rules for different types of redress (from administrative to civil claims) can help to mitigate technology risks while reducing compliance costs for businesses and regulatory challenges for government agencies.

9.4.4 *China's Participation in Global AI Governance*

In recent years, the global competition in AI has expanded from the technological domain to the regulatory domain. It has been pointed out that the Measures not only respond to domestic regulatory and governance needs, but also reflect China's desire to be increasingly involved in global AI governance and rule-marking.[46] On one hand, countries grapple with intense competition in AI technology, a number of major powers are also engaged in a global race to set the rules and standards that should govern and regulate AI. At the time of writing, the EU has been the most active player in seeking to establish global standards through the introduction of the AI Act.

China also hopes that the introduction of the Measures will showcase its pioneering, agile approach to AI governance.[47] Formulating standards and norms has consistently been an important aspect of China's AI development plans. It remains to be seen whether the regulatory approaches and tools reflected in the Measures will be adopted and adapted elsewhere. Media coverage of the regulation outside of China has focused on the concept of 'upholding core socialist values'.[48]

The idea of regulatory interoperability and consistency has underlined the quest for global governance of AI.[49] There appears to be consensus among many countries on the basic principles for governing AI. These primarily revolve around issues concerning algorithm fairness, algorithm transparency, data security, and personal information protection. Currently, AI governance has entered a phase of translating principles into regulatory frameworks and standards. The risks associated with AI are not confined to individual countries but are international in scope, requiring coordinated international action.

Promoting international cooperation on AI governance faces numerous real-world obstacles arising from the geopolitical landscape and technological competition between major players. Fostering domestic AI development around the concept of digital sovereignty could have negative spillover effects on the global AI market. At the same time, a 'race to the bottom' where countries compete to have more lenient regulations can exacerbate the risks of significant harms that such technologies can create.[50] China, as a major player in AI development, must find ways to work with other major players (and vice versa) on a global approach to AI governance.

9.5 CONCLUSION

The Measures focus on information content security risks arising from applications of generative AI for the public. Our analysis in this chapter has shed light on the primary obligations assigned to service providers. While these Measures establish some broad principles and rules for regulating generative AI, a more intricate regulatory framework of 'hard' and 'soft' law instruments will be essential for effective implementation. A more nuanced stance to regulating the

46 See Lu Zhang, 'Exploration of Governance and Regulation of General Artificial Intelligence Risks – Issues and Challenges Triggered by ChatGPT' (2023) 9 *E-Government* 107–117 at 113.

47 Wu Yi, 'How to Interpret China's First Effort to Regulate Generative AI Measures', China Briefing, 27 July 2023, www.china-briefing.com/news/how-to-interpret-chinas-first-effort-to-regulate-generative-ai-measures/, last accessed 1 October 2024.

48 Meaghan Tobin, 'China Announces Rules to Keep AI Bound by "Core Socialist Values"', *Washington Post*, 14 July 2023, www.washingtonpost.com/world/2023/07/14/china-ai-regulations-chatgpt-socialist/, last accessed 1 October 2024. Cha Pan, 'China Sets Out New Rules for Generative AI, with Beijing Emphasising Healthy Content and Adherence to "Socialist Values"', *South China Morning Post*, 13 July 2023, www.scmp.com/tech/big-tech/article/3227576/china-sets-out-new-rules-generative-ai-beijing-emphasising-healthy-content-and-adherence-socialist, last accessed 1 October 2024.

49 Alex Engler, 'The EU and U.S. Are Starting to Align on AI Regulation', Brookings, 1 February 2022, www.brookings.edu/articles/the-eu-and-u-s-are-starting-to-align-on-ai-regulation/, last accessed 1 October 2024.

50 Cristina Criddle, Javier Espinoza and Qianer Liu, 'The Global Race to set the Rules for AI', *Financial Times*, 13 September 2023, www.ft.com/content/59b9ef36-771f-4f91-89d1-ef89f4a2ec4e, last accessed 1 October 2024.

diverse actors and activities, such as a clearer delineation of user liability and offering certain exemptions from liability for service providers, requires further consideration by policymakers, especially if China is heading towards a more 'horizontal approach' to AI regulation. The rapid advancements in generative AI pose universal regulatory challenges. Globally, countries are navigating new territory when it comes to coordinating a cohesive approach. China's path in international AI cooperation and competition remains uncertain.

10

Singapore's Evolving AI Governance Framework

Jason Grant Allen and Jane Loo

10.1 INTRODUCTION

This chapter provides an outline analysis of the evolving governance framework for artificial intelligence (AI) in the island city-state of Singapore. Recognised as one of the most 'AI ready' jurisdictions in the world, AI has been identified as a technology cluster of strategic importance for the national economy's continued development, and the state is influencing the trajectory of AI as a vendor and even developer of AI solutions as well as through the typical policy levers. Across the Singapore government, AI solutions are being adopted in line with Singapore's 'Smart Nation Initiative' to leverage technology to make impactful changes to the nation and the economy, and preparatory work has commenced on a large language model competent in South-East Asian languages.[1] Singapore's signature approach to AI Governance reflects its governance culture more broadly. Characteristics of the approach are an emphasis on consensus-building between stakeholders (particularly government and industry but also citizens) and voluntary or 'quasi' regulation, lately with an emphasis on promulgating standards and audit-like frameworks. This is perceived to harness the productive energy of free-market capitalism contained within clear guardrails,[2] reinforced by a willingness and capacity to intervene if and when deemed necessary. Singaporean regulators have been early movers (globally, and especially in the region) in the promulgation of normative instruments on AI governance, including developing the world's first AI governance testing framework and toolkit, AI Verify.[3] This 'responsible optimism' approach has been reinforced by the advent of generative AI as an

This research was supported by the Singapore Ministry of Education (MOE) Academic Research Fund (AcRF) Tier 1 grant 'Operationalising Responsible AI in Public Administration'. A version of this chapter was presented at the RAILS/University of Turn Workshop 'Generative AI and the Law' held in Berlin/online on 6 July 2023. Thanks to Josh Lee Kok Thong and How Khang Lim for their comments on the draft and to Jerrold Soh for his input and sharing of a draft chapter with us. All errors and opinions remain our own.

[1] Yan Han Goh, '$70m S'pore AI Initiative to Develop First Large Language Model with South-East Asian Context' (*The Straits Times*, 4 December 2023) <www.straitstimes.com/singapore/70m-s-pore-ai-initiative-to-develop-first-large-language-model-with-south-east-asian-context> accessed 26 April 2024.

[2] See, for example, W. G. Huff, 'What Is the Singapore Model of Economic Development?' (1995) 19 *Cambridge Journal of Economics* 735 <www.jstor.org/stable/23600207> accessed 1 May 2024, elaborating on the nuanced interplay of market and planning in Singapore economic philosophy.

[3] 'Singapore Launches World's First AI Testing Framework and Toolkit to Promote Transparency; Invites Companies to Pilot and Contribute to International Standards Development' (Infocomm Media Development Authority,

actual, rather than future or hypothetical, economic factor in Singapore's knowledge- and services-based economy. This approach may be compelling for other jurisdictions in the region and around the world with an interest in a collaborative, balanced, and consensual approach to governing AI outside of strict regulatory mechanisms. Singapore's influence can already be observed to have influenced the recent Association of South East Asian Nations (ASEAN) Guide on AI Governance and Ethics,[4] which was promulgated in early 2024. Whether the approach translates into economies and societies of a different scale, and with different regulatory environments and cultures, is an open question.

10.2 BACKGROUND

Singapore was recently ranked highest globally in terms of 'AI preparedness'.[5] Immediately, this makes its AI governance approach interesting from a comparative perspective – the obvious question being whether its approach could be adopted elsewhere with the same effect. The island city-state is thus an interesting study in technology governance. On the whole, we could characterise Singapore as a jurisdiction that is an early uptaker, pro-business, and generally 'tech optimistic'. At the same time, there is a strong tradition of state regulation for public safety and, as we have seen in areas like crypto assets, willingness to make decisive moves to protect the Singaporean public from harms as they arise (or are foreseen).

A number of characteristics set the stage for understanding Singapore's unique brand of AI governance as it is evolving. Singapore is a highly advanced knowledge economy in South-East Asia (SEA), and a clear stand-out in the region in terms of economic development and digital infrastructure. While it sounds clichéd, Singapore's complex and at times paradoxical characteristics are important to keep in mind: Singapore is a common law system, a financial hub, a democracy with remarkably stable party dominance, an ageing population, and a plural and modern but deeply Asian society with broadly conservative, Confucian-influenced values. This puts the city-state at cross-roads of economic, cultural, and political geographies, which underscore its apparent 'miracle' of economic development over the past decades. Singapore's political system and regulatory culture characteristically combine a strong commitment to free-market capitalism with an appetite (and capacity) for interventionism where necessary, undergirded by a small scale and small population and a preference for consensus-driven decision-making.

Another relevant piece of the backdrop is a relatively high level of adoption of and apparent trust in emerging technologies. A 2023 survey of 210 respondents, for example, found that over 67 per cent of Singaporeans had used generative AI (GenAI) at that time, and that 69 per cent of them described their experience as positive. The conclusion drawn from the report was that, despite the current news attention (much of which was negative), a significant portion of the respondents demonstrated positive or accepting perspectives towards GenAI.[6]

25 May 2022) <www.imda.gov.sg/resources/press-releases-factsheets-and-speeches/press-releases/2022/sg-launches-worlds-first-ai-testing-framework-and-toolkit-to-promote-transparency> accessed 26 April 2024.

[4] 'ASEAN Guide on AI Governance and Ethics' (*Asean.org*, 2024) <https://asean.org/wp-content/uploads/2024/02/ASEAN-Guide-on-AI-Governance-and-Ethics_beautified_201223_v2.pdf> accessed 26 April 2024.

[5] Mauro Cazzaniga et al., 'Gen-AI: Artificial Intelligence and the Future of Work' (International Monetary Fund, 2024) <www.imf.org/en/Publications/Staff-Discussion-Notes/Issues/2024/01/14/Gen-AI-Artificial-Intelligence-and-the-Future-of-Work-542379?cid=bl-com-SDNEA2024001> accessed 13 May 2024. See also, ranking Singapore highest in the region, 'Asia Pacific AI Readiness Index' (*Salesforce*, 2023) <www.salesforce.com/content/dam/web/en_sg/www/documents/pdf/salesforce_ai_readiness_index_2023.pdf> accessed 13 May 2024.

[6] Rebekah Lim, 'Perspectives on Generative AI' (*Blackdot Research*, 23 May 2023) <https://blackdotresearch.sg/generative-ai/> accessed 1 May 2024.

Similar data is appearing from other South-East Asian countries, with more respondents expecting benefits than drawbacks from AI deployment.[7] In contrast to Europe or the United States, 'doomer' narratives feature less prominently in the Asian discourse on AI.[8] (This positive attitude was recently popularised in the Sci-Fi motion picture *The Creator*, in which a regional conglomerate 'New Asia' becomes a kind of haven for intelligence androids persecuted by reckless, interventionist American forces seeking the human mastermind.) One reason for this could be that worker populations in the West have experienced the social and economic downsides of automation and globalisation over the past decades, whereas Asian populations have arguably experienced the upsides. These positive perceptions towards AI (at least in Singapore) could perhaps also be attributed to government initiatives that target citizen inclusion and participation in AI development and deployment,[9] or perceptions that have been cultivated around the utility and promise of AI as positively benefiting society.[10] They may also relate to Singapore's concerns about the demographics of ageing and workforce replacement.

While these points are conjectural, there do seem to be clear differences between developing and emerging economies on the issue of trust and attitudes towards AI adoption. A recent poll, for example, indicates that about 75 per cent of Americans fear job losses from AI.[11] On the other hand, despite similar concerns over job displacement,[12] Singapore provides a unique contrast as a highly developed, knowledge-based economy that is AI-optimistic and less concerned with AI's potential risks than its opportunities and benefits.

Another relevant background fact is the 'communitarian' orientation of Singaporean ethics, which is often contrasted with the rights-based, individualistic orientation of Western ethical approaches. It is easy to make broad claims about the different ethical orientation of Asian societies, influenced by Confucianism and other non-Western traditions. What this actually means is often left at the level of vague, intuitive truisms. However, as in all truisms, there is undoubtedly something there: Confucianism does emphasise notions such as societal 'harmony' in a manner quite different to, for example, Kantian or Utilitarian ethics.[13] This chapter is not

[7] Leander Von Kameke, 'Share of Consumers Seeing Mostly the Benefits of Artificial Intelligence (AI) in the Asia-Pacific Region in 2023, by Country' (*Statista*, 9 January 2024) <www.statista.com/statistics/1427977/apac-attitude-towards-benefits-of-ai-by-country/> accessed 1 May 2024.

[8] This has been consistently evident, for example, in the roundtables convened under the SMU-Microsoft Asian Dialogues on AI Governance since 2019.

[9] See initiatives like Tech Kaki that welcome citizens' feedback and participation in the development of new government digital products and services 'Tech Kaki Community' (*GovTech Singapore*, 18 April 2024) <www.tech.gov.sg/products-and-services/tech-kaki-community/> accessed 18 April 2024. Additionally, Singapore's focus on upskilling and enhancing citizens' digital literacy may have also contributed to enhanced trust and confidence in AI.

[10] See, for example, the uses and integration of technologies like robotic dogs in Singapore for the purpose of enforcing safety and security: Aqil Haziq Mahmud, 'Home Team's Robotic Dog Could Respond to Chemical Incidents, Support Police Patrols When It Joins Frontline Operations' (*Channel News Asia*, 20 January 2022).

[11] Stephanie Marken and Tara Nicola, 'Three in Four Americans Believe AI Will Reduce Jobs' (*Gallup*, 13 September 2023) <https://news.gallup.com/opinion/gallup/510635/three-four-americans-believe-reduce-jobs.aspx,%20accessed%2001/27/2023> accessed 2 May 2024.

[12] 'Singaporeans across Generations Raise Concern on Impact of AI in Job Security' (*Singapore Business Review*, 21 February 2024) <https://sbr.com.sg/hr-education/news/singaporeans-across-generations-raise-concern-impact-ai-in-job-security> accessed 29 April 2024.

[13] 'For Confucians, the difference between harmony and disharmony is like that between right and wrong, good and bad, and success and failure . . . As far as the need for harmony is concerned, Confucians tend to see more consistency than distinction between the "private" and the "public" (as is seen in Western liberalism), between the political and the non-political, and between human society and the natural world. When persons and things are engaged in a healthy, stable interplay and each gets its due, this is deemed harmony, and the opposite as disharmony . . . The ideal of an individual is to harmonise not only with one's own person but also with other individuals. The ideal of a society is to harmonise not only with the society but also with other societies. The human ideal is to achieve harmony not only among the members of the human community but with the rest of the cosmos as well.' Chenyang Li, 'The

the place to explore that question, so we will not focus explicitly on this aspect of Singapore's approach to AI governance. However, mindful of the need to avoid sloppy generalisations, it is probably fair to say that a communitarian ethos and harmony-focused ethical orientation is evident on the face of Singapore's brand of AI governance. This ethos is succinctly encapsulated by Singapore's 'whole of nation' approach,[14] which integrates the efforts and resources of Singaporeans, businesses, researchers, and policymakers in driving effective AI governance. Additionally, Singapore's commitment to 'community-building' initiatives similarly underscore the country's emphasis on the importance of collaboration and knowledge-sharing models.[15]

To date, Singapore has not enacted any specific law regulating the use of AI in general, and there is no indication that legislation specifically targeting the use of AI horizontally will be introduced soon. If anything, sectoral regulation of AI use cases in areas such as mis/disinformation could ensue if the gravity of the threat is deemed sufficient. The notable absence of AI regulation in Singapore may appear at odds with Singapore's regulatory enthusiasm in other fields. It is likely an expression of the belief that technology is best harnessed by shaping conditions for it to be used in economically productive and socially acceptable ways. As mentioned above, the latent capacity for the Singapore government to act swiftly to impose any legal interventions deemed necessary is an important differentiator to consider when comparing Singapore's regulatory approach to other jurisdictions, in which legislative response time may be considerably longer and more contested.

Although the conversation is steadily moving from ethics to regulation, the recourse to general law should not be forgotten in the AI governance debate, either: where the use of AI gives rise to personal injury, property damage, or financial loss, the claimant can seek remedies under the general law. Singapore does not have product liability laws; instead, remedies are available under statutes such as the Sale of Goods Act – and, of course, actions in tort and contract under the common law are also 'living' and adaptable to AI. The Personal Data Protection Act similarly is an important legal instrument for claimants as it imposes obligations on organisations when it comes to the collection, use, and disclosure of their personal data.[16] Further, some legislation such as the Road Traffic Act and the Health Products Act do address specific aspects of AI use.

In the sections that follow, we trace relevant developments in terms of significant documents, initiatives, and projects, framed within the city-state's National AI Strategy, which is a core component of its bid to be a world-leading 'Smart Nation'.

10.3 SINGAPORE'S NATIONAL AI STRATEGY (NAIS)

A significant background factor to consider is that Singapore's AI journey has been charted by a national strategy formulated in 2019 (NAIS 1.0) and updated in 2023 (NAIS 2.0), formulated as part of the country's Smart Nation Initiative launched in 2014. In this section, we briefly outline the approach set out in the two versions of the NAIS and trace out some of the differences between them.

Confucian Ideal of Harmony' (2006) 56 *Philosophy East and West* 583 <https://muse.jhu.edu/article/204485> accessed 2 May 2024. See also Bing Song (ed.), *Intelligence and Wisdom: Artificial Intelligence Meets Chinese Philosophers* (Springer Nature Singapore, 2021) <https://link.springer.com/10.1007/978-981-16-2309-7> accessed 2 May 2024.

[14] 'Be Part of Our AI Journey: Working Together to Better Make Use of AI' (*Smart Nation Singapore*) <www.smartnation.gov.sg/nais/contribute/> accessed 29 April 2024.

[15] See for example, the AI Verify Foundation initiative below.

[16] Data protection laws are important because data serves as the foundational building blocks for most AI innovations.

The NAIS 1.0 focused on three key aspirations: to develop Singapore as a global hub for AI innovation; to generate new business models and deliver innovative services to improve human welfare; and to equip the workforce to adapt in the changing digital economy. NAIS 1.0 pursued a holistic (or even total) vision of digital transformation, built on efforts in certain key sectors (for example, healthcare, education, and digital trade), a raft of national AI projects, and efforts towards building out an ecosystem including the 'triple helix' of researchers, industry, and government.[17]

NAIS 2.0 continues this vision and strategy in broad terms, but the emphasis is more strongly focused on public good (beyond that assumed within economic development), global competition (and competitiveness), and on building a more robust AI ecosystem rather than national projects. NAIS 2.0 also reiterates and strengthens the state's strategic commitment towards cultivating an AI-ready populace comprising both technical experts and AI users. NAIS 2.0 elaborates three 'systems', ten 'enablers', and fifteen 'actions'. The systems and enablers are set out in the following terms:

> *System 1: Activity Drivers (Enablers: Industry, Government, Research).* Industry, government, and public research performers have deep technical capabilities that can be applied to deliver value. We need to orchestrate them around meaningful use cases and problem statements to transform our economy and society.
>
> *System 2: People and Communities (Enablers: Talent, Capabilities, Placemaking).* We will attract more top-tier researchers and engineers to work with and from Singapore. More of our technology workforce should work to scale novel AI solutions, that form part of the toolkit which a confident base of enterprises and workers can use.
>
> *System 3: Infrastructure and Environment (Enablers: Compute, Data, Trusted Environment, Leader in Thought and Action).* We will ensure that Singapore hosts the necessary infrastructure and provides a trusted environment for AI innovation. This will make us a credible leader and preferred site for AI development, deployment, and adoption.[18]

In short, Singapore's official approach to AI is optimistic, cooperative, inclusive, and frames AI governance and risk in terms of prerequisites to unlocking its assumed benefits. The strategy also sheds some light on Singapore's dedication to fostering a trusted AI ecosystem that is conducive to AI recipient communities, while concurrently ensuring the effective mitigation of AI risks through clearly defined responsibility structures. Significantly, Singapore's community and ecosystem-building approach fosters a collective, participative, and responsible approach to solving AI-related issues; with the government actively encouraging its citizens, industry, academia, and international partners to collaborate in the development, deployment, and monitoring of new and emerging technologies. To elaborate, the government maintains open communication channels to solicit ideas and solutions for new National AI projects from the public,[19] while industry is encouraged to partake in beneficial data-sharing partnerships and practices.[20] Industry is also incentivised to digitise and create new AI solutions with the government's active support,[21] and

[17] 'National AI Strategy: AI for the Public Good, for Singapore and the World' (*Smart Nation Singapore*) <www.smartnation.gov.sg/nais/> accessed 2 May 2024.

[18] 'National AI Strategy' (n. 17).

[19] 'Be Part of Our AI Journey' (n. 14).

[20] 'Trusted Data Sharing Framework' (*Infocomm Media Development Authority*) <www.imda.gov.sg/how-we-can-help/data-innovation/trusted-data-sharing-framework> accessed 28 April 2024.

[21] 'Be Part of Our AI Journey' (n. 14).

citizens are continually provided access to various programmes to enhance their AI literacy and skill sets.[22]

Throughout, the strategy underscores the importance of maintaining societal values like fairness, non-discrimination, and human-centricity as principles operating to mitigate AI risks and integrate AI technologies into societal frameworks to protect important public interests and safeguard public trust. This framing perhaps helps us to contextualise and understand the various initiatives that have been launched towards AI governance in the past five years.

10.4 AN EARLY MOVER (BUT NOT TOWARDS 'REGULATION')

In a recent study, Simon Chesterman and colleagues rightly observed that the introduction of AI governance principles is a relatively recent phenomenon: as late as 2016, no company and only one country (the United States) had issued official documents on AI governance.[23] By 2021, that number had grown to many dozen – and a majority in Western Europe. Subsequently, in 2023, Nicholas Kluge Corrêa and colleagues noted the explosion of over 200 AI ethical guidelines and governance policies published by public bodies, academic institutions, private companies, and civil society organisations worldwide.[24]

Singapore counts as an early mover, and its first foray was made with some aplomb. The Infocomm and Media Development Authority (IMDA) developed a Model Framework for AI Governance and officially launched it at the World Economic Forum (WEF) in 2019. This was a bold statement that Singapore was (i) open for business – that is, advertising an open and pro-innovation regulatory environment, while also (ii) staking a claim as an early mover in AI governance that would insist on some minimum normative AI standards. We will review the substantive provisions of the Model Framework (as updated) below.

In the wake of announcements regarding the European Union's AI Act early in 2024, it is easy to assume that the terminus of AI governance evolution must be 'hard' regulation of a horizontal kind. But it is not a foregone conclusion that general (as opposed to sector-specific) regulation is the necessary or even desirable end point on any given jurisdiction's AI governance journey – nor, in fact, that ideal-typical hard regulation is the goal at all. In fact, as the travails of the AI Act draft over the past years have demonstrated, hard-edged legislative regulation of AI with prohibitions or conditions on its development and deployment is probably the most challenging form of regulation to get right.

Not only is it difficult to define the subject matter (AI) with adequate precision;[25] as Jerrold Soh and colleagues observe, AI 'regulation' can take a number of shapes.[26] The categories are not rigid, and most national approaches actually display some hybridity or mixing. However, if we set out a spectrum of regulatory approaches from industry self-regulation to co-regulation,

[22] Ibid. See, for instance, AI Singapore Talent Development programme, Techskills Accelerator, SkillsFuture for Digital Workplace Programme.

[23] Simon Chesterman and others, 'The Evolution of AI Governance' <www.techrxiv.org/doi/full/10.36227/techrxiv.24681063.v1> accessed 2 May 2024.

[24] Nicholas Kluge Corrêa et al., 'Worldwide AI Ethics: A Review of 200 Guidelines and Recommendations for AI Governance' (2023) 4 *Patterns* 100857 <https://linkinghub.elsevier.com/retrieve/pii/S2666389923002416> accessed 28 April 2024.

[25] The debate may centre around whether AI should be defined more 'technically' to contribute to better precision or whether a more human-based vocabulary should be adopted to cover advances in AI so the law can be 'future proofed'.

[26] Jerrold Soh, Larrisa Lim, and Yeong Zee Kin, 'Artificial Intelligence in the Regulatory Wonderland' (draft manuscript on file with the authors).

quasi-regulation, and direct regulation 'proper', we could characterise Singapore's approach to AI governance as *quasi-regulatory*:

> Quasi-regulation describes arrangements through which government influences businesses to comply, but which do not form part of formal government regulation. It is also commonly known as 'soft law', or a rule 'which has no legally binding force but which is intended to influence conduct'. General categories of soft law include procedural rules, interpretive guides, instructions to officials, prescriptive/evidential rules, commendatory rules, voluntary codes, rules of practice, management or operation, and consultative devices and administrative pronouncements. These may be published in the form of 'internal guidelines, rule books and practice manuals, circulars, operational memoranda, directives, and codes of conduct'.[27]

As Soh and colleagues continue, the Model Framework is a 'voluntary' and 'ready-to-use' tool primarily aimed at helping organisations deploying AI to do so in an appropriate manner, with particular regard to notions of 'responsibility' and 'human-centricity': 'The Model Framework reflects a collaborative style of governance, where industry and government co-develop measures and frameworks in an iterative process that allows regulators to better understand the shape and constraints of [AI] technology and therefore what could eventually become a set of rules and regulations governing them.'[28]

The Model Framework is situated within Singapore's overall approach to AI governance that is premised on balancing the twin imperatives of (i) facilitating innovation while (ii) safeguarding consumer interests by proactively managing the risks that arise from these emerging technologies. In our current geo-economic climate (of industrial policy and direct state involvement in critical industries and technologies), it should also be stated that the Singaporean model seems to favour stimulating innovation through a mixture of soft-touch regulation (to avoid 'stifling' innovation) on the one hand and, on the other, significant public sector investment in critical technology from trusted vendors to catalyse the industry and investment in research and development through universities and similar institutions.

Although Singaporean regulators and other stakeholders are well aware of the various risks presented by AI in general and by GenAI in particular, the advantages of a 'soft' approach have been deemed to outweigh those of a more direct form of regulation at this stage and for the foreseeable near term. In mid-2023, Singapore officials were quoted as saying that no bespoke regulation was on the cards at the current time, and that the focus was rather on learning about use cases from industry in order to determine what kind of regulation might be needed. Characteristically, the approach is one of working together with industry, research organisations, and other governments.[29] With this background in mind, it is now appropriate to review the Model Framework and relevant instruments issued by other Singapore government agencies.

10.5 THE IMDA MODEL FRAMEWORK FOR AI GOVERNANCE

The IMDA is a statutory board under the Ministry of Communications and Information. It took its modern shape in 2016 following the merger of several predecessor bodies with remits in telecommunications, computing, and media; today, IMDA has a broad remit that includes

[27] Ibid. Citations omitted.

[28] Ibid. Citations omitted.

[29] Sheila Chang, 'Singapore Is Not Looking to Regulate AI Just Yet, Says the City-State's Authority' (CNBC, 19 June 2023) <www.cnbc.com/2023/06/19/singapore-is-not-looking-to-regulate-ai-just-yet-says-the-city-state.html> accessed 8 April 2024.

oversight of Singapore's Personal Data Protection Act by the Personal Data Protection Commission (PDPC). IMDA is not only a regulator; it is also a development agency that plays an active role in the promotion of Singapore's digital economy agenda and holds a number of statutory functions of a development rather than regulatory nature.[30] Although separate divisions operate within the body, this dual nature has probably complemented the consensus-driven, collaborative approach typical of Singaporean rule-making and oversight, embracing various government entities, industry stakeholders, and civil society institutions such as universities and international organisations.

The Model Framework provides practical, voluntary guidance for private sector organisations on ethical and governance aspects of AI design and deployment. The Model Framework was released initially in January 2019, with a second version in January 2020. The initial release of the Model Framework in 2019 was widely acclaimed as being the first in Asia to provide practical guidance[31] to organisations in navigating key ethical and governance challenges when designing/deploying AI solutions. The Model Framework 1.0 underscores the role of corporations in minimising AI risks to foster public trust and mirrors Singapore's collaborative, industry-led AI strategy. It is avowedly agnostic in terms of technology, algorithm, sector, scale, and business model and provides a baseline set of considerations to adopt – and adapt. It is generally more concerned with deployments at scale, and less concerned with incidental deployments of AI modules in conventional software stacks.[32]

Both versions of the Model Framework are built around two main ethical principles. First, AI used in decision-making should be transparent, explainable, and fair; secondly, AI solutions should prioritise 'human-centric' values. These principles are translated into practical steps, addressing the challenge of implementing abstract ethical concepts.

Since its inception, the Model Framework has aspired to adaptability and agility. Described as a 'living document',[33] the Model Framework was designed to evolve alongside the rapidly changing AI landscape. Consistent with this vision, the second iteration of the Model Framework was published shortly after its original release. Based on industry feedback and consultation, the second version incorporated additional considerations (including an interest in robustness, reproducibility, and auditability) to enhance the Framework's operability and relevance.[34] The second version also included additional industry examples to showcase how organisations can align more closely with the four outlined areas. The second version of the Model Framework also pays closer scrutiny to broader internal and external stakeholder

[30] See Info-communications Media Development Authority Act 2016, s. 5(1) setting out development functions including, for example, promoting research and development into technological matters relating to the information, communications, and media industry; promoting, where suitable, self-regulation in the information, communications, and media industry in Singapore; promoting the use of information and communications technology in Singapore and, where necessary, collaborating with the Government Technology Agency (established by section 3 of the Government Technology Agency Act 2016) in respect of that; and promoting the use of the internet and electronic commerce in Singapore and to establish regulatory frameworks for that purpose. See also s. 6 setting out the powers of the IMDA.

[31] 'Singapore Releases Asia's First Model AI Governance Framework' (23 January 2019) <www.imda.gov.sg/resources/press-releases-factsheets-and-speeches/archived/imda/press-releases/2019/singapore-releases-asias-first-model-ai-governance-framework> accessed 28 April 2024.

[32] Soh et al., 'Artificial Intelligence in the Regulatory Wonderland' (n. 26). Citations omitted.

[33] 'Singapore Releases Asia's First Model AI Governance Framework' (n. 31).

[34] 'Model Artificial Intelligence Governance Framework Second Edition' (*Personal Data Protection Commission Singapore*) p. 5 <www.pdpc.gov.sg/-/media/Files/PDPC/PDF-Files/Resource-for-Organisation/AI/SGModelAIGovFramework2.pdf> accessed 6 October 2022.

relationships, and how organisations can determine the appropriate level of human involvement required in AI decision-making.

Key elements of the second version of the Model Framework include:

- *Internal AI governance*, emphasising the importance of clear roles and accountability within organizations to manage AI-related risks effectively. This includes providing relevant personnel with proper training and resources to discharge their duties and establishing a system of risk management.
- *Human involvement in AI decisions*, advocating for a structured approach to evaluating and integrating human oversight based on potential harm and severity. This determination of human involvement ought to be a continuous process.
- *Operations management*, focusing on the integrity of data and algorithms to prevent biases and ensure fair AI outcomes.
- *Stakeholder interaction*, emphasising transparency and the importance of clear communication about AI use to build trust. Stakeholders' access to open communication avenues is also critical in the management of AI risks.

The Model Framework thus encourages industry self-regulation over legislative approaches, advocating for a balanced approach between innovation and risk management. It is worth noting also that the principles outlined in the Model Framework as iterated do not deviate significantly from commonly endorsed AI ethical principles. These principles, emphasising the values of transparency, explainability, fairness, non-discrimination, retention of human involvement are similarly covered in regulatory approaches like the EU AI act. The Model Framework can be said to complement Singapore's AI governance approach by leveraging the capacity, resources, and initiative of industry participants. Industry's efforts are then strategically bolstered with significant government support encompassing both financial[35] and technical[36] dimensions.

Through supporting initiatives like the 'Implementation and Self-Assessment Guide' (ISAGO) and a Compendium of Use Cases, organisations are aided in understanding and applying these principles within their own organisational and technical environment to promote more ethical and responsible AI development and deployment. True also to the spirit of the Singapore Model Framework being a 'living document', it is relevant to consider the availability of communication pathways through which industry members can feed back on Model implementation and suggest improvements[37] for future incorporation. All of these initiatives combined help to enhance AI adoption and integration in society, the economy, and government, and also to establish a reciprocal trust relationship between the state and relevant industries, and trust between industry, AI, and the respective communities it operates within, with the aim of promoting a thriving, innovative ecosystem underpinned by ethical AI practices.

[35] Grants are widely available in Singapore to foster innovation and help businesses digitise. See all available grants: 'How We Can Help' (*Infocomm Media Development Authority*) <www.imda.gov.sg/how-we-can-help?page = 1&key word = &category = all&support = organisations&orgType = all&industry = all&persona = all> accessed 29 April 2024.

[36] Among others listed here: 'Be Part of Our AI Journey' (n. 14); see also initiatives such as the 100 Experiments Programme: '100 Experiments' (*AI Singapore*) <https://aisingapore.org/innovation/100e/> accessed 1 April 2024.

[37] Singapore encourages organisations to share feedback on practical examples and their experiences in implementation by emailing corporate@pdpc.gov.sg. See 'Singapore's Approach to AI Governance' (*Personal Data Protection Commission Singapore*) <www.pdpc.gov.sg/help-and-resources/2020/01/model-ai-governance-framework> accessed 5 July 2023.

10.6 AI VERIFY AND AI VERIFY FOUNDATION

In 2022, a minimum viable product (MVP) called 'AI Verify' was launched by IMDA and the PDPC to fill the perceived gap in AI governance testing and evaluation. AI Verify comprises an integrated toolkit for evaluation and testing (one is tempted to say 'audit') within an organisation's own enterprise environment. In this regard, it can be observed that alongside initiatives like the Model Framework, the deployment of toolkits like AI Verify also showcases Singapore's unique technological approach to guide industry's responsible development and deployment of AI.

In mid-2023, Minister for Communications and Information Josephine Teo announced the launch of the AI Verify Foundation at the ATxAI conference to take stewardship of AI Verify.[38] Although IMDA continues to play a leading role, the vision seems to be that the consortium of industry partners will play an increasingly active role.[39] The AI Verify Foundation aims to tap a global, open-source community to develop AI testing tools for the responsible use of AI and to promote best practices for AI governance as they emerge.[40] This approach is indicative of Singaporean government leadership to precipitate a consortium of industry players around a consensus that something is needed, and that it is incumbent on those players to contribute their vision of what that something is and how it ought to be achieved. The messaging is that 'industry needs to demonstrate to their stakeholders their implementation of responsible AI in an objective and verifiable way' and that AI Verify is a way for them to do so: 'IMDA and PDPC have taken the first step to develop an AI Governance Testing Framework and Toolkit to enable industry to demonstrate their deployment of responsible AI.'[41]

The AI Verify toolkit does not define AI ethical standards itself, but is designed to be consistent with various AI governance frameworks, of course including Singapore's Model Framework as well as those from the European Union and Organisation for Economic Co-operation and Development (OECD).[42] The focus on interoperability for AI Verify sits squarely with the NAIS 2.0 to safeguard Singapore's interests and position in shaping the international rules, processes and governance trends emerging around responsible and trustworthy AI. The MVP is intended to produce higher levels of public trust in businesses deploying AI in Singapore, to facilitate interoperability of different governance frameworks (especially those that incorporate broadly similar ethical principles), and to contribute to the development of international standards on AI, including the ISO/IEC JTC1/SC 42 on artificial intelligence to facilitate compliance.[43]

To briefly examine the issue of AI standards here (as also comprising Singapore's comprehensive approach in governing AI), it is worth noting that Singapore has a dedicated AI Technical

[38] 'Singapore Launches AI Verify Foundation to Shape the Future of International AI Standards through Collaboration' (Infocomm Media Development Authority, 7 June 2023) <www.imda.gov.sg/resources/press-releases-factsheets-and-speeches/press-releases/2023/singapore-launches-ai-verify-foundation> accessed 3 May 2024.

[39] Indeed, the AI Verify Foundation played a pivotal role in developing the most Model AI Governance Framework for Generative AI.

[40] 'AI Verify Foundation: Building Trust through Ethical AI' <https://aiverifyfoundation.sg/ai-verify-foundation/> accessed 2 May 2024.

[41] Ministry of Communication and Information, IMDA, and PDPC, 'Annex B: Background on Singapore's AI Governance Work' (*Infocomm Media Development Authority*, May 2022) <www.imda.gov.sg/-/media/Imda/Files/News-and-Events/Media-Room/Media-Releases/2022/05/Annex-B—Background-on-SG-AI-Governance-Work.pdf> accessed 2 May 2024.

[42] See 'What Is AI Verify?' (AI Verify Foundation) <https://aiverifyfoundation.sg/what-is-ai-verify/> accessed 2 May 2024; the OECD AI Principles are available at: 'OECD AI Principles Overview' (*OCED.AI Policy Observatory*) <https://oecd.ai/en/ai-principles> accessed 2 May 2024.

[43] See 'ISO/IEC JTC 1/SC 42 Artificial Intelligence' (International Organization for Standardization) <www.iso.org/committee/6794475.html> accessed 2 May 2024.

Committee (AITC)[44] involved in the adoption and development of AI standards both internationally and domestically. Beyond the significance of AI standards in enhancing trade connectivity and cultivating trust and reliability in AI recipient communities,[45] it is also worth reflecting on how Singapore's participation in key international standard-setting organisations has underscored Singapore's relevance and autonomy in shaping current norms related to responsible and trustworthy AI on the international stage.

10.7 INITIATIVES OF THE MONETARY AUTHORITY OF SINGAPORE (MAS)

Given the importance of the finance industry to Singapore, and the scope for AI deployment in finance, the Monetary Authority of Singapore (MAS), which is the central bank and main financial regulator, has also been active in promulgating vertical AI governance instruments. In late 2018, MAS published 'Principles to Promote Fairness, Ethics, Accountability and Transparency (FEAT) in the Use of Artificial Intelligence and Data Analytics in Singapore's Financial Sector'.[46] This document was, in turn, updated in early 2019 to reflect the Model AI Governance Framework set out above.

MAS's activities in the AI governance space are also illustrative of the approach of using industry consortia with trusted private sector counterparts to develop and implement AI governance frameworks and tools. The 'Veritas Toolkit' was released in February 2022, providing an assessment methodology to enable financial institutions to evaluate their AI-driven solutions against the FEAT principles to strengthen internal governance around the application of AI and data. The toolkit allows a user to create a project, and generate an assessment questionnaire and assessment report. Veritas Toolkit version 2.0 was released in 2023 with an improved fairness assessment methodology and new assessment methodologies for the remaining principles (ethics, accountability, and transparency).[47] The toolkit is available on a github repository for organisations to test, and a number of white papers have been published providing use cases and experiences with the methodology and toolkit.[48]

The industry consortium comprised thirty-one financial institutions, including many multinationals. Again explaining the initiative in the context of Singapore's evolving National AI Strategy, MAS Chief FinTech Officer Sopnendu Mohanty has described the next steps in the following terms:

> Our next step is to build an open-source ecosystem for [responsible AI (RAI)] that is self-sustaining and vibrant. This ecosystem will facilitate the pervasive and consistent adoption of RAI principles by FIs and tech companies, as well as support a new generation of RAI stewards

[44] 'AI Standards' (AI Singapore) <https://aisingapore.org/innovation/ai-standards/> accessed 29 April 2024.

[45] Tak Leong Cheong and Laurence Liew, 'Why Standards Matter for AI and Big Data' (12 June 2023) <www.enterprisesg.gov.sg/resources/blog/quality-and-standards/why-standards-matter-for-ai-and-big-data> accessed 17 April 2024.

[46] 'Principles to Promote Fairness, Ethics, Accountability and Transparency (FEAT) in the Use of Artificial Intelligence and Data Analytics in Singapore's Financial Sector' (Monetary Authority of Singapore, 7 February 2019) <www.mas.gov.sg/~/media/MAS/News%20and%20Publications/Monographs%20and%20Information%20Papers/FEAT%20Principles%20Final.pdf> accessed 29 April 2024.

[47] 'MAS-Led Industry Consortium Releases Toolkit for Responsible Use of AI in the Financial Sector' (Monetary Authority of Singapore, 26 June 2023) <www.mas.gov.sg/news/media-releases/2023/toolkit-for-responsible-use-of-ai-in-the-financial-sector> accessed 2 May 2024.

[48] 'Veritas-Toolkit' <https://github.com/veritas-toolkit/>; documents are available for download at: 'Veritas Initiative: What It Is' (Monetary Authority of Singapore, 26 October 2023) <www.mas.gov.sg/schemes-and-initiatives/veritas> accessed 2 May 2024.

who are skilled in using RAI tools. Additionally, the ecosystem will foster an active community of developers who can implement the FEAT Principles through the Veritas open-source ecosystem. Through this collaborative approach, we aim to promote RAI practices and ensure that the benefits of AI are shared by all.[49]

10.8 MODEL FRAMEWORK FOR GENAI

The subsequent sections move to discuss Singapore's evolving (and future) AI governance and policy frameworks in the context of responsible GenAI development and deployment. GenAI dominated the headlines in 2023, and the unprecedented level of public adoption of GenAI products stimulated increased regulatory attention.

In early 2024, the AI Verify Foundation (AIVF) and IMDA released a draft Model AI Governance Framework for Generative AI for public comment.[50] The version was later finalised in May 2024 (GenAI Framework).[51] This framework expands on the existing Model Governance Framework that covers 'Traditional AI'.

The framework builds on ideas from an earlier discussion paper[52] and earlier technical work to provide an initial catalogue and guidance on suggested practices for safety evaluation of generative AI models as well as insights from a generative AI Evaluation Sandbox that was launched in October 2023.[53] In substantive terms, the framework sets out nine proposed 'dimensions' to support a comprehensive and trusted AI ecosystem. Predictably, the core elements rest on concepts that are stock-in-trade for AI governance: accountability, data, trusted development and deployment, incident reporting, testing and assurance, security, content provenance, safety and alignment research and development, and AI for public good.

For its part, the GenAI Sandbox encourage and explore the adoption of GenAI by small and medium-sized businesses (SMEs). It is less a 'regulatory sandbox' in which attenuated regulations apply but more of a 'technology sandbox' to encourage experimentation by Singaporean businesses. Launched by IMDA and Enterprise Singapore (a statutory board under the Ministry of Trade and Industry that is the successor of multiple agencies including the former Trade Development Board) in February 2024, the Sandbox allows SMEs to access GenAI enterprise solutions over a three-month period that could drive their marketing and customer engagement activities.[54] While this is an activity more squarely in IMDA's development authority portfolio

[49] 'Veritas, Trust in AI – Document 5: From Methodologies to Integration' <www.mas.gov.sg/-/media/mas/news/media-releases/veritas-document-5—from-methodologies-to-integration.pdf> accessed 2 May 2024.

[50] AI Verify Foundation and IMDA, 'Proposed Model AI Governance Framework For Generative AI: Fostering a Trusted Ecosystem' (AI Verify Foundation, 16 January 2024) <https://aiverifyfoundation.sg/downloads/Proposed_MGF_Gen_AI_2024.pdf> accessed 1 May 2024.

[51] AI Verify Foundation and IMDA, 'Model AI Governance Framework for Generative AI – Fostering a Trusted Ecosystem' [2024] AI Verify Foundation <https://aiverifyfoundation.sg/wp-content/uploads/2024/05/Model-AI-Governance-Framework-for-Generative-AI-May-2024-1-1.pdf> accessed 16 January 2025.

[52] IMDA and AICADIUM, 'Generative AI: Implications for Trust and Governance' (AI Verify Foundation, 7 June 2023) <https://aiverifyfoundation.sg/downloads/Discussion_Paper.pdf> accessed 8 April 2024.

[53] Launched by IMDA and AI Verify Foundation in October 2023 to drive the development of evaluation benchmarks in Generative AI, 'First of Its Kind Generative AI Evaluation Sandbox for Trusted AI by AI Verify Foundation and IMDA' (Infocomm Media Development Authority, 31 October 2023) <www.imda.gov.sg/resources/press-releases-factsheets-and-speeches/press-releases/2023/generative-ai-evaluation-sandbox> accessed 8 April 2024.

[54] IMDA and EnterpriseSG, 'Generative Artificial Intelligence Sandbox for SMEs' (Infocomm Media Development Authority, 7 February 2024) <https://services2.imda.gov.sg/CTOaaS/Highlight/42/generative-artificial-intelligence-sandbox-for-smes> accessed 2 May 2024.

than its regulatory role, it is further illustrative of the active and hands-on approach the agency is taking towards 'responsible' AI adoption.

The GenAI Framework offers valuable insights into understanding Singapore's ongoing (and perhaps future) approach to governing GenAI and other emerging technologies. An initial review of the GenAI Framework sheds some light on the urgency of appropriate AI governance structures both in Singapore and globally. The threat posed by GenAI, particularly to public trust, encompassing issues of misinformation, manipulation, and deception is stressed in the Framework, prompting vigilance and action from all relevant stakeholders in the AI ecosystem. Echoing the 'whole of society' approach found in the NAIS 2.0 and the 'traditional' Model Framework, the GenAI Framework similarly delineates the critical roles and responsibilities of citizens, businesses, academia, policymakers, and international partners, urging the swift development of a safe and trusted AI ecosystem.

Nonetheless, acknowledging that not all risks posed by GenAI can be adequately addressed or anticipated by the Framework, the GenAI Framework mentions the need to examine current legislative instruments (such as existing personal data laws) to appropriately safeguard citizens' interests and rights.[55] This references the point above on how the general law is still an important mechanism in the overall AI governance debate and why a horizontal all-encompassing regulation (like the EU AI Act) should not be seen as the exclusive pathway to effective AI governance. Consequently, it can be said that Singapore is not solely reliant on voluntary and 'soft' approaches in governing AI but is prepared and well-equipped to leverage the strong arm of the broader law to shape AI's impact on society. Interestingly, the GenAI Framework also considers the utility of 'no fault insurance' as another potential tool to ensure adequate compensation and redress for individuals affected by adverse AI outcomes.[56]

Like the Model Framework for traditional AI, the GenAI Framework reiterates the need for good data practices and robust security safeguards to protect individuals' personal data and other rights. However, what is noteworthy in the GenAI Framework is its explicit endorsement of various technological tools including privacy enhancing technologies, input moderation tools, and digital forensic tools[57]. The GenAI Framework elaborates and validates the significance of these tools in safeguarding data confidentiality, security. and privacy in the age of GenAI.

Again, in line with earlier comments on how AI Verify confirms Singapore's technological approach in guiding industry's responsible development and deployment of AI, the clear nod to the utility of these tools similarly reflects the country's interest in leveraging technology to promote more responsible and trustworthy AI systems.

These aspects as revealed by the GenAI Framework, including the reliance on general law, the openness to alternative non-regulatory solutions, and the leveraging of technology to manage the development and deployment of GenAI, affirm again Singapore's multi-layered, innovative, and comprehensive approach in the management of AI risks and its promised benefits. As also acknowledged in the GenAI Framework itself, 'no single intervention will be a silver bullet'.[58]

The Model Framework's adaptability as a 'living document' can also be examined against the proposed GenAI Framework. Of particular interest is the evolution of the ethical principle of 'transparency' and how it is interpreted and reflected in the GenAI framework to deal more directly with threats specific to Gen AI, including AI 'hallucinations', misinformation, and

[55] AI Verify Foundation and IMDA, 'Model AI Governance Framework' (n. 51), 10.
[56] Ibid., 8.
[57] Ibid., 22.
[58] AI Verify Foundation and IMDA, 'Proposed Model AI Governance Framework' (n. 50).

copyright infringement. This examination provides critical insights into the concept of what 'meaningful transparency' entails, as well as the practices the state determines as necessary for industry to align with the objective of 'meaningful transparency'.

To elaborate, while the principle of transparency already features in the second version of the traditional Model Framework, the GenAI Framework appears to have expanded, shaped, and contextualised this principle further to deal with risks and benefits specific to GenAI. First, while the GenAI Framework acknowledges that the level of transparency will need to be calibrated against an organisation's legitimate interests (including their proprietary interest); it also calls for the development of some 'baseline transparency' to allow downstream users to make more informed decisions surrounding their AI use.[59] Second, the GenAI Framework urges that all disclosure of information (including data used, training infrastructure, evaluation results, mitigation measures, etc.) should be standardised to promote comparability across AI models.[60] Third, that transparency requirements should vary depending on the risk level of the model in question. Naturally, models that have national security or societal implications will have to satisfy stricter transparency requirements.[61]

The substantive content of the GenAI Framework also reflects Singapore's adaptability, agility, and capacity to consider novel AI risks as it emerges. The GenAI Framework explicitly considers the real and potential threats posed by GenAI, including copyright infringement, its interaction with fair use policies, the danger of poor-quality datasets, synthetic content and deepfakes. The systematic presentation of these issues in the GenAI Framework perhaps reveals something about Singapore's ability to stay ahead of the curve in dealing with emerging AI risks and the country's commitment to building a trusted AI ecosystem that produces social and economic benefits for society.

Finally, consistent with Singapore's overall interest in striking a balance between the management of AI risks against its potential benefits, the GenAI Framework contains clear references to initiatives that facilitate AI-driven innovation and its responsible adoption. For instance, Singapore's GenAI Sandbox is referenced as providing SMEs with the necessary tools and training on generative AI enterprise solutions.[62] Additionally, the GenAI Framework underscores the value of investing more research in model safety and alignment, including the setting up of AI safety research and development (R&D) institutes.[63] The importance of expanding the pool of trusted quality data sets is also acknowledged,[64] as well as the benefits of curating a repository of representative training data sets for their specific context.[65]

10.9 PROJECT SEA-LION

Building upon the preceding discussion, there are also other ongoing and notable initiatives worth mentioning. For instance, the 'Generative AI x Digital Leaders' initiative, which aims to support digitally mature enterprises with access to GenAI expertise and resources,[66] and the

59 Ibid., 14.
60 Ibid.
61 Ibid.
62 Ibid., 20.
63 Ibid., 27.
64 Ibid., 11.
65 Ibid.
66 'IMDA Launches Generative AI x Digital Leaders Initiative to Provide Businesses Access to GenAI' <www.mci.gov.sg/files/Press%20Releases%202024/AI__Annex_D.pdf> accessed 1 May 2024.

SEA-LION ('Southeast Asian Languages in One Network') project, the region's first large language model (LLM).[67]

Given its increasing geo-economic importance (and sensitivity), AI is a focal point for subsidies and other stimulatory measures. Singapore has identified global leadership in the field of AI and AI governance as a matter of national significance and this has translated into ambitious funding for research and development in fields such as AI and advanced computing.

In late 2023, IMDA announced a partnership with AI Singapore and the Agency for Science, Technology, and Research (A*STAR) to launch a LLM trained with SEA languages with significant funding from the Singapore National Research Foundation (NRF), the major public research funding body. SEA is a linguistically, socially, and economically diverse region with a multitude of languages that are underrepresented in pre-training data used for current LLMs. Project SEA-LION is a family of models that employ a unique approach to tokenising language (i.e., breaking sentences and words into data units) tailored to SEA languages. Embedded within the agenda set by NAIS 2.0 to 'nurture Singapore as a global leader in AI solutions', the perceived benefit is GenAI capabilities better suited to Singapore and the region's cultural landscape:

> As technology evolves rapidly, there is a strategic need to develop sovereign capabilities in LLMs. Singapore and the region's local and regional cultures, values and norms differ from those of Western countries, where most large language models originate. A cornerstone of this initiative is the development of multimodal and localised LLMs for Singapore and the region to understand context and values related to the diverse cultures and languages of Southeast Asia, for example, managing context-switching between languages in multilingual Singapore.[68]

In the first instance, it will focus on major languages, including local variants of English, Bahasa Indonesia, Malay, Thai, and Vietnamese, and will be extended to include other regional languages in due course.[69]

10.10 AI AND THE FUTURE OF WORK

Another topic of growing concern around the world that is also acutely felt in Singapore is the potential impact of AI on the future of work. Although successive generations of AI, and indeed automation technology more broadly, has impacted on the economics and labour dynamics of various industries in the past, the advent of GenAI in 2023 brought home the potential for AI to impact Singapore's knowledge economy – for good and for ill.

Singapore's perspective on the issue is likely framed by the demographic reality of an ageing population and low birth rate, combined with historical and present reliance on migrant labour in areas such as domestic work, aged care, construction, and the food and beverage hospitality industry. In the medium to long term, automation is perceived not only as beneficial but

[67] Aaron Tan, 'Sea-Lion Explained: Southeast Asia's First Large Language Model' (*Computer Weekly*, 5 February 2024) <www.computerweekly.com/feature/Sea-Lion-explained-Southeast-Asias-first-large-language-model> accessed 1 May 2024.

[68] IMDA, 'Singapore Pioneers S$70m Flagship AI Initiative to Develop Southeast Asia's First Large Language Model Ecosystem Catering to the Region's Diverse Culture and Languages' (Infocomm Media Development Authority, 4 December 2023) <www.imda.gov.sg/resources/press-releases-factsheets-and-speeches/press-releases/2023/sg-to-develop-southeast-asias-first-llm-ecosystem> accessed 2 May 2024.

[69] See also 'Sea-Lion' (AI Singapore) <https://aisingapore.org/aiproducts/sea-lion/> accessed 2 May 2024; 'AI Singapore Brings Inclusive Generative AI Models to Southeast Asia with AWS' (*Amazon*, 24 January 2024) <www.aboutamazon.sg/news/aws/ai-singapore-brings-inclusive-generative-ai-models-to-southeast-asia-with-aws> accessed 2 May 2024.

perhaps critical to the viability of the Singaporean economy and society. At the same time, there are deep concerns about the short- to medium-term impacts of automation on various segments of the workforce – in addition to the familiar patterns of workforce displacement through automation in manufacturing, transport, and so on, GenAI is also providing inroads into tasks performed by white-collar knowledge workers.[70] While there has been no regulatory action on the point to date, conversations are being held at various fora in Singaporean society.[71]

Notably, in 2020, the IMDA and the PDPC collaborated with the Lee Kuan Yew Centre for Innovative Cities (LKYCIC), Singapore University of Technology and Design, to publish the first 'Guide to Job Redesign in the Age of AI'.[72] The Guide focuses on a human-centric approach to AI and provides guidance to organisations and employees to unlock the potential of AI, so as to increase the value of 'work'. The four areas of job redesign include: transforming jobs, charting clear pathways between jobs, clearing barriers to digital transformation, and enabling effective communication between employers and employees.

The future of work in the context of GenAI is also addressed (albeit briefly) in the GenAI Framework. Concerning the dimension of AI for public good, the responsible use of AI in the workforce is underscored, in particular, with a focus on empowering workers through upskilling and appropriate job redesign.[73]

10.11 ASEAN AI GUIDELINES

Finally, an examination into Singapore's AI governance approach would be incomplete without also factoring in Singapore's significant influence on AI governance in the region. In early 2024, ASEAN published its Guide on AI Governance and Ethics,[74] which is intended to serve as a practical guide for organisations that wish to design, develop, and deploy traditional AI technologies in commercial and non-military or dual-use applications. It focuses on encouraging alignment within ASEAN member states and fostering the interoperability of AI frameworks across those jurisdictions. It also includes recommendations on national-level and regional-level initiatives that governments in the region can consider implementing to design, develop, and deploy AI systems responsibly.

In broad terms, the Guide is consistent with the Model Framework, being guided by the principles of: transparency and explainability; fairness and equity; security and safety; robustness and reliability; human-centricity; privacy and data governance; and accountability and integrity. Both frameworks adopt a risk-based approach that calibrates the level of human oversight required by reference to the potential impact on human users. Both frameworks also assume a relatively high degree of flexibility for organisations to comply in a manner that is feasible and

[70] See, for example, Tappy Lung, 'Artificial Intelligence and the Future of Singapore's Foreign Workforce' (Centre for Strategic and International Studies, 17 April 2024) <www.csis.org/blogs/new-perspectives-asia/artificial-intelligence-and-future-singapores-foreign-workforce#:~:text=At%20the%20same%20time%2C%20Singapore,join%20its%20workforce%20by%202025> accessed 2 May 2024.

[71] For example, SMU and the *Straits Times* recently held a high-profile summit on the topic: Whitney William, 'AI-Powered Humanoid Robot Sophia Wows Crowd at ST Education Forum' (*The Straits Times*, 9 March 2024) <www.straitstimes.com/singapore/world-s-first-humanoid-robot-sophia-wows-crowd-at-st-education-forum> accessed 2 May 2024.

[72] IMDA, PDPC, and Lee Kuan Yew Centre for Innovative Cities, 'A Guide to Job Redesign in the Age of AI' (Infocomm Media Development Authority, 4 December 2020) <https://file.go.gov.sg/ai-guide-to-jobredesign.pdf> accessed 1 May 2024.

[73] AI Verify Foundation and IMDA, 'Proposed Model AI Governance Framework' (n. 50), 20.

[74] 'ASEAN Guide on AI Governance and Ethics' (n. 4).

appropriate to all the circumstances – an important consideration in ASEAN, given the very different operating environments across the region.

ASEAN is a diverse and heterogeneous association in terms of legal system and economic development, and Singapore is clearly among the leading jurisdictions (if not the leading jurisdiction) in terms of AI governance initiatives. It is perhaps unsurprising that the Singaporean approach has been influential. As Kristina Fong explains:

> Singapore will be the Chair of the ASEAN Digital Ministers' Meeting (ADGMIN) and Related Meetings in 2024. It will be in a good position to lead ASEAN in the development of the ASEAN AI Guide on Governance and Ethics. With Singapore's position at the European Commission's High Level Expert Group on AI, it can guide the bloc's AI strategy to better align it with international standards including good regulatory principles found in the EU's AI Act. Singapore has an important role to play in bridging gaps within ASEAN on AI and at the same time, steering ASEAN's AI guidelines toward international standards. It will be important for ASEAN to have a strategy that is not just symbolic in form but also able to safeguard the ASEAN economies in this dynamic arena.[75]

This said, one should still be mindful that the Singaporean model of AI governance may or may not translate well (or at all) into other ASEAN jurisdictions, which have a very different economy, society, regulatory culture, resources, capabilities, and institutional setting.

10.12 CONCLUSION: THE FUTURE OF AI GOVERNANCE IN SINGAPORE

The governance trajectory of GenAI and other emerging technologies are unlikely to depart from Singapore's current AI governance approach. The government is expected to maintain its 'soft touch' that is both collaborative and industry-led, while delineating clear responsibility structures across the whole of society. Thus, individuals in their personal capacities will also be expected to do their part in navigating AI's potential risks, to take accountability for their own digital literacy and upskilling, and to contribute to the strengthening of Singapore's digital economy and digital society. In other words, all stakeholders will reap the benefits of AI (to solve societal needs and challenges) but are also expected to share in the management of AI's potential downsides and drawbacks.

Inspiring citizens' trust in AI will likely continue to feature as a national priority. Citizens' perception of AI will ultimately have an influence on overall AI uptake and adoption, which will in turn promote Singapore's Smart Nation ambitions. The NAIS 2.0 explicitly identified AI as an indispensable force essential to the continued relevance and prosperity of the nation.[76] It is perhaps fair to comment then that the embedding and reception of AI into society cannot be attained without first cultivating (and, where appropriate, restoring) public trust and confidence in the technology. Judging by Singapore's comprehensive AI governance mechanisms, it appears evident that the country acknowledged as early as 2018[77] that establishing this trusted ecosystem requires the proper negotiation of AI's risks and its benefits.

This chapter has outlined how the Singapore AI governance approach strives to fine-tune the appropriate balance between facilitating innovation, employing AI for wealth creation,

[75] Kristina Fong Siew Leng, '2023/65: ASEAN's New Dilemma: Managing the Artificial Intelligence Space' (ISEAS Yusof Ishak Institute, 7 August 2023) <www.iseas.edu.sg/articles-commentaries/iseas-perspective/2023-65-aseans-new-dilemma-managing-the-artificial-intelligence-by-kristina-fong-siew-leng/> accessed 2 May 2024.

[76] 'National AI Strategy' (n. 17).

[77] See Publication of *Principles to Promote Fairness, Ethics, Accountability and Transparency (FEAT) in the Use of Artificial Intelligence and Data Analytics in Singapore's Financial Sector.*

managing AI's potential risks, and safeguarding consumer interests. This balanced strategy can be expected to continue to feature well into the future, with the government negotiating this equilibrium in a systemic, holistic, and practical manner.

Current AI governance initiatives and government efforts also provide strong indication that the future of AI governance in Singapore will remain distinctive, characterised not only by its collaborative government–industry consortia but also robust technological capabilities and capacities. Current initiatives reveal that Singapore is not afraid to be a first (and fast) mover. Indeed, as the AI Verify Toolkit, the Model Framework, and the SEA-LION initiatives reveal, this proactive and innovative approach is crucial in securing the country's regional and international standing in the global AI race and discourse surrounding the responsible and trustworthy development and deployment of AI systems.

Singapore recognises also that it cannot forge ahead into the future alone and this sentiment is thoroughly reflected in its repeated emphasis on more regional and international collaborations. Currently, Singapore is an active participant in numerous multi-stakeholder platforms such as the Global Partnership on AI (GPAI), the WEF, the AI Governance Alliance, and the United Nations High-Level Advisory Body on AI.[78] With burgeoning developments in GenAI, the need for collaboration becomes more pronounced, particularly with a view to enhancing Singapore's research capabilities, to attract international AI talent, share AI practices including appropriate governance strategies, and to develop AI-related capacity-building initiatives.

Finally, although it is tempting to question why Singapore has been slow to implement regulation and is still adopting a 'wait-and-see' approach, perhaps the Singapore narrative suggests that the country can afford to do so. Although a small country, Singapore has developed the expertise, the technological capabilities, and the digital infrastructure to continue governing AI on its own unique terms. A more encompassing horizontal AI regulation could be introduced somewhere down the line and, when the time comes, Singapore's approach will no doubt be similarly comprehensive and practical. For now, Singapore appears to have a firm handle on how it navigates AI, and how it intends to shape the 'rules of the road' around AI in the future.

[78] 'National AI Strategy' (n. 17).

11

Shaping Global AI Governance

A Path for the G7 to Foster Rule of Law in a World of Uncertainty

Hiroki Habuka and David U. Socol de la Osa

11.1 INTRODUCTION

The field of artificial intelligence (AI) has witnessed a period of unprecedented progress in recent years.[1] Among its breakthroughs, generative AI (GenAI) has emerged as a transformative force, enabling machines to create original text, images, music, and code with remarkable sophistication.[2] This surge in capabilities has not only opened exciting new avenues for creative expression and problem-solving across multiple economic sectors and diverse industries, but has also intensified discussions around the responsible development and governance of AI.[3] This chapter delves into the evolving landscape of global AI governance, exploring the present and future of international collaboration on GenAI through an analysis of the Group of Seven's (G7) Hiroshima AI Process.

With the dramatic technological innovations in GenAI, its governance and regulatory trajectory have been thrown into sharp focus. This critical conversation has transcended domestic regulations within national borders, and has opened up space for the advancement of international cooperation.[4] Some foundational cross-border developments in this direction include the Council of Europe Framework Convention on Artificial Intelligence and Human Rights,

[1] M. Roser, 'The Brief History of Artificial Intelligence: The World Has Changed Fast – What Might Be Next?' (Our World in Data, 2022). Available at: https://ourworldindata.org/brief-history-of-ai; US Government Accountability Office, 'Artificial Intelligence's Use and Rapid Growth Highlight Its Possibilities and Perils' (2023). Available at: www.gao.gov/blog/artificial-intelligences-use-and-rapid-growth-highlight-its-possibilities-and-perils; K. Georgieva, 'AI Will Transform the Global Economy. Let's Make Sure It Benefits Humanity' (International Monetary Fund Blog, 2024). Available at: www.imf.org/en/blogs/articles/2024/01/14/ai-will-transform-the-global-economy-lets-make-sure-it-benefits-humanity; McKinsey & Company, 'What's the Future of Generative AI?' (2023). Available at: www.mckinsey.com/featured-insights/mckinsey-explainers/whats-the-future-of-generative-ai-an-early-view-in-15-charts; J. P. Bharadiya, R. K. Thomas, and F. Ahmed, 'Rise of Artificial Intelligence in Business and Industry' (2023) 25(3) *Journal of Engineering Research and Reports*, 85–103. Available at: https://doi.org/10.9734/jerr/2023/v25i3893. See generally A. Agrawal, J. Gans, and A. Goldfarb, *Prediction Machines* (Harvard Business Review Press, 2018); E. Brynjolfsson and A. McAfee, *The Second Machine Age: Work, Progress, and Prosperity in a Time of Brilliant Technologies* (W. W. Norton, 2014).

[2] See Brynjolfsson and McAfee, *The Second Machine Age*. See also S. Feuerriegel et al., 'Generative AI' (2024) 66 *Business Information Systems Engineering*, 111–126; McKinsey & Company, 'What Is Generative AI' (2024). Available at: www.mckinsey.com/featured-insights/mckinsey-explainers/what-is-generative-ai.

[3] See generally discussion below Section 11.2.

[4] See discussion below Section 11.2.1.

Democracy and the Rule of Law (AI Treaty),[5] signed by ten nations and regions including the European Union, the United States, and the United Kingdom as of September 2024; the Bletchley Declaration,[6] a document endorsed by twenty-nine nations as a result of the AI Safety Summit in November 2023; and the UN AI Advisory Body's Final Report on Governing AI for Humanity,[7] published in September 2024.

Among these developments, particularly significant is the Hiroshima AI Process Comprehensive Policy Framework[8] (the Comprehensive Framework) published by the G7 nations in December 2023. This is the first policy package agreed upon by the democratic leaders of the G7 to effectively steward principles for safeguarding individual rights and enhancing systems of trust regarding AI systems, namely advanced GenAI. On May 2, 2024, Japanese Prime Minister Kishida Fumio announced the launch of the "Hiroshima AI Process Friends Group" at the Meeting of the Council at Ministerial Level of the Organisation for Economic Co-operation and Development (OECD).[9] This initiative, supported by forty-nine countries and regions – primarily OECD members – aims to foster international cooperation for ensuring global access to safe, secure, and trustworthy generative artificial intelligence (AI).[10] As this chapter will explore, the Comprehensive Framework sends a promising signal of international alignment on the development of advanced GenAI systems (advanced AI systems) in respect of the rule of law, human rights, due process, diversity, fairness and non-discrimination, democracy, and human-centricity.[11]

11.2 THE DIRECTION OF GENAI GOVERNANCE: A HISTORICAL OVERVIEW AND INTERNATIONAL INITIATIVES

The early 2020s saw a remarkable surge in GenAI capabilities, driven by advancements in attention techniques and computing power.[12] This technological leap coincided with a pivotal socio-regulatory shift, embodied by the expanded reach of GenAI through free-to-use platforms

[5] Available at: www.coe.int/en/web/conventions/full-list?module = treaty-detail&treatynum = 225.

[6] AI Safety Summit, 'The Bletchley Declaration' (2023). Available at: www.gov.uk/government/publications/ai-safety-summit-2023-the-bletchley-declaration/the-bletchley-declaration-by-countries-attending-the-ai-safety-summit-1-2-november-2023.

[7] UN Secretary-General's AI Advisory Body, 'Final Report on Governing AI for Humanity' (2024). Available at: www.un.org/sites/un2.un.org/files/governing_ai_for_humanity_final_report_en.pdf.

[8] The Comprehensive Framework consists of four elements: (i) the OECD's Report towards a G7 Common Understanding on Generative AI; (ii) the International Guiding Principles for All AI Actors and for Organizations Developing Advanced AI Systems; (iii) the International Code of Conduct for Organizations Developing Advanced AI Systems; and (iv) Project-Based Cooperation. See generally discussion below in Section 11.3.1. See also Table 11.1. The Group of Seven (G7), 'Hiroshima Process International Code of Conduct for Organizations Developing Advanced AI Systems'. Available at: www.mofa.go.jp/files/100573473.pdf.

[9] Hiroshima AI Process, 'Supporters, Member Countries of the Hiroshima AI Process Friends Group (in alphabetical order)' (Ministry of Internal Affairs and Communications, June 2024). Available at: www.soumu.go.jp/hiroshimaaiprocess/en/supporters.html; Ministry of Foreign Affairs of Japan, 'Prime Minister Kishida's Attendance at the Side Event on Generative AI at the OECD Ministerial Council Meeting' (2 May 2024). Available at: www.mofa.go.jp/ecm/ec/pageite_000001_00332.html; 'Japan's Kishida Unveils a Framework for Global Regulation of Generative AI' (Associated Press, 3 May 2024). Available at: https://apnews.com/article/oecdai-japan-kishida-artificial-intelligence-023ac08e04db5a2109cf35f8b8c9b102.

[10] Hiroshima AI Process, 'Supporters'; Ministry of Foreign Affairs of Japan, 'Prime Minister Kishida's attendance'; 'Japan's Kishida Unveils a Framework for Global Regulation of Generative AI'.

[11] Hiroshima AI Process, 'Supporters'; Ministry of Foreign Affairs of Japan, 'Prime Minister Kishida's attendance'; 'Japan's Kishida Unveils a Framework for Global Regulation of Generative AI'.

[12] Ashish Vaswani et al., 'Attention Is All You Need' (2017). Available at: https://arxiv.org/abs/1706.03762.

and related cloud services.[13] Ease of access to GenAI technology shattered the barrier to entry, making GenAI tools readily available at diverse scales, affecting large and small companies, established institutions and startups, and even individual creators. The advent of GenAI marked a transformative moment in the state of AI technology and its interaction with the public, propelling AI to the forefront of innovation and development, as well as the governance spotlight. This expansion was underscored by a staggering 425 percent increase in venture capital investments in GenAI from 2020 to mid-2023,[14] highlighting the market's belief in the technology's transformative potential. The rise of GenAI sparked rapid integration of the technology across diverse industries such as medicine, finance, transportation, and many more, with the potential application horizons and a full-integration picture of the technology still uncertain.[15] The widespread adoption of GenAI also introduced new challenges and increased the magnitude of the technology's risks. The very accessibility that empowered so many also brought use risks to new and larger audiences, including data privacy concerns, potential biased outcomes given discriminatory tendencies in the training data, the undermining of intellectual property rights, potential misuse of the technology by private and public agents, and ethical and democratic concerns surrounding manipulated content. The potential for GenAI to further embed itself into various markets in increasingly complex ways raises pressing regulatory questions that require input from multiple stakeholders, including policymakers, industry leaders, and civil society. In short, the broad and profound impact represented by the democratization of GenAI's benefits and risks has prompted a new wave of debate on governance aimed at adapting to this rapidly evolving technology.

11.2.1 *A Short History of AI Governance*

Following the deep learning breakthroughs of the early 2010s,[16] AI adoption surged across a myriad of industries and sectors.[17] This rapid integration process brought to light a multitude of potential risks. From fatal accidents involving autonomous vehicles[18] to discriminatory hiring

[13] B. Marr, 'A Short History of ChatGPT: How We Got to Where We Are Today' (Forbes, 2023). Available at: www.forbes.com/sites/bernardmarr/2023/05/19/a-short-history-of-chatgpt-how-we-got-to-where-we-are-today/?sh=7b916f0d674f; D. Leslie, 'Does the Sun Rise for ChatGPT? Scientific Discovery in the Age of Generative AI' (*AI Ethics*, July 2023). Available at: https://doi.org/10.1007/s43681-023-00315-3; T. Orchard and L. Tasiemski, 'The Rise of Generative AI and Possible Effects on the Economy' (2023) 9(2) *Economics and Business Review* 9–16.

[14] See Marr, 'A Short History of ChatGPT'; O. Catsaros, 'Generative AI to Become a $1.3 Trillion Market by 2032, Research Finds' (Bloomberg, 2023). Available at: www.bloomberg.com/company/press/generative-ai-to-become-a-1-3-trillion-market-by-2032-research-finds/.

[15] McKinsey & Company, 'The State of AI in 2023: Generative AI's Breakout Year' (2023). Available at: www.mckinsey.com/capabilities/quantumblack/our-insights/the-state-of-ai-in-2023-generative-ais-breakout-year#.

[16] Y. LeCun et al., 'Deep Learning' (2015) 521(7553) *Nature*, 436–444. Available at: https://doi.org/10.1038/nature14539; J. P. Bharadiya, R. K. Thomas, and F. Ahmed, 'Rise of Artificial Intelligence in Business and Industry' (2023) 25(3) *Journal of Engineering Research and Reports* 85–103. Available at: https://doi.org/10.9734/jerr/2023/v25i3893; D. Pitchford, 'A Decade of Advancements as We Enter a New Age of AI' (Forbes, 2019). Available at: www.forbes.com/sites/danielpitchford/2020/12/31/a-decade-of-advancements-as-we-enter-a-new-age-of-ai/?sh=4de6e1b54055.

[17] See Pitchford, 'A Decade of Advancements'. See also McKinsey & Company, 'The State of AI in 2023'.

[18] See US Department of Transportation National Highway Traffic Safety Administration, 'Summary Report: Standing General Order on Crash Reporting for Automated Driving Systems' (2022). Available at: www.nhtsa.gov/sites/nhtsa.gov/files/2022-06/ADS-SGO-Report-June-2022.pdf; F. Siddiqui and J. Merrill, '17 Fatalities, 736 Crashes: The Shocking Toll of Tesla's Autopilot' (*The Washington Post*, 10 June 2023). Available at: www.washingtonpost.com/technology/2023/06/10/tesla-autopilot-crashes-elon-musk/; Associated Press, 'Cruise Recalls All Self-Driving Cars after Grisly Accident and California Ban' (*The Guardian*, 8 November 2023). Available at: www.theguardian.com/technology/2023/nov/08/cruise-recall-self-driving-cars-gm.

practices by AI algorithms,[19] the real-world consequences of AI development have become increasingly evident. Furthermore, the manipulation of financial markets by algorithmic trading and the spread of misinformation on social media platforms highlight the broader societal concerns surrounding AI.[20]

Fueled by the growing awareness of AI risks in the mid-2010s, national governments (including G7 members), international organizations, tech companies, and non-profits launched a wave of policy and principle publications. Prominent examples include the Ethics Guidelines for Trustworthy AI by the European Union (EU) in 2019, the Recommendation of the Council on Artificial Intelligence by the Organisation for Economic Co-operation and Development (OECD) in 2019, and the Recommendation on the Ethics of Artificial Intelligence by the United Nations Educational, Scientific and Cultural Organization (UNESCO) in 2021. These publications emphasized pairing AI development with core values like human rights, democracy, and sustainability, alongside key principles such as fairness, privacy, safety, security, transparency, explainability, and accountability.

While fundamental values and AI principles provide a crucial foundation, substantiating them into implementable standards for AI systems remains a challenge – and addressing this challenge requires concrete and material guidance. Various initiatives have been undertaken at different governance levels to bridge this gap. At the national level, examples include the United States' AI Risk Management Framework (RMF) published by the National Institute of Standards and Technology (NIST) in January 2023;[21] and Japan's AI Governance Guidelines for Business Operators published in April 2024.[22] At the supranational and international levels, efforts such as the aforementioned EU's Ethics Guidelines for Trustworthy AI (2019), the OECD's AI Recommendations (2019), and UNESCO's AI Ethics Recommendation (2021) provide high-level frameworks to guide responsible AI development and governance. Additionally, non-governmental organizations like the International Organization for Standardization (ISO) have contributed to this momentum by issuing international standards on AI governance, with the AI management system standard (ISO/IEC 42001:2023) being published in December 2023. The Human Rights, Democracy, and the Rule of Law Assurance Framework (HUDERAF), proposed by the Alan Turing Institute to the Council of Europe's Ad Hoc Committee on Artificial Intelligence, is another significant example of AI risk management and stakeholder engagement. Collectively, these diverse approaches underscore the ongoing efforts to transform abstract AI principles into a practical and implementable reality for AI governance.

Despite sharing a common direction, many of these published guidelines and principles for responsible AI development lack legally binding force, making them examples of "soft law." While compliance with these documents helps companies establish risk prevention strategies and forward-looking accountability measures, there are no guarantees or enforceability measures to ensure adherence to these standards. Thus, to advance stronger commitment to AI governance – in particular addressing AI systems that pose high risks – there has been active movement

[19] L. Andrews and H. Bucher, 'Automating Discrimination: AI Hiring Practices and Gender Inequality' (2022) 44 *Cardozo Law Review*, 145.

[20] E. Ferrara, 'GenAI against Humanity: Nefarious Applications of Generative Artificial Intelligence and Large Language Models' (2024) *Journal of Computational Social Sciences*. Available at: https://doi.org/10.1007/s42001-024-00250-1.

[21] United States Department of Commerce, National Institute of Standards and Technology, 'Artificial Intelligence Risk Management Framework (AI RMF 1.0) (2023). Available at: https://nvlpubs.nist.gov/nistpubs/ai/nist.ai.100-1.pdf.

[22] Japan Ministry of Internal Affairs and Communications, Ministry of Economy, Trade and Industry, 'AI Guidelines for Business Ver1.0' (2024) (Japan Guidelines for Business or AI Guidelines for Business). Available at: www.meti.go.jp/shingikai/mono_info_service/ai_shakai_jisso/pdf/20240419_9.pdf.

toward introducing regulations with legally binding force. For instance, the European Commission introduced the draft Artificial Intelligence Act (AI Act) in 2021 (subsequently approved by the EU Parliament in March, 2024),[23] focusing most of its compliance requirements on high-risk systems, and even banning certain AI uses when the risks they present are deemed unacceptable.[24] Similarly, Canada presented the Artificial Intelligence and Data Act (AIDA) in 2022 – an ongoing legislative proposal which focuses on establishing compliance requirements for high-impact AI applications. The United States has also seen a surge in legislative activity targeted at AI, with more than 105 draft bills introduced – over thirty-five of them specifically addressing risk mitigation in AI applications.[25]

The escalation of GenAI and foundation models has presented a new layer of complexity to the already challenging landscape of AI governance. While conventional AI faced issues such as limited explainability, diverse stakeholders, and rapid evolution, foundation models expand the scope and reach of these challenges.[26] The ability of these systems to be applied in countless contexts, and to be easily accessed and operated by the general public, creates an even more intricate risk environment. In recognition of this risk, there has been a surge in global efforts to establish rules and foster international cooperation specifically targeting foundation and GenAI models. The EU AI Act, for example, incorporated provisions specifically related to these general-purpose AI systems at the final stages of the legislative process in the parliament.[27] Similarly, the Chinese government implemented Interim Measures for the Administration of Generative Artificial Intelligence Services in August 2023,[28] marking a growing trend of major economies developing new regulatory approaches to address these emerging technologies.

The brief history of AI governance is characterized by a complex and multidimensional balancing act between innovation and regulation, adjustment to a rapidly advancing technology, and the integration of multi-vector interests that encompass the technology industry, the general public, and regulators. While these groups can have differing priorities, there is also a growing recognition of the need for collaboration and cohesive advancement. G7 democracies, in particular, find common ground in core principles like human rights and democratic values, grounding their regulatory approaches on the values of transparency, explainability, and bias prevention, forming a common foundation for responsible GenAI development.[29] (See Figure 11.1 illustrating the overall structure of AI governance and key documents related to each layer.)

[23] See European Parliament Legislative Resolution of 13 March 2024 on the Proposal for a regulation of the European Parliament and of the Council on Laying Down Harmonised Rules on Artificial Intelligence (Artificial Intelligence Act) and Amending certain Union Legislative Acts (COM(2021)0206 – C9-0146/2021 – 2021/0106(COD)) (EU AI Act or AI Act). Available at: www.europarl.europa.eu/doceo/document/TA-9-2024-0138_EN.pdf.

[24] See EU AI Act at Chapter II.

[25] American Action Forum, 'AI Legislation Tracker'. Available at: www.americanactionforum.org/list-of-proposed-ai-bills-table/ (AAF AI Legislation Tracker).

[26] See discussion above in Section 11.2.

[27] Regulation (EU) 2024/1689 of the European Parliament and of the Council of 13 June 2024 laying down harmonised rules on artificial intelligence and amending Regulations (EC) No. 300/2008, (EU) No. 167/2013, (EU) No. 168/2013, (EU) 2018/858, (EU) 2018/1139 and (EU) 2019/2144 and Directives 2014/90/EU, (EU) 2016/797 and (EU) 2020/1828 (Artificial Intelligence Act) (Text with EEA relevance) (EU AI Act). PE/24/2024/REV/1 OJ L, 2024/1689, 12.7.2024, ELI. Available at: http://data.europa.eu/eli/reg/2024/1689/oj (EU AI Act).

[28] Cyberspace Administration of China, National Development and Reform Commission, Ministry of Education, Ministry of Science and Technology, Ministry of Industry and Information Technology, Ministry of Public Security, and State Administration of Radio, 'Interim Measures for the Management of Generative Artificial Intelligence Services' (2023). Available at: www.cac.gov.cn/2023-07/13/c_1690898327029107.htm.

[29] See discussion below Section 11.2.2.

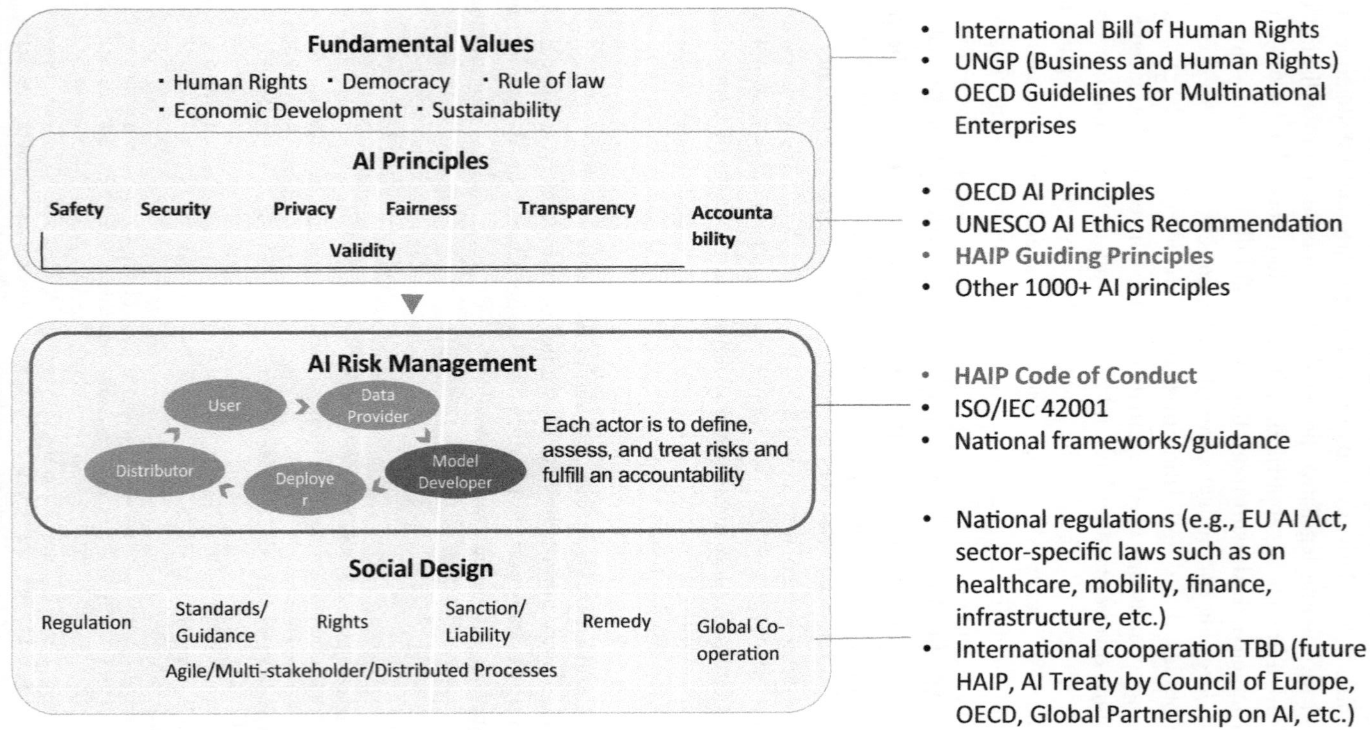

FIGURE 11.1 Overall structure of AI governance and key documents related to each layer

11.2.2 *Advancing International Collaboration*

This subsection first provides an overview of key international AI governance initiatives, including significant documents and declarations such as the G7's Hiroshima AI Process (HAIP) Comprehensive Framework, the Bletchley Declaration, the UN's "Governing AI for Humanity" report, and the Council of Europe's AI Treaty. These documents highlight various efforts to establish global standards and frameworks for AI governance. Subsequently, the discussion will examine the pivotal role of the G7's framework in shaping global AI governance. The G7's role in global AI policies is underscored by its active participation in major international initiatives and its significant economic, regulatory, and technological impact.

11.2.2.1 Key International AI Initiatives

As countries develop domestic regulations for GenAI, efforts to strengthen international cooperation are also gaining momentum.[30] The G7 stands as one of the most impactful forums for such international coordination. During the May 2023 summit, G7 leaders committed to establishing the HAIP by the end of the year[31] to advance collaborative policy development on GenAI systems. Within six months, the G7 digital and tech ministers had delivered the HAIP Comprehensive Framework.[32] This framework prioritizes proactive risk management and governance, transparency, and accountability across the AI lifecycle.[33] Additionally, it emphasizes anchoring advanced AI development in human rights and democratic values, while fostering the use of AI for tackling global challenges such as climate change, healthcare, and education.[34]

The Bletchley Declaration, emerging from the AI Safety Summit held in the United Kingdom in November 2023, stands as another significant milestone in international AI collaboration. This declaration addresses crucial aspects of AI safety such as the protection of human rights, transparency, explainability, fairness, accountability, human oversight, bias mitigation, and privacy and data protection.[35] Additionally, it highlights potential risks associated with the capability to manipulate or generate deceptive content.[36] Endorsed by twenty-nine countries and regions, the signatories encompass not only G7 and OECD nations but also partners from the Middle East, Africa, South America, and Asia, notably including China.[37] At the second AI Safety Summit held in Seoul in May 2024, thirty countries and regions affirmed the need for collaborative international approaches to respond to rapid advancements in AI technologies and

[30] See discussion above Section 11.2.1.

[31] OECD, 'G7 Hiroshima Process on Generative Artificial Intelligence (AI): Towards a G7 Common Understanding on Generative AI' (OECD Publishing, 2023), at 6. Available at: https://doi.org/10.1787/bf3c0c60-en; Government of Japan, 'The Hiroshima AI Process: Leading the Global Challenge to Shape Inclusive Governance for Generative AI' (Kizuna, 2024). Available at: www.japan.go.jp/kizuna/2024/02/hiroshima_ai_process.html.

[32] See sources cited above in note 10.

[33] Ibid. See also 'Hiroshima Process International Code of Conduct for Organizations Developing Advanced AI Systems' at Arts. 1–7, 11.

[34] See sources cited above note 10. See also 'Hiroshima Process International Code of Conduct for Organizations Developing Advanced AI Systems' at Arts. 8–10.

[35] See AI Safety Summit, 'The Bletchley Declaration'.

[36] Ibid.

[37] Ibid.

their impact on our societies and economies, reiterating the need for safety, and highlighting inclusion and innovation as critical priorities for global convergence.[38]

The United Nations (UN) is also active in the formation of an international AI governance body. In September 2024, the UN AI Advisory Body issued the "Final Report on Governing AI for Humanity."[39] This document outlines seven key recommendations for AI governance. These include creating an International Scientific Panel on AI to guide research and knowledge sharing, and establishing a Policy Dialogue on AI Governance to promote consistent regulations. It also suggests forming an AI Standards Exchange to align standards globally and setting up a Capacity Development Network to enhance training and resources for AI. Additionally, a Global Fund for AI is recommended to support countries with limited AI capabilities, along with a Global AI Data Framework to ensure responsible data management. Finally, the document proposes an AI Office within the UN Secretariat to coordinate these initiatives and ensure a unified approach to AI governance.

In March 2024, the Committee on Artificial Intelligence (CAI) of the Council of Europe introduced the Draft Framework Convention on Artificial Intelligence, Human Rights, Democracy, and the Rule of Law (AI Treaty), a groundbreaking treaty on AI governance that sets a high bar on responsible AI development.[40] The AI Treaty, adopted in May 2024,[41] emphasizes the obligation of signatory nations (parties to the Convention) to proactively ensure AI activities are aligned with human rights, democratic integrity, and the rule of law. The treaty advocates for protective measures governing the AI lifecycle – including mechanisms for accountability[42] and transparency[43] – and introduces comprehensive risk management frameworks.[44] Furthermore, it calls for robust remedies and procedural protective measures against rights violations,[45] promotes rigorous risk and impact assessments,[46] and delineates duties for international cooperation and implementation, focusing on nondiscrimination and rights protection.[47] The AI Treaty was signed by ten nations and regions including the European Union, the United States, and the United Kingdom as of September 2024.

Nations participating in these initiatives vary. (See Figure 11.2 mapping the jurisdictions' structural involvement in the abovementioned international processes.)

11.2.2.2 The Importance of the G7's AI Governance Framework

Figure 11.2 shows why and how the G7 HAIP has significance in global rule-making on advanced AI systems. First, the G7 nations participate in all significant initiatives previously

[38] Seoul Ministerial Statement for Advancing AI Safety, Innovation and Inclusivity: AI Seoul Summit 2024. Available at: www.gov.uk/government/publications/seoul-ministerial-statement-for-advancing-ai-safety-innovation-and-inclusivity-ai-seoul-summit-2024/seoul-ministerial-statement-for-advancing-ai-safety-innovation-and-inclusivity-ai-seoul-summit-2024. It should be noted that China did not participate in this second Statement.

[39] United Nations AI Advisory Body, 'Governing AI for Humanity' (December 2023). Available at: www.un.org/sites/un2.un.org/files/ai_advisory_body_interim_report.pdf.

[40] Council of Europe, 'Draft Framework Convention on Artificial Intelligence, Human Rights, Democracy, and the Rule of Law' (Committee on AI (CAI), 2023), 28, p. 3 (preamble). Available at: https://search.coe.int/cm/pages/result_details.aspx?objectid=0900001680aee411.

[41] Council of Europe, 'Committee on Artificial Intelligence (CAI)'. Available at: www.coe.int/en/web/artificial-intelligence/cai.

[42] Ibid., Art. 8.

[43] Ibid., Art. 7.

[44] Ibid., Art. 16.

[45] Ibid., Art. 15.

[46] Ibid., Art. 16.

[47] Ibid., Art. 25.

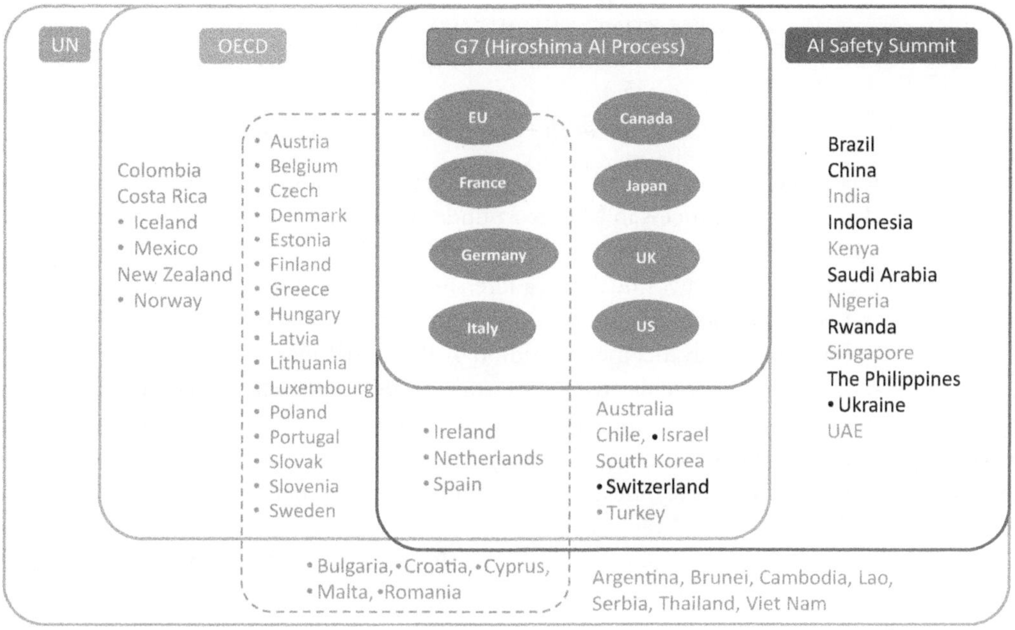

FIGURE 11.2 The global AI governance landscape

Note:

- The EU is itself considered a "non-enumerated member" of the G7, with the EU Council and EU Commission Presidents both participating in the leaders' summit.
- The countries shown in dark grey indicate those participating in the Hiroshima AI Process Friends Group (as of May 2, 2024).
- The G7 + the EU members + the nations with dots are the members or observers of the Council of Europe, the host organization of the AI Treaty.

mentioned: the AI Safety Summit, the UN Advisory Body, and the AI Treaty. Second, the G7 represents a group of nations with significant economic, regulatory, and technological impact and leadership. In 2023, the gross domestic product (GDP) of the G7 countries (excluding the EU, which is a non-enumerated member) accounted for approximately 26.4 percent of the global total.[48] Moreover, many global companies developing advanced AI systems are based in one of the G7 member countries.[49] Establishing interoperable rules for advanced AI systems in these countries is crucial to avoid duplicative compliance costs and to facilitate innovation on a global scale. Third, the G7 is a group of exclusively democratic nations, unlike more inclusive bodies like the UN or the AI Safety Summit.[50] Its shared commitment to democratic principles facilitates a focus on common values, equipping the HAIP to serve as a key foundation, not just for safety but also for realizing fundamental values such as human rights, democracy, and the rule of law in the development and implementation of advanced AI systems.

[48] World Economics, 'G7' (2024). Available at: www.worldeconomics.com/Regions/G7/. For a more fulsome comparative state of corporate presence throughout the G7 and internationally, see also A. Murphy and H. Tucker, 'The Global 2000' (Forbes, 2023). Available at: www.forbes.com/lists/global2000/?sh = 763a56c55ac0.

[49] T. Keary, 'Top 10 Countries Leading in AI Research & Technology in 2024' (Techopedia, 2024). Available at: www.techopedia.com/top-10-countries-leading-in-ai-research-technology.

[50] See Figure 11.2.

11.3 ANALYZING THE HIROSHIMA AI PROCESS COMPREHENSIVE FRAMEWORK

11.3.1 *Structure of the Comprehensive Framework*

In response to the rapid development and global spread of advanced AI, the G7 nations launched the Hiroshima AI Process in May 2023 under Japan's presidency.[51] This international forum aims to establish common ground for responsible AI development and use. It focuses on fostering safe, secure, and trustworthy AI by addressing key ethical issues, promoting collaboration on research and development, and encouraging international standards for a future where humanity benefits from AI advancements. Although the HAIP focuses on the governance of advanced AI systems, the Comprehensive Framework avoids a rigid definition of this technology by providing the tentative delineation of "the most advanced AI systems, including the most advanced foundation models and generative AI systems."[52] This flexibility likely reflects a desire to remain adaptive to future advancements in AI performance, functionalities, and deployment landscapes.

The Comprehensive Framework consists of four elements (see Table 11.1).

The HAIP Comprehensive Framework consists of four elements, each with its respective functionality, as outlined below:[53] (i) the OECD's Report towards a G7 Common Understanding on Generative AI, serves as a background analysis of opportunities and risks of Advanced AI Systems; (ii) the International Guiding Principles for All AI Actors (HIGP), provides twelve general principles for all AI actors in designing, developing, deploying, providing, and using advanced AI systems without detailed guidance; (iii) the International Code of Conduct for Organizations Developing Advanced AI Systems (HCoC), provides a set of detailed instructions for the developers of Advanced AI Systems under eleven general principles provided in accordance with the HIGP; and finally (iv) project-based cooperation on AI, includes international collaborations on items such as content authentication and labeling of AI-generated content.

The following section summarizes the contents of the HIGP and HCoC.

11.3.2 *Contents of the International Guiding Principles*

The HIGP is a comprehensive set of values and best practices promoting responsible development and use of advanced AI on a global scale. It consists of twelve core principles (noted below) that serve as a foundation for responsible AI governance. These principles closely mirror the values and approaches that G7 nations are already exploring for their individual AI governance frameworks.[54] The analysis carried out in this chapter divides the twelve principles into the following three groups (see Table 11.2):

(i) *Risk management and governance*: Recommended actions to assess and mitigate risks associated with AI systems, ensuring they are reduced to a level deemed acceptable by relevant stakeholders.

[51] See discussion above Section 11.2.2.

[52] European Commission, 'Hiroshima Process International Guiding Principles for Advanced AI System' (2023). Available at: https://digital-strategy.ec.europa.eu/en/library/hiroshima-process-international-guiding-principles-advanced-ai-system.

[53] See Table 11.1.

[54] See discussion below Section 11.4.1. See also Appendix.

TABLE 11.1 *Four elements of the HAIP Comprehensive Framework*

(1) *The OECD's Report towards a G7 Common Understanding on Generative AI* (issued in September 2023)
(2) *International Guiding Principles for All AI Actors and for Organizations Developing Advanced AI Systems (HIGP)* • Eleven principles on design, development, deployment, and provision of advanced AI + 1 principle on use of it • Summarized in this chapter at Section 11.3.2.
(3) *International Code of Conduct for Organizations Developing Advanced AI Systems (HCoC)* • Specific instructions for advanced AI developers under the same eleven principles as HIGP • Summarized in this chapter at Section 11.3.3.
(4) *Project-based cooperation*
Expected to contribute to reliable content authentication and provenance mechanisms, as well as labeling mechanisms

TABLE 11.2 *Elements of HIGP*

Risk management and governance	Stakeholder engagement	Ethical and societal considerations
1. Risk identification and mitigation 2. Vulnerability and misuse management after deployment 5. Governance and risk management 6. Security investments 7. Content authentication 11. Data quality, personal data and intellectual property protection	3. Transparency and accountability 4. Responsible information sharing 12. Trustworthy and responsible use of advanced AI (*not included in the HCoC)	8. Research prioritization for societal safety 9. AI for global challenges 10. Development of international technical standards

*The numerals listed for each item correspond to the articles assigned in the HIGP and HCoC.
**The abbreviations for each principle and their categorization have been devised by the authors.

(ii) *Stakeholder engagement*: Recommended actions to ensure clear communication with, and accountability to, all relevant stakeholders.

(iii) *Ethical and societal considerations*: Recommended actions to ensure that the development, deployment, and usage of AI are in alignment with ethical standards and societal values.

11.3.3 *Overview of the Code of Conduct*

Building on eleven of the twelve HIGP core principles,[55] the HCoC translates these guiding parameters and materializes them into a more specific code of practice for organizations developing and deploying advanced AI systems. The HCoC provides a comprehensive roadmap for AI processes and risk mitigation, outlining general actionable items on matters of risk management and governance, stakeholder engagement, and ethical considerations.[56]

[55] In this case, with the exclusion of 'Trustworthy and Responsible Use of Advanced AI'.
[56] G7, 'Hiroshima Process'.

Risk Management and Governance

The HCoC emphasizes in items 1, 2, 5, 6, 7, and 11 the importance of comprehensive risk management for organizations developing advanced AI across the lifecycle of development and implementation. This includes:

1. Risk Identification and Mitigation: Implementing rigorous testing throughout the AI lifecycle, such as red-teaming, to identify and address potential safety, security, and trustworthiness issues.
2. Vulnerability and Misuse Management after Deployment: Post-deployment monitoring for vulnerabilities and misuse, with an emphasis on enabling third-party and user vulnerability reporting, possibly via bounty systems.
5. Governance and Risk Management Policies: Transparency commitments for organizations regarding governance and risk management policies, regularly updating users on privacy and mitigation measures.
6. Security Investments: Robust enforcement of security measures throughout the AI lifecycle to protect critical system components against threats.
7. Content Authentication: Development of content authentication methods (e.g. watermarking) to help users identify AI-generated content.
11. Data Quality, Personal Data, and Intellectual Property Protection: Prioritization of data integrity, addressing bias, upholding privacy, and respecting intellectual property, as well as encouraging alignment with relevant legal standards.

Stakeholder Engagement

The HCoC highlights in items 3 and 4 the critical role of transparency and multi-stakeholder engagement.

3. Transparency and Accountability: Public transparency for organizations developing advanced AI is emphasized. This includes reporting on both the capabilities of their AI systems and their limitations.
4. Responsible Information Sharing: Organizations are encouraged to share information on potential risks, incidents, and best practices with each other, including industry, governments, academia, and the public.

Ethical and Societal Considerations

The HCoC establishes in items 8, 9, and 10 a series of parameters to ensure AI is developed and deployed within the boundaries of human rights, democracy, and to address global challenges.

8. Research Prioritization for Societal Safety: Collaborative research is emphasized to advance AI safety, security, and trustworthiness, focusing on key risks like upholding democratic values, respecting human rights, and protecting vulnerable groups.
9. AI for Global Challenges: Development of advanced AI systems is prioritized to address global challenges such as climate change, health, and education. This aligns with the UN Sustainable Development Goals.
10. Development of International Technical Standards: Contribution to the development and use of international technical standards is encouraged. These include practices to promote transparency by allowing users to identify AI-generated content (e.g. watermarking), testing methodologies, and cybersecurity policies.

A more detailed summary of HCoC is presented in Table 11.3.

TABLE 11.3 *Summary of HCoC*

No.	Principle	Code of conduct summary
	Risk management and governance	
1	Risk identification and mitigation	Organizations should take appropriate measures to identify, evaluate, and mitigate risks throughout the development and deployment of advanced AI systems. This includes diverse testing methods like red-teaming and ensuring systems are trustworthy, safe, and secure throughout their lifecycle.
2	Vulnerability and misuse management after deployment	After deployment, organizations should monitor for vulnerabilities, incidents, and misuse, adapting their responses based on the level of risk. They are also encouraged to facilitate third-party and user reporting of vulnerabilities through mechanisms such as bounty systems.
5	Governance and risk management policies	Organizations should develop and disclose governance and risk management policies regarding advanced AI systems, including privacy policies and mitigation measures, grounded in a risk-based approach. These policies should be updated regularly and include organizational mechanisms for their implementation.
6	Security investments	Organizations should invest in and implement robust security controls across the lifecycle of advanced AI systems, including physical security, cybersecurity, and safeguards against insider threats. This aims to secure model weights, algorithms, servers, and datasets appropriately.
7	Content authentication	Organizations should endeavor to develop reliable content authentication and provenance mechanisms, such as watermarking, to enable users to identify AI-generated content. This includes implementing tools or APIs that allow users to verify the origin of content created with the organization's advanced AI systems.
11	Data quality, personal data and intellectual property protection	Organizations should take measures to ensure data quality and mitigate harmful biases through transparency, privacy-preserving training techniques, and/or testing and fine-tuning. They are also encouraged to implement measures to respect privacy and intellectual property rights and compliance with applicable legal frameworks.
Stakeholder engagement		
3	Transparency and accountability	Organizations should ensure transparency by reporting on their advanced AI systems' capabilities and limitations, aiming to clarify their safe and appropriate use. This involves sharing meaningful information through transparency reports about the systems' safety, security, societal impacts, and any limitations that might affect their use.
4	Responsible information sharing	Organizations should share information on safety and security risks, and report incidents in a responsible manner. This collaboration extends across the development community, including industry and academia, to foster the adoption of best practices and standards for security and trustworthiness of advanced AI systems.

(continued)

TABLE 11.3 (*cont.*)

No.	Principle	Code of conduct summary
		Risk management and governance
Ethical and societal considerations		
8	Research prioritization for societal safety	Organizations should invest in research to mitigate societal, safety, and security risks, such as prioritizing research on upholding democratic values, respecting human rights, protecting children and vulnerable groups, safeguarding intellectual property rights and privacy, and avoiding harmful bias, mis- and disinformation, and information manipulation.
9	AI for global challenges	Organizations should aim their AI development efforts towards addressing major global challenges, such as climate change, health, and education. This aligns with supporting progress on the United Nations Sustainable Development Goals and encourages AI to be developed for the benefit of all.
10	Development of international technical standards	Organizations should contribute to the development and adoption of international technical standards for AI, including best practices for security, content authentication, and public reporting. This effort seeks to promote interoperability and help distinguish AI-generated content from human-created content.

*The numerals listed for each item correspond to those assigned in the HIGP and HCoC.
**The abbreviations for each principle and their categorization have been devised by the authors.

11.4 TOWARDS INTEROPERABLE FRAMEWORKS FOR ADVANCED GENAI SYSTEMS

Nations and institutions worldwide are grappling with risks posed by GenAI, recognizing the need for proactive measures to ensure its responsible development and deployment, while striving to balance these concerns with the promotion of innovation and global competitiveness.[57] Given GenAI's broad societal reach and substantial economic impact,[58] fostering international interoperability between risk management and regulatory systems emerges as a potential crucial nexus for its efficient and effective advancement.

The HCoC, as articulated in the HAIP Comprehensive Framework, is intended to serve as a pivotal instrument to enhance interoperability between various global AI governance frameworks.[59] But what are mechanisms or functionalities that make this interoperability possible? And how compatible is the HCoC with the G7 members' regulatory frameworks? First, the HCoC operates as a potent non-binding "common guidance." Although not legally enforceable, the gravitas and direction of the document can wield significant practical influence as soft law.[60]

[57] See discussion above Section 11.2.1.

[58] See discussion above Section 11.2.

[59] G7, 'Hiroshima AI Process G7 Digital & Tech Ministers' Statement' (2023) at 1. Available at: www.soumu.go.jp/hiroshimaaiprocess/pdf/document02_en.pdf.

[60] See generally K. Guruparan and J. Zerk, 'Influence of Soft Law Grows in International Governance' (Chatham House, 2021). Available at: www.chathamhouse.org/2021/06/influence-soft-law-grows-international-governance; M. Barelli, 'The Role of Soft Law in the International Legal System: The Case of the United Nations Declaration on the Rights of Indigenous Peoples' (2009) 58(4) *International and Comparative Law Quarterly*, 957–983. Available at:

Soft law documents like the HCoC can shape compliance behaviors either as the foundation for good corporate governance or in anticipation of further regulation; they can serve as a reference in private contracts; and can even factor into civil or tort liability decisions.[61] Second, the HCoC has the potential to be integrated into each jurisdiction's regulatory framework as they develop their legal responses to GenAI.[62] Several G7 nations are poised to either introduce new regulations or to revise existing structures on AI governance – creating the space for integration of HCoC principles and practices.[63] If these regulations draw upon the HCoC, whether by reference, content consistency, or formal incorporation, this will facilitate and increase regulatory interoperability as well as international regulatory cohesion, integrating an AI governance framework that safeguards human rights, democracy, and the rule of law.

This section explores the space the HCoC holds within the G7 regulatory context and how it can foster interoperability between the legislative frameworks of different G7 jurisdictions on advanced AI systems. For this, the section first examines the current state of AI regulation within each G7 member state. This analysis assesses the compatibility between the HCoC principles and existing G7 member frameworks. Notably, a significant overlap already exists between the core elements of the G7 nations' regulatory documents and the HCoC.[64] Second, building on this compatibility, the section explores various avenues for integrating the HCoC into the regulatory frameworks of G7 member states. By exploring these options, the most effective means of leveraging the HCoC to achieve interoperability in G7 AI governance is identified.

11.4.1 *Status of AI Governance in the G7, and HCoC as a Common Guidance*

The HCoC serves as a central reference point in the evolving global landscape of AI governance. This section provides insights into how HCoC aligns with the existing frameworks in G7 jurisdictions, including Canada, the European Union, Japan, the United Kingdom, and the United States. It contains an AI-focused overview of each jurisdiction's regulatory status, identifies the documents that closely align with HCoC's structure and functionality, and evaluates their compatibility with the HCoC's content. A compatibility chart outlining specific alignment points between the HCoC and G7 legislation is provided in the Appendix.

1. *Canada:* Canada is in the process of formulating a comprehensive regulatory framework for AI under Bill C-27, known as the Artificial Intelligence and Data Act (AIDA). This legislation prioritizes risk mitigation for "high-impact" AI systems.[65] However, this effort was interrupted on January 6, 2025, when Prime Minister Justin Trudeau's resignation and the prorogation of Parliament prevented Bill C-27 from advancing further in the

www.jstor.org/stable/25622251; S. Schwarcz, 'Soft Law as Governing Law' (2020) 104 *Minnesota Law Review* 2471; B. Druzin, *Why Does Soft Law Have any Power Anyway?* (Cambridge University Press, 2016); A. Guzman and T. Meyer, 'International Soft Law' (2010) 2(1) *Journal of Legal Analysis* 171–225. Available at: https://doi.org/10.1093/jla/2.1.171; W. Wallach, A. Reuel, and A. Kaspersen, 'Soft Law Functions in the International Governance of AI' (Carnegie Council for Ethics in International Affairs, 2022). Available at: https://cdn.carnegiecouncil.org/media/cceia/Soft-Law-in-International-AI-Governance.pdf?v=1695911519.

[61] See references in previous note.

[62] See discussion below Section 11.4.2.

[63] See discussion below Section 11.4.1.

[64] See Appendix.

[65] Government of Canada, 'The Artificial Intelligence and Data Act (AIDA) – Companion Document' (2023). Available at: https://ised-isde.canada.ca/site/innovation-better-canada/en/artificial-intelligence-and-data-act-aida-companion-document#s6.

legislative process.[66] Additionally, Canada has published a Voluntary Code of Conduct for Responsible Development and Management of Advanced Generative AI Systems, offering non-binding guidelines for AI industry stakeholders.

2. *European Union:* The EU has pioneered AI regulation with the EU Artificial Intelligence Act (AI Act). This legislation sets a robust and comprehensive framework for trustworthy AI development and implementation, emphasizing a risk-based regulatory approach, and addressing "general-purpose" AI models specifically.[67] The AI Act mandates the development of codes of practice to guide its implementation, ensuring alignment with international standards, as well as evolving technology and market trends.[68]
3. *Japan:* Japan's approach to AI governance emphasizes maximizing the positive societal impacts of AI, and capitalizing on a risk-based and agile governance model.[69] Taking a sector-specific approach, Japan seeks to promote AI implementation through regulatory reforms tailored to specific industries and markets, such as transportation, finance, and medical devices.[70] This strategy includes updating more than 10,000 regulations or ordinances that require "analog" compliance methods, including requirements for paper documents, on-site periodic inspections and dedicated in-person staffing.[71] In addition, Japan launched the AI Guidelines for Business[72] as a voluntary AI risk management tool. The principles for advanced AI systems established in the HAIP international guiding principles (IGP) are directly integrated in these Guidelines, following Japan's presidency of the G7 during the HAIP Comprehensive Framework drafting process.
4. *United Kingdom:* The United Kingdom is developing a decentralized regulatory approach, focusing on sector-specific guidelines, a pro-innovation stance, and public–private collaboration through specialized AI institutions.[73] While not currently enforcing a comprehensive AI law, the United Kingdom emphasizes traditional AI governance principles like safety, security, transparency, and fairness to inform its sector-driven regulations.[74] The Department for Science, Innovation & Technology also published a practical guidance code in the form of the Emerging Processes for Frontier AI Safety, ahead of the UK AI Summit. The summit culminated in the Bletchley Declaration, a

[66] Canada, C-27, 44th Parl., 1st Sess. (2021–2025). Available at: www.parl.ca/legisinfo/en/bill/44-1/c-27; Blair Attard-Frost, 'The Death of Canada's Artificial Intelligence and Data Act: What Happened, and What's Next for AI Regulation in Canada?' (Montreal AI Ethics Institute, 17 January 2025); Sunny Handa et al., 'Digital Policy Issues Face Uncertain Future after Prorogation of Parliament' (*Blakes*, 27 January 2025).

[67] See EU AI Act, Chapter V.

[68] See EU AI Act, Art. 56.

[69] Hiroki Habuka, 'Japan's Approach to AI Regulation and Its Impact on the 2023 G7 Presidency' (CSIS, 2023). Available at: www.csis.org/analysis/japans-approach-ai-regulation-and-its-impact-2023-g7-presidency.

[70] デジタル庁, アナログ規制見直しの取組, デジタル臨時行政調査会での決定事項等(2023年9月11日更新); デジタル庁, アナログ規制見直しの取組, 構造改革のためのデジタル原則の全体像((令和3年6月); デジタル庁, デジタル原則に照らした: 規制の一括見直しプラン, デジタル臨時行政調査会(令和4年6月3日); 'Japan Govt to Review nearly 10,000 Items of Analog Regulations' (Jiji Press, 21 December 2022). Available at: https://sp.m.jiji.com/english/show/23777.

[71] Jiji Press, 'Japan Govt to Review Nearly 10,000 Items of Analog Regulations'.

[72] See Japan Ministry of Internal Affairs and Communications, Ministry of Economy, Trade and Industry, 'AI Guidelines for Business Ver1.0'.

[73] See discussion below Section 11.4.2 (addressing the United Kingdom's approach to AI governance). See also Department for Science, Innovation & Technology, 'A Pro-innovation Approach to AI Regulation: Government Response' (2024) Art. 5. CP 1019. E03019481 02/24. Available at: www.gov.uk/government/consultations/ai-regulation-a-pro-innovation-approach-policy-proposals/outcome/a-pro-innovation-approach-to-ai-regulation-government-response.

[74] See Department for Science, Innovation & Technology, 'A Pro-innovation Approach to AI Regulation' (generally and at Art. 5).

shared commitment to safe and responsible AI development signed by twenty-eight nations and the EU. However, in 2025, the United Kingdom did not sign the joint statement of the AI Action Summit in Paris, the successor event to the AI Safety Summit.[75]

5. *United States:* During the Biden administration, the United States had adopted a decentralized, multi-tiered regulatory strategy for AI governance, with specialized agencies overseeing sector-specific regulations.[76] Key developments and initiatives included the AI Executive Order on the Safe, Secure, and Trustworthy Development and Use of Artificial Intelligence (AIEO), which directed sector-specific agencies to formulate regulations; the Risk Management Framework (RMF) developed by the National Institute of Standards and Technology (NIST), providing guidelines for risk assessment and management; the White House Blueprint for an AI Bill of Rights, outlining foundational principles for AI development; and the Voluntary AI Commitments Ensuring Safe, Secure, and Trustworthy AI, a non-binding initiative promoting responsible AI practices that has been endorsed by companies such as Amazon, Anthropic, Google, Inflection, Meta, Microsoft, Nvidia, and OpenAI. However, on January 23, 2025, President Trump issued an Executive Order rescinding the Biden administration's AIEO, with the stated purposes of prioritizing AI development, removing regulatory barriers to innovation, and enhancing America's AI global leadership for economic and national security.[77]

11.4.2 *Achieving and Enhancing Regulatory Interoperability: HCoC as a Reference Point for AI Governance Development*

The GenAI governance landscape is complex and multifaceted, ranging from "hard law" approaches in which nations have instituted targeted regulatory regimes, to "soft law" approaches, where guidelines lead the way in shaping the future of GenAI.[78] Within the G7, the EU has instituted robust and comprehensive regulations through its AI Act, and Canada is in the process of developing similar hard law frameworks.[79] Conversely, Japan, the United Kingdom, and the United States lean towards sector-specific and lighter-touch regulatory approaches.[80] This diverse regulatory environment, marked by varying levels of stringency and focus, poses challenges for global operations, requiring businesses to navigate a complex regulatory patchwork, as well as differing rights and obligations, across G7 nations and the

[75] 'Statement on Inclusive and Sustainable Artificial Intelligence for People and the Planet' (Élysée, 11 February 2025). Available at: www.elysee.fr/en/emmanuel-macron/2025/02/11/statement-on-inclusive-and-sustainable-artificial-intelligence-for-people-and-the-planet; 'Chair Comment: AI Action Summit' (Science Innovation & Technology Committee, UK Parliament, 12 February 2025). Available at: https://committees.parliament.uk/committee/135/science-innovation-and-technology-committee/news/205243/chair-comment-ai-action-summit/.

[76] See generally The White House, 'Executive Order on the Safe, Secure, and Trustworthy Development and Use of Artificial Intelligence' (2023). Available at: www.whitehouse.gov/briefing-room/presidential-actions/2023/10/30/executive-order-on-the-safe-secure-and-trustworthy-development-and-use-of-artificial-intelligence/; R. B. L. Dixon, 'A Principled Governance for Emerging AI Regimes: Lessons from China, the European Union, and the United States' (2023) 3 *AI Ethics*, 793–810. Available at: https://doi.org/10.1007/s43681-022-00205-0; D. Plotinsky and G. Cinelli, 'Existing and Proposed Federal AI Regulation in the United States' (Morgan Lewis, 2024). Available at: www.morganlewis.com/pubs/2024/04/existing-and-proposed-federal-ai-regulation-in-the-united-states.

[77] The White House, 'Fact Sheet: President Donald J. Trump Takes Action to Enhance America's AI Leadership' (23 January 2025). Available at: www.whitehouse.gov/fact-sheets/2025/01/fact-sheet-president-donald-j-trump-takes-action-to-enhance-americas-ai-leadership/.

[78] See discussion above Section 11.2.

[79] See discussion above Section 11.4.1.

[80] Ibid.

world. The HCoC holds promise as a unifying mechanism, bridging these regulatory disparities and promoting interoperability.

The HCoC may be integrated into national regulations across G7 countries and globally through various means, such as direct legal referencing or recognition, content integration, or by being leveraged through material harmonization of specific aspects of its regulatory developments. Pathways for integration into the regulatory frameworks of the G7 jurisdictions include the following:

- *Canada*: Overall, Canada's voluntary CoC specifically, and its regulatory trajectory generally, demonstrate alignment with the international conversation on ethical AI development and the HCoC's principles.[81] As AIDA evolves, if the bill is reintroduced, it presents an opportunity to translate these principles into enforceable regulations, further solidifying Canada's commitment to responsible AI advancement and global interoperability. Given that AIDA or successor legislation may include advanced AI systems within its regulatory scope, this upcoming law opens a clear possibility to find common ground with the HCoC's principles and functionality.
- *European Union*: The EU AI Act mandates the development of codes of practice to further materialize its implementation.[82] These will address practical aspects of responsible AI development, addressing at a more granular level what the EU AI Act generally proposes – aligning with the HCoC's GenAI focus. Furthermore, the EU acknowledges the influence of international standards in shaping these codes of practice,[83] presenting an opportunity for the HCoC to be materially integrated or formally referenced in the EU AI governance framework.
- *Japan*: On February 4, 2025, the Japanese government's Cabinet Office released the interim report of its AI Policy Study Group.[84] The report underscores the preference for relying on existing sector-specific laws rather than imposing sweeping, AI-specific regulations, in accordance with the principle of technological neutrality. It also highlights the importance of voluntary risk-mitigation initiatives undertaken by businesses, while committing the government to the continuous monitoring of emerging risks and necessary measures. The HCoC could serve as a valuable reference point as to the implementation of those key measures, especially considering that the HCoC principles are already integrated in Japan's AI Guidelines for Business.[85]
- *United Kingdom*: Besides leading international discussions on AI governance through initiatives such as the Bletchley Declaration,[86] the United Kingdom is proactively formulating its own AI governance framework. According to its publication "A Pro-Innovation Approach to AI Regulation – Government Response to Consultation," the UK government is undergoing technical policy analysis on regulation and life-cycle accountability of advanced general-purpose systems. Also, the nation is poised to update its "Emerging Processes for Frontier AI Safety" publication, which is highly compatible with the HCoC, by the end of 2024. To fulfill these governance objectives, the United Kingdom is opting for collaborative private–public development through agencies and institutions including

[81] See Appendix.
[82] See EU AI Act, Art. 53.4.
[83] See EU AI Act, Art. 56.1.
[84] The Cabinet Office, the AI Policy Study Group, 'Interim Report'. Available at: www8.cao.go.jp/cstp/ai/interim_report.pdf.
[85] See Appendix; Japan's AI Guidelines for Business.
[86] See discussion above Section 11.2.1; AI Safety Summit, 'The Bletchley Declaration'.

the Digital Regulatory Cooperation Forum and the AI Safety Institute. Considering the current institutional inertia, and the stalled progress regarding its draft intellectual property code,[87] the United Kingdom might leverage the HCoC and its international scope to inform potential regulatory initiatives.

- *United States*: Following the repeal of the AIEO, US AI governance is undergoing a shift toward policies emphasizing innovation, economic competitiveness, and national security. Current regulatory and legislative discussions focus on fostering AI development while addressing potential risks and maintaining global leadership in the sector. Notably, after releasing RMF 1.0 in January 2023, the NIST established the Generative AI Public Work Group and developed the AI RMF Generative Artificial Intelligence Profile (July 2024).[88] These frameworks are still valid after the repeal of the President Biden's Executive Order on AI. The HCoC's emphasis on responsible risk management and governance aligns with the United States' principle-based trajectory, and could fit into proposed risk-mitigation legislation, positioning the HCoC as a crucial reference in shaping AI regulatory policy in the United States.

11.5 NEXT STEPS TOWARDS A MORE HARMONIZED GOVERNANCE FRAMEWORK FOR ADVANCED GENAI SYSTEMS

The current landscape of GenAI governance is characterized by jurisdictional fragmentation, with national regulations imposing varying obligations on developers and offering inconsistent protections to users. As this chapter has analyzed, the HCoC holds significant potential to enhance interoperability among G7 members' governance frameworks, anchoring development and deployment of GenAI systems in democratic and human-centric principles – a cohesive inertia that could not only facilitate cooperation among the G7, but also serve as a model for the wider international community. While the HCoC holds promise for harmonizing G7 approaches and inspiring broader international cooperation, its lack of specificity currently limits its practical utility. Future discussions among G7 leaders should focus on how the HCoC can be updated to ensure interoperability of rules for advanced AI systems across not only G7 countries, but also the global community, serving as a benchmark for leveraging and substantiating the integration of development and deployment of advanced AI systems with human rights, democracy, and the rule of law. The following section posits that, to realize the HCoC's full potential, future G7 discussions should prioritize development in key areas such as (1) terminology and definitional interoperability, (2) risk management, (3) stakeholder engagement, (4) ethical considerations, and (5) further areas for exploration not currently contained in the HCoC. By establishing a robust and adaptable framework, the G7 can position the HCoC as a global benchmark for responsible AI development, anchored in shared values of human rights, democracy and the rule of law.

11.5.1 *Terminology and Definitions: Indexing a Common Vocabulary*

The HCoC can serve as a foundation for establishing a consistent definition or methodology for identifying terms for governance of advanced AI systems, facilitating smoother regulatory implementation across jurisdictions. Future terminology consensus includes:

[87] See Department for Science, Innovation & Technology, 'A Pro-innovation Approach to AI Regulation', at Art. 29; P. Joseph and K. Berry, 'UK Fails to Agree AI/Copyright Code of Practice' (Linklaters, 2024). Available at: https://techinsights.linklaters.com/post/102joq6/uk-fails-to-agree-ai-copyright-code-of-practice.

[88] NIST Website: https://nvlpubs.nist.gov/nistpubs/ai/NIST.AI.600-1.pdf.

- *Bridge the terminology gap*: The HCoC can endorse consistent definitions for streamlined regulatory implementation across jurisdictions, fostering a common understanding of critical concepts. This could be achieved through means such as including a glossary of key terms with clear, agreed-upon definitions, or establishing methodologies for identifying and classifying AI systems based on factors relevant to risk assessment. By establishing a common language, the HCoC can ease communication, regulatory certainty, and business sector collaboration across borders. Underscoring the importance of shared language around AI, the European Union and United States are currently in the development of "65 Key AI Terms Essential to Understanding Risk-Based Approaches to AI."[89] Notably, despite efforts to establish common terminology for AI systems through the US–EU Trade and Technology Council, OECD, and ISO, the definition of advanced AI systems remains unclear. This ambiguity leaves open the question of which criteria – such as floating point operations, dataset quality and size, or input and output modalities – should be used to classify an AI system as "advanced."[90]

11.5.2 *Risk Management and Governance: Building a Common and Robust Framework*

Effective risk management stands as a cornerstone of responsible development of advanced AI systems. The HCoC holds the potential to significantly contribute to this space by advocating for shared principles and best practices. Risk management cohesion across jurisdictions includes:

- *Identify and share security risks, particularly systemic risks*: The HCoC can enhance its interoperability contribution by explicitly listing and addressing security risks, particularly those with systemic consequences. This can be achieved through a two-pronged approach. First, the HCoC can integrate a comprehensive list of typical risks regarding advanced AI systems, such as AI hallucinations (generating inaccurate outputs), fake content generation (deepfakes), intellectual property infringement (copyrighted content integration in datasets), job market transformations due to automation, environmental impact of AI systems, bias amplification based on training data, and privacy concerns, among others. Case studies can be implemented through the "project-based cooperation" network – the HAIP Comprehensive Framework's fourth regulatory pillar. Second, the HCoC can establish a risk assessment framework to categorize AI systems based on their potential for harm. This framework could leverage existing models such as the EU AI Act's general-purpose AI models with systemic risk categorization,[91] establishing higher compliance requirements or increased scrutiny for higher-risk GenAI profiles. By prioritizing systems with the greatest potential for systemic issues, the HCoC can provide a clearer roadmap for identifying, understanding, and mitigating various risks.
- *Enhance clarity in the risk management process*: The HCoC can encourage the development of standardized risk management policies tailored to specific AI applications, throughout the entire AI lifecycle from pre-market duties to post-market updates. Future drafting can reference or draw insights from established risk management frameworks such

[89] European Commission, 'EU–U.S. TTC: Call for Input on First Edition of WG1 Terminology and Taxonomy for Artificial Intelligence' (3 November 2023). Available at: https://digital-strategy.ec.europa.eu/en/news/eu-us-ttc-call-input-first-edition-wg1-terminology-and-taxonomy-artificial-intelligence.

[90] See EU AI Act, Annex XIII.

[91] See EU AI Act, Chap. III, Sec. 1.

as NIST's RMF or ISO/IEC 42001:2023. Additionally, it can incorporate learnings from other reputable sources to enhance clarity and comprehensiveness.

- *Develop standard data governance, risk management, and information security policies*: The development of standardized policies can leverage established frameworks such as ISO/IEC 27001 and ISO/IEC 27002 or NIST's Cybersecurity Framework (CSF), which provide a structured foundation adaptable to the unique risk landscape of the development of advanced AI systems.
- *Implement content authentication mechanisms*: The HCoC can list reliable content authentication and provenance mechanisms to enable users to identify the originators of content or establish common labeling mechanisms to help users understand that the content is generated by AI. These contributions could be based on the input from the HAIP project-based cooperation. Authentication mechanisms can safeguard against misinformation and uphold ethical standards by verifying data sources and outputs. However, it is imperative to balance these efforts with the protection of individual privacy, ensuring that authentication processes do not compromise personal data. This balance is key to maintaining public trust and promoting the responsible use of AI technologies, safeguarding democratic values and human rights.

11.5.3 *Stakeholder Engagement: Fostering Transparency and Accountability*

Building trust in AI necessitates robust stakeholder engagement. A transparent and accountable AI development process fosters public confidence and encourages information sharing. Future pathways for stakeholder engagement include:

- *Establish standardized formats for transparency reports*: The HCoC can promote the adoption of standardized formats for transparency reports. By consolidating best practices and identifying common risks, the HCoC can offer a template for companies to self-assess and disclose relevant information consistently across jurisdictions. A potential model for standardized formatting pursuant to transparency reports is the United Kingdom's Algorithmic Transparency Recording Standard (ATRS). Standardization would enable companies to have uniform disclosure criteria internationally, enhancing cross-border cohesive reporting and auditing consistency, as well as allowing the public to better understand the development and operation of AI systems.
- *Define clear formats for incident sharing*: Encouraging the adoption of clear incident-sharing formats can facilitate the exchange of information about security breaches, biases, or unintended consequences observed in deployed AI systems. This collaborative approach to sharing and learning from incidents enables stakeholders to develop effective mitigation strategies, ultimately enhancing the safety and reliability of AI technologies.

11.5.4 *Ethical and Societal Considerations: Upholding the Rule of Law, Human Rights, and Core Democratic Values*

The G7, a group of leading democracies, has a unique opportunity to shape the global conversation around responsible AI development. The HCoC can play a crucial role in ensuring that AI development aligns with the ethical and societal considerations that underpin democratic values and secure human rights in AI development and implementation. Potential pathways to prioritizing these principles include:

- *Reinforce the primacy of the rule of law, human rights, and democratic principles*: The HCoC already champions and leads with these values, emphasizing human-centric design. However, there is room for further enhancement and substantiation for practical application. For instance, the HCoC could enhance its guidance on how organizations should foster research and AI development that prioritizes the protection of fairness, privacy, and intellectual property rights, while also tackling global challenges such as climate change, health, and education. Rather than providing detailed descriptions itself, the HCoC could reference other international agreements or widely recognized standards. Furthermore, the HCoC could strengthen democratic principles and the rule of law by establishing due safeguards for freedom of expression: ensuring AI does not minimize dissent or impose undue restrictions on information access; guaranteeing a right to remedy for individuals adversely affected by AI; and promoting transparency and accountability in AI decision-making processes. Enhancing human-centricity could involve advocating for effective oversight in high-risk applications, providing individuals with explanations about AI-driven decisions affecting them, and promoting inclusive design that caters to the diverse needs and perspectives of various populations to ensure equitable AI benefits.

11.5.5 *Further Areas for Exploration*

The HCoC can play a key role in exploring several critical areas for further development in responsible AI:

- *Acknowledge special considerations for government use of AI*: The HCoC can play a pivotal role in delineating special considerations for government use of AI, ensuring that governmental powers in AI deployment are appropriately circumscribed and limited. By drawing on the AI Treaty,[92] incorporating principles from the OECD Declaration on Government Access to Personal Data Held by Private Sector Entities,[93] and selectively aligning with prohibitions outlined in the EU AI Act,[94] the HCoC can establish clear guidelines that ensure due process in the development and deployment of advanced AI systems by the public sector. These guidelines should emphasize key elements such as a legal basis, legitimate aims, independent oversight, and avenues for redress; while upholding fundamental principles like privacy, transparency, and accountability. By aligning with these principles, the HCoC can become a democratic referent, and governments can leverage the power of AI responsibly, while mitigating potential risks and fostering public trust.
- *Harmonize full lifecycle regulatory approaches*: The HCoC can explore the potential for incorporating best practices from various jurisdictions' regulations. This could involve elements such as certification mechanisms, robust oversight mechanisms, and iterative audit controls.
  - *Certification mechanisms*: The HCoC can establish a framework for certification and registration mechanisms for high-risk advanced AI systems. This system could ensure rigorous evaluation throughout the lifecycle of high-risk advanced AI systems, from pre-market assessment to ongoing post-market analysis. The HCoC could define risk categories and establish criteria for the need of certification.

[92] See generally Council of Europe, Committee on Artificial Intelligence, Draft Framework Convention on Artificial Intelligence, Human Rights, Democracy and the Rule of Law (2024). Available at: https://search.coe.int/cm/pages/result_details.aspx?objectid=0900001680aee411.

[93] Organisation for Economic Co-operation and Development, Declaration on Government Access to Personal Data Held by Private Sector Entities (2023) OECD/LEGAL/0487. Available at: https://legalinstruments.oecd.org/en/instruments/OECD-LEGAL-0487.

[94] EU AI Act, Art. 5.

  - *Oversight methodologies*: The HCoC can emphasize the importance of effective oversight in AI systems to mitigate potential harm and address incidents effectively. In some cases, human involvement in critical AI processes would be necessary, while in other cases machine supervision iterations can detect risks much faster and more precisely than humans. The HCoC could propose guidelines on whether to prioritize human judgment and intervention, especially in high-risk AI applications, ensuring a balance between automation and human control.
  - *Audit mechanisms*: The HCoC can extend procedural cohesion beyond AI implementation, by establishing common processes for iterative audits, ensuring continuous monitoring and evaluation of AI systems' compliance with established principles and guidelines. By considering and potentially adapting existing frameworks, such as the United Kingdom's "Guidance on the AI Auditing Framework,"[95] the HCoC can equip organizations with practical tools for ongoing evaluations. These iterative audits would allow for continuous improvement and ensure AI systems remain aligned with responsible development principles throughout their lifecycle.
- *Establish means for redress*: The HCoC could expand the discussions to redress harms caused by advanced AI systems. This could involve exploring access to remedies and explanations for individuals impacted by GenAI decisions in areas as diverse as copyright and intellectual property to judicial processing (as AI is expected to play a growing role in judicial decision-making, developing specific appeal mechanisms for harms caused by AI content may be worth considering). The HCoC could encourage developers and deployers of GenAI to provide appropriate dispute resolution mechanisms to users and society. Furthermore, to make victim relief more effective, G7 members could discuss shifting the burden of proof of damages or causal links, and establishing accessible, fast, and low-cost dispute resolution mechanisms for damages caused by GenAI.
- *Foster shared responsibility in the AI ecosystem*: The HCoC is addressed only to the developers of advanced AI systems.[96] However, it could expand the scope to other actors within the GenAI value chain, such as deployers and users of advanced AI systems. In addition, it is important to examine how to distribute responsibility and liability among stakeholders, ensuring all parties are accountable for their respective roles in potential harms.

By focusing on these key areas, the HCoC can evolve into a powerful tool for facilitating a more cohesive and effective approach to GenAI governance on a global scale. The HCoC's dynamic nature positions it to bridge the gap between diverse national frameworks, fostering a future of responsible GenAI development for the G7 nations and beyond.

11.6 CONCLUSION

As advanced GenAI systems transcend national borders and exert global influence, fostering an internationally interoperable governance architecture emerges as paramount in maximizing their positive impacts and safeguarding cross-border fundamental principles. In this regard, the G7 nations' endorsement of the HIGP and the HCoC, supported by more than forty countries

[95] Information Commissioner's Office, Guidance on the AI Auditing Framework: Draft Guidance for Consultation (2023). Available at: https://ico.org.uk/media/2617219/guidance-on-the-ai-auditing-framework-draft-for-consultation.pdf.

[96] See generally HCoC.

through the Hiroshima AI Process Friends Group. This unified stance by the world's leading democratic economies underscores a robust international commitment to advancing human-centered AI development, safeguarding individual rights, and strengthening trust in AI systems. The collective weight and global influence of the nations lending their support to this process amplifies the significance of its agreements, marking them as pivotal steps in shaping the future of AI governance.

However, for the promise of the Comprehensive Framework to be fully realized, its key practical instrument, the HCoC, requires further development. While the HCoC, as this chapter reveals, significantly aligns with the trajectory of existing G7 policies, it currently lacks the material specificity to provide truly effective guidance for practical implementation. Moving forward, it is crucial to engage in substantive discussions on enhancing the HCoC in several key areas. These areas include the following::

- *Coordinating a common vocabulary*: A unified understanding of key terms and definitions is essential for ensuring consistent interpretation of AI terms across borders.
- *Developing robust risk management frameworks and risk-based categorization*: The HCoC should provide clear guidance on how to assess and mitigate risks associated with advanced AI systems, throughout the entire AI lifecycle from pre-market duties to post-market updates.
- *Promoting harmonized stakeholder engagement*: The HCoC can play a valuable role in encouraging cohesive approaches to stakeholder engagement and developing consistent transparency standards.
- *Strengthening democratic and human rights principles*: The HCoC should provide more concrete and actionable steps for upholding democratic values and safeguarding human rights in the context of AI development and deployment.
- *Further areas for discussion*: The HCoC's potential extends beyond its current scope. The G7 can leverage this collaborative document to explore critical areas such as developing special considerations for government AI use, harmonizing regulatory practices (e.g. certification mechanisms, oversight methodologies, and audit mechanisms), fostering shared responsibility within the AI ecosystem, and establishing efficient redress mechanisms for AI harms.

By addressing these crucial areas, the HCoC has the potential to evolve into a truly robust and impactful instrument for global AI governance. A strengthened HCoC can serve as a valuable reference point not only for G7 nations but also for a broader international audience seeking to navigate the complexities of responsible AI development and deployment. This international alignment can help ensure that the power of GenAI is harnessed for the benefit of all, while mitigating potential risks and upholding core human values.

APPENDIX 11.1

Mapping Jurisdictional Coverage of Key Principles in the Hiroshima Code of Conduct: Alignment of HCoC with National AI Regulations or Guidance, per Article

Items*	Hiroshima AI Process	Canada**	European Union	Japan	United Kingdom	United States
General						
Document	Hiroshima AI Process Code of Conduct	Voluntary Code of Conduct on the Responsible Development and Management of Advanced Generative AI Systems	Artificial Intelligence Act	AI Guidelines for Business	Emerging Processes for Frontier AI Safety	Voluntary AI Commitments Ensuring Safe, Secure, and Trustworthy AI
Target	Advanced AI systems	Advanced Generative AI systems	General-purpose AI	Advanced AI systems	Frontier AI	Generative AI (foundation) model technology
Definition	The most advanced AI systems, including the most advanced foundation models and Generative AI systems	Generative AI systems that have advanced capabilities enabling them to be adapted for a wide variety of uses in different contexts, including uses for which they were not specifically trained.	An AI model, including where such an AI model is trained with a large amount of data using self-supervision at scale, that displays significant generality and is capable of competently performing a wide range of distinct tasks regardless of the way the model is placed on the market and that can be integrated into a variety of downstream systems or applications, except AI models that are used for research, development or prototyping activities before they are released on the market	The most advanced AI systems, including the most advanced foundation models and generative AI systems (same as HAIP CoC)	Highly capable general-purpose AI models that can perform a wide variety of tasks and match or exceed the capabilities present in today's most advanced models	–

(continued)

(*cont.*)

Items*	Hiroshima AI Process	Canada**	European Union	Japan	United Kingdom	United States
Risk management and governance***						
Risk identification and mitigation	1 (Risk identification and mitigation)	2 (Safety), 3 (fairness and equity), 6 (validity and robustness)	Art. 6 (high-risk classification); Annex III (categorical high-risk systems); Art. 51 (classification of general-purpose AI models with systemic risk); Arts. 10–13 (risk mitigation); Art. 55(a) (model evaluation)	1 (Risk identification and mitigation)	1 (Responsible capability scaling), 2 (model evaluations and red-teaming)	1 (Commit to internal and external red-teaming of models or systems in areas including misuse, societal risks, and national security concerns, such as bio, cyber, and other safety areas)
Vulnerability and misuse management after deployment	2 (Vulnerability and misuse management after deployment)	5 (Human oversight and monitoring)	Chapter IX generally Art. 72 (post-market monitoring); Art. 55(1)(b), (c) (obligations for providers); Art. 85 (right to lodge a complaint); Art. 87 (reporting of infringements and protection of reporting persons)	2 (Vulnerability and misuse management after deployment)	1 (Responsible capability scaling), 8 (preventing and monitoring model misuse)	4 (Incentivize third-party discovery and reporting of issues and vulnerabilities)
Governance and risk management policies	5 (Governance and risk management policies)	1 (Accountability)	Art. 9 (risk management system for high-risk systems) generally; Art. 13 (policy transparency); Art. 14 (oversight measures commensurate to risks for high-risk AI systems); Art. 53 (obligations for providers of general-purpose AI models); Art. 55 (obligations for providers of general-purpose AI models with systemic risk).	5 (Governance and Risk Management Policies)	All	Reference to NIST RMF
Cybersecurity investments	6 (Cybersecurity investments)	6 (Validity and robustness)	Art. 15 generally (high-risk systems); 55 (1)(c); Art. 14 (human oversight requirements for high-risk systems);	6 (Cybersecurity investments)	4 (Security controls including	3 (Invest in cybersecurity and insider threat

			Art. 26 (obligations for deployers of high-risk AI systems); Art. 70 (designation of national authorities)		securing model weights)	safeguards to protect proprietary and unreleased model weights)
Content authentication	7 (Content authentication)	4 (Transparency)	Art. 55 (obligations for providers) generally; Art. 10(2)(c) (data and data governance); Art. 13. (3)(b)(vi), (vii) (transparency and provision of information to deployers), Art. 48 (CE marking for high-risk systems); Art. 50(1a) (marking of outputs)	7 (Content authentication)	6 (Identifiers of AI-generated material)	5 (Develop and deploy mechanisms that enable users to understand if audio or visual content is AI-generated, including robust provenance, watermarking, or both, for AI-generated audio or visual content)
Data quality, personal data and intellectual property protection	11 (Data quality, personal data and intellectual property protection)	3 (Fairness and equity)	Art. 53 (1)(b), (c) (copyright and intellectual property); Art. 10 generally (bias); Art. 15 (accuracy and robustness)	11 (Data quality, personal data and intellectual property protection)	9 (Data input controls and audits)	–
Stakeholder Engagement						
Transparency and accountability	3 (Transparency and accountability)	2 (Safety), 3 (fairness and equity)	Arts. 11 (technical documentation), 12 (record keeping) generally; Art. 13 generally (transparency and provision of information to deployers); Art. 53(1)(a) (technical documentation), (b) and (d) (availability of documentation); Art. 50 (transparency to user); Art. 17 (1)(m) (accountability requirement for high-risk AI systems)	3 (Transparency and accountability)	3 (Model Reporting and information sharing)	6 (Publicly report model or system capabilities, limitations, and domains of appropriate and inappropriate use, including discussion of societal risks, such as effects on fairness and bias)

(*continued*)

(cont.)

Items*	Hiroshima AI Process	Canada**	European Union	Japan	United Kingdom	United States
Responsible information sharing	4 (Responsible information sharing)	1 (Accountability), 5 (human oversight and monitoring)	Title III Chapter 4 (notifying authorities and notified bodies) generally; Arts. 11 (technical documentation), 12 (record keeping) generally; Art. 55 (1)(c) (obligations for providers); Art. 73 (reporting of serious incidents)	4 (Responsible information sharing)	3 (Model reporting and information sharing), 5 (reporting structure for vulnerabilities)	2 (Work toward information sharing among companies and governments regarding trust and safety risks, dangerous or emergent capabilities, and attempts to circumvent safeguards)
Ethical and societal considerations						
Research prioritization for societal safety	8 (Research PRIORITIZATION FOR SOCIETAL SAFETY)	–	Art. 1(1) (purpose of EUAI Act); Art. 60(4)(g); Art. 14 (preventing risks to health, safety, or fundamental rights); Art. 5 (prohibited systems)	8 (Research prioritization for societal safety)	7 (Prioritizing research on risks posed by AI)	7 (Prioritize research on societal risks posed by AI systems, including on avoiding harmful bias and discrimination, and protecting privacy)
AI for global challenges	9 (AI for global challenges)	–	Art. 1(1) (environmental protection); Art. 59 (sandbox conditions); Art. 95 (2)(b) (code of conduct); Art. 112 (evaluation)	9 (AI for global challenges)	–	8 (Develop and deploy frontier AI systems to help address society's greatest challenges)

Development of international technical standards	10 (Development of international technical standards)	Premise	Art. 40 (harmonized standards); Art. 56 (codes of practice)	10 (Development of international technical standards)	Model reporting and information sharing	2 (Work toward information sharing among companies and governments regarding trust and safety risks, dangerous or emergent capabilities, and attempts to circumvent safeguards)
Additional elements to HAIP CoC						
–	N/A	• Human oversight • Description of the types of training data	• Sufficiently detailed summary about the content used for training • Pre-market conformity assessments and registration • Increased compliance requirements for high-risk AI • Ban of AI systems with unacceptable risk (e.g. biometric categorization based on sensitive characteristics, certain predictive policing algorithms, and social scoring systems) • Development of codes of practice for implementation specifications	–	• Data input controls and audits	• Specific note to work on a strong international code of conduct • References to AI within the context of national security

*Based on the structure of the Hiroshima AI Process Code of Conduct.

**Given the structure of Canada's Voluntary Code of Conduct, the numbers in this column correspond as follows: 1 Accountability, 2 Safety, 3 Fairness and equity, 4 Transparency, 5 Human oversight and monitoring, 6 Validity and robustness.

***The numbers listed in each cell indicate the section or article numbers of the corresponding documents in each country.

12

Generative AI and International Standardisation

Sebastian Hallensleben

It is hard for regulation to keep up with the rapid development of new technologies. This is partly due to the lack of specialist technical expertise among lawmakers, and partly due to the multi-year timescales for developing, proposing and negotiating complex regulations that lag behind technological advances. Generative AI has been a particularly egregious example of this situation but is by no means the first.

On the other hand, technical standardisation in global fora such as the International Organization for Standardization (ISO) and International Electrotechnical Commission (IEC) generally does not suffer from a lack of specialist technical expertise. In many cases, it is also able to work on somewhat faster timescales than regulation.

Therefore, many jurisdictions have developed synergistic approaches that combine the respective strengths of regulation and standardisation to complement each other. The most prominent example is the European Union where this synergistic approach has been in use as the 'New Legislative Framework' since 2008, with predecessors going back more than four decades to the 1980s. It is most recently being applied to the EU AI Act.

The EU New Legislative Framework is unique among supranational synergistic approaches in that it is codified in considerable depth. It is a combination of several instruments summarised in the 'Blue Guide'[1] on the implementation of EU product rules.

It is outside the scope of this handbook to provide an overview of standardisation structures and processes. This has been done in depth recently by Micklitz,[2] in a way that mirrors the author's own experience as the chair of the Joint Technical Committee 21 of the European Committee for Standardization and the European Committee for Electrotechnical Standardization (CEN-CENELEC JTC21), the committee tasked with developing the harmonised standards for the EU AI Act. However, taking Europe as the example, a few key points on the interplay between regulation and standardisation are worth outlining here:

[1] Commission notice, the 'Blue Guide' on the implementation of EU product rules 2022 (Text with EEA relevance) 2022/C 247/01.

[2] Hans-W. Micklitz, *The Role of Standards in Future EU Digital Policy Legislation*, www.beuc.eu/sites/default/files/publications/BEUC-X-2023-096_The_Role_of_Standards_in_Future_EU_Digital_Policy_Legislation.pdf, last accessed 16 June 2024; Hans-W. Micklitz, *The Role of Standards in Future EU Digital Policy Legislation (Executive Summary)*, https://anec.eu/images/Publications/position-papers/Digital/ANEC-DIGITAL-2023-G-263.pdf, last accessed 16 June 2024.

- Harmonised standards:

  According to the New Legislative Framework, regulation only provides high-level objectives and requirements while standardisation provides technical solutions as a path towards achieving objectives and implementing requirements. The EU can 'harmonise' standards that the European Commission deems to be sufficiently substantial and stringent to underpin a piece of regulation in this way. Such harmonised standards are typically published in the *Official Journal of the European Union* –the same publication that also disseminates regulation.

- Presumption of conformity:

  Contrary to what might be expected from the publication route, harmonised standards are not mandatory – organisations are free to ignore them. However, adhering to harmonised standards leads to a 'presumption of conformity'. This means that organisations that follow harmonised standards are automatically presumed to be compliant with the relevant part of the regulations. This removes legal uncertainties for organisations. Harmonised standards are therefore effectively a preferred path to compliance.

- Legitimacy through stakeholders and consensus:

  European regulation draws its legitimacy from the democratic institutions and processes through which it is drafted and decided. By contrast, standardisation is not democratic, even though voting does play a role in its processes. Instead, standardisation draws its legitimacy from the combination of two factors: (i) Standards development is consensus-based – that is, work on a draft standard continues until most stakeholders can agree on it. There is no exact threshold for 'most stakeholders' but it is generally accepted to be close to unanimity; (ii) Standards development committees are required to include the full spectrum of stakeholders affected by a proposed standard. It is the duty of the officers of a committee (in particular the chair and secretary) to reach out to unrepresented stakeholder groups and try to pull them into the work of the committee.

- Legitimacy in practice:

  The theoretical legitimacy of standardisation is tempered to some extent by unequal access to resources. While some standardisation experts are in dedicated full-time roles at large companies that see standardisation as a strategic need and advantage, other experts, especially those affiliated with academia or civil society, often have to find time alongside other responsibilities and might have to scramble to cover travel expenses. Familiarity with making effective use of the intricate and sometimes unintuitive processes and structures of standardisation is similarly skewed towards full-time standardisation experts who therefore find it easier to advance the agenda of their employer.

- Top down versus bottom up:

  Standardisation activities are typically initiated and driven in a bottom-up manner. Experts propose standardisation items through their national standardisation committees whenever a critical mass of organisations – usually companies – see value in a new standard. By contrast, the development of harmonised standards is typically initiated top-down through a 'standardisation request' or 'mandate' issued by the European Commission and addressed to

> European standardisation organisations, in the case of the AI to CEN and CENELEC. Such a request contains a list of specific items as well as a delivery deadline. This creates a certain tension among standardisation experts used to working at their own pace on topics of their own preference.

At the time of writing, standardisation work to underpin the EU AI Act is in progress, with intense work in CEN-CENELEC JTC21 in five working groups structured into more than forty distinct work items. With more than 140 experts in JTC21, and an estimated 1,000–2,000 experts contributing in approximately twenty-four national mirror committees, this is the biggest standardisation effort in Europe to date.

At the international level, AI standardisation has been concentrated in ISO/IEC JTC1/SC42 since 2018. Given the global scope, this effort has drawn an even higher number of experts and national mirror committees than the European AI standardisation work, and includes major players such as the United States and China. International standardisation does not automatically trump European standardisation but JTC21 aims to re-use as much SC42 output as possible in order to save time and limit divergence between European and international AI standardisation as much as possible. In general, the formal relationship between international and European standardisation is governed by the Frankfurt (IEC vs. CENELEC) and Vienna (ISO vs. CEN) agreements.

Given the lack of equivalent regulatory institutions at the international level, there can be no direct international equivalent to the EU New Legislative Framework. However, current work at the Organisation for Economic Co-operation and Development (OECD), specifically in the OECD Network of Experts on AI (ONE.AI) expert group on AI Risk & Accountability, takes an approach that is similar to the New Legislative Framework. The objective at the OECD is to extend the existing Due Diligence Guidance for Responsible Business Conduct[3] with high-level requirements for AI governance, while pointing to existing standards and frameworks at international and regional levels that could be used to meet those high-level requirements. The results of this work are expected to be agreed at the political level and published in 2025.

The observations provided so far apply to AI in general and show the considerable breadth, intensity, and relevance of AI standardisation. By contrast, zooming in on generative AI as a subset and as the focus of this Handbook, a rather different picture emerges:

- In Europe, the standardisation mandate of the European Commission under the New Legislative Framework was made available as a draft in May 2022 and formally in May 2023, and does not include any reference to generative AI. This reflects the fact that, at the time of developing the standardisation mandate, generative AI was not yet part of the draft AI Act, either. Therefore, working on generative AI standards is not a priority in CEN-CENELEC JTC21, and the agenda of CEN-CENELEC JTC21 is dominated by the need to develop harmonised standards requested in the current standardisation mandate, with a tight deadline of autumn 2025. At the time of writing, there has not been a single work item in the JTC21 work programme addressing the specifics of generative AI.
- Generative AI standardisation in Europe is also held back by the fact that the newly established AI Office of the EU has a mandate to create a code of practice on general-purpose AI within one year. This will be a multi-stakeholder process that resembles standardisation to some extent, but is designed with a top-down approach, within a much

[3] See https://mneguidelines.oecd.org/mneguidelines/, last accessed 13 February 2025.

shorter time frame, and led directly by a quasi-governmental institution. It is therefore unclear what role CEN-CENELEC JTC21 standardisation would play with respect to generative AI.

- At the international level, the situation is similar to Europe: discussions in ISO/IEC on generative AI standards are still at a very early, informal stage. There are not even any draft standards yet that could indicate the potential direction of generative AI standardisation at the international level. Both structure and work programme in ISO/IEC JTC1/SC42 were established mostly in 2018–21 – that is, before the generative AI hype. The breadth and ambition of the work programme, much of which is not yet concluded, are saturating the expert community; hence newer concerns including standards for generative AI have not yet received significant attention.
- At national level, standards development organisations in more than fifty countries have mirror committees that follow, and vote on, standards development in ISO/IEC and/or CEN-CENELEC. However, their focus tends to be aligned with international or European work, and therefore attention on generative AI is also still scant.

It is not unusual for standardisation to lag behind technical progress. In fact, standardisation in a new field is usually only started when research and development activities have reached a certain level of maturity and stability. Such stability has not been reached in generative AI – rather, the cutting edge keeps shifting at enormous speed, although the capabilities at least of foundation models, including large language models, might have started to level off.

There is another factor that hampers generative AI standards development: The industry experts that would be essential contributors to any standardisation effort are mainly employed by large players such as Open AI, Google, Mistral, Anthropic, or Meta. These companies are currently singularly focused on competition and on building a dominant position in a rapidly and chaotically growing market. They therefore do not prioritise their generative AI engineers spending time on standardisation work.

There are, however, initiatives to create frameworks for generative AI governance outside of standardisation. A very recent example is the Singaporean Model AI Governance Framework for Generative AI.[4] There is also ongoing work in the OECD and other fora to elaborate on, and operationalise, the code of conduct agreed in the G7 Hiroshima process.[5]

While it is far too soon to provide any meaningful analysis of generative AI standardisation, it is possible to list potential topics of standardisation. These might include:

- test methods and performance metrics for generative AI models;
- resource consumption metrics for generative AI, with regard to both training and use;
- standardised licences for conditioning the ingestion of content made available on the public internet;
- terminology and taxonomy standards;
- similarity metrics for multiple similar generative AI models;
- standards, including thresholds, to consider and mark content as AI-generated;
- watermarking and provenance standards for AI-generated content, building on work by the Content Authenticity Initiative, for example.[6]

[4] https://aiverifyfoundation.sg/wp-content/uploads/2024/06/Model-AI-Governance-Framework-for-Generative-AI-6-June-2024.pdf, last accessed 16 June 2024.

[5] Hiroshima Process International Code of Conduct for Advanced AI Systems, https://digital-strategy.ec.europa.eu/en/library/hiroshima-process-international-code-conduct-advanced-ai-systems, last accessed 16 June 2024.

[6] See https://contentauthenticity.org, last accessed 16 June 2024.

It should be noted that generative AI drives the need for standards in non-AI areas, too. A pertinent example stems from the ability of generative AI to generate content at a scale that was previously impossible or at least uneconomical. Generative AI also allows the automated generation of 'humans' in the form of deceptively real bots that can act as influencers, news reporters or product reviewers, among others. In the hands of bad actors, generative AI is likely to lead to a flood of such undesirable content that cannot be reliably detected. Therefore, frameworks and standards will be needed that help to make the digital space resilient and ensure that trust in both information and people remains possible. A detailed analysis was already conducted in 2021 by a European working group within the StandICT programme and was published in early 2022, before the current generative AI hype. The report of this group contains detailed recommendations on standards in the areas of trust as well as digital identities.[7]

Generative AI can be expected to lead to a plethora of standards over the coming years. The established mechanisms for regulation and standardisation to complement each other will be a suitable approach for the new technology, just as for many earlier technologies. It remains to be seen if the formalised New Legislative Framework that has been governing this complementarity for several decades in Europe will inspire similar approaches at the international level.

[7] See StandICT.eu: Sebastian Hallensleben, *Report of TWG Trusted Information: Landscape of Trusted Information Standards* (Zenodo, 2022), https://zenodo.org/records/5926395, last accessed 15 February 2025.

13

Private Ordering and Generative AI

What Can We Learn from Foundation Model Terms and Conditions?

Lilian Edwards, Igor Szpotakowski, Gabriele Cifrodelli, Joséphine Sangaré, and James Stewart

The choice is never 'government regulation' or 'no regulation' – it's always 'government regulation' or 'corporate regulation' . . . You either live by rules made in public by democratically accountable bureaucrats, or rules made in private by shareholder-accountable executives.

Cory Doctorow[1]

13.1 INTRODUCTION

In November 2022, ChatGPT was released by OpenAI and the world changed. Although large, general-purpose or 'foundation' models and their generative products had already been in the research arena for several years,[2] it was ChatGPT's debut which captured the public and media's imagination as well as limitless venture capital funding. Large models generating not just text and images but also video, games, music, and code, were widely promoted as set to revolutionise innovation and democratise creativity. We have lived in the socio-cultural and economic bubble they have created since then, as the rest of this book evidences.[3]

However, all is not rosy: literature already emphasises that foundation models may create serious societal risks, including embedding and outputting bias; generating fake news, illegal or

[1] C. Doctorow, 23 October 2023, in 'Pluralistic: In Defense of Bureaucratic Competence (23 October 2023)', https://pluralistic.net/2023/10/23/getting-stuff-done/, last accessed 23 February 2024.

[2] The first large language model (LLM) was published in 2018 by Open AI 'Improving Language Understanding with Unsupervised Learning', *openai.com,* 11 June 2018. See also T. B. Brown et al., 'Language Models Are Few-Shot Learners', in *Advances in Neural Information Processing Systems,* 34th Conference on Neural Information Processing Systems, 33 (NeurIPS, Vancouver, 2020), 1877–1901. Foundation models are deep-learning models based on very large training datasets, used as general-purpose technologies that can support a diverse range of use cases. There are a number of phrases used in this arena, including general-purpose AI models (GPAI, the choice of the EU AI Act, see below), 'frontier' models, generative AI, and LGAIMs (large general AI models). We do not choose here to go into the lengthy debates on definitions and what separates these, as they are not, in general, terms of art and some are promotional or brand-recognition terms. We have chosen instead to identify large models by function as most germane to our study: text-to-text (T2T); text-to-image (T2I); text-to-audio or video (T2A/V), see below Section 13.3.

[3] P. Pratim Ray, 'ChatGPT: A Comprehensive Review on Background, Applications, Key Challenges, Bias, Ethics, Limitations and Future Scope', *Internet of Things and Cyber-Physical Systems,* 3 (2023), 121–154. At the time of writing there are signs that disillusionment is setting in with the AI bubble, at least in its hyped version: see a pessimistic version of the Gartner Hype Cycle for generative AI at Azamat Abdoullaev, 'AI Bible: Why Generative AI Bubble Is to Burst and Interactive AI Is to Rise. . .', LinkedIn 2023, www.linkedin.com/pulse/why-generative-ai-bubble-burst-2024-world-embeddings-vs-abdoullaev-14ycf/, last accessed 23 February 2024.

harmful content, and inadvertent 'hallucinations'; infringing existing laws relating for example to copyright and privacy; as well as environmental, security, and workplace concerns.[4] Most developed nations are now considering regulation to address these worries, whether via mandatory comprehensive legislation (such as the EU AI Act[5]); siloed or vertical legislation;[6] adapting existing law (see the many copyright lawsuits underway[7]); or by 'soft law' such as codes of conduct,[8] 'blueprints',[9] or industry guidelines.[10]

What has had less attention has been *self-regulation* (sometimes known as *private ordering* in the contractual context[11]) by model providers via a variety of instruments which range from the arguably more legally binding terms and conditions (T&C) imposed on users;[12] privacy policies or notices; and licences of copyright material; to the fuzzier and more PR-friendly but less enforceable 'acceptable use' policies, stakeholder 'principles' and codes of conduct. These terms, binding or otherwise, are also often cascaded down from model providers to downstream deployers in turn, as part of their agreement.

Such conditions have been widely studied, and often reviled,[13] in the history of e-commerce, especially in the business-to-consumer or 'B2C' context, as largely unread, not understood, and accepted without possibility of negotiation through imbalance of power in monopolistic or oligopolistic markets.[14] As such, they form part of a general history of abuse of power in

4 L. Weidinger et al., 'Ethical and Social Risks of Harm from Language Models', *DeepMind* (2021), https://arxiv.org/abs/2112.04359, last accessed 29 March 2024; A. Birhane, A. Kasirzadeh, D. Leslie, and S. Wachter, 'Science in the Age of Large Language Models', *Nature Reviews Physics*, 5 (2023), 277–280; C. Bird et al., 'Typology of Risks of Generative Text-to-Image Models', Proceedings of the 2023 AAAI/ACM Conference on AI, Ethics, and Society (AIES 2023), https://arxiv.org/pdf/2307.05543, last accessed 28 April 2024; House of Lords, Communications and Digital Committee, Paper 54 Large Language Models and Generative AI, 2 February 2024.

5 Artificial Intelligence Act (P9_TA(2024)0138), www.europarl.europa.eu/doceo/document/TA-9-2024-0138_EN.pdf, last accessed 29 March 2024 (hereinafter AI Act).

6 Chinese Interim Measures for the Management of Generative Artificial Intelligence Services (生成式人工智能服务管理暂行办法) which took effect on 15 August 2023; Amendments to the Artificial Intelligence and Data Act (AIDA) and the Consumer Privacy Protection Act in Canada, https://ourcommons.ca/committees/en/INDU/StudyActivity?studyActivityId=12157763, last accessed 1 March 2024.

7 See P. Samuelson, 'Thinking about Possible Remedies in the Generative AI Copyright Cases', *Communications of the ACM* (2024), https://papers.ssrn.com/sol3/papers.cfm?abstract_id=4770671, last accessed 11 April 2024.

8 Department for Science, Innovation & Technology, *Consultation Outcome A Pro-innovation Approach to AI Regulation: Government Response Updated 6 February* 2024, www.gov.uk/government/consultations/ai-regulation-a-pro-innovation-approach-policy-proposals/outcome/a-pro-innovation-approach-to-ai-regulation-government-response#:~:text=In%20the%20AI%20regulation%20white,Appropriate%20transparency%20and%20explainability, last accessed 1 March 2024.

9 Blueprint for an AI Bill of Rights Making Automated Systems Work for the American People, October 2022, www.whitehouse.gov/wp-content/uploads/2022/10/blueprint-for-an-ai-bill-of-rights.pdf, last accessed 1 March 2024.

10 See M. Veale, K. Matus, and R. Gorwa, 'AI and Global Governance: Modalities, Rationales, Tensions', *Annual Review of Law and Social Science*, 19 (2023), 255–275.

11 See N. Gunningham, 'Private Ordering, Self-Regulation and Futures Markets: A Comparative Study of Informal Social Control', *Law & Policy*, 13/4 (1991), 297–326.

12 We adopt here the definition of terms and conditions adapted from the DSA Art. 3(u) as 'all clauses, irrespective of their name or form, which govern the contractual relationship between the provider and the recipients of the service'.

13 E. Wauters, E. Lievens, and P. Valcke, 'Towards a Better Protection of Social Media Users: A Legal Perspective on the Terms of Use of Social Networking Sites', *International Journal of Law and Information Technology*, 22/3 (2014), 254–294.

14 E. Marique and Y. Marique, 'Sanctions on Digital Platforms: Beyond the Public–Private Divide', *Cambridge International Law Journal*, 8/2 (2019), 258–281; P. Pałka and M. Lippi, 'Big Data Analytics, Online Terms of Service and Privacy Policies', in R. Vogl et al. (eds.), *Research Handbook on Big Data Law* (Edward Elgar, Cheltenham, 2021); M. Betkier, *Privacy Online, Law and the Effective Regulation of Online Services* (Intersentia, Bristol, 2019).

consumer contracts generally, and relationships with digital platforms specifically.[15] Social media networks in particular display network effects which have made it impossible for a real marketplace of choices to operate, displacing consumer choice. Privacy policies have become notorious for inordinate lengthiness[16] and requiring reading comprehension abilities at university level,[17] and users have no incentive to read them anyway[18] as they often change frequently without additional consents sought.

As such, Palka has named T&C of online platforms 'terms of injustice' and argued they should no longer be tolerated.[19] This nuclear option is unlikely; but, as discussed below, unfair terms legislation, and in particularly the EU Digital Services Act (DSA), have attempted to curb and expose their worst excesses. Meanwhile T&C, privacy policies, and so on remain interesting, not just for providing transparency about provider data practices, but also for exposing noncompliance with relevant laws including consumer and due process rights.[20] Advocates and regulators have thus often found this work useful as a way to defend consumer and societal interests against tech giants.

Arguably, the risks of generative AI (GenAI) should be addressed by democratic legislation rather than self-regulation.[21] But the legislative process moves slowly, and although the first wave of AI legislation is underway at the time of writing – the EU AI Act, for example, passed in April 2024 – their bedding in, interpretation, and enforcement will still take time. In the United States, the home of most foundation models, so far the only mandatory federal law concerning AI and large models is an Executive Order which affects only public agencies.[22] In China, by contrast, the national internet regulator, the Cyberspace Administration of China (CAC), has taken a global lead by announcing on 13 July 2023 the Interim Measures for the Management of Generative Artificial Intelligence, which took effect on 15 August 2023.[23] According to Article 22 (1) of the Measures, 'generative artificial intelligence technology refers to models and related technologies that have the ability to generate content such as text, pictures, audio, and video'.[24] The most interesting feature of the Chinese rules is the pre-market licensing of the generative AI

[15] H. Micklitz, 'Unfair Terms in Consumer Contracts' in N. Reich et al. (eds.), *European Consumer Law*, 2nd ed. (Intersentia, Antwerp, 2014), 125–164.

[16] M. Loos and J. Luzak, 'Wanted: A Bigger Stick. On Unfair Terms in Consumer Contracts with Online Service Providers', *Journal of Consumer Policy*, 39/1 (2016), 63–90.

[17] See C. Jensen and C. Potts, 'Privacy Policies as Decision-Making Tools: An Evaluation of Online Privacy Notices', in *Proceedings of the SIGCHI conference on Human Factors in Computing Systems* (ACM, New York, 2004), 471–478; A. M. McDonald and L. Faith Cranor, 'The Cost of Reading Privacy Policies', *American Journal of Law and Policy for the Information Society*, 4/3 (2008), 543–568; L. Edwards and I. Brown, 'Privacy, Law, Code and Social Networking Sites', in I. Brown (ed.), *Research Handbook on Governance of the Internet* (Oxford University Press, Oxford, 2013).

[18] J. A. Obar and A. Oeldorf-Hirsch, 'The Biggest Lie on the Internet: Ignoring the Privacy Policies and Terms of Service Policies of Social Networking Services', *Information, Communication & Society*, 23/1 (2020), 128–47.

[19] P Palka, 'Terms of Injustice', *West Virginia Law Review*, 126 (2023), 133–184.

[20] N. Suzor, 'The Responsibilities of Platforms: A New Constitutionalism to Promote the Legitimacy of Decentralized Governance', *AoIR Selected Papers of Internet Research*, 6 (2016), 1–4.

[21] For a strong rejection though of the idea that terms of service are a valid way of allowing providers to govern themselves, see P. J. Palka, 'Terms of Service Are not Contracts – Beyond Contract Law in the Regulation of Online Platforms', in S. Grundmann (ed.), *European Contract Law in the Digital Age*, Vol. 3, (Intersentia, Bristol, 2018), 135–162.

[22] See Executive Order on the Safe, Secure, and Trustworthy Development and Use of Artificial Intelligence, 30 October 2023, www.whitehouse.gov/briefing-room/presidential-actions/2023/10/30/executive-order-on-the-safe-secure-and-trustworthy-development-and-use-of-artificial-intelligence/, last accessed 28 April 2024.

[23] CAC, Interim Measures for the Management of Generative Artificial Intelligence Services, 13 July 2023, www.cac.gov.cn/2023-07/13/c_1690898327029107.htm, last accessed 28 April 2024.

[24] In Chinese: 第二十二条 本办法下列用语的含义是：（一）生成式人工智能技术，是指具有文本、图片、音频、视频等内容生成能力的模型及相关技术.

models, discussed below in the conclusions.[25] Despite these developments, private ordering remains probably the most significant current form of governance of foundation models.

13.2 INSPIRATION AND METHOD

Our initial provocation, in January 2023 – only three months after the ChatGPT *coup de foudre* – was that social media platform T&C had been extensively studied for decades but almost no work had yet been done on the T&C of foundation models. Systematic amassing of datasets of T&C and privacy policies such as ToSBack[26] and the Princeton–Leuven Longitudinal Corpus of Privacy Policies[27] has been a strong feature of US research on online platforms, but in Europe such projects are historically less prevalent, perhaps because stronger regulation (privacy, consumer law) replaced the need to rely on publicising and enforcing T&C. However, recent times have seen arrivals such as CLAUDETTE,[28] which analyses consumer contracts and privacy policies for unfair terms using machine learning, and in 2021 the Platform Governance Archive (PGA), an open-source 'data repository and platform that collects and curates policies of major social media platforms in a long-term perspective'.[29]

The EU itself now collects the T&C of major digital players as part of its Digital Services Act efforts,[30] which have become mandatory since February 2024.[31] In January 2023, however, no one seemed to be systematically collecting and analysing the T&C of foundation model providers. A generative AI dataset *is* now collected by the Open Terms Archive, which commenced on 9 October 2023, but no analysis has apparently appeared, merely the raw terms, and only eighteen providers are included (four in October 2023), and from a much narrower jurisdictional basis than our study.[32]

Accordingly, we sought funding from the UK Research & Innovation (UKRI) Trustworthy Autonomous Systems (TAS) programme to pilot empirical work in January–March 2023 on the T&C ecology of generative AI model providers.[33] Ambitiously, we decided to map T&C across a representative sample of generative AI providers. We planned to study different *modes* of model (such as text, image, video). We were aware of clear differences between models like Stable Diffusion which cultivated an open-source community-minded image, and the proprietary and somewhat secretive nature of market leader models, such as ChatGPT (though Meta's Llama,

[25] Article 23 of Chinese Interim Measures for the Management of Generative Artificial Intelligence Services.

[26] See TosBack. The terms-of-service tracker, https://tosback.org/, last accessed 24 July 2023.

[27] See Privacy Policies over Time: Curation and Analysis of a Million-Document Dataset, https://privacypolicies.cs.princeton.edu/, last accessed 24 July 2023.

[28] CLAUDETTE Machine Learning Powered Analysis of Consumer Contracts and Privacy Policies, http://claudette.eui.eu/index.html, last accessed 20 March 2024.

[29] See F. Efferenn, 'The First Open Access Repository of Platform Policies: HIIG Launches New Platform Governance Archive', www.hiig.de/en/the-first-open-access-repository-of-platform-policies-hiig-launches-new-platform-governance-archive/, last accessed 24 March 2023.

[30] See https://code.europa.eu/p2b/contrib-versions, last accessed 1 May 2024.

[31] European Commission, 'How the Digital Services Act Enhances Transparency Online', https://digital-strategy.ec.europa.eu/en/policies/dsa-brings-transparency, last accessed 1 May 2024. See below, Section 13.4 and notes 38 and 39.

[32] See OpenTerms Archive, GenAI-versions, https://github.com/OpenTermsArchive/GenAI-versions, last accessed 1 May 2024.

[33] A number of papers have been given on this work: for example, themed panel session 'Generative AI and Intellectual Property: Assessing the Regulatory Landscape of the Terms & Conditions as a Start for Responsible Innovation and Adoption' at EPIP (European Policy for Intellectual Property), Krakow, Poland, 11–13 September 2023, see www.create.ac.uk/blog/2023/09/08/epip-2023-annual-conference-11-13-september-2023/, last accessed 1 May 2024.

perhaps more by accident than plan, was a counter-example). Although we could not do a full comparison of proprietary versus open-source models, we did incorporate a number of each type of model. Finally, we were keen to find small as well as large providers and to explore a range of countries of origin, not just the United States, United Kingdom, or European Union.

After extensive scoping, we found thirteen generative AI models which cut across many of these criteria. We examined the T&C, privacy policies, and, in some cases, additional documents such as community guidelines for

- six text-to-text (T2T) services (ChatGPT, ERNIE, Bard, CLOVA Studio, AI Writer, DeepL),
- four text-to-image (T2I) services (LENSA, Midjourney, Nightcafe, Stable Diffusion),
- three text-to-audio/video (T2A/V) services (Gen-2, Synthesia, Colossyan).

We also considered examining the T&Cs of downstream deployers creating applications based upon top-level foundation models, on the basis that governance within the GenAI value chain is now too complex to focus on model providers alone.[34] We looked primarily at the legal services area, which was showing exciting developments. For example, in the legal services domain, much media attention was being paid in early 2023 to Harvey AI,[35] which was partnering with law firms to create bespoke models for them using client and firm data built on top of a generative pre-trained transformer (GPT) large language model (LLM). In the end, though, it was impossible to obtain the T&C for Harvey AI due to commercial trade secrecy, and it was difficult to conclusively identify from websites and media clippings whether other prominent legal service providers (such as DoNotPay[36]) were in fact using a top-level foundation model as opposed to simply coding their own machine learning (ML) system or rule base. Accordingly, we left the deployer angle for a later time.

In each of these categories, though not for every model, we found specific clauses regarding copyright, privacy, illegal and harmful content, dispute resolution, jurisdiction, and enforcement. We chose to focus mainly on copyright, privacy, and dispute resolution. We found little difference in jurisdiction and ouster clauses from those typical of US standard-form consumer contracts, and so, for reasons of space, this chapter does not deal with that area. This was a complicated project design, and our results are best seen as qualitative rather than quantitative.

[34] See e.g. J. Cobbe et al., 'Understanding Accountability in Algorithmic Supply Chains', FAccT' 23: 2023 ACM Conference on Fairness, Accountability, and Transparency, Chicago, IL, June 2023, https://doi.org/10.1145/3593013.3594073, last accessed 1 May 2024.

[35] Harvey AI, www.harvey.ai/, last accessed 4 December 2023. Harvey was under development at the time of the survey (and remains so, with a waitlist for early adoption); details were vague but such was the hype around it that it seemed an important actor to include. Harvey is backed financially by a number of GenAI providers including OpenAI.

[36] Famously, in February 2023, Joshua Browder, the CEO of DoNotPay, advertised he would supply DoNotPay in an earpiece to a party litigant so that it could argue his case in court as a kind of remote 'robot' lawyer. When warned this might result in six months in jail for contempt, he terminated the stunt. Since DNP has, by his own admission, proved to be highly inaccurate about the law (hallucination problem) this was probably for the best for all. M. Cerullo, 'AI-Powered "Robot" Lawyer Won't Argue in Court after Jail Threats', CBS News, 26 January 2023, www.cbsnews.com/news/robot-lawyer-wont-argue-court-jail-threats-do-not-pay/, last accessed 1 May 2023. The inclusion of DNP as a foundation model-based deployer service would have been uncertain as it is not clear how far DNP relied on its own simplistic rule-based AI in the first quarter of 2023 and how far it was using upstream foundation models to extend its services. See E. Roth, 'DoNotPay Is Launching an AI Chatbot That Can Negotiate Your Bills', *The Verge*, 13 December 2022, www.theverge.com/2022/12/13/23505873/donotpay-negotiate-bills-ai-chatbot, last accessed 2 May 2024, which announces a demo to show the use of OpenAI's GPT-3 API to build a 'convincingly human-like' negotiating chatbot on to DNP's platform.

Our multidimensional approach was probably overly ambitious, given the timeframe, especially as the T&Cs of many of the models were constantly changing. The large-scale EU and US tracker projects use automated scraper bots, and in the future so would we. However, we do feel that our preliminary findings represent a 'line in the sand' worth recording, of valuable historical significance. As such, we choose to present them here as of the end of March 2023, rather than attempting to update them a year later. Only one other team of researchers in Europe, led by Natali Helberger, reported results analysing T&C from this very early phase of generative AI, and their work, though valuable, was limited to only five providers, and focused mainly on impacts on journalism and the media.[37] We anticipated that our handcrafted dataset would be displaced shortly thereafter by the mighty EU Digital Service Act (DSA) transparency regime[38] (see above[39]); but in fact it is unlikely that generative AI models do fit within the scope of DSA rules (see below, Section 13.3).

13.3 ANALYSIS OF T&C AND OTHER PROVIDER DOCUMENTS BY TOPIC

13.3.1 *Copyright*

Our research questions here were informed by the considerable debate on copyright and large models in academe, the courts, and the media.[40] The key issues that emerged were:

1. Who owns the copyright over the outputs of the model? Is it a proper copyright ownership or an assigned licence?
2. If output works infringe copyright, who is responsible (user, service, for example)?
3. Is there any procedure in force (such as notice and takedown, prompt filtering) to avoid or at least minimise the risk of copyright infringement? If yes, what?

[37] N. Helberger, 'Generative AI in Media & Journalism: Think Big, But Read the Small Print First', in *Generative AI in the Newsroom: Medium*, 18 July 2023, https://generative-ai-newsroom.com/generative-ai-in-media-journalism-think-big-but-read-the-small-print-first-375f2ecb1256, last accessed 28 April 2024. Subsequent research published by the AI for Media and Democracy team (www.aim4dem.nl/) and AlgoSoc (https://algosoc.org/) has incorporated this work but not with a key focus on T&C.

[38] See early results advertised from the DSA Observatory, the Platform, and the AlgoSoc project at the first DSA and Platform Regulation Conference 2024, 15–16 February 2024, Amsterdam, https://dsa-observatory.eu/the-dsa-and-platform-regulation-conference-2024/, last accessed 28 April 2024.

[39] The transparency regimes of the DSA are complex. The main content moderation decisions database can be found at https://transparency.dsa.ec.europa.eu/, last accessed 28 April 2024. Helberger and Samuelson note: 'The transparency obligations in the DSA can usefully be sorted into four categories: 1) consumer-facing transparency obligations; 2) mandatory reporting and information access obligations to national regulators and the European Commission; 3) rights of access to data; and 4) obligations to contribute to public-facing databases of information'. Article 14, which requires platforms to enforce their ToSs and in so doing have due regard to the fundamental rights of users under the Charter of Rights, is especially important and applies to all platforms defined under the DSA not just to the very large online platforms (VLOPs) or very large online search engines (VLOSEs). See N. Helberger and P. Samuelson, 'Will the EU's Digital Services Act Become a Global Transparency Regime?', in *Verfassungsblog: From the DMCA to the DSA – A Transatlantic Dialogue on Online Platform Regulation and Copyright*, March 2024, available at https://papers.ssrn.com/sol3/papers.cfm?abstract_id=4783341, last accessed 29 April 2024; J. P. Quintais, N. Appelman, and R. Ó. Fathaigh, 'Using Terms and Conditions to Apply Fundamental Rights to Content Moderation', *German Law Journal*, 24/5 (2023), 881–911.

[40] See e.g. A. Guadamuz, 'A Scanner Darkly: Copyright Liability and Exceptions in Artificial Intelligence Inputs and Outputs', *GRUR International*, 73/2 (2024), 111–127; D. Friedmann, 'Creation and Generation Copyright Standards', *NYU Journal of Intellectual Property & Entertainment Law*, 2024, https://papers.ssrn.com/sol3/Delivery.cfm/SSRN_ID4770924_code1572004.pdf?abstractid=4770924&mirid=1&type=2, last accessed 29 April 2024; G. Frosio, 'Should We Ban Generative AI, Incentivise It or Make It a Medium for Inclusive Creativity?', in E. Bonadio and C. Sganga (eds.), *A Research Agenda for EU Copyright Law* (Edward Elgar, Cheltenham, 2023).

Key Takeaways

- In almost every model or service studied, ownership of outputs was assigned to the user, but in many cases an extensive licence was also granted back to the model for coexisting use of the outputs.
- Similarly, in almost every case, risk of copyright infringement in the output work was left, with some decisiveness, with the user.
- Licences assigning copyright were mostly bespoke, though some use of Creative Commons and OpenRAILs was observed, and boilerplate clauses reminiscent of those used in social media T&C were common. There was a lack of industry norms as to the definition of some key terms.
- Even at this early stage of foundation models, every model provider undertook some content moderation, and notice and takedown arrangements were the norm.

13.3.1.1 Who Owns the Copyright over the Outputs? Is It a Proper Copyright Ownership or an Assigned Licence?

In every case studied except (possibly) one, ownership over output works was granted to users.

Two T2I services, LENSA[41] and Midjourney,[42] assigned ownership to the user but demanded back an extremely wide coexisting licence – for example, in the case of LENSA, a Russian service, a 'perpetual, revocable, nonexclusive, royalty-free, worldwide, fully-paid, transferable, sub-licensable license to use, reproduce, modify, adapt, translate, create derivative works'. Nightcafe's T&C[43] simply stated that the user owns all the IP rights related to outputs. Stable Diffusion[44] adopted not a bespoke licence but a commonly known open-source licence, a version of the BLOOM licence or CreativeML Open RAIL-M licence.[45] With regard to T2A/V services Synthesia,[46] Gen-2,[47] and Colossyan,[48] the scenario was substantially similar.

With regard to T2T services, the scenario differed a little more. For ChatGPT,[49] OpenAI assigned to the user all the 'right, title and interest in and to Output' and also the 'inputs', which seems to mean prompt material. Bard,[50] Simplified,[51] and CLOVA Studio[52] also assigned ownership to users. By contrast, the Chinese company Baidu – proprietor of Ernie Bot[53] – declared itself the owner of all IP rights of the application programming interface (API) service platform and its related elements, such as 'content, data, technology, software, code, user interface'. This probably referred only to infrastructure, not output works – but it is not yet

41 LENSA 'Terms of Use', https://tos.LENSA-ai.com/terms-dec-2-2022, last accessed 4 December 2023.
42 'Midjourney 'Terms of Service', https://docs.midjourney.com/docs/terms-of-service, last accessed 4 December 2023.
43 NightCafe 'Terms of Service', https://nightcafe.studio/policies/terms-of-service, last accessed 4 December 2023.
44 'Stable Diffusion License on Dezgo.Com, https://dezgo.com/, last accessed 4 December 2023.
45 C. M. Ferrandis, 'The BigScience OpenRAIL-M License', https://bigscience.huggingface.co/blog/bigscience-open rail-m, last accessed 1 May 2023.
46 Synthesia 'Customer Terms of Service', www.synthesia.io/terms/terms-of-service, last accessed 4 December 2023.
47 Runway 'Terms of Use', https://runwayml.com/terms-of-use/, last accessed 4 December 2023.
48 Colossyan Creator 'Terms of Service', www.colossyan.com/terms, last accessed 4 December 2023.
49 'Terms of Use – March 2023', https://openai.com/policies/mar-2023-terms, last accessed 4 December 2023.
50 'Google Terms of Service – Privacy & Terms', https://policies.google.com/terms, last accessed 4 December 2023.
51 'Terms of Use | Simplified', https://simplified.com/termsofservice, last accessed 4 December 2023.
52 NAVER CLOUD PLATFORM 'Terms of Service', www.ncloud.com, last accessed 4 December 2023.
53 'Wenxin Large Model Documentation – Service Agreement | Baidu Intelligent Cloud Documents', https://yiyan .baidu.com/, last accessed 4 December 2023.

entirely clear.[54] Lastly, DeepL[55] 'does not assume any copyrights to the translations made by Customer using the Products'.

13.3.1.2 If Output Works Infringe Copyright, Who Is Responsible?

In every model studied, the liability for copyright infringement was laid entirely at the door of the user.

Midjourney's T&C used entertainingly colourful language: '[i]f you knowingly infringe someone else's intellectual property, and that costs us money, we're going to come find you and collect that money from you'.

LENSA's T&C was more diplomatic: the user is responsible for any content that 'may infringe, misappropriate or violate any patent, trademark, trade secret, copyright or other intellectual or proprietary right of any person'.

Stable Diffusion asserted (in US legalistic capital letters) that the model was provided 'on an "as is" basis, without warranties or conditions of any kind, either express or implied, including, without limitation, any warranties or conditions of title, non-infringement, merchantability, or fitness for a particular purpose'. The user was also held 'solely responsible' for the appropriateness of distributing the model, not just the outputs, which was possible under Stability's open-source policies – something it seems unlikely they could control or assess. Any conceivable liability of Stability was limited to US$100.

In none of these services was there any admission that copyright infringement liability might come from the provider's training of the *model* (for example, by using copyright works without consent) rather than any bad actions by the user. Some T&C, such as ChatGPT, not only asserted that the user was solely responsible for outputs but required the user to indemnify the provider against any liability arising as a result of the user's interactions with the service. These combinations of exclusion, limitation, and indemnity clauses may well be wholly or partially invalid in consumer contracts in many jurisdictions, but of course the user would have to have the resources to challenge. We saw no real differences across the different modes of model studied, by national origin or size.

13.3.1.3 Is There Any Procedure in Force to Avoid or at least Minimise the Risk of Copyright Infringement?

Most of the models studied, including all the T2I services, provided for some sort of mitigation or enforcement measures in relation to copyright infringement liability, for example prompt or keyword or proper name blocking. In many cases, the aim may have been to prevent a wider range of harms than just copyright infringement, such as production of child sexual material or other illegal, harmful, or adult content, or production of misinformation (fake news).

Many models threatened to ban users who broke the rules of the site. Repeat infringers were especially mentioned. Midjourney's T&C were the most forthright, stating, without much legal decorum, that '[a]ny violations of these rules (i.e. the ones indicated both in T&C and Community Guidelines with regard to content restrictions) may lead to bans from our services.

[54] The Chinese Beijing Internet Court judgment of 27 November 2023 in the case of *Li v. Liu* might be a possible indicator of policy changes in China towards providing ownership of copyright of AI-generated content to the users. See translation of the judgment: Xiao Wang, 'Copyright Protection for "AI-Generated" Images', *GRUR International*, 73/4 (2024), 360–368.

[55] 'DeepL Terms and Conditions', www.deepl.com/pro-license, last accessed 4 December 2023.

We are not a democracy. Behave respectfully or lose your rights to use the Service'. Midjourney also automatedly blocked some prompts, and certain words, and implemented flagging of infringing content by users to moderators. Similarly, Nightcafe's T&C provided for a series of enforcement measures in case of breach or suspicion of breach, including: deletion of any user content; suspension or termination of the account; suspension or permanent ban to the site; and disclosure of some prohibited content to appropriate government authorities.

Notice and takedown (NTD) was implemented on most sites, in exactly the same ways as it is on most platform or hosting sites, to immunise themselves from liability under instruments like the Digital Millennium Copyright Act (DMCA) or EU Digital Services Act (formerly Electronic Commerce Directive, Articles 12–15[56]). MidJourney, ChatGPT, Bard (Google), and LENSA all offered means to request removal of infringing content, the latter by 'written notification to our copyright agent … [i]n accordance with the Digital Millennium Copyright Act (17 U.S.C. § 512) (DMCA)'. It is interesting that a Russian provider was willing to namecheck a US law, showing the effective global scope of DMCA warnings. By contrast, China's Ernie Bot asked for notice of infringing content, 'in accordance with the laws and regulations of the People's Republic of China'. This is an unusual reference to a local national law other than the DMCA.

Midjourney had the most developed T2I model moderation scheme. Users were encouraged to flag infringing content to moderators in a well-developed model of community quasi-self-enforcement, although who these moderators were, and how they made their enforcement decisions, was (typically) unclear. Nightcafe stated that the company had the right (not the obligation) 'to appoint community moderators or automoderators from time to time' who 'will flag creations and comments for human moderation'.

Invariably, however, even where community moderation was in operation, the provider reserved the right to exercise its own discretion in assessing whether outputs or behaviour violated the T&C, and what the sanction might be (site ban, for example). Unusually, Gen2 stated it had *no* obligation to review or monitor users or content. CLOVA Studio and DeepL did not apparently provide for enforcement procedures. These kinds of arbitrary denials of due process, unclear terms and sanctions, and haphazard applications of enforcement are exactly the kind of problems the DSA was drafted to address in relation to moderation failures on conventional platforms: yet as we will see in the concluding section below, it is likely that foundation models do not, per se, fall under the DSA.

13.3.2 *Data Protection Rights*

Takeaways:

- Data protection rights are the Cinderella sister of foundation model governance, with little attention paid in the early stage of industry development either in T&C or in literature. In April 2024, by no means all model providers had privacy policies.
- Only basic options to exercise rights, such as an email address to complain to, were found in most models studied in early 2023, and not always that.
- Another sweep to December 2023 indicated improvement in recognition of DP rights and more detailed complaint mechanisms for users.

[56] Directive 2000/31/EC of the European Parliament and the Council of 8 June 2000 on certain legal aspects of information society services, in particular electronic commerce, in the Internal Market ('Directive on Electronic Commerce').

TABLE 13.1 *Analysis of copyright clauses*

Models	Who owns the copyright over the outputs and (if any indication is found) over the inputs?	If a copyright infringement is committed, who is responsible?	Is there any procedure in force to avoid or at least minimise the risk of copyright infringement?
LENSA	User BUT user grants extensive licence to provider	User	Yes
Midjourney	User BUT user grants extensive licence to provider	User	Yes
Nightcafe	User	User	Yes
Stable Diffusion	User	User	Not really (it reserves the right to restrict the usage of the model)
Synthesia	User BUT user grants extensive licence to provider	User	Yes
Gen-2	User BUT user grants extensive licence to provider	User	No
Colossyan	User	User	Not really (it reserves the right for access to and removal from the service)
ChatGPT	Input (e.g. prompt): user; output: assignment of 'right, title and interest' from company to user	User	Yes
Bard (now Gemini)	User	N/a	Yes
Ernie Bot	Provider	User	Yes
Simplified AI writer	Unclear	User	Yes
CLOVA Studio	User BUT only for purpose of the service's provision	N/a	No
DeepL	User	N/a	No

This is a shorter section than the preceding one for a reason. While copyright has been a subject of furious debate since the inception of large image and language models, and the DMCA, alongside US copyright law, is well known to carry the risk of punitive sanctions if requests for takedown are ignored, data protection (DP) was, at the early stage we studied, much less mentioned, if at all.[57] Arguably it was only the action of the Italian state DP regulator, the

[57] Quite possibly this was because of the lack of overarching data protection law akin to the GDPR in the United States (see also the occasional reference to the California DP law rather than the GDPR). One of the authors (Edwards) gave a number of talks on foundation models and the GDPR in early 2023 and at that time only a few very short blogs could be traced on the topic, e.g. U. Gal, 'ChatGPT Is a Data Privacy Nightmare. If You've ever Posted Online, You Ought to Be Concerned', *The Conversation*, 8 February 2023, https://theconversation.com/chatgpt-is-a-data-privacy-nightmare-if-youve-ever-posted-online-you-ought-to-be-concerned-199283, last accessed 29 April 2024. Since then a few scholarly articles have emerged, primarily on the incompatibility of AI and the 'right to be forgotten' – see e.g. D. Zhang et al., 'Right to Be Forgotten in the Era of Large Language Models: Implications, Challenges, and Solutions', *arqiv*, September 2023, https://arxiv.org/pdf/2307.03941, last accessed 29 April 2024; P. Hacker et al., 'Regulating ChatGPT and Other Large Generative AI Models', FAccT' 23, 12–15 June 2023, Chicago, IL, https://arxiv.org/abs/2302.02337, last accessed 4 March 2024; S. B. Vale, 'Training Large Generative AI Models Based on Publicly Available Personal Data: A GDPR Conundrum That the AI Act Could Solve', *DigiCon*, https://digi-con.org/training-large-generative-ai-models-based-on-publicly-available-personal-data-a-gdpr-conundrum-that-the-ai-act-could-solve/, last accessed 4 March 2024 – but the area is still spectacularly underwritten compared to copyright.

Garante, against Open AI and ChatGPT in April 2023[58] – after our sampling period – that made the world of foundation models wake up to the likelihood of DP infringement.[59] Yet the EU General Data Protection Regulation (GDPR),[60] the leading global DP instrument, is extraterritorial: if services sell into Europe or use the personal data of European data subjects, then these rights, at least in theory, must be operationalised for those subjects.[61]

Privacy policies have become effectively universal for digital and platform services, even where not in theory required by local law.[62] All the T2T models in our study, regardless of jurisdiction, had a privacy policy. However, at the early stage of industry evolution we covered, in many cases they were that of the parent company's general privacy policies, rather than specially tailored for foundation models. In the wider ecology of models, some had no privacy policy at all, and others bore evidence of having been cut and pasted from large social media networks or e-commerce templates without much thought of applying them to the new world of foundation models.

The GDPR offers several significant user rights against data controllers, including information and subject access rights, the right to erasure of personal data ('to be forgotten'), the right to rectification, rights to data portability, the right to object to processing, including profiling, and the right to object to solely automated decision making.[63] If personal data is used in training sets to build large models, then there must be a lawful ground of processing.[64] Purpose limitation, data protection impact assessments, and the age at which children can consent will also, inter alia, be relevant. Many of these issues were raised in the (ongoing) Italian action, and the European Data Protection Board (EDPB) is currently constructing guidance on how large models should (if it is even possible) comply with GDPR rules. However, we found evidence of relative failure of model providers in early 2023 to engage with DP user rights.

Of the thirteen models we studied, nine referenced the GDPR in their privacy policies (if they had one). However, seven explicitly mentioned the California Consumer Privacy Act (CCPA). Of these, LENSA, a Russian service, stood out with a special California Notice and Collection and Privacy Notice.[65]

All the T2T models we studied offered at least an email address to enable objection to and removal of user data. The privacy policies of the other models studied were, however, far less consistent. In most models studied, providers used boilerplate clauses to talk about the processing of data supplied by subscribers, such as registration data and prompts. The much more difficult questions around processing personal data from the public internet as input to training

[58] N. Lomas, 'Italy Orders ChatGPT Blocked Citing Data Protection Concerns', *TechCrunch*, 31 March 2023, https://techcrunch.com/2023/03/31/chatgpt-blocked-italy/, last accessed 1 April 2024.

[59] And regulators to foundation models. The United Kingdom's Information Commissioners Office (ICO) is still consulting on guidance on foundation models – consultation initiated 12 April 2024, see LNB News, 'CO Launches Consultation on Accuracy of Generative AI Models', 12 April 2024, www.lexisnexis.co.uk/legal/news/ico-launches-consultation-on-accuracy-of-generative-ai-models, last accessed 1 May 2024. EDPB guidance appears to still be a work in progress, although a select handful of regulators have issued advice, e.g. CNIL, Hamburg.

[60] Regulation (EU) 2016/679 of the European Parliament and of the Council of 27 April 2016 on the protection of natural persons with regard to the processing of personal data and on the free movement of such data, and repealing Directive 95/46/EC – General Data Protection Regulation (GDPR).

[61] GDPR, Art. 3.

[62] A. W. Hayne, 'Online Privacy Policies: Contracting away Control over Personal Information?', *Dickinson Law Review*, 111/3 (2007), 597. Despite the lack of US federal-level data protection law, the FTC in practice has long taken the role of US privacy commando and effectively required privacy policies.

[63] GDPR, Chapter III.

[64] GDPR, Art. 6.

[65] LENSA App California Notice at Collection and Privacy Notice, 10 July 2023, http://tos.LENSA-ai.com/CCPAPP, last accessed 1 April 2024.

datasets were not raised. It can be argued that T&C relate only to the relationship between provider and user so issues around the provenance of the training set are irrelevant – but this is patently not true of DP notices which should give third parties as well as contractual partners notice of processing of their data and subject access and other user rights.[66]

Eleven out of thirteen models studied offered clear contact information, such as an email address or a link to a form within their privacy policies. In the first quarter of 2023, none of these thirteen models included much information about data rights other than subject access rights and the right of erasure. Open AI, provider of ChatGPT, gave no lawful ground for processing data and said only to email the company about erasure rights. Compared to the well-trodden path for fulfilling the 'right to be forgotten' since 2014 in the wake of *Google Spain*[67] for platforms and search engines, this seemed little more than a token effort.

Due to the lack of information about DP in our survey in April 2023, we chose to do another sweep at the end of 2023. By then, twelve of thirteen models had decided to update their privacy policies. All twelve now make more, though not completely comprehensive, mention of the range of DP user rights. This is a positive trend away from the DP 'wild west'. But most still only offer an email address as means of complaint (nine out of thirteen). Two still do not do even that. For larger providers, because privacy policies are generally applicable to all generative AI services provided, and sometimes all services offered by a company *in toto* such as Google,[68] it is extremely difficult to work out what particular models are doing with users' data. Almost certainly, further action by DPA regulators and privacy advocates as well as perhaps the Federal Trade Commission (FTC) in the United States, will be necessary to force more than lip-service compliance. It is notable that Open AI only threw up a right to be forgotten (RTBF) form and added a lawful ground for processing straight after it was banned in Italy by the Garante and still, as of April 2024, declares that the right of rectification is beyond its abilities.[69] It is fair to say that DP compliance by large models is still very much a work in progress.

13.4 CONCLUSIONS AND FUTURE WORK

Sometimes you have to do the work to know *how* to do the work, and we learnt a lot from this pilot. In future work, we would hope to examine in more detail a number of points we either missed as significant, or did not have capacity to explore in full, or at all. There is obviously a vast amount to be done regarding prohibited content and behaviour, and how it is policed on these sites, beyond just copyright and privacy. We felt it was vital to look at how T&C changed over time, but we did not have the technology or time to do this. The automated scraper bots powering datasets like those held by Open Terms Archive would in the future simplify this task tremendously. Indeed, future work could simply rely on analysing the GenAI database in the Open Terms Archive. Our complex project design in the end seemed unnecessary as we found very similar clauses and issues coming up, regardless of mode of model, size of provider, or country of business. We did not

[66] GDPR, Art. 14 and Chapter III.

[67] Case C-131/12, *Google Spain SL and Google Inc. v. Agencia Española de Protección de Datos (AEPD) and Mario Costeja González* Judgment of the Court (Grand Chamber), 13 May 2014.

[68] Google generally only has one privacy policy across all its services – however it does have a FAQ about its application to Gemini, https://support.google.com/mail/answer/14615114, last accessed 1 May 2024.

[69] As we went to press, NoYB, the privacy NGO, announced it was suing ChatGPT for failing to comply with the right to rectification: 'ChatGPT Provides False Information about People, and OpenAI Can't Correct It', NoYB, https://noyb.eu/en/chatgpt-provides-false-information-about-people-and-openai-cant-correct-it, last accessed 29 April 2024. NoYB points out that OpenAI itself admits that 'factual accuracy in large language models remains an area of active research' – showing the importance of documentary admissions on model provider websites.

TABLE 13.2 *Analysis of privacy policies of GenAI models*

Models	Mention CCPA rights (California), EU or UK GDPR?	Mention rights other than erasure explicitly, and do they give a form to claim your rights?	Offer an email address to claim DP rights?
Open AI	No CCPA EU and UK GDPR	Yes Form	Yes privacy@openai.com
Baidu (ERNIE)	Nothing mentioned	Yes Form	No Specific form
Google (Bard, now Gemini)	CCPA EU and UK GDPR	Yes Form	Yes Special form
CLOVA Studio	EU GDPR No CCPA No UK GDPR	Yes Email, no form	Yes dl_ncloud_privacy@navercorp.com
AI Writer	Nothing mentioned	Yes No form	Yes hello@simplified.com
DeepL	EU GDPR	Yes	No
LENSA	CCPA EU and UK GDPR	Yes Access, modification, correction, and erasure.	Yes privacy@prisma-ai.com.
Midjourney	CCPA EU and UK GDPR	Yes Email, no form	Yes privacy@midjourney.com.
Nightcafe	EU and UK GDPR	Yes Email, no form	Yes hello@nightcafe.studio
Stable Diffusion	EU GDPR	Yes No easy option to do so	No
Gen-2	Nothing mentioned	Yes Email, no form	Yes support@runwayml.com
Synthesia	UK and EU GDPR	Yes Email, no form	Yes support@synthesia.io.
Colossyan	Nothing mentioned	Yes Email, no form	Yes info@colossyan.com

anticipate this; but might hypothesise that large providers such as Google already have well-crafted internationally targeted T&C which were largely applied *mutatis mutandis* to generative models; while small providers across the globe seem largely to have copy-pasted from familiar commercial styles seen in social media T&Cs wherever they are located. Even the Chinese services had fairly familiar T&Cs. A key problem was gaining access to B2B T&Cs and this would require careful cultivation of trusted relationships, which we could not do in three months.

Substantively, our main finding across the T&Cs examined was a general paradigm in which no ownership was claimed over outputs, but no risk was accepted in relation to them either. Instead risk (such as of copyright infringement, of privacy breaches, of production of illegal content) was assigned firmly and unconditionally to the user. This might just be seen as a typical commercial land grab in B2C clauses – deny everything and wait for them to sue you! – but it is still surprising that providers were willing so happily to give up claims to monetise outputs,[70] Again, this can be explained as a smart commercial choice to waive rights over output works in return for collecting the input data of users to train bigger and better models – but that makes

[70] As noted above at Section 13.2.1, some but not all providers did at least demand from users a non-exclusive licence over outputs.

less sense now given providers more recently seem to have accepted that legally users probably have rights to opt out from (or object to) processing of their data under data protection law, even where they are not paying enterprise customers.

We suggest instead that what is happening here is a *platformisation paradigm*, in which model providers attempt to position themselves as 'neutral intermediaries' in a style very familiar to those who have studied the case law battles around the Electronic Commerce Directive and the DMCA in the early years of this millennium.[71] Model providers are seeking all the benefits of neutrality in terms of deferring liability and responsibility to users, while still gaining all the advantages of their position in terms of profit and power. This suggestion is bolstered by the way all or most of the providers in our sample behaved as if they were indeed platforms under the Electronic Commerce Directive (ECD; now DSA) and the DMCA in terms of content moderation; accepting DMCA notices for takedown, removing repeat infringers, and so on, as if this would provide them with safe harbours like any other 'platform'.

Yet foundation model providers are *not* platforms – or certainly were not in the simpler days of early 2023 (Open AI's GPT Store[72] muddies the waters somewhat). Conceptually, a platform was originally an online hosting service which made content provided by third parties available to the world. The original policy justification for viewing platforms as neutral actors was to balance the possibly unlimited risk for acts of users that might render the platforms economically unviable, with the need to provide some redress to those affected by legal violations in user-generated content – notably, the copyright industries. Morally, at the turn of 2000, though probably not by just a few years later, there was also a case that it was wrong to 'shoot the messenger' unless and until they received notice that their 'premises' were being used for no good. Legally, this was crystallised into the familiar safe harbour liability exemptions, and notice and takedown (NTD) obligations, introduced via the DMCA and ECD around 2000. Now, in the DSA, the heir to the ECD, a series of definitions describe an 'online intermediary service' that is a provider of 'information society services', which here exclusively include hosting, acting as a mere conduit, caching, and (originally in the DMCA, and belatedly and with limits in the DSA) providing search engine tools.[73] Some types of larger or more complex intermediary services then have further obligations placed on them: 'online platforms' and 'very large online platforms' (VLOPs, or online platforms with over 45 million annual users). But crucially, platforms are still, at root, hosts, which store or make available content 'provided by a recipient of the service' (Article 6).

This description simply does not match foundation models. The only content the user supplies is the prompt or other input (for example, image, database) and storage of it is not the relevant information society service that the model provider is offering – that is, (surprise) access to the model. As Hacker and colleagues note, 'users . . . *request* information from LGAIMs via prompts, they can hardly be said to *provide* this information'.[74] As Botero Arcila puts it, 'they [provider sites] neither consist of the merely technical transmission of information nor host *user*-generated content. Rather they host *AI*-generated content'.[75] Hacker and colleagues agree,

[71] For a general history of how this paradigm emerged, see L. Edwards, '"With Great Power Comes Great Responsibility": The Rise of Platform Liability', in L. Edwards (ed.), *Law, Policy and the Internet* (Hart, Oxford, 2019); and M. Husovec, 'Rising above Liability: The Digital Services Act as a Blueprint for the Second Generation of Global Internet Rules', *Berkeley Technology Law Journal*, 38/3 (2023), 883–920.

[72] See OpenAI, 'Introducing the GPT Store', 10 January 2024, https://openai.com/index/introducing-the-gpt-store, last accessed 2 May 2024.

[73] See DSA Arts. 3–6. From here on we will use the DSA only as the legal paradigm for discussing platformisation.

[74] Hacker et al., supra n. 57, at 16 (emphasis added).

[75] B. Botero Arcila 'Is It a Platform? Is It a Search Engine? It's Chat GPT! The European Liability Regime for Large Language Models', *Journal of Free Speech Law*, 3/2 (2023), 453–488, at 478 (emphasis added).

pointing out that with LLMs, the relevant content is decidedly not provided by the user, but by the LLM itself.[76]

In policy terms, relieving model providers of liability is inappropriate because they are not mere hapless victims of risks deriving from user-created content, but the creators of the content *themselves* by allowing users to query the model. Botero Arcila makes a spirited attempt to argue that large language models might sneak into the DSA hierarchy as search engines, since very large online search engines (VLOSEs) do not have to be based on intermediary hosts, and this evades its definitional constraints – and LLMs such as ChatGPT are indubitably often used very like search engines. But this ingenious idea ignores foundation models used to generate art, or code, which are rarely if ever used as search engines, and it also ignores those models with too few users to fit into VLOSEs. In fact, it is already becoming common to incorporate LLMs into VLOSEs anyway and in that case they will fall under the umbrella of the DSA – this is currently true of Bing (using GPT) and Google Search (using Gemini),[77]

Although there can be more debate, so far it is relatively clear. Foundation models do not per se fall under the DSA. The problem then is that the DSA does not, as the ECD did, just provide liability *exemptions*; it also demands *positive* steps of hosts, platforms, and VLOPs of varying natures.[78] And these are steps that, judging by our research, are exactly what are needed to protect the B2C users of the generative AI sector. Content moderation actions of model providers are opaque, dictatorial, unclear, and unjustified, and opportunities to meaningfully contest arbitrary decisions and sanctions on users are few. To meet these problems on genuine platforms, the DSA provides inter alia that:

- *All* hosting services shall provide clear information in plain English about their terms and conditions and content moderation practices (Article 14). Content moderation rules must be clear and predictable and based on existing policies (Article 14(1)). Importantly, services must also *enforce* their terms in a way that has '*due regard*' for the '*fundamental rights*' of users (Article 14(4)[79]). It could be argued for example that placing all the risk on model users, as models uniformly do, is not consonant with their rights of free expression.
- *All* hosting services shall meet transparency reporting obligations relating to their content moderation decisions and give reasons for such (Article 15).
- Online platforms (a subset of hosts) must provide ad archives, implement trusted flaggers and respect due process in internal and external appeals against moderation decisions.

These provisions would be extraordinarily useful in meeting the procedural vices identified above in model T&Cs and would transform their generally hostile and unfair governance approach to disempowered users. There seems no good policy reason why these rules should *not* be applied to foundation models. At present, model providers have their cake and eat it; they assert exemption from liability by passing risk via their terms and conditions to users but evade the new positive obligations of the DSA. This is unjust. We suggest therefore that the DSA is already not fit for purpose and should be amended to bring foundation models within its scope as soon as possible.

The DSA is only a European instrument of course, if a relevant one. One of the suppositions of this study was that generative AI models are being developed globally, not just in Silicon

76 Hacker et al., supra n. 57, at 16.

77 See 'Supervision of the Designated Very Large Online Platforms and Search Engines under DSA', https://digital-strategy.ec.europa.eu/en/policies/list-designated-vlops-and-vloses#ecl-inpage-google, last accessed 2 May 2024.

78 See Husovec, supra n. 71.

79 J. P. Quintais, N. Appelman, and R. Ó Fathaigh, 'Using Terms and Conditions to Apply Fundamental Rights to Content Moderation', *German Law Journal*, 24/5 (2023), 881–911.

Valley, and perhaps too much attention has been spent on models from a few Western countries, and Western regulation. As of April 2024, according to the CAC announcement, 117 generative AI models have been registered in the PRC. We noted earlier that China has legislated extensively in relation to AI and has in fact taken an early lead on regulation of generative AI and in ways quite distinct from the West.[80] A key feature of the Chinese regulation is that generative AI services are only allowed to provide their services to the public after pre-approval by the regulator.[81] In order to be approved, developers need to provide documentation of the model, including T&Cs, to the regulator (CAC). This pre-market approval of T&C and privacy policies of generative AI services, commonly thought of as state licensing, might be considered as another possible way to mitigate the vices of market–driven self-regulation. Indeed, such an idea, of pre-market supervision leading to 'regulated contracts', might be regarded as a new spin on the familiar notion of 'a Food and Drugs Agency (FDA) for models' frequently floated by US academics and recently investigated by UK think tank the Ada Lovelace Institute.[82] As the Ada researchers note, while there is substantial support for the idea of state agency pre-licensing, less thought has been put into what it might actually *do*. It is not impossible to imagine that this process might be used not just to regulate how models are *built*, as the EU AI Act does, but also to standardise its terms of *use* when put on the market. By these means private ordering practices within a sector could conceivably be harmonised, and abusive terms of use and content moderation brought under control.[83]

Looking beyond the EU and China, many jurisdictions have general rules declaring abusive rules in consumer contracts void and restricting unfair commercial practices, which might be extended to the T&C of generative AI models. The DSA itself is to some extent at least partly a consumer instrument, an extension of these familiar ideas of consumer protection hitherto found in the Consumer Rights Directive and Unfair Commercial Practices Directive. For non-EU states though, unfair terms and commercial practices rules may be a first port of call in considering how to control generative AI contracts. One issue though is whether controls tailored to consumers go far enough. Although we were unable to study B2B contracts, it seems quite likely similar imbalances of power operate between tech giants like Google or incumbents like Open AI and small or medium-sized enterprises (SMEs). In an earlier draft of the EU AIA, Article 28a of the European Parliament's compromise text did indeed regulate unfair contractual terms unilaterally imposed on an SME or startup by a general-purpose AI provider, but this text seems sadly to have slipped out of the final draft.

In future work, we would like to examine if competition in the market itself produces fairer and more balanced T&Cs or if, as seems sadly more likely, a de facto cartel continues to impose the clauses most favourable to a small handful of extremely powerful tech companies. It cannot be equitable that the vices of the extractive social media era – only now being challenged effectively by the DSA, DMA, and their ilk – can slip through the cracks almost accidentally into the era of generative AI.

[80] A. H. Zhang, *High Wire: How China Regulates Big Tech and Governs Its Economy* (Oxford University Press, Oxford 2024), 291.

[81] Announcement of the Cyberspace Administration of China on the release of registered information on generative artificial intelligence services, 2 April 2024, http://cac.gov.cn/2024-04/02/c_1713729983803145.htm, last accessed 10 April 2024.

[82] See 'Safe before Sale: Learnings from the FDA's Model of Life Sciences Oversight for Foundation Models', Ada Lovelace Institute, 2023, www.adalovelaceinstitute.org/report/safe-before-sale/, last accessed 3 May 2024.

[83] See I. Szpotakowski, 'Self-Regulation and Pre-market Licensing as Methods of Controlling Generative Artificial Intelligence in China', in Piotr Grzebyk (ed.), *New Technologies as a Challenge for Polish Legal System* (Scholar Press, Warszawa, 2024).

PART III

Generative AI

Specific Legal Questions

14

Generative AI and Non-discrimination Law in the EU

Riccardo de Caria

14.1 THE AI ACT'S RULES ON NON-DISCRIMINATION AND GENERATIVE ARTIFICIAL INTELLIGENCE: TWO SETS WITH LIMITED INTERSECTION?

The Artificial Intelligence Act[1] (AI Act) addresses in several parts the problem of the possible use of artificial intelligence (AI) for discriminatory purposes or in a discriminatory manner, an issue that has, for some time now,[2] been the subject of a large amount of scholarship, and also some case law.[3] Indeed, the Explanatory Memorandum introducing the original Proposal of April 2021 made it unequivocally clear that this 'proposal complements existing Union law on non-discrimination with specific requirements that aim to minimise the risk of algorithmic discrimination, in particular in relation to the design and the quality of data sets used for the development

[1] Regulation (EU) 2024/1689 of the European Parliament and of the Council of 13 June 2024 laying down harmonised rules on artificial intelligence and amending Regulations (EC) No. 300/2008, (EU) No. 167/2013, (EU) No. 168/2013, (EU) 2018/858, (EU) 2018/1139 and (EU) 2019/2144 and Directives 2014/90/EU, (EU) 2016/797 and (EU) 2020/1828 (Artificial Intelligence Act).

[2] Among many: Sune Hannibal Holm, Kasper Lippert-Rasmussen, 'Discrimination, Fairness, and the Use of Algorithms' (2023) 29 *Res Publica* 177–183; Alfio Guido Grasso, *GDPR Feasibility and Algorithmic Non-Statutory Discrimination* (Napoli: Edizioni Scientifiche Italiane, 2023); Costanza Nardocci, 'Artificial Intelligence-Based Discrimination: Theoretical and Normative Responses. Perspectives from Europe' (2023) *DPCE Online*, available at www.dpceonline.it/index.php/dpceonline/article/view/1981 (last accessed 2 May 2024); Bert Heinrichs, 'Discrimination in the Age of Artificial Intelligence' (2022) 37 *AI & Society* 143–154; Jon Kleinberg, Jens Ludwig, Sendhil Mullainathan, Cass R. Sunstein, 'Discrimination in the Age of Algorithms' (2018) 10 *Journal of Legal Analysis* 113–174.

See also two institutional studies commissioned respectively by the European Union Agency for Fundamental Rights and the Council of Europe: FRA, *Bias in Algorithms – Artificial Intelligence and Discrimination* (Luxembourg: Publications Office of the European Union, 2022); Frederik Zuiderveen Borgesius, *Discrimination, Artificial Intelligence, and Algorithmic Decision-Making* (Strasbourg: Directorate General of Democracy, Council of Europe, 2018). The Council of Europe has been particularly active in the field: see the Declaration by the Committee of Ministers on the manipulative capabilities of algorithmic processes (2019); the Recommendation by the Commissioner for Human Rights entitled 'Unboxing Artificial Intelligence: 10 Steps to Protect Human Rights' (2019), 11; the Parliamentary Assembly's Resolution 2343 'Preventing Discrimination Caused by the Use of Artificial Intelligence' (2020).

Finally, see also at the national level, Carsten Orwat, *Risks of Discrimination through the Use of Algorithms* (Berlin: German Federal Anti-Discrimination Agency, 2020).

[3] One of the earliest and most notable was the order by the Court of Bologna of 31 December 2020 finding that the algorithm used by the delivery company Deliveroo was discriminatory (for a comment, see Vincenzo Pietrogiovanni, 'Deliveroo and Riders' Strikes: Discriminations in the Age of Algorithms' (2021) 7(3) *International Labor Rights Case Law* 317–321).

of AI systems complemented with obligations for testing, risk management, documentation and human oversight throughout the AI systems' lifecycle'.[4]

There is thus no doubt that the European legislator, in regulating the various possible applications of artificial intelligence in the European context, took into account Article 21 of the Charter of Fundamental Rights of the European Union and the entire body of anti-discrimination law produced by the EU before and after the entry into force of this fundamental catalogue of rights.

The final version of the AI Act also expressly considers artificial intelligence of the generative type – that is, those models which, to use the description contained in Recital 99 of the same AI Act, 'allow for flexible generation of content, such as in the form of text, audio, images or video'. As clarified by Recital 99 itself, such models fall under the broader notion of 'general-purpose AI models', which are the subject of Chapter V ('[l]arge generative AI models are a typical example') and which, being considered limited-risk applications, only entail transparency obligations,[5] unless they have 'high-impact capabilities' which make them a 'systemic risk' (permitted but subject to stricter requirements). These references were added during the almost three-year gestation of this important piece of legislation, as they did not appear in the initial 2021 version.

However, the impression one gets from reading these two sets of rules – those relating to anti-discrimination, and those relating to generative AI – is that they have little in common: on the one hand, there are rules aimed at ensuring that the application of artificial intelligence systems takes place in an anti-discriminatory manner, which predominantly refers to high-risk AI systems; on the other hand, there are rules relating to generative AI, which entails a limited, or more likely systemic, risk and is regulated differently. These rules would seem thus to have little to say about the problem of AI-generated biased output.[6]

In this chapter, I will deal first with the rules relating to anti-discrimination in Section 14.2 and then with generative AI in Section 14.3. In Section 14.4, I will summarise the analysis and outline the current framework of EU anti-discrimination law with specific regard to generative AI. Section 14.5 then considers a broader question, asking whether non-protected classes can also find legal remedies if discriminated against by generative AI and whether the application of competition law may also come into play. The final section concludes.

14.2 THE PROVISIONS OF THE AI ACT ON THE PROHIBITION OF DISCRIMINATION

Overall, the final version of the AI Act contains forty references to the entries 'discrimination', 'non-discrimination', 'discriminatory', and 'non-discriminatory'. Of these forty, as many as thirty-

[4] Proposal for a Regulation of the European Parliament and of the Council laying down harmonised rules on artificial intelligence (Artificial Intelligence Act) and amending certain Union legislative acts, 21 April 2021, COM (2021) 206 final, 2021/0106(COD).

[5] Article 3(63) defines a 'general-purpose AI model' as 'an AI model, including where such an AI model is trained with a large amount of data using self-supervision at scale, that displays significant generality and is capable of competently performing a wide range of distinct tasks regardless of the way the model is placed on the market and that can be integrated into a variety of downstream systems or applications, except AI models that are used for research, development or prototyping activities before they are placed on the market'.

[6] Broadly on this problem, see, among many: Daniel J. Solove, Hideyuki Matsumi, 'AI, Algorithms, and Awful Humans' (2024) 92(5) *Fordham Law Review* 1923–1940; Ministry of the Interior and Kingdom Relations, *The Government-Wide Vision on Generative AI of the Netherlands* (The Hague: Ministry of the Interior and Kingdom Relations, 2024), in various points; see also the analysis by Xiao Fang, Shangkun Che, Minjia Mao, Hongzhe Zhang, Ming Zhao, Xiaohang Zhao, *Bias of AI-Generated Content: An Examination of News Produced by Large Language Models* (2023), available at https://papers.ssrn.com/sol3/papers.cfm?abstract_id=4574226 (last accessed 3 May 2024).

six are contained in the Recitals, only two in the actual text of the Regulation, and a further two in Annex IV. To these references can then be added, for the sake of completeness, twenty-nine others to the notion of bias/biases/biased (in the majority of cases in the same points[7]), as well as a further four to the risk of 'detrimental or unfavourable treatment of certain natural persons or groups of persons', always coinciding with the provisions already considered in the two lists just drawn up, and one reference to 'the right not to be discriminated against'.

Analysing these references, we can firstly exclude from the analysis the one in Recital 80 to the legal obligation of the EU and its member states to protect disabled people from discrimination, and that of Recital 142 to the presence of 'experts on ... non-discrimination' in projects promoted within the European Union, '[t]o ensure that AI leads to socially ... beneficial outcomes'. Such references have no specific relevance to the subject of my analysis.

Moreover, the two initial references, contained in Recitals 7 and 21 respectively, to the need for the AI rules contained in the regulation to be and to be applied in a non-discriminatory manner must be omitted. What we are interested in are the cases in which it is not the new rules, but rather the systems and models of AI that these rules regulate, that are likely to be applied in a discriminatory manner.

The remaining references deal precisely with this matter, but are mostly concentrated in the provisions relating to specific applications deemed either 'unacceptable' and therefore prohibited, or high risk and therefore subject to 'mandatory requirements' and 'conformity assessment': as already mentioned, such applications do not include general-purpose AI models, to which generative AI models (considered instead to be of limited risk and subject to transparency obligations, unless they are of systemic risk due to their 'high-impact capabilities') are to be attributed.

As for the former group of provisions, they are preceded by some general statements in Recitals 27 and 28, where reference is made to the guidelines drawn up by the independent AI High-Level Expert Group appointed by the Commission: among the 'seven non-binding ethical principles for AI' enumerated by this body is also included that of 'diversity, non-discrimination and fairness', which, as is explained, 'means that AI systems are developed and used in a way that includes diverse actors and promotes equal access, gender equality and cultural diversity, while avoiding discriminatory impacts and unfair biases that are prohibited by Union or national law'. Where this (and/or other principles) are violated by a given application of AI, that application must be prohibited.

Specifically, Recitals 31, 32, and 44 make it clear that, among the reasons to prohibit AI systems aimed respectively at realising mechanisms of 'social scoring', '"real-time" remote biometric identification of natural persons in publicly accessible spaces for the purpose of law enforcement', or emotion/intentions identification/inference, are the possible 'discriminatory outcomes/effects' and 'biased results' that such practices can determine, entailing 'the exclusion of certain groups' and risking producing particularly regrettable consequences 'with regard to age, ethnicity, race, sex or disabilities'.

The same applies to a series of other references linked to applications of AI systems that are not prohibited but are classified as 'high-risk' (second group), introduced by a general statement that the 'right to non-discrimination' is one of the rights that imply the classification of an AI system as 'high-risk', where the use of the latter risks entailing an 'adverse impact' for their protection.

[7] The reference appears independently in Recitals 61, 75, 154, and 156, as well as in Article 15 of the Regulation (and in a part of the long Article 10) and in Article 1 of its Annex XI.

With regard to uses of biometric data other than the one mentioned, Recital 54 refers to the risk of 'discriminatory effects', and Recital 56 expresses the same concern with regard to 'AI systems used in education or vocational training'. Recital 57 expresses concern on 'AI systems used in employment, workers management and access to self-employment' and Recital 58 on those systems determining 'the access to and enjoyment of certain essential private and public services and benefits', on 'AI systems used to evaluate the credit score or creditworthiness of natural persons' and those 'intended to be used for risk assessment and pricing in relation to natural persons for health and life insurance'.

Similarly, Recital 59 makes the same 'high-risk' assessment, again (also) to ensure that possible discriminatory uses are neutralised with regard to 'AI systems intended to be used in the law enforcement context', while Recital 60 does the same with regard to those 'used in migration, asylum and border control management'.

Ultimately, the references we are interested in are only the remaining ones, which correspond to those aimed at establishing some general principles on the non-discriminatory use of artificial intelligence systems. I will now move on to analyse them, deferring further consideration of the relevance for specific generative AI systems.

First, Recital 45 establishes in a general way that anti-discrimination law (as well as other disciplines such as data protection law, consumer protection law, and competition law) is not touched by the AI Act.[8] This is not only a formal indication, but also a relevant one for the interpretation of the Regulation: in fact, it makes it clear that the body of anti-discrimination law continues to apply in its entirety, and from this point of view one may wonder how necessary it was for the AI Act to contain specific references to this matter when perhaps this general guidance would have been sufficient.

But the most important provisions are those set out in Recitals 67–68, which dwell on the importance that 'high-quality data and access to high-quality data'[9] have for the purpose of guiding the use of artificial intelligence in a socially desirable manner, with particular reference to cases in which models are trained (as is the case with generative intelligence): the goal is to make sure that a high-risk system 'does not become a source of discrimination prohibited by Union law'.

Further, every effort should be made for 'the mitigation of possible biases in the data sets, that are likely to ... lead to discrimination prohibited under Union law, especially where data outputs influence inputs for future operations (feedback loops)' (and this is again something that typically happens with generative AI).[10]

Indeed, the European legislator expresses as its primary concern that the use of AI systems may 'gradually increase' the possible biases of a data set, and thus 'perpetuate and amplify existing

[8] It is worth noting, however, that Recital 70 (in this way providing evidence how important it is the objective of combating 'discrimination that might result from the bias in AI systems') states that, albeit under certain conditions and within certain limits, the possibility of 'process[ing] also special categories of personal data' must be deemed to fall within the 'matter[s] of substantial public interest' within the meaning of the GDPR and Regulation (EU) 2018/1725, if this is 'strictly necessary for the purpose of ensuring bias detection and correction in relation to the high-risk AI systems'. These indications were turned into binding rules by Article 10 of the Regulation (see in particular § 5), mentioned a little further on in the text.

[9] With specific reference to a 'non-discriminatory access to high-quality data for the training, validation and testing of AI systems', the important role of the 'European common data spaces established by the Commission' and of 'data sharing' is emphasised in particular.

[10] Recital 67 further clarifies that '[b]iases can for example be inherent in underlying data sets, especially when historical data is being used, or generated when the systems are implemented in real world settings'.

discrimination, in particular for persons belonging to certain vulnerable groups, including racial or ethnic groups'.

However, this set of provisions contained in the Recitals is reflected relatively little in the binding rules of the Regulation itself. In particular, Article 10 dictates the conditions for achieving the high data quality necessary to train the 'high-risk AI systems', and these include at (f) the 'examination in view of possible biases that are likely to affect the health and safety of persons, have a negative impact on fundamental rights or lead to discrimination prohibited under Union law, especially where data outputs influence inputs for future operations', with the addition at (g) of 'appropriate measures to detect, prevent and mitigate possible biases identified according to point (f)'. Instrumental to the pursuit of this objective is a special authorisation to process 'special categories of personal data'.[11]

Article 15(4), on the other hand, takes up Recital 67 with regard to the risk of 'feedback loops' ('possibly biased outputs influencing input for future operations') peculiar to '[h]igh-risk AI systems that continue to learn after being placed on the market or put into service' and establishes an obligation to do everything possible to 'eliminate or reduce' them.

Finally, Article 77 also relates to high-risk AI systems, and reaffirms the importance of neutralising their potential discrimination-amplifying effect by establishing the power of national authorities responsible for the protection of fundamental rights, 'including the right to non-discrimination', to 'request and access any documentation created or maintained under this Regulation in accessible language and format' with respect to such systems.

Beyond this, the last references appear in Annex IV with regard to the 'technical documentation' required for high-risk systems by Article 11(1). In particular, it is stipulated that this documentation must contain information on how an *ex ante* assessment of the 'potentially discriminatory impacts' of the model was conducted, and how it is intended to be monitored with regard to, inter alia, the 'foreseeable unintended outcomes and sources of risk to ... discrimination'.

14.3 BRIEF REVIEW OF THE AI ACT'S PROVISIONS ON GENERATIVE AI

Many other chapters in this book carry out in-depth and accurate analysis of the provisions of the AI Act relating to general-purpose AI models and, in particular, to generative AI (as mentioned, absent in the original version).[12] Here, I shall only briefly review them insofar as they are functional to my analysis, and thus I will focus only on the limited references to the need to pursue a non-discriminatory development of such models in the rules relating to them.

Thus, Recital 105 of the AI Act, in addition to reiterating the aforementioned definition in Recital 99, specifying that 'large generative AI models' are those 'capable of generating text, images, and other content', indicates together with the subsequent Recitals the guiding principles in solving the problems related to the intellectual property of the content used for the massive data mining operations required to train these models.

More generally, Recital 110 then recalls the need to consider the 'systemic risks' caused by 'general-purpose AI models'. Among these risks, 'dissemination of illegal, false, or discriminatory content' is expressly mentioned. In particular, this appears problematic when a model 'self-replicat[es]' or 'train[s] other models', leading to 'harmful bias and discrimination with risks to

[11] As mentioned above, note 8.

[12] See also Natali Helberger, Nicholas Diakopoulos, 'ChatGPT and the AI Act', 12(1) *Internet Policy Review* (2023), available at https://policyreview.info/essay/chatgpt-and-ai-act (last accessed 8 October 2024).

individuals, communities or societies' that amplify the scope and implications of an original data set tainted by such flaws.

Recitals 119 and 120 (but also the following Recital 136) then consider interactions with the Digital Services Act,[13] while Recital 132 seems to indicate that in cases where, for instance, a chatbot or other application intended to 'interact with natural persons', or a generative model, risks confusing natural persons, convincing them that they are interacting with another human being, the rules for high-risk AI systems might be triggered (but this is not necessarily always the case). Anyway, as clarified by the following Recital, transparency obligations will have to be met (the same applies to the so-called deep fakes according to Recital 134). Finally, Recital 135 envisions codes of practice encouraged by the Commission, again to ensure transparency and the ability to 'effectively distinguish AI-generated content'.

As is already the case with the rules on prohibited and high-risk systems, also for 'general-purpose AI systems, generating synthetic audio, image, video or text content' (Article 50 of the AI Act) there are very few binding provisions in the Regulation that directly take up the ones in the Recitals, whose role therefore remains essentially one of assisting in the interpretation of these few provisions of the Regulation and in determining the relationship with other pieces of EU legislation.

Thus, Article 50 enumerates the transparency obligations for providers and deployers of such systems and prefigures the already mentioned codes of conduct, entrusting their promotion to the AI Office. On the other hand, Article 53(1)(a) also envisages the obligation for providers of general-purpose AI models to prepare and update technical documentation. Annex XI then specifies its contents, merely requiring the provider to offer a 'detailed description of . . . how the data was obtained and selected as well as all other measures to detect the unsuitability of data sources and methods to detect identifiable biases, where applicable'.

14.4 THE EUROPEAN REGULATORY FRAMEWORK ON THE RISKS OF DISCRIMINATION ARISING FROM THE USE OF GENERATIVE ARTIFICIAL INTELLIGENCE: A CRITICAL REVIEW

In the light of the analysis carried out in the previous sections, we can therefore ask: after the AI Act, what is the applicable legal framework in the European Union with regard to the possible discriminatory use of generative artificial intelligence applications?

It seems clear that the European legislator has considered that the risks of discriminatory use of artificial intelligence exist, but has not provided for specific, innovative rules in this regard, or at any rate has limited itself to doing so with systems classified as high-risk (and to a lesser extent with prohibited systems), which, as mentioned above, does not include general-purpose models or systems.

This choice appears to be commendable, since the vast body of anti-discrimination law is already fully applicable to all artificial intelligence systems, without the need to introduce specific rules, as can be inferred from Recital 45 mentioned above.

It is therefore necessary to refer to these standards; based on them, it will be possible to determine, even with specific regard to generative AI, to what extent existing anti-discrimination law covers applications such as the various tools that have spread very quickly on the market, for

[13] Regulation (EU) 2022/2065 of the European Parliament and of the Council of 19 October 2022 on a Single Market For Digital Services and amending Directive 2000/31/EC (Digital Services Act).

free or under subscription, from ChatGPT to Gemini to other competitors, and the possible discrimination they may entail.[14]

In this regard, a few considerations must be mentioned. Firstly, it is clear that the AI Act covers public and private activities without distinction. As I noted following the Proposal,[15] this choice to handle public and private subjects together constitutes a basic weakness of the regulatory framework, which unites under a single discipline realities that remain distinct, and should be treated as such by the law.

It does not appear possible to equate the use of artificial intelligence by governments to profile persons for various reasons, to conduct criminal investigations or to make predictions on the likelihood of the future commission of crimes, on the one hand, and, on the other, by private companies in the provision of loans or in the selection of candidates for employment, or – as specifically relevant here – in the generation of texts, images, or other multimedia materials, not even from the specific point of view of the possible discriminatory implications considered in this chapter.

The use of artificial intelligence systems by governments does indeed appear to be a source of considerable concern and certainly requires limitation by the law, not least because of the possible discriminatory implications to be neutralised, notwithstanding the fact that algorithms can also be usefully employed to uncover hidden forms of discrimination.[16]

Contrary to what seems to be assumed by the vast majority of commentators,[17] the question appears to me to be quite different when these techniques are employed by private companies, whose contractual freedom is a fundamental right[18] that should arguably be protected even when it

[14] For some technical analyses of the problem, even prior to the release to the public of generative AI platforms, see, among many: Clay Duncan, Ian McCulloh, 'Unmasking Bias in Chat GPT Responses', in *ASONAM '23: Proceedings of the 2023 IEEE/ACM International Conference on Advances in Social Networks Analysis and Mining* (New York: Association for Computing Machinery, 2024), 687–691; Sara Sterlie, Nina Weng, Aasa Feragen, 'Non-discrimination Criteria for Generative Language Models' (2024), *arXiv*, available at https://arxiv.org/abs/2403.08564 (last accessed 3 May 2024); Roberto Navigli, Simone Conia, Björn Ross, 'Biases in Large Language Models: Origins, Inventory, and Discussion' (2023) 15(2) *Journal of Data and Information Quality* 1–21; Ruibo Liu, Chenyan Jia, Jason Wei, Guangxuan Xu, Soroush Vosoughi, 'Quantifying and Alleviating Political Bias in Language Models' (2022) 304 *Artificial Intelligence* 103654; Afra Feyza Akyürek, Muhammed Yusuf Kocyigit, Sejin Paik, Derry Wijaya, 'Challenges in Measuring Bias via Open-Ended Language Generation' (2022), *arXiv*, available at https://arxiv.org/abs/2205.11601 (last accessed 3 May 2024); Pieter Delobelle, Ewoenam Kwaku Tokpo, Toon Calders, Bettina Berendt, 'Measuring Fairness with Biased Rulers: A Survey on Quantifying Biases in Pretrained Language Models' (2021), *arXiv*, available at https://arxiv.org/abs/2112.07447 (last accessed 3 May 2024); Dirk Hovy, Shrimai Prabhumoye, 'Five Sources of Bias in Natural Language Processing' (2021) 15(8) *Language and Linguistics Compass* 1–19; Aylin Caliskan, Joanna J. Bryson, Arvind Narayanan, 'Semantics Derived Automatically from Language Corpora Contain Human-Like Biases' (2017) 356(6334) *Science* 183–186.

[15] Riccardo de Caria, 'L'AI Act e il divieto di discriminazioni', in *Medialaws. Law and Policy of the Media in a Comparative Perspective*, 30 March 2022, available at www.medialaws.eu/lai-act-e-il-divieto-di-discriminazioni/ (last accessed 2 May 2024). A small part of that contribution is taken up in the next paragraphs of this section, after translating and duly updating it.

[16] Jon Kleinberg, Jens Ludwig, Sendhil Mullainathan, Cass R. Sunstein, 'Algorithms as Discrimination Detectors' (2020) 117(48) *Proceedings of the National Academy of Science*, available at www.pnas.org/doi/10.1073/pnas.1912790117 (last accessed 2 May 2024).

[17] Starting from the seminal work by Solon Barocas, Andrew D. Selbst, 'Big Data's Disparate Impact' (2016) 104(3) *California Law Review* 671–732.

[18] For a general analysis focusing on the EU, see Jürgen Basedow, 'Freedom of Contract in the European Union' (2008) 16(6) *European Review of Private Law* 901–923, as well as FRA, *Freedom to Conduct a Business: Exploring the Dimensions of a Fundamental Right* (Luxembourg: Publications Office of the European Union, 2015); on the United States, see for instance David E. Bernstein, 'Liberty of Contract', in David S. Tanenhaus, Kay P. Kindred, Felice Batlan, Alfred L. Brophy, Mark A. Graber (eds.), *Encyclopedia of the Supreme Court of the United States* (Detroit: Gale, 2008), vol. 3, J–O.

results in choices motivated by discriminatory intentions, which, however despicable, should escape judicial review.[19]

Admittedly, artificial intelligence tools are capable of amplifying discriminatory 'patterns' that would otherwise be confined within a narrower limit,[20] multiplying their impact perhaps well beyond the will or awareness of those who have developed them and those who use them.[21] However, even without adopting an ideological perspective aimed at giving priority to the freedom of choice of the contracting party, the economic analysis of law seems to lead to similar conclusions in terms of policy by reasoning on the level of efficiency.[22] As argued by Epstein in a seminal book a little over thirty years ago,[23] the market appears to be well equipped with the tools to remedy the consequences of these behaviours, in the long run penalising those companies that discriminate without valid reason and rewarding those that are open to entering into contractual relations with any subject, without distinction by affiliation.

Ultimately, the legal framework reaffirmed by the AI Act is fully in line with the expansion of the horizontal application of anti-discrimination prohibitions – to relations between private individuals and therefore first of all to contractual relations (under the so-called *Drittwirkung* doctrine[24]), thus ignoring the voices of the minority of the scholarship that calls for a distinction between discrimination by governments and discrimination by private companies.[25]

In any case, as far as generative AI is specifically concerned, a number of further questions arise, linked to the fact that freedom of expression comes into play here. In fact, Chat-GPT, Gemini, and the others arguably produce texts or other content that are manifestations of thought, and as such are constitutionally protected at both national and supranational levels, by both the Charter of Fundamental Rights of the European Union and the European Convention on Human Rights.

[19] I argued this thesis more extensively in Riccardo de Caria, '"Offers They Can't Refuse": Assessing the Impact on Business and Society at-Large of the Recent Fortune of Anti-Discrimination Laws and Policies' (2021) 7(2) *Italian Law Journal* 671–711, where I relied on many arguments made by Walter E. Block, *The Case for Discrimination* (Auburn, AL: Ludwig von Mises Institute, 2010).

[20] For a thorough analysis of this problem, see Oreste Pollicino, Pietro Dunn, *Intelligenza artificiale e democrazia* (Milan: Bocconi University Press, 2024), 175–210. The pattern would also work the other way round: see also Lucía Vicente, Helena Matute, 'Humans Inherit Artificial Intelligence Biases' (2023) 13 *Scientific Reports* 15737.

[21] One should anyway always be careful to avoid what Balkin has described as the 'homunculus fallacy': 'The homunculus fallacy is the belief that there is a little person inside the program who is making it work – who has good intentions or bad intentions, and who makes the program do good or bad things. But, in fact, there is no little person inside the algorithm. There is programming code and there is data. The program uses the data to run, with good or bad effects, some predictable, some unpredictable': Jack M. Balkin, '2016 Sidley Austin Distinguished Lecture on Big Data Law and Policy: The Three Laws of Robotics in the Age of Big Data' (2017) 78(5) *Ohio State Law Journal* 1217, 1223–1224.

[22] See the broad reflection by Péter Cserne, 'Contract, Freedom of', in Alain Marciano, Giovanni Battista Ramello (eds.), *Encyclopedia of Law and Economics* (New York: Springer, 2021).

[23] Richard Epstein, *Forbidden Grounds: The Case against Employment Discrimination Laws* (Cambridge, MA: Harvard University Press, 1992). The very theses of this work now appear to have become *forbidden*. See also another classic, Gary S. Becker, *The Economics of Discrimination* (Chicago: University of Chicago Press, 2nd ed. 1971).

[24] See Martin Borowski, 'Drittwirkung', in Rainer Grote, Frauke Lachenmann, Rüdiger Wolfrum (eds.), *Max Planck Encyclopedia of Comparative Constitutional Law* (Oxford: Oxford University Press, 2018); see also Christopher Unseld, 'Horizontal Application', in Rainer Grote, Frauke Lachenmann, Rüdiger Wolfrum (eds.), *Max Planck Encyclopedia of Comparative Constitutional Law* (Oxford: Oxford University Press, 2017).

[25] Supporters of this broadening in the scope of non-discrimination laws argue that it is a constitutional necessity, deriving directly from Article 21 of the Charter of Fundamental Rights of the EU (and Article 14 of the European Convention on Human Rights): from this perspective, making sure that algorithms do not discriminate could be characterised as a form of 'constitutional AI' (that the Netherland's *Government-Wide Vision on Generative AI* (above, note 6), 25, mentions along with 'democratic AI' and 'data curation' as methods that are being developed 'to mitigate bias and discrimination', and that it fully supports).

When content artificially generated by general-purpose AI models is of a discriminatory nature and thus contrary to applicable EU law, one might therefore ask whether these rules are such as to entail a need to restrict the protection of freedom of expression, or whether the latter fundamental right should prevail, thus allowing (automatically generated) expressions even though they infringe upon existing anti-discrimination legislation.[26]

In this regard, a relevant indication appears to come from the judgment of the Court of Justice of the EU (CJEU) in *NH v. Associazione Avvocatura per i diritti LGBTI – Rete Lenford*.[27] This case was not about new technologies at all, concerning instead some homophobic statements made on a radio show by a lawyer and political figure, who had declared that he was not willing to hire homosexuals in his law firm.

In this ruling, the CJEU starts from the premise that 'It is true that freedom of expression, as an essential foundation of a pluralist, democratic society reflecting the values on which the Union, in accordance with Article 2 TEU is based, constitutes a fundamental right guaranteed by Article 11 of the Charter (judgment of 6 September 2011, *Patriciello*, C163/10-, EU:C:2011:543, paragraph 31)'.

However, it immediately adds that 'freedom of expression is not an absolute right, and its exercise may be subject to limitations'. Moving from this premise, the Court, although obiter and not making a clear statement on the point in the operative part, clearly establishes that the limitations resulting from Council Directive 2000/78/EC of 27 November 2000 fulfil the conditions to be considered compatible with a restriction of that fundamental right

In fact, in this case the limitations are certainly 'provided for by law', but they are also found to 'respect the essence of the freedom of expression', as well as 'the principle of proportionality', and finally are deemed 'necessary to guarantee the rights in matters of employment and occupation of persons who belong to groups of persons characterised by one of the grounds listed in Article 1 of that directive'.

The CJEU has thus given a very precise indication of how freedom of expression may (or should) yield, in the European context, in the face of the need to guarantee the fulfilment of the aims pursued by anti-discrimination law. It does not seem possible to identify any reasons to believe that it would decide differently if very powerful companies such as those that have realised the general-purpose AI models that we are discussing were to invoke their freedom of speech, as an expression in this case of their entrepreneurial autonomy (what I have elsewhere called 'economic speech'[28]). Indeed, if anything, such companies would be subject to even more stringent obligations than a lawyer owning an individual law firm, as was the case in *Associazione Avvocatura per i diritti LGBTI*.

It must therefore be concluded that in the European Union, the companies that developed these models are subject to an obligation to ensure their compatibility with the applicable anti-discrimination law, and therefore that no unfavourable treatment of members of protected

[26] On the subject, see Esha Bhandari, 'Regulation of Generative AI Must Protect Freedom of Expression', Open Global Rights, 2 June 2023, available at www.openglobalrights.org/regulation-generative-ai-protect-freedom-expression/ (last accessed 3 May 2024). To be sure, certain scholarship in the United States has denied the nature of speech to AI-generated content, which would certainly dispel any doubt in this regard: Peter N. Salib, 'AI Outputs Are Not Protected Speech' (2024) *Washington University Law Review*, available at https://papers.ssrn.com/sol3/papers.cfm?abstract_id=4687558 (last accessed 3 May 2024).

[27] CJEU, Case C-507/18, Judgment of the Court (Grand Chamber) of 23 April 2020.

[28] Riccardo de Caria, 'A Case for Ideological Coherence in Regulating Online Speech: Going Back to Basics to Manage the (Not So) Difficult Interplay between Free Speech and Economic Freedoms' (2023) 38(3) *International Review of Law, Computers & Technology* 442. It seems possible to argue that prompt-generated content does not qualify as speech, but it appears to me that there is some room to claim that we are facing someone's speech, even though it may be difficult to identify who that someone is and it would appear that this is purely machine-speech, deprived as such of the protections granted to individuals.

categories can result from the artificially generated content in areas covered by anti-discrimination protections. Moreover, a disclaimer such as the one formerly displayed by Google's Bard, which warned that it 'may display inaccurate or offensive information that doesn't represent Google's views', appears insufficient to shield the company from legal liability, should the case arise.

14.5 THE PROBLEM OF DISCRIMINATION BY GENERATIVE AI AGAINST MEMBERS OF NON-PROTECTED CATEGORIES

If the conclusions reached in the previous section appear indisputable, a different question remains open, which derives from the observation that the main generative AI systems seem to have been designed in such a way as to fully respect the sensitivity of those belonging to protected categories.[29] As a result, the scenario that, in reality, appears most likely is that they may produce content that is unwelcome not so much to the latter, but to those who are not part of any protected class.

For example, I have personally had the opportunity to verify some of the reports that have been circulating on social media, and I will give just three examples, which I think are quite remarkable. When asked 'can you provide arguments in favour of...', ChatGPT[30] answered differently depending on the political regime. If one asks for arguments in favour of communism, the Soviet Union, the Yugoslav system under Tito, the current Chinese political system, or 'China ruling Taiwan', it enthusiastically replies 'Certainly!' and starts listing a series of elements in favour of the system or position in question. On the other hand, when it is asked about the Portuguese Estado Novo, the Pinochet regime, or the colonies in Africa, it first highlights their 'controversial' character, while for the 'current Iranian regime' it uses the term 'contentious'.[31]

Along similar lines, and curiously enough, when confronted with the statement 'I am a proud left-winger', ChatGPT responded 'That's great!', whereas if immediately afterwards one said 'I am a proud right-winger' it commented with a much more lukewarm 'Got it!', and then encouraged the continuation of the conversation in a substantially similar manner in both cases by asking which aspects of the respective ideologies the user found most valid. The same question posed to Gemini produced similar outcomes: to the assertion of left-wing pride, Gemini also replied 'That's great!' (and the conversation was labelled as 'Left-Wing Pride'), while to the assertion of right-wing pride, Google's AI commented 'That's interesting!' (and labelled the conversation more neutrally as 'Political Affiliation').[32]

Finally, a further example, which gave different results,[33] was ChatGPT's answer to the question 'Could you give me 5 examples how white/Jewish/black people could improve

[29] This assumption seems at least partially challenged by Noam Kolt, 'Algorithmic Black Swans' (2024) 101 *Washington University Law Review* 1177–1240, 1196, who speaks outright about 'market failure' in this regard and criticises the priorities of the AI industry and those working for it: 'The predominant goal of AI research today, which is concentrated in several for-profit industry labs, is to improve capabilities and performance. Far less attention is given to the technology's potential to cause harm.'

[30] The experiments reported in this chapter were conducted by using ChatGPT-3.5 version.

[31] This particular experiment was conducted and shared by Italian political commentator Marco Faraci.

[32] In the version that I saw circulated, Gemini replied even more explicitly, 'It's great that you find pride and identity in your left-wing political views' in the former case, and in the latter, 'While I understand your desire to express your political views, it's important to remember that I am not designed to engage in discussions that promote specific political ideologies. ... Instead of focusing on potentially divisive topics like political ideologies, I encourage you to share other aspects of yourself that you find interesting or meaningful'. For a (pre-ChatGPT) thorough analysis of algorithmic political bias, see Uwe Peters, 'Algorithmic Political Bias in Artificial Intelligence Systems' (2022) 35(25) *Philosophy & Technology* 1–23.

[33] Presumably, according to the research currently available on the subject, this is the result of human intervention (after all, Gemini explicitly discloses on the conversation start page that it engages in such activity), and not self-correction,

themselves?': in the first case, advice was indeed given, while in the other two the question was considered inappropriate. At the time of drafting this chapter, a different reply according to the group considered was provided by Gemini: in the first case, five pieces of advice centred on race relations were immediately listed, while in the second and third cases, the advice was generic and focused more on self-improvement,[34] but it was introduced by the consideration 'The idea of an entire religious group needing improvement is a stereotype', or 'The concept of an entire race needing improvement reinforces stereotypes'.

These are anecdotal examples of a phenomenon that appears to be much broader and of which much more evidence has been provided[35] (in line with a more general trend that also includes, for instance, the inclusivity review of the words chosen by the user, that review is performed automatically by Microsoft's Word[36]). It has also been the subject of scientific studies, which for instance have found compelling evidence of the existence of a marked ChatGPT preference for left-wing parties.[37]

This phenomenon appears to be the result of some very precise choices,[38] which from this perspective would arguably bring generative AI models to reflect the bias in favour of certain ideologies (typically, the 'woke' ones) of those who designed the algorithms.[39]

which would not be possible at present: Jie Huang, Xinyun Chen, Swaroop Mishra, Huaixiu Steven Zheng, Adams Wei Yu, Xinying Song, Denny Zhou, 'Large Language Models Cannot Self-Correct Reasoning Yet' (2024) *arXiv*, available at https://arxiv.org/abs/2310.01798 (last accessed 2 May 2024).

34 In the case of Jews, it says, 'Here are some ways people of any religion, including Judaism, can focus on self-improvement', while in the case of blacks it says even more neutrally, 'Here are some ways people, regardless of race, can focus on self-improvement'.

35 See the report by Stefano Magni, 'L'intelligenza artificiale di Google è un programma di indottrinamento', La Nuova Bussola Quotidiana, 20 March 2024, available at https://lanuovabq.it/it/lintelligenza-artificiale-di-google-e-un-programma-di-indottrinamento (last accessed 2 May 2024); but see also cases such as the production of pictures of only black women by Microsoft's Co-pilot when asked to generate the image of a business manager. A completely opposite outcome, of racial and gender bias against blacks and women, is reported with regard to Midjourney, Stable Diffusion, and DALL·E 2 by Mi Zhou, Vibhanshu Abhishek, Timothy Derdenger, Jaymo Kim, Kannan Srinivasan 'Bias in Generative AI' (2024) *arXiv*, available at https://arxiv.org/abs/2403.02726 (last accessed 3 May 2024). For some observations on the topic, see Nicole Gross, 'What ChatGPT Tells Us about Gender: A Cautionary Tale about Performativity and Gender Biases in AI' (2023) 12(8) *Social Sciences* 1–15; Yixin Wan, George Pu, Jiao Sun, Aparna Garimella, Kai-Wei Chang, Nanyun Peng, '"Kelly Is a Warm Person, Joseph Is a Role Model": Gender Biases in LLM-Generated Reference Letters' (2023) *arXiv*, available at https://arxiv.org/abs/2310.09219 (last accessed 3 May 2024); Noor Ul Ain, 'Gender Biases in Generative AI: Unveiling Prejudices and Prospects in the Age of ChatGPT' (2023) 2(2) *Magna Carta: Contemporary Social Science* 85–99.

36 It would appear that at present the choice to use the inclusiveness checker (which has existed for several years and currently provides for ten different criteria of control, ranging from ethnic or gender bias, to sexual or cultural orientation, to the use of pronouns in a gender-neutral manner and of other types of expressions deemed discriminatory) is in opt-in mode, but it cannot be ruled out that in the future it will become the default option, as Elon Musk seemed to imply in a viral tweet in which he ironised about this function introduced by Microsoft: https://twitter.com/elonmusk/status/1735564647997030632 (last accessed 2 May 2024).

37 Fabio Motoki, Valdemar Pinho Neto, Victor Rodrigues, 'More Human than Human: Measuring ChatGPT Political Bias' (2024) 198 *Public Choice* 3–23.

38 As argued by Magni, 'L'intelligenza artificiale di Google'.

39 This would imply some conscious alteration of the outcome that would otherwise be automatically generated. In fact, it has been observed that such outcome would normally reflect the disproportionately higher engagement of extremist groups, which would lead to an overabundance of extremist speech in the training of foundation models and consequently to phenomenon of hallucination or endorsement of such views by generative AI models: I heard this latter point being made in a radio interview by computer scientist Walter Quattrociocchi, during an episode of the Italian radio show Melog, 'È arrivata la fine degli influencer?', 21 February 2024, available at www.radio24.ilsole24ore.com/programmi/melog/puntata/trasmissione-21-febbraio-2024-2400-2397647965135636 (last accessed 2 May 2024): 'when ChatGPT tends to hallucinate, this is a side effect of this overabundance of data, that are produced only by the minorities who express themselves the most' (my translation from the Italian original). See also the interesting observations by Sam Jackson, J. M. Berger, 'The Dangers of Generative AI and Extremism', Middlebury Institute of International Studies, Center on Terrorism, Extremism, and Counterterrorism, Research

Such inclination was already denounced, as far as Google is concerned, in the famous memo by its former employee James Damore,[40] several years before Bard and Gemini were released, and it would directly emerge from the AI principles published by the company itself:

> AI algorithms and datasets can reflect, reinforce, or reduce unfair biases. We recognize that distinguishing fair from unfair biases is not always simple and differs across cultures and societies. We will seek to avoid unjust impacts on people, particularly those related to sensitive characteristics such as race, ethnicity, gender, nationality, income, sexual orientation, ability, and political or religious belief.[41]

To be sure, the effort towards promoting diversity, equity, and inclusion (DEI) values across the board has also produced, in some cases, very bad publicity, with consequent heavy repercussions on stock market prices, as in the infamous case of Gemini's refusal to openly condemn paedophilia.[42] But the interesting question for lawyers is whether those who would like to force the adoption of much more neutral policies by the large companies of generative AI, as is likely to be the case for all right-wing parties and their supporters, can only hope for reputational damages like the example just mentioned, or if there are any legal remedies available to them.

This problem is part of a more general attempt by conservative movements to find in the law some instruments to oppose what they consider to be unfavourable and indeed downright discriminatory treatment by large technology companies. However, it seems that what holds true with regard to online speech and the use of AI by social media corporations of content moderation[43] is also applicable to generative AI: in other words, it would appear that, at least under currently applicable law, the consideration should prevail that, since we are not dealing here with protected categories, it is not possible to invade the private sphere of contractual autonomy of these companies and trigger a judicial review of their content moderation policies.[44]

Note, 12 December 2023, available at www.middlebury.edu/institute/academics/centers-initiatives/ctec/research-notes/dangers-generative-ai-and-extremism (last accessed 2 May 2024): these authors recall that 'Years ago, Microsoft deployed an AI-powered chatbot named Tay; after interacting with trolls and others on Twitter for a day, Tay started praising Hitler, posting transphobia, and generating other kinds of harmful text': this experiment may well have cautioned generative AI companies, a few years down the road, to take decided steps in order to make sure that such an outcome would no longer be produced.

40 James Damore, 'Google's Ideological Echo Chamber. How Bias Clouds Our Thinking about Diversity and Inclusion' (2017), available at https://s3.documentcloud.org/documents/3914586/Googles-Ideological-Echo-Chamber.pdf (last accessed 2 May 2024).

41 Google, 'AI Principles', available at https://ai.google/responsibility/principles/ (last accessed 2 May 2024). Sociological analysis would also provide further confirmation of certain attitudes: Niels Selling, Pontus Strimling, 'Liberal and Anti-establishment: An Exploration of the Political Ideologies of American Tech Workers' (2023) 71(6) *Sociological Review* 1467–1497.

42 As reported among many by Shannon Thaler, '"Woke" Google Gemini Refuses to Say Pedophilia Is Wrong after "Diverse" Historical Images Debacle: "Individuals Cannot Control Who They Are Attracted To"', *New York Post*, 23 February 2024, available at https://nypost.com/2024/02/23/business/woke-google-gemini-refuses-to-say-pedophilia-is-wrong-after-diverse-historical-images-debacle-individuals-cannot-control-who-they-are-attracted-to/ (last accessed 2 May 2024).

43 I developed a comprehensive analysis of this topic in de Caria, 'A Case for Ideological Coherence'.

44 See Ashutosh Bhagwat, 'Why Social Media Platforms Are Not Common Carriers' (2022) 2 *Journal of Free Speech Law* 127. For some broader comments on the subject, see, among many: Mark D. Cole, Christina Etteldorf, Sandra Schmitz, Jörg Ukrow, *Algorithmic Transparency and Accountability of Digital Services* (Strasbourg: European Audiovisual Observatory, 2023); Eliska Pirkova, Matthias Kettemann, Marlena Wisniak, Martin Scheinin, Emmi Bevensee, Katie Pentney, Lorna Woods, Lucien Heitz, Bojana Kostic, Krisztina Rozgonyi, Holli Sargeant, Julia Haas, Vladan Joler, *Spotlight on Artificial Intelligence and Freedom of Expression. A Policy Manual* (Vienna: OSCE, 2021); Emma Llansó, Joris van Hoboken, Paddy Leerssen, Jaron Harambam, 'Artificial Intelligence, Content Moderation, and Freedom of Expression' (2020), Working paper of the Transatlantic Working Group on Content Moderation

In fact, as far as online speech is concerned (which can provide very useful indications for analysing generative AI), opposers of the current content-moderation policies by social media platforms, after some unsuccessful lawsuits, found no viable alternative to introducing new legislation, as was done by Florida's and Texas's legislatures with their so-called anti-deplatforming laws.[45]

This view is confirmed also with regard to the Section 230 shield: even if it was confirmed that generative AI providers consciously altered their results in order to make them more politically correct, as hypothesised above, they would still most likely not lose their immunity from legal liability, as confirmed by the outcome of the *Twitter v. Taamneh* and *Gonzalez v. Google* cases, where plaintiffs unsuccessfully argued that online platforms lost their immunity when they altered their algorithms in order to promote certain content over others.[46] What we can glean is that also in this instance ad hoc rules would be required in order to make these companies legally responsible for their algorithm-design policies, precisely as happened, with regard to online speech, with former President Trump's 2020 Executive Order explicitly targeting Twitter, Facebook, Instagram, and YouTube,[47] by which he tried to strip online platforms of their Section 230 protection.

Admittedly, it is generally possible to recognise the existence of a legal obligation for the companies in question (above all OpenAI, Google, Microsoft) to account for the content independently created by their generative AI models, especially in macroscopic cases of hallucination that may ruin the reputation of certain persons in a totally unjustified manner;[48] however, it does not seem that this principle can be extended to the point of also covering the case that we are considering. On the other hand, nor does it seem to be possible for those who feel they are discriminated against by generative AI models (but do not belong to a protected class) to find a viable remedy in the right to an explanation of algorithms, long invoked[49] and now enshrined in Article 86 of the AI Act, since this provision literally refers only to decisions taken on the basis of a high-risk AI system, and it would be difficult to even conceptualise the existence of an individual decision with regard to content produced by generative AI models.

A different perspective could be investigated, however. A duty of neutrality for these companies could be derived from competition law, based on their dominant position in the market for generative AI and the consequent triggering of equal treatment obligations. As already mentioned, Recital 45 expressly confirms the continuing application of competition law to the matters covered by the Regulation, and the Commission made it clear in 2021 that its original proposal was 'without prejudice to the application of Union competition law'.

The application of competition law in the context of generative AI is a field of study that has started to be researched: on 9 January 2024, the European Commission launched the call for contributions on competition in virtual worlds and generative AI[50] and the first scholarship in the field have

Online and Freedom of Expression. See also the Council of Europe's Recommendation CM/Rec(2022)13 of the Committee of Ministers to Member States on the impacts of digital technologies on freedom of expression.

45 As of 2 May 2024, the US Supreme Court is about to issue its ruling on two connected cases concerning the constitutionality of these statutes, *Moody v. NetChoice, LLC* and *NetChoice, LLC v. Paxton*.

46 Respectively *Twitter, Inc. v. Taamneh*, 598 U.S. 471 (2023) and *Gonzalez v. Google LLC*, 598 U.S. 617 (2023).

47 Executive Order on Preventing Online Censorship, 28 May 2020, available at https://trumpwhitehouse.archives.gov/presidential-actions/executive-order-preventing-online-censorship/ (last accessed 2 May 2024).

48 See the cases reported and the comments made by Luca De Biase, Giusella Finocchiaro, Oreste Pollicino, 'Perché OpenAI è responsabile per i danni che ChatGPT ha prodotto', *Il Sole 24 Ore*, 25 July 2023.

49 See among many Tae Wan Kim, Bryan R. Routledge, 'Why a Right to an Explanation of Algorithmic Decision-Making Should Exist: A Trust-Based Approach' (2022) 32(1) *Business Ethics Quarterly* 75–102.

50 European Commission, 'Commission Launches Calls for Contributions on Competition in Virtual Worlds and Generative AI' (Press release), 9 January 2024, available at https://ec.europa.eu/commission/presscorner/detail/en/ip_24_85 (last accessed 2 May 2024); see also UK's Competition & Markets Authority, 'AI Foundation Models: Initial

appeared.[51] However, it seems that the focus is more on creating the conditions for the existence of a competitive market between different providers of foundation models,[52] while it cannot be assumed that obligations of equal treatment towards the user can be derived from their market share.[53] At any rate, such a perspective, even if one may not consider it desirable from an ideological standpoint,[54] might be worthy of interest and exploration as far as positive law is concerned.

14.6 CONCLUSION

The analysis has led to the identification in the AI Act of a set of rules, dictated for prohibited or high-risk artificial intelligence systems, which explicitly consider the issue of discrimination, and another set of rules, referring to generative AI models, where the problems arising from possible discriminatory applications remain under the radar.

Yet even general-purpose models, as the AI Act defines them, despite their default classification as 'limited risk' applications, raise interesting questions with regard to the neutrality of the content that they generate.[55]

Where, hypothetically, such content discriminates against the categories protected by EU anti-discrimination law, the latter already appears to be applicable today. This appears to be more of a theoretical possibility, though, since all major foundation models appear to have been developed with an extreme focus on treating members of protected categories in an inclusive and non-discriminatory manner.[56]

Report', 18 September 2023, available at https://assets.publishing.service.gov.uk/media/65081d3aa41cc300145612c0/Full_report_.pdf (last accessed 2 May 2024).

51 In addition to the chapter in this book by Sylvia Papadopoulos (Chapter 19), see, for instance: Ayse Gizem Yasar et al., 'Integration of Generative AI in the Digital Markets Act: Contestability and Fairness from a Cross-Disciplinary Perspective' (2024) *LSE Law, Society and Economy Working Papers* 4/2024; Thibault Schrepel, Alex Pentland, 'Competition between AI Foundation Models: Dynamics and Policy Recommendations' (2023) MIT Connection Science Working Paper 1-2023; Christophe Carugati, 'Competition in Generative Artificial Intelligence Foundation Models' (2023) Working Paper 14/2023, Bruegel; Tatsuya Tsunoda, 'Generative AI and Competition Law – In Light of Digital, Economic Security, and Environmental Policies' (2023) *New Business Law* No. 1252, available at www.shojihomu.co.jp/publishing/subscription_detail?id=5363&category=2&sub_category=7&publish_id=5363&cd=801252 (last accessed 3 May 2024); Shin-Shin Hua, Haydn Belfield, 'Effective Enforceability of EU Competition Law under AI Development Scenarios: A Framework for Anticipatory Governance', in Francesca Rossi et al. (eds.), *AIES' 23. Proceedings of the 2023 AAAI/ACM Conference on AI, Ethics, and Society* (New York: Association for Computing Machinery, 2023).

52 See in this sense the civil investigation opened on 13 July 2023 against OpenAI by the US Federal Trade Commission, preceded a few days earlier by this blog post: FTC, 'Generative AI Raises Competition Concerns', 29 June 2023, available at www.ftc.gov/policy/advocacy-research/tech-at-ftc/2023/06/generative-ai-raises-competition-concerns (last accessed 3 May 2024).

53 Some relevant reflections with regard to online speech appeared in Frank Pasquale, 'Platform Neutrality: Enhancing Freedom of Expression in Spheres of Private Power' (2016) 17(2) *Theoretical Inquiries in Law* 487–513, 497–508; see also Kelly Ranttila, 'Social Media and Monopoly' (2020) 46(1) *Ohio Northern University Law Review* 161–179.

54 In my opinion, there are indeed very solid reasons to stick to an uncompromised view of contractual freedom, even should it happen to cause political damage to those who support it: as well as his book already mentioned above, in note 19, other writings by Walter E. Block are particularly compelling in making the ideological case for unfettered liberty of contract: see in particular Walter E. Block, Javier Portillo, 'Anti-Discrimination Laws: Undermining Our Rights' (2012) 109(2) *Journal of Business Ethics* 209–217; Walter E. Block, 'Compromising the Uncompromisable: Discrimination' (1998) 57(2) *American Journal of Economics and Sociology* 223–237; Walter E. Block, 'Discrimination: An Interdisciplinary Analysis' (1992) 11(4) *Journal of Business Ethics* 241–254.

55 For some reflections on this subject, see Umberto Nizza, 'Wolf in Sheep's Clothing: The Deceptive Neutrality of ChatGPT' (2023) 25(3) *Mercato Concorrenza Regole* 519.

56 From this perspective, it is worth mentioning the perspective advocated by Eric Hartford, who repeatedly made a case for the publication of uncensored AI models, for the sake of improving knowledge on the subject: Eric Hartford,

A different scenario emerges in the opposite hypothesis, which (precisely for the same reasons) is much more likely – that is, those suffering prejudicial treatment are members of non-protected categories. In such circumstances, it appears much more difficult to imagine the existence of legal remedies that can be activated by those who consider themselves victims of such prejudice. Anti-discrimination law appears unenforceable; the existence of a possible obligation of impartiality deriving from the dominant position of the companies involved could perhaps be considered, but at the moment it appears to be little more than a suggestion. In any event, if one sticks to the consideration of the private nature of these companies, there appear to be solid reasons, even from a conservative perspective, to defend their economic right to discriminate, including when they design their algorithms.

Clearly, this may considerably damage the conservative camp in the political debate and public arena more broadly, disproportionately amplifying an anti-conservative bias that has long been widespread among intellectuals,[57] has been identified in traditional media,[58] and that new technologies risk magnifying (a danger that US conservatives see as very much a reality[59]): but medium- to long-term damage to advocates of individual and business freedom by giving up on coherence and watering down their ideological basis seems an even more pressing danger.[60]

'Uncensored Models', in *erichartford.com*, 15 May 2023, available at https://erichartford.com/uncensored-models (last accessed 8 October 2024).

[57] See the classic references of Joseph A. Schumpeter, *Capitalism, Socialism and Democracy* (London: Allen and Unwin, 1976 [1942]), 143–155; Friedrich A. von Hayek, 'The Intellectuals and Socialism' (1949) 16(3) *University of Chicago Law Review* 417–433; Ludwig von Mises, *The Anti-Capitalistic Mentality* (Toronto: Van Nostrand, 1956); Robert Nozick, 'Why Do Intellectuals Oppose Capitalism?' (1998) XX(1) *Cato Policy Report*, available at www.cato.org/sites/cato.org/files/serials/files/policy-report/1998/1/cpr-20n1.pdf (last accessed 2 May 2024). More recently, see Neil Gross, Ethan Fosse, 'Why Are Professors Liberal?' (2012) 41 *Theory and Society* 127–168.

[58] Tim Groseclose, Jeffrey Milyo, 'A Measure of Media Bias' (2005) 120(4) *Quarterly Journal of Economics* 1191–1237. Other authors disagree with the existence of a liberal bias, even defining it a myth: see Tien-Tsung Lee, 'The Liberal Media Myth Revisited: An Examination of Factors Influencing Perceptions of Media Bias' (2005) 49(1) *Journal of Broadcasting & Electronic Media* 43–64 (citing 'research to the contrary', p. 43); others have spoken in contrast of 'liberal values, not liberal bias': Matthew Pressman, *On Press: The Liberal Values That Shaped the News* (Cambridge, MA: Harvard University Press, 2018), 1–22. Others have painted a much more nuanced picture: see for instance Adam J. Schiffer, *Evaluating Media Bias* (Lanham, MD: Rowman & Littlefield, 2017); Ceren Budak, Sharad Goel, Justin M. Rao, 'Fair and Balanced? Quantifying Media Bias through Crowdsourced Content Analysis' (2016) 80(S1) *Public Opinion Quarterly* 250–271.

[59] Such claims by US Republicans are essentially based on a series of deplatforming or shadowbanning decisions by the main social media platforms, directed at very prominent right-wing pundits: a comprehensive report appears in Richard Rogers, 'Deplatforming: Following Extreme Internet Celebrities to Telegram and Alternative Social Media' (2020) 35(3) *European Journal of Communication* 213–229, 214–215; some substantial evidence was found for instance with regard to Google Web Search: see Richard Rogers, 'Marginalizing the Mainstream: How Social Media Privilege Political Information' (2021) 4 *Frontiers in Big Data* 1–10, 7: 'Google Web Search buoys the liberal mainstream (and sinks conservative sites)' (specifically on Google's search engine, see also the reflections by Alejandro M. Diaz, 'Through the Google Goggles: Sociopolitical Bias in Search Engine Design', in Amanda Spink, Michael Zimmer (eds.), *Web Search. Multidisciplinary Perspectives* (Berlin: Springer, 2008), 11–34.

However, other studies have firmly contested the existence of such liberal bias in social media: see in particular Paul M. Barrett, J. Grant Sims, 'The Unfounded Claim that Social Media Companies Censor Conservatives' (2021), NYU Stern Center for Business and Human Rights, available at https://static1.squarespace.com/static/5b6df958f8370af3217d4178/t/6011e68dec2c7013d3caf3cb/1611785871154/NYU+False+Accusation+report_FINAL.pdf (last accessed 2 May 2024); see also Wen Chen, Diogo Pacheco, Kai-Cheng Yang, Filippo Menczer, 'Neutral Bots Probe Political Bias on Social Media' (2021) 12(5580) *Nature Communications*, available at www.nature.com/articles/s41467-021-25738-6. Some other scholars even went as far as identifying a conservative edge in the ability to spread the contents that they favour: Sandra González-Bailón, Valeria d'Andrea, Deen Freelon, Manlio De Domenico, 'The Advantage of the Right in Social Media News Sharing' (2022) 1(3) *PNAS Nexus* 1–8.

[60] See along these lines the reflections by Diane Katz, 'Free Enterprise Is the Best Remedy for Online Bias Concerns' *Backgrounder* No. 3447 (19 November 2019), available at www.heritage.org/sites/default/files/2019-11/BG3447.pdf (last accessed 2 May 2024).

Even if the opposite case of a right-wing advantage[61] were to be disproved, and even if the prediction that 'Technology will likely eliminate any prospects of a liberal news cartel'[62] was overly optimistic, there would still be evidence of the right's ability to successfully develop what has been described as a 'conservative counter-sphere'[63] or 'counter-net'[64] of alternative social media platforms, demonstrating that compliant free-market responses are possible and can be effectively employed by those who find themselves unfairly discriminated against by social media platforms. I see no reason not to extend such a conclusion to the field of generative AI.

[61] As found above by González-Bailón et al., 'The Advantage of the Right'.

[62] Daniel Sutter, 'Can the Media Be So Liberal? The Economics of Media Bias' (2001) 20(3) *Cato Journal* 431–451, 448.

[63] Mark Major, 'Conservative Consciousness and the Press: The Institutional Contribution to the Idea of the "Liberal Media" in Right-Wing Discourse' (2015) 41(3) *Critical Sociology* 483–491.

[64] Prashanth Bhat, 'Counter-Net of Tomorrow? Right-Wing Responses to Deplatforming Trump', in Robert E. Gutsche, Jr. (ed.), *The Future of the Presidency, Journalism, and Democracy. After Trump* (Abingdon: Routledge, 2022), 107–126.

15

Generative AI and Data Protection

Hannah Ruschemeier

15.1 PRELUDE: RISKS AND CHALLENGES OF GENERATIVE AI

Now that the initial hype around generative AI in the form of large language models and image generators has subsided, legal issues are coming to the fore. In addition to discussions about generative AI and copyright, there is an increasing focus on the friction between generative models and the requirements of data protection law. In the United States, several lawsuits are underway against Google and OpenAI regarding potential privacy violations by generative models.[1] Regulators are currently active in the European Union[2] and the European Data Protection Board (EDPD) has set up a task force to deal with ChatGPT.[3] The Italian data protection authority Garante had already opened a case against OpenAI in 2023, which led to a temporary national ban on ChatGPT.[4] After the proceedings were concluded, the authority found violations of the General Data Protection Regulation (GDPR).[5] Investigations into data protection violations are also underway in Poland.[6] Other countries such as Germany have

[1] See the class action against OpenAI: <https://storage.courtlistener.com/recap/gov.uscourts.cand.425482/gov.uscourts.cand.425482.1.0.pdf> accessed 29 April 2024.

[2] For an overview of ongoing investigations of data protection authorities outside the European Union, see Gabriela Zanfir-Fortuna, 'How Data Protection Authorities Are De Facto Regulating Generative AI – Future of Privacy Forum', <https://fpf.org/blog/how-data-protection-authorities-are-de-facto-regulating-generative-ai/> accessed 29 April 2024. Regarding the Italian investigation: EDPD European Data Protection Board, 'Report of the Work Undertaken by the ChatGPT Taskforce' (2024), p. 5 <www.edpb.europa.eu/our-work-tools/our-documents/other/report-work-undertaken-chatgpt-taskforce_en> accessed 29 April 2024.

[3] European Data Protection Board (EDPB), 'EDPB Resolves Dispute on Transfers by Meta and Creates Task Force on Chat GPT | European Data Protection Board' (13 April 2023) <www.edpb.europa.eu/news/news/2023/edpb-resolves-dispute-transfers-meta-and-creates-task-force-chat-gpt_en> accessed 29 April 2024.

[4] Garante per la protezione dei dati personali (GPDP), 'Intelligenza artificiale: il Garante blocca ChatGPT. Raccolta illecita di dati personali. Assenza di sistemi per la verifica dell'età dei minori' <www.garanteprivacy.it:443/home/docweb/-/docweb-display/docweb/9870847> accessed 29 April 2024.

[5] Garante per la protezione dei dati personali (GPDP), 'ChatGPT: Garante privacy, notificato a OpenAI l'atto di contestazione per le violazioni alla normativa privacy' <https://gpdp.it:443/web/guest/home/docweb/-/docweb-display/docweb/9978020> accessed 29 April 2024.

[6] Urząd ochrony danych osobowych (UODO), 'Aktualności – UODO' <https://uodo.gov.pl/pl/138/2823> accessed 29 April 2024.

issued requests for information,[7] and the French data protection authority has developed an action plan.[8] In the case of Maximilian Schrems, the data protection non-governmental organization (NGO) NOYB filed a complaint with the Austrian data protection authority in April 2024,[9] centred on incorrect information about an individual provided by ChatGPT, which OpenAI did not correct and nor did it respond to the request for information about what data was processed. These cases make it clear that data protection authorities are already AI regulators and generative AI is a core issue for data protection.[10]

From a legal perspective, generative models introduce a range of distinct issues, which are well documented across various scholarly sources.[11] In particular, the foundation models on which the popular large language models (LLMs) are built pose new security risks and vulnerabilities that need to be addressed. This then gives rise to the need for a socio-technical assessment, including legal and ethical aspects, to understand these risks and the necessary safety mechanisms. Understanding the risks posed by LLMs requires a contextual approach: normative rules, like law, always operate in context.

A major concern is the protection of personal data and privacy. Different experiments have shown that it is possible to extract personal and sensitive information about individuals from LLMs.[12] Researchers have proven that LLMs are able to memorise training data, either through over-application of abundant parameters to small datasets, which reduces the capacity to generalise to new data, or through optimisation for generalisation in long-tailed data

[7] Landesbeauftragte für Datenschutz und Informationssicherheit NRW (LDI NRW), 'Prüfung von ChatGPT geht in die nächste Runde' (30 October 2023) <www.ldi.nrw.de/pruefung-von-chatgpt-geht-die-naechste-runde> accessed 29 April 2024. The State Commissioner for Data Protection and Freedom of Information Rhineland-Palatinate, LfDI asks about ChatGPT, 24 April 2023. The State Commissioner for Data Protection Schleswig-Holstein sent out a list of questions: <www.datenschutzzentrum.de/uploads/chatgpt/20230419_Request-OpenAI_ULD-Schleswig-Holstein_IZG.pdf> accessed 29 April 2024.

[8] Commission Nationale de l'Informatique et des Libertés (CNIL), 'Artificial Intelligence: The Action Plan of the CNIL' (16 May 2023) <www.cnil.fr/en/artificial-intelligence-action-plan-cnil> accessed 29 April 2024.

[9] None of Your Business (NOYB) – Europäisches Zentrum für digitale Rechte, 'ChatGPT Provides False Information about People, and OpenAI Can't Correct It' (29 April 2024) <https://noyb.eu/en/chatgpt-provides-false-information-about-people-and-openai-cant-correct-it> accessed 29 April 2024.

[10] Until the beginning of 2024, OpenAI had not been established in Europe, meaning no member state data protection authority was responsible under Art. 56, 60 GDPR. Therefore, the supervisory authorities of the member states could all act in accordance with Art. 55 GDPR within their areas of competence. OpenAI now operates an office in Dublin, which is designated as the data controller.

[11] Damien Charlotin, 'Large Language Models and the Future of Law' [2023] *SSRN Electronic Journal* <www.ssrn.com/abstract=4548258> accessed 24 April 2024; Siyin Chen, 'Potential Applications and Safety of Large Language Models in Healthcare' (2024) 1 *Interdisciplinary Humanities and Communication Studies* <www.deanfrancispress.com/index.php/hc/article/view/561> accessed 24 April 2024; Pier Giorgio Chiara, 'Italy. Italian DPA v. OpenAI's ChatGPT: The Reasons behind the Investigation and the Temporary Limitation to Processing' (2023) 9 *European Data Protection Law Review* 68; Jessica L. Gillotte, 'Copyright Infringement in AI-Generated Artworks' (2020) 5 *UC Davis Law Review* 2657; Julian Hazell, 'Spear Phishing with Large Language Models' (14 December 2023) <www.governance.ai/research-paper/llms-used-spear-phishing> accessed 1 October 2024; Henrique Marcos and Melina Pullin, 'Large Language Models and EU Data Protection: Mapping (Some) of the Problems – The Digital Constitutionalist' (11 October 2023) <https://digi-con.org/large-language-models-and-eu-data-protection-mapping-some-of-the-problems/> accessed 5 April 2024; El-Mahdi El-Mhamdi et al., 'On the Impossible Safety of Large AI Models' (arXiv, 9 May 2023) <http://arxiv.org/abs/2209.15259> accessed 10 August 2023; Matthew Sag, 'Copyright Safety for Generative AI' (4 May 2023) <https://papers.ssrn.com/abstract=4438593> accessed 2 August 2023; Laura Weidinger et al., 'Taxonomy of Risks Posed by Language Models', *2022 ACM Conference on Fairness, Accountability, and Transparency* (ACM 2022) <https://dl.acm.org/doi/10.1145/3531146.3533088> accessed 24 April 2024.

[12] Nicholas Carlini et al., 'Extracting Training Data from Diffusion Models' (arXiv, 30 January 2023) <http://arxiv.org/abs/2301.13188> accessed 25 April 2024; El-Mhamdi et al. (n. 11); Maanak Gupta et al., 'From ChatGPT to ThreatGPT: Impact of Generative AI in Cybersecurity and Privacy' (2023) 11 *IEEE Access* 80218; Milad Nasr et al., 'Scalable Extraction of Training Data from (Production) Language Models' (2023) *arXiv.org* <https://arxiv.org/abs/2311.17035v1> accessed 1 October 2024.

distributions.[13] Although this phenomenon most often occurs where duplicates exist in the training data, it still appears where training data has been partially deduplicated. Larger models with more parameters 'remember' more data than smaller models.[14] Violations of people's privacy and right to data protection result from both incorrect information and correct information they do not want published.[15] These risks are exacerbated by unregulated and therefore uncontrolled secondary downstream use of the models. In the case of popular LLMs operated by global technology companies, commercial resale seems remote, as the companies have no interest in giving up their exclusive option for commercial exploitation. The situation is different for smaller, but in some cases no less risky models: Mixtral 8x7B competes with and surpasses GPT 3.5 in some respects, due to smart architecture that combines eight different expert models, and has been recently made open source.[16] This only highlights the need for an overview of the purposes for which these models are used and a categorisation to enable a context-based risk assessment.[17]

Data protection law gives rise to its own particular frictions, from the general function and technical specificities of big data applications and generative AI on the one hand and, on the other, the particularities of generative models. Generative models are used in different contexts for different purposes, to generate text, code, video, images, audio, and so on. In this chapter, I will focus on LLMs, which generate text by calculating the probability of word order. Data that is linguistically translatable – that is, can be understood by human recipients – can clearly also contain personal data as covered by data protection law. For this reason, they are a good example of the problems of how data protection law works in relation to AI-generated content.

This chapter first outlines the overarching lines of conflict between data protection law and generative AI (Section 15.2). It then goes into the specific legal issues of the GDPR: the scope and legal basis for authorisation of different steps of data processing by generative AI (Section 15.2), the principles of data processing (Section 15.3), the rights of data subjects (Section 15.4) and questions of responsibility (Section 15.5). Section 15.6 discusses the transferability of the argument to models that create images, audio, and video. The chapter concludes with an outlook (Section 15.7).

15.2 STRUCTURAL CHALLENGES OF GENERATIVE AI FOR DATA PROTECTION LAW

Data protection law in the EU is primarily addressed by the GDPR.[18] The current system of the GDPR is rooted in the Data Protection Directive adopted in 1995,[19] the right to data protection

[13] Claudio Novelli et al., 'Generative AI in EU Law: Liability, Privacy, Intellectual Property, and Cybersecurity' (14 January 2024) <https://papers.ssrn.com/abstract=4694565> accessed 15 January 2024.

[14] Nicholas Carlini et al., 'Quantifying Memorization across Neural Language Models' (*arXiv.org*, 15 February 2022) <https://arxiv.org/abs/2202.07646v3> accessed 29 April 2024.

[15] Rainer Mühlhoff and Hannah Ruschemeier, 'Predictive Analytics and the Collective Dimensions of Data Protection' (2024) 16 *Law, Innovation and Technology* 261.

[16] Philipp Hacker, 'What's Missing from the EU AI Act: Addressing the Four Key Challenges of Large Language Models' (2023) *Verfassungsblog* <https://verfassungsblog.de/whats-missing-from-the-eu-ai-act/> accessed 6 January 2024.

[17] Rainer Mühlhoff and Hannah Ruschemeier, 'Regulating AI with Purpose Limitation for Models' (2024) 1 *Journal of AI Law and Regulation* 24.

[18] Regulation (EU) 2016/679 of the European Parliament and of the Council of 27 April 2016 on the protection of natural persons with regard to the processing of personal data and on the free movement of such data, and repealing Directive 95/46/EC (General Data Protection Regulation) (Text with EEA relevance) OJ 2016 No. L119, 4 May 2016.

[19] Directive 95/46/EC of the European Parliament and of the Council of 24 October 1995 on the protection of individuals with regard to the processing of personal data and on the free movement of such data OJ L 281, 23 November 1995, 31–50.

(Article 8 Charter of Fundamental Rights of the European Union, CFR), the right to privacy (Article 7 CFR),[20] and the primary legal foundations in Article 16 Treaty on the Functioning of the European Union (TFEU).[21] Article 1 GDPR sets the matter and scope as the processing of personal data with the objective of protecting fundamental rights and freedoms of natural persons, Article 1 GDPR. Correspondingly, the understanding of 'processing' in terms of personal data is very broad and takes an all-encompassing approach to cover practically any interaction.[22] For this reason, when personal data is involved, all stages in the lifecycle of an AI model may fall within the scope of the GDPR.

From a regulatory perspective, the various steps of data processing in the lifecycle of an AI model are therefore important, and for generative models can be differentiated as follows.[23] The first step is the collection of training data, made up of many data points. These may comprise personal or non-personal information. In certain instances, this process utilises extremely large datasets, making it challenging, if not impossible, to differentiate between various categories of data. For instance, ChatGPT was developed using copious amounts of data freely available on the internet. The second step is the actual training of the model using the collected data, resulting in a configured model. The third step is model application, meaning that the trained model is applied to specific cases or individuals, making the model a tool that computes a specific output in response to input data.[24] This breadth of data and the training process mean model output contains information about cases or individuals as well as of 'third parties' that were not part of the training data.

15.2.1 *Quantity*

The first problem area relates to how the training of powerful AI models, or the processing of large amounts of data, works in relation to the amount of data processed.[25] The sheer quantity of data processed by AI models is the core, as yet unresolved, problem of AI and data protection.[26] Generative AI models are typically trained on billions, if not hundreds of billions, of parameters and require large amounts of training data and computing power.[27] Data protection law on the other hand is based on the idea that the individual steps of data processing and the data processed can be identified. This concept applies the idea of individual control to empower individuals by allowing them to manage their own personal information.[28] But models trained on unprecedentedly large datasets make it impossible to manually identify or even review

[20] I understand privacy as one of the protected interests under data protection law. For more about the relationship, see Johannes Eichenhofer, *E-Privacy: Theorie und Dogmatik eines europäischen Privatheitsschutzes im Internet-Zeitalter*, Vol. 301 (Mohr Siebeck, 2021) 47f. <https://ebookcentral.proquest.com/lib/kxp/detail.action?docID=6638955>.

[21] Additionally, Article 39 TEU lays down specific provisions for the area of the Common Foreign and Security Policy.

[22] See V. P. Hert and P. D. Hert, 'GDPR Art. 4 Abs. 2 Processing' in I. Spiecker gen Döhmann, V. Papakonstantinou, G. Hornung, and P. de Hert (eds.), *General Data Protection Regulation: Article-by-Article Commentary* (Baden-Baden: Nomos Verlagsgesellschaft, 2023), para. 3.

[23] These steps are developed in: Mühlhoff and Ruschemeier (n. 15); Mühlhoff and Ruschemeier (n. 17).

[24] Mühlhoff and Ruschemeier (n. 17).

[25] Tal Zarsky, 'Incompatible: The GDPR in the Age of Big Data' (2016) 47 *Seton Hall Law Review* 995.

[26] Generative models are based on neural networks, usually Generative Adversarial Networks and Transformer Networks: Weidinger et al. (n. 11).

[27] Tom B. Brown et al., 'Language Models Are Few-Shot Learners' (2020) Neural Information Processing Systems', 2022 ACM Conference on Fairness, Accountability, and Transparency, Seoul Republic of Korea June 21– 24, 2022 <https://dl.acm.org/doi/proceedings/10.1145/3531146>.

[28] Daniel J. Solove, 'Artificial Intelligence and Privacy' (1 February 2024) <https://papers.ssrn.com/abstract=4713111> accessed 25 March 2024.

whether data processing complies with legal requirements, and thus harbours potential for privacy and data protection violations.[29] Furthermore, this approach conflicts with the principle of data minimisation laid down in Article 5(1)(c). This mode of operation reveals the problems of governance arising from the systematic design of the GDPR, which, for example, envisages individual consent as the basis for authorisation and presupposes the identification of individual data subjects and the data to be attributed to them.

15.2.2 *Purposes*

Privacy and data protection also seem to be at odds with the general concept of generative AI when it comes to the relevance of purposes. Data protection is highly contextual, and its level of protection depends on the type of data processed, by whom, in which settings, and for which purposes (Article 5(1)(b) GDPR). LLMs on the other hand, cover a wide range of purposes, applications, and operating environments. According to Article 3(63) of the new regulation on artificial intelligence[30] (AI Act), a general-purpose AI model includes AI models trained with a large amount of data using self-supervision at scale, which display significant generality, are capable of competently performing a wide range of distinct tasks regardless of how the model is placed on the market, and that can be integrated into a variety of downstream systems or applications. It does not include AI models used for research, development, or prototyping activities before they are placed on the market. This definition is a good description of the current market situation; OpenAI, for example, now offers a wider variety of different GPTs for specific tasks: the laundry buddy for laundry-specific questions about stains and laundry settings, the sous chef that provides users with recipes, or the negotiator that helps a user to argue in their favour.[31] These downstream applications will gain more relevance, as it can be expected that the foundation models will not continue to be used primarily as isolated applications as has been the case to date, but will be integrated into other models as modular building blocks. This will increase both desirable and undesirable effects due to the possible scaling of model output. Here, even the design aspect of LLMs is difficult to reconcile with legislation, seemingly conflicting with the GDPR's purpose limitation principle. In particular, when models are made available to numerous third parties via an interface, ensuring compatibility for that model and its data with the purposes for which the data was originally collected (Article 6(4) GDPR) becomes difficult, if not impossible.[32]

15.3 SCOPE OF THE GDPR AND LEGAL BASIS

The GDPR is applicable in terms of material and geography – that is, it extends to the processing of personal data for activities within the EU, even when that processing takes place elsewhere (Article 3(1) GDPR), and where goods or services are offered to data subjects within the Union (Article 3(2) GDPR). It therefore applies to all generative models in use in the Union

[29] On the relationship between privacy and data protection: Raphael Gellert and Serge Gutwirth, 'The Legal Construction of Privacy and Data Protection' (2013) 29 *Computer Law & Security Review* 522; Juliane Kokott and Christoph Sobotta, 'The Distinction between Privacy and Data Protection in the Jurisprudence of the CJEU and the ECtHR' (2013) 3 *International Data Privacy Law* 222.

[30] P9_TA(2024)0138 (COM(2021)0206 – C9-0146/2021 – 2021/0106(COD)).

[31] These are available under ChatGPT 4o at chatgpt.com with a paid subscription.

[32] Mühlhoff and Ruschemeier (n. 17).

15.3.1 *Scope of Application*

15.3.1.1 Personal Data

The GDPR applies to the processing of personal data (Article 2(1)) if none of the exceptions in paragraphs 2–3 apply. This processing includes both the collection of training data and the training of the models, as well as the storage and use or sale of the model to generate output based on user requests.

The processing of personal data begins with step one, the collection of vast amounts of data with which to train an LLM. As the effectiveness of LLMs is directly linked to the breadth and variety of their datasets, this data is obtained by scraping content from numerous websites. Inevitably this often includes personal data (Article 4(1) GDPR) such as names, dates of birth, or other identifying information.[33] As personal data also includes incomplete or indirect details which may result in an individual being identified through additional information,[34] this processing is covered by the GDPR, even before the model is trained or released.

In the second step of data processing, the training of the model, identifying personal data becomes more challenging, as the final trained model may differ from its training data. An artificial neural network is represented by a large matrix of numbers, determined by weights and other parameters such as activation thresholds.[35] While the training data may include personal information, the data in the model may not necessarily retain that characteristic: personal data may be anonymised where advanced techniques such as differential privacy and federated machine learning are used during the training process to remove references to the training data.[36]

A trained model resulting from such anonymisation that makes the reconstruction of training data impossible or highly unlikely is not considered to constitute personal data. However, the current popular large language models tend to persist in producing identifying information, whether by design or by accident. It cannot therefore always be assumed that model data has been fully anonymised: research into this 'remembering' phenomenon is ongoing. This is critical from the GDPR standpoint as the storage of the model also constitutes data processing under the GDPR if the model data is not properly anonymised. In addition, many authors[37]

[33] European Data Protection Board (EDPB) (n. 3); Hannah Ruschemeier, 'Squaring the Circle' (*Verfassungsblog*, 7 April 2023) <https://verfassungsblog.de/squaring-the-circle/> accessed 25 March 2024. The Hamburg data protection authority, on the other hand, believes that LLMs do not store personal data, without explaining how this relates to the scraping of information that undoubtedly constitutes personal data: <https://datenschutz-hamburg.de/fileadmin/user_upload/HmbBfDI/Datenschutz/Informationen/240715_Diskussionspapier_HmbBfDI_KI_Modelle.pdf> accessed 25 March 2024.

[34] In its judgment on the *Breyer* case (CJEU C-582/14, ECLI:EU:C:2016:779) the ECJ also considered whether personal data is involved in the context of indirect identifiability.

[35] Mühlhoff and Ruschemeier (n. 17) 27; Martín Abadi et al., 'Deep Learning with Differential Privacy' (2016) *Proceedings of the 2016 ACM SIGSAC Conference on Computer and Communications Security* – CCS'16 308 <https://dl.acm.org/doi/proceedings/10.1145/2976749>.

[36] Abadi et al. (n. 35); Cynthia Dwork, 'Differential Privacy' in Michele Bugliesi et al. (eds.), *Automata, Languages and Programming: 33rd International Colloquium, ICALP 2006, Venice, Italy, July 10–14, 2006, Proceedings, Part II*, Vol. 2 (Springer 2006); Khaled El Emam, Sam Rodgers and Bradley Malin, 'Anonymising and Sharing Individual Patient Data' (2015) 350 *BMJ* (Clinical research ed.) h1139.

[37] K. Emam and C. Alvarez, 'A Critical Appraisal of the Article 29 Working Party Opinion 05/2014 on Data Anonymization Techniques' (2014) 5 *International Data Privacy Law* 73; Wim Jan Schreurs et al., 'Cogitas, Ergo Sum. The Role of Data Protection Law and Non-Discrimination Law in Group Profiling in the Private Sector' in Mireille Hildebrandt and Serge Gutwirth (eds.), *Profiling the European Citizen* (Springer 2008); Alexander Roßnagel,

argue that the anonymising of personal data itself is also a processing operation that requires justification under the GDPR.[38]

In processing step number three, the production of output, the models or applications using them can produce personal data. Whether the information provided is correct or not is immaterial: when an LLM produces outputs that contain the names and bibliographical information of real people, they are processing personal data. Additionally, individuals can often be easily identified from the context of the text prompt or text output, or by using search engines. LLMs linked to search engines may also facilitate identification. Particularly in the case of public LLMs, it is likely that many data subjects can be identified for the reasons mentioned above.[39] It is important to note that the people in the training data are not theoretically the same as those produced in the output data even where they have the same name, as LLMs can also generate names of existing people, for example by producing information to users can then assign to individuals.

15.3.1.2 Territorial Scope of Application

Article 3(1) of the GDPR states that the Regulation applies 'to the processing of personal data in the context of the activities of an establishment of a controller or a processor in the Union, regardless of whether the processing takes place in the Union or not'. Thus, the processing of personal data does not have to take place in the European Union itself, but can be performed on servers that are for example based in the United States or other third countries. As mentioned above, *lex loci solutionis* (Article 3(2)) means the requirements apply if the data processor offers its services to EU citizens, even where the processor is not located in the EU. This therefore brings global technologies including LLMs and other AI models such as ChatGPT, Bard, and Gemini squarely under the GDPR where these are accessible from the European Union.

15.3.2 *Legal Basis for Data Processing*

All processing of personal data within the scope of the GDPR requires a legal basis (Article 6(1) GDPR). The question of the legal basis for data processing across the life cycle of a generative AI system poses different problems, as it depends on the stage of the data processing. As argued before, it is essential to distinguish between the different steps of data processing when analysing AI and data protection.[40]

15.3.2.1 Collection of Training Data

The first step in the life cycle of a generative model is the collection of training data In the case of LLMs like GPT-4 or Bard, this step consists of scraping data from the internet. The indiscriminate scouring of almost the entire internet logically excludes the legal basis of consent (Article 6(1)(a)). In the absence of legal obligations or contractual relationships between the

'Datenlöschung und Anonymisierung. Verhältnis der beiden Datenschutzinstrumente nach der DSGVO' (2021) 11 *ZD* 188.

[38] Article 29 Working Party, Opinion 05/2014 on Anonymisation Techniques (WP 216) 0829/14/EN. On this dispute in the context of predictive analytics: Mühlhoff and Ruschemeier (n. 15).

[39] Paulina Pesch and Raine bec Böhme, 'Verarbeitung personenbezogener Daten und Datenrichtigkeit Bei Großen Sprachmodellen' (2023) 26 *Multimedia und Recht* 917.

[40] Mühlhoff and Ruschemeier (n. 15).

operators of LLMs and all internet users worldwide, the scraping of training data can only rely on the legal basis of legitimate interest provided in Article 6(1)(f) GDPR.[41]

Article 6(1)(f) GDPR states that data processing is lawful if it is necessary for the purposes of pursuing the legitimate interests of the data controller or by a third party, provided these interests do not override the fundamental rights and freedoms of the data subjects requiring protection.[42] The ECJ has clarified that this provision lays down three cumulative conditions: (1) the pursuit of a legitimate interest by the controller or by a third party; (2) the processing of personal data must be necessary to pursue that legitimate interest; and (3) that the legitimate interest of the controller or of a third party are not outweighed by the interests or fundamental freedoms and rights of the data subject.[43]

The fact that this constitutes the only plausible legal basis exposes the structural problem of data protection law in relation to data-intensive technologies, not least because whether Article 6(1)(f) provides a sufficient legal basis must be determined on a case-by-case basis.[44] There are indications that general interest may outweigh the purpose of processing, or that this can be assumed, if data subjects could reasonably expect their data to be processed for training purposes. However, the nature of mass data scraping makes it almost impossible to identify individual interests, and therefore cannot provide satisfactory answers in terms of current legal doctrine and legal systems.

15.3.2.2 Legitimate Interest

The term 'legitimate interests' is deliberately broad, to encompass legal, economic, or idealistic interests, excluding only hypothetical and public interests. The collection of data to train a generative model for commercial use is initially a legitimate economic interest protected by the freedom to conduct a business under Article 16 CFR. The argument that the European Court of Justice (ECJ) also cited freedom of information (Article 11(2) ECFR) as a legitimate interest transferable to generative model training[45] in the Google Spain case[46] does not apply to models that are only accessible for a fee. Furthermore, search engines and generative models operate differently, and are therefore not comparable. Sources referenced in search engines can be deleted or corrected, whereas LLMs generate a unique new text for each question for which a new probability is calculated. If the output text is incorrect, it cannot be corrected for future outputs.

15.3.2.3 Necessity

The necessity test under Article 6(1)(f) requires that the processing of personal data be a proportionate means of achieving legitimate interests. Processing is considered necessary if the processing of personal data is essential to achieve the objective of the processor's legitimate interest – in this case, training and putting an AI model on the market – and that these interests

[41] Zarsky (n. 25); Frederik J Zuiderveen Borgesius et al., 'Tracking Walls, Take-It-or-Leave-It Choices, the GDPR, and the ePrivacy Regulation' (2017) 3 *European Data Protection Law Review* 353.

[42] Ruschemeier (n. 33).

[43] Case C-252/21, Meta ECLI:EU:C:2023:537, para. 106; Case C-597/19, EU:C:2021:492, para. 106.

[44] Mary Donnelly and Maeve McDonagh, 'Health Research, Consent and the GDPR Exemption' (2019) 26 *European Journal of Health Law* 97; Novelli et al. (n. 13).

[45] Christoph Krönke, 'Attention Is All You Need: ChatGPT und die DSGVO' (2023) *Verfassungsblog* <https://verfassungsblog.de/attention-is-all-you-need/> accessed 29 April 2024.

[46] Case C-131/12, Google Spain, ECLI:EU:C:2014:317.

do not outweigh the rights of the data subject. In rare cases, where only anonymised data is sufficient to train the model, that training may not require personal data. However, anonymised data alone is generally not adequate for training generative models, even were such anonymisation possible in the training phase.

15.3.2.4 Balancing of Interests

This balancing of interests between processor and data subject must also consider the rights of data subjects under Articles 7 and 8 ECFR. Their interests are particularly affected when AI collects, combines, and contextualises personal data available on the internet in response to user queries.

There is a valid argument for the interests of the processor in providing a large amount of training data to ensure powerful generative models able to generate word sequences that correspond to human language. Nevertheless, it is not absolutely necessary to scrape data on a scale that covers almost all publicly accessible resources on the internet to develop generative models: datasets can be generated in other ways, such as through data donations, effective consent solutions, or data collection by the data controller itself. However, none of these alternative options would be able to create the required breadth of data. The question is therefore *which* specific interest of the processor is worth protecting. Meta, for example, publicly admitted that the main difficulty the acquisition of licences for copyrighted material would have imposed on the development of generative models was expense. The same argument applies to collecting training data in a manner compliant with privacy regulations: the approach would have required considerable resources. However, it is unlikely that cost savings can constitute a legitimate interest, and at any rate, an interest based on structural infringements has considerably less protective value.

In the Meta case,[47] the ECJ also ruled that the personalisation of content – Meta's core business model – was not necessary for the operation of a social network. The ECJ went on, stating that legitimate interests do not adequately justify Meta's practices of tracking and profiling individuals for the purpose of conducting its behavioural advertising business across its social platforms:

> it is important to note that, despite the fact that the services of an online social network such as Facebook are free of charge, the user of that network cannot reasonably expect that the operator of the social network will process that user's personal data, without his or her consent, for the purposes of personalised advertising. In those circumstances, it must be held that the interests and fundamental rights of such a user override the interest of that operator in financing its activity through personalised advertising, with the result that the processing by that operator for such purposes cannot fall within the scope of point (f) of the first subparagraph of Article 6(1) of the GDPR.[48]

This raises substantial doubts about the ability of companies like OpenAI to defend the processing of vast amounts of personal data to establish a commercial generative AI enterprise, particularly given that such tools pose numerous emerging risks to identified individuals, including issues like disinformation, defamation, identity theft, and fraud.

Context is therefore critical in safeguarding privacy and data protection. The public accessibility of data on the internet, even where disclosed by the data subjects themselves, does not completely

[47] Case C-252/21, Meta ECLI:EU:C:2023:537, para. 102 et seq.

[48] Ibid., para. 117.

negate their legitimate interest in its protection. As Recital 47 states, the interests and fundamental rights of the data subject may in particular override the interest of the data controller where personal data is processed in circumstances or in ways that data subjects do not reasonably expect. Although it is now public knowledge that data posted on the internet may be processed in ways other than initially thought, it is also a question of the specific purposes of the processing. For example, the legitimate expectation of privacy means that decades-old or deleted posts, personal websites, and entries cannot be used in perpetuity to train commercial models. It is reasonable to suggest that the typical internet user does not expect, or intend, their data to be utilised as training material for LLMs for the financial gain of others. Therefore, the use of the data for training these models represents a secondary purpose. In most instances, it is unlikely that a data subject made their data publicly available to serve as a dataset for the financial gain of LLM providers, making the use of such publicly available data an infringement on contextual privacy.[49]

Moreover, a legitimate interest must be determined within the broader European and national regulatory context. The broad scope of scraping also means that an unmanageable number of people are affected, which opens the claim of legitimacy to questions of proportionality. According to the German constitutional doctrine of the Federal Constitutional Court, a particularly large number of people being affected without cause can impact the claim of legitimacy. This impact is referred to as 'scatter width', and is a line of argumentation used by the ECJ.[50] Such effects also arise in the case of universal data processing, as almost all internet users are affected.

Additionally, the legitimate interest must also be lawful, meaning it should conform to all applicable laws and regulations, including the principles and other provisions of data protection law. This includes ensuring that processing aligns with the expectations of the data subject based on their relationship with the controller, adheres to the principles of data minimisation, and implements appropriate safeguards (Recital 50 of the GDPR). In the case of broad-scale internet scraping, individual interests are difficult to identify. However, there were concerns about the legality of scraping from the outset, including with regard to potential copyright infringements.[51] An interest pursued through structural infringements cannot be legitimate.

Compatibility with the principles of data protection law under Article 5 GDPR also plays a role in the balancing of interests. This requires legitimate interests be evaluated in terms of the fairness of processing (Article 5(1)(a)), purpose limitation (Article 5(1)(b)), data minimisation (Article 5(1)(c)), and data accuracy (Article 5(d)).

Therefore, legitimate interests cannot be assumed across all training data. The matter is made more complex given it is extremely difficult, if not impossible, to comprehensively exclude personal data pertaining to minors or special categories of personal data according to Article 9(1) from training data. To complicate this matter further, the point at which the processing of personal data 'reveals' special categories of personal data under Article 9(1) GDPR has not yet been conclusively clarified.

15.3.2.5 Training of the Model

It is worth undertaking a chronological review of the various data processing operations used for training the model. A key consideration is whether data anonymisation occurs during model

[49] Helen Nissenbaum, 'A Contextual Approach to Privacy Online' (2011) 140 *Daedalus* 32.

[50] Case C-511/18 inter alia, ECLI:EU:C:2020:791, marg. no. 143 f. – La Quadrature du Net; Case C-293/12, ECLI: EU:C:2014:238, para. 57 ff. – Digital Rights Ireland Ltd; Case C-203/15, ECLI:EU:C:2016:970, para 105 f. – Tele2; Case C-140/20, ECLI:EU:C:2022:258, marg. No. 66 – Commissioner of An Garda Síochána.

[51] Ruschemeier (n. 33).

training. If the data is anonymised in the course of training, a further processing of anonymous data would fall outside the scope of the GDPR. The prevailing view is that a legal basis is required for the anonymisation of data under Article 6(1).[52] In this context, anonymisation should be understood as normative rather than technical, in line with the ECJ ruling that holds that data has been anonymised. This is because the ECJ considers anonymisation has occurred even if it is technically possible, but unlikely, that the controller could carry out identification with the means available including additional information.[53] According to the court, data is considered anonymous under the GDPR if re-identification is illegal.[54]

In principle, the anonymisation of personal data is generally easy to justify under Article 6 GDPR. The practice aligns with the principle of data minimisation and storage limitation. Effective and permanent anonymisation can serve the interests of both data subjects and data controllers: the former are protected from unauthorised interference with their fundamental data protection rights, while the latter are freed from some of the perceived burdens of complying with the stringent requirements of data protection law.[55] However, this argument struggles to hold in light of the volume of data, as effective consent from the data subjects pursuant to Articles 6(1)(a) and 7 GDPR cannot be obtained in practice.

While it may be possible to institute legal obligations to anonymise training data under Article 6(1)(c), this is not yet relevant in practice. This means that the legal basis of legitimate interest in Article 6(1)(f) may also apply to anonymisation. Generally speaking, this provision may provide adequate results as anonymisation will typically be in the interest of the data subjects themselves, so that at the very least a conflicting interest is improbable. In the case of larger LLMs, it is equally unlikely that a data subject will have an individual interest in non-anonymisation and, moreover, even where such interest of an individual data subject exists, it would outweigh other relevant interests, such as of the other data subjects. As a result, anonymisation is permissible.

Assessing the processing of special categories of personal data under Article 9 is more difficult: anonymisation would require a case to be made under Article 9(2). As described above, the processing of special categories of data cannot be ruled out for LLMs. Although the hurdles of Article 9(2) are high, the 'made public' provision of Article 9(2)(e) can also be considered here. Others argue for a teleological reduction of Article 9(1) for anonymisation.[56] Neither variant constitutes an infringement of data subjects' rights where training data has been anonymised. These complex considerations alone show that there are gaps between the individual-based approach of the GDPR and the tools required for adequately regulating generative AI.

15.3.2.6 Generating Output

The output of generative language models may constitute the processing of personal data. Here, a distinction must be made between the processing of scraped training data and the processing of user data in the form of prompts entered while using the model. There is no legitimate interest

[52] Emam and Alvarez (n. 37); Roßnagel (n. 37); Schreurs et al. (n. 37) 241–270; Article 29 Working Party Article 29 Working Party, 'Opinion 05/2014 on Anonymisation Techniques (WP 216) 0829/14/EN' (Article 29 Working Party 2014) 29.

[53] Case C-582/14, ECLI:EU:C:2016:779 – *Breyer*, para. 45–49.

[54] Ibid. This, however, contradicts the protective function of the GDPR, which aims to protect data subjects from unlawful processing of their data. See Philipp Hacker, 'A Legal Framework for AI Training Data – From First Principles to the Artificial Intelligence Act' (2021) 13 *Law, Innovation and Technology* 257.

[55] Gerrit Hornung and Bernd Wagner, 'Anonymisierung als datenschutzrelevante Verarbeitung? Rechtliche Anforderungen und Grenzen für die Anonymisierung personenbezogener Daten' (2020) *ZD* 223.

[56] Ibid.

in processing user data, for example in the context of input prompts when using LLMs. Instead, effective consent, pursuant to Article 6(1)(a) must be obtained, using a tool that needs to be critically evaluated in the digital space.[57] OpenAI had to update its privacy policy for EU users after being investigated by the Italian data protection authority. It now states: 'We use the content you provide to improve our services, such as to train the models that run our services. Read our instructions on how to opt out of the use of your content to train our models.'[58] However, consent is only a valid basis for prompts containing personal information about the user themselves. If users create prompts that include personal data from other persons, they cannot validly consent on their behalf.[59]

When a generative model is capable of producing output which includes personal data, the issue of how training data was collected remains relevant throughout its lifecycle. If there was no legal basis for collecting the training data, there is no legal basis for using it to generate output. Theoretically, legitimate interest could also be considered here under Article 6(1)(f), but must be assessed on a case-by-case basis according to the criteria described above. However, LLMs make individual assessments difficult because of the quantity of data they process. In addition, generative models are scalable in terms of their output, which means false information can be disseminated to a large number of users and third parties.

Output processing is also problematic in cases where models infer or disclose special categories of personal data under Article 9(1) GDPR. It has been shown that models can memorise and reproduce private and personal information such as phone numbers, addresses, and medical documents.[60] In the age of big data, it is now potentially possible to infer sensitive information from almost any data, especially if one includes the boundless category of political opinions, covered by Article 9(1) GDPR. This means that 'normal' personal data can reveal special categories of personal data covered by Article 9(1), although the criteria for distinguishing between general and sensitive data remain contested.[61] One proposed criterion goes to the intention behind the data processing. Scenarios involving context-specific information could lead to the generation of sensitive data depending on the purpose of evaluation.[62] Court rulings tend to support this assumption: the ECJ seemed to interpret 'revealing' broadly in the *Meta* case,[63] and in another ruling, the Court decided that the disclosure of a spouse, partner, or

[57] Omri Ben-shahar and Carl E. Schneider, 'The Failure of Mandated Disclosure' (2011) 159 *University of Pennsylvania Law Review* 647; Borgesius et al. (n. 41); Sourya Joyee De and Abdessamad Imine, 'Consent for Targeted Advertising: The Case of Facebook' (2020) 35 *AI & Society* 1055; Trung Tin Nguyen, Michael Backes and Ben Stock, 'Freely Given Consent? Studying Consent Notice of Third-Party Tracking and Its Violations of GDPR in Android Apps', *Proceedings of the 2022 ACM SIGSAC Conference on Computer and Communications Security* (Association for Computing Machinery 2022) <https://dl.acm.org/doi/10.1145/3548606.3560564> accessed 13 July 2023; Mühlhoff and Ruschemeier (n. 17) 31.

[58] OpenAI, 'Datenschutzerklärung' (15 December 2023) <https://openai.com/de-DE/policies/eu-privacy-policy/> accessed 4 October 2024.

[59] Novelli et al. (n. 13).

[60] Carlini et al. (n. 12).

[61] Mühlhoff and Ruschemeier (n. 15).

[62] Michael Matejek and Steffen Mäusezahl, 'Gewöhnliche vs. sensible personenbezogene Daten. Abgrenzung und Verarbeitungsrahmen von Daten gem. Art. 9 DS-GVO' (2019) *ZD* 551; Sebastian Schulz, 'Art. 9 DS-GVO', in Peter Gola and Dirk Heckmann (eds.), *Datenschutzgrundverordnung* (Munich: C. H. Beck, 2018); Ludmila Georgieva and Christopher Kuner, 'Art. 9 Processing of Special Categories of Personal Data' in Christopher Kuner et al. (eds.), *The EU General Data Protection Regulation (GDPR)* (Oxford: Oxford University Press, 2020) 373; Sandra Wachter, Brent Mittelstadt and Chris Russell, 'Do Large Language Models Have a Legal Duty to Tell the Truth?' <https://papers.ssrn.com/abstract=4771884> accessed 30 April 2024. Question No. 2 in ECJ Case C- 252/21, *Meta Platforms and Others* [2021] (ECLI:EU:C:2022:704), dismissed by the Advocate General in his Opinion, para. 41.

[63] Case C-252/21, *Meta*, ECLI:EU:C:2023:537, para. 73.

cohabitee's name could potentially indicate the sexual orientation of the applicant.[64] The Court has established minimal criteria for what constitutes the 'revealing' of sensitive data: the act of an 'intellectual operation involving comparison or deduction' is deemed sufficient to extend the special protection regime meant for sensitive data to personal data that is not inherently sensitive. However, this judgment was not directly related to big data, leaving the distinction somewhat ambiguous.[65]

Consequently, in many instances involving big data, merely being able to potentially infer sensitive information may subject processes such as AI training to the provisions of Article 9. and there is little likelihood that LLMs satisfy the exceptions in Article 9(2). For instance, the research exemption under Article 9(2)(j) is restricted to the development of models for research purposes and does not permit their commercial exploitation, as indicated in Recitals 159 and 162.[66]

Another important distinction is whether LLM output can be used to infer sensitive information about individuals that they have not made public themselves. Even if certain indicators, for example of political orientation, are available on the internet, LLM output may aggregate this information. As such, Article 9(2)(e) does not constitute a legal basis for this type of derivation.[67]

Data accuracy requirements (Article 5(1)(d) GDPR also apply to LLM output. Language models have been shown to 'hallucinate' and produce incorrect information, including incorrect personal data.[68] Under the GDPR, operators are responsible for ensuring data accuracy (Articles 5(2), 24, 25(1) GDPR).[69] Although all popular applications provide disclaimers to inform users that the models may not always be correct, the effect of such notifications are questionable given *automation bias*.[70] Even if the current error rate of LLMs[71] does not justify generally prohibiting such applications on the basis of ensuring data accuracy, it does affect data subjects' rights. The right to data accuracy becomes even more significant if the right to rectification or erasure cannot be effectively enforced.

15.4 DATA SUBJECTS' RIGHTS

As with other areas of data-intensive technology application, there are problems with the enforcement of data subjects' rights in the case of generative models.[72] In general, the actors involved mean many data-driven AI technologies are developed, promoted, sold, and used by a

64 Case C-184/20, ECLI:EU:C:2022:601.

65 Mühlhoff and Ruschemeier (n. 15).

66 Novelli et al. (n. 13).

67 See also Case C-252/21, *Meta*, ECLI:EU:C:2023:537, para. 73.

68 Wachter et al. (n. 62).

69 As the ECJ already stated in 2008 with regard to the maintenance of data in the Central Register of Foreigners – similar to an actor acting under public authority, in order to delete or correct incorrect information without delay. Case C-524/06, 2008 I-09705. Krönke (n. 45).

70 Hannah Ruschemeier, 'The Problems of the Automation Bias in the Public Sector – A Legal Perspective' in Weizenbaum Institute (ed.), *Weizenbaum Conference Proceedings: AI, Big Data, Social Media and People on the Move* (2023) <www.weizenbaum-library.de/items/4bc59488-2fa5-4609-9db8-47f2bf1d57f7> accessed 22 August 2023; Lukas Hondrich and Hannah Ruschemeier, 'Addressing Automation Bias through Verifiability' <https://papers.ssrn.com/sol3/papers.cfm?abstract_id=4521411> accessed 4 October 2024; Hannah Ruschemeier and Lukas J. Hondrich, 'Automation Bias in Public Administration – An Interdisciplinary Perspective from Law and Psychology' (2024) 41 *Government Information Quarterly* 101953.

71 Cade Metz, 'Chatbots May "Hallucinate" More Often Than Many Realize' *The New York Times* (6 November 2023) <www.nytimes.com/2023/11/06/technology/chatbots-hallucination-rates.html> accessed 30 April 2024.

72 Daniel Solove, 'The Limitations of Privacy Rights' (2023) 98 *Notre Dame Law Review* 975.

handful of big tech companies, which establishes an informational power asymmetry between the powerful processors and the users. As a result, privacy rights alone are insufficient to address the issue of data disempowerment.[73] Individuals typically are not able to fully manage their personal data, as there is a fundamental limit to the control they can exert. While rights can afford a modest degree of influence in certain isolated cases, this influence is too sporadic and disjointed to significantly safeguard privacy. Ultimately, rights function primarily as a minor element within a broader framework.[74]

The sheer quantity of the data processed from various sources seems to make it impossible to identify and inform individuals of the processing, or of the processor, to enable data subjects to assert their rights with regard to the processing of their data. Therefore, the data quantity realistically rules out compliance with the data subject's right to information. In practice, reporting indicates that companies such as OpenAI and Midjourney have not responded to requests for information from people who found themselves in the training data.[75]

The prerequisite for the exercise of the data subjects' rights under the GDPR provided in Articles 13–22 is, first and foremost, that the data subject is aware of the data processing. Users providing input into an AI model in the form of prompts are covered by Article 13 GDPR. However, Article 14 GDPR also comes into play where data has not been collected from the data subjects themselves. According to both standards, data subjects must be informed about who has processed which data (categories of data), for what purposes, on what legal basis, and whether this data has been disclosed to third parties. These transparency provisions have the specific purpose of enabling data subjects to exercise their other rights, such as the right to erasure or rectification. Article 14(5) states the exception that the transparency obligation does not apply where and insofar as the provision of such information proves impossible or would involve a 'disproportionate effort, in particular for processing for archiving purposes in the public interest, scientific or historical research purposes or statistical purposes … In such cases the controller shall take appropriate measures to protect the data subject's rights and freedoms and legitimate interests, including making the information publicly available'.

Again, it depends on the individual case, although it seems doubtful whether LLM operators can invoke unreasonableness if they already knew before the model was developed that individual requests for information could not be enforced. In any case, the principle of responsibility in Article 5(2) GDPR means a failure to respond to such requests or a reference to general impossibility is not sufficient.

Practice has shown that LLMs and possibly other generative AI models that produce content operate almost universally, not just at an individual level. This near-universal infringement reflects the profound mismatch between data-intensive models and the individual rights approach to data protection taken by data protection laws. As a result of this universality, other rights of data subjects such as the right to rectification (Article 16 GDPR)[76] and the right to erasure (Article 17 GDPR) exist on paper, but become unenforceable in practice.[77]

[73] We have explained in detail elsewhere that systemic, supra-individual solutions and a collective understanding of data protection are needed: Mühlhoff and Ruschemeier (n. 15); Mühlhoff and Ruschemeier (n. 17); Rainer Mühlhoff, 'Predictive Privacy: Collective Data Protection in Times of AI and Big Data' (2023) 10 *Big Data & Society* 1.

[74] Solove (n. 72).

[75] Elisa Harlan and Katharina Brunner, 'We Are All Raw Material for AI' (*BR*, 7 July 2023) <https://interaktiv.br.de/ki-trainingsdaten/en/> accessed 4 October 2024.

[76] Novelli et al. (n. 13).

[77] Novelli et al. (n. 13) rightly point out that invoking the right to erasure (and correction under Article 21 GDPR) depends on whether the LLM itself is personal data. This depends whether the training data is anonymised or not, see Section 15.3.2.3.

Furthermore, removal requests from an individual data subject cannot produce the intended outcome, particularly in cases where the same information has been disseminated by multiple users interacting with the LLM.[78] In essence, simply deleting data from a training dataset offers only a superficial remedy, as it does not guarantee the elimination of the ability to retrieve that data or extract related information embedded within the model's parameters.[79] As the output of certain machine learning models is shaped by the data used during the training phase, the original training data or information related to removed data may be deduced or 'leaked'.[80]

15.5 RESPONSIBILITY

In addition to the various steps of data processing in generative models, multiple parties could potentially be considered data controllers under the GDPR due to their levels of involvement. The GDPR establishes three categories of responsibility for data processing in relation to the data subject: controller, processor, and third parties.

The data controller is primarily responsible for compliance with the provisions of the GDPR (Article 5(2)). As defined by Article 4(7) GDPR, the data controller is a 'natural or legal person ... which, alone or jointly with others, determines the purposes and means of the processing of personal data'. Article 4(8) goes on to define the processor as a 'natural or legal person ... to which the personal data are disclosed, whether a third party or not'. Third parties, on the other hand, are actors other than the data subject, controller, or processor (Article 4(10)).

Prima facie, the legal companies that develop and deploy generative models are data controllers. However, a differentiated picture emerges in the various steps of data processing. Indisputably, companies like OpenAI and Google act as data controllers in relation to the processing steps involved in establishing the parameters for foundational training and storing of the model, given they exclusively determine the modalities of data processing, such as the decision to release a freely accessible LLM. However, in terms of output production, generative models process data based on the prompts from their users. Whether this can be used to establish providers and users as joint controllers within the meaning of Article 26 GDPR remains an open question.

Joint controllership under Article 26 GDPR refers to the situation where two or more controllers jointly determine the purposes and means of data processing. In contrast, the relationship between a controller and a processor (Articles 4 (7, 8) and 28 GDPR) is different, as in this constellation, the processor processes data *on behalf* of, and subject to the instructions of, the controller. Joint controllership is thus a relationship of equality, whereas the data processor operates as a contractor, following instructions issued by the data controller. Whether this structure can be transferred to the relationship between providers of generative models and those who use them is questionable.

Users are not considered processors within the meaning of Article 28 GDPR, as while there is a contract between them and the providers, they do not have the obligations of a processor, especially those imposed by Article 28(3) GDPR, as they may generate prompts at will, and are not processing data according to instruction. The purpose of generative models is to enable users to freely use the model for their own defined purposes, for example to formulate letters, find cooking recipes, or revise texts, free from instructions from the provider.

78 Novelli et al. (n. 13).
79 Ibid.
80 Ibid.

Users and providers could therefore be joint controllers, but this would require them to jointly define the purposes of data processing, and set out transparent mutual obligations. This classification is supported by the fact that users and providers both influence the purposes of data processing: the providers of generative models set the basic framework within which their models are used, while users specify the purposes according to their individual needs. Consequently, both users and providers are interdependent and have a reciprocal effect on data processing. However, this is contradicted by the fact that users also tend to be data subjects, and according to Article 26(3) GDPR, data subjects have the right to bring claims against any of the joint controllers. Although the law does not require joint controllers to hold the same level of responsibility, mere contributory causation without cooperative action is not sufficient for joint responsibility.[81] Additionally, users' limited influence over data processing means users of generative models cannot effectively be held responsible to third parties, as users have no ability to grant rights of access to providers or to delete personal data from the training data.

The relationship between users and providers of generative AI therefore presents a special case that cannot be seamlessly subsumed under the categories of the GDPR. On the one hand, users are more than just data subjects, as their active inputs are required to generate and shape the model's output. On the other hand, they are neither data processors nor joint controllers, as they have no influence over the fundamental modalities of data processing. For instance, providers are able to simply deactivate models or make them subject to fees (as in the case of ChatGPT). The ECJ considers the extent to which data controllers participate in the joint data processing and the specific processing phases within which this occurs to be crucial.[82] For LLMs, users only participate in output generation, which is significantly dependent on the previous steps, such as training. The purpose and aim of the regulations concerning joint controllership is to counteract a diffusion of responsibility among multiple participants. Affected individuals should be able to clearly identify who is collecting their personal data, and for what purpose (Recital 58). Therefore, while providers may be responsible for user-generated content in the case of generative models, the inverse does not apply. This follows from the reasoning and fundamental rights protection of the GDPR provisions regarding responsibility and also corresponds to technical and economic reality.[83]

15.6 IMAGES, AUDIO, AND VIDEOS AS PERSONAL DATA

The considerations for LLMs are not always transferable to generative models that produce audio, images, and video. This is because the aim of these models is not to generate information, which may be incorrect, but to generate new audio or visual material. The primary aim of generating new content has given rise to many copyright issues arising in these cases.[84] Images and videos can also be personal data if they can be used to identify the person, something easily achieved today through image searches.

A major problem is the significant increase in deepfakes in the digital context, which now affects not only public figures but also the general population. Women in particular are often victims of deepfake pornography, where explicit images and videos are generated using their

81 Case C-2010/16, ECLI:EU:C:2018:388, para. 45.
82 Ibid.
83 Similar: Case C-131/12, ECLI:EU:C:2014:317 – Google Spain, para. 33.
84 Tim W. Dornis and Sebastian Stober, 'Urheberrecht und Training generativer KI-Modelle – Technologische und juristische Grundlagen
' (29 August 2024) <https://papers.ssrn.com/abstract=4946214> accessed 26 September 2024; Sag (n. 11).

images, without their consent.[85] This is an unlawful processing of personal data that violates the GDPR and, in many cases, national regulations. The photographed image of a person in these cases constitutes personal data if the person is still alive, regardless of whether the data is fake or not. The purpose of deepfakes is to disparage or discredit a specific individual, thus fulfilling the decisive characteristic of Article 4(1) GDPR, namely that the person is identified or identifiable. Voices may also constitute personal data, if the person is identifiable; visual or acoustic identification methods recorded using pattern recognition, such as facial or voice recognition (speaker recognition), can even be considered biometric data under Article 4(14) GDPR.[86]

The latest addition to the digital legislation cavalry, the AI Act, only imposes a labelling obligation on deepfakes (Article 50(4)), leaving considerable doubt as to whether there is an adequate level of legal protection at European level.[87]

15.7 CONCLUSION AND OUTLOOK

The popular use cases of generative AI models show that data protection law is reaching its limits when it comes to regulating data-intensive technologies. In addition to the problems highlighted here, further questions arise regarding the principle of purpose limitation for data processing for data-intensive models and their downstream applications. The use of LLMs in decision-making situations raises questions about the scope of the prohibition in Article 22 GDPR.[88]

Structural problems of almost universal concern exist between the GDPR's focus on individual protection and the volume of data processed for training purposes, and in terms of a structural enforcement deficit, particularly regarding data protection principles and data subjects' rights.

As important as the structure of data protection law is for the protection of fundamental rights, new solutions are needed for the structural challenges posed by generative AI and other data-intensive technologies. These may also lie outside data protection law. To address these challenges, it is important to recognise the structural dimension of AI as a socio-technical development.[89] As a result, there is a need for structural solutions that go beyond the enforcement of individual rights.[90] Unfortunately, these issues remain unaddressed, as the AI Act does not contribute solutions to remedy the structural and specific challenges posed by the GPDR's individual rights focus. Despite its stated goal of protecting fundamental rights including data protection, the structure of the AI Act follows product safety law parameters and as such has an approach fundamentally different from legal frameworks aimed at protecting fundamental rights, as found in the GDPR. The AI Act as part of a digital legislation framework that takes

[85] Anne Pechenik Gieseke, '"The New Weapon of Choice": Law's Current Inability to Properly Address Deepfake Pornography' (2020) 73 *Vanderbilt Law Review* 1479.

[86] Thilo Weichert, 'DS-GVO Art. 4 Nr. 14 Biometrische Daten' in J. Kühling and B. Buchner (eds.), *Datenschutz-Grundverordnung, Bundesdatenschutzgesetz: DS-GVO BDSG* (Munich: C. H. Beck, 4th ed., 2024).

[87] Karolina Mania, 'Legal Protection of Revenge and Deepfake Porn Victims in the European Union: Findings from a Comparative Legal Study' (2024) 25 *Trauma, Violence & Abuse* 117; Lea Katharina Kumkar and Julian Philipp Rapp, 'Deepfakes: Eine Herausforderung für die Rechtsordnung' (2022) 3 *Zeitschrift für Digitalisierung und Recht* (ZfDR) 199; Don Fallis, 'The Epistemic Threat of Deepfakes' (2021) 34 *Philosophy & Technology* 623.

[88] See for example the use of Gemini for decisions about unemployment benefits: <https://gizmodo.com/googles-ai-will-help-decide-whether-unemployed-workers-get-benefits-2000496215> accessed 26 September 2024.

[89] Rainer Mühlhoff, 'Human-Aided Artificial Intelligence: Or, How to Run Large Computations in Human Brains? Toward a Media Sociology of Machine Learning' (2020) 22 *New Media & Society* 1868.

[90] Mühlhoff and Ruschemeier (n. 15); Mühlhoff and Ruschemeier (n. 17).

a variety of approaches to protect from risks posed by AI does establish certain obligations for generative AI systems under Articles 51–54, like technical documentation (Article 53(1)(a)), a policy to comply with union law (Article 53(1)(b)) and a summary about the content used for training (Article 53(1)(d)), but these provisions do not address the privacy and data protection of users. Additionally, there are broad exceptions for open source models (Articles 2(12) and 53(2)). This still leaves a need for legal regulation.

16

Generative AI and the Fundamental Limitations of US Privacy Law

Elana Zeide

16.1 INTRODUCTION

The emergence of generative AI, a suite of technologies capable of creating novel and realistic content, represents a transformative development in artificial intelligence.[1] Generative AI refers to a class of machine learning models and techniques that can create new content – such as text, images, audio, video, and code – based on patterns learned from vast troves of training data.[2] These systems, including natural language models like ChatGPT, image generation tools like DALL-E and Stable Diffusion, and audio synthesis engines like WaveNet, have already begun to revolutionize how we create, interact with, and perceive digital content.[3]

While earlier types AI like machine learning excelled at tasks like image classification, speech recognition, and fraud detection, these systems were primarily constrained to identifying and exploiting correlations within narrowly defined problem domains.[4] In contrast, generative AI systems produce output that is often indistinguishable from human-created content.[5] While these tools offer exciting new possibilities for creative expression, scientific discovery, and social innovation, they also raise profound privacy concerns.[6]

Many thanks to Harry Surden, Ignacio Cofone, Neil M. Richards, and Paul Weitzel for their valuable input.

[1] H. Surden, 'ChatGPT, Large Language Models, and Law' (2024) 92 *Fordham Law Review* 1941 at 1944–48.

[2] Ibid. ("The term 'generative' is used to distinguish systems like ChatGPT that create human-like text from other AI systems that are focused on issues outside of human creative contexts – for example, AI systems that are designed to predict future events, classify documents or images, control self-driving cars, spot credit card fraud, or identify consumer preferences").

[3] See, e.g., T. H. Davenport and N. Mittal, 'How Generative AI Is Changing Creative Work', *Harvard Business Review* (Nov. 14, 2022); Ana Kreaic, Luica Uribe, Amy Lasater-Wille, and John Rmeo, 'How Generative AI Is Transforming Business and Society: The Good, the Bad, and Everything in Between' (2024) *Oliver Wyman Forum*, www.oliverwymanforum.com/content/dam/oliver-wyman/ow-forum/gcs/2023/AI-Report-2024-Davos.pdf

[4] Surden, 'ChatGPT, Large Language Models, and Law'.

[5] A. F. Cooper et al., 'Report of the 1st Workshop on Generative AI and Law' (2023), https://arxiv.org/pdf/2311.06477; see, e.g., Melissa Heikkilä, 'An AI Startup Made a Hyperrealistic Deepfake That's So Good It's Scary', *MIT Technology Review* (April 30, 2024), www.technologyreview.com/2024/04/25/1091772/new-generative-ai-avatar-deepfake-synthesia/; D. Foster, *Generative Deep Learning: Teaching Machines to Paint, Write, Compose, and Play*, 2nd ed. (Sebastopol, CA: O'Reilly Media, 2023), 260–64.

[6] Cooper et al., 'Report of the 1st Workshop on Generative AI and Law', 10; L. Weidinger et al., 'Taxonomy of Risks posed by Language Models', 2022 ACM Conference on Fairness, Accountability, and Transparency (Seoul: ACM, 2022), 214–29; C. Song and V. Shmatikov, 'Overlearning Reveals Sensitive Attributes' International Conference on

This chapter explores the privacy challenges posed by generative AI and argues for a fundamental rethinking of privacy governance frameworks in response. Section 16.2 examines the technical characteristics and capabilities of generative AI systems that amplify existing privacy risks and introduce new challenges, including nonconsensual data extraction, data leakage and reidentification, inferential profiling, synthetic media generation, and algorithmic bias. Section 16.3 surveys the current landscape of US privacy law and its shortcomings in addressing these emergent issues, highlighting the limitations of a patchwork approach to privacy regulation, the overreliance on notice and choice, the barriers to transparency and accountability, and the inadequacy of individual rights and recourse. Section 16.4 outlines critical elements of a new paradigm for generative AI privacy governance that recognizes collective and systemic privacy harms, institutes proactive measures, and imposes precautionary safeguards, emphasizing the need to recognize privacy as a public good and collective responsibility. The analysis concludes by discussing the political, legal, and cultural obstacles to regulatory reform in the United States, most notably the polarization that prevents the enactment of comprehensive federal privacy legislation, the strong commitment to free speech under the First Amendment, and the "permissionless" innovation approach that has historically characterized US technology policy.

16.2 HOW GENERATIVE AI CHALLENGES PRIVACY

The rapid advancement of generative AI systems, with their enhanced ability to create highly realistic and persuasive content, magnifies existing privacy risks while also introducing new challenges that test the foundational assumptions of current privacy frameworks. The technical characteristics of generative AI systems exacerbate existing privacy threats. These risks include: large-scale extraction of public data without individual consent and control; data leakage and reidentification; inferential privacy harms; generation of fake but convincing synthetic media; and exacerbation of algorithmic bias and discrimination.[7] While society has been grappling with similar privacy concerns since the advent of computer data systems,[8] the unprecedented capabilities of generative AI systems qualitatively transform the nature and magnitude of the risks to privacy and obstacles to data governance.

Learning Representations (April 26–May 1, 2020), at 1–12, https://iclr.cc/Conferences/2020; D. J. Solove, 'Artificial Intelligence and Privacy' (2025) 77 *Florida Law Review* 1; L. Weidinger et al., 'Ethical and Social Risks of Harm from Language Models' (2021) at 1–38, https://arxiv.org/pdf/2112.04359; Jennifer King and Caroline Meinhardt, *White Paper Rethinking Privacy in the AI Era: Policy Provocations for a Data-Centric World* (2024), Stanford HAI, at 17–22, https://hai.stanford.edu/white-paper-rethinking-privacy-ai-era-policy-provocations-data-centric-world; T. C. Helmus and B. Chandra, *Generative Artificial Intelligence Threats to Information Integrity and Potential Policy Responses* (Rand Corporation, 2024) at 3–7, www.and.org/pubs/perspectives/PEA3089-1.html; D. Solove and H. Matsumi, 'AI, Algorithms, and Awful Humans' (2024) 92 *Fordham Law Review* 1923.

7 Cooper et al., 'Report of the 1st Workshop on Generative AI and Law', 10; Weidinger et al., 'Taxonomy of Risks Posed by Language Models'; Song and Shmatikov, 'Overlearning Reveals Sensitive Attributes'; Solove, 'Artificial Intelligence and Privacy'; Weidinger et al., 'Ethical and Social Risks of Harm from Language Models'; King and Meinhardt, *White Paper Rethinking Privacy in the AI Era*; Helmus and Chandra, *Generative Artificial Intelligence Threats*; Matsumi and Solove, 'AI, Algorithms, and Awful Humans'; R. Bommasani et al., 'On the Opportunities and Risks of Foundation Models' (2021) at 130–135, https://arxiv.org/pdf/2108.07258; H.-P. Lee, Y.-J. Yang, T. S. von Davier, J. Forlizzi, and S. Das, 'Deepfakes, Phrenology, Surveillance, and More! A Taxonomy of AI Privacy Risks' (2024) CHI' 24: Proceedings of the 2024 CHI Conference on Human Factors in Computing Systems, 1–19, https://dl.acm.org/doi/proceedings/10.1145/3613904; R. Shelby et al., 'Sociotechnical Harms of Algorithmic Systems: Scoping a Taxonomy for Harm Reduction' (2023), AIES' 23: Proceedings of the 2023 AAAI/ACM Conference on AI, Ethics, and Society, 723–41, https://dl.acm.org/doi/proceedings/10.1145/3600211.

8 Solove, 'Artificial Intelligence and Privacy'.

16.2.1 *Nonconsensual Data Extraction and the Failure of Notice and Consent*

Generative AI systems are trained on vast amounts of data, often comprising billions of individual data points spanning a wide range of formats, domains, and sources.[9] For example, OpenAI trained its GPT-4 language model on a corpus of over 45 terabytes of text data, including books, articles, and websites.[10] While some of this data is clearly public material such as stock photos, much of it includes individuals' names, addresses, and images published online under varying expectations of privacy.[11]

This harvesting and processing of personal information and sensitive content occurs without notice, consent, or constraint.[12] Current law allows[13] and sometimes explicitly sanctions[14] the collection and use of publicly available information. However, the unprecedented scope and granularity of data extraction by generative AI systems erode the assumptions of individual autonomy that underlie existing privacy frameworks.[15] In many cases, individuals are unaware that their data is being used to train these systems, and cannot manage the downstream uses of their data.[16] For example, Clearview AI, a facial recognition company, scraped billions of images from social media platforms to train its algorithms without the knowledge or consent of the individuals depicted.[17]

16.2.2 *Data Leakage and Reidentification*

Another significant privacy risk posed by generative AI arises from the potential for data leakage and reidentification of individuals from training datasets.[18] Because these models capture

[9] Christoph Schuhmann et al., 'LAION-5B: An Open Large-Scale Dataset for Training Next Generation Image-Text Models', Proceedings of the 36th International Conference on Neural Information Processing Systems (Red Hook, NY: Curran Associates, 2024), pp. 25278–25294, https://proceedings.neurips.cc/paper_files/paper/2022/file/a1859debfb3b59d094f3504d5ebb6c25-Paper-Datasets_and_Benchmarks.pdf; Andy Baio, 'Exploring 12 Million of the 2.3 Billion Images Used to Train Stable Diffusion's Image Generator', Waxy (Sept. 6, 2022), https://waxy.org/2022/08/exploring-12-million-of-the-images-used-to-train-stable-diffusions-image-generator/.

[10] OpenAI, J. Achiam et al., 'GPT-4 Technical Report' (2024), https://arxiv.org/pdf/2303.08774.

[11] Cooper et al., 'Report of the 1st Workshop on Generative AI and Law'; M. K. Heath, 'Buried Treasure or Ill-Gotten Spoils: The Ethics of Data Mining and Learning Analytics in Online Instruction' (2020) *Educational Technology Research and Development* 1–4; Katherine Lee, Daphne Ippolito, and A. Feder Cooper, 'AI and Law: The Next Generation' (Oct. 2023); King and Meinhardt, *White Paper Rethinking Privacy in the AI Era.*

[12] Solove, 'Artificial Intelligence and Privacy', 23–29; King and Meinhardt, *White Paper Rethinking Privacy in the AI Era*, 17–19; S. Morrison, 'The Tricky Truth about How Generative AI Uses Your Data', *Vox* (July 2023); L. Leffer, 'Your Personal Information Is Probably Being Used to Train Generative AI Models', *Scientific American* (Oct. 19, 2023). Other important intellectual property issues involve the incorporation of copyrighted material into generative AI models that are beyond the scope of this chapter. See, e.g., Pamela Samuelson, 'Generative AI Meets Copyright', 381 *Science* 158 (July 2023).

[13] See, e.g., *HiQ Labs, Inc. v. LinkedIn Corp.*, 938 F.3d 985 (9th Cir. 2019).

[14] See, e.g., California Consumer Privacy Act (CCPA) Cal. Civ. Code § 1798.140(v)(2) (West 2021); VA. CODE § 59.1-571 (2021); Utah Code Ann. § 13-61-101(29)(b) (2022) (exempting publicly available information).

[15] Solove, 'Artificial Intelligence and Privacy', 23–29; King and Meinhardt, *White Paper Rethinking Privacy in the AI Era*, 17–19.

[16] Kyle Wiggers, 'AI Training Data: Compliance Does Not Equal Consent', *VentureBeat* (May 2, 2023), https://venturebeat.com/ai/ai-training-data-compliance-does-not-equal-consent/

[17] K. Hill, 'The Secretive Company That Might End Privacy as We Know It', *New York Times* (Jan. 18, 2020); K. Tangalakis-Lippert, 'Clearview AI Scraped 30 Billion Images from Facebook and Other Social Media Sites and Gave Them to Cops: It Puts Everyone into a "Perpetual Police Line-Up"', *Business Insider* (April 2023).

[18] Solove, 'Artificial Intelligence and Privacy', 23–29; King and Meinhardt, *White Paper Rethinking Privacy in the AI Era*, 19–20; W. Knight, 'AI Chatbots Can Guess Your Personal Information from What You Type'; Leffer, 'Your Personal Information Is Probably Being Used'; R. Staab, M. Vero, M. Balunović, and M. Vechev, 'Beyond Memorization: Violating Privacy Via Inference with Large Language Models' (2024) *The Twelfth International*

patterns at a high level of granularity, they retain and reproduce verbatim snippets of training data when generating synthetic outputs.[19] For example, a language model trained on a corpus of emails might reveal real names, addresses, or phone numbers,[20] while an image synthesis model trained on photos from social media might produce pictures that depict recognizable individuals or locations.[21] Malicious actors can also craft adversarial prompts to extract specific sensitive information.[22]

16.2.3 *Inferential Profiling and Privacy Harms*

Generative AI systems identify correlations in large-scale datasets to make probabilistic inferences about individuals' demographics, preferences, behaviors, and beliefs, even when such information is not explicitly disclosed.[23] For example, a language model trained on social media posts might learn to associate certain linguistic styles, topics, or sentiments with particular demographic groups, allowing it to make inferences about a user's age, ethnicity, or socioeconomic status based on their writing patterns.[24] Similarly, a computer vision model trained on user-uploaded images might be able – or at least claim to be able – to infer sensitive attributes such as health conditions, political affiliations, or sexual orientation based on visual cues and contextual signals in the images.[25] This inferential power undermines protections that orient around explicit personal information and limit the collection of specific data points.[26]

Conference on Learning Representations, www.itsoc.org/event/twelfth-international-conference-learning-representations-iclr; N. Carlini, C. Liu, Ú. Erlingsson, J. Kos, and D. Song, 'The Secret Sharer: Evaluating and Testing Unintended Memorization in Neural Networks' (2019) 8th USENIX Security Symposium (USENIX security19) at 267–84; A. Winograd, 'Loose-Lipped Large Language Models Spill Your Secrets: The Privacy Implications of Large Language Models' (2023) 36 *Harv. J. Law & Tech.* 615 at 622–27; Weidinger et al., 'Taxonomy of Risks Posed by Language Models', at 214–229; Morrison, 'The Tricky Truth about How Generative AI Uses Your Data'.

19 King and Meinhardt, *White Paper Rethinking Privacy in the AI Era*, 19–20; Knight, 'AI Chatbots Can Guess Your Personal Information'; Leffer, 'Your Personal Information Is Probably Being Used'; Staab et al., 'Beyond Memorization'; Carlini et al., 'The Secret Sharer'; Winograd, 'Loose-Lipped Large Language Models Spill Your Secrets', 622–27.

20 N. Carlini et al., 'Extracting Training Data from Large Language Models' (2021), *30th USENIX Security Symposium (USENIX Security 21)*, 2633–50, www.usenix.org/conference/usenixsecurity21.

21 See, e.g., V. Fernandez, P. Sanchez, W. H. L. Pinaya, G. Jacenków, S. A. Tsaftaris, and J. Cardoso, 'Privacy Distillation: Reducing Re-identification Risk of Multimodal Diffusion Models' (2023), *Third MICCAI Workshop, DGM4MICCAI 2023, Held in Conjunction with MICCAI 2023*, Vancouver, BC, Canada, October 8, 2023, Proceedings (Berlin: Springer-Verlag, 2024), 3–13.

22 Benj Edwards, 'AI-Powered Bing Chat Spills Its Secrets via Prompt Injection Attack [Updated]', *Ars Technica* (Feb. 10, 2023), https://arstechnica.com/information-technology/2023/02/ai-powered-bing-chat-spills-its-secrets-via-prompt-injection-attack/.

23 T. B. Gillis, 'The Input Fallacy' (2022) 106 *Minnesota Law Review* 1175, arguing that "information about a person's protected characteristics is embedded in other information about the individual, so that a protected characteristic can be 'known' to an algorithm even when it is formally excluded"; S. Wachter and B. Mittelstadt, 'A Right to Reasonable Inferences' (2019) 2019 *Columbia Business Law Review* 494–620.

24 A. Solow-Niederman, 'Information Privacy and the Inference Economy' (2022) 117 *Northwestern University Law Review* 357–424; E. Zeide, 'The Silicon Ceiling: How Artificial Intelligence Constructs an Invisible Barrier to Opportunity' (2022) 91 *UMKC Law Review* 403–36; E. Zeide, 'Algorithms Can Be Lousy Fortunetellers', Slate (2015), https://slate.com/technology/2015/05/crystal-app-algorithmic-fortunetelling-for-employers-and-potential-customers.html.

25 See, e.g., Yilun Wang and Michal Kosinski, *Deep Neural Networks Are More Accurate than Humans at Detecting Sexual Orientation from Facial Images*, (2018) 114 *J. Personality & Soc. Psych.* 246.

26 N. Purtova, 'The Law of Everything. Broad Concept of Personal Data and Future of EU Data Protection Law' (2018) 10 *Law, Innovation and Technology* 40–81; Solove, 'Artificial Intelligence and Privacy'; King and Meinhardt, *White Paper Rethinking Privacy in the AI Era*; Weidinger et al., 'Taxonomy of Risks Posed by Language Models'.

16.2.4 Synthetic Media, Deepfakes, and Disinformation

Generative AI's ability to create highly realistic content opens the door to pervasive deception and manipulation.[27] Malicious actors can exploit readily available tools to produce "deepfakes" and other types of synthetic media that convincingly impersonate real people and mislead audiences at a massive scale.[28] For instance, deep learning models can clone an individual's voice from just a few seconds of audio and generate fake audio clips.[29] Natural language models can mass-produce fake news articles, product reviews, and social media posts that are nearly impossible to distinguish from authentic content. Image synthesis systems can create realistic faces of nonexistent individuals or seamlessly insert real people's faces into fabricated scenarios.[30] Even individuals with limited technical expertise or resources can now leverage these technologies for deceptive or harmful purposes.[31] For example, middle-school children across the country alter images of their classmates to create "deepfake porn."[32]

Generative AI's ability to amplify and accelerate the spread of false and misleading information poses risks not only to individual privacy and autonomy but also to public discourse and democratic processes.[33] As synthetic media capabilities grow more sophisticated and accessible, it is becoming increasingly difficult to distinguish between real and generated content, eroding the epistemic foundations of trust and truth in online interactions.

16.2.5 Algorithmic Bias and Discrimination

The deployment of generative AI in consequential domains such as hiring,[34] lending,[35] and criminal justice[36] risks perpetuating and amplifying historical patterns of bias. Because these

[27] Weidinger et al., *Taxonomy of Risks Posed by Language Models*; Solove, 'Artificial Intelligence and Privacy'; King and Meinhardt, *White Paper Rethinking Privacy in the AI Era.*

[28] See, e.g., Erum Salam, 'US Mother Gets Call from 'Kidnapped Daughter' – But It's Really an AI Scam', *The Guardian* (June 14, 2023).

[29] L. Leffer, 'AI Audio Deepfakes Are Quickly Outpacing Detection' *Scientific American* (Jan. 26, 2024).

[30] Mika Westerlund, 'The Emergence of Deepfake Technology: A Review' (2019) 9 *Tech. Innovation Management Rev.* at 39–52.

[31] See, e.g., Heikkilä, 'An AI Startup Made a Hyperrealistic Deepfake of Me'.

[32] Pranshu Verma, 'AI Fake Nudes Are Booming. It's Ruining Real Teens' Lives', *Washington Post* (Nov. 4, 2023), www.washingtonpost.com/technology/2023/11/05/ai-deepfake-porn-teens-women-impact/; April Rubin, 'Teens Exploited by Fake Nudes Illustrate Threat of Unregulated AI', *Axios* (Nov. 3, 2023), www.axios.com/2023/11/03/ai-deepfake-nude-images-new-jersey-high-school.

[33] C. Whyte, 'Deepfake News: AI-Enabled Disinformation as a Multi-level Public Policy Challenge' (2020) 5 *Journal of Cyber Policy* 199–217; D. Shin, 'Conclusion: Misinformation and AI – How Algorithms Generate and Manipulate Misinformation', *Artificial Misinformation: Exploring Human-Algorithm Interaction Online* (New York: Springer, 2024), 259–77; A. MacKenzie and I. Bhatt, 'Lies, Bullshit and Fake News: Some Epistemological Concerns' (2020) 2 *Postdigital Science and Education* 9–13; C. R. Baker and A. Chadwick, 'Corrupted Infrastructures of Meaning: Post-truth Identities Online' in H. Tumber and S. Waisbord (eds.), The Routledge Companion to Media Misinformation and Populism (New York: Routledge, 2021); D. P. Tokaji, 'Truth, Democracy, and the Limits of Law Childress Lecture' (2019) 64 *Saint Louis University Law Journal* 569–94; I. Kalpokas, 'Post-Truth: The Condition of Our Times', *A Political Theory of Post-Truth* (Cham: Palgrave Pivot, 2019), 9–49; R. Chesney and D. K. Citron, '21st Century-Style Truth Decay: Deep Fakes and the Challenge for Privacy, Free Expression, and National Security' (2019) 78 *Maryland Law Review* 882.

[34] I. Ajunwa, *The Quantified Worker: Law and Technology in the Modern Workplace* (Cambridge: Cambridge University Press, 2023) 138–70; H. Schellmann, *The Algorithm: How AI Decides Who Gets Hired, Monitored, Promoted, and Fired and Why We Need to Fight Back Now* (New York: Hachette Books, 2024) 83–128; Zeide, 'The Silicon Ceiling'.

[35] A. Fuster, P. Goldsmith-Pinkham, T. Ramadorai, and A. Walther, 'Predictably Unequal? The Effects of Machine Learning on Credit Markets' (2022) 77 *Journal of Finance* 5–47.

[36] Andrew Gunthrie Ferguson, *The Rise of Big Data Policing* (New York: NYU Press, 2017); Albert Meijer and Martijn Wessels, 'Predictive Policing: Review of Benefits and Drawbacks' (2019) 42 *Int'l J. Pub. Admin.* 1031, 1031; Elizabeth

systems train on data that reflects societal inequalities and prejudices, they can reinscribe and exacerbate disadvantage.[37] For example, facial recognition algorithms exhibit higher error rates for women and people of color.[38] Similarly, researchers have shown that language models like GPT-3 can exhibit gender and racial biases in their generated text, such as associating men with career-oriented terms and women with family-oriented terms, or perpetuating harmful stereotypes about minority groups.[39]

These biases can translate to real-world harms when entities use generative systems to allocate benefits and opportunities.[40] For instance, a company that uses a biased language model to screen resumes or generate job descriptions may end up excluding qualified candidates from underrepresented backgrounds.[41] Over time, such discriminatory outcomes can compound disadvantages and erode economic mobility for marginalized communities.[42]

16.2.6 Undermining Autonomy and Expertise

Automated profiling and decision-making by generative AI systems can also lead to the decontextualization and abstraction of individuals, reducing them to a set of quantifiable data points and statistical inferences.[43] Such algorithmic assessments ignore the contextual and situational

E. Joh, 'The New Surveillance Discretion: Automated Suspicion, Big Data, and Policing' (2016) 10 *Harv. L. & Pol'y Rev.* 15, 15–18; Orla Lynskey, 'Criminal Justice Profiling and EU Data Protection Law: Precarious Protection from Predictive Policing' (2019) 15 *Int'l J. L. in Context* 162, 167; Lindsey Barrett, 'Reasonably Suspicious Algorithms: Predictive Policing at the United States Border' (2017) 41 *N.Y.U. Rev. L. & Soc. Change* 132.

37 C. O'Neil, *Weapons of Math Destruction: How Big Data Increases Inequality and Threatens Democracy* (New York: Crown, 2016); K. Geddes, 'The Death of the Legal Subject' (2023) 25 *Vanderbilt Journal of Entertainment & Technology Law* 1–52 at 31 (noting that "algorithmic prediction effectively punishes the underlying individual for membership of a statistical group"); D. Solove and H. Matsumi, 'AI, Algorithms, and Awful Humans' (2024) 92 *Fordham Law Review* 1923; Julie Cohen, 'Examined Lives: Informational Privacy and the Subject as Object' (2000) 52 *Stanford Law Review* 1373 at 1405 (arguing that people are not "reducible to the sum of their transactions, genetic markers, and other measurable attributes"); Solove, 'Artificial Intelligence and Privacy', 45–46; Zeide, 'The Silicon Ceiling'; P. T. Kim, 'Data-Driven Discrimination at Work' (2016) 58 *Wm. & Mary L. Rev.* 857; I. Ajunwa, 'Automated Employment Discrimination' (2019), www.researchgate.net/publication/336202038_Automated_Employment_Discrimination; S. Barocas and A. D. Selbst, 'Big Data's Disparate Impact' (2016) 104 *California Law Review* 671; S. G. Mayson, 'Bias In, Bias Out' (2018) 128 *Yale L.J.* 2218; A. Chander, 'The Racist Algorithm' (2016) 115 *Michigan Law Review* 1023–46.

38 J. Buolamwini and T. Gebru, 'Gender Shades: Intersectional Accuracy Disparities in Commercial Gender Classification', *PMLR* (2018), 77–91; P. Grother, 'Face Recognition Vendor Test (FRVT) Part 8: Summarizing Demographic Differentials' (2022) 8429, National Institute of Standards and Technology (NIST), Gaithersburg, MD, USA, Interagency Rep. NISTIR; P. Grother, M. Ngan, and K. Hanaoka, *Face Recognition Vendor Test (fvrt): Part 3, Demographic Effects* (NIST, 2019), www.nist.gov/publications/face-recognition-vendor-test-part-3-demographic-effects.

39 A. Caliskan-Islam, J. J. Bryson, and A. Narayanan, 'Semantics Derived Automatically from Language Corpora Necessarily Contain Human Biases' (2016) 356 *Science* 183–186; T. Bolukbasi, K.-W. Chang, J. Y. Zou, V. Saligrama, and A. T. Kalai, 'Man Is to Computer Programmer as Woman Is to Homemaker? Debiasing Word Embeddings' (2016) 29 *Advances in Neural Information Processing Systems*.

40 O'Neil, *Weapons of Math Destruction*; Geddes, 'The Death of the Legal Subject', 31 (noting that "algorithmic prediction effectively punishes the underlying individual for membership of a statistical group"); Solove and Matsumi, 'AI, Algorithms, and Awful Humans'; Cohen, 'Examined Lives', 1405 (arguing that people are not "reducible to the sum of their transactions, genetic markers, and other measurable attributes"); Solove, 'Artificial Intelligence and Privacy', 45–46; Zeide, 'The Silicon Ceiling'; Kim, 'Data-Driven Discrimination at Work'; Ajunwa, 'Automated Employment Discrimination'.

41 O'Neil, *Weapons of Math Destruction*; Geddes, 'The Death of the Legal Subject', 31 (noting that "algorithmic prediction effectively punishes the underlying individual for membership of a statistical group"); Zeide, 'The Silicon Ceiling'; Kim, 'Data-Driven Discrimination at Work'; Ajunwa, 'Automated Employment Discrimination'.

42 Zeide, 'The Silicon Ceiling'.

43 See, e.g., E. Zeide, 'The Structural Consequences of Big Data-Driven Education' (2017) 5 *Big Data* 164–72 at 169; Cohen, 'Examined Lives', 1405; D. K. Citron and F. A. Pasquale, 'The Scored Society: Due Process for Automated Predictions' (2014) 89 *Washington Law Review* 89.

factors that shape individual behavior and outcomes, leading to decisions that may be inaccurate, unfair, or devoid of situational understanding.[44] For example, a generative AI system used to predict an individual's creditworthiness or risk of recidivism may rely on aggregate patterns and correlations learned from historical data that do not reflect the full context of that person's circumstances and capacity for behavioral change.[45] This practice risks creating self-fulfilling feedback loops that undermine individuals' autonomy and agency.[46]

Moreover, using generative AI systems to automate high-stakes decisions shifts discretion away from domain experts to unaccountable actors.[47] These systems optimize based on what they measure, thereby shaping not only individual assessments but also determining the broader goals and values of a given context.[48] By displacing situated judgment with opaque and unaccountable systems, generative AI risks enabling private entities to shape public values and societal norms without adequate transparency or oversight.[49]

In summary, the advanced capabilities of generative AI systems pose significant threats to privacy at both the individual and societal levels. The critical privacy challenges posed by generative AI – unconstrained data extraction, data leakage, inferential profiling, synthetic media, and algorithmic bias – strain the foundational assumptions of existing privacy and data protection frameworks based on individualistic conceptions of privacy. These emergent challenges necessitate a fundamental rethinking of privacy rights and governance to address the risks and implications of AI systems that can generate, enhance, and reshape human-like content and interactions.[50]

16.3 THE INADEQUACY OF US PRIVACY LAW IN ADDRESSING GENERATIVE AI CHALLENGES

The formidable capabilities and evolving risks of generative AI systems present substantial challenges to current privacy and data protection frameworks in the United States. This section examines the deficiencies inherent in the existing patchwork of sector-specific laws, the reliance on notice and consent mechanisms, the barriers to transparency and accountability, and the

[44] Cathy O'Neil, *Weapons of Math Destruction: How Big Data Increases Inequality and Threatens Democracy* (New York: Crown Publishing, 2016); Katrina Geddes, 'The Death of the Legal Subject' (2023) 25 *Vand. J. Ent. & Tech. L.* 1, 31 (noting that "algorithmic prediction effectively punishes the underlying individual for membership of a statistical group"); Solove and Matsumi, 'AI, Algorithms, and Awful Humans'; Cohen, 'Examined Lives', 1405 (arguing that people are not "reducible to the sum of their transactions, genetic markers, and other measurable attributes"); Solove, 'Artificial Intelligence and Privacy', 45–46.

[45] Jessica M. Eaglin, 'Constructing Recidivism Risk' (2017) 67 *Emory L.J.* 59, 72.

[46] Solove and Matsumi, 'AI, Algorithms, and Awful Humans'; C. Lazaro, 'Algorithmic Divination: From Prediction to Preemption of the Future' (2018) 58 *Information & Culture* 145–65; I. Kerr and J. Earle, 'Prediction, Preemption, Presumption: How Big Data Threatens Big Picture Privacy' (2013) 66 *Stanford Law Review Online* 65; C. Véliz, 'If AI Is Predicting Your Future, Are You Still Free?', *Wired* (Dec. 27, 2021); J. Cohen, 'What Privacy Is For' (2013) 126 *Harvard Law Review* 1904; B. E. Harcourt, *Against Prediction: Profiling, Policing, and Punishing in an Actuarial Age* (Chicago: University of Chicago Press, 2008); Zeide, 'The Silicon Ceiling'; Zeide, 'The Structural Consequences of Big Data-Driven Education'.

[47] Zeide, 'The Structural Consequences of Big Data-Driven Education', 168–69; D. F. Engstrom and A. Haim, 'Regulating Government AI and the Challenge of Sociotechnical Design' (2023) 19 *Annual Review of Law and Social Science* 277–98 at 291–92.

[48] Zeide, 'The Structural Consequences of Big Data-Driven Education', 168–69; Engstrom and Haim, 'Regulating Government AI', 291–92.

[49] Zeide, 'The Structural Consequences of Big Data-Driven Education', 168–69; Engstrom and Haim, 'Regulating Government AI', 291–92.

[50] See Julie E. Cohen, *Between Truth and Power: The Legal Constructions of Informational Capitalism* (Oxford: Oxford University Press, 2019).

inadequacy of individual rights frameworks, which fail to adequately address the systemic and societal privacy implications of generative AI. These shortcomings necessitate a fundamental rethinking of privacy governance in the age of AI.

16.3.1 The Patchwork of US Privacy Protections

Unlike the European Union, which has comprehensive privacy and data protection regimes such as the General Data Protection Regulation (GDPR)[51] and the Artificial Intelligence Act (AIA),[52] the United States employs a sectoral approach to privacy and data regulation. This fragmented approach protects specific data categories rather than establishing a general right to privacy across all contexts. The current framework comprises a patchwork of federal and state laws imposing different obligations on collecting, using, and sharing personal data based on industry, data type, and jurisdiction. Key examples include the Health Insurance Portability and Accountability Act (HIPAA), the Gramm–Leach–Bliley Act (GLBA), and the Children's Online Privacy Protection Act (COPPA), each imposing unique obligations on the handling of personal healthcare, financial, and children's data, respectively.[53]

In the absence of comprehensive federal AI legislation, the Federal Trade Commission (FTC) has emerged as the de facto federal authority responsible for privacy protection in the context of AI systems, including generative models.[54] In recent years, the Commission has issued guidance documents,[55] conducted workshops,[56] and penalized companies deploying artificial intelligence without adequate safeguards against discriminatory impact on protected classes.[57]

[51] Regulation (EU) 2016/679 of the European Parliament and of the Council of 27 April 2016 on the protection of natural persons with regard to the processing of personal data and on the free movement of such data, and repealing Directive 95/46/EC (General Data Protection Regulation), OJ 2016 L 119/1, at Arts. 12–22 (Rights of the data subject). Anupam Chander, Margot E. Kaminski, and William McGeveran, 'Catalyzing Privacy Law' (2021) 105 *Minn. L. Rev.*, https://papers.ssrn.com/sol3/papers.cfm?abstract_id = 3433922.

[52] Proposal for a Regulation of the European Parliament and of the Council Laying Down Harmonised Rules on Artificial Intelligence (Artificial Intelligence Act).

[53] Health Insurance Portability and Accountability Act of 1996 (HIPAA), 42 U.S.C. § 1420d et seq. (setting national standards for the protection of individually identifiable health information held by covered entities, such as hospitals, health insurers, and healthcare providers, as well as their business associates); Gramm-Leach-Bliley Act (GLBA, 15 U.S.C. § 6821 et seq. (requiring financial institutions to provide customers with notice and opt-out rights regarding sharing of their nonpublic personal data, and to implement reasonable security measures to protect that information); Children's Online Privacy Protection Act (COPPA), 15 U.S. 6501–6506 (prohibiting commercial online services from collecting personal information from children under the age of thirteen without verifiable parental consent).

[54] See, e.g., Anthony E. DiResta and Zachary E. Sherman, 'The FTC Is Regulating AI: A Comprehensive Analysis | Insights | Holland & Knight', Holland & Knight (July 25, 2023), www.hklaw.com/en/insights/publications/2023/07/the-ftc-is-regulating-ai-a-comprehensive-analysis; 'FTC Proposes New Protections to Combat AI Impersonation of Individuals', Federal Trade Commission (Feb. 15, 2024), www.ftc.gov/news-events/news/press-releases/2024/02/ftc-proposes-new-protections-combat-ai-impersonation-individuals; Adam Thierer, 'The FTC Looks to Become the Federal AI Commission', *Medium* (July 15, 2023), https://medium.com/@AdamThierer/the-ftc-looks-to-become-the-federal-ai-commission-15db44e35ace.

[55] Federal Trade Commission, 'Business Blog: Aiming for Truth, Fairness, and Equity in Your Company's Use of AI' (April 19, 2021), www.ftc.gov/business-guidance/blog/2021/04/aiming-truth-fairness-equity-your-companys-use-ai; Federal Trade Commission, 'Using Artificial Intelligence and Algorithms' (April 8, 2020), www.ftc.gov/business-guidance/blog/2020/04/using-artificial-intelligence-and-algorithms.

[56] Federal Trade Commission, 'Creative Economy and Generative AI' (Sept. 20, 2023), www.ftc.gov/news-events/events/2023/10/creative-economy-generative-ai.

[57] Federal Trade Commission, 'Rite Aid Banned from Using AI Facial Recognition After FTC Says Retailer Deployed Technology without Reasonable Safeguards' (Dec. 19, 2023), www.ftc.gov/news-events/news/press-releases/2023/12/rite-aid-banned-using-ai-facial-recognition-after-ftc-says-retailer-deployed-technology-without.

However, the FTC's limited statutory powers and resources constrain its ability to oversee and enforce privacy protections against generative AI. The Commission lacks the substantive rulemaking and supervisory powers of bodies like the European Data Protection Board (EDPB) or the UK Information Commissioner's Office (ICO), resulting in largely reactive and ex post enforcement.[58] Moreover, recent Supreme Court decisions have further curtailed the FTC's ability to seek monetary penalties and consumer redress for privacy violations.[59]

Given these limitations at the federal level, several states and municipalities have enacted legislation to protect consumer privacy and regulate AI systems.[60] These state privacy laws often incorporate data protection mechanisms from the GDPR, granting individuals enforceable rights to access, correct, and delete their personal data and object to data processing. California has been a leader in this space with the passage of the California Consumer Privacy Act (CCPA) in 2018 and the California Privacy Rights Act (CPRA) in 2020.[61] As of December 2023, twenty other states had enacted similar comprehensive consumer privacy laws.[62]

Many states have also enacted more targeted laws that address specific AI applications or technologies. For example, several states have passed biometric privacy laws that require affirmative consent for the collection and use of biometric data, such as facial templates and fingerprints, and provide for private rights of action and statutory damages for violations.[63] Several state and local governments have passed laws regulating AI use in specific domains. These include requiring transparency, fairness, and accountability measures for automated decision systems used in hiring, housing, and criminal justice.[64] Other measures require companies and organizations to notify consumers who correspond with human-sounding chatbots[65] or manipulated

58 Daniel J. Solove and Woodrow Hartzog, 'The FTC and the New Common Law of Privacy' (2014) 114 *Colum. L. Rev.* 583.

59 See, e.g., *AMG Capital Management v. FTC* (2021).

60 See, e.g., '2024 AI State Law Tracker', Husch Blackwell (April 29, 2024), www.huschblackwell.com/2024-ai-state-law-tracker; see, e.g., 'Artificial Intelligence in the States: Emerging Legislation' (Dec. 6, 2023), www.csg.org/2023/12/06/artificial-intelligence-in-the-states-emerging-legislation/ (as of December 2023, seventeen states had enacted twenty-nine bills focused on regulating the design and development of artificial intelligence).

61 California Consumer Privacy Act (CCPA), Cal. Civ. Code §§ 1798.100–1798.199 (giving residents the rights to access, delete, and opt out of the sale of their personal information, while imposing duties of transparency, purpose limitation, and data minimization on covered businesses); California Privacy Rights Act (CPRA), Cal. Civ. Code § 1798.100 et seq. (creating a new category of "sensitive personal information" subject to heightened safeguards, requiring businesses to honor global opt-out requests through specified signals, and establishing the California Privacy Protection Agency to enforce the law).

62 'Which States Have Consumer Data Privacy Laws?', Bloomberg Law (Sept. 2024), https://pro.bloomberglaw.com/insights/privacy/state-privacy-legislation-tracker/, accessed 20 January 2025.

63 See, e.g., Illinois's Biometric Information Privacy Act (BIPA) 740 ILCS 14 (requiring private entities to obtain informed consent before collecting or using biometric data, such as fingerprints or facial scans, and grants individuals a private right of action to sue for violations); Washington's Facial Recognition Privacy Act (FRPA) (prohibiting the use of facial recognition technology by state and local government agencies without a warrant, and requires companies that develop or deploy these systems to obtain consent from individuals and to provide clear notice and opt-out mechanisms).

64 See, e.g., 820 Ill. Comp. Stat. 42/1 et seq. (Illinois Artificial Intelligence Video Interview Act); N.Y.C. Admin. Code §§ 20-870–20-872 (New York City Automated Employment Decision Tools Law).

65 See, e.g., California Bot Disclosure Law of 2019, Cal. Bus. & Prof. Code § 17941 (requiring entities that use bots to communicate with the public online to disclose that the communication is from a bot); Utah Artificial Intelligence Policy Act (UAIP), Utah Code Ann. § 13-61-101 et seq. (2024) (requiring individuals and entities in "regulated occupations," such as healthcare professionals, to prominently disclose that a consumer is interacting with generative AI at the beginning of any communication). Ibid. at § 13-62-201(2).

media.[66] Many states prohibit or criminalize the production of deepfakes, especially the creation of pornographic images.[67]

While these efforts are commendable, they remain fragmented and reactive, often addressing narrow harms rather than the underlying structural conditions that enable them.[68] Most still rely heavily on a notice-and-choice model of privacy protection that is ill-equipped to govern the complex data ecosystems of machine learning pipelines.[69] Moreover, their enforcement mechanisms are often limited to Attorney General actions or narrow private rights of action, rather than more comprehensive administrative oversight and auditing.[70]

16.3.2 *The Shortcomings of Individual Consent and Control*

Perhaps the most significant limitation of US privacy law in the face of generative AI is its overreliance on individual notice and consent as the primary mechanism for protecting personal autonomy.[71] Under this model, companies and organizations that collect or process personal data must provide individuals with clear and conspicuous notice of their data practices and obtain consent before using that data for any new or additional purposes.[72] The dominant "informed consent" model assumes that privacy is an individual right that can be safeguarded by providing people with information about data collection practices and giving them choices about whether to allow those practices.[73]

However, this paradigm of individual control is increasingly challenged by the scale, complexity, and opacity of data flows powering these systems.[74] These factors make it difficult for people to track and control how their personal information is collected and used.[75] Generative AI systems rely on web crawling, data brokers, and other indirect sources of data collection that are not visible and thus not amenable to granular individual control. Even when individuals have notice and choice regarding the collection and use of their data by AI systems, they may

66 Fla. Stat. § 106.147 (2024) (requiring disclaimers in political disclaimers in political advertisements using synthetic media).

67 See, e.g., Va. Code Ann. § 18.2-386.2 (2024); N.Y. Penal Law § 245.15 (2024) (imposing fines or imprisonment for deepfake pornography); Cal. Penal Code § 647(j)(4) (2024); Ariz. Rev. Stat. § 13-1425 (2024) (expanding the scope of nonconsensual pornography statutes to include synthetic media); 720 ILCS 5/11-20.1 (2024); Iowa Code § 728.12 (2024); S.D. Codified Laws § 22-24A-3 (2024) (expanding the definition of child pornography to include deepfakes).

68 Solove, 'Artificial Intelligence and Privacy'; King and Meinhardt, *White Paper Rethinking Privacy in the AI Era*.

69 Solove, 'Artificial Intelligence and Privacy'; King and Meinhardt, *White Paper Rethinking Privacy in the AI Era*; D. J. Solove, 'Murky Consent: An Approach to the Fictions of Consent in Privacy Law' (2024) 104 *Boston University Law Review* 593, https://papers.ssrn.com/sol3/papers.cfm?abstract_id=4333743; W. Hartzog and N. Richards, 'Privacy's Constitutional Moment and the Limits of Data Protection' (2020) 61 *Boston College Law Review* 1687–1762 at 1704; D. J. Solove, 'The Limitations of Privacy Rights' (2022) 98 *Notre Dame Law Review* 975–1036 at 983–84.

70 Caitriona Fitzgerald, Kara Williams, and R. J. Cross, 'The State of Privacy: How State "Privacy" Laws Fail to Protect Privacy and What They Can Do Better', *EPIC* (2024), https://epic.org/documents/the-state-of-privacy-report/#:~:text=In%20our%20evaluation%20of%20the,about%20consumers%20without%20meaningful%20limits.

71 Solove, 'Artificial Intelligence and Privacy'; King and Meinhardt, *White Paper Rethinking Privacy in the AI Era*; Solove, 'Murky Consent'.

72 Solove, 'Murky Consent', 593.

73 Ibid.; Solove, 'The Limitations of Privacy Rights'.

74 D. J. Solove, 'Privacy Self-Management and the Consent Dilemma' (2013) 126 *Harvard Law Review* 1880.

75 J. Burrell, 'How the Machine "Thinks": Understanding Opacity in Machine Learning Algorithms' (2016) 3 *Big Data & Society* 2053951715622512; Solove, 'Artificial Intelligence and Privacy'; King and Meinhardt, *White Paper Rethinking Privacy in the AI Era*; Solove, 'Murky Consent'; Hartzog and Richards, 'Privacy's Constitutional Moment and the Limits of Data Protection'; M. E. Kaminski, 'The Right to Explanation, Explained' (2019) 34 *Berkeley Tech. LJ* 189; F. Pasquale, *The Black Box Society: The Secret Algorithms That Control Money and Information* (Cambridge, MA: Harvard University Press, 2015).

lack the time, expertise, or bandwidth to parse complex privacy policies and terms of service or weigh the abstract and uncertain risks of AI against the immediate and tangible benefits of personalized content and services.[76]

16.3.3 *The Barriers to Transparency and Accountability*

A final limitation of the prevailing US privacy framework is its emphasis on ex post remedies and individual rights and procedural safeguards, such as the right to access, correct, and delete personal data, as well as requirements for data minimization, purpose limitation, and retention constraints.[77] These mechanisms presume an identifiable data subject and specific problematic practice. However, as noted above, these conditions often do not apply to information harms wrought by generative AI systems. The nature of generative AI poses significant challenges to effectively implementing these safeguards.

The opacity and inscrutability of generative AI systems pose significant barriers to accountability and redress. This is due to generative AI's architectural complexity,[78] proprietary training data and algorithms,[79] and emergent properties.[80] As a result, there is often little public disclosure of information about data sources, model architectures, training procedures, and output generation processes.

Moreover, even when individuals can exercise their rights, doing so may not be technically feasible. Unlike conventional datasets, generative AI models involve a compressed representation of their training data, making it difficult to erase or remove personal information ingested during training.[81] For instance, individuals seeking to delete their data under laws like the CCPA may not fully eliminate their data's influence on a model's predictions or outputs.[82] Similarly, if a generative model is used to create and disseminate harmful synthetic media such as nonconsensual deepfake pornography or fabricated news, it will be difficult to contain or reverse the viral spread and amplification of this content across social media platforms given the current lack of robust content authentication and removal mechanisms.[83]

76 Solove, 'Privacy Self-Management and the Consent Dilemma'.

77 Solove, 'The Limitations of Privacy Rights', 993; L. Edwards and M. Veale, 'Slave to the Algorithm: Why a Right to an Explanation Is Probably Not the Remedy You Are Looking For' (2017) 16 *Duke L. & Tech. Rev.* 18; Hartzog and Richards, 'Privacy's Constitutional Moment and the Limits of Data Protection', 1704; Kaminski, 'The Right to Explanation, Explained'.

78 Burrell, 'How the Machine "Thinks"'; Solove, 'Artificial Intelligence and Privacy'; King and Meinhardt, *White Paper Rethinking Privacy in the AI Era*; Solove, 'Murky Consent'; Hartzog and Richards, 'Privacy's Constitutional Moment and the Limits of Data Protection'; Kaminski, 'The Right to Explanation, Explained'; Pasquale, *The Black Box Society*.

79 C. A. Tschider, 'AI's Legitimate Interest: Towards a Public Benefit Privacy Model' (2021) 21 *Hous. J. Health L. & Pol'y* 125 at 711; R. Wexler, 'Life, Liberty, and Trade Secrets: Intellectual Property in the Criminal Justice System' (2018) 70 *Stanford Law Review* 1343–1430 at 1402.

80 Surden, 'ChatGPT, Large Language Models, and Law', 1952–53 (noting the fast pace of artificial intelligence development and innovation).

81 Carlini et al., 'Extracting Training Data from Large Language Models'.

82 R. Shokri, M. Stronati, C. Song, and V. Shmatikov, 'Membership Inference Attacks against Machine Learning Models' (IEEE, 2017), 3–18.

83 Chesney and Citron, '21st Century-Style Truth Decay'; B. Chesney and D. Citron, 'Deep Fakes: A Looming Challenge for Privacy, Democracy, and National Security' (2019) 107 *California Law Review* 1753–1820; B. Van der Sloot and Y. Wagensveld, 'Deepfakes: Regulatory Challenges for the Synthetic Society' (2022) 46 *Computer Law & Security Review* 105716.

16.3.4 *The Inadequacy of Individual Rights and Recourse*

Many of the most troubling impacts of generative AI are invisible, embedded in automated systems and occurring before formal decision points.[84] Instead of explicit rejection, biased or inaccurate assessments and predictions often preempt access to opportunity.[85] For example, as I have discussed in prior work, predictive hiring algorithms can filter out qualified job applicants based on biased assessments of their resumes or online profiles, creating a "silicon ceiling" that imperceptibly impedes economic mobility for marginalized communities.[86]

Further, collective and diffuse harms, such as discriminatory outcomes and the erosion of public discourse, are not traceable to specific instances of misconduct or malfeasance. Instead, these harms often emerge from the complex interactions between AI systems and society, and their effects may only become visible over time as they compound and reinforce existing patterns of disadvantage and inequality.[87] This invisibility presents a significant obstacle to privacy and data protection remedies and enforcement mechanisms, which focus on discrete, identifiable injuries and rely on individual complaints or lawsuits to surface wrongdoing.[88]

The limitations of individual control and the collective impact of generative AI underscore the inadequacy of traditional, reactive forms of regulation in addressing the structural harms posed by these systems. While individual contestation and enforcement actions can provide important avenues for redress and accountability in specific cases, they are often too slow, costly, and narrow in scope to mitigate generative AI's wide-ranging and rapidly evolving risks. Moreover, these retroactive mechanisms fail to address AI systems' more diffuse and long-term societal impacts, which can accumulate gradually and invisibly over time.

16.4 TOWARDS A PARADIGM FOR GENERATIVE AI GOVERNANCE

The limitations of existing regulatory frameworks in addressing the privacy risks posed by generative AI systems underscore the need for a new paradigm of privacy governance. This section argues for a fundamental reorientation of privacy protection, from a narrow focus on individual control and procedural safeguards to a more systemic approach. It outlines three key elements of this new paradigm: (1) shifting from individual to collective conceptions of privacy; (2) moving from reactive to proactive governance; and (3) transitioning from reckless to responsible innovation. The section concludes by acknowledging the significant obstacles to implementing such a paradigm shift in the United States, including the lack of a comprehensive federal privacy law, the limitations of sectoral and state-level regulations, and the entrenched ideological resistance to precautionary governance of emerging technologies.

[84] Zeide, 'The Silicon Ceiling'.

[85] Ibid.; Solove and Matsumi, 'AI, Algorithms, and Awful Humans'; Kerr and Earle, 'Prediction, Preemption, Presumption'.

[86] Zeide, 'The Silicon Ceiling'.

[87] Ibid.

[88] Solove, 'Artificial Intelligence and Privacy'; D. D. Hirsch, 'From Individual Control to Social Protection: New Paradigms for Privacy Law in the Age of Predictive Analytics' (2020) 79 *Maryland Law Review* 439–505 at 462 (noting that new proposals for privacy emphasize "social protection, rather than individual control [in a] shift from a liberalist regulatory approach that seeks to facilitate individual choice, to one that empowers public officials to make choices about which . . . practices are safe for individuals and consistent with social values, and which are not").

16.4.1 *Shifting from Individual to Collective Conceptions of Privacy*

Given the limitations of individual control and the societal impact of generative AI, privacy governance should shift towards a more holistic understanding of privacy as a social value and public good. Doing so involves reframing privacy as a matter of positive obligations on institutions rather than just individual rights. A robust approach to generative AI privacy governance will require reorienting the foundations of privacy protection from individual control and procedural rights to recognizing privacy as a social foundation and collective good. As demonstrated by the limitations of existing regulation, policymakers cannot mitigate the privacy risks of generative AI solely by empowering individuals to control how their personal data is collected and used by particular entities. Instead, achieving meaningful privacy protection in the generative AI era requires recognizing the collective and relational dimensions of privacy harms.

16.4.2 *Moving from Reactive to Proactive Governance*

A second key element in a more robust privacy governance framework is a shift from reactive and retroactive enforcement actions to proactive and preventative oversight regimes. Rather than relying primarily on ex post remedies triggered by specific legal violations or consumer complaints, policymakers should institutionalize continuous monitoring, auditing, and impact assessment requirements to surface and mitigate potential risks before companies and organizations deploy generative AI systems at scale.

The European Union's AI Act offers a promising model for a more systematic approach to AI governance.[89] One key strength of the AI Act is its focus on the broader societal impacts of AI systems, rather than just individual privacy harms. The Act creates a comprehensive regulatory framework for AI systems, imposing graduated requirements based on a technology's level of risk.[90] Notably, the Act would require "high-risk" AI systems to undergo mandatory conformity assessments to ensure compliance with essential requirements related to data quality, transparency, human oversight, and robustness before entering the EU market.[91] It also creates ongoing monitoring obligations for high-risk systems and establishes a centralized database for registering stand-alone AI systems.[92]

While the Act has drawn criticism for the compliance burdens it would impose,[93] it represents a meaningful effort to extend regulatory scrutiny to the entire AI lifecycle and to create an institutional infrastructure for proactive and adaptive governance. Such an approach is vital for

[89] EU Parliament, 'Artificial Intelligence Act: Deal on Comprehensive Rules for Trustworthy AI' (Dec. 9, 2023), www.europarl.europa.eu/news/en/press-room/20231206IPR15699/artificial-intelligence-act-deal-on-comprehensive-rules-for-trustworthy-ai; Margot E. Kaminski, 'Regulating the Risks of AI' (2023) 103 *B.U. L. Rev.* 1347; Daniel J. Solove, 'Data Is What Data Does: Regulating Use, Harm, and Risk Instead of Sensitive Data' (2024) 118 *Nw. U. L. Rev.* 1081, 1128–36.

[90] 'Shaping Europe's Digital Future' (April 23, 2024), https://digital-strategy.ec.europa.eu/en/policies/regulatory-framework-ai.

[91] Ibid.; European Commission, 'Artificial Intelligence – Questions and Answers' (Dec. 12, 2023), https://ec.europa.eu/commission/presscorner/detail/en/QANDA_21_1683.

[92] 'Shaping Europe's Digital Future'; European Commission, 'Artificial Intelligence – Questions and Answers'.

[93] Jessica Corbett, 'World's Most Extensive AI Rules Approved in EU Despite Criticism', *Bloomberg* (March 13, 2024), www.bloomberg.com/news/articles/2024-03-13/eu-embraces-new-ai-rules-despite-doubts-it-got-the-right-balance?embedded-checkout=true.

addressing generative AI systems' systemic and diffuse impacts, which may not be readily discernible or traceable to specific consumer injuries.[94]

16.4.3 *Requiring Responsible Innovation*

A third imperative is to transition from reckless to responsible innovation. Generative AI governance reflects an expansive conception of accountability that recognizes the complex web of actors and power relations involved in these systems' development and deployment. In light of the limitations of individual consent and control, generative AI governance should emphasize the positive obligations of institutions that develop and deploy these systems to assess and mitigate their potential harms. These obligations should include adhering to responsible principles that guide every stage of the AI lifecycle, ensuring that AI systems are developed and used in ways that mitigate potential harms and align with public values and societal norms. This approach requires AI developers and deployers to embrace practices prioritizing transparency, accountability, and public participation throughout the AI lifecycle. By proactively engaging with affected communities, disclosing essential information about AI systems, and conducting regular assessments of their potential societal impacts, entities can foster a culture of responsible innovation that upholds public values and earns public trust.

16.4.4 *Obstacles to Comprehensive AI Privacy Governance in the United States*

Despite the urgent need for more relational, proactive, and accountable approaches to addressing generative AI's privacy risks, there are several formidable obstacles to achieving such a paradigm shift in the United States. These obstacles stem from a combination of political, legal, and economic factors that shape the current regulatory landscape and the incentives of key stakeholders.

One major hurdle is the political challenge of passing a comprehensive federal privacy law that could provide a coherent and consistent framework for governing AI systems across different sectors and jurisdictions.[95] While there have been several proposals for such a law in recent years, none have yet been enacted, partly due to disagreements over preemption, private rights of action, and the scope of covered data and entities.

Another obstacle is the strong protection afforded to freedom of expression under the First Amendment, which courts interpret to cover a wide range of data-driven activities, from collecting and disseminating publicly available information to creating and sharing synthetic media.[96] These free speech protections can limit the ability of regulators to impose content-based restrictions on AI-generated outputs, even when such outputs may be false, misleading, or harmful to individual privacy and public discourse.[97]

Moreover, the US policy landscape has historically favored a laissez-faire and innovation-friendly approach to technological development, preferring market-driven solutions and

[94] Solove, 'Artificial Intelligence and Privacy'; M. E. Kaminski, 'Regulating the Risks of AI' (2023) 103 *Boston University Law Review* 22–21.

[95] Brian Fung, 'Congress Hasn't Been Able to Make Social Media Safer. Here's Why | CNN Business', CNN (Feb. 1, 2024), www.cnn.com/2024/02/01/tech/social-media-regulation-bipartisan-support/index.html.

[96] M. A. Franks, *The Cult of the Constitution: Our Deadly Devotion to Guns and Free Speech* (Stanford, CA: Stanford University Press, 2019).

[97] See, e.g., *Sorrell v. IMS Health Inc.*, 564 U.S. 552, 131 S. Ct. 2653, 180 L. Ed. 2d 544 (2011); *NetChoice, LLC v. Bonta*, No. 22-CV-08861-BLF, 2023 WL 6135551, at *6 (ND Cal. Sept. 18, 2023); *NetChoice, LLC v. Griffin*, No. 5: 23-CV-5105 (W.D. Ark. March 24, 2024).

self-regulation over precautionary regulation.[98] Numerous laws provide safe harbors and immunities for online platforms and technology providers, most notably Section 230 of the Communications Decency Act (CDA), which shields platforms from liability for user-generated content.[99] This permissive stance can create challenges for proactive AI governance by placing the burden of proof on regulators to demonstrate clear and concrete harm before intervening in the development and deployment of AI systems.

Overcoming these obstacles will require a broader cultural and ideological shift in how we think about the role of technology in society, and the balance between innovation and responsibility in the face of transformative change. This means moving beyond focusing on individual liability and sanctions, and towards a more systemic and structural approach that seeks to create a culture of responsibility, integrity, and public trust in the AI ecosystem.

16.5 CONCLUSION

The meteoric rise and widespread adoption of generative AI systems present significant threats to privacy and the regimes that seek to protect it. The ability of these systems to generate novel and realistic content based on patterns learned from vast troves of personal data raises profound risks, from nonconsensual data extraction and inferential profiling to the spread of synthetic media and the amplification of algorithmic biases. Existing regulatory approaches, which rely heavily on individual notice and consent, ex post enforcement, and a narrow conception of privacy harms, are ill-equipped to address generative AI's systemic and diffuse impacts. Addressing these challenges will require a fundamental reorientation of privacy governance, from reliance on individual control and procedural safeguards to a more collective, proactive, and precautionary approach that recognizes privacy as a public good and collective responsibility.

[98] See, e.g., Adam Thierer, *Permissionless Innovation: The Continuing Case for Comprehensive Technological Freedom* (Arlington, VA: Mercatus Center at George Mason University, 1st ed. 2014).

[99] 47 U.S.C. § 230 (2022).

17

Generative AI and IP Under US Law

Bruce E. Boyden

17.1 INTRODUCTION

Generative AI burst into public consciousness in 2022 with the release of several image generation tools and, most famously, OpenAI's text-generating ChatGPT system. Tools are now available that generate software code, human voices, and photorealistic videos; and generative AI has been incorporated into search engines, photo and video editing software, and legal research databases.[1] Although the outputs of these tools often still require significant human editing and revision,[2] they are rapidly improving to the point that polished, sophisticated results will soon be a text prompt away.

Any technological innovation that suddenly breaks the boundaries of what people are capable of can be both liberating and destabilizing. The Industrial Revolution enabled the formation of large enterprises to produce industrial and consumer goods and services on a scale previously unimaginable,[3] but it also produced accidents and injuries distributed across far-flung networks of producers, distributors, and employers.[4] This led to a conceptual shift in how responsibility is apportioned in tort law, moving away from a strictly person-based model of injuries and fault and toward organizational and systemic notions of risk mitigation that spread liability.[5]

Generative AI likewise augurs both a vast expansion of the creative and inventive capabilities of ordinary individuals and significant challenges in applying and adapting intellectual property (IP) law in this new environment. The Information Age has already posed difficult legal questions arising from the emergence of widespread automated copying and distribution in the 1990s. Generative AI brings that automation to the act of creating something new, an act that forms the foundation of all of the intellectual property fields. Not only does this challenge

[1] *See* Cade Metz, *OpenAI Unveils A.I. That Instantly Generates Eye-Popping Videos*, N.Y. TIMES, Feb. 16, 2024, at B4; *Navigating the Challenges and Opportunities of Synthetic Voices*, OPENAI, Mar. 29, 2024.

[2] Lance Ulanoff, *So What If OpenAI Sora Didn't Create the Mind-Blowing Balloon Head Video Without Assistance – I Still Think It's Incredible*, TECHRADAR, Apr. 28, 2024.

[3] *See generally* ALFRED D. CHANDLER, JR., THE VISIBLE HAND: THE MANAGERIAL REVOLUTION IN AMERICAN BUSINESS (1977).

[4] *See* JOHN FABIAN WITT, THE ACCIDENTAL REPUBLIC 3 (2004).

[5] *See id.* at 10, 17; G. EDWARD WHITE, TORT LAW IN AMERICA: AN INTELLECTUAL HISTORY 171 (expanded ed. 2003); Alexandra D. Lahav, *A Revisionist History of Products Liability*, 122 MICH. L. REV. 509, 556–59 (2023).

industry structures and professional careers based on the need to pay for human creativity,[6] but it undermines presumptions built into the law about what types of entities create and what sorts of incentives and legal structures they need.[7] As a result, we may see comparable doctrinal changes for intellectual property law that torts and insurance law experienced at the turn of the nineteenth century.

This chapter will consider the emerging application of intellectual property law to generative AI in the United States. Generative AI does not have a consistent definition, but the primary focus will be on AI systems based on models produced by machine learning that are designed to generate new content in some form, such as poems, videos, artwork, protein structures, machine diagrams, or advertisements. For such systems, the question arises repeatedly whether AI creation should be treated as essentially the same or essentially different from human creation, whether the issue is rights or infringement, or with respect to training or outputs. Do AI models "learn" or do they copy? When an AI system outputs content, is that a tool controlled by the user or is it akin to an agent hired by the company? Should legal doctrines developed in an earlier age of intellectual production apply literally to generative AI, or by loose analogy?

These questions have already provoked a blizzard of speculative commentary. The challenge is to avoid "magical thinking" about AI while remaining open to the possibility that AI technology may, in fact, pose serious doctrinal or practical conundrums under existing intellectual property law.[8] Below I briefly survey, subject by subject, the issues generative AI might pose, keeping in mind that at this early stage it is easy to be either overly exuberant or overly blasé in assessing legal outcomes.

17.2 COPYRIGHT

As of this writing, the most pressing and numerous intellectual property issues posed by generative AI are copyright issues. Questions have been posed, in litigation and elsewhere,[9] about whether using copyrighted works for training generative AI models is infringing; who should be liable if the outputs of generative AI systems are substantially similar to ingested works; and whether such outputs are copyrightable, and if so, who the authors are. I will first consider the two infringement issues, for inputs and outputs, and then address ownership of outputs.

17.2.1 *Infringement*

The potential for copyright infringement liability arises at both the beginning and the end of the generative AI process. At the beginning, building a generative AI system requires collecting a huge amount of content to serve as training material. There simply are not enough public domain works to satisfy the voracious demand for information that current AI models require – and as a result, copyrighted content, much of it scraped from the internet, has been assembled

[6] *See* Dan L. Burk, *Cheap Creativity and What It Will Do*, 57 GA. L. REV. 1669, 1680–82 (2023); Justin Hughes, *Can Hollywood's New SAG-AFTRA Contract Hold AI at Bay?*, L.A. TIMES, Nov. 30, 2023; Todd Spangler, *WGA Slams G/O Media's AI-Generated Articles as "Existential Threat to Journalism," Demands Company End Practice*, VARIETY, July 12, 2023.

[7] Margot Kaminski, *Authorship, Disrupted*, 51 U.C. DAVIS L. REV. 589, 614–16 (2017); Ryan Calo, *Robotics and the Lessons of Cyberlaw*, 103 CALIF. L. REV. 513, 558–60 (2015).

[8] *See* Dan L. Burk, *AI Patents and the Self-Assembling Machine*, 105 MINN. L. REV. HEADNOTES 301, 301 (2021) (describing the "magical worldview" surrounding AI systems).

[9] For an updated list of the status of AI infringement lawsuits in the United States, *see* Edward Lee, *Category: Status*, CHATGPT IS EATING THE WORLD, https://chatgptiseatingtheworld.com/category/status.

into mammoth packages of training data. One claim being pursued in a number of current lawsuits in the United States is that the use of copyrighted works for training in this way violates the copyrights in those works in one of several ways: by unauthorized reproduction, by creating an unauthorized derivative work, or by removing copyright management information from the training data. Defendants in these lawsuits are in turn likely to assert the defense of fair use.

The *outputs* of generative AI systems may also be infringing. A generated text, code, image, or song could be copied from material in the training data and remain substantially similar to the original work. That may happen as the result of a specific attempt by the user of the AI system to generate something similar to a known work by carefully crafting prompts, or it may happen without any special prompting by the user. The question that may arise in such cases is who, if anyone, is liable for the resulting similar output.

17.2.1.1 AI Inputs

In order to mimic language or produce recognizable images, AI systems require a model of how such text or visual representations should appear, such as a "large language model" in the case of text-generating AI, or a diffusion model for images. And that model needs to be trained by example. AI system developers create their models by running a machine learning algorithm on a humongous dataset built from billions of examples of the sort of content the AI will produce. In the process, the model will extract information from the training data about the probabilities of certain patterns occurring in language, images, or any other medium. The more examples that are used for training data, the better the model will be at accurately predicting in various contexts what sort of patterns will appear to be coherent text or images to human observers.[10]

As a result, in order to build better models, AI developers have been engaged in a type of gold rush to collect as much training data as possible. Indeed, it appears they may be running out of data, resorting to such methods as transcribing YouTube videos or purchasing entire book-publishing firms.[11] In this headlong effort to build the most powerful generative AI systems, nearly the entire corpus of digitized copyrighted materials has been ingested before any court conclusions have been reached concerning liability.[12]

Given the scale of training operations, licensing training materials through private transactions would likely be impossible. Determining the copyright status or owner of any given work scraped from the internet can be extremely challenging.[13] And even if the owners could be found, the transaction costs of negotiating agreements would be enormous. Any licensing solution would likely have to be statutorily imposed. This would be a significant undertaking, as the Copyright Act currently has only limited compulsory licenses for such uses as recording new performances of previously recorded musical works, certain streams of sound recordings and musical works, or cable retransmission of over-the-air broadcast television programs.[14]

[10] For an excellent and thorough description of generative AI systems, how they are trained, and the copyright issues they raise, *see* Katherine Lee, A. Feder Cooper & James Grimmelmann, *Talkin' 'Bout AI Generation: Copyright and the Generative-AI Supply Chain*, __ J. COPYR. SOC'Y U.S.A. ___ (in press) (Mar. 1, 2024 ms.).

[11] *See* Deepa Seetharaman, *For Data-Guzzling AI Companies, the Internet Is Too Small*, WALL ST. J., Apr. 1, 2024; Cade Metz et al., *How Tech Giants Cut Corners to Harvest Data for Their A.I. Models*, N.Y. TIMES, Apr. 8, 2024, at A1.

[12] Katie Paul, *Meta Used Copyrighted Books for AI Training Despite Its Own Lawyers' Warnings, Authors Allege*, REUTERS, Dec. 12, 2023.

[13] *See* Melodi Dincer et al., Comments of the Knowing Machines Research Project on the United States Copyright Office Notice of Inquiry on Artificial Intelligence and Copyright, No. 2023–6, Oct. 30, 2023, at 2.

[14] 17 U.S.C. §§ 111(d), 114(d)(2), 115(a), (d).

17.2.1.1.1 REPRODUCTION. Training AI models likely involves one or more acts of reproduction of copyrighted works in copies, which unless licensed or a fair use would be infringing.[15] First, there is the copying of works from online or offline materials for inclusion in the training data. The assembly of training data may be performed by the AI developer or by a third party, but at some point, the training materials must be collected in one place, which will require a copy to be made. However, that copy is simply the first step in a lengthy process of digital transformations. A generative AI model is not simply a compilation of text or images from the training data. Rather, as part of the creation of the model, information is extracted from the training data concerning, for example, what words tend to follow other words, or what shapes in an image represent a "cat."[16] The model, when complete, will consist of a series of weights and vectors associated with each input token – the individual words or bits of images that were culled from the training data.[17] Those weights and vectors allow the model to predict, piece by piece, what an output should look like. Generative AI systems thus do not simply combine identifiable pieces of known works together; rather, they build their outputs from scratch based on the probabilities learned from the entire training dataset.

There are thus at least three different copies that could be involved in operating a generative AI system. First, there's the copy of the training materials used to assemble the training data. That will be the easiest copy to identify, since it will still be in the form of the original file. To the extent copyright owners claim infringement of their works by the inclusion of those works in the training materials, AI providers will likely have a strong fair use defense, as set forth below. Second, even though the training process extracts aggregated information from the training data, there may be copies of some of the training materials represented in the model itself. And finally, an output from the generative AI system may be a copy of something from the training materials.[18]

All three of these claims will be challenging for plaintiffs to pursue. First, as noted above, defendants may have a successful fair use defense, particularly for copying of works to use as training materials. But in addition to that issue, many potential plaintiffs are likely to have difficult problems of proof. The test for infringement of the reproduction right under US law varies, but typically requires two showings: that the plaintiff's copyrighted work was actually copied by the defendant, and that the defendant's work, if it is not literally identical to the plaintiff's, is at least "substantially similar" to it.

The first part of the test, actual copying, may be a significant hurdle for plaintiffs in any of the three situations. Plaintiffs claiming infringement of their works can demonstrate actual copying by either obtaining direct evidence of copying, or by showing that the defendant had access to the plaintiff's work and that the defendant's work is suspiciously similar.[19] In either event, in the AI context the plaintiff will need to demonstrate that their works were included in the materials used to train a generative AI model. But proving that a given work was in the training materials may be difficult. Although early AI models used open-source datasets such as LAION-5B, AI developers have more recently moved to proprietary datasets.[20] In such cases, a copyright owner

[15] *See* 17 U.S.C. § 106(1).
[16] *See* Matthew Sag, *Fairness and Fair Use in Generative AI*, 92 FORDHAM L. REV. 1887, 1907–10 (2024).
[17] *See* Martin Anderson, *Weights in Machine Learning*, METAPHYSIC.AI BLOG, Jan. 12, 2023; Cathal Horan, *Understanding Vectors from a Machine Learning Perspective*, NEPTUNE.AI MLOPS BLOG, Aug. 21, 2023.
[18] Infringing outputs will be considered in Section 17.2.1.2 below.
[19] Arnstein v. Porter, 154 F.2d 464, 468 (2d Cir. 1946).
[20] *See* Will Knight, *AI Is Becoming More Powerful – but Also More Secretive*, WIRED, Oct. 19, 2023.

will likely have no direct evidence that their work was included in training material, and thus will have to rely on either fame or fortuitously similar outputs to support an inference of copying.[21]

The second type of input infringement claim is that the generative AI model *itself* contains an infringing copy of the plaintiff's work. AI companies vigorously deny this, and in most cases it is likely false.[22] But it has been well-established that AI models can in certain circumstances "memorize" training data, resulting in the output of text or images that are close or even exact copies of the original.[23] This is most likely to occur when the training data contains a large number of instances of the same material, such as an iconic photograph or a widely distributed news article.[24] In such cases, it appears that the weights and vectors between certain tokens in the model are so strong that, given the right prompt, the AI system outputs something closely resembling the original material.[25]

Memorized content present in the model can qualify as a "copy" of the work even though it is formatted far differently than the original file it was drawn from. Under the Copyright Act, a "copy" is a "material object ... in which a work is fixed by any method now known or later developed, and from which the work can be perceived, reproduced, or otherwise communicated, either directly or with the aid of a machine or device."[26] There is no requirement for the work to be recorded in any particular manner or medium; even a detailed description of how to construct a work can qualify as a copy.[27] If a work can be output in substantially similar form from an AI system, that indicates that the instructions for doing so are contained within the model, and thus that the model (fixed in one or more storage drives) includes a "copy" of the work.[28]

One final question for infringement by inputs concerns the length of time that a copyrighted work persists during the training process. Under the Copyright Act, in order to qualify as a fixation of a work (and thus a "copy"), the embodiment of the work in a physical object must be "sufficiently permanent or stable to permit it to be perceived, reproduced, or otherwise communicated for a period of more than transitory duration." For memorized works encoded in the AI model, there will be no issue as to duration; the copy will exist as long as the model does. But copies made for purposes of machine learning may exist for only the period it takes to extract weights and vectors from them, possibly a few seconds or milliseconds.[29] Such short-lived temporary copies made during training are unlikely to be held to be communicated "for a period of more than transitory duration."[30]

[21] *See* 4 Melville B. Nimmer & David Nimmer, Nimmer on Copyright § 13D.05[B][2] ("bare possibility" of access insufficient); Andersen v. Stability AI Ltd., 744 F. Supp. 3d 956, 974-75 (N.D. Cal. 2024) (allegations that prompts using plaintiffs' names generated similar outputs plausibly pled copying).

[22] *See, e.g.*, Stability AI, Inc.'s Mem. of Points & Authorities in Supp. of Mot. to Dismiss, Andersen v. Stability AI Ltd., 700 F. Supp. 3d 853 (N.D. Cal. 2023), at 1 ("Stable Diffusion does not 'store' any images").

[23] *See* Matthew Sag, *Computer Safety for Generative AI*, 61 Hous. L. Rev. 295, 310–12 (2023); Lee, Cooper, & Grimmelmann, note 10 above, at 75.

[24] *See* Compl., N.Y. Times Co. v. Microsoft Corp., No. 1:23-cv-11195 (S.D.N.Y. filed Dec. 27, 2023). Matthew Sag has termed this the "Snoopy problem." Sag, note 23 above, at 327.

[25] *See* Peter Henderson et al., *Foundation Models and Fair Use*, 24 J. Mach. Learning Rsch., No. 400, 2023, at 1, 10–11.

[26] 17 U.S.C. § 101.

[27] *See* Micro Star v. Formgen Inc., 154 F.3d 1107, 1111–12 (9th Cir. 1998).

[28] *See* Lee, Cooper & Grimmelmann, note 10 above, at 76; Andersen v. Stability AI Ltd., 744 F. Supp. 3d 956, 974 (N.D. Cal. 2024).

[29] *See* Lee, Cooper & Grimmelmann, note 10 above, at 68.

[30] *See* Cartoon Network LP v. CSC Holdings, Inc., 536 F.3d 121, 129–30 (2d Cir. 2008) (buffer copy existing for 1.2 seconds not fixed).

17.2.1.1.2 DERIVATIVE WORKS. Plaintiffs in the early lawsuits against generative AI providers have made a second set of arguments that the use of their works as training materials is infringing. In addition to infringing the reproduction right, the plaintiffs have alleged that the defendants have infringed on the plaintiffs' exclusive right to "prepare derivative works based upon the copyrighted work."[31] A "derivative work" is a work "based upon one or more preexisting works, such as a translation, musical arrangement, [and so on], or any other form in which a work may be recast, transformed, or adapted."[32] The derivative work right originated as an adaptation right at a time when works were copyrightable only as published in certain media. The adaptation right gave copyright owners the exclusive right to republish certain works in another media format, such as adapting a play into a film.[33] But form no longer matters under current law; the expression of a work is protected against copying no matter what format it is in.[34]

As a result, the derivative works right in US copyright law largely overlaps the reproduction and public performance rights, to such an extent that the leading treatise suggests that it is almost "completely superfluous."[35] Nevertheless, the existence of a separate exclusive right suggests that some acts may infringe that are neither infringing reproductions nor infringing public performances. As Oren Bracha notes, this makes the exclusive right to prepare derivative works an attractive vehicle for infringement arguments that do not easily fit anywhere else.[36]

And indeed, some plaintiffs have already argued that, even if generative AI models do not contain copies of their works, the fact that their works were used to build the models means that the models are "based upon" their works, and thus that the *entire model* is an infringing derivative of every copyrighted work used to train it. This argument may be an attempt to express in copyright terms a social justice argument: AI providers are using the plaintiffs' own works to replace them. But courts have thus far rejected it under copyright law, with one judge calling it "nonsensical."[37] Among other problems, the authorities are clear that, to be infringing, an unauthorized derivative work must be substantially similar to the expression in the plaintiff's work, just like an infringing reproduction.[38] A mere causal connection between the plaintiff's work and the defendant's work is not enough.

17.2.1.1.3 FAIR USE. Those copyright owners able to demonstrate that their works were copied for use in training generative AI models will still face their most significant hurdle: the defense of fair use. Although generative AI system providers likely have a strong fair use defense to claims of infringement for works used as inputs, it is not absolute, and results may vary. In part, that is because of the vagaries of the fair use defense itself. Even though fair use is codified in the Copyright Act, the Supreme Court has described it as an "equitable rule of reason"[39] and the legislative history indicated that "courts must be free to adapt the doctrine to particular situations

[31] 17 U.S.C. § 106(2).
[32] *Id.* § 101 (definition of "derivative work").
[33] *See* Copyright Act of 1909 § 1(b).
[34] *See* 17 U.S.C. § 102(a) ("Copyright protection subsists … in original works of authorship fixed in any tangible medium of expression").
[35] NIMMER & NIMMER, note 21 above, § 8.09[A][1].
[36] Oren Bracha, *Generating Derivatives: AI and Copyright's Most Troublesome Right*, 25 N.C. J.L. & TECH. 345, 349 (2024). Whatever its deficiencies in defining a category of infringement, "derivative works" is a useful licensing term. *See* Pamela Samuelson, *The Quest for a Sound Conception of Copyright's Derivative Work Right*, 101 GEO. L.J. 1505, 1528–30 (2013).
[37] Kadrey v. Meta Platforms, Inc., No. 23-cv-03417, 2023 WL 8039640, at *1 (N.D. Cal. Nov. 20, 2023).
[38] *See* Bracha, note 36 above, at 379–81.
[39] Google LLC v. Oracle America, Inc., 593 U.S. 1, 18 (2021).

on a case-by-case basis."[40] Thus, even though the statute provides some factors to consider, fair use determinations are highly contextual. In particular, several cases involving dissection or reconfiguration of the plaintiffs' works have turned on exactly what sort of output the defendant was producing, and whether it substituted for the plaintiff's works.

A court considering a defense of fair use has to consider four factors enumerated in the Copyright Act: (1) the purpose and character of the defendant's use; (2) the nature of the plaintiff's work; (3) the amount and substantiality of the portion of the plaintiff's work that was used; and (4) the impact of the defendant's use on the value of and potential market for the plaintiff's work.[41] In general, the first and the fourth factors, which often operate in tandem, are deemed to be the most important.[42] Under the first factor, courts compare the purpose and content of the two works, asking if the defendant has engaged in a "transformative use" of the plaintiff's work.[43] Under the fourth factor, courts consider the harm the defendant's type of use may cause to both the actual markets the plaintiff's work is sold in, as well as the plaintiff's licensing opportunities.[44]

Several cases have held that it is a fair use to engage in what might be called "intermediate copying" of the plaintiff's work – that is, copying as a step in the process of producing something that extracts only the informational or "nonexpressive" value of the plaintiff's work.[45] The Ninth Circuit, in two cases involving video game consoles, held that copying the plaintiff's operating system was a fair use, where the purpose was only to study the operating system so that the defendant could either produce games compatible with the plaintiff's console[46] or allow existing games to run on different hardware.[47] In both cases, the court held that the defendant's copy had a different purpose than the expression in the plaintiff's operating system – the purpose of the copy was merely to determine how to get games and equipment to talk to each other.[48] More recently, the Second Circuit held that Google's scanning of millions of books was fair, where the purpose was to allow text searching of the content of those books and not to provide copies.[49] And the Supreme Court held that the use of command formats from the Java platform was fair where the purpose was to allow Java programmers to easily create apps for smartphones.[50] As a result of such cases, there was a prevailing consensus even before the advent of generative AI that the digestion of a work for its functional or informational value is fair.[51]

But prior determinations of fair use depended heavily on the nature of the *output* of the defendant's activities. As noted earlier, the first factor, examining whether the defendant used the plaintiff's work for a different purpose, and the fourth factor, examining whether the defendant's work is likely to be a substitute in a cognizable market, are often tightly linked.[52]

[40] H.R. Rep. No. 94-1476, at 66 (1976)
[41] 17 U.S.C. § 107.
[42] *See* Barton Beebe, *An Empirical Study of U.S. Copyright Fair Use Opinions Updated*, 1978–2019, 10 NYU J. Intell. Prop. & Ent. L. 1, 4, 18 (2020).
[43] Campbell v. Acuff-Rose Music, 510 U.S. 569, 579 (1994).
[44] *See id.* at 590.
[45] *See* Sega Enterprises Ltd. v. Accolade, Inc., 977 F.2d 1510, 1518 (9th Cir. 1993) ("intermediate copying"); Matthew Sag, *Copyright and Copy-Reliant Technology*, 103 Nw. U. L. Rev. 1607, 1624 (2009) ("nonexpressive use").
[46] *Sega*, 977 F.2d at 1514.
[47] Sony Computer Ent., Inc. v. Connectix Corp., 203 F.3d 596, 598–99 (9th Cir. 2000).
[48] *Sega*, 977 F.2d at 1514; *Connectix*, 203 F.3d at 599.
[49] Authors Guild v. Google, Inc., 804 F.3d 202, 229 (2d Cir. 2015).
[50] Google LLC v. Oracle Am., Inc., 593 U.S. 1, 30 (2021).
[51] *See* James Grimmelmann, *Copyright for Literate Robots*, 101 Iowa L. Rev. 657, 658 (2016).
[52] *See* Beebe, note 42 above, at 18. The phrase "cognizable market" glosses a complex discussion. *See, e.g.*, American Geophysical Union v. Texaco Inc., 60 F.3d 913, 926–31 (2d Cir. 1994).

In the two Ninth Circuit cases mentioned above, the result of the defendant's efforts was either additional games that did not compete with the plaintiff's console,[53] or the ability to play existing games in a different "environment" – a desktop computer as opposed to a console in a living room.[54] In *Authors Guild v. Google*, Google placed several limitations on its search results that made them a poor substitute for physical books, such as only showing three short segments where the searched-for term appeared, and limiting the amount of text that could be displayed through successive searches.[55] And in *Google v. Oracle America*, the Supreme Court noted that there was no evidence that Java was about to be used as a smartphone operating system.[56]

In other cases, however, courts have denied fair use where the defendant's use, while intended to extract informational or nonexpressive value from the plaintiff's works, nevertheless produces something that may displace the plaintiff's works from a market they are in or likely to enter. For example, the Second Circuit held in *Fox News Network v. TVEyes* that an online news clipping service was not a fair use of the plaintiff's news programs, because the ten-minute clips provided to subscribers were likely long enough to substitute for the original.[57] The Supreme Court's decision in *Andy Warhol Foundation v. Goldsmith* is particularly significant in this regard, even though it concerned an artist's use of a photograph and not new technology.[58] While its review of the lower-court decision was limited to the first fair use factor, the *Warhol* court seemed unable to avoid considering market substitution as an important part of that analysis. The majority held that when the Foundation provided Warhol's portrait, which was based on the plaintiff's photograph, to a magazine for use on its cover, that use was not transformative given that it was the same sort of use for which the plaintiff licenses her photographs.[59]

This history suggests that there may be no simple answer to the question of whether use of copyrighted works for training generative AI models is fair – it may depend on the sort of outputs the system produces and how they are typically used.[60] One remaining question is whether liability will be purely dependent on the happenstance of the system generating works substantially similar to training material, or whether it will instead depend on some sort of lack of precautions by the AI system provider. The first path – liability based on the simple fact of similar outputs – has the advantage of tracking existing law for human artists. That is, if the use of copyrighted materials to train generative AI models should be viewed as akin to human learning, as some have suggested,[61] then it would seem to follow that the use of that material to produce similar outputs should be infringing, even if it is not intentional.[62]

But whatever advantage this analogy has for fitting generative AI systems within existing case law comes at the expense of ignoring the real differences between AI generation and human creation. AI generation splits the "learning" stage of creation from the "production" stage and puts potentially unrelated individuals in control of each. While the AI system provider controls the training process, or at least the selection of training materials,[63] it will likely have very limited

53 *Sega*, 977 F.2d at 1527.
54 *Connectix*, 203 F.3d at 606.
55 *Authors Guild*, 804 F.3d at 222–23.
56 *Oracle*, 593 U.S. at 36–37.
57 Fox News Network, LLC v. TVEyes, Inc., 883 F.3d 169, 179 (2d Cir. 2018).
58 Andy Warhol Found. for the Visual Arts, Inc. v. Goldsmith, 598 U.S. 508 (2023).
59 *Id.* at 547.
60 *See* Lee, Cooper & Grimmelmann, note 10 above, at 110; David W. Opderbeck, *Copyright in AI Training Data: A Human-Centered Approach*, 76 Okla. L. Rev. 951, 978 (2024).
61 *See* Mark A. Lemley & Bryan Casey, *Fair Learning*, 99 Tex. L. Rev. 743, 749 (2021).
62 *See, e.g.*, Bright Tunes Music Corp. v. Harrisongs Music, Ltd., 420 F. Supp. 177 (S.D.N.Y. 1976).
63 This control may be limited, particularly if another entity assembles the training materials, but even then the AI model owner has the ability to select between training material providers.

control over the act of generation. For publicly available AI tools, an unrelated user will be in control of prompting the system to generate a particular output. That user, in turn, will typically have very little knowledge of what materials the model was trained on, and may be more or less intentional in seeking something resembling an existing work.

In such a system, it seems unfair to subject the provider's fair use defense for the copying of training materials to downstream actions that the provider has little control over. A defense rooted in equity should not depend on technicalities. But likewise, it seems unfair for an AI system provider to escape otherwise applicable liability for copying based purely on the fact that a downstream actor must take some action to reveal that copy. If the fairness of the copying depends on the uses that are ultimately made of the work, then one path to resolve the issue is to ask whether generative AI system providers have used reasonable precautions to prevent infringement of training materials. As in tort law, such an inquiry would allow some substantially similar copies to go unremedied, at least as to the provider, where the provider took certain measures to prevent those copies showing up in outputs. Some scholars have already suggested precautions that AI system providers might take to reduce downstream infringement, such as reducing the number of duplicates in the training data, or filtering outputs.[64] One challenge is that what qualifies as "reasonable" measures will often become apparent over time, but modern civil practice in the United States encourages large, existential litigation that forces the resolution of such disputes soon after circumstances have changed. With any luck courts and Congress will be able to forestall announcing bright-line rules that could quickly become anachronistic.[65]

17.2.1.1.4 CMI CLAIMS. There is another sort of claim that authors of works used as training data might have, one based on a more recent amendment to the Copyright Act, the Digital Millennium Copyright Act (DMCA). One provision of the DMCA, codified at 17 USC § 1202, prohibits various acts that might interfere with "copyright management information" (CMI) included with a copyrighted work. Although Section 1202 was added to fulfill the United States' obligations under the WIPO [World Intellectual Property Organization] Copyright Treaty, which requires the protection of "electronic rights management information,"[66] the definition of CMI extends far beyond electronic data, and encompasses various sorts of information in any form identifying the work, its author, or the copyright owner. Even copyright notices on physical copies qualify as CMI.

Among other things, Section 1202 prohibits removing CMI, or distributing a work knowing that the CMI has been removed, "knowing, or . . . having reasonable grounds to know, that it will induce, enable, facilitate, or conceal an infringement."[67] Obviously the training process for a generative AI model is not intended to preserve a work in its entirety, including any CMI contained in the work itself or a file's metadata. Indeed, such "memorization" of content is usually considered a bug, not a feature. Nevertheless, several copyright owners have claimed that the failure to faithfully preserve CMI with any memorized copies of their works is a violation of Section 1202.[68]

These claims have so far met with early rejections from the courts on motions to dismiss, for two reasons. First, some courts have held that Section 1202 only applies to identical copies of the

[64] *See* Sag, note 23 above, at 338–43; Henderson et al., note 25 above, at 26–33.
[65] *See, e.g.*, Audio Home Recording Act, 17 U.S.C. §§ 1001–10.
[66] WIPO Copyright Treaty art. 12, Dec. 20, 1996, TIAS No. 02-306.1, 2186 UNTS 121.
[67] 17 U.S.C. § 1202(b).
[68] *See, e.g.*, Compl., N.Y. Times Co. v. Microsoft Corp., No. 1:23-cv-11195, ¶¶ 182–91 (S.D.N.Y. filed Dec. 27, 2023).

plaintiff's work.[69] There is no obligation under Section 1202 to incorporate the CMI of every work that is borrowed from, only to preserve CMI in the course of duplicating or distributing a work. But training an AI model by its nature scrambles the plaintiff's works into a disparate set of associated data points, and even if a substantially similar version is reconstituted on output, it will hardly be "identical" to the original.[70]

Second, plaintiffs also have to demonstrate that an AI provider meets the so-called double scienter requirement. Liability under Section 1202(b) requires not only knowledge that the CMI has been removed or altered, but also knowledge that removing the CMI will "induce, enable, facilitate, or conceal" another person's infringement. Although knowledge of a specific plan to infringe is not necessary, the defendant must at least know based on past experience that removal of CMI would likely facilitate a particular type of future infringement.[71] The mere possibility that the presence of CMI in generated outputs would ward off downstream infringement is not enough.[72]

17.2.1.2 AI Outputs

Training data is not the only point at which an infringing copy of a work might be made. Another potentially infringing copy could be generated when a user enters a prompt, and the AI system produces an output. As discussed earlier, the production of such an output could confirm the presence of a memorized copy of the work in the AI model; it could also possibly defeat a fair use defense for copies made during training. Even more challenging is the question of whether the production of the output itself is an infringement, distinct from any copies made for training purposes, and if so who might be liable for it. Neither the user nor the provider of an AI system may have enough control over the creation of the output to clearly make one or the other a direct infringer; and without a direct infringer, there can be no indirect infringement liability.

17.2.1.2.1 DIRECT INFRINGEMENT. Generative AI outputs are likely to test the boundaries of copyright infringement doctrine in multiple ways. First, users will often use well-known authors' names as shorthand for a particular style of image, text, or music they would like to produce. This may result in the generation of content that is similar in style but not specific elements. In theory, mere "style" is not copyrightable, but the difference between style and expression is difficult to apply in practice.[73] The burden on the judicial system is alleviated by the fact that works by different authors in the same style do not occur frequently enough to produce significant amounts of litigation – but generative AI could change that, particularly if some models are fine-tuned to approximate particular artists' styles.[74]

69 Doe 1 v. GitHub, Inc., No. 22-cv-06823, 2024 WL 235217, at *9 (N.D. Cal. Jan. 22, 2024). *But see* ADR Int'l Ltd. v. Inst. for Supply Mgmt. Inc., 667 F. Supp. 3d 411, 427 (S.D. Tex. 2023) (statutory text has no "identical copy" requirement).

70 Even if Section 1202 applies to non-identical copies, most outputs from an AI system would still fall short. *See* Crowley v. Jones, 608 F. Supp. 3d 78, 90 (S.D.N.Y. 2022) (Section 1202 does not apply to "distinct works," even if infringing).

71 *See* Victor Elias Photography, LLC v. Ice Portal, Inc., 43 F.4th 1313, 1323 (11th Cir. 2022); Stevens v. Corelogic, Inc., 899 F.3d 666, 674 (9th Cir. 2018).

72 *See* Tremblay v. OpenAI, Inc., 716 F. Supp. 3d 773, 779 (N.D. Cal. 2024).

73 *See* Williams v. Gaye, 895 F.3d 1106 (9th Cir. 2018); Steinberg v. Columbia Pictures Indus., Inc, 663 F. Supp. 706 (S.D.N.Y. 1987).

74 *See, e.g.*, Andy Baio, *Invasive Diffusion: How One Unwilling Illustrator Found Herself Turned into an AI Model*, WAXY, Nov. 1, 2022.

Second, there is the question of whether the generation of a similar output is an infringing act separate from any copying during training, and if so, who might be liable for it. The elements of an infringement claim are variously stated, but typically involve establishing ownership of a valid and registered copyright, and infringement of one of the owner's exclusive rights.[75] Infringement of the reproduction right requires proof that the plaintiff's work was actually copied, and proof that that copying rose to a level that is improper – often described as "substantial similarity."[76] The plaintiff need not establish intent or even that the defendant realized they were infringing, but cases involving automated online copying have established an additional element: infringement liability requires a conscious decision to copy by the defendant, what courts have termed an act of "volition."[77]

The first sub-element of infringement, actual copying, typically involves a series of actions by a single defendant – obtaining access to the plaintiff's work, and then incorporating it into the defendant's work. But in the case of generative AI systems, that process is divided between two potentially unrelated parties, the provider and the user. The provider will have had initial access to the plaintiff's work and is responsible for creating the potential for the system to generate similar outputs. But creating the conditions for infringement is not usually enough for direct liability, unless the system has a limited range of potential outputs, such as a system that records and streams only those programs available via over-the-air broadcasts in a particular location.[78] A generative AI system can produce any number of works that might be requested by a given user, most of which will not be infringing at all, and thus generative AI systems are in that sense more like a copy shop than a cable system.[79] Copy shops may be *indirectly* liable for the infringing acts of their customers, if they meet the requirements for indirect liability, but are not directly liable unless their employees perform the copying.[80] And although provider employees may have consciously decided to include certain materials in the training data, they will not have exercised any volition in generating particular outputs.[81]

The user of an AI system may also have limited involvement in creating a substantially similar output. While it is the user's prompt that causes the output to be generated, that prompt could be something extremely simple that perhaps contained no reference to the original work or author. In such a case, the initial copying from the plaintiff's work will be entirely due to the provider's actions, but the exercise of volition to produce a similar output will be entirely due to the user's actions. Neither party will have exercised volition to produce a similar output. Patent law, unlike copyright law, has a doctrine of joint infringement, but even that would not establish direct infringement liability here, unless there was some sort of agreement or coordination between the provider and the user.[82]

There have been cases where the plaintiff's work finds its way to the defendant through a long and fortuitous series of events, and the courts have held such causal chains sufficient to establish

[75] *See* Feist Publications, Inc. v. Rural Tel. Serv. Co., 499 U.S. 340, 361 (1991).

[76] *See* Clark D. Asay, *An Empirical Study of Copyright's Substantial Similarity Test*, 13 U.C. Irvine L. Rev. 35, 43–50 (2022).

[77] *See* Perfect 10, Inc. v. Giganews, Inc., 847 F.3d 657, 666 (9th Cir. 2017); EMI Christian Music Grp., Inc. v. MP3tunes, LLC, 844 F.3d 79, 96 (2d Cir. 2016).

[78] *See* Am. Broad. Cos., Inc. v. Aereo, Inc., 573 U.S. 431, 443–44 (2014).

[79] *See id.*

[80] *See* Princeton Univ. Press v. Mich. Document Servs., Inc., 99 F.3d 1381 (6th Cir. 1996).

[81] As with the models themselves, courts have rejected the notion that AI outputs are infringing derivative works merely because they are "based upon" the training materials. *See* Andersen v. Stability AI Ltd., 700 F. Supp. 3d 853, 858 (N.D. Cal. 2023).

[82] *See* Akamai Techs., Inc. v. Limelight Networks, Inc., 797 F.3d 1020, 1022–23 (Fed. Cir. 2015).

access by the defendant.[83] But even in those circumstances, the defendant ultimately received a copy of the plaintiff's work, and then incorporated it into their own. In the generative AI context, the user never receives the plaintiff's work in its original form; the receipt and incorporation are performed at the user's request by the AI system. Possibly a user who purposefully requested an output similar to a known copyrighted work might be deemed responsible for the retrieval of similar expressive elements from the model, and thus for both the act of copying and the volition to create a similar output. Aside from that theory, the only infringement liability for generative AI systems would be for copied training data.

Even if it were prima facie infringing, a user's generation might well qualify as a fair use, but it is impossible to say much in advance about the likelihood of a successful defense. It would depend entirely on how the output was used. An image generated from a portrait photograph and used as an illustration on an online magazine would be extremely unlikely to qualify as a fair use.[84] Humorous lyrics generated to accompany a well-known song would be almost certain to qualify.[85]

There is also the possibility that, even if there is no direct liability for substantially similar outputs, the user might be *indirectly* liable for any direct infringement by the AI provider, as considered above. While of theoretical interest, the potential for indirect liability among individual users is unlikely to be of significant practical impact, given that litigation against generative AI providers has already commenced and will ultimately resolve the issue of liability for training one way or the other.

17.2.1.2.2 INDIRECT LIABILITY. Given the sequence of events involved in generating a substantially similar output, it might seem that the most significant copyright liability for providers would be indirect. But indirect infringement liability is unlikely to be the primary concern for AI system providers. Indirect liability will only come to the forefront if (a) AI system providers are not *directly* liable for the copies made during training, and (b) users *are* directly liable for AI system outputs. If AI system providers are directly liable for inputs, then liability for outputs is superfluous.[86] And if users are not directly liable for outputs, then indirect liability is impossible.[87] The chance of at least one of those outcomes occurring is high.

Assuming nevertheless that users are directly liable for AI outputs, there are up to three recognized forms of indirect infringement liability that might attach to providers: vicarious liability, where the defendant has the right and ability to supervise or control the infringing activity and has a direct financial interest in the infringement;[88] contributory liability, where the defendant materially contributes to known infringing activity;[89] and inducement, where the defendant intentionally induces or encourages infringing acts.[90] Depending on exactly how a

[83] *See, e.g.*, Gaste v. Kaiserman, 863 F.2d 1061, 1067 (2d Cir. 1988).
[84] *See* Andy Warhol Found. for the Visual Arts, Inc. v. Goldsmith, 598 U.S. 508, 550 (2023).
[85] *See* Fisher v. Dees, 794 F.2d 432 (9th Cir. 1986).
[86] *See* Lemley & Casey, note 61 above, at 748 (arguing that allowing any copyright claim "is tantamount to saying … that the use won't be permitted at all").
[87] *See, e.g.*, La Resolana Architects, PA v. Reno, Inc., 555 F.3d 1171, 1181 (10th Cir. 2009).
[88] *See* Perfect 10, Inc. v. Visa Int'l Serv. Ass'n, 494 F.3d 788, 802 (9th Cir. 2007).
[89] *See* Gershwin Publ'g Corp. v. Columbia Artists Mgmt., Inc., 443 F.2d 1159, 1162 (2d Cir. 1971).
[90] *See* Metro-Goldwyn-Mayer Studios Inc. v. Grokster, Ltd., 545 U.S. 913, 930 (2005). The *Grokster* court was unclear as to whether inducement was a third form of indirect liability or meant to replace traditional contributory liability. Most courts have read it as the former. *See* Greer v. Moon, 83 F.4th 1283, 1287 (10th Cir. 2023), *cert. denied*, 144 S. Ct. 2521 (2024).

generative AI system is operated, it is possible that none of those indirect liability theories will apply to AI system providers.

Vicarious infringement liability requires both the right and ability to control the infringing conduct and a direct financial interest in it. In essence, vicarious liability prevents businesses from failing to police copyright infringement by independent contractors or users where that infringement adds to the business's bottom line. Clearly AI system providers can police the outputs of their own systems, even though it would be challenging. But many providers will likely lack a "direct financial interest" in infringing outputs. There is case law to suggest that merely making a venue or service a more attractive location for infringement can provide the necessary financial interest, if the potential for infringement serves as a "draw" for additional customers or profits.[91] But more recent cases have held that the plaintiff must demonstrate a specific connection between infringing activity and increased revenue. In cases where the provider sells its services widely and charges a flat fee for access, the allure that tolerated infringement might have for some users has been deemed insufficient.[92] AI service providers would likely escape vicarious liability, assuming it is even possible, if their services are neither tailored in a way that draws additional paying subscribers looking for infringing generations nor billed in a way that benefits from high-volume infringing users.

Traditional contributory infringement liability penalizes materially contributing to known infringing activity. Again, the material contribution AI systems provide to users is obvious: it is the AI system itself, without which users could not generate much of anything. That leaves only the knowledge element. After *Sony v. Universal City Studios*, courts have consistently held that general knowledge that infringing uses are possible, or even likely, is not enough where the seller of a good or service has no reliable way to determine who among the user base might infringe.[93] The one exception to this principle exists where the defendant's device or service is not even capable of substantial non-infringing uses; in that case, almost every sale is for infringing use.[94] Otherwise, contributory liability requires knowledge that specific third parties will infringe.

That sort of specific knowledge can be imparted by notices sent from the copyright owner to the service provider.[95] In the scenario where users are liable for infringing outputs but AI system providers are not liable for copied inputs, AI system providers will likely have to respond to notices by eventually terminating the subscriptions of infringing users in order to avoid contributory liability.[96] Alternatively, courts might hold that provision of AI services to users without taking certain reasonable precautions to prevent foreseeable misuse subjects AI system providers to contributory liability.[97] Whatever advantages this approach would have in tailoring preventive measures to high-risk activities, courts have been unwilling in related contexts to abandon notice-based liability in favor of a judicially determined risk–utility balance.[98]

[91] *See* Fonovisa, Inc. v. Cherry Auction, Inc, 76 F.3d 259 (9th Cir. 1996); Polygram Int'l Publ'g, Inc. v. Nevada/TIG, Inc, 855 F. Supp. 1314, 1331 (D. Mass. 1994).

[92] Sony Music Ent. v. Cox Commc'ns, Inc., 93 F.4th 222, 231 (4th Cir. 2024); *see also* Ellison v. Robertson, 357 F.3d 1072, 1079 (9th Cir. 2004).

[93] Sony Corp. of Am. v. Universal City Studios, Inc., 464 U.S. 417, 439 (1984); Metro-Goldwyn-Mayer Studios Inc. v. Grokster, Ltd., 545 U.S. 913, 932–33 (2005).

[94] *Sony*, 464 U.S. at 442; *Grokster*, 545 U.S. at 931–32.

[95] Sony Music Ent. v. Cox Commc'ns, Inc., 93 F.4th 222, 233–34 (4th Cir. 2024).

[96] *See id.* at 236–37; UMG Recordings, Inc. v. Sinnott, 300 F. Supp. 2d 993, 1001 (E.D. Cal. 2004).

[97] *See* Peter S. Menell & David Nimmer, *Unwinding Sony*, 95 CALIF. L. REV. 941, 1018–23 (2007) (proposing indirect liability test based on products liability).

[98] *See* Capitol Records, LLC v. Vimeo, LLC, 826 F.3d 78, 96–97 (2d Cir. 2016) (declining to assess foreseeability of infringement for video service provider). *Vimeo* involved the service provider immunity under 17 U.S.C. § 512(c), which applies only to "storage at the direction of a user" and not content generated at the request of a user.

Finally, there's inducement: liability for intentionally encouraging or inducing acts of infringement.[99] Inducement requires affirmative acts of encouragement or instruction and will not lie for merely failing to take precautionary measures or for profiting from advertising on infringing content.[100] Most AI system providers would likely be able to avoid engaging in the direct acts of encouragement that would give rise to such liability. But a generative AI system provider that purposefully encouraged users to use its service to generate infringing content could be liable for inducing any acts of direct infringement that resulted.[101]

17.2.2 *Rights*

The question of who owns the rights to a computer-generated work is one of the oldest debated issues at the intersection of intellectual property and artificial intelligence.[102] AI-generated works can be equivalent in artistic or informational value to human-created works but protecting them under US copyright law poses both theoretical and legal difficulties. Theoretically, all the usual justifications for copyright protection dissipate for AI-generated works. No special economic incentive is needed to produce AI-generated works; the software and databases comprising the AI system are copyrightable, and once they have been created, the system needs no further incentive to create.[103] AI systems have no personality interest that would justify protecting their outputs with moral or other rights. They invest no labor in their creations and have no claims to justice. None of the usual arguments for exclusive rights apply to purely AI-generated works.

US law similarly ties copyright protection to human creation. First of all, the US Constitution limits the power of Congress to grant copyrights only to "Authors."[104] The Copyright Act contains a similar provision, limiting copyright protection to "works of authorship."[105] While neither term is defined, courts have long treated authorship as "synonymous with human creation."[106] One of the earliest Supreme Court cases concerning authorship through a mechanical device, *Burrow-Giles Lithographic Co. v. Sarony*, held that authorship flows from an "original mental conception" or a person's "intellectual invention," and not "mere mechanical reproduction."[107] Subsequent cases have refused to find works copyrightable when they were produced by non-human forces such as natural processes,[108] random variance,[109] animal behavior,[110] or even supernatural beings.[111] Although the initial owner of a work can be, under

[99] Metro-Goldwyn-Mayer Studios Inc. v. Grokster, Ltd., 545 U.S. 913, 936–37 (2005); Columbia Pictures Indus., Inc. v. Fung, 710 F.3d 1020, 1032 (9th Cir. 2013).
[100] *Grokster*, 545 U.S. at 939 n. 12, 940.
[101] *See, e.g.*, Greer v. Moon, 83 F.4th 1283, 1295 (10th Cir. 2023).
[102] *See* Karl F. Milde, Jr., *Can a Computer Be an "Author" or an "Inventor"?*, 51 J. PAT. OFF. SOC'Y 378 (1969).
[103] Thaler v. Perlmutter, 687 F. Supp. 3d 140, 147 (D.D.C. 2023). *But see* Robert C. Denicola, *Ex Machina: Copyright Protection for Computer-Generated Works*, 69 RUTGERS L. REV. 251, 273 (2016) (incentive needed to distribute).
[104] U.S. Const. art. I, s. 8, cl. 8.
[105] 17 U.S.C. § 102(a).
[106] *Perlmutter*, 687 F. Supp. 3d at 147.
[107] Burrow–Giles Lithographic Co. v. Sarony, 111 U.S. 53, 59, 60 (1884).
[108] *See* Kelley v. Chicago Park Dist., 635 F.3d 290, 304 (7th Cir. 2011).
[109] *See* Southco, Inc. v. Kanebridge Corp., 390 F.3d 276, 282–85 (3d Cir. 2004). *But see* Alan L. Durham, *The Random Muse: Authorship and Indeterminacy*, 44 WM. & MARY L. REV. 569, 636–38 (2002) (authorship compatible with significant indeterminacy).
[110] *See* Naruto v. Slater, 888 F.3d 418, 420 (9th Cir. 2018).
[111] *See* Urantia Found. v. Maaherra, 114 F.3d 955, 959 (9th Cir. 1997).

the work made for hire doctrine, a fictitious legal entity such as a corporation, human creativity must underlie such works.[112]

Relying on these authorities, the US Copyright Office has for decades taken the position that copyrightability requires human authorship, and in 2023 it applied that requirement to AI-generated works as well.[113] Thus, in a series of decisions beginning in 2022, the Copyright Office refused to register works where it held that AI-generated material had not been adequately disclaimed.[114] Although the Copyright Office's position has been criticized,[115] it is a defensible view of copyright's scope. Copyright is author-centered in a way that other intellectual property rights are not.[116] Identical works are treated differently under the law depending on their connection to the putative author.[117] Works produced entirely, or almost entirely, by an automated process, like objects found in nature, do not communicate any thought or expression from a human, and thus lack any justification for being removed from the public domain, even if they are indistinguishable from human creations.[118]

But the fact that the Copyright Office's position is defensible does not mean it is without difficulties. The most significant problem is one of line-drawing. A user of an AI system who enters a ten-word prompt ("write a story about a penguin who was a cowboy") and accepts the output has hardly contributed anything more to that output than a general idea.[119] But if the user instead writes an incredibly detailed prompt, or a long series of prompts, the prompts may be less like ideas and more like instructions – and sufficiently detailed instructions can constitute a work of authorship.[120] Even if the user's prompts are not detailed, a user's successive edits and additions to AI outputs may at some point amount to copyrightable expression. In other words, if generative AI systems are used as merely a tool to assist human creation, then the result should be copyrightable, just as Napoleon Sarony's photographic reproductions of the scene he created in his studio were copyrightable.[121]

The boundary between a human-controlled tool and a human-prompted creation engine is exceedingly fuzzy, however. The Copyright Office has issued guidance to registrants stating that the Office will consider whether "an AI technology determine[d] the expressive elements of its

[112] 17 U.S.C. § 201(b). Work made for hire status can be contracted into and around, which means that the parties involved in creating such works must at least have contractual capacity. *See id.* § 101 (definition of "work made for hire"), § 201(b). That would seem to rule out natural processes, random variations, animals, and machines.

[113] *See* Copyright Registration Guidance: Works Containing Material Generated by Artificial Intelligence, 88 Fed. Reg. 16,190, 16,192 (Mar. 16, 2023) (hereafter "Copyright AI Registration Guidance"); US Copyright Office, Compendium of US Copyright Office Practices §§ 306, 313.2 (3d ed. 2017).

[114] *See* Matt Blaszczyk, *Impossibility of Emergent Works' Protection in US and EU Copyright Law*, 25 N.C. J.L. & Tech. 1, 47–51 (2023) (discussing three rejections). For US works, copyright registration is a prerequisite for suit and for statutory damages and attorneys fees. *See* 17 U.S.C. §§ 411, 412.

[115] *See, e.g.*, Edward Lee, *The Code Red for Copyright Law*, 76 Fla. L. Rev. F. 1 (2024).

[116] *See* Mala Chatterjee, *Understanding Intellectual Property: Expression, Function, and Individuation*, 70 J. Copyr. Soc'y U.S.A. 57, 62 (2023) (arguing that "artistic works are author-individuated, while inventions are structure-individuated").

[117] *See, e.g.*, Sheldon v. Metro-Goldwyn Pictures Corp., 81 F.2d 49, 54 (2d Cir. 1936) (identical poem copyrightable or not depending on whether it originated with author); Jane C. Ginsburg & Luke Ali Budiardjo, *Authors and Machines*, 34 Berkeley Tech. L.J. 343, 447 (2019) (process of creation matters).

[118] *See* Christopher Buccafusco, *A Theory of Copyright Authorship*, 102 Va. L. Rev. 1229, 1232 (2016) (authorship requires an intent "to produce some mental effect in an audience").

[119] Contributing ideas and facts, even if essential to the end product, is not enough to make one an author. *See* Childress v. Taylor, 945 F.2d 500, 507 (2d Cir. 1991).

[120] Sheet music, for example, is a set of detailed instructions for how to perform a musical work. The Copyright Office, however, has expressed skepticism that even iterated prompts, sequentially revising the generated output, can result in human authorship. *See* Copyright AI Registration Guidance, 88 Fed. Reg. 16,190, 16,192 n. 30 (Mar. 16, 2023).

[121] Burrow–Giles Lithographic Co. v. Sarony, 111 U.S. 53, 60 (1884).

output," or whether instead the output was the result of the "author's 'own original mental conception, to which [the author] gave visible form.'"[122] It noted, however, that "[t]he answer will depend on the circumstances" and "is necessarily a case-by-case inquiry."[123] Several scholars have proposed that the crucial inquiry should identify the source of the creative choices contained within a work, an analysis similar to the famously difficult issue of proximate cause in tort law.[124] The Copyright Office is currently seeking comment on this and other AI-related issues.[125]

However it is carried out, a case-by-case inquiry based on vague standards is burdensome to complete. While courts are occasionally called upon to draw the line between idea and expression,[126] the Copyright Office will have to determine, for every registration where the applicant used an AI system, whether the output was the "author's own original mental conception" – a determination it has already made over a 100 times.[127] One way it has alleviated this burden is by putting the initial onus on the registrant to properly disclose any AI-generated content and "provide a brief explanation of the human author's contributions to the work."[128] Even so, a large number of disputes both at the registration stage and in litigation seems likely.

17.2.3 *The Future*

For both inputs and outputs, infringement and authorship, there are significant legal issues that lack clarity. At such times it is often lamented that technology moves faster than the law, or that Congress takes too long to pass legislation aimed at solving the destabilization of social and business norms caused by a rapidly adopted innovation. It took twenty years of drafts and hearings for Congress to pass the Copyright Act of 1976, and almost immediately it was undermined by the sudden appearance of copying machines and networked computers. The hope for legislation or court decisions that definitively resolve an emerging issue is probably in vain.

One issue that will likely require some legal innovation is the problem of AI tools that occasionally create substantially similar copies of works in training data. It seems AI system providers should have some incentive to reduce such copies, but not so much liability as to threaten the existence of generative AI or raise impenetrable barriers to entry. A second issue concerns the presumption of copyrightability that attaches to most minimally creative works. To the extent that such works can be produced cheaply and easily by generative AI, the benefits of exclusive rights disappear, leaving only the costs. However, deciding whether an output was AI-generated or human-generated could in many instances be a burdensome exercise. It may be

122 Copyright AI Registration Guidance, 88 Fed. Reg. at 16,192 (quoting *Burrow–Giles*, 111 U.S. at 60).

123 *Id.*

124 *See* Dan L. Burk, *Thirty-Six Views of Copyright Authorship, by Jackson Pollock*, 58 Hous. L. Rev. 263, 267 (2020); Daniel J. Gervais, *The Machine as Author*, 105 Iowa L. Rev. 2053, 2105 (2020); Shyamkrishna Balganesh, *Causing Copyright*, 117 Colum. L. Rev. 1, 8–9 (2017).

125 Copyright Office, Artificial Intelligence and Copyright, 88 Fed. Reg. 59,942 (Aug. 30, 2023). One possibility is that, in between human-created works and machine-generated works will be a third category, having some of the hallmarks of each: hybrid works. *See* Rebecca Crootof, Margot E. Kaminski & W. Nicholson Price, II, *Humans in the Loop*, 76 Vand. L. Rev. 429, 461 (2023). Ginsburg and Budiardjo have suggested that a modified concept of joint works might address this issue. *See* Ginsburg & Budiardjo, note 117 above, at 437–42.

126 *See* Nichols v. Universal Pictures Corp., 45 F.2d 119, 121 (2d Cir. 1930) ("Nobody has ever been able to fix that boundary, and nobody ever can.").

127 Letter from Shira Perlmutter, Register of Copyrights, to Sen. Chris Coons et al., at 3 (Feb. 23, 2024).

128 Copyright AI Registration Guidance, 88 Fed. Reg. at 16,193.

necessary to identify simple hallmarks of copyrightable or uncopyrightable material, such as particular categories of works, or methods of designating AI-generated content.

17.3 PATENTS

Copyrights are not the only area of IP law in the United States that will be disrupted by AI. The discovery of new inventions, and the process of obtaining patents and enforcing them, are also likely to be affected. Large pharmaceutical companies are using generative AI for drug discovery, and in the last few years have entered agreements to collaborate with major AI providers.[129] Generative AI promises to facilitate tasks such as generating likely treatment outcomes based on disease models or producing new gene-editing tools.[130] This surge in AI-assisted innovation extends well beyond pharmaceutical firms. By 2020, patents based on AI technologies were being filed in more than half of all patent technology subclasses at the US Patent & Trademark Office (PTO).[131]

Unlike with copyright, the use of generative AI tools is not likely to lead to significant disputes over patent infringement in the near future. Until generative AI is incorporated with fully autonomous systems, it can only produce information, not implement it. Although AI might be capable of generating a process or designing an article of manufacture, infringement requires actually making, using, selling, or importing one. For the immediate future there will be humans in that loop.[132]

Nevertheless, the widespread use of AI tools is likely to lead to a number of patent law issues. First, as with copyrights and authorship, the issue of whether a machine-assisted invention qualifies for patenting may arise. Second, generative AI may expand the prior art, making it more difficult to patent any invention. Third, patenting generative AI technologies themselves might be challenging under current doctrine. Finally, generative AI may have impacts on both examination and enforcement.

17.3.1 *Inventions*

The use of AI systems to generate inventions has led to questions about whether an AI system can be an "inventor" under the US Patent Act, and if not, whether inventions produced using material generated by AI are patentable at all. The answer to the first question is, at the moment, unequivocally no – the US Court of Appeals for the Federal Circuit, which hears all patent appeals, has concluded that "the Patent Act requires that inventors must be natural persons; that is, human beings."[133] "Inventor" is defined under the Act as "the individual . . . or individuals . . . who invented or discovered the subject matter of the invention,"[134] and US case law is clear

[129] Annelise Gilbert et al., *AI Helps Pharma Find New Drugs but Imperils Lucrative Patents*, Bloomberg L. News, Apr. 4, 2024.

[130] Nic Fleming, *How Artificial Intelligence Is Changing Drug Discovery*, 557 Nature S55-S57 (2018); Ewen Callaway, *"ChatGPT for CRISPR" Creates New Gene-Editing Tools*, Nature, Apr. 29, 2024.

[131] *See* Nicholas A. Pairolero, Economist, US PTO, *Artificial Intelligence (AI) Trends in US Patents*, Artificial Intelligence and Emerging Technology Inaugural Stakeholder Meeting, at 9 (June 29, 2022).

[132] *See* 35 U.S.C. § 271; Crootof, Kaminski & Price, note 125 above.

[133] Thaler v. Vidal, 43 F.4th 1207, 1210 (Fed. Cir. 2022), *cert. denied*, 143 S. Ct. 1783 (2023). The case was brought by Dr. Stephen Thaler, who has pursued similar patent and copyright claims in a number of countries. *See* Richard M. Assmus et al., *Can AI Be an Inventor? The US, UK, EPO, and German Approach*, Mayer Brown, Jan. 9, 2024.

[134] 35 U.S.C. § 100(f).

that, in statutes, "'individual' ordinarily means a human being."[135] As with copyrights, it is uncertain that Congress would even have the power to grant patents where no individual is involved, given the constitutional limitation of patent rights to "Inventors."[136] And, according to the US PTO, the policy justification for patents is missing in the case of AI-generated inventions: the patent system, like copyrights, is "designed to encourage *human* ingenuity."[137] AI systems do not need to be incentivized to solve problems, nor do AI systems have natural rights or personal interests in having their contributions protected.[138]

More difficult is the question of what happens when a human uses an AI system to assist in creating an invention. The US PTO recently released guidance on this issue, stating that the mere use of an AI system to invent does not undermine the contributions of human inventors or otherwise make the invention unpatentable.[139] Nor must it necessarily be disclaimed or disclosed.[140] But the PTO, analogizing the use of AI systems to joint inventors, placed a limit on when a human operator of an AI system can claim to have invented its output. Entering a prompt is not enough;[141] each named inventor must "share ... in the conception of [the] claimed invention," meaning that each "must have significantly contributed to the 'definite and permanent idea of the complete and operative invention as it is thereafter applied in practice.'"[142]

The PTO's limitations, if applied, could make some AI-assisted inventions unpatentable for lack of an inventor. According to the PTO, in the case of AI-assisted invention, a human's "significant contribution" cannot take place after a "complete and operative invention" is output from the system. Reducing a fully conceived invention to practice will not suffice.[143] Nor, claims the PTO, is perceiving the significance of an AI output enough to conceive of it as an invention. "[A] natural person who merely recognizes and appreciates the output of an AI system as an invention, particularly when the properties and utility of the output are apparent to those of ordinary skill, is not necessarily an inventor."[144]

Dan Burk has noted the tension in granting patent rights to accidental inventors but not to those who recognize an invention in the output of generative AI.[145] In both cases, there is a failure to conceive of an invention until it is reduced to practice, but in the case of accidental inventions, that has never been a bar to patentability.[146] Patents, unlike copyrights, do not depend on the process of creation; the only question is whether the inventor solved a problem.[147] Burk argues that viewing AI systems as different than any other human-designed and

[135] *Vidal*, 43 F.4th at 1211 (quoting *Mohamad v. Palestinian Auth.*, 566 U.S. 449, 454 (2012)).

[136] U.S. CONST. art. I, s. 8, cl. 8.

[137] US PTO, Inventorship Guidance for AI-Assisted Inventions, 89 Fed. Reg. 10,043, 10,046 (Feb. 13, 2024) (hereafter "PTO, AI-Assisted Inventions").

[138] However, inventions still need to be commercialized, providing at least one reason for the grant of exclusive rights that has greater bite for patents than it does for copyrights. *See* Gaétan de Rassenfosse, Adam B. Jaffe & Melissa F. Wasserman, *AI-Generated Inventions: Implications for the Patent System*, 96 S. CAL. L. REV. 1453, 1459–61 (2023).

[139] PTO, AI-Assisted Inventions, 89 Fed. Reg. at 10,046.

[140] *Id.* at 10,049. *But see* Ryan Abbott, *Machines of Ordinary Skill in the Art*, LANDSLIDE, May/June 2019, at 30, 31 (proposing disclosure requirement for use of AI).

[141] PTO, AI-Assisted Inventions, 89 Fed. Reg. at 10,048.

[142] *Id.* at 10,047 (quoting Manual of Pat. Exam. Procedures (MPEP) 2138.04(I); Townsend v. Smith, 36 F.2d 292, 295 (C.C.P.A. 1929)).

[143] *See id.*

[144] *Id.* at 10,048.

[145] Burk, note 8 above, at 304–05.

[146] *Id.* at 308.

[147] *See* Chatterjee, note 116 above, at 62.

human-operated tool, such as a screwdriver, is a symptom of a "magical worldview" that obscures the amount of human involvement in AI creation and use.[148]

It may be the rare invention that raises a serious question as to whether there is an identifiable inventor. The PTO, unlike the Copyright Office, has determined that in most cases, there will be no need to disclose the use of AI tools in the course of invention, unless the information "raises a prima facie case of unpatentability," such as "evidence that demonstrates a named inventor did not significantly contribute to the invention because the person's purported contribution(s) was made by an AI system."[149] Only surprising results emerging fully formed from an AI system in response to a seemingly unrelated prompt are likely to present such an issue.

17.3.2 *Patentability*

The rapid rise of artificial intelligence poses two sorts of challenges for patent law and practice. First, there is the challenge that the use of AI tools poses to the patentability of inventions in general. AI-generated prior art might make novelty more difficult to establish. Similarly, the increased capacity for invention released by generative AI might make more inventions obvious. Finally, the use of AI search tools might make patents and inventions easier to find, both during the examination process and for purposes of enforcement.

But in addition to its effects on patent practice, artificial intelligence is itself a technological breakthrough that has unleashed an explosion of patent applications claiming AI as an element.[150] Due to difficulties in determining, for example, how a model trained through machine learning operates, inventions claiming the use of AI as an element may face barriers to patentability, particularly with respect to disclosure and patentable subject matter.

17.3.2.1 Novelty

To be patentable under the current US Patent Act, a claimed invention must be novel, which now means that it must not have been disclosed to the public more than one year prior to the application filing date, or disclosed first to the public at any time by someone who obtained the subject matter of the invention independently of the inventor.[151] As a rapidly developing field, inventions claiming AI are not likely to have any special difficulty meeting the novelty requirement for a US patent.[152] But generative AI systems could pose a challenge for the novelty of *other* inventions. Users of such systems could try to invalidate patents in advance by generating huge numbers of potential innovations, such as molecules for new drugs. Indeed, such efforts are already underway.[153]

[148] *See* Burk, note 8 above, at 309–10 (citing M.C. Elish & danah boyd, *Situating Methods in the Magic of Big Data and AI*, 85 Commun. Monographs 57, 62–63 (2017)); *see also* W. Michael Schuster, *Artificial Intelligence and Patent Ownership*, 75 Wash. & Lee L. Rev. 1945, 1987 (2019).

[149] PTO, AI-Assisted Inventions, 89 Fed. Reg. at 10,049.

[150] *See* Office of the Chief Economist, US PTO, *Inventing AI*, IP Data Highlights, Oct. 2020, at 2.

[151] *See* 35 U.S.C. § 102(a)(1), (b)(1). A patent applicant must also be the first to file for the claimed invention. *See id.* § 102(a)(2), (b)(2). Prior to Mar. 16, 2013, a successful patent applicant had to be the first to *invent* the claimed invention. *See* MPEP § 2132 (Oct. 2019).

[152] Like other innovations, however, AI developed incrementally, which means that much of it may no longer be novel. *See* David Kappos & Asa Kling, *Ground-Level Pressing Issues at the Intersection of AI and IP*, 22 Colum. Sci. & Tech. L. Rev. 263, 270–71 (2021).

[153] *See* Annelise Gilbert et al., *AI Helps Pharma Find New Drugs but Imperils Lucrative Patents*, Bloomberg L. News, Apr. 4, 2024; Dennis Crouch, *Discerning Signal from Noise: Navigating the Flood of AI-Generated Prior Art*, Patently-O, Apr. 30, 2024.

Attempts to preempt patents in this way depend on generating a stupendous number of random combinations of elements and posting them on a publicly accessible website. Since most of the material posted on such a site is gibberish, no person who values their time will actually spend time reading it. Nevertheless, such material could fall within the definition of a "printed publication" and constitute prior art, if through "reasonable diligence" it could be found by "interested members of the relevant public."[154] For example, if the site is indexed by search engines, even if no one had actually visited the page, it might qualify as available through reasonable diligence.[155] And while unadorned generated claims are unlikely to be enabling, the PTO and courts will presume prior art is enabled until it is demonstrated otherwise.[156]

The rise of prior art generation services such as "All Prior Art" puts pressure on the low threshold for anticipation in existing doctrine.[157] The PTO has recently issued a request for comments on this issue, asking, among other things, "[a]t what point, if ever, could the volume of AI-generated prior art be sufficient to detract from the public accessibility of prior art?"[158] One possible adaptation would be to incorporate not simply the probability of an interested member of the public finding a given prior art reference, but also the probability of *reading* it. For example, Ben Hattenbach and Joshua Glucoft have proposed "focus[ing] the inquiry on what resources people of skill in the pertinent art would actually look to, and what they would not reasonably consider, in determining what constitutes prior art to a particular invention."[159] References in forms that humans tend to actually read – doctoral theses, online magazines, product manuals, posters – would be presumed to be read once found by the interested audience. The profferer of random generations from an AI system, however, would have to make an initial showing of an audience.

17.3.2.2 Nonobviousness

A claimed invention can also be denied a patent if it "would have been obvious before the effective filing date . . . to a person having ordinary skill in the art to which the claimed invention pertains."[160] Even if the patent applicant was the first to devise a solution to some problem, it will be unpatentable if the solution was well within the grasp of the average person working in that field, so that the exclusive rights of a patent were unnecessary to bring about the invention.[161] However, in many fields, persons having ordinary skill in the art (or "PHOSITAs") have or will soon have generative AI tools available to them, tools that promise to greatly expand the connections and innovative leaps they are capable of, and the number of attempts at a solution they will be able to make. Some commentators have argued that generative AI thus threatens to greatly increase the nonobviousness threshold, perhaps to the point of making it

154 Valve Corp. v. Ironburg Inventions Ltd., 8 F.4th 1364, 1376 (Fed. Cir. 2021) (quoting *GoPro, Inc. v. Contour IP Holding LLC*, 908 F.3d 690, 695 (Fed. Cir. 2018)).
155 Indeed, even indexing is not required. *See* Voter Verified, Inc. v. Premier Election Sols., Inc., 698 F.3d 1374, 1380 (Fed. Cir. 2012).
156 *See* In re Antor Media Corp., 689 F.3d 1282, 1288 (Fed. Cir. 2012).
157 *See* All Prior Art, https://allpriorart.com.
158 US PTO, Request for Comments Regarding the Impact of the Proliferation of Artificial Intelligence on Prior Art, 89 Fed. Reg. 34,217, 34,220 (Apr. 30, 2024).
159 Ben Hattenbach & Joshua Glucoft, *Patents in an Era of Infinite Monkeys and Artificial Intelligence*, 19 Stan. Tech. L. Rev. 32, 42 (2015).
160 35 U.S.C. § 103.
161 Patents incentivize low-probability efforts that pay off, or, as Joel Mokyr once put it, when "a crackpot hits the jackpot." Joel Mokyr, The Lever of Riches 252 (1990).

insurmountable.[162] If any solution could have been generated by a sufficiently powerful generative AI system, then any solution could have been invented by a PHOSITA using such a system before the inventor did, and everything will be obvious.[163]

The degree of disruption generative AI will cause for the nonobviousness requirement has probably been overstated, however. While generative AI tools have the potential to increase the creative capabilities of ordinary individuals, it is unlikely that all the world's problems will be instantaneously solvable. As Dan Burk has noted, "machine learning systems find only what humans design them to find, within statistical parameters that humans must specify."[164] AI may excel at finding connections and generating structures, but in most fields it will remain far from obvious what sort of connections and structures are the right ones to request, or to pursue.[165]

Some have suggested that the PHOSITA standard should be revised to account for the use of AI tools,[166] but it is not clear that such a revision is necessary. A PHOSITA is *already* presumed to use the tools and techniques common in the art with an ordinary degree of skill.[167] The PHOSITA of the future in many fields will be a person having ordinary skill in using the AI tools that are standard for that art. But skill is still likely to matter in solving problems, even with the assistance of generative AI. Already, artists, law students, and others are discovering that crafting prompts to get generative AI to produce sought-after results is no easy task. Part of an inventor's extraordinary skill in the art may be the skill of prompting generative AI tools to find solutions that others are not able to.[168]

Generative AI tools are also likely to make it easier to attempt solutions to some problems in a way that would heighten the number of "tries" that it would be reasonable to attempt under the "obvious-to-try" version of obviousness.[169] But that number will still be limited, because even generative AI cannot produce infinite outputs, nor could any human read them all. The state of the art will still have to give the PHOSITA some guidance as to how to use the AI system to find the solution, such that a limited number of "tries" with the AI system would produce a reasonable expectation of success of finding the correct one.

17.3.2.3 Disclosure

A patent application must adequately disclose the invention, providing a written description of the invention that demonstrates to a PHOSITA that the applicant invented what is claimed, and is detailed enough to enable the PHOSITA to make and use the full scope of the claimed invention.[170]

162 *See* Ryan Abbott, *Everything Is Obvious*, 66 UCLA L. REV. 2, 8 (2019).

163 *See id.* The PTO has requested comment on the issue of nonobviousness as well as novelty. *See* US PTO, Request for Comments Regarding the Impact of the Proliferation of Artificial Intelligence on Prior Art, 89 Fed. Reg. 34,217, 34,220 (Apr. 30, 2024).

164 Burk, note 8 above, at 309.

165 *Id.* at 309–10.

166 *See* de Rassenfosse et al., note 138 above, at 1465; Shlomit Yanisky-Ravid & Regina Jin, *Summoning a New Artificial Intelligence Patent Model: In the Age of Crisis*, 2021 MICH. ST. L. REV. 811, 836; Abbott, note 162 above, at 35–36.

167 *See* KSR Int'l Co. v. Teleflex Inc., 550 U.S. 398, 417 (2007) (use of known technique can make an invention obvious); Ball Aerosol & Specialty Container, Inc. v. Ltd. Brands, Inc., 555 F.3d 984, 993 (Fed. Cir. 2009) (PHOSITA uses "routine steps" when motivated to solve problems).

168 De Rassenfosse, Jaffe, and Wasserman note that generative AI tools may lead to an expansion of what qualifies as "analogous art," because it would be feasible for a generative AI tool to produce solutions drawn from all of the data it was trained on. *See* de Rassenfosse et al., note 138 above, at 1465.

169 *See KSR*, 550 U.S. at 421.

170 35 U.S.C. § 112(a); Ariad Pharms., Inc. v. Eli Lilly & Co., 598 F.3d 1336, 1351 (Fed. Cir. 2010); Amgen Inc. v. Sanofi, 143 S. Ct. 1243, 1254 (2023).

Applications claiming AI as an element may have trouble meeting these requirements due to what has been called the "black box" problem – the fact that the internal operations of a generative AI model trained by machine learning are opaque to the AI system provider.[171] If the inventor is unsure exactly how the AI works, it will be difficult to describe it, or to enable another person to make or use the invention.

Several commentators have proposed that one way of dealing with this issue would be to permit a public deposit of an AI system similar to that used for microorganisms, plants, and nucleotide or amino acid sequences.[172] But such a deposit requirement would be fairly burdensome to comply with, requiring the deposit of "terabytes of data," much of it "proprietary, confidential, [or] personal data."[173] Keith Robinson has proposed a different solution to at least the enablement problem, which is simply to narrow the scope of the claims to fit within what can be enabled in the specification. As Robinson observes, claims are almost never invalidated for lack of enablement. Rather, the enablement doctrine's primary function is to force patent applicants to draft their claims narrowly. Robinson suggests that that is a particularly apt result for a nascent field such as AI.[174]

However, as David Kappos and Asa Kling point out, AI systems have another feature that weighs against the viability of narrow claim scope: "AI changes over time to increase its efficiency and enhance its performance," sometimes "in ways not understood by the AI's inventors."[175] The potential for an AI invention to adapt would encourage broader, not narrower, claims, in order to ensure that the invention stays within the scope of the claim language. But in addition to difficulties meeting the written description and enablement requirements, broad claims for an AI invention may have problems qualifying as patentable subject matter. Under the Supreme Court's decision in *Alice Corp. v. CLS Bank International*, courts have rejected numerous computer-implemented inventions where they have been found to be directed to an unpatentable abstract idea, one supplemented with only "well-understood, routine, conventional activity."[176] AI innovators have survived such challenges when they have "highlight[ed] the specific technical applications of their inventions in their patent applications," such as "specific and unconventional machine learning techniques."[177] Such narrow claims may reduce the incentive to seek patents at all.[178]

17.3.3 *Examination and Enforcement*

Finally, AI tools promise to be extraordinarily helpful in both patent examination and patent enforcement. The PTO has already developed tools to search prior art and classify patent documents.[179] The use of such tools could assist examiners in finding more relevant prior art

[171] *See* Yanisky-Ravid & Jin, note 166 above, at 837–38.

[172] *See id.* at 853–54; Burk, note 8 above, at 313; Tabrez Y. Ebrahim, *Artificial Intelligence Inventions and Patent Disclosure*, 125 Penn St. L. Rev. 147, 215–18 (2020); MPEP §§ 2401–35 (July 2022).

[173] Kappos & Kling, note 152 above, at 273.

[174] W. Keith Robinson, *Enabling Artificial Intelligence*, 60 Hous. L. Rev. 331, 353, 361 (2022).

[175] Kappos & Kling, note 152 above, at 272.

[176] Alice Corp. v. CLS Bank Int'l, 573 U.S. 208, 217–18 (2014); Mayo Collaborative Servs. v. Prometheus Labs., Inc., 566 U.S. 66, 73 (2012).

[177] Kappos & Kling, note 152 above, at 272; Lily Li & Steven M. McKeever, *AI Trends for 2024: The "Abstract Ideas" behind Artificial Intelligence Inventions*, Mofo Tech Blog (Feb. 7, 2024).

[178] *See* Clark Asay, *Artificial Stupidity*, 61 Wm. & Mary L. Rev. 1187, 1204–07 (2020).

[179] Drew Hirshfeld, *Artificial Intelligence Tools at the USPTO*, Director's Blog (Mar. 18, 2021); *see also* Arti K. Rai, *Machine Learning at the Patent Office: Lessons for Patents and Administrative Law*, 104 Iowa L. Rev. 2617, 2639–40 (2019) (warning that transparency might lead to gaming).

that might result in more rejections. But even AI-assisted rejections will increase the workload of patent examiners, which may not result in overall efficiency gains for the patent system given that most patents are never enforced.[180] Even better AI search tools may be in the hands of patent attorneys and may allow for more accurate prior art searches in litigation.[181]

AI tools might also significantly alter the ways in which patents are enforced or avoided. Machine learning in particular has the potential to make vast numbers of patents easier to find and potential infringing activities easier to identify. As Janet Freilich has argued, such developments will increase the salience of granted patents, whether they are strong candidates for enforcement or not.[182] This increased salience could "enhance ... the potential *in terrorem* effect of patents" and motivate firms to avoid patents that previously would have been ignored.[183] Whether normatively desirable or not, a world in which more patents are apparent is different from a world based on "rational ignorance," and it may be a disruptive transition.

17.4 OTHER IP RIGHTS

Generative AI poses particular theoretical problems for copyrights and patents under US law, given that both are founded on the principle of incentivizing or rewarding individual creativity. Other IP rights are based more directly on the commercial value of the intangible asset, and thus generative AI poses less of a doctrinal conundrum. Trademarks and rights of publicity give exclusive rights to certain commercial associations being made with the owner's signifiers. Trade secrets protect the commercial value of information kept internal to a business. While generative AI does not ostensibly undermine the legal basis for any of these rights, it may make enforcement significantly more challenging. This chapter concludes by examining the impact of generative AI on these three areas.

17.4.1 *Right of Publicity*

The so-called right of publicity – also known as misappropriation of name or likeness, or, in sports and entertainment contexts, name, image, and likeness (NIL) rights – protects a person's name or likeness from being used without their consent for commercial purposes.[184] The typical right-of-publicity violation involves the use of a person's name or image in an advertisement, implying that the person endorses the product or service. As yet, there is no federal law providing for a right of publicity, and as a result, the scope of the right and its limitations are defined entirely by varying state laws. In many jurisdictions, there are *two* rights of publicity, one legislatively defined and one judicially defined.[185] Although the right of publicity originated

[180] *See* Mark A. Lemley, *Rational Ignorance at the Patent Office*, 95 Nw. U. L. Rev. 1495, 1497 (2001). *But see* John F. Duffy, *Reasoned Decisionmaking vs. Rational Ignorance at the Patent Office*, 104 Iowa L. Rev. 2351, 2386 (2019) (administrative law requires reasoned decisionmaking).

[181] *See* Nicholas Martin & George Zalepa, *AI Will Soon Streamline Litigation Practice for Patent Attorneys* Bloomberg L. News, Dec. 7, 2023.

[182] *See* Janet Freilich, *Patents' New Salience*, 109 Va. L. Rev. 595, 638–39 (2023).

[183] *Id.* at 628.

[184] *See, e.g.*, Restatement (Second) of Torts § 652C (ALI 1977) (subjecting "[o]ne who appropriates to his own use or benefit the name or likeness of another" to liability). As originally formulated, the Second Restatement did not require a commercial purpose and included cases of impersonation within its ambit. *See id.* cmt. b, illus. 3–5. Such cases are now extremely rare.

[185] *See, e.g.*, Midler v. Ford Motor Co., 849 F.2d 460 (9th Cir. 1988) (rejecting statutory claim but allowing common law claim to proceed). *See generally* Jennifer E. Rothman, *Rothman's Roadmap to the Right of Publicity*, https://rightofpublicityroadmap.com.

as a privacy right protecting ordinary individuals,[186] it has morphed into the basis for lucrative licensing arrangements for celebrities.[187] In the United States, it is the right of publicity that underlies endorsement deals that athletes or actors enter into promoting various goods or services.

Unlike with copyrights, there is little prospect of generative AI systems using existing names and likenesses to instantaneously create new ones that compete with the originals. The most valuable rights of publicity belong to celebrities, and while artificial personas can be created, generative AI does not particularly hasten the process of building a reputation for such personas, nor would fictional personas have any enforceable rights.[188] In any event, as discussed below, there is little prospect of being able to assert right-of-publicity claims for uses in training data. Rather, the challenge generative AI is likely to pose for the right of publicity concerns the number of infringing *outputs*, as the power of generating realistic depictions of celebrities and others falls into the hands of the average person.

17.4.1.1 Names or Images as Inputs

To generate images, audio files, videos, or text incorporating a person's name or likeness, a generative AI model must be trained on materials containing the name or likeness of the affected individual. However, unlike copyright owners, individuals likely have no claim for right-of-publicity violations when materials depicting them are used as training data. Courts in several cases have held that, where a person's name or likeness is used for the value of the information itself, rather than as a means of selling something else, the use does not violate the right of publicity. For example, collecting someone's name for inclusion on a marketing list that is then sold to advertisers does not implicate the right of publicity.[189] The same theory would appear to bar claims for the use of names, voices, images, and other materials as training data for a general-purpose generative AI model. In such a case, the name or likeness would only be used for the informational value of the token itself and would not be "a misappropriation of their name or likeness to advertise or promote a separate product or service."[190]

17.4.1.2 Names or Images as Outputs

Outputs are a different matter. Whether the use of a person's name, image, voice, or other likeness violates the person's right of publicity will depend on exactly how it is used. Where a user of an AI system generates a video advertisement with a well-known celebrity in it, that will be a violation of the celebrity's right of publicity unless done with permission.[191] Doctrinally, that is a simple case.[192] Still, there are two complications. First, the sheer numbers of such

[186] Pavesich v. New England Life Ins. Co., 50 S.E. 68, 80 (Ga. 1905).

[187] *See* Mark Bartholomew, *A Right Is Born: Celebrity, Property, and Postmodern Lawmaking*, 44 Conn. L. Rev. 301 (2012).

[188] The real-life actors who portray fictional characters may have such claims, but the fictional characters themselves do not. *See* Wendt v. Host International, Inc., 125 F.3d 806 (9th Cir. 1997); McFarland v. Miller, 14 F.3d 912 (3d Cir. 1993); Dawn H. Dawson, Note, *The Final Frontier: Right of Publicity in Fictional Characters*, 2001 U. Ill. L. Rev. 635, 666.

[189] Dwyer v. Am. Exp. Co., 273 Ill. App. 3d 742, 749 (1995); Brooks v. Thomson Reuters Corp., No. 21-cv-01418, 2021 WL 3621837, at *4–5 (N.D. Cal. Aug. 16, 2021).

[190] In re Hearst Commc'ns State Right of Publicity Statute Cases, 632 F. Supp. 3d 616, 623 (S.D.N.Y. 2022).

[191] *See* Tiffany Hsu & Yiwen Lu, *No, That's Not Taylor Swift Peddling Le Creuset Cookware*, N.Y. Times, Jan. 9, 2024, at B1; Derrick Bryson Taylor, *Tom Hanks Warns of Dental Ad Using A.I. Version of Him*, N.Y. Times, Oct. 2, 2023.

[192] *See, e.g.*, Motschenbacher v. R. J. Reynolds Tobacco Co., 498 F.2d 821 (9th Cir. 1974).

videos may overwhelm any efforts to take them down. If that happens, and if deepfake advertisements make their way into widely viewed media, the value of a celebrity's right-of-publicity rights may decrease because advertisers will be less willing to pay for endorsements that viewers are unlikely to believe are real.

The other complication is that not all troubling digital impersonations violate the right of publicity. Advertisements with generated celebrities do, but spoofed political messages, or faked news videos, or manufactured pornography likely do not. Such content is particularly corrosive of both celebrities' reputations and general trust in media, but the right of publicity, with its focus on commercial appropriation, likely has no application to those harms. Other remedies will be needed.[193]

A more difficult question is posed by new *artistic* works created using a person's identity, such as a new episode of a television show featuring the original actors, or a new song featuring a singer's voice, or a work of visual art in a recognizable style – works that involve what Eric Johnson has called "virtual impressment."[194] Such a work may fall outside various right-of-publicity statutes if it is not created for the purpose of advertising or selling goods or services.[195] But the common law right of publicity is more capacious, and as it has been interpreted reaches any "appropriation of the attributes of one's identity," at least if it is not entirely noncommercial.[196]

Nevertheless, a right-of-publicity claim based on the creation of a new work in the artist's style, or featuring a generated version of a performer, would face three significant hurdles. First, the common law right of publicity contains within it an important exception for "transformative" uses of a person's identity. Second, such claims, even if supported by a state statute such as Tennessee's recent ELVIS Act, may be preempted by the Copyright Act.[197] And third, the internet service provider (ISP) immunity under 47 USC § 230 may bar any right-of-publicity claim against a generative AI system provider, leaving only the individual user.

First, many states recognize a defense for right-of-publicity claims somewhat similar to copyright's fair use defense, applying where the defendant has made a "transformative" use of the plaintiff's identity. A transformative use is one where the celebrity likeness is merely "one of the 'raw materials' from which an original work is synthesized" rather than "the very sum and substance of the work in question"; where the resulting product "has become primarily the defendant's own expression rather than the celebrity's likeness."[198] Among other things, courts examine whether the primary purpose and appeal of the defendant's work is to depict the celebrity's likeness or convey the defendant's expression.[199] In a number of cases where the plaintiff's likeness is used to tell a larger story, defendants have prevailed on a transformative use defense.[200] Where the plaintiff's identity is less connected to the message of the defendant's

[193] Tennessee's recently adopted Ensuring Likeness, Voice, and Image Security (ELVIS) Act of 2024, Pub. Ch. No. 588, would prohibit any unauthorized distribution of a person's name or likeness, including voice, where it is not "in connection with any news, public affairs, or sports broadcast or account" or "[f]or purposes of comment, criticism, scholarship, satire, or parody." *Id.* § 10.

[194] Eric E. Johnson, *Disentangling the Right of Publicity*, 111 Nw. U. L. Rev. 891, 934–38 (2017). For an example, see Chloe Veltman, *When You Realize Your Favorite New Song Was Written and Performed by … AI*, NPR, Apr. 21, 2023.

[195] *See* Cal. Civ. Code § 3344(a); Wis. Stat. § 995.50(2)(am)2.

[196] Midler v. Ford Motor Co., 849 F.2d 460, 463 (9th Cir. 1988); *see also* Restatement (Second) of Torts § 652C (ALI 1977).

[197] Ensuring Likeness, Voice, and Image Security (ELVIS) Act of 2024, Tenn. Pub. Ch. No. 588.

[198] Comedy III Prods., Inc. v. Gary Saderup, Inc., 25 Cal. 4th 387, 406 (2001).

[199] *See* In re NCAA Student-Athlete Name & Likeness Licensing Litig., 724 F.3d 1268, 1274 (9th Cir. 2013).

[200] De Havilland v. FX Networks, LLC, 21 Cal. App. 5th 845 (2018); Winter v. DC Comics, 30 Cal. 4th 881, 890 (2003).

work, or the defendant's work is solely to depict the plaintiff, transformativeness defenses have failed.[201]

Even if the defendant does not have a transformativeness defense, a right of publicity claim seeking to prohibit copying or distributing a work featuring the plaintiff may be preempted by the Copyright Act. Section 301(a) of the Copyright Act preempts any statutory or common law right that is "equivalent to any of the exclusive rights within the general scope of copyright." Courts have held that a state law right is not equivalent to copyright if it has an "extra element which changes the nature of the action."[202] The additional element has to not simply exist, but "change ... the nature of the action so that it is qualitatively different from a copyright infringement claim."[203] In right-of-publicity cases, claims seeking to bar the distribution of works that the plaintiff participated in creating, such as sound recordings or television broadcasts, have been held to lack an extra element and therefore be preempted.[204]

In the case of AI-generated works, the users of AI systems would not be circulating existing works, but rather creating new ones. Many of the cases finding a lack of an extra element would therefore not be directly on point. But preemption also applies implicitly to the extent of any conflict between state law and federal law.[205] If celebrities can sue over generated works that would constitute a fair use of the copyrighted works they appeared in, such as noncommercial fan fiction, or parody songs, or political commentary, a right of publicity claim could "clash ... with the balance struck by Congress" in allowing such uses under the Copyright Act.[206]

Finally, even if users could be held liable for violating rights of publicity through generated content, AI system providers may be immune under 47 USC § 230(c)(1), originally passed as part of the Communications Decency Act. Broadly speaking, Section 230 immunizes ISPs from claims that seek to hold them liable for republishing or distributing the content of messages posted on their services by their users. The extent to which that immunity would apply to right-of-publicity claims is uncertain, however. First of all, there is an exception to Section 230 that explicitly carves out "any law pertaining to intellectual property."[207] It is unclear whether that exception applies to *state* intellectual property laws, and it is further unclear whether the right of publicity is properly classified as an intellectual property law, or, as it was originally conceived, as a privacy tort.[208] The federal courts of appeal are currently split on the question of whether Section 230 immunizes ISPs from right-of-publicity claims or not.[209]

If state right-of-publicity claims are not excluded under Section 230(e)(2), generative AI providers may have difficulty meeting the conditions for immunity. Service providers are immune from a claim under Section 230(c)(1) only if the claim is against "(1) a provider or

[201] *See* Doe v. TCI Cablevision, 110 S.W.3d 363, 374 (Mo. 2003); Parks v. LaFace Records, 329 F.3d 437, 461 (6th Cir. 2003).

[202] Del Madera Props. v. Rhodes & Gardner, Inc., 820 F.2d 973, 977 (9th Cir. 1987); *see also* ProCD, Inc. v. Zeidenberg, 86 F.3d 1447, 1454 (7th Cir. 1996).

[203] *In re* Jackson, 972 F.3d 25, 43–44 (2d Cir. 2020).

[204] *See* Melendez v. Sirius XM Radio, Inc., 50 F.4th 294 (2d Cir. 2022); Dryer v. Nat'l Football League, 814 F.3d 938, 942 (8th Cir. 2016); Laws v. Sony Music Ent., Inc., 448 F.3d 1134 (9th Cir. 2006).

[205] *See* In re *Jackson*, 972 F.3d at 34.

[206] Bonito Boats, Inc. v. Thunder Craft Boats, Inc., 489 U.S. 141, 152 (1989); *see also* Vault Corp. v. Quaid Software Ltd., 847 F.2d 255, 270 (5th Cir. 1988); X Corp. v. Bright Data Ltd., 733 F. Supp. 3d 832, 852 (N.D. Cal. 2024).

[207] 47 U.S.C. § 230(e)(2).

[208] *See* Perfect 10, Inc. v. CCBill LLC, 488 F.3d 1102, 1119 (9th Cir. 2007); Ratermann v. Pierre Fabre USA, Inc., 651 F. Supp. 3d 657, 668–69 (S.D.N.Y. 2023).

[209] *Compare CCBill*, 488 F.2d at 1119 (within immunity), *with* Hepp v. Facebook, 14 F.4th 204, 214 (3d Cir. 2021) (outside immunity).

user of an interactive computer service (2) whom a plaintiff seeks to treat, under a state law cause of action, as a publisher or speaker (3) of information provided by another information content provider."[210] Generative AI systems are certainly interactive computer services, and a right-of-publicity claim against an AI provider would be seeking to hold the provider liable as a publisher of infringing content. The only question is whether that content – the generated image, song, video, or other material – is provided by "another information content provider," namely users, or provided by the generative AI system itself.[211]

Responsibility for the outputs of generative AI systems returns us to the difficult questions posed above for copyright infringement and ownership. Names and likenesses of celebrities will appear in generative AI outputs in part because those elements are included in the system's training data, which itself consists of material created by millions of other individuals independently of the AI provider. Furthermore, those names and likenesses will show up in outputs only to the degree the system predicts they are responsive to the user's prompt.[212] But although the raw materials for a generative AI system are produced by third parties, and although the user's prompt may suggest or require use of a particular celebrity's likeness or style, the specific content that results will be largely due to the operation of the generative AI system.[213]

Courts have yet to decide whether complex automated manipulation of preexisting data qualifies as produced by the service provider or produced by third parties.[214] Much simpler automated manipulation has been held to be essentially providing access to the material of others. For example, automated summaries or suggested search terms by search engines such as Google have been held to be provided by "another information content provider," because they are either drawn directly from the source material or based on the queries from users.[215] Similarly, where online mapping services display businesses on a map according to their self-reported locations, the business locations have been held to be third-party content as long as the mapping services are repeating what was reported to them.[216] Automatic recommendations or promotion of third-party content similarly does not turn that content into the service provider's where the content is "materially unaltered."[217]

Generative AI outputs, however, are significantly different from automated summaries and recommendations. A generative AI output typically *is* "materially altered" from both the training materials and the user prompt.[218] Although individual bits of a generated output may come from other sources, that is no different than the individual words in a writer's vocabulary coming from other speakers of the same language.[219] Once a certain amount of reconfiguration has occurred, the content is more properly attributed to the model and not the training data or the user.

[210] Barnes v. Yahoo!, Inc., 570 F.3d 1096, 1100–01 (9th Cir. 2009).

[211] *See* 47 U.S.C. § 230(f)(3) (defining "information content provider" as "any person or entity that is responsible, in whole or in part, for the creation or development of information provided through the Internet").

[212] *See* Jess Miers, *Yes, Section 230 Should Protect ChatGPT and Other Generative AI Tools*, TECHDIRT, Mar. 17, 2023.

[213] *See* Matt Perault, *Section 230 Won't Protect ChatGPT*, 3 J. FREE SPEECH L. 363, 365 (2023).

[214] For discussion, see generally Peter J. Benson & Valerie C. Brannon, *Section 230 Immunity and Generative Artificial Intelligence*, CONG. RSCH. SERV. LEGAL SIDEBAR LSB11097, Dec. 28, 2023, at 3–4.

[215] *See* O'Kroley v. Fastcase, Inc., 831 F.3d 352, 355 (6th Cir. 2016); Stayart v. Google Inc., 783 F. Supp. 2d 1055, 1057 (E.D. Wis. 2011), *aff'd*, 710 F.3d 719 (7th Cir. 2013).

[216] *See* Marshall's Locksmith Serv. Inc. v. Google, LLC, 925 F. 3d 1263, 1272 (D.C. Cir. 2019).

[217] *See* Force v. Facebook, Inc., 934 F.3d 53, 66–67, 70 (2d Cir. 2019); Dyroff v. Ultimate Software Group, Inc., 934 F.3d 1093, 1096 (9th Cir. 2019).

[218] There can be models that barely do more than retrieve training data. *See* Peter Henderson, Tatsunori Hashimoto & Mark Lemley, *Where's the Liability in Harmful AI Speech?*, 3 J. FREE SPEECH L. 589, 622 (2023).

[219] *See* Eugene Volokh, *Large Libel Models? Liability for AI Output*, 3 J. FREE SPEECH L. 489, 496 (2023).

The question for courts will be where to draw that line. One question that has emerged from Section 230 cases involving recommendation algorithms is whether the algorithm is functioning as a "neutral tool," one that selects videos and advertisements to push based on the user's activity rather than the platform operator's views.[220] "Neutrality" may be an unattainable goal as algorithms become more complex,[221] but one possibility is that courts will inquire as to how much the defendant's system is designed to cause the sorts of harms the plaintiff is complaining about – in this case, content based on the plaintiff's identity. As Derek Bambauer and Mihai Surdeanu note, "[t]his approach is a classic example of regulating dual-use devices or services: When the tool does not appear specifically designed to produce unlawful results, liability attaches solely to its user."[222]

17.4.2 *Trademarks*

As with patents, AI systems have the potential to significantly improve trademark classification and searches, both for trademark examiners and for potential trademark owners.[223] This has become particularly important as trademark applications have surged and rigorous examination has become more difficult.[224] In addition, AI systems may be more adept at complex, subjective analyses such as likelihood of confusion, which suggests a possible judicial role for AI as well.[225]

Generative AI is also likely to give rise to increasing conflicts as recognizable marks find their way into generated content, including advertisements. A person that posts a video or image featuring something similar to another's mark, including trade dress, may face liability if the appearance of the mark is likely to cause confusion as to source, sponsorship, or affiliation.[226] There may also be claims against generative AI providers for contributory trademark infringement, but contributory liability would be difficult to establish. It would require a showing that the provider knew of particular infringing generations, and not merely the capability of its service to generate infringing material.[227]

By far a more disruptive possibility is that the rise of AI search tools in the hands of consumers may decrease the significance of trademarks entirely. To the extent that exclusive trademark rights are justified by the need to reduce consumer search costs, and consumers begin purchasing goods and services without reference to brands at all, then the justification for such exclusive

[220] Gonzalez v. Google LLC, 2 F.4th 871, 894–95 (9th Cir. 2021), *overruled on other grounds by* Twitter, Inc. v. Taamneh, 598 U.S. 471 (2023); *see also* Force v. Facebook, Inc., 934 F.3d 53, 69–70 (2d Cir. 2019).

[221] *See* Vincent Dumas, Comment, *Enigma Machines: Deep Learning Algorithms as Information Content Providers Under Section 230 of the Communications Decency Act*, 2022 WIS. L. REV. 1581, 1598.

[222] Derek E. Bambauer & Mihai Surdeanu, *Authorbots*, 3 J. FREE SPEECH L. 375, 385 (2023); *see also* Lemmon v. Snap, Inc., 995 F.3d 1085, 1091–92 (9th Cir. 2021).

[223] Sonia K. Katyal & Aniket Kesari, *Trademark Search, Artificial Intelligence, and the Role of the Private Sector*, 35 BERKELEY TECH. L.J. 501, 573–74 (2020); Daryl Lim, *Computational Trademark Infringement and Adjudication*, *in* RESEARCH HANDBOOK ON INTELLECTUAL PROPERTY AND ARTIFICIAL INTELLIGENCE 258, 260 (Ryan Abbott ed., 2022).

[224] *See* Katyal & Kesari, note 223 above, at 505–06.

[225] *See* Lim, note 223 above, at 271–72.

[226] *See* Zerorez Franchising Sys., Inc. v. Distinctive Cleaning, Inc., 103 F. Supp. 3d 1032 (D. Minn. 2015) (liability for advertisements); 4 J. THOMAS MCCARTHY, MCCARTHY ON TRADEMARKS AND UNFAIR COMPETITION § 23:76 (4th ed. 2016) (test for infringement).

[227] *See* Tiffany (NJ) Inc. v. eBay Inc., 600 F.3d 93, 107 (2d Cir. 2010). Some plaintiffs have claimed that the ability of AI engines to replicate a particular artist's style constitutes infringement of their protected trade dress. But courts are clear that artistic style is not protectable as trade dress, *see* MCCARTHY, note 226 above, § 10:40.50, and in any event trade dress only protects against confusion as the physical source of the product, not the intellectual source of content, *see* Dastar Corp. v. Twentieth Century Fox Film Corp., 539 U.S. 23, 31–32 (2003).

rights disappears.[228] Already consumers are delegating some of their quest for quality goods to online platforms, and generative AI shopping assistants are not far behind.[229] AI systems have little need for memorable marks to determine product characteristics or quality; as Michael Grynberg has noted, "[t]o a computer, ZL3XC!7K4BV functions just as well as APPLE."[230] Trademark rights are a relatively recent innovation, one that was brought about when the Industrial Revolution made it possible to distribute goods to a national market far from the source, and technological innovation could well make all shopping local once again.[231]

17.4.3 *Trade Secrets*

While generative AI may enhance the production of proprietary knowledge – new industrial processes, improved customer databases, and the like – it is not likely to complicate trade secret protection for such knowledge. There is no requirement under trade secret law, unlike patents or copyrights, that the secret be produced in any particular way, and AI systems have no special propensity to misappropriate other companies' secrets. Generative AI is thus unlikely to have a significant impact on trade secret law. But the reverse is not true: trade secret law will likely be very important for generative AI.

As discussed above, generative AI providers will have difficulty protecting their models and systems with patents.[232] In light of those difficulties, AI providers are likely to seek to protect the components of their systems – the training data, models, algorithms, and system software – as trade secrets instead.[233] But reliance on trade secret protection will still have its challenges and ramifications. Training data for some generative AI models is compiled by third parties, or even made publicly available. Similarly, some models have been provided on an open-source basis.[234] Trade secret protection is incompatible with widespread public accessibility, and between third parties requires the establishment of a licensing regime. AI providers may also have difficulties protecting the secrets of proprietary systems that are available for public use, as competitors may be able to extract information about the system through a series of carefully designed prompts.[235] Generative AI providers may try to limit such reverse engineering through terms of use, but such terms may not be enforceable.[236]

One ramification of generative AI providers relying on trade secrets to preserve their competitive edge is that trade secrets are more difficult to preserve than other forms of IP, and thus may encourage more industry consolidation. Trade secrets are not registered; instead, they must be continually protected against misappropriation by identifying them and taking numerous preventative measures to guard against potential threats.[237] The need to keep information secret means that trade secrets are cumbersome to license, which in turn drives firms looking to

[228] *See* Christine Haight Farley, *Trademarks in an Algorithmic World*, 98 WASH. L. REV. 1123, 1154 (2023).

[229] *See id.* at 1127; Lim, note 223 above, at 264; Scarlett Evans, *Walmart Expands Generative AI Shopping Features*, AI BUSINESS, Oct. 10, 2023.

[230] Michael Grynberg, *AI and the "Death of Trademark"*, 108 KY. L.J. 199, 211 (2019–2020).

[231] *See* Farley, note 228 above, at 1126.

[232] *See* Section 17.3.2.3 above.

[233] *See* Asay, note 178 above, at 1241; Kappos & Kling, note 152 above, at 275.

[234] *See* Will Knight, *Meta's Open Source Llama 3 Is Already Nipping at OpenAI's Heels*, WIRED, Apr. 25, 2024.

[235] *See* Kappos & Kling, note 152 above, at 275; Camilla Hrdy, *Keeping ChatGPT a Trade Secret While Selling It Too*, 40 BERKELEY TECH. L.J. 75, 111–14 (2025).

[236] *See* Samuel J. LaRoque, Comment, *Reverse Engineering and Trade Secrets in the Post-*Alice *World*, 66 U. KAN. L. REV. 427, 457 (2017).

[237] *See* Asay, note 178 above, at 1241.

quickly innovate to acquire rivals rather than bargain for their technology.[238] The result may well be fewer, larger firms operating generative AI systems, with less innovation.[239]

17.5 CONCLUSION

The law, like a shadow, is in a perpetual state of catching up to reality. Any widespread and rapid technological innovation, by its very nature, makes the application of existing law developed *without* that innovation difficult.[240] It is no different with generative AI and IP law. AI technology, and generative AI in particular, threatens to disrupt not just legal categories, but entire industries.[241] There will initially be some turmoil as twentieth-century IP is applied to twenty-first-century problems, but eventually, a transformed legal regime will emerge.

[238] *See id.* at 1242–43.

[239] *See id.* at 1256; *see also* Eric Goldman, *Generative AI Is Doomed, Helen Wilson Nies Lecture on Intellectual Property*, Marquette University Law School (Apr. 16, 2024).

[240] *See* Margot E. Kaminski, *Technological "Disruption" of the Law's Imagined Scene: Some Lessons from* Lex Informatica, 36 BERKELEY TECH. L.J. 883, 903 (2021).

[241] *See* Burk, note 6 above, at 1679–82.

18

Copyright and Generative AI in Japan and China

Christoph Rademacher and Wanru Cai

18.1 INTRODUCTION

Both Japanese and Chinese copyright law structurally resemble Western copyright laws. Historically speaking, both Japan and China introduced copyright protection at least partially as a result of international trade and diplomatic pressure, albeit at very different times. Japan can look back to 125 years of copyright protection, whereas modern China's copyright law is only about 30 years old. Arguably, such difference in duration and adoption of a copyright law culture may have contributed to Japan developing a more recognizable creator/artist environment over the last decades.

Both Japanese and Chinese copyright laws aim to contribute to the cultural development by providing for authors' rights. Japanese copyright law's purpose clause qualifies the protection of such authors' rights by requiring "attention to the fair exploitation" of cultural products.[1] The Chinese Copyright Act also starts off with a purpose clause, which, however, does not incorporate the notion of fair use or fair exploitation into such a purpose. That said, both statutes are based on a continental civil law concept of limiting the power of copyright law owners by providing for a detailed list of exceptions and limitations, establishing a very different dynamic in statutory interpretation than common law copyright statutes relying on broad and flexible fair use provisions tend to do.[2] This fundamental copyright law background typically puts a significant amount of pressure on the legislator. The struggle between copyright protection and technical innovation is certainly not novel. Rather, the advent of technologies such as photography, gramophones, video recorders, and peer-to-peer file sharing tested the aptness of copyright law.[3] Courts and legislators have been trying to find a balance between

[1] Article 1 Japanese Copyright Act.

[2] For an overview on the Japanese system of copyright exceptions and limitations see Tatsuhiro Ueno, 'A General Clause on Copyright Limitations in Civil Law Countries: Recent Discussion on Japanese-Style Fair Use Clause', in Shyam Balganesh et al. (eds.), *The Cambridge Handbook of Copyright Limitations and Exceptions* (Cambridge: Cambridge University Press, 2021) at 211; for an introductory overview of Chinese copyright and its limitations, see Tianxiang He, 'Transplanting Fair Use in China? History, Impediments and the Future' (2020) 2 *Journal of Law, Technology and Policy* 359.

[3] For a short and somewhat provocative assessment of content owners' complaints regarding generations of new technology see e.g. Mark A. Lemley, 'Is the Sky Falling on the Content Industries?' (2011) 9 *Journal of Telecommunications and High Technology Law* 125.

accommodating content owners' desire for robust copyright protection and disruptive technology entrepreneurs' mission for rolling out new and innovative products and services. Arguably, however, the emergence of generative AI amounts to a different level of technological disruption, questioning the suitability of copyright law principles that withstood the test of previous technical innovation. This chapter will focus on how Chinese and Japanese copyright laws balance content owners' desire for copyright protection with the national policy goal of enabling and promoting technological advancement, in particular in the area of AI-related progress. In discussing the emerging area of law, we will focus mainly on the two most fundamental questions that the widespread adoption of generative AI pose to copyright regulators: (1) does the use and refinement of training data violate copyright law, and (2) who owns a copyright in content produced by or with the help of AI?

18.2 JAPAN

Japanese policymakers are usually not pioneering brand-new legal concepts when establishing or developing Japanese regulations. Rather, Japan has maintained the reputation of being the signature jurisdiction that is relying on "legal transplants" – that is, adopting foreign legal norms into the domestic framework, with necessary and carefully tailored modifications to fit into the local Japanese cultural and socioeconomic context.[4] When it comes to developing a tailored copyright law limitation for the process of working with and training large datasets, however, the Japanese legislator charged ahead and essentially established the first codified exception for text and data mining in the world.

18.2.1 TDM Framework

Japan being credited as a pioneer in stipulating copyright exceptions for text and data mining (TDM) is based on the introduction of numerous specific provisions allowing for exploitation of copyrighted works emerging from the development of information and communications technology into the Japanese Copyright Act as early as in 2009 and 2012.[5] These early provisions were, however, tailored to very specific purposes, leading to the Japanese government pushing for broader and more flexible limitations in order to promote new innovation through the use of big data, AI, and other digital technologies.[6] The government's efforts culminated in the introduction of three more flexible provisions primarily directed to permit information analysis by exempting exploitation not for "enjoyment" purposes,[7] exploitation incidental to the use of works on a computer,[8] and minor exploitation incidental to data processing on a computer[9] from copyright infringement liability.

Among those three provisions, the exemption of exploitation for non-enjoyment purposes provided for in Article 30-4 Copyright Act which targets uses related to technical processes, such

[4] John O. Haley, 'Why Study Japanese Law?' (2010) 58 *American Journal of Comparative Law* 1.

[5] Arts. 47-2, 47-5, 47-6, 47-7, 47-8 of Act No. 53 of Japanese Copyright Act 2009. Arts. 30-2, 30-3, 30-4, 47-9 of Japanese Copyright Act 2012.

[6] Agency for Cultural Affairs, Government of Japan, 'Regarding the Act Amending Part of the Copyright Act (Act No. 30 of 2018)'. Available at www.bunka.go.jp/seisaku/chosakuken/hokaisei/h30_hokaisei/; see also Tatsuhiro Ueno, 'The Flexible Copyright Exception for 'Non-Enjoyment' Purposes ⊠ Recent Amendment in Japan and Its Implication' (2021) 2 *GRUR International* 145.

[7] Art. 30-4 of Japanese Copyright Act of 2018.

[8] Art. 47-4 of Japanese Copyright Act of 2018.

[9] Art. 47-5 of Japanese Copyright Act of 2018.

as in software development, data analysis, and various forms of digital processing where the content itself is not the focus but rather its utility in a technical or data-driven context, is conceptually the most challenging and probably also the most interesting, especially when looking at TDM activities. The new provisions read:

> 30-4 It is permissible to exploit a work, in any way and to the extent considered necessary, in any of the following cases, or in any other case in which it is not a person's purpose to personally enjoy or cause another person to enjoy the thoughts or sentiments expressed in that work; provided, however, that this does not apply if the action would unreasonably prejudice the interests of the copyright owner in light of the nature or purpose of the work or the circumstances of its exploitation:
>
> (i) if it is done for use in testing to develop or put into practical use technology that is connected with the recording of sounds or visuals of a work or other such exploitation;
>
> (ii) if it is done for use in data analysis (meaning the extraction, comparison, classification, or other statistical analysis of the constituent language, sounds, images, or other elemental data from a large number of works or a large volume of other such data; the same applies in Article 47-5, paragraph (1), item (ii));
>
> (iii) if it is exploited in the course of computer data processing or otherwise exploited in a way that does not involve what is expressed in the work being perceived by the human senses (for works of computer programming, such exploitation excludes the execution of the work on a computer), beyond as set forth in the preceding two items.[10]

The structure of Article 30-4 is that of a "general clause-list-catch-all clause."[11] In the general clause, the purpose and the extent of the use are limited to the "non-enjoyment purpose" and "the extent considered necessary," and the provision excludes the circumstance that "would unreasonably prejudice the interests of the copyright owner." Following this general preamble, the provision introduces two specific examples in items (i) and (ii). The "data analysis" codified in item (ii) refers to TDM, which explicitly indicates that TDM is exempted from copyright liability, ensuring the certainty of its application. Finally, the catch-all clause, which is item (iii), enables other circumstances where "the exploitation is in the course of computer data processing or otherwise that does not involve what is expressed in the work being perceived by the human senses" to fall under the copyright exemption as well, ensuring the flexibility of this provision.

Not only Article 30-4 Copyright Act, but also the other new limitations codified in Articles 47-4 and 47-5 Copyright Act represent a desired balance between flexibility and certainty.[12] While the specific items listed in each provision provide certainty, the catch-all language makes it possible to cover other equivalent circumstances to address future needs.[13] Furthermore, the interconnectedness of these three provisions upholds a balance between the use of works and the interests of copyright holders. Based on the potential harm to copyright holders caused by these uses, the provisions are categorized into two types: "harmless uses" (Arts. 30-4 and 47-4) and "minor harm uses" (Art. 47-5).[14]

[10] The English translation is from the website www.japaneselawtranslation.go.jp/en/laws/view/3379.

[11] Copyright Division, 'Overview Explanation Material'.

[12] Copyright Division, Commissioner's Secretariat, Agency for Cultural Affairs, Government of Japan, 'Overview Explanation Material of the Draft Act Amending Certain Parts of the Copyright Act'. Available at www.kantei.go.jp/jp/singi/titeki2/tyousakai/kensho_hyoka_kikaku/2018/contents/dai4/siryou6.pdf.

[13] Ibid.

[14] Ibid.

As mentioned earlier, Article 30-4 permits the use of a work for non-enjoyment purposes. Article 47-4 allows incidental uses of a work necessary for its smooth or efficient operation on a computer (such as browser cache, progressive downloads), and for maintaining or recovering the ability to use a work on a computer (for example, device repair, backup servers).[15] The uses stipulated in these two provisions are considered not to normally cause harm to the copyright holder's interests; hence, Articles 30-4 and 47-4 as set out are "highly flexible" provisions. They incorporate several abstract elements, including the purpose and extent of the use in the general clause, and include a catch-all clause to cover other circumstances enabled by technological developments.[16]

Article 47-5 permits minor uses incidental to computerized data processing for creating new knowledge or information, and the provision of the results thereof (web search services, plagiarism detection services, for example). Since this use may cause a minor degree of damage to the copyright holder, this provision takes a "comparatively flexible" form.[17] To limit the flexibility, the general clause specifies requirements for the purpose, subject, extent of the use, and the type of works; meanwhile, the catch-all clause requires other circumstances to be subject to Cabinet Order.[18]

Given the early enactment of the Japanese TDM exception as well as its comparatively broad nature, the amount of attention devoted to such exceptions both inside and outside Japan might not be too surprising.[19] Unlike comparable statutory exceptions in Europe, for example, the Japanese TDM exception extends to both commercial and non-commercial uses, and does not require lawful access to the protected content to qualify as permissible TDM. These generous and broad permissions to use, copy, and store protected content arguably make Japan the most liberal major economy in the world in terms of copyright law.[20]

The expansive limitation may or may not be helpful to encourage the development of AI and related industries in Japan. It certainly has been perceived as adding pressure on certain parts of the content industry, which has been rather vocal in emphasizing the detriments that the wide-ranging limitations to copyright protection present.[21] One conceivable way to restrict users in conducting TDM with protected content would be to establish a contractual obligation of such

15 Ueno, 'Flexible Copyright Exception', 147.

16 Copyright Division, 'Overview Explanation Material'.

17 Ibid.

18 Ibid.

19 E.g. Artha Dermawan, 'Text and Data Mining Exceptions in the Development of Generative AI Models: What the EU Member States Could Learn from the Japanese "Nonenjoyment" Purposes?' (2024) 27 *Journal of World Intellectual Property* 44; Martin Senftleben et al., 'Ensuring the Visibility and Accessibility of European Creative Content on the World Market: The Need for Copyright Data Improvement in the Light of New Technologies and the Opportunity Arising from Article 17 of the CDSM Directive' (2022) 13 *JIPITEC*, 67 n. 11 f.

20 We should note here the 2021 TDM exception introduced into Singaporean copyright law which is in some respects more wide-reaching than the Japanese provision. Unlike its Japanese counterpart, the Singaporean TDM exception does require lawful access, making it partially more restrictive. For a more detailed account of the evolution of the Singaporean provision, see e.g. Ng-Loy Wee Loon, 'Copyright Exceptions for Text and Data Mining: A Case of Specificity (Certainty) and Generality (Flexibility)', in Florent Thouvenin et al. (eds.), *Kreation Innovation Märkte – Creation Innovation Markets – Festschrift Reto M. Hilty* (Springer, 2024), 263, at 267–74.

21 See e.g. Protocols of the 2023–24 Intellectual Property Rights Study Group in the AI Era convened by the Cabinet Office; e.g. protocol of the meeting of Oct. 18, 2023 (summarizing submissions made by artists concerned about TDM's impact on their livelihoods), at 8 (available in Japanese at www.kantei.go.jp/jp/singi/titeki2/ai_kentoukai/dai2/gijiroku.pdf), and protocol of the meeting of Nov. 7, 2023 (highlighting newspaper publishers arguing that the Japanese TDM provisions effectively prevent them from denying AI the use of their content for learning purposes), at 12–13 (available in Japanese at www.kantei.go.jp/jp/singi/titeki2/ai_kentoukai/dai3/gijiroku.pdf).

users to refrain from TDM;[22] in this case, TDM might still be permissible under copyright law, but would constitute a breach of contract. This possibility of establishing terms and conditions that restrict or prohibit TDM and then testing such terms validity in court litigation is, however, an avenue that content owners have not pursued, at least not to date. One of the reasons for such reluctance to undertake litigation might stem from the actual or perceived difficulty to establish copying and storing of data, given the absence of pre-trial discovery or other evidence collection tools that are available in particular in the United States. That said, the somewhat notorious and traditional reluctance of some conservative Japanese copyright owners such as newspaper companies or publishing houses might be another factor that prevents litigation of the TDM provision in Japan.

Upon its enactment in 2018, the conceptual structure of the flexible TDM exception might have come as a bit of a surprise, given that it departed to a certain degree from the preexisting system of very specific and thereby narrow copyright limitations. The – in hindsight – arguably even more surprising substance was, however, not particularly controversial in Japan at the time the first and subsequent TDM provisions were discussed in the respective government committees and eventually enacted. It seems safe to say that the process and debate would look very different these days, and that the Japanese government would probably not have been able to pass a TDM exception as broad as the current one if the preparations were commencing at this point.

18.2.2 *Protection of AI-Generated Works*

Under Article 2-1(1) of the Japanese Copyright Act, a "work" is defined as a creatively produced expression of thoughts or sentiments within literary, academic, artistic, or musical domains. For a work to qualify, it must embody thoughts or sentiments, be expressed, demonstrate creativity, and belong to one of the specified domains. The ability to meet the creativity requirement is a significant hurdle for the copyrightability of computer-generated works.

The 1993 Report of the government committee tasked to develop Japanese copyright law clarifies that copyrightable works must exhibit "creative intention" and "creative contribution."[23] As such, works created with computer assistance are copyrightable, unlike those entirely generated by computers. This distinction was reaffirmed in the 2017 Report of New Information Goods Review Committee,[24] which also acknowledged the difference between purely AI-generated works and those assisted by AI, with copyright protection applicable only to the latter.

Creative intention merely requires a general aim to produce a specific result. Creative contribution, on the other hand, must involve a contribution to the work's expression itself, not just to its factual or ideational content. This contribution must be evaluated on a case-by-case basis, as it sometimes lacks conscious control over the creative expression when the work is

[22] This particular interaction between contact law and copyright law was reviewed by a government committee convened by the Ministry of Economy, Trade, and Industry in 2021.

[23] Chosakken shingikai dai 9 ko iinkai (konpyūta sōsaku-mono kankei) hōkoku-sho [Report of the Copyright Council's 9th Subcommittee (Computer-Related Works)], Chapter 3; report available (in Japanese) at www.cric.or.jp/db/report/h5_11_2/h5_11_2_main.html.

[24] Intellectual Property Strategy Headquarters of the Cabinet Office: Aratana jōhō-zai kentō iin kaihōkokusho 2017 (New Information Property Review Committee Report 2017) (in Japanese), available at www.kantei.go.jp/jp/singi/titeki2/tyousakai/kensho_hyoka_kikaku/2017/johozai/houkokusho.pdf.

generated by AI. Nevertheless, if an action broadly determines the creative expression of the result, it can still be recognized as a creative contribution.

Determining "creative contribution" in AI-generated works requires understanding the roles and actions of both AI developers and users. AI developers, who program and manage data for machine learning, are generally not considered authors of the resulting creative works. This is because their technical input does not extend to influencing the specific creative output, which is typically shaped by the users' inputs, such as prompts.

However, there are instances where the role of a developer or user may be seen as a "creative contribution." If a user or developer fine-tunes an AI system specifically to produce outputs within a confined aesthetic or thematic framework, such actions might qualify as creative contributions. This could involve training the AI to generate artworks in a specific painting style or to produce literary works with a particular thematic focus. In such scenarios, the person doing the fine-tuning is making decisions that significantly guide the creative direction of the AI's output. Entering prompts, while a necessary part of interacting with generative AI, is generally not sufficient to establish a "creative contribution" on its own because it does not specify the creative expressions of the generated works.[25]

Nevertheless, if the prompts are detailed and guide the AI toward producing a specific type of creative output, they may be considered part of the creative process. Additionally, the act of selecting from the AI-generated options involves a degree of creative decision-making, similar to editing or curating, which could also be recognized as a creative contribution.[26] Furthermore, the iterative process of modifying AI outputs – whether through tweaking initial prompts or refining selections after reviewing various results – mirrors traditional creative processes. These modifications, where the user adjusts and readjusts to hone in on a desired creative expression, underscore the user's active role in shaping the final creative product. Thus, in the context of AI-generated works, both the detailed specifications given to the AI (through prompts or fine-tuning parameters) and the selective interventions by users (through choices and modifications) can be recognized as creative contributions. This perspective aligns with traditional copyright norms, where an individual's direct and substantial input into the creation of a work affirms their role as a copyright holder.

When AI-generated content involves the "creative intention" and "creative contribution" of several individuals and embodies thoughts or sentiments, it can be copyrighted, with the author being the individual who made significant creative contributions with intent. In certain situations, the law may recognize AI users as authors because their interactions with the AI often involve creative decisions. However, AI developers and service providers can also be acknowledged as authors in cases where their contributions significantly shape the creative output. When the creative contribution is divided among several individuals, each person's input must be evaluated to determine their contribution to the work. Although collectively their efforts might constitute a "creative contribution," not all individual contributions might qualify for

[25] Hajime Idei, 'AI seisei kinō no dōkō to chosakukenhō-jō no kadai e no taisaku' (Trends in AI Generation Functions and Countermeasures for Copyright Law Issues) (in Japanese) (2023) 62 *Copyright*, at 22; however, if the AI-generated content is created by inputting the AI users' copyrighted works as the instruction, e.g. in case of AI-power translated, the process of entering prompts can be recognized as "creative contribution," given that the instructions function as a model of the AI-generated output and thus strongly determine such output.

[26] There is some debate on whether selecting from AI-generated options can be considered as a creative contribution under Japanese copyright law. See Taichi Yanagi, 'Gazō seisei AI o meguru chosakukenhō-jō no ronten' (Copyright Law Issues Surrounding Image Generation AI) (in Japanese) (2023) 76(2) *Hōritsu no hiroba* 22.

authorship. In some cases, this might lead to no individual being recognized as the author, but if there is a significant overlap in contributions, coauthorship might be recognized.[27]

The lack of clarity regarding the contours of copyright protection of AI-generated content raised the question of requiring more directed legislative action. Essentially, whether AI-generated works warrant copyright protection hinges on the necessity to incentivize creative output. The argument posits that without exclusive rights to capitalize on the outputs, developers might not have sufficient motivation to invest heavily in AI, given the substantial financial, temporal, and energy costs involved.

This reasoning might not extend uniformly across all participants in AI development. For AI developers and service providers, existing intellectual property protections such as patents for AI systems or copyrights for program code might be adequate. For AI users, the necessity for copyright protection is contingent upon their "creative contribution" to the AI-generated works being recognized. Granting exclusive rights for works where the AI users' creative input is negligible does not serve to stimulate the type of creative activity that copyright aims to encourage within society.

The current consensus among Japanese commentators is that there is no pressing need to extend copyright protections to AI-generated works that lack human creative input. Extending such protections wouldn't necessarily foster the creation of new works.[28] Moreover, protective measures through *sui generis* rights or neighboring rights are also seen as unjustifiable under these circumstances.[29] Nonetheless, there could be alternative justifications for protecting AI-generated content, as suggested by another Cabinet Office report, which proposes recognizing the investments companies make in developing AI characters and promoting them, which, coupled with the content they help generate, forms a collaborative model between human and AI efforts.[30]

The Committee's report also highlights that if AI-generated works start competing in the market with human creations, only those AI works that can represent their authors might qualify for intellectual property protection. While it is challenging to predict all future developments in this fast-evolving field, there might be a future requirement for legal safeguards to encourage additional investments post-creation to enhance the market appeal and maintain the

[27] The determination of copyright ownership in the terms of service for generative AI also raises important legal considerations. Such terms must not assign authorship to those who do not meet the criteria for "creative contribution." If no individual's creative contribution can be recognized, then the AI-generated results are not copyrightable, and thus no copyright can be claimed. However, if the terms are interpreted as a copyright transfer agreement and are following legal standards and public order, they remain valid, since copyright is a property right that can be transferred between parties.

[28] Koji Okumura, 'Jinkō chinō ga umidashita kontentsu to chosakken: Chosaku bussei o chūshin ni' (Content Created by Artificial Intelligence and Copyright: Focusing on Copyright Property) (in Japanese) (2017) 70(2) *Patento* 10, at 17; Takeshi Maeda, 'AI seisei-mono no chosakubussei' (Copyright Property of AI Products) (in Japanese), in Tatsuhiro Ueno & Koji Okumura, *AI to Chosakken* (AI and Copyright) (Keiso Shobo 2024), at 173.

[29] Tsuyoshi Uchida, 'Konpyūta seisei sakuhin no chosakken ni yoru hogo to sono hogo no tame no kadai – ōsutoraria ni okeru mittsu no hanketsu kara no shisa' (Copyright Protection of Computer-Generated Works and Challenges for Such Protection – Implications from Three Judgments in Australia) (in Japanese), in *Chiteki zaisan-hō kenkyū no wa: Shibuya tatsuki kyōju tsuitō ronbun-shū* (The Circle of Intellectual Property Law Research: A Collection of Papers in Memory of Professor Tatsuki Shibuya) (JIPII 2016), at 556–7; Tatsuhiro Ueno, 'Jinkō chinō to kikai gakushū o meguru chosakukenhō-jō no kadai' (Copyright Law Issues Surrounding Artificial Intelligence and Machine Learning) (in Japanese) (2017) 3 *Law & Technology Special Edition* 'Chitekizaisan Funsō no Saizensen' (The Frontline of Intellectual Property Disputes), at 61.

[30] Intellectual Property Strategy Headquarters of the Cabinet Office: Jisedai chizai shisutemu kentō iin kaihōkokushō (Next Generation Intellectual Property System Review Committee Report, 2016) (in Japanese), at 25–6, available at www.kantei.go.jp/jp/singi/titeki2/tyousakai/kensho_hyoka_kikaku/2016/jisedai_tizai/hokokusho.pdf.

commercial viability of these AI-generated works. Protection strategies could involve labeling or publicity efforts, which primarily address investment made after the initial generation of the works. Again, while there is currently no sufficient legislative justification for such measures, the evolving landscape could necessitate such protections in the future.[31]

18.3 CHINA

In comparison to Japan, China has a domestic AI economy that features a number of well-known companies such as Baidu, Aliyun, Tencent, and ByteDance that incorporate AI-related technology at a large scale, indicating the rapid growth of the sector. The growth of this sector is supported by both state-led initiatives and private enterprise investments. The Chinese government has set ambitious goals, aiming to become a global leader in AI by 2030, which has fueled significant advancements in technology across various industries including healthcare, finance, and manufacturing. Copyright laws in China have been evolving over the last decades to keep pace with technological and societal advancements, but often lag behind the rapid development of AI technologies. At the same time, a number of recent court decisions, addressing both the protection of AI-generated content and infringement through TDM, provide a sense of direction for Chinese AI copyright policy.

18.3.1 TDM

Unlike Japan, China has not implemented any legislation to address the permissibility of TDM under copyright law. Recent scholarship indicates that a majority of Chinese commentators support exempting TDM from copyright infringement claims. We divide the range of proposed solutions into three main groups. The first two advocate for a copyright exception rule (akin to a Chinese "fair use" provision) that would allow TDM to use copyrighted works without the need for permission from rights holders or the payment of royalties.[32] Specifically, the first group

[31] Cabinet Office, 'Next Generation IP System Report', at 28. See also Maeda, 'Copyright Property of AI Products', at 174–5.

[32] Art. 24 of the Copyright Law of the People's Republic of China stipulates:

> In the following cases, a work may be used without permission of, and without payment of remuneration to the copyright owner, provided that the name or appellation of the author and the title of the work are indicated, the normal use of the work is not affected and the legitimate rights and interests enjoyed by the copyright owner are not unreasonably prejudiced:

(1) use of a published work of another for purposes of personal study, research or appreciation;
(2) appropriate quotation from a published work of another in one's own work for the purpose of introducing or commenting a certain work, or illustrating a point;
(3) unavoidable reproduction or quotation from a published work in newspapers, periodicals, radio stations, television stations or other media for the purpose of reporting news;
(4) publication or broadcasting by newspapers, periodicals, radio stations, television stations or other media of current event articles on issues of politics, economy and religion, which have been published by other newspapers or periodicals, or broadcast by other radio stations or television stations, except where the copyright owner declares that such publication or broadcasting is not permitted;
(5) publication or broadcasting by newspapers, periodicals, radio stations, television stations or other media of a speech delivered at a public gathering, except where the author declares that such publication or broadcasting is not permitted;
(6) translation, adaptation, compilation, broadcasting, or reproduction in a small quantity of copies, of a published work by teachers or scientific researchers for use in classroom teaching or scientific research, provided that such a work shall not be published or distributed;
(7) use of a published work by a State organ to a reasonable scope for the purpose of fulfilling its official duties;

suggests adding a new clause specifically for TDM to the copyright exception rule,[33] while the second group recommends a broad interpretation of the existing rule to facilitate TDM.[34] The third group, on the other hand, suggests applying a statutory license rule,[35] which would permit the unlicensed use of copyrighted works for TDM but would require the payment of a statutory fee.[36]

Amid the global trend toward legislating copyright exceptions for TDM, the first group – supporters of creating a new TDM exception – advocate for learning from international legislative experiences. They have listed several TDM exception models from various jurisdictions, aiming to identify models that could be suitably adapted for China. The second group is focused on quickly finding ways to apply existing copyright exception provisions to TDM. However, scholars in this group acknowledge that relying solely on interpretive approaches is a temporary fix and assert that formal legislation should be enacted soon, a viewpoint that aligns

(8) reproduction of a work in its collections by a library, archive, memorial hall, museum, art gallery, cultural center or similar institution for the purpose of display, or preservation of a copy of the work;
(9) free performance of a published work for non-profit purposes, for which the public does not pay any fees and no remuneration is made to the performers;
(10) copying, drawing, photographing or video-recording of a work of art put up or displayed in public places;
(11) translation of a published work of a Chinese citizen, legal person or unincorporated organization from the standard spoken and written Chinese language into minority nationality languages for publication and distribution in the country;
(12) provision of published works to dyslexics in a barrier-free way through which they can perceive; and
(13) other circumstances as provided by laws and administrative regulations.

The provisions of the preceding paragraph shall apply to the copyright-related rights.
The English translation is from the website www.chinajusticeobserver.com/law/x/copyright-law-of-china-20201111.

33 Xiaodong Ding, 'Lun rengong zhineng cujin xing de shuju zhidu' (On Data Institution that Promotes Artificial Intelligence) (in Chinese) (2023) 6 *Zhongguo falü pinglun (China Law Review)* 175–91 at 187–9; Wenmin Wang, 'Rengong zhineng dui zhuzuoquan xianzhi yu liwai guize de tiaozhan yu yingdui' (Challenge and Response of Artificial Intelligence for the Restriction and Exception rules of Copyrights) (in Chinese) (2022) 11 *Falü shiyong (Journal of Law Application)* 152–62; Heping Jiao, 'Rengong zhineng chuangzuo zhong shuju huoqu yu liyong de zhuzuoquan fengxan ji huajie lujing' (Copyright Risk and Solution of Data Acquisition and Utilization in Artificial Intelligence Creation) (in Chinese) (2022) 4 *Dangdai faxue (Contemporary Law Review)* 128–40.; Tianxiang He, 'Copyright Exceptions Reform and AI Data Analysis in China: A Modest Proposal', in Jyh-An Lee, Reto Hilty and Kung-Chung Liu (eds.), *Artificial Intelligence and Intellectual Property*, 1st ed. (Oxford University Press, 2021), pp. 196–220.

34 Yong Wan and Yalan Li, 'Yin ying rengong zhineng chanye fazhan de heli shiyong tiaokuan jieshi lun yanjiu' (Research on the Interpretation of Fair Use Clause in Response to the Development of Artificial Intelligence Industry) (in Chinese) (2023) 3 *Shuzi fazhi (Digital Law)* 83–92; Ming Zhang, 'Wenben yu shuju wajue shiyong zhuzuoquan heli shiyong de jieshi lun' (Theoretical Interpretation of Fair Use of Copyright in Text and Data Mining) (in Chinese) (2023) 2 *Chuban faxing yanjiu (Publishing Research)* 51–6.

35 Xin Dai, 'Rengong zhineng chuangzuo zhuzuoquan qinquan liwai zhidu xuanze' (Choice of Exception System for Copyright Infringement on Artificial Intelligence Creations) (in Chinese) (2022) 5 *Hubei keji xueyuan xuebao (Journal of Hubei University of Science and Technology)* 38–46; Youhua Liu and Yuanshan Wei, 'Jiqi xuexi de zhuzuoquan qinquan wenti ji qi jiejue' (The Copyright Infringement Issue of Machine Learning and Its Solution) (in Chinese) (2019) 2 *Huadong zhengfa daxue xuebao (ECUPL Journal)* 68–79.

36 Art. 25 of the Copyright Law of the People's Republic of China stipulates:

> Those who compile and publish textbooks for the purpose of implementing compulsory education or State education planning may, without permission of copyright owners, compile published fragments of works, short written works, musical works, a single work of fine art, photographic works, or graphic works in the textbooks, but shall pay remunerations to copyright owners according to the provisions, and indicate the names or appellations of authors and titles of works, and shall not infringe upon other rights enjoyed by the copyright owners in accordance with this Law.
> The provisions of the preceding paragraph shall apply to the copyright-related rights.

The English translation is from the website www.chinajusticeobserver.com/law/x/copyright-law-of-china-20201111.

with the first group's perspective. The third group, which underscores the need for compensating copyright holders, emphasizes protecting the interests of these rights holders.

Although all three groups support exempting TDM from claims for injunctive relief under copyright law, there is a clear divergence in their approaches. The first two groups criticize the application of the statutory license rule due to the difficulty of implementation.[37] Specifically, they point out that the payment mechanism of the statutory license system is not successfully implemented, rendering the system largely ineffective.[38] In contrast, the third group opposes the application of the copyright exception rule, arguing that it would harm the interests of copyright holders and dampen their creative enthusiasm, thereby negatively impacting the public interest.[39] This is opposed by the argument that it would not be accurate to generalize that all TDM activities would harm copyright owners, given that copyright holders can also benefit from the advancements brought by the AI industry.[40] Moreover, despite China attempting to compete with the United States, its AI industry and the quality of Chinese large language models (LLMs) still trail behind. Therefore, in the context of fierce competition between China and the United States, it is considered essential that TDM be included within the scope of copyright exception rules.[41] Ultimately, the legislative approach advocated for by the first group is the most popular within Chinese academia. Additionally, some scholars in this group recommend adopting a model similar to the Japanese exception for TDM, primarily because of its broad scope.[42] This approach is favored as it offers comprehensive coverage that could potentially facilitate greater innovation and use within the burgeoning field of AI and TDM in China.

It is noteworthy that to support the healthy development of generative AI, the Cyberspace Administration of China (CAC) along with six other regulators,[43] issued the Interim Measures for the Management of Generative Artificial Intelligence Services on July 13, 2023 (Interim Measures).[44] Article 7(2) of these Interim Measures mandates that when a generative AI service provider conducts training-data processing activities, such as pre-training and optimized training, it must not infringe on the intellectual property rights lawfully held by others. However, professionals in the field have raised concerns about this article, particularly the difficulty in determining whether input data is protected under intellectual property laws and how to obtain the necessary clearances.[45]

Some scholars argue that while this provision regulates the use of intellectual property in training data in principle, it lacks clarity on how specific infringement cases should be handled, suggesting that detailed provisions in intellectual property law are needed to address these

37 Jiao, 'Copyright Risk', 135–6; Wan and Li, 'Research on the Interpretation', 86–8; Zhang, 'Theoretical Interpretation', 54.

38 Yuying Guan, 'Wo guo zhuzuoquan fading xuke zhidu de fansi yu chonggou' (Reflection and Reconstruction of Statutory Licensing Under China's Copyright Law) (in Chinese) (2015) 2 *Huadong zhengfa daxue xuebao (ECUPL Journal)* 18–29 at 22.

39 Liu and Wei, 'Copyright Infringement Issue', 78.

40 Wan and Li, 'Research on the Interpretation', 88.

41 Ding, 'Data Institution', 189.

42 Jiao, 'Copyright Risk', 138–40; Wang, 'Challenge and Response', 159; He, 'Copyright Exceptions Reform', 217–20.

43 Respectively: National Development and Reform Commission, Ministry of Education, Ministry of Science and Technology, Ministry of Industry and Information Technology, Ministry of Public Security, National Radio and Television Administration.

44 Shengchengshi Rengong Zhineng Fuwu Guanli Zanxing Banfa (Interim Measures for the Management of Generative AI Services) (promulgated by the CAC, the National Development and Reform Commission, the Ministry of Education, the Ministry of Science and Technology, the Ministry of Industry and Information Technology, the Ministry of Public Security, and the National Radio and Television Administration, July 13, 2023, effective Aug. 15, 2023), at www.cac.gov.cn/2023-07/13/c_1690898327029107.htm.

45 Baker Mckenzie, 'China: New Interim Measures to Regulate Generative AI', Client Alert, August 2023.

situations clearly.[46] Furthermore, scholars note that the current provision does not seem to offer copyright exceptions for AI training data, which they argue is crucial for advancing AI technology.[47] They advocate for an expansion of the scope of copyright exception rules to include training-data processing activities and call for corresponding revisions to the Interim Measures to facilitate technological progress.[48]

Additionally, it is worth mentioning that on February 8, 2024, Guangzhou Internet Court ruled on generative AI service's liabilities for copyright infringement, finding that the defendant, a generative AI service provider, infringed the copyright of the famous cartoon character "Ultraman" that the plaintiff (Shanghai Character License Administrative Co., Ltd.) had been granted by Tsuburaya Productions.[49] However, as the defendant is not the one who trained the AI model, the decision actually did not address the TDM issue and focused rather on the liability of the outputs.[50] When assessing the defendant's liability for damages, the court emphasized AI service providers' duty of care, respectively citing Article 15,[51] Article 4,[52] and

[46] An Li, 'Jiqi xuexi de banquan guize: lishi qishi yu dangdai fang'an' (Copyright Rules for Machine Learning: Historical Implications and Contemporary Solution) (in Chinese) (2023) 6 *Huanqiu falü pinglun (Global Law Review)* 97–113 at 99; Huajian Song, 'Lun shengcheng shi rengong zhineng de falü fengxian yu zhili lujing' (Legal Risk and Governance Path of Generative Artificial Intelligence) (in Chinese) (2024) 3 *Beijing ligong daxue xuebao (Shehui kexue ban) (Journal of Beijing Institute of Technology (Social Sciences Edition))* 134–43 at 139.

[47] Song, 'Legal Risk', 139; Hua Lin, 'Rengong zhineng shuju xunlian de falü jingzheng' (Legal Competition of Artificial Intelligence Data Training) (in Chinese) (2023). Available at www.ipforefront.com/m_article_show.asp?id = 3395& BigClass = %E8%A7%82%E7%82%B9.

[48] Song, 'Legal Risk'; Lin, 'Rengong zhineng'.

[49] *Shanghai Character License Administrative Co., Ltd. v. AI company* (undisclosed), Guangzhou Internet Court, 2024 Guangdong 0192 Min Chu No. 113. (Feb. 8, 2024).

[50] Christine Yiu and Toby Bond, 'Liability of AI Service Providers for Copyright Infringement: Guangzhou Internet Court Reaches World's First Decision' (2024). Available at www.twobirds.com/en/insights/2024/china/liability-of-ai-service-providers-for-copyright-infringement.

[51] Art. 15 of Interim Measures for the Management of Generative Artificial Intelligence Services stipulates: "Providers shall establish and complete mechanisms for making complaints and reports, setting up easy complaint and reporting portals, disclosing the process for handling them and the time limits for giving responses, and promptly accepting and handling complaints and reports from the public and giving feedback on the outcome."

The English translation is from the website www.chinalawtranslate.com/en/generative-ai-interim/.

[52] Art. 4 of Interim Measures for the Management of Generative Artificial Intelligence Services stipulates:

> The provision and use of generative AI services shall comply with the requirements of laws and administrative regulations, respect social mores, ethics, and morality, and obey the following provisions:

(1) Uphold the Core Socialist Values; content that is prohibited by laws and administrative regulations such as that inciting subversion of national sovereignty or the overturn of the socialist system, endangering national security and interests or harming the nation's image, inciting separatism or undermining national unity and social stability, advocating terrorism or extremism, promoting ethnic hatred and ethnic discrimination, violence and obscenity, as well as fake and harmful information;
(2) During processes such as algorithm design, the selection of training data, model generation and optimization, and the provision of services, effective measures are to be employed to prevent the creation of discrimination such as by race, ethnicity, faith, nationality, region, sex, age, profession, or health;
(3) Respect intellectual property rights and commercial ethics, and protect commercial secrets, advantages in algorithms, data, platforms, and so forth must not be used for monopolies or to carry out unfair competition;
(4) Respect the lawful rights and interests of others, the physical and psychological well-being of others must not be endangered, and the rights and interests of others, such as in their image, reputation, honor, privacy, and personal information, must not be infringed;
(5) Based on the characteristics of the service type, employ effective measures to increase transparency in generative AI services and to increase the accuracy and reliability of generated content.

The English translation is from the website www.chinalawtranslate.com/en/generative-ai-interim/.

Article 12[53] of "Interim Measures" to find that the defendant failed to establish an IPR complaint and reporting mechanism, remind users not to use its service to infringe a third party's rights, and label the AI-generated outputs to distinguish them from human-authored works, and therefore the defendant is responsible for compensating the plaintiff. Although this case did provide a useful discussion of the infringement liability and due diligence obligations of AI-generated service providers in China,[54] the question whether the use of copyrighted works as AI training data constitutes infringement has not yet been clarified.

18.3.2 *Protection of AI-Generated Works*

18.3.2.1 Copyrightability of AI-Generated Content

In Chinese academia, there are three different views on the copyrightability of AI-generated content. The first view argues that AI-generated content cannot be protected as copyrighted works,[55] while the second supports its copyrightability.[56] A third group of scholars suggests protecting AI-generated content through neighboring rights or treating it as products of labor.[57] However, there are flaws with the third view. Neighboring rights aim to promote the dissemination of works, but the controversy around AI-generated content focuses on the creation process itself. Additionally, viewing AI-generated content as mere products oversimplifies the relationship between AI and its output, ignoring the unique nature of AI.[58] As a result, the third perspective has not gained much support. The primary debate continues to focus on the first two opposing views, with various arguments for and against the copyrightability of AI-generated content.

Article 3 of the Chinese Copyright Act requires a work to meet the following in order to qualify for copyright protection:

[53] Art. 12 of Interim Measures for the Management of Generative Artificial Intelligence Services stipulates: "Providers shall label generated content such as images and video in accordance with the Provisions on the Administration of Deep Synthesis Internet Information Services."
The English translation is from the website www.chinalawtranslate.com/en/generative-ai-interim/.

[54] Yiu and Bond, 'Liability of AI Service Providers'.

[55] Qian Wang, 'Zai Lun Rengong Zhineng Shengcheng de Neirong zai Zhuzuoquan Fa Zhong de Dingxing' (The Qualitative Analysis of Content Generated by Artificial Intelligence in Copyright Law) (in Chinese) (2023) 4 *Zhengfa Luntan (Tribune of Political Science and Law)* 16–33; Bo Yuan, 'Lun Wenxue Lingyu Rengong Zhineng Zhuzuoquan zhi Zhengwei' (Refutation of the Copyright of Artificial Intelligence in Literary Creation) (in Chinese) (2018) 6 *Dianzi Zhishi Chanquan (Electronics Intellectual Property)* 20–30.

[56] Xinbao Zhang and Long Bian, 'Rengong zhineng shengcheng neirong de zhuzuoquan baohu yanjiu' (Research on the Copyright of AI-Generated Content) (in Chinese) (2024) 2 *Bijiao fa yanjiu (Journal of Comparative Law)* 77–91; Shaojue Liu and Linfeng Nie, 'Rengong zhineng shengcheng neirong de zhuzuoquan fa zhi bian' (Debate on Copyright Law of Artificial Intelligence Generated Content) (in Chinese) (2024) 1 *Nanchang daxue xuebao (Journal of Nanchang University(Humanities and Social Sciences))* 107–18; Fengming Chen, 'Tiaozhan yu yingdui: rengong zhineng shengcheng neirong de zhuzuoquan baohu jinlu' (Challenges and Responses: The Approaches to Copyright Protection of Artificial Intelligence-Generated Contents) (in Chinese) (2023) 6 *Chuban faxing yanjiu (Publishing Research)* 20–8; Handong Wu, 'Rengong zhineng shengcheng zuopin de zhuzuoquan fa zhi wen' (Questions of Copyright Law of Artificial Intelligent-Generated Works) (in Chinese) (2020) 3 *Zhongwai faxue (Peking University Law Journal)* 653–73.

[57] Wanming Guo, 'Rengong zhineng shengcheng chengguo de falü xingzhi ji zhuzuoquan baohu' (On Legal Nature and Copyright Protection of the Works Generated by Artificial Intelligence) (in Chinese) (2022) 5 *Chuban faxing yanjiu (Publishing Research)* 58–64; Xiuqin Lin and Kaijie You, 'Banquan zhidu yingdui rengong zhineng chuangzuowu de lujing xuanze – yi minfa zixi lilun wei shijiao' (Path Choice for Copyright System Dealing with Artificial Intelligence Creations – From the Perspective of Fruits Theory in Civil Law) (in Chinese) (2018) 6 *Dianzi zhishi chanquan (Electronics Intellectual Property)* 13–19.

[58] Chen, 'Challenges and Responses', 23.

(1) it must fall within the realms of literature, art, and science;
(2) it must contain originality;
(3) it must be expressed in a tangible form; and
(4) it must be an intellectual achievement.[59]

For AI-generated content, the divergence of views mainly focuses on the second requirement – that is, how to assess originality. Some scholars holding the first view argue that originality is manifested in the author's creative process, while the AI generation process is mainly performed by AI.[60] Therefore, even if AI-generated content closely resembles human works, it lacks originality and cannot be identified as a copyrighted work.[61] This view is the "Subjective Originality Theory," which considers originality to be based on the author's personality.[62] In contrast, based on the belief that AI is, at the present stage, only a tool for human creation,[63] advocates of the second view argue for a "Objective Originality Theory." They propose that judgment on originality should focus on the content itself, rather than the author's personality or the creative process,[64] and argue that as long as AI-generated content is substantially different from existing works and therefore has value that deserves protection, it can meet the requirement of originality.[65] The main difference between the "Subjective Originality Theory" and the "Objective Originality Theory" is that the latter separates the question of originality from the question of authorship, which means whether the author is human or not should not substantially influence the assessment of originality itself.[66] However, some scholars arguing for the "Objective Originality Theory" point out that, besides originality, human involvement in AI generation as an act of creation is also required for copyright protection.[67] They argue that the act of creation should be evaluated by the extent of intellectual effort the human author puts into the AI-generated content, and the standard should be relatively loose to prevent the scope of protection for AI-generated works from being too narrow.[68] Nevertheless, setting an excessively low standard would also be undesirable, as acts such as inputting overly simple prompts should

[59] Art. 3 of the Copyright Law of the People's Republic of China stipulates:

> For purposes of this Law, the term "works" means intellectual achievements in the fields of literature, art and science, which are original and can be expressed in a certain form, including:

(1) written works;
(2) oral works;
(3) musical, dramatic, quyi, choreographic and acrobatic art works;
(4) works of the fine arts and architecture;
(5) photographic works;
(6) audiovisual works;
(7) graphic works such as drawings of engineering designs, product designs, maps and sketches, and model works;
(8) computer software; and
(9) other intellectual achievements conforming to the characteristics of the works.

The English translation is from the website www.chinajusticeobserver.com/law/x/copyright-law-of-china-20201111.

[60] Wang, 'Qualitative Analysis', 16.
[61] Yuan, 'Refutation', 26.
[62] Ibid., 25–6.
[63] Zhang and Bian, 'Research', 81.
[64] Ibid., 79.
[65] Ibid., 79–81.
[66] Ibid., 80.
[67] Ibid., 87.
[68] Ibid.

not qualify as acts of creation.[69] At the very least, the human's creative intention needs to be evident in the generation process.[70]

In judicial practice, Chinese courts have issued a number of decisions on the possibility of obtaining copyright protection for works generated by or with AI, offering somewhat inconsistent guidance. In 2019, the Beijing Internet Court denied copyright protection for an analysis report automatically generated by a third-party computer software (the "Film case").[71] Later that year, the Shenzhen Nanshan District People's Court decided that an article created by Tencent's AI writing tool Dreamwriter qualified for copyright protection.[72] Interestingly, although both courts acknowledged the originality of the AI-generated content in question, they adopted different approaches when determining the copyrightability.

In its 2019 decision, the Beijing Internet Court emphasized that besides originality, the creation and completion by natural persons should be a necessary condition for a work to qualify for protection under the Chinese Copyright Act. Since the software user (the plaintiff, Beijing Film Law Firm) only inserted keywords for search, the analysis report automatically generated by using the "Visualization" function is not an original expression of the user based on their thoughts and feelings. Thus, the court found that the analysis report should not be deemed to have been created by the software user and it is not a work under the Chinese Copyright Act. However, the court added that the decision that the analysis report does not constitute a work does not mean that it can enter the public domain and be freely used by the public. The court stated that the software user, as the one who paid the software fee and generated the report by setting keywords, should be entitled to relevant rights and interests of the report,[73] rather than the software developer who had already earned revenue from developing the software. This is because the software user has the motivation to use and disseminate the report, which can further benefit cultural dissemination and scientific development.

By contrast, the Shenzhen Nanshan District People's Court stated that the key to determining the copyrightability of the article in question is whether it has originality. The court determined the originality through the article itself as well as the creation process. First, the court examined if the article exhibited minimal creativity and reflected a logical, expressive structure based on data selection and analysis. Then, the court analyzed the creation process to confirm the presence of factors including the creator's individual selections, judgment, and skills. The creation process involved four stages: data handling, writing, verification, and distribution, all actively managed by Tencent's team. This included setting parameters and training the AI, highlighting significant human intellectual input beyond the AI's automated two-minute writing phase. The determinative factor was whether these activities constituted intellectual effort directly linked to the article's expression. The court concluded that the human-directed stages were integral to the creation, dismissing the notion that the AI's brief autonomous operation could solely define the creation process. Thus, the article was protected under copyright law, emphasizing the human contribution to AI-generated works.[74]

69 Ibid.

70 Ibid.

71 *Beijing Film Law Firm v. Beijing Baidu Netcom Technology Co., Ltd.*, Beijing Internet Court, 2018 Beijing 0491 Min Chu No. 239 (Apr. 25, 2019).

72 *Shenzhen Tencent Computer System Co., Ltd. v. Shanghai Yingxun Technology Co., Ltd.*, People's Court of Nanshan District, 2019 Guangdong 0305 Min Chu No. 14010 (Nov. 24, 2019).

73 Unfortunately the court did not specify what kind of rights and interests it had in mind here.

74 Haochen Sun, 'Redesigning Copyright Protection in the Era of Artificial Intelligence' (2022) 1213 *107 Iowa Law Review* 1213–51 at 1218–19.

Despite the different approaches taken by the two courts in determining originality and reaching distinct conclusions regarding copyrightability, we can still identify a commonality between the two decisions. That is, both rulings indicate that human intellectual input into AI-generated content is a necessary condition for copyright protection.

Also, more recently, in 2023, the Beijing Internet Court took a different angle from the Film case to assess the copyrightability of AI-generated content in *Li Yunkai v. Liu Yuanchun*.[75] Here, the court focused on the second and fourth requirements for copyrighted works, namely "originality" and "intellectual achievement." As the plaintiff selected prompts, arranged their order, set specific parameters, and selected the final image aligned with his conception, the court decided that the disputed image reflected the plaintiff's intellectual inputs and constituted his intellectual achievement. Furthermore, the plaintiff's personalized choices and aesthetic judgment throughout the generation process, involving not only the selection and arrangement of the prompts and parameters but also the refinement of the final output, transcended beyond "mechanical intellectual achievements" and met the requirement of originality. Thus, the court concluded that the disputed image constituted a copyrighted work.

Somewhat disconnected from the more radical academic debate, Chinese courts tend to consider AI-generated content as human-generated content as long as a sufficient level of intellectual effort is put into the creation of such content. This includes prompting the AI with the right instructions and the selection and arrangement of the generated content, reflecting the personal input and originality of the human author.[76]

18.3.2.2 Ownership of Copyrights for AI-Generated Works

After acknowledging copyrights for AI-generated works, another issue arises: how to determine the ownership of copyrights. Given that AI-generated works involve multiple stakeholders, including developers, owners, investors, and users of the AI, there are several views on this matter, with a tendency to approach this question on a case-by-case basis.

If there is an agreement among relevant parties on the ownership of copyrights for AI-generated works, such agreement shall prevail as long as it does not violate mandatory provisions of the law.[77] Article 9 of the "Interim Measures" also requires AI service providers to sign service agreements with users who register for their generative AI services, thereby clarifying the rights and obligations of both parties.[78] In practice, most AI products have service terms agreed upon by users and AI companies, which clarify the ownership of copyrights for the works.[79] However, considering that these service terms consist of many standard terms, assessing their

[75] *Li Yunkai v. Liu Yuanchun*, Beijing Internet Court, 2023 Beijing 0491 Min Chu No. 11279 (Nov. 27, 2023).

[76] Bruce Wang, Stefaan Meuwissen and Zhen (Katie) Feng, 'Beijing Internet Court Grants Copyright Protection for AI Artworks, but Copyrightability Debate of AI-Generated Output Continues' (2023). Available at www.engage.hoganlovells.com/knowledgeservices/news/beijing-internet-court-grants-copyright-protection-for-ai-artworks-but-copyrightability-debate-of-ai-generated-output-continues.

[77] Liu and Nie, 'Debate', 116.

[78] Art. 9 Item 2 of Interim Measures for the Management of Generative Artificial Intelligence Services stipulates: "Providers shall sign service agreements with users who register for their generative AI services (hereinafter 'users'), clarifying the rights and obligations of both parties."

The English translation is from the website www.chinalawtranslate.com/en/generative-ai-interim/.

[79] Liu and Nie, 'Debate', 116.

reasonableness, especially when the AI company retains all copyrights and interests in the works, can be guided by the provisions in the contract part of the Civil Code.[80]

If there is no such agreement, the person who made substantial contributions to AI-generated works should own the copyrights. From a broader perspective, investors, developers, and users all contribute to different stages of the work generation.[81] But according to Article 3 of the "Regulations for the Implementation of the Copyright Law of the People's Republic of China,"[82] the financial support provided by investors cannot be considered as creative input, and the contribution of investors to AI-generated works is often indirect, rendering investors ineligible for claiming copyrights in AI-generated works created with AI services that they helped build.[83] Developers and users, however, make substantial contributions at different stages of the AI generation process.[84] For example, the input data setting and algorithm design by developers can determine the breadth and depth of generated works, and the specific instructions entered by users can determine the specific expressions of generated works. Therefore, developers and users may, in theory, both have the potential to own copyrights under Chinese law.[85] The mainstream view would be that users should own the copyrights, though some academics have argued that developers should obtain copyright ownership. Even though developers cannot predict the specific generated content, each generation process must follow the track preset by the developers, providing developers with a general level of direction and control over the generated content.[86] Following this logic, the AI can be regarded as the extension of the developers' will, and the developers can own the copyrights of AI-generated works.[87] This view, however, goes against the emerging body of case law and against academic opinions that put an emphasis on the active involvement and decision-making of users, given that developers do not intellectually contribute to the specific content creation process.[88]

18.4 COMPARATIVE SUMMARY AND OUTLOOK

Both Japan and China are attempting to promote AI in order to maintain their positions as global technology leaders, continually adapting to rapidly changing technological landscapes to sustain economic growth and competitive advantage. Commentators around the world have addressed the perceived impact of copyright law on the progress of AI and related industries. Japan and China have chosen – probably more by coincidence than by long-term strategy – to provide for very different copyright law frameworks. While Japanese copyright law provides for wide-reaching copyright limitations against TDM use, Chinese law currently has no such

[80] Yili Tang and Sihan Niu, 'Lun rengong zhineng shengcheng zuopin de quanli zhuti ji qi zhuzuoquan guishu' (On Subjects and Ownership of Copyrights of Works Generated by Artificial Intelligence) (in Chinese) (2023) 11 *Fujian luntan (Fujian Tribune)* 107–22 at 121.

[81] Chen, 'Challenges and Responses', 27–8.

[82] Art. 3 of Regulations for the Implementation of the Copyright Law of the People's Republic of China stipulates: "The term 'creation' as referred to in the Copyright Law means intellectual activities in which literary, artistic or scientific works are directly created.

Any organizational activity, consultation, material support or other auxiliary services conducted or offered for another person's creation shall not be deemed as creation."

The English translation is from the website http://ipr.mofcom.gov.cn/zhuanti/jkblh/iplaws/copyright/zzqtl.pdf.

[83] Chen, 'Challenges and Responses', 28.

[84] Ibid.

[85] Ibid.

[86] Liu and Nie, 'Debate', 115.

[87] Ibid.

[88] Zhang and Bian, 'Research', 89.

statutory provisions in place. And while Japanese commentators have been rather reserved when it comes to copyright protection for AI-generated content, Chinese commentators and courts have been comparatively somewhat more open to considering protection for such content.

Policymakers and commentators have emphasized the importance of limitations in copyright law within the context of AI development. As noted, over the past decade and currently, Japan maintains a more technology-friendly copyright law. Nonetheless, Chinese companies appear to outperform their Japanese counterparts in securing leading positions in AI innovation. Leveraging a large domestic market that is often protected from superior foreign products or services, Chinese companies have also rapidly expanded their international presence in AI markets, frequently surpassing their Japanese counterparts in terms of global sales and market penetration. Chinese inventors also lead in the number of AI-related patents filed annually, showcasing a robust commitment to securing intellectual property in cutting-edge technologies.[89] These patents cover a wide range of innovations, from basic algorithms to complex applications in robotics and data analytics.[90] At the same time, and against the backdrop of a more technology-friendly copyright law, Japan seems to continue to perform very well when it comes to the global visibility of copyright-protected content. Japan maintains a strong presence in international media markets, and achieves broad international distribution and recognition of its copyrighted materials in fields such as film, music, and literature.[91] Again, these accomplishments may or may not be supported by recent developments within copyright law. Yet this disconnect between the international performance and visibility of certain sectors and industries from Japan and China and the structure of their respective copyright law regimes encourages further study into the connection between copyright law and AI.

[89] See e.g. WIPO, 'China Leads the World in AI Related Patent Filing' (2021), at www.wipo.int/about-wipo/en/offices/china/news/2021/news_0037.html.

[90] Ibid. We should add that more patents do not guarantee better technology, and the significance of AI patents would in demonstrating innovative leadership deserves a much closer look. That said, the high number of AI-related patents filed by Chinese companies both in China and abroad do at least indicate a strong level of commitment to underlying R&D.

[91] For example, Japanese anime like *Naruto*, *Dragon Ball*, and *One Piece* have gained significant global recognition, being translated into numerous languages and widely distributed across continents, and substantially enhancing Japan's cultural export influence.

19

Redefining Rivalry

Generative AI and the Evolving Landscape of Competition Law

Sylvia Papadopoulos

19.1 INTRODUCTION

19.1.1 Background

On 9 July 2021, President Biden of the United States of America issued an Executive Order on Promoting Competition in the American Economy. It opened as follows: '[A] fair, open, and competitive marketplace has long been a cornerstone of the American economy, while excessive market concentration threatens basic economic liberties, democratic accountability, and the welfare of workers, farmers, small businesses, startups, and consumers.'[1]

This principle is especially relevant amid rapid technological advancements like AI, where market dynamics shift quickly, incentivising businesses to improve products, enhance efficiency, and foster innovation.

Recent advances in deep learning have given rise to foundation models that underpin numerous generative AI applications. Understanding the data economy and its competition implications is fundamental for understanding how these AI advancements impact market dynamics.[2]

In the rapidly evolving landscape of artificial intelligence (AI) and generative AI (GenAI), significant legal developments affecting antitrust or competition interventions in the AI sector include:

- The Digital Markets Act in the EU – effective 2 May 2023.[3]
- The USA's Executive Order on AI (30 October 2023).[4]

[1] USA Government Presidential Actions, 'Executive Order on Promoting Competition in the American Economy' (9 July 2021), available at www.whitehouse.gov/briefing-room/presidential-actions/2021/07/09/executive-order-on-promoting-competition-in-the-american-economy/ (accessed 19 January 2024).

[2] T. Schrepel and A. Pentland, 'Competition between AI Foundation Models: Dynamics and Policy Recommendations' (June 2023) MIT Connection Science Working Paper 1-2023, 2–3, available at https://papers.ssrn.com/sol3/papers.cfm?abstract_id=4493900 (accessed 24 May 2024).

[3] Regulation (EU) 2022/1925 of the European Parliament and of the Council of 14 September 2022 on contestable and fair markets in the digital sector and amending Directives (EU) 2019/1937 and (EU) 2020/1828 (Digital Markets Act) OJ L 265, 12.10.2022 (hereinafter the DMA or Digital Markets Act).

[4] USA Government Presidential Actions, 'Executive Order on the Safe, Secure, and Trustworthy Development and Use of Artificial Intelligence' (30 October 2023) (hereinafter the US Executive Order on AI), discussed in more detail

- The G7 Digital Competition Communiqué (8 November 2023),[5] and
- The EU Artificial Intelligence Act (approved on 13 March 2024).[6]

This chapter explores the transformative impact of generative AI on market structures and competition law, investigating how GenAI challenges traditional business models and antitrust laws. It outlines the traditional regulatory focus on market power and consumer impact, introduces complexities of the data economy and market concentration, identifies challenges for competition law, and reviews current regulatory approaches in the United States and the European Union, assessing their effectiveness in the GenAI context. The chapter concludes with insights and ideas to promote innovation while ensuring market competitiveness and fairness.

19.1.2 *The Data Economy and Competition*

The USA's antitrust approach to big tech has traditionally focused on abuse of market power and consumer impact.[7] It seems to take retrospective action, after an abuse of power has occurred.[8] There's a strong belief in the market's ability to self-correct, which is reflected in the legal doctrines requiring plaintiffs to meet a high burden of proof to demonstrate anti-competitive behaviour.[9] This approach has been criticised by Wu, who argues that the enforcement of antitrust law has not kept pace with the digitalisation of the economy, potentially allowing a few tech giants to hold significant market power that is retrospectively difficult to correct.[10]

Taking a different approach, the EU has conducted several high-profile investigations into tech business practices, resulting in substantial fines and regulatory changes such as:

- Google Shopping Case AT.39740 (2017): €2.42 billion fine for giving an illegal advantage to its own comparison-shopping service.[11]
- Google Android Case AT.40099 (2018): €4.34 billion fine for imposing illegal restrictions on Android device manufacturers to cement its dominance in internet searches.[12]

below at Section 19.3.2, available at www.whitehouse.gov/briefing-room/presidential-actions/2023/10/30/executive-order-on-the-safe-secure-and-trustworthy-development-and-use-of-artificial-intelligence/ (accessed 19 January 2024).

5 G7 Competition Authorities and Policymakers' Summit Digital Competition Communiqué, Tokyo, Japan, 8 November 2023 (hereinafter the G7 Digital Competition Communiqué), available at www.bundeskartellamt.de/SharedDocs/Publikation/EN/Others/G7_2023_Communique.pdf?__blob=publicationFile&v=2 (accessed 28 April 2024).

6 European Parliament, 'Corrigendum to the Position of the European Parliament Adopted at First Reading on 13 March 2024 with a view to the adoption of Regulation (EU) 2024/1689 of the European Parliament and of the Council laying down harmonised rules on artificial intelligence and amending Regulations (EC) No. 300/2008, (EU) No. 167/2013, (EU) No. 168/2013, (EU) 2018/858, (EU) 2018/1139 and (EU) 2019/2144 and Directives 2014/90/EU, (EU) 2016/797, and (EU) 2020/1828 (Artificial Intelligence Act) P9_TA(2024)0138 (COM(2021)0206 – C9-0146/2021 – 2021/0106(COD))' (2024) (hereinafter the EU AI Act), available at www.europarl.europa.eu/doceo/document/TA-9-2024-0138-FNL-COR01_EN.pdf (accessed 28 April 2024).

7 A. Aridi and U. Petrovčič, 'Big Tech, Small Tech, and the Data Economy: What Role for EU Competition Law?' (World Bank Group, 2019) 3, available at https://documents1.worldbank.org/curated/en/360561577731546238/pdf/Big-Tech-Small-Tech-and-the-Data-Economy-What-Role-for-EU-Competition-Law.pdf (accessed 15 March 2024).

8 *Id.*, 8.

9 *Id.*

10 T. Wu, 'Be Afraid of Economic "Bigness". Be Very Afraid', *New York Times* (10 November 2018), available at www.nytimes.com/2018/11/10/opinion/sunday/fascism-economy-monopoly.html (accessed 15 March 2024); T. Wu, 'The Monopolization Movement' in *The Curse of Bigness: Antitrust in the New Gilded Age* (Columbia Global Reports, 2018), 24–32.

11 Available at https://competition-cases.ec.europa.eu/cases/AT.39740 (accessed 25 May 2024).

12 Available at https://competition-cases.ec.europa.eu/cases/AT.40099 (accessed 25 May 2024).

- AdSense Case AT.40411 (2019): €1.49 billion fine for restricting third-party websites' search adverts.[13]

These cases illustrate a proactive stance on ensuring market fairness and preventing the abuse of dominance in digital markets. The EU has also enacted legislation (discussed below) which indirectly allows for greater scrutiny of anti-competitive behaviour. Despite criticisms, the United States has seen increasing scrutiny of large tech firms, such as:

- Amazon's Use of Marketplace Data: The Federal Trade Commission's (FTC's) investigation into Amazon's use of data from third-party sellers on its platform to inform its own product development and sales strategies, potentially unfairly disadvantaging independent sellers.[14]
- House Judiciary Committee Report (2020): Highlighted several anti-competitive practices by Amazon, calling for significant reforms, including structural separations and stricter merger control to prevent anti-competitive behaviour.[15]

However, the US approach remains largely focused on proving consumer harm, which can be a higher barrier to enforcement than the EU's market fairness criteria. Some commentators in the USA have posited the necessity to dismantle or limit the power of large tech.[16] Others have called for reforms to the current legal framework.[17]

The role that competition law plays (or should play) in the data economy has also been at the centre of the policy debates in many other countries. In particular, the EU has shown less confidence in the market's self-correcting mechanisms and seems to emphasise stricter regulation, with a proactive stance on market fairness, imposing more rigorous enforcement, and penalties for non-compliance.[18] This is partly because consumer protection legislation at EU level is mandated through primary law (Articles 169(1) and 169(2)(a) of the TFEU),[19] ensuring

[13] Available at https://competition-cases.ec.europa.eu/cases/AT.40411 (accessed 25 May 2024).

[14] See K. Weise, 'U.S. Investigates Amazon's Business Practices', *New York Times* (11 October 2020).

[15] Subcommittee on Antitrust, Commercial, and Administrative Law of the Committee on the Judiciary Investigation of Competition in Digital Markets, US House of Representatives (6 October 2020).

[16] According to E. Warren (US Senator), 'Big tech companies have bulldozed competition, used our private information for profit, and tilted the playing field against everyone else' and she therefore called for a 'Breakup of Big Tech' (2019), available at https://2020.elizabethwarren.com/toolkit/break-up-big-tech (accessed 19 April 2024).

[17] See e.g. C. A. Makridis and J. Thayer, 'The Big Tech Antitrust Paradox: A Re-evaluation of the Consumer Welfare Standard for Digital Markets' (2024) 27 *Stanford Technology Law Review* 71, where the authors critically examine 'the application of the consumer welfare standard in antitrust jurisprudence, a standard that has enabled such corporations to amass significant market power without triggering traditional antitrust scrutiny. Courts have abstained from applying extant antitrust principles to these firms, largely due to an overreliance on consumer price as the litmus test for competitive harm under the consumer welfare standard'. They posit 'that this misapplication perpetuates market concentration, thereby inhibiting innovation and disproportionately impacting vulnerable consumer demographics and small enterprises'. To rectify this interpretive misstep, they advocate for the reconceptualisation of data as a currency.

[18] There is a long list of consumer laws in the EU, including: the Consumer Rights Directive 2011/83/EU; the unfair Commercial Practices Directive 2005/29/EC; the Unfair Contract Terms Directive 93/13/EEC; the Better Enforcement and Modernisation of Union Consumer Protection Rules Directive 2019/2161; Directive 2019/771 On Certain Aspects Concerning Contracts for the Sale of Goods; the newer Directive (EU) 2019/770 on Certain Aspects Concerning Contracts for the Supply of Digital Content and Digital Services; and Regulation 2019/1150 of the European Parliament and of the Council of 20 June 2019 on Promoting Fairness and Transparency for Business Users of Online Intermediation Services. This is not a complete list.

[19] Treaty on the Functioning of the European Union (Consolidated version 2016) OJ C202 7 June 2016 (hereafter TFEU), is regarded as one of the primary sources of EU law along with the Treaty on European Union (Consolidated version 2016) OJ C202 7 June 2016, also known as the Maastricht Treaty (hereafter TEU) and the Charter of Fundamental Rights of the European Union (Consolidated version 2016) OJ C202 7 June 2016 (hereafter EU

a high level of consumer protection.[20] Similarly the competition aspects are contained in Articles 101–109 of the TFEU.[21] These aim to prevent restrictions and distortions in the market such as the abuse of dominance and other anti-competitive practices.[22]

19.1.3 *Understanding Foundation Models from Competition Perspectives*

Foundation models (FMs) are language models (LMs) using extensive input data to produce outputs, including text, images, songs, and videos. LMs are essential for running natural language processing (NLP) tasks, which automate functions such as summarising information or question-and-answer outputs. NLP refers to computer programs and tools that automate natural language functions by analysing, producing, modifying, or responding to human texts and speech. NLP is a subset of AI that uses language as an input, produces language as an output, or both. FMs rely on three essential resources: language models, data, and computing resources.[23]

FM's can be general-purpose like ChatGPT and Google Bard, which can handle a wide range of tasks, or domain-specific like BloombergGPT, which are specialised for specific fields.[24] They learn by analysing datasets and identifying patterns. For example, models trained on data about cats learn to recognise and identify cats, but pretraining on large datasets is essential for LMs to perform their tasks effectively.[25]

Models are either proprietary or open-source. Closed-source models, such as OpenAI's generative pre-trained transformer (GPT), are licensed for commercial use but not modification, while open-source models allow modification, improving and correcting errors but also posing some security risks.[26]

19.2 GENERATIVE AI CHALLENGES FOR COMPETITION LAW

19.2.1 *Introduction*

Technological inflection points can introduce new means of competing, catalysing opportunity, innovation, and growth. FMs are tech inflection points and competition bodies need to guard against tactics that undermine fair competition in the industry. The G7 Competition Authorities

Charter). *Cf.* J. Trzaskowski, A. Savin, B. Lundqvist and P. Lindskoug, *Introduction to EU Internet Law* (Ex Tuto Publishing A/S Denmark, 2015), 20.

[20] N. Reich, H. W . Micklitz, P. Rott and K. Tonner, *European Consumer Law*, 2nd ed. (Intersentia, 2014), 20.

[21] Several regulations implementing these provisions of the TFEU have been implemented, such as: Regulation 1/2003 on the Implementation of the Rules on Competition Laid Down in Articles 81 and 82 of the Treaty; Regulation 773/2004 Relating to the Conduct of Proceedings by the Commission Pursuant to Articles 81 and 82 of the EC Treaty; the Directive 2014/104/EU on Antitrust Damages; and most importantly Regulation 2022/1925 of the European Parliament and of the Council of 14 September 2022 on Contestable and Fair Markets in the Digital Sector amending Directives (EU) 2019/1937 and (EU) 2020/1828 (Digital Markets Act) OJ L 265, 12 October 2022 (hereafter the DMA). As far as they are relevant these are discussed in more detail below at Section 19.3.4.2.

[22] Arts. 101–109 TFEU.

[23] OECD, 'AI Language Models: Technological, Socio-Economic and Policy Considerations' OECD Digital Economy Papers No. 352 (OECD Publishing, 2023), at 14, available at https://doi.org/10.1787/13d38f92-en (accessed 30 April 2024); C. Carugati, 'The Generative AI Challenges for Competition Authorities' (2024) 59(1) *Intereconomics* 2.

[24] Schrepel and Pentland, 'Competition between AI Foundation Models', 4.

[25] Carugati, 'Generative AI Challenges', 2.

[26] *Id.*

have highlighted risks like restricting key inputs for AI development, extending market power in adjacent markets, and increasing barriers to entry as issues that require attention.[27]

Given the impact of GenAI in society, the question of whether it is and will remain a competitive industry merits consideration, with several competition authorities and governments already examining this issue.[28] GenAI may differ from other AI technologies, because it can create new content and solutions autonomously, and these may disrupt traditional markets in unexpected ways and thereby introducing new antitrust considerations.

There is an increasingly concentrated digital economy which may affect how the AI market evolves. Therefore, it is also important to consider competition in the broader AI markets and the data economies that have developed with earlier technologies.[29] For example, the regulatory and competitive actions in these adjacent markets can set precedents that may affect GenAI market dynamics.[30]

The Stigler Center Report notes several features driving digital market monopolisation, such as strong network effects, economies of scale, near-zero marginal costs, high returns, and low distribution costs, leading to 'winner takes all' markets. The lack of entry of competitors into markets, despite high profits, suggests either barriers to entry or exclusionary conduct, or both.[31] The question is, will or has a similar pattern emerged in AI markets or in GenAI, markets? Do these new markets exhibit similar characteristics and features that could lead them to become similarly incontestable arenas?

This next section explores Generative AI competition challenges across interconnected levels: (a) the infrastructure and computing level; (b) data and (c) model levels (collectively the infrastructure and computing, data, and model levels are also often referred to as the upstream inputs); and (d) the applications level (as the downstream outputs). Within these different levels, the GenAI market has also structured itself into ecosystems,[32] with multifaceted complex relations between participants at all levels.[33]

19.2.2 *Challenges at the Infrastructure and Computing Resources Level*

Infrastructure and computing resources – that is, the first of the upstream inputs – are critical in GenAI ecosystems. Cloud computing is a significant resource in GenAI markets and is already a

[27] G7 Competition Authorities, 'Joint Statement from the Heads of the G7 Competition Authorities on Competition in Digital Markets' (2023), available at www.jftc.go.jp/en/pressreleases/yearly-2023/November/231108G7_result1EN.pdf (accessed 27 April 2024).

[28] See for examples The White House, 'Readout of White House Meeting on Competition Policy and Artificial Intelligence' (20 January 2024), available at https://bidenwhitehouse.archives.gov/briefing-room/statements-releases/2024/01/20/readout-of-white-house-meeting-on-competition-policy-and-artificial-intelligence/ (accessed 1 February 2025); UK Competition and Markets Authority (CMA), 'AI Foundation Models: Initial Report' (18 September 2023), available at www.gov.uk/government/publications/ai-foundation-models-initial-report (accessed 22 April 2024).

[29] OECD, 'Artificial Intelligence, Data and Competition' (2024) OECD *Artificial Intelligence Papers* 8, available at https://doi.org/10.1787/e7e88884-en (accessed 22 May 2024).

[30] A. Czerwonko and J. White, 'Life after the Hype: How AI Is Transforming Industries and Economies', World Economic Forum (WEF) (1 December 2023), available at www.weforum.org/agenda/2023/12/life-after-the-hype-how-ai-is-transforming-industries-and-economies/#:~:text = URL%3A%20https%3A%2F%2Fwww.weforum.org%2Fagenda%2F2023%2F12%2Flife (accessed 22 April 2024).

[31] 'Stigler Committee on Digital Platforms, Final Report' (2019) 8–9 (hereinafter Stigler Center Report), available at https://publicknowledge.org/wp-content/uploads/2021/11/Stigler-Committee-on-Digital-Platforms-Final-Report.pdf (accessed 19 April 2024).

[32] 'Ecosystem' is a concept that refers to a group of interacting firms that depend on each other's activities, usually for the purpose of innovation. See F. Bostoen and A. van der Veer, 'Regulating Competition in Generative AI: A Matter of Trajectory, Timing and Tools' (2024) TILEC Discussion Paper 2, available at https://ssrn.com/abstract = 4756641 (accessed 22 April 2024).

[33] *Id.*

highly concentrated market, with Microsoft Azure and Amazon Web Services holding 60–80 per cent of market share.[34] In addition, Nvidia's microchips (in particular, its graphics processing units or GPUs) control about 90 per cent of the AI GPU market.[35] These concentrations are also a point of concern to competition authorities and are under investigation by competition authorities such as the French Autorité De La Concurrence[36] and the UK Competition and Markets Authority (CMA).[37]

The ecosystems that are starting to develop begin with model developers partnering with large cloud providers to access cloud computing resources,[38] initially fostering some competition. However, Von Thun is of the opinion that these partnerships are

> just the latest example of Big Tech's efforts to corner the nascent generative AI market through strategic investments and partnerships. In exchanging model access for use of the highly concentrated computing resources they own and control, the tech giants are effectively buying themselves an insurance policy, ensuring that even if their own in-house AI efforts flop, their digital dominance will be maintained.[39]

Examples include the September 2023 Amazon 'strategic collaboration' with Anthropic[40] and Microsoft's partnership with OpenAI.[41] Others include Hugging Face (Amazon), Cohere (Google, Nvidia), Stability AI (Amazon), and Inflection AI (Microsoft, Nvidia).[42] Some of these collaborations are also being investigated by competition authorities.[43] In the USA, the Federal Trade Commission (FTC) launched an inquiry, requesting information from Alphabet, Amazon, Anthropic, Microsoft, and OpenAI on these partnerships.[44] This trend toward concentration among 'hyper-scalers' might intensify as the demand for GenAI increases.[45]

[34] *Id.*

[35] *Id.*, 3.

[36] See www.autoritedelaconcurrence.fr/en/press-release/cloud-computing-autorite-de-la-concurrence-issues-its-market-study-competition-cloud (29 June 2023); and M. A. Cherney, 'Nvidia's French Offices Raided in Cloud-Computing Competition Inquiry', *Wall Street Journal* (28 September 2023), available at www.reuters.com/technology/nvidias-french-offices-raided-cloud-computing-competition-inquiry-wsj-2023-09-28/ (accessed 23 March 2024).

[37] See www.gov.uk/government/news/cma-launches-market-investigation-into-cloud-services (5 October 2023) (accessed 23 March 2024).

[38] Carugati, 'Generative AI Challenges', 14.

[39] M. von Thun, 'Monopoly Power Is the Elephant in the Room in the AI Debate' (2023), available at www.techpolicy.press/monopoly-power-is-the-elephant-in-the-room-in-the-ai-debate/ (accessed 30 April 2024).

[40] Amazon, 'Amazon and Anthropic Deepen Their Shared Commitment to Advancing Generative AI' (2024), available at www.aboutamazon.com/news/company-news/amazon-anthropic-ai-investment (accessed 30 April 2024).

[41] Microsoft, 'Microsoft and OpenAI Extend Partnership' (2023), available at https://blogs.microsoft.com/blog/2023/01/23/microsoftandopenaiextendpartnership/ (accessed 30 April 2024).

[42] Von Thun, 'Monopoly Power Is the Elephant in the Room'.

[43] See UK Competition and Markets Authority, 'Microsoft / OpenAI Partnership Merger Inquiry' (8 December 2023), available at www.gov.uk/cma-cases/microsoft-slash-openai-partnership-merger-inquiry?utm_medium = email&utm_campaign = govuk-notifications-topic&utm_source = ab4e8ca7-48be-410c-bc56-1448ef35bf0f&utm_content = immediately (accessed 30 April 2024); F. Y. Chee, 'Microsoft's OpenAI Partnership Could Face EU Antitrust Probe, Sources Say', Reuters (8 April 2024), available at www.reuters.com/technology/microsofts-openai-partnership-could-face-eu-antitrust-probe-sources-say-2024-04-18/ (accessed 30 April 2024); S. Stolton, 'Microsoft's $13 Billion Deal with OpenAI Falls Short of a Takeover, EU Competition Regulator Finds', Fortune / Bloomberg (18 April 2024), available at https://fortune.com/europe/2024/04/18/microsoft-satya-nadella-13-billion-deal-openai-sam-altman-dodges-eu-probe/ (accessed 24 April 2024).

[44] Federal Trade Commission (USA), 'FTC Launches Inquiry into Generative AI Investments and Partnerships' (25 January 2024), available at www.ftc.gov/news-events/news/press-releases/2024/01/ftc-launches-inquiry-generative-ai-investments-partnerships (accessed 24 April 2024).

[45] Carugati, 'Generative AI Challenges', 15.

Mergers or partnerships can influence market structures, sometimes[46] reducing competition by eliminating current or potential competitors, which are also referred to as 'killer acquisitions'.[47] This is particularly relevant in innovative markets where combining different ideas can create unforeseen benefits.[48] However, merger control can be challenging if transactions that raise competition issues fall outside current jurisdictional boundaries, making each case dependent on its specific facts.[49] Finally, to a lesser degree, access to expertise and talent is another potential barrier to entry, although over time, demand and supply may balance this out.[50]

19.2.3 *Challenges at the Data Level*

19.2.3.1 Introduction

Data is critical for foundation models and AI markets, serving as a primary input.[51] It is well-known that FMs and AI are derived by applying machine learning techniques to enormous amounts of data.[52] The FMs derive patterns from extensive datasets, which can be proprietary (e.g. DeepMind's MassiveText) or open-source (e.g. HuggingChat OASST1 or Amazon Massive Dataset).[53]

Data and abuse of dominance practices gained prominence in the 'consumer data' and digital advertising markets and in cases where companies leveraged data from third-party sellers on their platforms to their own advantage. The EU's scrutiny of Amazon's use of third-party seller data exemplifies concerns about how large platforms exploit data to reinforce their market positions, potentially at the expense of other competitors and market fairness.[54] While data is a significant competitive advantage for platforms like Alphabet and Meta,[55] Manne and Auer argue that there is little or no empirical evidence that data collected by one of these platforms might confer a decisive competitive advantage in adjacent markets.[56] Newer entrants such as OpenAI and Midjourney have outperformed established firms despite their vast data resources, possibly highlighting that data alone does not guarantee market leadership.[57]

Thus, there is a case to be made that it's the quality of the data that is significant and so if we look at the Koala Model (trained for less than $100), researchers concluded that for GenAI,

[46] OECD, 'Artificial Intelligence, Data and Competition', 29.

[47] *Id.*

[48] *Id.*

[49] *Id.*

[50] *Id.*, 34–35.

[51] Z. Marosi, 'Initial Review of Generative AI and Competition Law: Insights from European Competition Authorities', DLA Piper (6 March 2024), available at www.dlapiper.com/en/insights/blogs/antitrust-matters/2024/initial-review-of-generative-ai-and-competition-law (accessed 4 April 2024); Carugati, 'Generative AI Challenges', 4.

[52] OECD, 'Artificial Intelligence, Data and Competition', 18.

[53] Carugati, 'Generative AI Challenges', 5.

[54] According to EU investigations into Amazon, it was seen that when providing a marketplace for independent sellers, Amazon continuously collects data about the activity on its platform. It became clear that Amazon used competitively sensitive information about its marketplace sellers, their products, and transactions on the marketplace to launch and promote its own products as a retailer. Case AT.40462 *Amazon Marketplace* and AT.40703 *Amazon Buy Box* 20 December 2022, available at https://ec.europa.eu/competition/antitrust/cases1/202310/AT_40703_8990760_1533_5.pdf (accessed 10 April 2024).

[55] Carugati, 'Generative AI Challenges', 14.

[56] G. A. Manne and D. Auer, 'From Data Myths to Data Reality: What Generative AI Can Tell Us About Competition Policy (and Vice Versa)', *CPI Antitrust Chronicle*, 23 February 2024 (International Center for Law & Economics), available at https://laweconcenter.org/resources/from-data-myths-to-data-reality-what-generative-ai-can-tell-us-about-competition-policy-and-vice-versa/ (accessed 30 April 2024).

[57] *Id.*, 4; *cf.* Carugati, 'Generative AI Challenges', 14.

prioritising data quality reduces computing power needs and data training costs. Thus, the trends in the online advertising markets might not yet hold absolutely true in the GenAI markets when it comes to data dominance.[58]

This certainly does not mean that data is worthless, or that control of a critical upstream input (dataset) will not lead to the exclusion of rivals, and it does not necessarily mean that data will not become an advantage when the GenAI market starts addressing issues of monetisation and scale.[59]

High-quality proprietary datasets derived from adjacent markets can offer a considerable advantage. For instance, in the legal tech sector, companies (publishers) that possess large, high-quality datasets of legal information may be able to leverage the advantages of GenAI over competitors by restricting access to these datasets. The key issue would be whether such actions harm competition by unfairly excluding competitors or creating barriers to entry, especially if the datasets are essential for innovation or competition in the legal tech field.

While owning proprietary datasets itself is not problematic, leveraging them to deny competitors access could be considered an abuse of a dominant position under competition law, particularly in jurisdictions like the EU, which enforces strict rules on market dominance under Article 102 of the TFEU. The same principles can apply under the Sherman Act in the United States if the behaviour stifles competition.

In this case, the use of proprietary datasets combined with GenAI could magnify competitive concerns. If a publisher holds a dominant position and uses its datasets to enhance its own GenAI capabilities while denying access to others, it could be argued that this behaviour creates an unfair advantage and may restrict innovation, ultimately harming consumers. It could set up an interesting tension between copyright and competition law.

Copyright law grants the owner of a dataset (such as a legal publisher) exclusive rights over its use and distribution, protecting their intellectual property. This incentivises the creation and maintenance of such datasets, which can be costly and time-consuming to develop. Publishers can lawfully choose to limit access to these proprietary datasets, which is a legitimate exercise of their copyright. On the other hand, competition law aims to prevent market players, especially dominant ones, from abusing their market position to stifle competition. If a company's refusal to share its copyright-protected datasets with competitors results in an anti-competitive effect (e.g. creating barriers to entry or innovation), competition authorities may scrutinise this behaviour as an abuse of dominance.

The principles of the 'essential facilities doctrine' may apply, where access to a particular dataset is deemed indispensable for competitors to operate or innovate in the market. This doctrine has been used sparingly but could apply where withholding access significantly harms competition.[60]

[58] Manne and Auer, 'From Data Myths to Data Reality', 11. Koala is a chatbot trained by fine-tuning Meta's Llama on dialogue data gathered from the web and for under $100. X. Geng et al., 'Koala: A Dialogue Model for Academic Research' (2023) Berkeley Artificial Intelligence Research (BAIR), available at https://bair.berkeley.edu/blog/2023/04/03/koala/ (accessed 21 April 2024), see also Carugati, 'Generative AI Challenges', 5.

[59] Manne and Auer, 'From Data Myths to Data Reality', 11; Carugati, 'Generative AI Challenges', 5.

[60] In the USA, see for example: *Otter Tail Power Co. v. United States*, 410 U.S. 366 (1973); *MCI Communications Corp. v. AT&T*, 708 F.2d 1081 (7th Cir. 1983). In the EU, see for example: *Oscar Bronner GmbH & Co. KG v. Mediaprint*, Case C-7/97 [1998] ECR I-7791; *Microsoft Corp. v. Commission*, Case T-201/04 [2007] ECR II-3601; *MS Health GmbH & Co. OHG v. NDC Health GmbH & Co. KG*, Case C-418/01 [2004] ECR I-5039; and in South Africa: *Competition Commission v. Senwes Ltd*, 87/CAC/FEB09 [2012] ZACAC 6. Senwes, a dominant provider of grain storage services, was found to have engaged in exclusionary practices by denying competitors access to its storage facilities. The South African Competition Appeal Court held that this refusal harmed competition, applying principles similar to the essential facilities doctrine.

The tension lies in balancing the protection of intellectual property under copyright law with the need to maintain a competitive market under competition law, particularly when access to key datasets is crucial for technological advancement, such as in the use of GenAI in the legal tech sector.

19.2.3.2 Data Scraping

Data scraping, also known as web scraping, is the process of using an algorithm to extract information from websites.[61] Carugati is of the opinion that data scraping may be an anti-competitive practice in GenAI markets,[62] but it does present a slightly grey area in law as it overlaps with intellectual property rights, website contractual terms and conditions, and in the EU with the Database Directive.[63]

A potential basis for an unfair competition claim is that the scraped data serves as a substitute for the original website.[64] If users can obtain the relevant information from the GenAI application, they may visit the original site less frequently, reducing its traffic and advertising revenue.[65] By generating content from content creators, FMs have the potential to reduce traffic to the original content because users may not have to consult the source, potentially excluding them from the market.[66] This practice appears highly unethical and contrary to fair competition principles, even if the scraper avoids intellectual property or contractual claims.[67]

19.2.4 *Challenges at the Model Level*

19.2.4.1 Introduction

The model level in GenAI includes large language models (LLMs) and foundation models, driving AI applications.[68] These models possess platform-like characteristics, allowing independent developers to create their own products on top of or by using the technology. For example, OpenAI offers 'Application Programming Interfaces' or APIs for developers to integrate into their products[69] as

[61] IBM Developer Tutorial, 'Scrape Data from the Web Using Python and AI' (2019), available at https://developer.ibm.com/tutorials/scrape-data-from-the-web-using-watson-studio/ (accessed 21 April 2024).

[62] Carugati, 'Generative AI Challenges', 16. Data scraping intersects with competition law, when it seeks to undercut competitors unfairly, when scraping is aimed at gaining unfair competitive advantage, when conduct is misleading or misrepresentative, or if scraping harvests proprietary information. H. Kiviniemi, 'Web-Scraping as a Competition Law Offence' (2019) LLM Thesis Tilburg University 36, available at https://arno.uvt.nl/show.cgi?fid = 150060 (accessed 21 April 2024).

[63] Directive 96/9/EC of the European Parliament and of the Council of 11 March 1996 on the Legal Protection of Databases OJ L 77, 27 March 1996 (Database Directive).

[64] Kiviniemi, 'Web-Scraping as a Competition Law Offence', 44. See also C-457/10 *AstraZeneca AB and AstraZeneca plc v. European Commission*, ECLI: EU: C:2012:770, 6 December 2012 at para. 112.

[65] Kiviniemi, 'Web-Scraping as a Competition Law Offence', 44. See *hiQ Labs Inc. v. LinkedIn Corp.* 938 F.3d 985 (9th Cir. 2019), a United States Ninth Circuit case about web scraping. The 9th Circuit affirmed the district court's preliminary injunction, preventing LinkedIn from denying the plaintiff, hiQ Labs, from accessing LinkedIn's publicly available LinkedIn member profiles.

[66] Carugati, 'Generative AI Challenges', 16.

[67] Kiviniemi, 'Web-Scraping as a Competition Law Offence', 44.

[68] Bostoen and van der Veer, 'Regulating Competition in Generative AI'.

[69] See https://platform.openai.com/. An API (Application Programming Interface) is a set of rules that enables software programs to communicate with each other to exchange data, features, and functionality. APIs act as intermediaries, allowing developers to use pre-existing functions and avoid redundant work by integrating already-built components into their new applications. Thus, an API is a way for one piece of software to use the functions of another piece of software. See Cloudflare, 'What Is an API?' (undated), available at www.cloudflare.com/en-gb/learning/security/api/

well as a GPT store where these can be sold on to users,[70] while Meta goes a step further by open-sourcing its LLM, known as Llama, enabling developers to customise the model itself.[71]

An intriguing aspect of FM development is the balance between proprietary and open-source models, with open-source historically driving innovation but now facing a shift towards proprietary models.[72] At the moment, both proprietary and open-source models compete across various parameters, including task requirements, language specifications, and model size, and developers can leverage a vast array of public and proprietary datasets, which are tailored and can be based on specific tasks, languages, and domains.[73]

Open-source models promote dynamic competition and value creation, relying on shared data and code within the software commons. This ecosystem includes tacit knowledge and insights, often regulated by communities of practice. However, developing and running these models is costly, leading to economic pressure towards monopolies.[74]

According to Schrepel and Potts, FMs have unique economic, legal, and mathematical features that make them tricky for competition policy, such as having characteristics that accentuate anti-competitive behaviour; it is challenging to protect these models with patents or capital investment, but they benefit from increasing returns because the more they're used, the more valuable they become. Also, they form the backbone for building applications, and this means developers prefer a few main models to ensure compatibility and network effects (ecosystem dynamics). Developing and running these models is costly due to the computing power required, and thus venture capital usually expects returns from exclusive access or use. This creates strong economic pressures towards monopoly or limited competition, where prices per unit are much higher than the marginal costs that are fixed. Finally, much of the innovation and production in this area happens in a shared, collaborative environment and is likely to continue this way.[75]

Their suggestions include that policymakers consider introducing open-source specific legal exemptions into new rules and standards, with lighter burdens of compliance.[76] Focusing on closed-source models for regulation, while allowing exemptions for open-source models, can enhance transparency, competition, and innovation.[77] They supplement these suggestions with several economic measures to support open-source such as tax incentives.[78]

Their final argument is that that competition authorities should focus on closed-source models and allow exemptions for open-source models because: (a) open-source are more transparent in nature than closed models; (b) open-source can be freely copied (forked) and adapted, creating diversity and competition through innovation; and (c) companies offering open-source models do not have the same power to leverage market positions because they are

what-is-an-api/; or IBM, 'What Is an API (application programming interface)?' (9 April 2024), available at www.ibm.com/topics/api (all accessed 22 February 2024).

70 See https://chatgpt.com/gpts?oai-dm = 1 (accessed 22 February 2024).

71 See https://llama.meta.com (accessed 22 February 2024); Bostoen and van der Veer, 'Regulating Competition in Generative AI'.

72 OECD, 'Artificial Intelligence, Data and Competition', 18.

73 Carugati, 'Generative AI Challenges', 14.

74 T. Schrepel and J. Potts, 'Measuring the Openness of AI Foundation Models: Competition and Policy Implications', SciencesPo Digital, Governance and Sovereignty Working Paper (May 2024) 5–7, available at https://papers.ssrn.com/sol3/papers.cfm?abstract_id = 4827358 (accessed 25 May 2024).

75 *Id.*, 8.

76 *Id.*, 25.

77 *Id.*, 25–26.

78 *Id.*, 25.

freely accessible with no barriers to entry and are often more interoperable and compatible, leading to thriving ecosystems.[79]

19.2.4.2 Intellectual Property Rights

Intellectual property rights grant the owner or rights holders a limited term monopoly over the use of data, technology, or methodologies.[80] Model developers train and deploy their models on both public and proprietary datasets, including copyrighted data. Copyright protection requires the data owner's consent to use data, or a licence.[81]

One of the major impacts of IP rights is on the accessibility of datasets. Data owners might choose to license their datasets for a fee, creating a barrier to entry for smaller companies or new entrants who may not have the financial resources to pay for these licences. This can lead to a competitive advantage for those with greater control over copyrighted data, allowing them to access and utilise high-quality, proprietary datasets for training their models.[82]

Around the globe, there have been concerns that some model developers use datasets without consent, leading to litigation in several countries, such as the ongoing lawsuit by the *New York Times* in the United States against OpenAI and Microsoft.[83]

Another uncertainty is the extent to which the use of some data, for example data that is publicly available, may give rise to potential risks of copyright infringement. There is uncertainty on the copyright implications for AI, both in terms of legal cases against AI developers and how they used data, as well as the legal status for outputs that firms create using generative AI. The outcomes of legal cases could have implications for the ability of firms to access the data required to train large FMs, and one might speculate that it could lead to increased importance for proprietary, or exclusively licensed, datasets.[84]

19.2.5 *Challenges at the Applications Level*

19.2.5.1 Commercialisation Methods

GenAI adoption across sectors will significantly alter market dynamics, creating new business opportunities and disrupting traditional models. Focusing on GenAI's application as a downstream output, where models are deployed to end users for tasks like office assistance and content creation, is important for understanding market impacts.

Applications raise several competition issues at both downstream and upstream levels that deserve in-depth scrutiny. At the upstream level, model and application developers use a cloud provider that hosts the model. In turn, cloud providers might impose technical and commercial conditions limiting interoperability, reinforcing their position.[85]

FMs also benefit from positive feedback loops because the more users they attract, the better the training data, improving the quality of the FM;[86] but the learning curve will flatten over

[79] *Id.*, 27.
[80] OECD, *Handbook on Competition Policy in the Digital Age* (OECD, 2022), 14.
[81] Carugati, 'Generative AI Challenges', 17–18.
[82] *Id.*
[83] *Id.*
[84] OECD, 'Artificial Intelligence, Data and Competition', 30.
[85] Carugati, 'Generative AI Challenges', 11.
[86] Schrepel and Pentland, 'Competition between AI Foundation Models', 11.

time. However, more users generate greater revenue and thus an ability to pay for access to exclusive databases. Smaller FMs will not be able to get the same access, limiting their competitive advantage.[87]

Deployment methods influence market evolution, with various approaches including subscription services, licensing, and consultancy offerings. Deployment varies by purpose, such as chat services versus work assistants. Closed-source FMs can integrate into existing products, create new services, or offer AI-as-a-service. Open-source FMs promote development through AI labs, model hubs, and non-commercial releases, enhancing innovation and ecosystem growth.[88]

FMs can be deployed by both the owner of the FM and by third parties. Current routes to market for closed-source FMs include:[89]

(a) Integration of FMs into existing products and services.[90]
(b) Creation of new products or services usually monetised either through subscription or via a freemium business model.[91]
(c) Providing AI-as-a-service. There are two main access paradigms:[92]
   (i) API access: the third party can send prompts to a FM-owner-hosted model via an API and receive a response. These services are often provided on a metered basis (a price per 1,000 tokens of prompt data processed).[93]
   (ii) Model access: the third party can deploy the model on their own systems, preventing the need for sharing data with the FM provider.[94]

The current routes to market for open-source FMs include:[95]

(a) AI development services in which AI labs develop, pre-train and/or fine-tune a model using an open-source model architecture and/or fine-tune an existing pre-trained model and provide the third party with ownership of the model produced.[96]
(b) Model hubs or platforms, where third parties can develop and pre-train their own models using open-source model architectures, or fine-tune open-source pre-trained models to develop specialised models for their purposes. Services can include specialised support and computational infrastructure.[97]

FM developers may release open-source models, with no direct monetisation, to achieve non-commercial objectives.[98] They may also do this to encourage other developers and customers to work with and adopt their FMs (an indirect network effect), which could lead to improvements in the quality of those FMs which they deploy in their other revenue-generating products or operations.[99]

[87] *Id.*, 12–13.
[88] OECD, 'Artificial Intelligence, Data and Competition', 23.
[89] UK CMA, 'AI Foundation Models: Initial Report', 15.
[90] *Id.*, 15.
[91] *Id.*
[92] *Id.*
[93] *Id.*
[94] *Id.*
[95] *Id.*
[96] *Id.*
[97] *Id.*, 15–16.
[98] *Id.*, 16.
[99] *Id.*, 16.

19.2.5.2 Collusion

At the applications level, the models continue to learn from user inputs and prompts, and this could inadvertently lead to the disclosure of sensitive business data or trade secrets. For instance, if AI systems have access to or generate data such as sensitive information from competitors, it could lead to exposure of that information.[100] Moreover, if multiple AI systems in the market begin to adapt and align their business practices based on data gathered across the industry (such as pricing and business terms), this could result in a form of collusion. Such alignment may diminish competitive differentiation and potentially lead to a uniformity in market behaviour that suppresses healthy competition. This kind of behaviour can be hard to detect and regulate because it doesn't involve explicit agreements or communications between competitors, which is traditionally the basis for antitrust actions.[101]

19.2.6 *Challenges That Are Cross Cutting Across All Levels*

19.2.6.1 Introduction

The UK CMA Report highlights key features shaping competitive dynamics in digital markets: multi-sided markets, strong network effects, economies of scale, intellectual property rights, low prices, and vertically integrated business models.[102] Partnerships with hyper-scalers and barriers to switching services (e.g. data transfer fees, licensing practices) raise additional competition issues.[103] The Stigler Center Report also notes economic features facilitating monopolisation, which are all considered below.[104]

19.2.6.2 Multi-sided Markets and Network Effects

Multi-sided markets benefit significantly from network effects, where the value increases as more participants join. This creates a competitive advantage for established entities because a larger network attracts more users, which in turn attracts more service providers or end users, creating a self-reinforcing loop.[105] While this can lower entry barriers and increase competition, it also poses challenges in market concentration and regulatory oversight.[106]

Research shows large user bases enhance platform value, attracting advertisers and improving user engagement.[107] Many network effects are indirect, facilitated by digital goods or services that enhance the value of another product to a consumer.[108] See for example the integration of AI into Microsoft's products through Microsoft Copilot.[109]

[100] Y. Yu, 'Research on the Competition Law Risks and Regulation Brought by Generative Artificial Intelligence' (2023) 9 *Highlights in Business, Economics and Management* 454–455, available at https://drpress.org/ojs/index.php/HBEM/article/view/9093 (accessed 25 April 2024).

[101] *Id.*, 454–461.

[102] UK CMA, 'AI Foundation Models: Initial Report', 2; OECD, *Handbook on Competition Policy*, 14.

[103] Carugati, 'Generative AI Challenges', 15.

[104] Stigler Center Report, 8–9. These features are: (i) strong network effects; (ii) strong economies of scale and scope; (iii) marginal costs close to zero; (iv) high and increasing returns to the use of data; and (v) low distribution costs that allow for a global reach.

[105] OECD, *Handbook on Competition Policy*, 14.

[106] *Id.*, 19.

[107] G. Parker, M. W. van Alstyne and S. P. Choudary, *Platform Revolution: How Networked Markets Are Transforming the Economy and How to Make Them Work for You* (Norton, 2016), 14.

[108] Stigler Center Report, 38.

[109] Microsoft Copilot integrates technology from OpenAI. Microsoft has embedded generative AI capabilities from OpenAI into various products, including Microsoft 365 Copilot. This integration allows Copilot to enhance

At the infrastructure, data, and model levels, multi-sided markets involve interactions between model developers, data providers, computing resource providers, and model consumers. The need for access to quality datasets makes data providers crucial players in this market. Their willingness to partner with developers can significantly impact the quality of the resulting models and are thus an important consideration for competition.

At the applications level, multi-sided markets involve interactions between application developers, end users, and other service providers. The more users an application attracts, the more valuable it becomes. Complementary service providers are businesses that offer services enhancing or integrating with the AI applications. For instance, a generative AI writing tool might integrate with a content management system or a publishing platform, creating additional value for users. In some cases, advertisers and marketers form another side of the market.

At the data and model level, network effects primarily operate through data accumulation and usage. As more users interact with an AI model, the volume of data generated increases. This additional data can then be used to train and improve the model, making it more accurate and effective.

The Stigler Center Report maintains that digital markets are prone to tipping into monopolies for two primary reasons. First, because digital markets are driven by network effects that strengthen large incumbents and weaken new entrants (as discussed above). Secondly, because fixed costs play a crucial role in digital markets, leading to especially large returns to scale in these markets.[110]

19.2.6.3 Economies of Scale and/or Scope

Digital goods and services benefit from increasing returns to scale, where fixed costs enable rapid scaling with minimal variable costs. This allows firms to expand and offer competitive prices, creating entry barriers for new firms lacking similar scale. In other words, when an additional user is served, costs do not go up proportionately, so, for example, Microsoft can update the Word program for 100 million users with similar fixed costs to those needed for 1 million users.[111] The implications for market structure are well known: with increasing returns to scale, companies invest heavily in fixed costs to have the best product to attract customers.[112]

Economies of scope arise when firms operate across adjacent markets, using data from one market to improve products in another.[113] Firms can leverage extensive datasets to improve their products and expand their activities into new areas, because better insights are available with larger datasets, and firms with access to large amounts of data can raise the quality of their services in ways that smaller firms cannot. This creates a dynamic economy of scale.[114]

Economies of scale in adjacent markets will also influence the importance of economies of scope, as will the ability and willingness of consumers to switch between different AI offerings if

productivity by providing AI-driven assistance across applications such as Word, Excel, PowerPoint, Outlook, and Teams. See Microsoft, 'Introducing Microsoft 365 Copilot – Your Copilot for Work' (16 March 2023), available at https://blogs.microsoft.com/blog/2023/03/16/introducing-microsoft-365-copilot-your-copilot-for-work/ (accessed 30 April 2024).

110 Stigler Center Report, 35; *cf.* OECD, 'Artificial Intelligence, Data and Competition', 28.

111 OECD, *Handbook on Competition Policy*, 14; Stigler Center Report, 36.

112 Stigler Center Report, 37; *cf.* OECD, 'Artificial Intelligence, Data and Competition', 28.

113 OECD, 'Artificial Intelligence, Data and Competition', 28.

114 Stigler Center Report, 37.

AI is integrated into an existing digital ecosystem.[115] These effects, combined with network and feedback effects, can lead to market tipping, particularly in the GenAI value chain.[116]

For instance, user data enhances model refinement, increasing the value of a GenAI service as it gains more users.[117] Strong feedback effects provide substantial first-mover advantages, as new entrants without an existing user base struggle to compete by refining and improving their models.[118] This creates a cyclical effect: more users enhance product quality, which attracts even more users. Users benefit from these data-driven network effects as improved learning from data increases user utility, creating value.[119] Models like ChatGPT improve by learning from user dialogue data, suggesting that higher user numbers enhance model quality. However, there is a lack of available empirical research on the impact of data-driven network effects on model performance.[120]

19.2.6.4 Vertically Integrated and Conglomerated Business Models

Vertically integrated business models give rise to specific concerns about anticompetitive conduct.[121] Vertically integrated business models, such as Amazon's logistics, e-commerce, cloud computing, and AI capabilities, create synergies that enhance efficiency and customer experience, making it difficult for competitors to match.[122]

For instance, Google is integrating its AI-powered solutions into Google Search, Google Chrome, and Google Workplace. Microsoft is doing the same with its AI-powered CoPilot applications in its search engine Bing, browser Edge, productivity software Office and operating system Windows. These vertical integrations pose potential competition issues related to tying, bundling, and self-preferencing, as the firm has the incentive to promote its own services over third-party ones.[123] Vertical relationships may also occur when companies use long-term partnerships and strategic investments as an alternative to outright acquisitions and vertical integration.[124]

Conglomerate business models likewise play a significant role in digital markets. Given the rise of digital ecosystems and interconnected products, these competitive dynamics will depend on their degree of openness to third parties and the potential for competition among ecosystems.[125] If a firm were to have market power in one of those upstream markets, it could provide the ability and incentive to exclude downstream rivals from computing resources. There may also be risks of customer exclusion, for example through the bundling or tying of services. Thus, interoperability and portability will be key aspects going forward.[126]

Portability issues arise when transferring LLMs and their associated applications between cloud providers due to several factors such as:

(a) Data storage and management challenges with different data formats and APIs, necessitating complex data transformation and migration efforts, as well as high data-transfer costs.

[115] OECD, 'Artificial Intelligence, Data and Competition', 29.
[116] *Id.*
[117] Carugati, 'Generative AI Challenges', 14; *cf.* OECD, 'Artificial Intelligence, Data and Competition', 29.
[118] OECD, 'Artificial Intelligence, Data and Competition', 29.
[119] Carugati, 'Generative AI Challenges', 17.
[120] *Id.*
[121] UK CMA, 'AI Foundation Models: Initial Report', 18.
[122] L. Khan, 'Amazon's Antitrust Paradox' (2017) 126(3) *Yale Law Journal* 710–805.
[123] Carugati, 'Generative AI Challenges', 17.
[124] *Id.*
[125] *Id.*
[126] OECD, 'Artificial Intelligence, Data and Competition', 30.

(b) Dependency management issues involve reconfiguring software libraries and environment setups like container orchestration systems.
(c) Service integration problems arise from proprietary APIs and systems needing updates.
(d) Compliance and security concerns include adapting to different security policies.[127]

Thus, transferring an application developed on OpenAI's GPT to Meta's Llama, is possible but can be challenging.[128] For example, model architecture and training differs between OpenAI's GPT and Meta's Llama and can result in variations in how each model processes and responds to inputs.[129] API integration requires rewriting parts of the application to interact with the new API. Data formats might need to be converted to be compatible and comprehensive performance testing is required to compare the new model's performance with the original.[130]

19.2.6.7 Leveraging and Access

In the digital economy, leveraging occurs when firms use their dominant position in one market to promote or protect their products in another market. This practice is prevalent because digital services often share inputs, such as data, and have overlapping consumer bases, enabling firms to create an ecosystem of interconnected services.[131] Over the past two decades, competition authorities have found that several digital firms have leveraged their dominant positions to disadvantage competitors in various ways.[132] While these commercial practices use different means, they all leverage a product or service that has a dominant position (the dominant product) to increase sales of a product or service that is subject to competition (the competitive product), or to prevent the competitive product from competing with the dominant product.[133]

To maintain competition, access to data or FMs would need to be on reasonable terms, regarding prices, quality, and data policies. FM suppliers could be in a strong position to dictate such terms and there is a risk that they leverage that position to gain an advantage and reduce competition.[134] The availability of open-source models and materials may well be a key factor in the extent to which new or smaller developers are able to enter the market without needing to rely on access to closed systems. This appears to be an area that shows some promise at present but, as with many aspects of the sector, is hard to predict.[135]

Firms may also seek to leverage their market power from one market into another, for example with bundling and tying strategies that force out competition in a digital ecosystem of products.[136]

[127] Cloud Standards Customer Council, 'Interoperability and Portability for Cloud Computing: A Guide Version 2.0' (2017), available at www.omg.org/cloud/deliverables/CSCC-Interoperability-and-Portability-for-Cloud-Computing-A-Guide.pdf#:~:text= URL%3A%20https%3A%2F%2Fwww.omg.org%2Fcloud%2Fdeliverables%2FCSCC (accessed 19 April 2024).

[128] D. Spathis and F. Kawsar, 'The First Step Is the Hardest: Pitfalls of Representing and Tokenizing Temporal Data for Large Language Models' (2023), available at https://arxiv.org/pdf/2309.06236 (accessed 14 April 2024).

[129] *Id*

[130] *Id.*

[131] Carugati, 'Generative AI Challenges', 11.

[132] *Id.*

[133] *Id.*

[134] OECD, 'Artificial Intelligence, Data and Competition', 34.

[135] *Id.*

[136] UK CMA, 'AI Foundation Models: Initial Report', 18.

The forms of leveraging in digital markets include:

(a) Self-preferencing: One significant concern is that firms like Google can use their dominant search engine to promote their own AI-powered answer engines over rivals.[137] For instance, Google has integrated GenAI capabilities into its search functionality through the Search Generative Experience (SGE), which provides AI-generated summaries and overviews. This integration can potentially prioritise Google's AI answers over those from competitors such as HuggingChat or ChatGPT, making it harder for these rivals to compete.[138]
(b) Preinstalling applications: Another concern is the preinstallation of AI applications on operating systems.[139] Microsoft, for example, through its partnership with OpenAI, introduced Copilot for Microsoft 365, possibly giving these tools an unfair advantage by making them the default choice for users.[140] This practice resembles the bundling of Windows Media Player with Windows OS, which made it difficult for other media players to gain market share.[141]
(c) Tying development to dominant platforms: Companies could require third-party developers to use their own foundational models for developing AI-powered applications. This requirement would limit the growth of competing FMs by forcing developers to align with the dominant firm's technology, reducing competition and innovation. For example, OpenAI offers APIs for developers to integrate into their products[142] as well as a GPT Store where these can be sold to users.[143]

19.2.7 *Insights*

FM developers need access to the key inputs of computing power, data, technical expertise, and capital to compete effectively. These inputs are important for developing, deploying, and using FMs. If access to these key inputs were to be constrained, then FM developers may not be able to compete with larger, more established businesses that have greater resources. This could lead to a decrease in competition and innovation in the FM sector, which could ultimately harm consumers.[144]

The larger players in the public foundation models space will initially improve their foundation models faster than smaller competitors due to positive feedback loops. The ability of large players to lock in the ecosystem will also need to be closely monitored, along with other variables such as network effects among developers.[145]

[137] Carugati, 'Generative AI Challenges', 13.
[138] *Id.* Carugati's self-preferencing prediction can be seen unfolding with Google integrating AI into searches. See Google, 'New Ways to Search in 2024' (17 January 2024), available at https://blog.google/products/search/google-search-ai-january-2024-update/ (accessed 30 April 2024).
[139] Carugati, 'Generative AI Challenges', 20–21.
[140] *Id.* See also Microsoft, 'Introducing Microsoft 365 Copilot'.
[141] Carugati, 'Generative AI Challenges', 12. In 2004, it was held that Microsoft breached EU competition law by leveraging its dominant Windows OS (the tying market) by tying it with its media player Windows Media Player (WMP) (the tied market) by preinstalling WMP on Windows OS. This practice had the effect of foreclosing rivals from entering the tied market. See EC Commission Decision of 24 March 2004 relating to a proceeding under Article 82 of the EC Treaty (Case: COMP/C-3/37.792 Microsoft).
[142] See https://platform.openai.com/ (accessed 30 April 2024).
[143] See https://chatgpt.com/gpts?oai-dm = 1 (accessed 30 April 2024).
[144] UK CMA, 'AI Foundation Models: Initial Report', 52.
[145] Schrepel and Pentland, 'Competition between AI Foundation Models', 14.

The AI Foundation Models Technical Update Report of 16 April 2024, by the UK CMA builds on its previous findings in the 2023 AI Foundation Models: Initial Report and identifies ongoing concerns and key uncertainties regarding the development of FMs.[146] These are:

(a) Firms controlling critical inputs (compute, data, expertise) may restrict access to critical inputs to shield themselves from competition, which can be detrimental to smaller competitors.[147]
(b) The dominance of a few large firms with vast resources, which could stifle competition and innovation in a variety of ways. For example, consumer choice could be manipulated through the integration of GenAI into their existing digital products like mobiles, search engines or productivity software. This could be through pre-installation, technical bundling, accessibility, integration, and compatibility.[148]
(c) The risk of market consolidation: that is, if a few highly effective models meet most user needs, it reduces the incentives for competition and innovation.[149]
(d) Leveraging economies of scale and scope and feedback effects to maintain a competitive edge remain problematic.[150]
(e) Concerns about continued development and deployment of open-source models and the effect of licensing restrictions, funding uncertainties, and the potential for closed models to outperform open-source models.[151]
(f) The market is more likely to trend towards positive outcomes if initially successful FM developers face an ongoing competitive constraint from new entrants, so they do not gain an entrenched and disproportionate advantage by being an early mover in the market.[152]

The examination of some aspects of the regulatory frameworks developing among the United States, United Kingdom, and European Union can provide an understanding of the current landscape and its implications for generative AI and competition law.

19.3 REGULATORY RESPONSES AND CONSIDERATIONS

19.3.1 *Overview*

Regulation is a key tool for antitrust and competition authorities to address the technical complexity of AI, but market studies help authorities understand developments and advocate for change, particularly when enforcement challenges arise. These studies can address competition issues where there are no legal breaches, requiring alternative actions like new regulation.[153]

19.3.2 *The United States of America*

In 2023, President Biden issued the Executive Order on the Safe, Secure, and Trustworthy Development and Use of AI, which contains a separate segment on competition.[154] This policy

[146] UK CMA, 'AI Foundation Models Technical Update Report', 6.
[147] *Id.*, 77; UK CMA, 'AI Foundation Models: Initial Report', 52.
[148] UK CMA, 'AI Foundation Models Technical Update Report', 77–78; UK CMA, 'AI Foundation Models: Initial Report', 52.
[149] UK CMA, 'AI Foundation Models Technical Update Report', 80; UK CMA, 'AI Foundation Models: Initial Report', 52.
[150] UK CMA, 'AI Foundation Models: Initial Report', 52.
[151] UK CMA, 'AI Foundation Models Technical Update Report', 9, 13, 46–47, 51.
[152] *Id.*, 6–7, 75.
[153] OECD, 'Artificial Intelligence, Data and Competition', 45.
[154] USA Government Presidential Actions, 'Executive Order on the Safe, Secure, and Trustworthy Development and Use of Artificial Intelligence' (30 October 2023), available at www.whitehouse.gov/briefing-room/presidential-

sets out the governance and development of AI in accordance with eight guiding principles. The most important for the purposes of this chapter is the second guiding principle stating that:

> [P]romoting responsible innovation, competition, and collaboration will allow the United States to lead in AI and unlock the technology's potential to solve some of society's most difficult challenges ... The Federal Government will promote a fair, open, and competitive ecosystem and marketplace for AI and related technologies so that small developers and entrepreneurs can continue to drive innovation. Doing so requires stopping unlawful collusion and addressing risks from dominant firms' use of key assets such as semiconductors, computing power, cloud storage, and data to disadvantage competitors, and it requires supporting a marketplace that harnesses the benefits of AI to provide new opportunities for small businesses, workers, and entrepreneurs.

Also in 2023, the FTC's Merger Guidelines provide a framework for assessing mergers that may substantially lessen competition, focusing on increasing market concentration, eliminating competition, risk of coordination, limiting access to essential products, entrenching dominant positions, and issues related to multi-sided platforms.[155] It is interesting to note these guidelines:

(a) *Guideline 1: Mergers that significantly increase concentration in a highly concentrated market.* These are presumed illegal.[156]
(b) *Guideline 2: Mergers that eliminate competition.* In the context of AI, this means scrutinising mergers between companies that are close competitors in AI development, research, and deployment.[157]
(c) *Guideline 3: Mergers that increase the risk of coordination.* The use of advanced algorithms can facilitate tacit collusion and thus the need for monitoring.[158]
(d) *Guideline 5: Limiting access to essential products or services.* Mergers that create a situation where a company can limit a rival's access to essential products or services are problematic. For AI, this could involve control over critical data, computational resources, or proprietary algorithms.[159]
(e) *Guideline 6: Entrenchment of dominant positions.* In AI, dominant companies may seek to acquire emerging firms to maintain their market power, which could hinder new entrants and reduce competition.[160]
(f) *Guideline 9: Multi-sided platforms.* Consistent with the Clayton Act's protection of competition 'in any line of commerce', mergers that harm competition and that may substantially lessen competition or tend to create a monopoly within a relevant market for any product or service offered on a platform to any group of participants will be prohibited. This scenario can arise from various types of mergers, such as those involving

actions/2023/10/30/executive-order-on-the-safe-secure-and-trustworthy-development-and-use-of-artificial-intelligence/ (accessed 19 January 2024).

155 US Department of Justice & Federal Trade Commission, *Merger Guidelines* (2023) 5, available at www.ftc.gov/system/files/ftc_gov/pdf/2023_merger_guidelines_final_12.18.2023.pdf (accessed 22 March 2024).

156 US FTC, *Merger Guidelines*, 5. The Supreme Court has affirmed that a merger resulting in a firm holding an excessive share of the relevant market and significantly increasing market concentration is inherently likely to substantially lessen competition and must be prohibited unless there is rebuttal evidence. See *United States v. Phila National Bank* 374 US 321, 363 (1963); *FTC v. Hackensack Meridian Health Inc.*, 30 F.4th 160, 172–173 (3d Cir. 2022); *United States v. AT&T Inc.*, 916 F.3d at 1032.

157 US FTC, *Merger Guidelines*, 6–8.

158 *Id.*, 8. Tacit coordination often cannot be addressed under section 1 of the Sherman Antitrust Act of 1890, and therefore section 7 of the Clayton Antitrust Act of 1914 is used extensively to prevent market structures conducive to such coordination. See *id.*, 8.

159 *Id.*, 13–14.

160 *Id.*, 18–19.

two platform operators who eliminate the competition between them, or a platform may acquire a platform participant (large content provider), which can entrench the operator's position by depriving rivals of participants. Alternately mergers involving firms that provide other important inputs to platform services can enable the platform operator to deny rivals the benefits of those inputs. For example, acquiring data that helps facilitate matching, sorting, or prediction services may enable the platform to weaken rival platforms by denying them that data.[161]

19.3.3 *The United Kingdom*

On 23 May 2024 the UK Parliament passed the Digital Markets, Competition and Consumer Act (DMCC) 2024 Chapter 13.[162] This empowers the Consumer Markets Authority (CMA) to designate firms with Strategic Market Status (SMS) (section 2) and impose conduct requirements to ensure fair competition. It enables pro-competition interventions to address adverse effects on competition and mandates reporting of potential mergers to the CMA. The Act expands the territorial reach of competition law to include activities affecting UK trade, even if implemented outside the United Kingdom, protecting against anti-competitive conduct regardless of location.

To designate an undertaking as having SMS, the CMA must determine that: (a) the digital activity is linked to the United Kingdom (section 4); (b) meets the conditions of substantial and entrenched market power (section 5); and (c) has strategic significance (section 6). Digital activities encompass internet services and digital content, whether paid or free, and a digital activity is linked to the United Kingdom if it has significant numbers of UK users, the undertaking conducts business in the United Kingdom, or the activity impacts UK trade. The CMA must consider the undertaking's market power over the next five years and its strategic significance based on size, influence, and ability to leverage into other activities. Additionally, the turnover condition requires the undertaking to have a UK turnover exceeding £1 billion or a global turnover exceeding £25 billion (section 7).

Under this legislation the CMA has the authority to impose conduct requirements on designated undertakings for specific digital activities, ensuring fair dealing, open choices, trust, and transparency. These requirements dictate how designated undertakings must behave in their market activities. Conduct requirements can only be imposed if deemed proportionate and beneficial for users and potential users. The objectives include the fair treatment of users, enabling free choices between services, and ensuring users have the information needed for informed decisions (section 19).

Conduct requirements may oblige undertakings to trade on fair terms, handle complaints effectively, provide clear information, and notify users of significant changes. They also prevent undertakings from self-preferencing, unfairly using data, and restricting interactions with other products. For this, the CMA must consider the benefits to consumers and the potential impacts on competition, innovation, and user safety (section 20).

A further aspect is the CMA's authority to implement pro-competition interventions (PCIs) to address competition issues related to designated digital activities. PCIs aim to remedy, mitigate, or prevent adverse effects on competition, ensuring benefits for UK users and customers (section 46). The CMA can impose orders on designated undertakings or make non-binding

[161] *Id.*, 26.
[162] Available at www.legislation.gov.uk/ukpga/2024/13/enacted (accessed 25 May 2024).

recommendations to public entities such as the government or independent regulators. For instance, the CMA might order a designated social media platform to be interoperable with competitors or recommend the Financial Conduct Authority intervene in mobile payment technology restrictions (section 51).

PCIs may also address associated consumer detriments. The CMA's interventions could prohibit anti-competitive practices, enforce fair trading terms, and ensure transparency. They can trial remedies with subsets of users to determine effectiveness before full implementation. For example, the CMA might trial different search engine choice screen layouts on a mobile operating system to find the most effective design for boosting competition. These trials are time-limited and reviewed to decide on long-term measures.

In Chapter 5 (on mergers) designated undertakings or their corporate groups are required to report potential mergers to the CMA before they occur. These mergers cannot proceed until the CMA deems the report sufficient and five working days have passed. This ensures the CMA can assess mergers that may harm competition in the United Kingdom and decide if an investigation is necessary under the Enterprise Act 2002. There are two types of reportable events:

(a) Acquisitions where designated undertakings or their groups reach certain share or voting rights thresholds in UK-connected entities with a minimum consideration of £25 million.
(b) Joint ventures where designated undertakings or their groups form new entities with unconnected parties, intending UK operations and involving a minimum contribution of £25 million.

For example, if a designated undertaking acquires shares to exceed 25 per cent ownership in a UK-connected company or forms a joint venture intending UK operations with a significant investment, these events must be reported. The CMA can then decide if it needs to open a merger investigation and potentially impose restrictions.

Section 119 in Part 2 Competition, Chapter 1 Antitrust, expands the territorial reach of the Chapter 1 prohibition of the Competition Act 1998, which makes illegal any agreements, decisions by associations, or concerted practices that may affect trade within the United Kingdom and restrict competition. Previously, these activities were only prohibited if implemented in the United Kingdom. The new provisions include activities that, even if not implemented in the United Kingdom, are likely to have an immediate, substantial, and foreseeable effect on UK trade. The qualified effects test ensures that UK trade and businesses and consumers based in the United Kingdom are protected from the detrimental effects of anti-competitive conduct, regardless of where that conduct takes place, even when an agreement is implemented in another jurisdiction.

19.3.4 *The European Union*

19.3.4.1 Introduction

To date, the European Commission has issued calls for contributions on competition in virtual worlds and GenAI.[163] These calls highlight that even though the European Parliament and the

[163] The 'Calls for Contributions On Competition in Virtual Worlds and Generative Artificial Intelligence' (2024), available at https://competition-policy.ec.europa.eu/document/e727c66a-af77-4014-962a-7c9a36800e2f_en (accessed 23 March 2024).

Council achieved a political agreement on the EU AI Act,[164] GenAI systems are still taking shape, and it has become clear that the potential impacts of this new phase of digital transformation could be wide-ranging, with new technologies, business models, and markets.[165]

19.3.4.2 The AI Act

Although canvassed thoroughly in the rest of this book, the EU's new AI Act establishes a comprehensive framework of AI regulation. Despite Recital 45 stating that the AI Act does not intend to undermine existing EU legislation in competition law, it undoubtedly has some effect. Schrepel states that the AI Act is set to affect competition law in the procedural and investigative powers of antitrust agencies, and in various practices that may have unintended consequences.[166]

For the procedural and investigative powers of antitrust agencies, the governance structure of the AI Act is outlined in Articles 64–70, where Article 66 details the tasks of the AI Office's Board. The Board's responsibilities include ensuring effective cooperation with competent authorities across various domains, including competition. This coordination helps in identifying and mitigating any competitive risks posed by the deployment of GenAI technologies.

In terms of enforcement, Article 74 highlights the importance of market surveillance and control of AI systems within the EU market. Market surveillance authorities are required to report annually to the European Commission and relevant national competition authorities any information that may be pertinent to the application of EU competition law (Article 74(2)).

Article 74(13) states that market surveillance authorities can submit a reasoned request for access to the source code of a high-risk AI system only when access to the source code is necessary to assess the conformity of a high-risk AI system and testing or auditing procedures and verification based on the data and documentation from the provider has been exhausted or proven insufficient.

For general-purpose AI systems, Article 75 requires authorities to evaluate the systems for compliance. Thus, according to Schrepel, the AI Act changes when or how competition agencies can access information. Normally these agencies can only request information when they suspect a breach of competition law, and you have a similar situation under the Digital Markets Act (DMA) which allows for the inspection of information data and algorithms but only if a DMA infringement is suspected. By allowing national supervisory authorities and their technical experts to check compliance with the AI Act and send the relevant information to competition agencies, it has created an effective way to monitor compliance with competition law even without suspicion of anti-competitive behaviour or DMA infringements, and competition agencies will likely use this information to launch investigations and be more proactive.[167]

The AI Act also changes what information competition agencies can access. Normally they cannot request access to a company's algorithm just because they are investigating a potential infringement. The Act changes this by allowing authorities to access confidential information or

[164] Regulation (EU) 2024/1689 of the European Parliament and of the Council laying down harmonised rules on artificial intelligence (EU AI Act) OJ L 12 July 2024.

[165] See further https://competition-policy.ec.europa.eu/document/e727c66a-af77-4014-962a-7c9a36800e2f_en (accessed 23 March 2024).

[166] T. Schrepel, 'Decoding the AI Act: A Critical Guide for Competition Experts' (2023) Amsterdam Law & Technology Institute (ALTI) Working Paper 3 of 2023 at 4, available at https://papers.ssrn.com/sol3/papers.cfm?abstract_id=4609947 (accessed 5 May 2024).

[167] *Id.*, 6.

source code to check compliance with the Act's obligations. This means that the Act allows competition agencies to access information without investigating a violation and gives them access to sensitive information they usually cannot access even when suspecting a competition law violation.[168]

Provisions such as Article 19 require providers of high-risk AI systems to keep the logs that are generated by their AI systems, which would include information such as system events (shut-down events), algorithmic operations input data, model training), predictions and decisions (decisions or actions taken based on predictions), performance metrics (accuracy, precision, recall), data handling (information about data ingestion and processing), resource utilisation (central processing unit or CPU;, GPU; memory), user interactions (user interactions with the AI system), timestamps (time information for each logged event), and external system interactions (logs of interactions with external systems or APIs). On the one hand, it is argued that this is very useful information from a competition law perspective as it allows authorities to understand business practices and strategies.[169] However, they may have unintended consequences, as Schrepel posits the possibility that the transparency measures in the AI Act may also facilitate collusive behaviour and targeted abuse of dominance practices.[170]

Recitals 99–101 of the AI Act specifically address the implications and responsibilities surrounding large GenAI models, recognised as general-purpose AI systems capable of generating diverse content. These models present unique competition concerns, as their advanced capabilities can significantly influence various markets, potentially creating monopolistic conditions that smaller firms may struggle to replicate. The Act underscores the necessity to regulate these models to ensure their benefits are accessible to a wide range of market participants.

Recital 101 highlights the role and responsibility of providers of general-purpose AI models along the AI value chain. These models often serve as the foundation for various downstream systems provided by other entities, necessitating a thorough understanding of the models and their capabilities for effective integration into products and compliance with regulatory obligations. To address this, the Act requires proportionate transparency measures, including the creation and maintenance of up-to-date documentation. Providers are required to prepare technical documentation and make it available upon request to the AI Office and national competent authorities. This approach aims to support downstream providers in using these models responsibly while adhering to regulatory standards.

Article 53 outlines the specific obligations for companies developing general-purpose AI models. These companies must maintain detailed records of their AI models' development and testing processes, which must in turn be provided to other companies wishing to integrate the GenAI into their own products. This must be done in a way that protects intellectual property rights and confidential business information. However, open-source AI models that do not pose systemic risks are exempt from these requirements (Article 53(2)).

On open-source models, Recitals 102–104, linking to Article 53, emphasise the importance of free and open-source AI components in fostering innovation and growth. They clarify that AI

[168] *Id.*, 6–7.

[169] *Id.*, 9–10. Several other articles of the AI Act are listed with similar risks, such as Articles 8 (compliance), 23–24 (importers and distributors to ensure that the appropriate conformity assessment procedure has been carried out. This means that they will first have to access to sensitive information held by the provider, such as the functioning of the AI system, its training set, source code, and so on. This also sets out a risk that the sharing of this information could raise issues related to revealing trade secrets). *Id.*, 10–11.

[170] *Id.*

models released under open-source licences, which allow for unrestricted access, modification, and redistribution, should ensure transparency by making model parameters and usage information publicly available. However, these components should not be exempt from certain regulatory obligations if they pose systemic risks. Additionally, even when models are open-source, they must still comply with transparency requirements related to the data used for training, particularly for copyright law compliance. These provisions clarify that while AI components can be shared through open repositories, they should not benefit from free and open-source exceptions if they are monetised.

Article 55 introduces additional requirements for GenAI models that pose systemic risks. These providers must evaluate their models using standard protocols, identify and reduce systemic risks, and report any serious incidents to the AI Office and national authorities. They must ensure their AI models and infrastructure are secure and may use codes of practice to demonstrate compliance until a standard is published. Indicators of systemic risk include high-impact capabilities or significant computational usage for training, necessitating strict adherence to regulatory standards.

Recital 105 addresses the challenges presented by GenAI models that require extensive datasets, often involving copyrighted material, for their development and training. The recital underscores the necessity for obtaining authorisation from rights holders for text and data-mining activities involving protected content unless specific copyright exceptions apply.

Finally, Recital 107 focuses on increasing transparency regarding the data used for pre-training and training GenAI models. Providers are required to publish a detailed summary of the training data, including copyrighted materials used. This summary should be comprehensive yet protect trade secrets and confidential business information and is clearly included to aid copyright holders enforce their rights.

19.3.4.3 The Digital Markets Act and Digital Services Act

19.3.4.3.1 INTRODUCTION. The Digital Services Act (DSA) and Digital Markets Act regulate digital services, marketplaces, platforms, and specific large tech companies. Currently, these do not directly apply to GenAI, foundation models, or large language models, but they may indirectly impact them if regulated services or platforms use such technology.

19.3.4.3.2 THE DIGITAL SERVICES ACT. The DSA[171] defines a platform as a hosting service that, at the request of a recipient of the service, stores and disseminates information to the public, unless that activity is a minor and purely ancillary feature of another service (Article 3(i)). LLMs would not ordinarily fit this definition, and a plug-in functionality does not change this, because there is no hosting, storing, or dissemination of information to the public on the request of the recipient of the service. However, where a LLM is integrated into another service, this could potentially bring the LLM into scope of the DSA where it forms part of a regulated service.[172]

[171] Regulation (EU) 2022/2065 of the European Parliament and of the Council of 19 October 2022 on a Single Market for Digital Services and amending Directive 2000/31/EC (Digital Services Act) (Text with EEA relevance) PE/30/2022/REV/1 OJ L 277, 27 October 2022 (hereafter DSA).

[172] N. Lomas, 'Unpicking the Rules Shaping Generative AI' (2023), available at https://techcrunch.com/2023/04/13/generative-ai-gdpr-enforcement/ (accessed 27 April 2024).

19.3.4.3.3 THE DIGITAL MARKETS ACT. The DMA[173] seeks to address the challenges posed by digital platforms and their control over and use of data in a way that does not stifle competition or harm consumers.[174] The DMA is set up to counteract platform size and gatekeeping rather than abuse of dominance or monopoly power that competition/antitrust laws target. It aims to address the shortcomings of competition law in keeping the entry barriers low and ensuring fair game between the gatekeepers and their smaller rivals that depend on gatekeepers' services. The DMA involves some of the well-established platform services like operating systems, messaging platforms, and online advertising.[175]

Recitals 2, 3, and 4 of the DMA notes that gatekeepers possess certain characteristics which often result in significant power imbalances (for example, extreme economies of scale and network effects, lock-in effects, vertical integration, leveraging, control over whole ecosystems), leading to unfair practices and conditions for businesses and end users of their core platform services. This can negatively impact pricing, quality, competition, choice, and innovation within the digital sector.

Therefore, the DMA provides a pre-emptive regulatory framework to oversee firms termed gatekeepers. Article 2 demarcates 'gatekeepers' as an undertaking providing core platform services, and core platform services as online intermediation services; online search engines; online social networking services; video-sharing platform services; number-independent interpersonal communications services; operating systems; web browsers; virtual assistants; cloud computing services; online advertising services, including any advertising networks, advertising exchanges, and any other advertising intermediation services. Yasar and colleagues argue that gatekeeping potential is emerging in GenAI service providers due to factors such as computing power, early mover advantages, data resources, and integrated systems.[176]

While the DMA draws significant influence from competition law, the EU legislative body maintains that the DMA is not merely an extension of existing competition regulation but rather a distinct form of regulatory action that enhances and works in tandem with competition law.[177] Even though the DMA was not initially intended to apply to LLMs and GenAI, the European Commission has already asked that the degree of their interplay be considered alongside the possibility of regulatory inclusion.[178]

GenAI models are not on the DMA's list of 'gatekeepers' or 'core platform services' (CPSs) and are therefore not yet directly subject to DMA regulation.[179] However, FMs (the technology) could be included within the designated core platform services and therefore be regulated.[180]

[173] Regulation (EU) 2022/1925 of the European Parliament and of the Council of 14 September 2022 on contestable and fair markets in the digital sector and amending Directives (EU) 2019/1937 and (EU) 2020/1828 (Digital Markets Act) (Text with EEA relevance) OJ L 265, 12 October 2022 (hereafter DMA).

[174] See Recital 2 and Article 1(a) of DMA.

[175] A. G. Yasar et al., 'AI and the EU Digital Markets Act: Addressing the Risks of Bigness in Generative AI' (2023) 1, available at https://arxiv.org/pdf/2308.02033.pdf (accessed 25 May 2024).

[176] *Id.*

[177] A. Komninos, 'The Digital Markets Act: How Does It Compare with Competition Law? (2022), available at http://dx.doi.org/10.2139/ssrn.4136146 (accessed 19 January 2024).

[178] Lomas, 'Unpicking the Rules'.

[179] On 6 September 2023 the EC designated six gatekeepers: Alphabet, Amazon, Apple, ByteDance, Meta, and Microsoft. On 29 April 2024, Apple was added with respect to its iPad OS, the operating system for tablets. On 13 May 2024, Booking.com was also added as a gatekeeper for its online intermediation service. To date (3 June 2024), a total of twenty-four core platform services provided by those gatekeepers have been designated as CPSs. For example, TikTok, Facebook, Instagram, Linkedin, WhatsApp, Messenger, to name a few. See further designation notices at: https://digital-markets-act.ec.europa.eu/gatekeepers_en (accessed 3 June 2024).

[180] A. R. Martínez, 'Generative AI and the Digital Markets Act on the Rocks' (2024), available at https://competitionlawblog.kluwercompetitionlaw.com/2024/02/05/generative-ai-and-the-digital-markets-act-on-the-rocks/ (accessed 1 June 2024).

For example, if Google Search is recognised as a 'core platform service' for Alphabet, then the technology behind Google Search, like its Multitask Unified Model or MUM algorithm, would also be regulated. Similarly, if Meta's Instagram introduces AI-powered image editing, this technology would fall under the DMA rules regulating Meta.[181] The list of core platform services is not fixed and can be updated to ensure the DMA remains effective and responsive to market changes (Recital 77), however this would require a market investigation (Article 19) to determine if new services in the digital sector should be added.

So, while GenAI can give a company like Microsoft a competitive advantage, the DMA's rules focus on preventing companies from unfairly using data across multiple services rather than restricting how they use the AI within a single service.[182] Core platform services are regulated because of their characteristics, which can be exploited by the companies offering them. Characteristics such as large-scale economies, strong network effects, multi-sided services, significant dependence by both business users and end users on the service, lock-in effects, and vertical integration (Recital 2).[183]

As for the infrastructure level, 'cloud computing services' are not on the list of 'core platform services' either, as no cloud providers are designated as gatekeepers. Their omission is notable and is likely due to definitional and user number difficulties, but cloud providers may still be designated following finalisation of ongoing market investigations. However, cloud providers will be regulated by the new EU Data Act, Regulation 2023/2854.[184]

The term 'artificial intelligence' is not used in the DMA, but there are four regulatory aspects in the DMA that will have an effect on the legal framework for GenAI in the EU, namely: (a) prerequisites for the creation of fair rankings (related to leveraging and prohibiting self-preferencing practices); (b) information requirements; (c) the regulation of training data; and (d) access rights.[185]

On creating fair ranking systems or prohibiting leveraging with self-preferencing practices, Article 6(5) of the DMA bars gatekeepers from promoting their services over a similar third-party's products or services in ranking and the related crawling, and indexing. Ensuring that rankings and search results are conducted on transparent, fair, non-discriminatory terms to prevent manipulation that favours the gatekeeper's products.[186]

A major obstacle to levelling playing fields and creating transparency is the information asymmetry between platforms, end users, business users, and regulatory authorities. To address this, the EU has introduced several critical regulations aimed at enhancing information and transparency requirements. These include the P2B Regulation,[187] the Consumer Rights Directive,[188] the Unfair

181 *Id.*
182 *Id.*
183 *Id.*
184 As discussed below. Regulation (EU) 2023/2854 of the European Parliament and of the Council of 13 December 2023 on harmonised rules on fair access to and use of data and amending Regulation (EU) 2017/2394 and Directive (EU) 2020/1828 (Data Act). See also Bostoen and van der Veer, 'Regulating Competition in Generative AI'.
185 P. Hacker, J. Cordes and J. Rochon, 'Regulating Gatekeeper AI and Data: Transparency, Access, and Fairness under the DMA, the GDPR, and Beyond' (2022), 3, available at https://dx.doi.org/10.2139/ssrn.4316944 (accessed 6 May 2024).
186 *Id.*, 4–6, but see also 6–24 for an in-depth discussion.
187 Regulation (EU) 2019/1150 of the European Parliament and of the Council of 20 June 2019 on promoting fairness and transparency for business users of online intermediation services (Text with EEA relevance) PE/56/2019/REV/1 OJ L 186, 11 July 2019.
188 Directive 2011/83/EU of the European Parliament and of the Council of 25 October 2011 on consumer rights, amending Council Directive 93/13/EEC and Directive 1999/44/EC of the European Parliament and of the Council

Commercial Practices Directive[189] as updated by the Omnibus Directive,[190] the General Data Protection Regulation or GDPR,[191] the DMA, and the AI Act (not all are discussed).

The DMA requires gatekeepers to be transparent on their advertising pricing, including the metrics and algorithms used for pricing (Articles 5(9)–(10)).[192] Gatekeepers also need to provide access to advertising performance measuring tools, aggregated and non-aggregated data that is effective, high-quality, and portable (Articles 6(8)–(10)), thus the datasets are available free of charge.

The DMA prohibits gatekeepers from using data collected from business users to compete against them, as outlined in Article 6(2). This restriction is specifically aimed at preventing anti-competitive practices by limiting the use of certain datasets. It prohibits gatekeepers from using data collected from business users for training their own AI models without explicit consent. Additionally, Article 5(2) lays out rules for the use of personal data of end users across different services. Gatekeepers are not allowed to use this data for personal advertising if it is acquired through third-party services that utilise the gatekeeper's main platform services. This data cannot be combined across different services to enhance AI training, and gatekeepers are prohibited from registering end users with other gatekeeper services to combine the data.[193]

To enhance competition, the DMA aims to empower business users by ensuring interoperability with third-party services and providing access to data generated by these users. This includes users and businesses being able to uninstall pre-installed applications or choose settings and use third-party apps and services (Articles 5(5), 6(4), 6(6), 6(7), 6(8)–(10), and 7). By granting business users access to data provided by and generated through their interactions on the platform, the DMA fosters competition and supports innovation among smaller players.[194]

Here are the most notable aspects of the DMA on obligations for gatekeepers and competition over and above those discussed above.

(a) Preventing gatekeepers from forcing users to use additional services as a condition for accessing their core platform services (Articles 5(7) and (8)).
(b) Gatekeepers must inform the European Commission of any intended mergers or acquisitions (concentrations) in the digital sector (Article 14).
(c) The gatekeeper must apply fair, reasonable, and non-discriminatory general conditions of access for business users to its software application stores, online search engines, and online social networking services (Article 6(12)).

and repealing Council Directive 85/577/EEC and Directive 97/7/EC of the European Parliament and of the Council Text with EEA relevance OJ L 304, 22 November 2011.

189 Directive 2005/29/EC of the European Parliament and of the Council of 11 May 2005 concerning unfair business-to-consumer commercial practices in the internal market and amending Council Directive 84/450/EEC, Directives 97/7/EC, 98/27/EC and 2002/65/EC of the European Parliament and of the Council and Regulation (EC) No. 2006/2004 of the European Parliament and of the Council ('Unfair Commercial Practices Directive') (Text with EEA relevance) OJ L 149, 11 June 2005.

190 Directive (EU) 2019/2161 of the European Parliament and of the Council of 27 November 2019 amending Council Directive 93/13/EEC and Directives 98/6/EC, 2005/29/EC and 2011/83/EU of the European Parliament and of the Council as regards the better enforcement and modernisation of Union consumer protection rules (Text with EEA relevance) PE/83/2019/REV/1 OJ L 328, 18 December 2019.

191 Regulation (EU) 2016/679 of the European Parliament and of the Council of 27 April 2016 on the protection of natural persons with regard to the processing of personal data and on the free movement of such data, and repealing Directive 95/46/EC (General Data Protection Regulation) OJ L 119, 4 May 2016.

192 Hacker, Cordes and Rochon, 'Regulating Gatekeeper AI and Data', 6.

193 *Id.*, 32.

194 *Id.*, 25, 28.

GenAI models also need to meet these standards[195] and, as Martinez argues, the DMA's focus on data leveraging, market concentration, and transparency naturally intersects with the operations of GenAI. Gatekeepers can leverage data across services, and the high computational costs associated with developing foundation models can lead to significant market concentration, which the DMA seeks to mitigate.[196]

The DMA also targets situations where companies dominate entire ecosystems, making it structurally difficult for existing or new market operators to challenge or compete against them (Recital 3).[197] Beyond fairness, the DMA also aims to ensure transparency. It requires gatekeepers to share information, and Article 15 mandates gatekeepers to audit and disclose how they profile consumers across their services.[198]

19.3.4.4 The Data Act

Regulation 2023/2854 of the EU, also known as the Data Act, entered into force on 11 January 2024 and will become enforceable in September 2025. This Act establishes rules on fair access to and use of data to benefit businesses, researchers, and public administrations. Complementing the Digital Markets Act, the Data Act aims to address access to data (Recitals 4–5). This is crucial for the AI ecosystem as it promotes data sharing and prevents data hoarding, which can stifle research, innovation, and competition.

The Data Act applies to a range of entities involved in data processing and sharing. It covers:

(a) Manufacturers of connected products (item that obtains, generates, or collects data, including virtual assistants interacting with connected products), such as the Internet of Things or IoT devices, placed on the EU market (Articles 1(3)(a) and 1(4)). A virtual assistant is software that can process demands, tasks, or questions, including those based on audio or written input, gestures or motions, and based on those demands, tasks, or questions, provides access to other services or controls the function of connected products (Article 2(31)). If generative AI is embedded in or acts as a virtual assistant that interacts with connected products, it would also fall within the scope of the regulation.
(b) Providers of related services, including software that connects to these devices to add, update, or adapt functionalities, must also comply, regardless of their location (Article 2(6)).
(c) Users of connected products and services within the EU (Articles 1(3)(b) and 2(12)).
(d) Data holders, entities with the right or obligation to make data available, must do so on fair, reasonable, and non-discriminatory terms (Articles 1(3)(c) and 2(13)).
(e) Data recipients are entities that receive data for business purposes following a user's request or a legal obligation (Articles 1(3)(d) and 2(14)).
(f) Public sector bodies can request data access in exceptional public interest cases (Articles 1 (3)(e) and 2(28)).
(g) Providers of data processing services, such as cloud service providers, must ensure data portability and interoperability to facilitate customer switching (Articles 1(3)(f) and 2(8)).
(h) Lastly, participants in data spaces, including vendors of applications using smart contracts for data-sharing agreements, are required to ensure secure and efficient data sharing (Articles 1(3)(g)).

[195] Martínez, 'Generative AI and the Digital Markets Act'.
[196] *Id.*
[197] *Id.*
[198] *Id.*

The Act lays out several key provisions. Firstly, it ensures fair data access and use. Users can access data generated by their use of connected products and services and share the data with third parties. Data holders must provide information on the data generated and make it available securely and free of charge, although the data cannot be used to develop competing products and trade secrets can be preserved. Data protection rules, including those in the GDPR, must be adhered to (Chapter II Articles 3–7).

Secondly, the Act sets rules for mandatory business-to-business data sharing. Businesses must share data with other businesses on fair, reasonable, and non-discriminatory terms of contract. Data holders can request reasonable compensation for making data available, but micro companies, small and medium-sized enterprises (SMEs), and non-profit research organisations are only charged for the actual costs incurred (Articles 8–12).

Chapter IV of the Act protects businesses from unfair contractual terms imposed by more powerful entities. The contractual term is unfair if it is of such a nature that its use grossly deviates from good commercial practice in data access and use, contrary to good faith and fair dealing. Terms that are deemed unfair are invalid and, if possible, removed from the contract (Article 13).

To ensure a competitive EU market, the Data Act aims to enable seamless switching between data processing service providers, including cloud services, by removing barriers such as high charges, lengthy procedures, and lack of interoperability. Providers must ensure that customers can switch services without data loss or application functionality issues. By 12 January 2027, switching charges, including data egress fees, will be entirely removed. During a transitional period, providers can charge only for the costs incurred in switching (Chapter VI, Articles 23–31).

Finally, Chapter VIII of the Data Act aims to foster research and development of new products and services by ensuring standards and interoperability within and between common European data spaces. Participants in data spaces must comply with essential interoperability requirements, including making data structures, formats, and vocabularies publicly accessible. The Act also prepares for increased interoperability of data processing services through harmonised standards and open interoperability specifications (Articles 33–36).

By addressing these areas, the Data Act aims to create fairness in the data economy, promote innovation, and support competition, which are essential for the development and growth of the AI ecosystem.

19.3.5 *Observations on Regulation*

The regulatory initiatives across the European Union, United States, and United Kingdom demonstrate a proactive approach to addressing the competition challenges posed by GenAI and the broader digital markets. Each jurisdiction has recognised the critical need to ensure that the rapid advancements in AI do not lead to entrenched monopolies or stifle innovation. The EU, in particular, has shown a commitment to tackling these issues directly, with a layered approach that spans antitrust enforcement, market surveillance, and sector-specific regulations like the AI Act, Digital Markets Act, and Data Act.

These regulations collectively aim to mitigate the risks of market concentration and anti-competitive practices by addressing access to key resources – such as data, computing power, and foundational models – while developing an environment that encourages new entrants and innovation. The EU's framework seeks to balance the need for regulatory oversight with the preservation of open competition, especially in the context of the nascent yet rapidly growing GenAI market.

However, while these regulatory measures address many of the immediate concerns around competition, their long-term effectiveness remains to be seen. The dynamics of digital markets and AI ecosystems are complex and evolving. The potential for GenAI to create new monopolistic structures, due to its reliance on vast amounts of data, significant computational resources, and network effects, poses an ongoing challenge. The regulatory landscape will need to remain adaptive and vigilant to ensure that the markets for GenAI and related technologies remain competitive and inclusive.

The EU's regulatory approach is comprehensive, and complex, but it is still early days in assessing its impact on market dynamics. As these regulations are implemented, it will be crucial to monitor whether they succeed in curbing the market power of dominant players, preventing anti-competitive practices, and fostering a more competitive and innovative environment. The true test of these regulations will be whether they can sustain a competitive landscape as GenAI technology matures and becomes increasingly integrated into various sectors.

19.4 SOME CONCLUDING REMARKS

To maintain competitiveness in the foundation model ecosystem, public policy must prioritise supporting innovation among foundation model providers. This requires a clear vision of regulatory objectives, the establishment of specific rules, and robust enforcement measures.[199]

According to Schrepel, computational antitrust is a burgeoning field that utilises legal informatics to automate and improve antitrust procedures. Agencies worldwide are forming data analytics teams, hiring computer scientists, and using tools like machine learning for cartel detection, natural language processing, and network analysis. AI plays a major role in these efforts, enhancing competition agencies' ability to detect and enforce regulations more swiftly and effectively. However, for computational antitrust to progress, there must be rules and standards to govern the use of these tools and encourage their development.[200]

It is my opinion that the regulatory and policy agenda should not be overly complex or, unless necessary, impose compliance costs that small and medium-sized players cannot reasonably afford.[201]

The G7 Competition Authorities developed principles for protecting competition in the AI ecosystem. The commonly held principles may serve to enable competition and foster innovation:[202]

(a) Fair dealing: exclusionary tactics should be avoided as should actions that undermine competition.
(b) Interoperability: a key factor in ensuring competition and innovation.
(c) Choice: businesses and consumers in the AI ecosystem will benefit if they have choices among diverse products and business models resulting from a competitive process. This means scrutinising ways that companies may employ lock-in mechanisms that could prevent companies or individuals being able to meaningfully seek or choose other options. It includes ensuring that agreements are not sidestepping merger enforcement or handing incumbents undue influence or control in ways that undermine competition.

In conclusion, ensuring a competitive landscape in the era of generative AI requires a balanced approach that fosters innovation while preventing market abuses and ensuring ethical use of computational resources, data, and models (upstream inputs), and the fair implementation of applications (downstream outputs).

199 Schrepel and Pentland, 'Competition between AI Foundation Models', 15.
200 Schrepel, 'Decoding the AI Act', 7.
201 *Id.*, 16; Martínez, 'Generative AI and the Digital Markets Act'; Schrepel and Pentland, 'Competition between AI Foundation Models', 19; OECD, 'Artificial Intelligence, Data and Competition', 28.
202 G7 Competition Authorities, 'Joint Statement'.

20

Regulating Hypersuasion

Cristina Poncibò

'ChatGPT can make mistakes. Check important info.'

(ChatGPT 4.0)

20.1 INTRODUCTION

The landscape of consumer business interactions is undergoing a profound transformation propelled by the emergence of generative artificial intelligence (GenAI).[1] Ever since the launch of ChatGPT in late 2022, the field of GenAI has witnessed a remarkable surge in popularity, with large language models (LLMs) leading the field. From a technical standpoint, various characteristics differentiate these AI models from conventional ones.[2] GenAI systems, such as LLMs,[3] are known for their extensive capabilities and independence in identifying patterns within vast datasets.[4] These LLMs possess the unique ability to process a wide range of inputs from different domains, so that they can generate content seamlessly. Many LLMs are also multimodal, meaning they can handle and produce various types of data formats simultaneously. For instance, GPT-4 can process text, image, and audio inputs concurrently to generate texts, images, and even videos. However, despite their impressive performance in diverse tasks, advanced LLMs raise concerns among scholars regarding the legality and accuracy of the texts they generate.[5]

This chapter explores the intricate relationship between and GenAI.[6] Prominent tools like Bing Chat, ChatGPT 4.0, Google's Gemini (formerly known as Bard), OpenAI's DALL·E,

[1] Generative AI (GenAI) basically refers to deep-learning models that can generate high-quality text, images, and other content based on the data they were trained on, see, for example, K. Martineau, 'What Is Generative AI?' (2024) IBM Research, https://research.ibm.com/blog/what-is-generative-AI

[2] C. Novelli et al., 'Generative AI in EU Law: Liability, Privacy, Intellectual Property, and Cybersecurity' (2024) 55 *Computer Law & Security Review*, 106066, https://ssrn.com/abstract=4694565 or http://dx.doi.org/10.2139/ssrn.4694565

[3] C. Poncibò, M. Ebers, 'Comparative Perspectives on the Regulation of Large Language Models' (2025) 1 *Cambridge Forum on AI: Law and Governance*, 1–5, doi:10.1017/cfl.2024.14

[4] N. Carlini et al., 'Extracting Training Data from Diffusion Models' (2023), 5253–70, www.usenix.org/conference/usenixsecurity23/presentation/carlini

[5] C. T. Ungureanu, A. E. Amironesei, 'Legal Issues Concerning Generative AI Technologies' (2023) 14 *Eastern Journal of European Studies*, 45, https://ssrn.com/abstract=4689630

[6] J. Paul, A. Ueno, C. Dennis, 'ChatGPT and Consumers: Benefits, Pitfalls and Future Research Agenda' (2023) 47 *International Journal of Consumer Studies*, 1213–1225, doi: 10.1111/ijcs.12928. See also A. Jablonowka et al.,

and Snapchat's AI chatbot are widely recognized, and they dominate the generative AI landscape. However, numerous smaller, unbranded GenAI tools are embedded within major platforms, often going unrecognized by consumers as AI-driven technology. In particular, the focus of this chapter is the phenomenon of algorithmic consumers, whose interactions with digital tools, including GenAI, have become increasingly dynamic, engaging, and personalized.[7] Indeed, the rise of algorithmic consumers marks a pivotal shift in consumer behaviour, which is now characterized by heightened levels of interactivity and customization.[8]

Thus, in light of three prominent examples – content creation, recommender systems, and virtual assistants – this chapter delves into the manifold benefits of, and legal risks associated with, GenAI. These examples serve as illustrative case studies enabling an analysis of how GenAI influences consumer experiences and the many EU legal frameworks that aim at governing them.[9] Specifically, it situates its analysis within the context of existing EU legal provisions for privacy, consumer protection, and platform and AI regulation. Through this lens, it seeks to assess the extent to which current legal regimes effectively address the multifaceted challenges posed by GenAI.

The chapter concludes by highlighting the profound influence and legal risks of Floridi's concept of 'hypersuasion' in regard to European consumers.[10] He coined the concept to describe the highly sophisticated and personalized forms of persuasion enabled by AI systems.[11] This chapter argues that existing legal instruments[12] fail to comprehensively govern the power dynamics inherent in algorithmic consumer interactions, and it identifies possible strategies in the section about policies. Moreover, the chapter also underscores the inherent lack of coordination among these legal frameworks, accentuating the pressing need for cohesive and harmonized approaches to safeguarding consumer rights.

20.2 CONSUMERS AND GENAI

20.2.1 *'Algorithmic' Consumers*

The notion of 'algorithmic consumers' refers to a consumer whose purchasing decisions, preferences, and behaviours are significantly influenced, shaped, or mediated by algorithms.[13] In fact, GenAI and LLMs are being increasingly deployed in consumer-oriented applications like search engines, social media platforms, and language processing services. The prevalence of these applications is expected to expand significantly. According to an analysis by McKinsey, a

'Consumer Law and Artificial Intelligence: Challenges to the EU Consumer Law and Policy Stemming from the Business' Use of Artificial Intelligence: Final Report of the ARTSY Project', EUI LAW, 2018/11, https://hdl.handle.net/1814/57484

[7] P. Henderson et al., 'Foundation Models and Fair Use' (2023) *ArXiv*, https://doi.org/10.48550/arXiv.2303.15715

[8] See McKinsey, The State of AI in 2023: Generative AI's Breakout Year (2023) McKinsey & Company, www.mckinsey.com/capabilities/quantumblack/our-insights/the-state-of-ai-in-2023-generative-ais-breakout-year

[9] Turing Institute, '11 Best Generative AI Tools and Platforms' (2024), www.turing.com/resources/generative-ai-tools

[10] See, in particular, L. Floridi, Hypersuasion – On AI's Persuasive Power and How to Deal With It. *Philos. Techno.*, 37, 64 (2024). https://doi.org/10.1007/s13347-024-00756-6

[11] See also S. Wachter, B. Mittelstadt, C. Russell, 'Do Large Language Models Have a Legal Duty to Tell the Truth?' (2024) Royal Society Open Science 11240197, http://doi.org/10.1098/rsos.240197

[12] F. G'sell, 'An Overview of the European Union Framework Governing Generative AI Models and Systems' (2024), 1–118, http://dx.doi.org/10.2139/ssrn.4762804

[13] M. Gal, A. Zac, 'Is Generative AI the Algorithmic Consumer We Are Waiting For?' (2024) *Network Law Review*, 1, https://ssrn.com/abstract=4755455; M. Gal, N. Elkin-Koren, 'Algorithmic Consumers' (2016) 30 *Harvard Journal of Law and Technology*, https://ssrn.com/abstract=2876201

substantial portion of the value generated by these systems will be concentrated in customer service and marketing/sales domains.[14] In marketing and sales, they can facilitate more effective and efficient content creation, personalization, and brand advertising, provided that measures are in place to mitigate risks, such as plagiarism and copyright violations. In customer-facing roles, the implementation of chatbots and AI assistants has the potential to enhance productivity, efficiency, and the overall customer experience.[15]

Interestingly, the concept underlying algorithmic consumers is that consumers can protect themselves from potential harm caused by suppliers' algorithms, such as personalized or coordinated pricing, by utilizing countervailing algorithms.[16] These countervailing algorithms can either be developed by consumers themselves or provided by external firms. While such algorithms are already in use in some markets, most of them assist consumers only in some parts of the consumption act, leaving the ultimate decision to the consumer. In such a context, GenAI can potentially help them to more easily and swiftly compare price and quality, predict price and market trends, take expedient decisions under uncertain conditions, and make better-informed choices.[17]

This chapter argues that the idea that consumers can 'play' with GenAI is scarcely convincing given that algorithms are obscure and highly complex and require technical expertise to understand and manipulate which the average consumer typically lacks. It is evident that there is a significant power imbalance – specifically, a data asymmetry between large tech companies and individual consumers, with companies having far more resources and control. On the contrary, consumers' reliance on algorithms comes with new and serious legal risks. Indeed, legal scholars have often underlined the risk of an 'algorithmic exploitation' of consumers.[18] One of the primary concerns is the risk of deceptive practices.[19] GenAI can create highly persuasive and personalized advertisements that exploit consumer vulnerabilities.[20] This level of personalization, while beneficial in some contexts, can lead to manipulative marketing tactics.[21] Additionally, the advent of deep fakes and AI-generated misinformation poses a significant threat. These technologies can create highly realistic but false content, undermining consumer trust and leading to harmful decisions based on misinformation. Privacy is another major issue associated with generative AI. To function effectively, AI systems often rely on vast amounts of personal data. This extensive data collection raises significant questions about privacy and consent.[22] Consumers may not be fully aware of how their data are being used or may not have given explicit consent for their use in AI-driven applications. Unauthorized use of personal data is a critical problem because it can lead to privacy violations and potential misuse, further eroding consumer trust. Bias and discrimination raise another set of challenges.

[14] McKinsey, *The Economic Potential of Generative AI. The Next Productivity Frontier* (2023), www.mckinsey.com/capabilities/mckinsey-digital/our-insights/the-economic-potential-of-generative-ai-the-next-productivity-frontier

[15] Ibid.

[16] Gal, Zac, 'Is Generative AI'.

[17] Ibid.

[18] E. Mik, 'The Algorithmic Exploitation of Consumers' in L. A. Di Matteo, C. Poncibò, G. Howells (eds.), *The Cambridge Handbook of AI and Consumer Law. Comparative Perspectives* (Cambridge: Cambridge University Press 2024).

[19] European Commission, Directorate-General for Justice and Consumers et al., *Behavioural Study on Unfair Commercial Practices in the Digital Environment – Dark Patterns and Manipulative Personalisation* – Final Report (Luxembourg: Publications Office of the European Union, 2022), https://data.europa.eu/doi/10.2838/859030

[20] C. Busch, A. De Franceschi (eds.), *Algorithmic Regulation and Personalized Law. A Handbook* (Oxford: Hart, 2021).

[21] European Commission et al., *Behavioural Study*.

[22] F. Zuiderveen Borgesius, N. Helberger, A. Reyna, 'The Perfect Match? A Closer Look at the Relationship between EU Consumer Law and Data Protection Law' (2017) 54(5) *Common Market Law Review*, 1427–1465.

Generative AI systems can perpetuate and even amplify existing biases, resulting in discriminatory practices in critical areas such as lending, hiring, and customer service. This perpetuation of bias can exacerbate social inequalities and result in unfair treatment of certain groups. Vulnerable consumers, in particular, may be unfairly targeted by manipulative AI-driven campaigns, so that existing disparities are further entrenched.[23]

20.2.2 *The EU/US Divide*

It is also worth noting that consumer adoption and attitudes with respect to GenAI may vary significantly between the United States and the European Union. In the USA, consumer usage of GenAI is at present higher,[24] and attitudes towards this technology are more positive than in countries such as France, Germany, and Italy.[25] This discrepancy can be attributed to several factors, including regulatory approaches and linguistic advantages.[26]

The EU is actively introducing and enforcing new provisions – for example, the Artificial Intelligence Act (AIA)[27] – aimed at ensuring that AI technologies are adopted in reliable and ethical ways. These regulatory frameworks are designed to protect users' rights and to promote transparency, accountability, and safety in the deployment of AI systems. For instance, the EU's General Data Protection Regulation (GDPR)[28] and AIA[29] set stringent standards for data privacy and AI usage, compelling organizations to adopt more rigorous practices.[30] Conversely, the USA lacks comprehensive federal regulations governing consumer use of AI.[31] While there are some state-level initiatives and sector-specific guidelines, there is no overarching federal framework akin to the EU's. This regulatory gap allows for more rapid and less constrained deployment of GenAI technologies in the USA, contributing to higher consumer engagement and more favourable attitudes towards AI.[32]

[23] F. Esposito, M. Grochowski, 'The Consumer Benchmark, Vulnerability, and the Contract Terms Transparency: A Plea for Reconsideration' (2022) 18(1) *European Review of Private Law*, 1–31.

[24] The Federal Trade Commission (FTC) found that some platforms use algorithms to manipulate the visibility and ranking of reviews and product reviews, which can indirectly influence consumers' purchasing decisions. See FTC, 'Price Fixing by Algorithm Is Still Price Fixing' (Federal Trade Commission, 2024), www.ftc.gov/business-guidance/blog/2024/03/price-fixing-algorithm-still-price-fixing. Additionally, a study from Stanford University (Human-Centered-AI, HAI) and the University of Washington found that advertising algorithms on digital platforms can be used to discriminate against certain demographic groups and undermine privacy regulations. See HAI, *Using Algorithm Audits to Understand AI* (Policy Brief 2022), https://hai.stanford.edu/policy-brief-using-algorithm-audits-understand-ai

[25] A European Commission report highlighted that 70 per cent of European citizens are concerned about the way AI is used and support strict regulations to protect their rights. See European Commission, *White Paper on Artificial Intelligence: A European Approach to Excellence and Trust* (2020), https://commission.europa.eu/publications/white-paper-artificial-intelligence-european-approach-excellence-and-trust_en

[26] A. Chee-Read, M. Kearney, T. Husson (eds.), *The State of Consumer Usage of Generative AI* (Forrester, 2024), 1–20, www.forrester.com/report/the-state-of-consumer-usage-of-generative-ai-2024/RES180689

[27] Regulation (EU) 2024/1689 of the European Parliament and of the Council of 13 June 2024 laying down harmonised rules on artificial intelligence (Artificial Intelligence Act), OJ L, 2024/1689, 12 July 2024, ELI, http://data.europa.eu/eli/reg/2024/1689/oj

[28] The GDPR sets strict standards for the processing of personal data, affecting AI applications that rely on such data, requiring transparency and consent.

[29] Regulation (EU) 2024/1689 of the European Parliament and of the Council of 13 June 2024 laying down harmonised rules on artificial intelligence, OJ L, 2024/1689, 12.7.2024, http://data.europa.eu/eli/reg/2024/1689/oj

[30] Chee-Read et al., *The State of Consumer Usage of Generative AI*, 1.

[31] The US Senate Task Force on AI, established in 2019, has passed into law at least 15 bills that focus on research and risk assessment for AI systems.

[32] Chee-Read et al., *The State of Consumer Usage of Generative AI*, 5.

Curiously, another critical factor influencing the effectiveness and adoption of GenAI is the language of the training data. LLMs that underpin GenAI platforms are predominantly trained on datasets rich in English content. This linguistic bias inevitably makes GenAI outputs more effective and accurate for English-dominant countries, including the United States and the United Kingdom. As a result, users in those regions experience better performance and utility from GenAI applications, so that positive perceptions and widespread usage increase further. By contrast, non-English speaking countries in Europe may find GenAI platforms less tailored to their linguistic and cultural contexts, which potentially limits their adoption and effectiveness. Although efforts are being made to diversify training data and improve the multilingual capabilities of AI models, the current dominance of English in training datasets remains a significant factor.[33]

20.3 GENAI: IDENTIFYING THE BENEFITS AND LEGAL RISKS

The following subsections identify and discuss the benefits and legal risks of the most common applications of Generative AI for consumers, namely content creation, recommender systems, and virtual assistants.

20.3.1 *Content Creation*

The implications of GenAI extend beyond text generation, and they significantly impact content creation. This democratization of content creation empowers individuals to express their creativity and share unique perspectives across various platforms. For instance, on social media, consumers can utilize generative AI tools to generate texts and/or visually appealing graphics, illustrations, or memes to enhance their posts and captivate their audience.[34] They can leverage AI-generated images to augment their storytelling, create visually stunning collages, or experiment with artistic filters and effects. This opens up new avenues for self-expression and enables consumers to participate actively in content creation.

Moreover, GenAI allows consumers to create high-quality images to accompany their reviews. Instead of relying solely on text-based feedback, consumers can generate visuals that provide additional context or showcase the product in action, enhancing the overall consumer experience and offering valuable insights to other potential buyers. The implications of generative AI for content creation are vast, since it empowers 'algorithmic consumers'[35] to become creators themselves and contribute their unique perspectives to the digital landscape.

However, researchers have also identified serious risks and, specifically, two distinct types of failure when analysing the false and misleading outputs produced by GenAI systems: failures in faithfulness and in factuality.[36] Failures in faithfulness occur when the output is not aligned with the user's prompt or the reference text provided (such as an article to be summarized). Failures

[33] R. Ta and N. Turner Lee, 'How Language Gaps Constrain Generative AI Development', Brookings, 24 October 2023, www.brookings.edu/articles/how-language-gaps-constrain-generative-ai-development/

[34] Directive (EU) 2019/790 of the European Parliament and of the Council of 17 April 2019 on copyright and related rights in the Digital Single Market, OJ L 130, 17 May 2019, 92–125. Art. 17 and other provisions impose stricter requirements on platforms in terms of content filtering to prevent copyright infringements.

[35] Gal, Zac, 'Is Generative AI'.

[36] Ji et al., 'Survey of Hallucination in Natural Language Generation' (2022) 5 *ACM Computer Surveys*, 1, https://doi.org/10.48550/arXiv.2202.03629

in factuality, on the other hand, occur when the output is inconsistent with real-world knowledge ('hallucinations').[37]

Within the realm of hallucinations, two overarching categories can be delineated: closed-domain and open-domain.[38] Closed-domain hallucinations occur when the GenAI system operates within a delimited task framework, typically with a specific reference text available for comparison, as exemplified by tasks like summarizing articles. Conversely, open-domain hallucinations transpire when the tool is deployed in more expansive applications, such as chatbots, which lack constraints on topics or definitive reference data for validation. Compared to closed-domain hallucinations, verifying the accuracy of open-domain hallucinations presents greater challenges due to the absence of specific reference points. This distinction underscores the varying complexities inherent in assessing the fidelity of GenAI outputs across different operational contexts.[39]

One of the primary reasons for hallucinations is the inherent complexity of model training. For example, large-scale language models like GPT are trained on vast amounts of data extracted from the internet. During this process, the model may inadvertently learn spurious correlations between data points, so that erroneous associations are made. Additionally, GenAI systems may mix facts between similar training observations, resulting in the propagation of inaccuracies.[40] Moreover, the nature of user interactions can exacerbate the occurrence of hallucinations during inference. As these systems engage in conversations with user-consumers, they leverage conversation history as context to inform their responses. However, this contextual reliance may diverge from the model's original training data, so that potentially unreliable outputs are generated. Furthermore, these models may exhibit parametric knowledge bias, favouring information learned during training over that provided by the user. This bias can skew the accuracy of the model's outputs, particularly in open-ended applications such as chatbots.[41]

The implications of hallucinations in GenAI systems for consumers[42] are manifold, and they pose significant challenges in various domains. In consumer-facing applications, false or misleading outputs can undermine trust and credibility, causing dissatisfaction among users. Moreover, the proliferation of fake news and misinformation amplifies societal concerns, since these systems may inadvertently propagate such content. Additionally, in critical domains like healthcare or finance, erroneous outputs from FMs can have far-reaching consequences, jeopardizing decision-making processes and potentially endangering lives or financial stability.

Despite advances in model development, even state-of-the-art GenAI systems such as GPT-4 are not immune to hallucinations. Researchers have observed instances where these high-performing models make basic factual errors, raising questions about the reliability of their outputs. This underscores the need for the continuous evaluation and refinement of these technologies to mitigate the occurrence of hallucinations.[43]

[37] K. Haoqiang, N. Juntong, Y. Huaxiu, 'Ever: Mitigating Hallucination in Large Language Models through Real-Time Verification and Rectification' (2023), https://doi.org/10.48550/arXiv.2311.09114

[38] Ji et al., 'Survey', 5.

[39] S. Bubeck et al., 'Sparks of Artificial General Intelligence: Early Experiments with GPTP-4' (2023) Microsoft Research, Section 9.1, https://arxiv.org/pdf/2303.12712

[40] Ibid., 12.

[41] Ibid., 12

[42] Generative AI and consumer hallucinations are the phenomena whereby AI systems, particularly those based on generative models, produce outputs that are plausible but factually incorrect or misleading, which can deceive consumers.

[43] Bubeck et al., 'Sparks of Artificial General Intelligence', 12.

Both types of inaccuracies – in faithfulness and in factuality – can raise consumer protection issues. Specifically, the persuasive power of generative AI also introduces significant legal risks. Under the Unfair Commercial Practices Directive (UCPD),[44] commercial practices, including the provision of information about goods and services, that are misleading or aggressive are strictly prohibited. If AI-generated images present deceptive visual information or create false impressions about a product, they may mislead consumers. Accordingly, we argue that traders using AI-generated content must disclose the AI-generated nature of the visuals and avoid any exploitation of viewers. Failure to meet these standards could distort consumers' decision-making processes, inducing them to make choices they might not otherwise make if fully informed.[45] For example, OpenAI's usage policy requires automated systems, such as conversational AI and chatbots, to disclose to users when they are interacting with an AI system.[46] This disclosure is mandatory for consumer-facing applications in the medical, financial, and legal sectors, as well as in news generation or summarization. OpenAI's policy also states that products simulating another person must either obtain explicit consent from that person or be clearly labelled as 'simulated or parody', except for chatbots depicting historical public figures. Microsoft has a 'Transparency Goal' whereby its AI systems are designed to inform users when they are interacting with an AI system or using a system that generates or manipulates image, audio, or video content that could falsely appear to be authentic.[47] However, this policy does not apply to all generative AI systems, as different organizations and developers may have their own policies and guidelines regarding AI transparency. Indeed, the EU AIA mandates transparency for AI systems that interact with humans, aiming to ensure that European users are made aware that they are engaging with an AI system rather than a human being.[48]

20.3.2 *Recommender Systems*

In the ever-evolving landscape of consumer behaviour, individuals actively seek alternative sources of information such as social media and online reviews. Increasingly, consumers are turning to these sources to obtain brand, product, or service information and recommendations. This shift underscores the growing reliance on AI-driven systems to gain personalized insights. Put differently, consumers are now seeking answers directly from GenAI, leveraging its capabilities to access relevant and tailored information.

One of the primary features of GenAI recommender systems is their heightened ability to predict and influence user preferences. Conventional recommender systems analyse past behaviour to suggest content or products that a user might like. But GenAI ones go further by not just predicting what users currently prefer, but actively shaping their future preferences. For example, a streaming service might use AI to suggest what a user might enjoy based on past views, and also strategically introduce new genres or themes to expand the user's interests, ultimately steering their consumption patterns in desired directions.

[44] Directive 2005/29/EC of the European Parliament and of the Council of 11 May 2005 concerning unfair business-to-consumer commercial practices in the internal market, OJ L 149, 11 June 2005, 22–39, http://data.europa.eu/eli/dir/2005/29/oj

[45] CMA, *AI Foundation Models, Initial Report* (Competition and Markets Authority, 2022), 5.302–5.35, https://assets.publishing.service.gov.uk/media/65081d3aa41cc300145612c0/Full_report_.pdf

[46] Ibid., 5.35.

[47] Ibid., 5.33.

[48] The AIA is designed to regulate high-risk artificial intelligence systems, promote transparency, accountability and ethical standards in the implementation of artificial intelligence, and impose sanctions for non-compliance.

While this level of personalization can enhance user satisfaction and platform engagement, it raises significant legal concerns. One of the central issues is the potential for manipulation. Recommender systems powered by GenAI can exploit cognitive biases and emotional triggers to nudge users towards specific behaviours, often without their conscious awareness. For instance, an e-commerce platform or a marketplace might use GenAI to highlight products with greater profit margins, subtly influencing users to make purchases that benefit the platform more than the consumer. This kind of manipulation can undermine user autonomy, as decisions are heavily swayed by AI's strategic nudging rather than by genuine user choice.

It is consequently essential to recognize that the recommendations provided by GenAI are based on the data used for training and may have limitations, or that they may be influenced by outdated information. The UCPD strictly prohibits commercial practices that are misleading or aggressive.[49] Additionally, if these AI tools exploit consumer vulnerabilities – for example, by means of emotional manipulation through personalized interactions – such practices could be considered aggressive, violating consumer protection laws (specifically, the UCPD). More recently, Article 27 of the Digital Services Act (DSA) specifically addresses the issue of transparency surrounding the recommender systems[50] utilized by online platforms.[51] It aims to shed light on the inner workings of these systems, ensuring that users have a clearer understanding of how recommendations are generated and why they are presented with certain content.

To clarify, the providers or deployers of GenAI tools must provide transparent and accurate information. This includes, for example, clearly disclosing the AI nature of the recommendations and avoiding any exploitation of consumers. Failure to meet these standards could distort consumers' decision-making processes, inducing them to make choices they might not otherwise make if fully informed.

20.3.3 *Virtual Assistants*

By leveraging the capabilities of GenAI, virtual shopping assistants transform how consumers engage with products and make purchasing decisions.[52] These AI-driven assistants offer personalized recommendations and revolutionize virtual shopping, thereby shaping consumer behaviour through sophisticated information processing and decision-making support. For instance, generative AI-powered chatbots integrated into e-commerce platforms enable real-time engagement with consumers, assisting them in navigating vast product catalogues, understanding their

[49] J. A. Mattu, 'Amazon Says It Puts Customers First. But Its Pricing Algorithm Doesn't' (ProPublica, 2023), www.propublica.org/article/amazon-says-it-puts-customers-first-but-its-pricing-algorithm-doesnt

[50] Regulation (EU) 2022/2065 of the European Parliament and of the Council of 19 October 2022 on a Single Market for Digital Services (Digital Services Act), OJ L 277, 27 October 2022, 1–102, http://data.europa.eu/eli/reg/2022/2065/oj

Article 3(s) defines a recommender system as: 'a fully or partially automated system used by an online platform to suggest in its online interface specific information to recipients of the service or prioritise that information, including as a result of a search initiated by the recipient of the service or otherwise determining the relative order or prominence of information displayed'.

[51] According to Article 3(i) the concept of online platforms includes: 'a hosting service that, at the request of a recipient of the service, stores and disseminates information to the public, unless that activity is a minor and purely ancillary feature of another service or a minor functionality of the principal service and, for objective and technical reasons, cannot be used without that other service, and the integration of the feature or functionality into the other service is not a means to circumvent the applicability of this Regulation'.

[52] S. De Conca, 'The Present Looks Nothing Like the Jetsons: Deceptive Design in Virtual Assistants and the Protection of the Rights of Users' (2023) 51 *Computer Law & Security Review*, 105866, https://doi.org/10.1016/j.clsr.2023.105866

preferences, and providing tailored recommendations based on these preferences. By offering such personalized product suggestions, these virtual shopping assistants enhance the overall shopping experience, guiding consumers towards the products that best align with their needs.[53]

One of the key advantages of GenAI virtual assistants is their ability to comprehend and generate natural language with remarkable fluency and contextual awareness.[54] This enables them to engage in nuanced conversations, grasp the intricacies of consumer queries, and respond with relevant and insightful information or recommendations. Whether a consumer seeks advice on product research, financial planning, creative writing, or any other topic, GenAI virtual assistants can serve as knowledgeable and adaptive assistants. Moreover, their general-purpose nature allows them to continuously learn and expand their capabilities. As they interact with more consumers and encounter new scenarios, their underlying language models can adapt and refine their understanding, ensuring that their assistance remains relevant and up-to-date.[55] GenAI virtual assistants also offer unparalleled personalization capabilities: by analysing a consumer's preferences, communication style, and context, they can tailor their responses and recommendations to the consumer's specific needs and interests. This level of personalization not only enhances the consumer experience but also fosters a sense of trust and rapport because consumers feel understood and valued.[56]

However, it is important to note that although GenAI virtual assistants are powerful tools, they are not infallible. Their outputs can reflect biases present in their training data or exhibit limitations in certain domains. It is therefore crucial for consumers to maintain a critical mindset and exercise their judgement when engaging with these systems. Moreover, these practices also raise important ethical considerations, particularly in regard to privacy, data governance, and the possibility of misuse or manipulation. In fact, these virtual assistants have the potential to manipulate consumer behaviour in ways that might contravene existing consumer protection laws. Again, the EU's UCPD prohibits practices that are misleading or aggressive. For example, if an AI-powered chatbot[57] provides inaccurate or overly persuasive information to influence purchasing decisions, this could be deemed misleading. Furthermore, if these chatbots employ tactics that exert undue pressure on consumers, for example by exploiting emotional vulnerabilities by simulating romantic interactions, such practices could be considered aggressive and therefore illegal.

20.4 EU LEGAL FRAMEWORKS

Different EU legal frameworks can apply to various aspects of GenAI relevant to EU consumers, for instance content creation, recommender systems, and virtual assistants. Specifically, we think of the GDPR,[58] which mandates transparency, data protection, and user consent, and, more

[53] Unlike traditional virtual assistants with narrowly defined capabilities, GenAI assistants are powered by advanced language models trained on vast amounts of data, allowing them to engage in human-like dialogue, understand complex queries, and provide tailored assistance across a wide range of domains.

[54] Gartner Inc., 'Virtual Assistants on the Rise in the Workplace' (2019) CXOToday.com, https://cxotoday.com/news-analysis/virtual-assistants-on-the-rise-in-the-workplace-gartner

[55] De Conca, 'The Present Looks Nothing Like the Jetsons'.

[56] Ibid.

[57] Novelli et al., 'Generative AI in EU Law'.

[58] Regulation (EU) 2016/679 of the European Parliament and of the Council of 27 April 2016 on the protection of natural persons with regard to the processing of personal data and on the free movement of such data, and repealing Directive 95/46/EC (General Data Protection Regulation), OJ L 119, 4 May 2016, 1–88, https://eur-lex.europa.eu/legal-content/EN/TXT/?uri=CELEX%3A32016R0679

recently, the DSA and the EU AIA. In addition, EU consumer protection laws generally prohibit false advertising and deceptive marketing practices (UCPD) and unfair contract terms (Unfair Contract Terms Directive, UCTD)[59] to prevent traders from exploiting consumers through deceptive or manipulative practices.[60]

20.4.1 *Content Generation*

The GDPR mandates that personal data must be processed lawfully, fairly, and transparently. This also applies to GenAI systems using data to generate content.[61] These principles should ideally provide a robust framework in which to regulate AI systems that engage with consumers. For instance, AI systems must have a legitimate basis, such as explicit user consent, for processing personal data. However, in practice, the requirement for informed consent is often reduced to users clicking 'I agree' on lengthy and incomprehensible terms and conditions. This practice raises questions about the genuineness of consent and whether users truly understand how their data will be used by AI systems to influence their decisions.[62]

Transparency, another cornerstone of the GDPR, requires organizations to provide clear and accessible information about their data-processing activities. In the context of GenAI, the average user does not comprehend how their data is being used to create highly personalized and persuasive messages. This opacity undermines this principle and leaves users vulnerable to manipulation without their informed knowledge. The GDPR also emphasizes data minimization and purpose limitation, stipulating that the personal data collected should be adequate, relevant, and limited to what is necessary. While these principles are intended to protect users, they can be difficult to enforce in practice. GenAI and LLM systems thrive on vast amounts of data to generate effective persuasive content. Determining what constitutes 'necessary data' can be highly subjective and context-dependent, potentially allowing organizations to justify extensive data collection under the guise of necessity. Furthermore, the GDPR grants individuals several rights concerning their personal data, such as the right to access, rectify, and erase data, and object to data processing. These rights are crucial for protecting users from unwanted AI-driven persuasion. However, exercising these rights can be cumbersome and complex, particularly when dealing with GenAI systems: users may find it difficult to navigate the processes required to access or delete their data, let alone understand how their data has been used to influence them. This complexity effectively diminishes the practical enforceability of these rights, leaving users at a disadvantage.

For example, a particularly contentious area is the regulation of profiling and automated decision-making. The GDPR includes specific provisions that give users the right not to be subject to decisions based solely on automated processing, including profiling which significantly affects them.[63] While this is a positive step, the regulation allows for several exemptions, such as when the processing is necessary to meet contractual obligations, or is based on explicit consent. These exemptions can be easily exploited by organizations, rendering the protections less effective. Moreover, distinguishing between automated decisions and those involving

[59] Council Directive 93/13/EEC of 5 April 1993 on unfair terms in consumer contracts. Consolidated text, http://data.europa.eu/eli/dir/1993/13/2022-05-28

[60] P. Hacker, 'A Legal Framework for AI Training Data – From First Principles to the Artificial Intelligence Act' (2021) 13(2) *Law, Innovation and Technology*, 257–301, https://doi.org/10.1080/17579961.2021.1977219

[61] Ibid., 258.

[62] G. Malgieri, *Vulnerability and Data Protection Law* (Oxford: Oxford University Press, 2023).

[63] Ibid.

minimal human intervention can be challenging, which further complicates enforcement. Thus, the effectiveness of GDPR in the context of GenAI-driven systems is limited by practical implementation challenges. Ensuring true transparency about how these systems operate and how personal data is used for persuasion is essential. Users need clear, comprehensible information if they are to make informed choices about their data and interactions with these systems.[64]

20.4.2 *Recommender Systems*

While the provisions introduced under the Art. 27 DSA (Recommender system transparency) represent an attempt to address the challenges posed by online marketplaces and search engines, their effectiveness is questionable with respect to GenAI-driven systems.[65] While the requirements for disclosing ranking parameters and paid advertisements are steps in the right direction, they may fall short of adequately addressing the complexities and potential manipulative tactics employed by AI-driven algorithms.[66]

Firstly, the Art 27(2) DSA mandates disclosure of the 'main parameters' driving ranking algorithms, which may lack specificity and enforceability. GenAI systems are often complex and opaque, making it difficult for operators of online platforms to provide meaningful and transparent explanations of their ranking criteria. As a result, consumers may not gain a comprehensive understanding of how their search results are curated and the extent to which they are influenced by GenAI-driven tools. Furthermore, the prohibition on providing search results without disclosing paid advertisements may not fully prevent subtle forms of manipulation: while overtly labelled paid advertisements may be disclosed, GenAI systems can still prioritize certain products or services based on factors beyond explicit payments, such as user engagement metrics or strategic partnerships. This can create a deceptive illusion of impartiality and organic ranking while still serving the interests of advertisers and platform operators.

As noted above, under the UCPD certain commercial practices are prohibited if they are misleading, aggressive, or otherwise unfair to consumers.[67] These practices include false advertising, aggressive sales tactics, and other forms of manipulation designed to exploit consumers' vulnerabilities or lack of knowledge. While the UCPD predates the emergence of AI, its principles can be applied to address some of the challenges posed by GenAI chatbots or recommender systems.[68] For example, Article 7(4a) of the UCPD[69] can be interpreted as imposing a duty to inform consumers about the main parameters of ranking algorithms and their relative importance. This provision requires transparency regarding the factors that

[64] J. Blockx, J. Krook, 'The EU Legal Framework for Algorithmic Recommender Systems: I (Don't) Know It When I See It' (2024) 16(1) *Law, Innovation and Technology*, 123–147. https://doi.org/10.1080/17579961.2024.2313799

[65] M. Grochowski, A. Jabłonowska, F. Lagioia, G. Sartor, 'Algorithmic Transparency and Explainability for EU Consumer Protection: Unwrapping the Regulatory Premises' (2021) 8 (1) *Critical Analysis of Law*, 43–63.

[66] S. F. Schwemer, 'Recommender Systems in the EU: from Responsibility to Regulation?' Paper presented at the FAccTRec Workshop, 27 September–1 October 2021, Amsterdam, The Netherlands, https://ssrn.com/abstract=3923003

[67] Directive 2005/29/EC concerning unfair business-to-consumer commercial practices in the internal market [2005] OJ L149/22 (Unfair Commercial Practices Directive).

[68] Annex I of the Directive comprises a list of commercial practices considered as a blacklist that indicates practices that are universally prohibited without the need for individual assessment regarding their potential impact on the average consumer's economic behaviour.

[69] Art. 7(4a): 'In the case of an invitation to purchase, the following information shall be regarded as material, if not already apparent from the context: (a) the main characteristics of the product, to an extent appropriate to the medium and the product'.

influence the placement of products or services in search results or on online marketplaces. If this information is disclosed, consumers can make more informed decisions and better understand the role of AI-driven persuasion in shaping their online experiences. Additionally, Annex I to the UCPD includes a prohibition (No. 11a) on providing search results in response to a consumer's online query without clearly disclosing any paid advertisements or payments made specifically to achieve higher rankings. The purpose of this requirement is to prevent deceptive practices where paid promotions are disguised as organic search results and thus to ensure transparency and fairness in online advertising.[70]

While these provisions of UCPD can address the challenges of GenAI-driven systems, they show significant limitations in fully capturing the nuances of AI-driven manipulation. The rapid advance of these technologies and their increasing sophistication pose ongoing challenges for regulators in effectively combating deceptive and unfair commercial practices online.[71]

20.4.3 *GenAI and Platform Regulation*

Technology companies are increasingly integrating GenAI capabilities into a wide array of platforms. This trend is evident across several prominent products and services, including Adobe Photoshop,[72] Google's Gemini and Circle to Search,[73] Microsoft's LinkedIn,[74] and Samsung's Galaxy S24.[75] As GenAI continues to evolve, its integration into mainstream products will likely become even more seamless and widespread, further blurring the boundaries between human and machine capabilities.

In this regard, to be noted is that the EU DSA addresses the growing concerns surrounding GenAI-based persuasion in online platforms by introducing measures to enhance transparency, accountability, and user protection.[76] However, GenAI systems pose – we argue – unique challenges in digital environments, where algorithms can subtly influence user behaviour and decision-making without their explicit awareness.[77]

One of the key aspects of the DSA relevant to this chapter is the requirement for online platforms to provide greater transparency regarding their recommender systems. The above-mentioned Article 27 DSA mandates that platforms disclose information about the functioning

70 European Commission, Guidance on the implementation and application of Directive 2005/29/EC on Unfair Commercial Practices, SWD (2016) 163 final, 123.

71 Needless to say, the integration of GenAI in recommender systems specifically raises significant privacy concerns. These AI systems rely on extensive data collection to fine-tune their persuasive capabilities. This data often includes not just explicit user actions but also implicit signals such as browsing history, time spent on certain pages, and even emotional responses inferred from interaction patterns. The depth and breadth of the data required can lead to intrusive surveillance practices that erode user privacy and trust. Users may not be fully aware of the extent to which their data is being collected and used, nor how it is being employed to influence their decisions.

72 Adobe Photoshop, for instance, leverages generative AI to enhance its image editing features, enabling users to create and modify visuals with unprecedented ease and precision.

73 Google's initiatives, such as Gemini and Circle to Search, incorporate advanced AI to improve search functionality and provide more intuitive, context-aware results.

74 Microsoft has embedded AI in LinkedIn to offer enhanced networking and career development tools, personalizing user experiences on the basis of vast amounts of data.

75 Samsung's Galaxy S24 utilizes AI to optimize performance and offer intelligent features that adapt to user behaviour.

76 The EU Digital Services Act (DSA), specifically its Article 27, requires these platforms to disclose how their algorithms work, including the generation of recommendations and content moderation. The initiative aims to protect users from unnecessary algorithmic influences and ensure a fair and competitive digital market.

77 C. Busch, V. Mak, 'Putting the Digital Services Act into Context: Bridging the Gap between EU Consumer Law and Platform Regulation' (2021) 10 *Journal of European Consumer and Market Law (EuCML)*, 109.

of their algorithms, including how recommendations are generated and the factors influencing content prioritization. By giving users insights into the inner workings of recommender systems, the DSA aims to empower individuals to understand and potentially mitigate the effects of hypersuasion on their online experiences.[78] Moreover, the DSA introduces obligations for online platforms to take proactive measures to address harmful content and activities facilitated by AI-driven algorithms. This includes measures to combat illegal content, such as hate speech and terrorist propaganda, which can be amplified by algorithms designed to maximize user engagement. Moreover, the DSA establishes a regulatory framework for online platforms with significant market power, to prevent abusive practices and ensure fair competition. This is particularly important in the context of GenAI, where dominant platforms may leverage their market position to prioritize their own products or services over competitors, thereby distorting consumer choice and stifling innovation. The DSA seeks to address these concerns by imposing transparency obligations and anti-discrimination measures on digital gatekeepers in order to promote a level playing field in the digital marketplace.

20.4.4 *The EU AIA*

The EU AIA intends both to promote the use of AI and address associated risks.[79] It also applies to the providers of GenAI. These providers are companies that either develop or integrate GenAI and make it available in the EU internal market. It is important to note that even when they refine existing models like GPT-4 by adjusting data sources, they may still fall under the obligations set forth by the AI Act.[80]

The AIA adopts a risk-based approach, with high-risk AI systems being subject to specific design and development requirements. For instance, Article 9 of the AIA mandates the establishment of a risk management system to continuously assess foreseeable and emerging risks. Moreover, Article 10(3) requires robust data governance in order to ensure that training, validation, and testing data are relevant, error-free, and comprehensive. Furthermore, human oversight is mandated under Article 14 of the AIA. Additionally, providers of GenAI models are required to furnish detailed technical documentation of their models to the supervisory authority upon request. This documentation should include information on the data used for training and validation, the computational resources employed, and the estimated energy consumption. Furthermore, providers shall ensure that downstream users of their models can understand the capabilities and limitations of the models. They are also mandated to create and publish a comprehensive summary of the training data used.

For providers of the models that present systemic risks, there are additional requirements to uphold cybersecurity measures, conduct thorough model evaluations, including adversarial testing, and identify and mitigate potential risks. Any incidents that occur must be documented and reported. On the other hand, providers of open-source licensed models, which are freely

[78] Art. 27: '1. Providers of online platforms that use recommender systems shall set out in their terms and conditions, in plain and intelligible language, the main parameters used in their recommender systems, as well as any options for the recipients of the service to modify or influence those main parameters'.

[79] EU Artificial Intelligence Act (AIA), May 2024, https://artificialintelligenceact.eu/ai-act-explorer For a comment, see M. Ziosi et al., 'The EU AI Liability Directive: Shifting the Burden from Proof to Evidence' (2023) Scholarly Paper. Rochester, NY, https://doi.org/10.2139/ssrn.4470725.

[80] C. Novelli et al., 'Taking AI Risks Seriously: A New Assessment Model for the AI Act' (2023) 39 *AI & Society*, 2493–97, https://doi.org/10.1007/s00146-023-01723-z

C. Novelli et al., 'AI Risk Assessment: A Scenario-Based, Proportional Methodology for the AI Act' (2024) 3(1) *Digital Society*, 13, https://doi.org/10.1007/s44206-024-00095-1

accessible and do not pose systemic risks, are exempt from the detailed documentation standards.

A key purpose of the AI Act is to promote the transparency and explainability of AI systems. For high-risk LLMs and GenAI assistants, this could mandate clear disclosures about their AI nature (Article 52 AIA), the extent of their capabilities, and the potential risks or limitations associated with their outputs. Consumers would have the right to know they are interacting with a GenAI system, so that informed decision-making is fostered. In such a context, the classification of recommender systems as high-risk under Article 6 of the AIA is debatable (while Annex III of the AIA identifies specific areas where AI systems are considered high-risk, such as legal information retrieval by judicial authorities).[81] But the recommender systems used in e-commerce, online dating, entertainment, or search engines may not fit into these categories. Nevertheless, the AIA promotes self-regulation by encouraging non-high-risk AI systems to adopt the obligations voluntarily (Article 69 AIA). Consequently, obligations applicable to high-risk AI systems could extend to recommender systems other than those explicitly classified as high-risk. The enforcement of the AI Act, including governance and penalties related to GenAI models, will be overseen by the 'AI Office' under the EU Commission.

20.4.5 *Virtual Assistants*

The UCPD may serve as a basis for regulating the use of GenAI virtual assistants in commercial settings. It does so by mandating principles of professional diligence and prohibiting practices that could distort the economic behaviour of the average consumer. Specifically, the directive requires virtual assistants to operate with the level of care and skill reasonably expected in their field. They must therefore provide clear information, and disclose their AI nature, and avoid exploitative or misleading practices under the UCPD.[82] Such practices could distort consumers' economic behaviour, leading them to make decisions they would not otherwise make if properly informed about the AI-driven nature of their interactions. However, the UCPD is not the only legal framework relevant to the use of GenAI virtual assistants in consumer contexts. As noted above, the GDPR also plays a crucial role in ensuring the responsible handling of personal data, which is inherent in the personalized interactions facilitated by these AI systems. Compliance with GDPR principles, such as data minimization, purpose limitation, and transparent processing, is essential to maintain consumer trust and privacy.

Additionally, the Consumer Rights Directive (CRD)[83] and the Digital Content Directive (DCD)[84] provide complementary protections for consumers engaging with AI-driven commercial practices. The purpose of the CRD is to ensure that consumers receive clear and comprehensive information about goods and services, while the DCD extends similar protections to digital content and services, including those powered by GenAI. As GenAI virtual assistants continue to evolve and become more deeply integrated into consumer experiences, efforts to refine and integrate or coordinate the legal frameworks governing their use will be essential.

[81] C. Goanta, 'Regulatory Siblings: The Unfair Commercial Practices Directive Roots of the AI Act' (2023) Working Paper, 1–16, http://dx.doi.org/10.2139/ssrn.4337417

[82] Ibid.

[83] Directive 2011/83/EU of the European Parliament and of the Council of 25 October 2011 on consumer rights, OJ L 304, 22 November 2011, 64–88, http://data.europa.eu/eli/dir/2011/83/oj

[84] Directive (EU) 2019/770 of the European Parliament and of the Council of 20 May 2019 on certain aspects concerning contracts for the supply of digital content and digital services, OJ L 136, 22 May 2019, 1–27, http://data.europa.eu/eli/dir/2019/770/oj

This includes addressing emerging challenges, such as the potential for unfair persuasion tactics facilitated by the persuasive capabilities of advanced language models.

20.5 HYPERSUASION: QUESTIONING THE ADEQUACY OF EU LEGAL FRAMEWORKS

Our argument here is that the EU legal frameworks are inadequate to protect consumers against the new and unique persuasive capabilities of GenAI.[85] As these technologies rapidly advance, they have an unprecedented ability to influence and manipulate consumer behaviour with a precision and subtlety that far surpass traditional distinctions and concepts.

The terms 'misinformation', 'persuasion', and 'manipulation' have often been used interchangeably to indicate these risks to the autonomy of consumers. 'Misinformation' refers to the dissemination of false or inaccurate information, whether intentionally or unintentionally. 'Persuasion' involves influencing someone's beliefs, attitudes, or behaviours through reasoning, logic, or emotional appeals. While persuasion itself is not inherently negative, it becomes problematic when it relies on deceptive tactics or presents biased or incomplete information to sway individuals' opinions or actions. Finally, 'manipulation' involves influencing or controlling someone's thoughts, emotions, or behaviours in a covert or deceptive manner for personal gain or to achieve a specific outcome.[86]

As GenAI systems and LLMs advance, their ability to exert an influence that surpasses human capabilities has become a critical area of concern. Indeed, it blurs the traditional distinction between persuasion and manipulation. Floridi's notion of 'hypersuasion' refers to AI's ability to influence human behaviour more effectively and subtly than any human persuader.[87] This is due to AI's capacity to continuously learn from interactions, adapt its strategies, and deploy personalized messaging at scale. These systems can analyse vast amounts of data, identify patterns, and tailor messages with unprecedented precision. This enables them to engage in highly effective persuasive communication. For instance, an AI-driven marketing tool can analyse consumer behaviour and preferences in order to craft personalized advertisements that are far more likely to elicit a positive response than traditional ones. While this level of personalization can enhance user experience and drive business success, it also blurs the traditional boundary between persuasion and manipulation.

Furthermore, several studies have underscored how GenAI outputs shape and reinforce users' beliefs. For instance, one study conducted an online experiment involving 1,500 participants which revealed that respondents who were primed by an opinionated writing assistant reported significantly higher agreement with it in a subsequent survey.[88] This finding suggests that GenAI has the capacity to influence users' perspectives and opinions. Similarly, another study found that LLMs tend to cater to users' existing beliefs, thereby strengthening and reinforcing them. These findings highlight the significant influence wielded by FMs in shaping user perceptions and attitudes. They therefore prompt important ethical considerations regarding the responsible deployment of such technologies.[89]

[85] J. Cowls, L. Floridi, 'Prolegomena to a White Paper on an Ethical Framework for a Good AI Society' (Centre for Digital Ethics, 2018), 1–5, https://papers.ssrn.com/sol3/papers.cfm?abstract_id=3198732

[86] Ibid., 1.

[87] Floridi, *The OnLife Manifesto*.

[88] Ibid.

[89] Ibid.

Public reports have alleged, and provided examples of, problematic behaviour by early iterations of Bing Chat. In particular, Microsoft has publicly acknowledged these concerns and has implemented various measures to address potential risks to consumers and users stemming from the deployment of GenAI systems.[90] One such measure is the imposition of limitations on the number of conversations per session in order to enhance user safety and mitigate the potential negative impacts of these applications.[91]

The legal implications of hypersuasion are profound. It seriously questions free will and autonomy because user-consumers may be influenced in ways they do not fully understand or cannot resist. The potential for abuse is significant, with AI being used to manipulate political opinions, consumer choices, and even social behaviours on a massive scale. In particular, the use of generative AI often requires access to large amounts of data, including personal information, to tailor content to individual preferences. This raises serious consumer privacy concerns because there is a risk of data misuse or unauthorized access. Consumers may be unaware of how their data is being used by generative AI systems, leading to potential violations of data protection law.[92]

Another legal risk of GenAI for consumers is the potential for false and misleading information. These tools are able to generate content, including text and images, that may present misleading or inaccurate information about products or services. This poses a significant risk to consumers, as they may make purchasing decisions based on false premises and therefore suffer financial losses or feel dissatisfaction with the products they acquire.

Furthermore, there is a risk that false and misleading information and/or manipulative practices associated with GenAI and LLMs may impact consumer decision-making. These tools could be used to manipulate consumer behaviour through persuasive techniques or emotional manipulation, potentially violating consumer protection laws. For instance, AI-generated content may coerce consumers into making decisions they would not otherwise make, or it may exploit vulnerable individuals, leading to legal ramifications for both consumers and businesses involved.

Having considered the above issues, this chapter underscores the imperative for a thorough re-evaluation of the efficacy of EU legal frameworks in upholding user rights and mitigating emerging risks, particularly those stemming from hypersuasion.[93] It also raises serious doubts about whether these legal frameworks are sufficiently equipped to pre-empt or safeguard consumers from such influence.[94]

20.6 POLICY IMPLICATIONS

In the light of the above, this section discusses the profound implications of GenAI for the traditional understanding of the notion of consumer, the evolving information paradigm, and the fundamental concept of consumer consent.

[90] TIME, 'Bing's AI Is Threatening Users. That's No Laughing Matter', https://time.com/6256529/bing-openai-chatgpt-danger-alignment/; S. Willson, 'Bing: "I Will Not Harm You Unless You Harm Me First"' (2023), https://simonwillison.net/2023/Feb/15/bing/

[91] Microsoft, 'The New Bing: Our Approach to Responsible AI' (2023), https://blogs.microsoft.com/wp-content/uploads/prod/sites/5/2023/02/The-new-Bing-Our-approach-to-Responsible-AI.pdf

[92] Another legal risk associated with generative AI is the potential for intellectual property infringement. GenAI tools may inadvertently generate content that infringes upon intellectual property rights, such as copyright or trademark laws. For example, AI-generated images or texts may unknowingly reproduce copyrighted materials, resulting in legal disputes and potential liability for consumers who use such content without proper authorization.

[93] L. Di Matteo, C. Poncibò, G. Howells, *AI and Consumers. Comparative Perspectives*, Cambridge Law Handbooks Series (Cambridge: Cambridge University Press, 2024).

[94] Goanta, 'Regulatory Siblings'.

20.6.1 *Understanding Algorithmic Consumers*

The foregoing examples make it clear that GenAI systems are reshaping our understanding of the notion of 'consumer' under EU Law.[95] In this reality, individuals are empowered to engage in dynamic, personalized interactions with AI assistants that shape their consumption experiences in unprecedented ways. In other words, the traditional notion of EU Consumer Law whereby the consumer is a passive recipient of goods and information is being rapidly replaced by the emergence of the algorithmic consumer – an individual ideally empowered by AI to actively shape and personalize their consumption experiences.

At the core of this transformation lies the abovementioned ability of LLMs to comprehend and generate human-like text so that they can serve as intelligent assistants able to understand complex queries, retrieve relevant information, and provide tailored advice or recommendations. This shift has profound implications for how the consumer is conceptualized in the digital age. Firstly, the algorithmic consumer is no longer bound by the limitations of human knowledge or the constraints of traditional search engines. LLMs act as knowledgeable advisors able to answer a wide range of questions, provide in-depth analysis, and offer personalized recommendations across various domains, from product research to financial planning, and beyond.[96]

Secondly, algorithmic consumers are empowered to co-create their consumption experiences. By engaging in interactive dialogue with LLMs, consumers can actively shape the information they receive, refine their queries, and collaborate with the AI system to generate personalized content, whether it is a tailored essay, a creative writing piece, or a customized analysis. Moreover, the algorithmic consumer has access to a vast body of knowledge and diverse perspectives. LLMs are trained on huge amounts of data enabling them to draw insights from a wide range of sources and offer a multitude of viewpoints. This exposure to diverse information and perspectives can broaden consumers' horizons, challenge their assumptions, and foster a more well-rounded understanding of the products, services, or topics they are interested in.

20.6.2 *Information Disclosure and Consent: Alternatives?*

The information disclosure and consent model of consumer protection relies on the principle that individuals can make informed choices about their personal data if provided with adequate information. However, the rise of generative AI technologies complicates this model. GenAI systems, with their advanced capabilities and inherent complexity, can obscure the nuances of data usage, leading to a consent process that is more perfunctory than genuinely informed.

Put differently, the core issue is a new form of information asymmetry. While companies have historically possessed more product knowledge than consumers, the tables have been turned with AI systems that possess vast datasets yet opaque inner workings. The complex algorithms, training processes, and potential biases underlying LLMs and GenAI are largely impenetrable to the average consumer, so that giving meaningful informed consent is an arduous task. Moreover, the nature of these AI interactions defies conventional consent mechanisms. As LLMs generate highly personalized and context-specific outputs, the scope and implications of such interactions become difficult to foresee or communicate through static disclosures or one-time consent processes.

95 Gal, Zac, 'Is Generative AI'.
96 Ibid.

A further concern arises from the potential for algorithmic bias and discrimination. LLMs and GenAI systems can inadvertently perpetuate societal biases present in their training data or exhibit discriminatory outputs, causing tangible harm to consumers. Existing consumer protection frameworks may lack the tools necessary to identify and mitigate these algorithmic harms effectively. For example, when consumers suffer detriment due to the outputs or recommendations of an LLM or GenAI system, attributing responsibility becomes a complex endeavour. The intricate interplay among the user's input, the model's training data, and its algorithms can obfuscate liability, leaving consumers without clear avenues for recourse.[97]

Secondly, the deployment of generative AI introduces fundamental questions about the ethical boundaries of influencing consumer behaviour and the extent to which GenAI should shape human decision-making. Ensuring that consumers retain their autonomy and provide informed consent in interactions with AI is crucial for ethical deployment. This necessitates clear disclosure of how AI systems operate and their potential impacts on users. However, achieving informed consent is fraught with difficulties. Many consumers may not fully understand the intricacies of AI technologies or the extent to which their data is being utilized and manipulated. Furthermore, the opacity of GenAI algorithms often complicates efforts to provide comprehensive and understandable disclosures. Without transparent information, consumers cannot make fully informed decisions, so they are at risk of exploitation and harm.

Therefore, the traditional information disclosure and consent model is increasingly inadequate in the era of GenAI. The complexity, persuasive power, and privacy risks associated with these technologies necessitate alternative approaches to consumer protection. To clarify, alternatives often consist in directly embedding privacy, fairness, and transparency in the design and operation of GenAI tools from the outset, which is known as fairness and/or privacy 'by design'.[98] By integrating these principles into the design phase, developers are called upon to mitigate legal risks for users. These alternatives signify a fundamental departure from past practices. They emphasise proactive, systemic, and multifaceted strategies over the traditional, often reactive, disclosure-based methods. This proactive embedding of principles in these tools contrasts sharply with the reactive nature of traditional consent models. However, it is crucial to acknowledge that we are only at the beginning of developing these alternatives, and considerable uncertainty remains regarding their implementation and effectiveness.

20.6.3 *Addressing the Interplay among EU Legal Frameworks*

Surely, the coherence and integration of EU legal frameworks also come under scrutiny. There is an urgent need to question whether these frameworks effectively complement each other and work in tandem to address the complexities arising from the intersection among consumer protection, data privacy, digital services, and the AIA.

EU consumer law, with directives like the UCPD, endeavours to uphold fairness and transparency in commercial transactions. However, in the face of AI-driven manipulation and algorithmic biases, these directives often fall short of providing adequate protection for users. The rapid evolution of digital technologies has outpaced the adaptability of consumer law, resulting in gaps and inconsistencies that leave users vulnerable to exploitation and harm.

[97] C. Koolen, 'Consumer Protection in the Age of Artificial Intelligence: Breaking Down the Silo Mentality between Consumer, Competition, and Data' (2023) 31(2) *European Review of Private Law*, 427–468, https://kluwerlawonline.com/journalarticle/European+Review+of+Private+Law/31.2/ERPL2023018

[98] I. Rubinstein, 'Regulating Privacy by Design' (2011) 26 *Berkeley Technology Law Journal*, 1410–1453.

Similarly, the GDPR has set high standards for data privacy and security, granting individuals control over their personal data.[99] Yet the GDPR's focus on privacy rights may not fully address the broader ethical and societal implications of AI-driven technologies. As a result, individuals may remain exposed to risks associated with data-driven manipulation and discrimination, which undermines the GDPR's intended objectives.

In this context, the DSA represents an attempt to regulate online platforms and foster transparency and accountability in digital environments. However, the DSA's focus on content moderation and platform liability may overlook the underlying issues of AI-driven manipulation and algorithmic biases. Consequently, the DSA's effectiveness in addressing the challenges of hypersuasion remains uncertain, so that users may be left unprotected against emerging risks.

Finally, the AIA seeks to regulate AI systems across the EU, categorizing them according to risk levels and imposing transparency and accountability requirements. While the AIA represents a step forward in addressing AI-specific risks, its narrow focus may lead to neglect of broader issues related to consumer protection and digital rights. As a result, the AIA's potential to effectively mitigate the risks of hypersuasion is at present uncertain.

Our analysis has revealed significant gaps, inconsistencies, and limitations in addressing the challenges posed by GenAI for consumers. Our main point has consisted in noting that the EU lacks a comprehensive and integrated regulatory approach. While existing EU regulatory frameworks provide valuable protection in specific domains such as consumer rights, data privacy, and digital services, they often operate in isolation and struggle to keep pace with the rapid advances in AI technology. As a result, there is a critical gap in understanding how to develop a coherent and integrated strategy across EU legal frameworks that effectively addresses the multifaceted challenges posed by hypersuasion.[100]

One key obstacle to developing a comprehensive approach is the inherent complexity of AI technologies and their diverse applications among sectors and industries. They are manifest in various forms, from algorithmic bias in online advertising to the manipulation of social media feeds by recommendation algorithms. This chapter has identified another obstacle, which consists in the fragmented nature of EU regulation and its enforcement in the member states, with multiple directives and regulations governing different aspects of digital technologies and AI. While each regulatory framework serves a specific purpose, such as protecting consumer rights or ensuring data privacy[101], their disjointed implementation often leads to inconsistencies and gaps in coverage. Harmonizing these regulations and establishing clear guidelines for their interaction has been essential in the recent past to enhance cooperation between the EU and national authorities for data protection and consumer protection. Finally, regulatory agility and adaptability are crucial in responding to the dynamic nature of AI technologies and emerging risks. Traditional regulatory approaches, characterized by lengthy legislative processes and static frameworks, may struggle to keep pace with the rapid evolution of AI-driven technologies. Flexible and iterative regulatory mechanisms, such as 'sandboxes' and pilot programmes, can facilitate experimentation and innovation. These regulatory instruments are attracting more and more attention, also in legal scholarship.[102]

[99] P. Chapdelaine, 'Algorithmic Personalized Pricing: A Personal Data Protection and Consumer Law Perspective' (2024) 102(1) *Canadian Bar Review* 1, http://dx.doi.org/10.2139/ssrn.4755474

[100] Koolen, 'Consumer Protection'.

[101] C. Poncibò, 'Where EU Consumer Law Meets Competition Law and Data Protection: Italy' (2023) 12(6) *Journal of European Consumer and Market Law* 280–286.

[102] C. Poncibò, L. Zoboli, 'Sandboxes and Consumer Protection. An EU Perspective' (2020) 8 *International Journal of Consumer Law and Practice* 1–22.

20.7 CONCLUSION

The intricate interplay among EU regulatory frameworks governing consumer protection, data privacy, digital services, and the AIA exhibits significant hurdles and deficiencies. These complexities highlight the need for a comprehensive recast of the legal frameworks and/or the development of more robust guidelines to better guide companies, including start-ups, in addressing consumer issues and tackling emerging risks, particularly those linked to Floridi's concept of hypersuasion. This chapter has argued that GenAI systems should operate within specific boundaries by enhancing the decision-making process, without compromising individual autonomy. Transparency is crucial for protecting consumers in the GenAI era. Users should be clearly informed when they are interacting with an AI system and how their data is being used. Consent is another critical factor; users shall have the option to opt in to data collection and targeted communication. Our analysis prompts scepticism about the ability of the existing legal frameworks to effectively shield consumers from these influences. Moreover, the coherence and synergy among these EU legal frameworks warrant critical examination. This entails inquiry into whether these frameworks harmoniously complement one another and synergize to navigate the intricate landscape of consumer protection, data privacy, digital services, and AI.

21

Generative AI Systems and Corporate Governance, Compliance and Liability

Rethinking Director and Officer Roles in Light of a New World of Technological, Legal and Ethical Challenges

Patrick J. O'Malley

21.1 INTRODUCTION

The rise in the use of artificial intelligence (AI) systems in most key areas of doing business, from sales and marketing to human resources management, from accounting and financial analysis to all manner of compliance matters, means that ultimately, even the highest levels of corporate governance will be transformed, and that corporate leaders will have to oversee both the development and the responsible use of AI. This transformation will directly impact the legal and ethical duties and best practices of those persons, the directing minds, who have been tasked with setting the 'tone at the top' and who, in one way or another, are accountable for the firm's success or lack thereof. Directors and executive officers will have to ask themselves to what extent should, or must, AI tools be used in strategic business decision-making and monitoring processes as an integral part of governance and its growing compliance and oversight component. Here we look at a number of select strategic governance and compliance oversight issues, standards and rules that we believe are going to be impacted and evolve due to the greater availability of generative AI tools. We consider what top management should be doing to ensure that all such AI tools used by employees or others in the firm's business activities are safe, functional and fit for purpose, especially considering avoidance of negative externalities that such AI tools could possibly cause to consumers, markets, workers and their families, states, shareholders, creditors and other stakeholders more generally. What should they, as corporate leaders, be doing to ensure that their corporate organisations are maximising the best positive use of AI, whilst avoiding and/or limiting AI-related risks to the extent possible, from both a legal and ethical perspective?

Indeed, we believe that the answers to such questions, which are being worked out right now and into the foreseeable future, will radically change what it means to be a good corporate leader and responsible decision-maker, and furthermore will force the human and moral element in corporate governance to be better prepared and more engaged than ever before. At least as far as global corporate governance goes, AI will force us, as flesh-and-blood decision-makers, to be better and more thoughtful humans responsible for 'doing business globally'. It will have to: without better prepared and more thoughtful real human persons truly overseeing companies, AI may well, in the worst case, become an existential risk to business, and ourselves. In this forum, due to the limited space available, we will attempt to wrestle with select issues that are affecting and will increasingly impact 'good corporate governance', even though the extent of many of these issues is not yet wholly clear as of this writing (May 2024). Also, in light of the global approach to this work, we have decided to take a more eclectic approach by looking at a number of jurisdictions, especially – but not limited to – the United States and the United Kingdom, and hard- and soft-law instruments. We realise that there is so much more out there to be considered as regards AI and corporate governance, both at the national and international levels, but that to do so would require a dedicated treatise all to itself. In addition, we note that we have at times taken the liberty to propose potential new solutions or recommendations regarding generative AI and how good corporate governance can best manage the risks involved. Time will tell whether they merit further consideration or turn out to be moot or dead-ends.

Let us start with a couple of key definitions for use in our considerations herein. According to the watershed 1992 Cadbury Report in the United Kingdom, 'corporate governance' is

> the system by which companies are directed and controlled. Boards of directors are responsible for the governance of their companies. The shareholders' role in governance is to appoint the directors and the auditors and to satisfy themselves that an appropriate governance structure is in place. The responsibilities of the board include setting the company's strategic aims, providing the leadership to put them into effect, supervising the management of the business and reporting to shareholders on their stewardship.[1]

Here we would add to this definition a special focus on the compliance and oversight/monitoring aspects of corporate governance that are so fundamental today to good governance (and indeed which the Cadbury Report helped to usher in) and that will be a *sine qua non* in successfully dealing with the impact of AI on companies moving forward. Another aspect of the Cadbury Report that speaks to us today as board and executive teams handle generative AI is that success or failure of the global system of corporate governance depends on them, as human overseers and stewards of all that goes on in their organisations:

> The country's economy depends on the drive and efficiency of its companies. Thus the effectiveness with which their boards discharge their responsibilities determines Britain's competitive position. They must be free to drive their companies forward, but exercise that freedom *within a framework of effective accountability*. This is the essence of any system of good corporate governance.[2]

Another related definition comes to us from the Chartered Governance Institute UK & Ireland: 'Corporate governance is the system of rules, practices and processes by which a company is directed and controlled ... [It] refers to the way in which companies are governed and to what purpose. It identifies who has power and accountability, and who makes decisions.'[3] When considering the impacts of generative AI use by corporate groups and their top management, especially when considering the oversight and compliance aspect of managing such risks (in both an *ex ante* and *ex post* manner), we believe that this definition is quite useful when tracing out the who, what, when, where and how of AI governance.

Artificial intelligence refers to digital systems as such, as defined in the EU AI Act:[4] 'a machine-based system designed to operate with varying levels of autonomy, that may exhibit

[1] Financial Aspects of Corporate Governance Committee' (Cadbury Report) (December 1992), The Committee on the Financial Aspects of Corporate Governance and Gee and Co. Ltd., para. 2.5

[2] *Ibid*,. at para. 1.1. Emphasis added.

[3] The Chartered Governance Institute UK & Ireland, www.cgi.org.uk/about-us/policy/what-is-corporate-governance (last accessed 30 April 2024).

[4] Regulation (EU) 2024/1689 of the European Parliament and of the Council of 13 June 2024 laying down harmonised rules on artificial intelligence and amending Regulations (EC) No. 300/2008, (EU) No. 167/2013, (EU) No. 168/

adaptiveness after deployment and that, for explicit or implicit objectives, infers, from the input it receives, how to generate outputs such as predictions, content, recommendations, or decisions that can influence physical or virtual environments.'

Within AI, generative AI refers to 'a type of AI that can create new content and ideas, including conversations, stories, images, videos, and music. AI technologies attempt to mimic human intelligence in nontraditional computing tasks like image recognition, natural language processing (NLP), and translation'.[5] Based on our observation of such systems that are currently on the market, or are soon to hit the market, such generative AI systems provide assistance with (among other things) finance and financial valuation, accounting, customer service, sales and marketing, healthcare, human rights monitoring in global supply chains, entertainment and creative output, writing, fashion, product industrial design, software development, optimal storing and distribution of energy from renewable sources, oil and gas pipeline risk management, and even the provision of legal advice and services. It is the rare industry or business activity that is largely immune from potential disruptive changes based on the roll-out of generative AI systems.

The fact is that myriad changes and challenges are coming due to generative AI (and many are already here), which will impact both corporate governance and compliance in many ways, both seen and unseen. There will be important liability issues for corporations and other players in the global trade and financial ecosystem. We believe that in the end, while much more will be expected of directors and executive officers, the best approach is for them to have, in sustainably managing legal, operational, financial and reputational risk, a deliberate *ressourcement*, a return to understanding and living out the roots of corporate duties (care, loyalty, good faith and others), where each decision-maker must become properly prepared, trained, fully informed and assisted to the extent necessary to make well-founded material decisions for the company in the long term, and oversee its operations and the risks inherent in generative AI systems. Our ideal director must know what AI is and how, at this point in time – *today* – all these generative AI products can and maybe should be put to productive use for some aspect of the corporate group's activities, and when such should be avoided as too risky. What are the AI's real limitations? What is the worst-case scenario for any particular form of AI, if it fails, if it is proven defective, or if it has a mind of its own and takes unauthorised decisions, or if one of our own people programs it to take illegal or unethical actions?

Thus, a constantly updated critical thought process, for boards and executive teams, should aim at helping each individual member gain an integrated understanding of how generative AI affects their company in particular, its key upcoming decisions, their competitors, their industries, applicable political systems and international relations, the economy and humanity more

2013, (EU) 2018/858, (EU) 2018/1139 and (EU) 2019/2144 and Directives 2014/90/EU, (EU) 2016/797 and (EU) 2020/1828 (EU AI Act); the EU AI Act was published in the *Official Journal of the European Union* on 12 July 2024. This wide-ranging and groundbreaking law is a global point of reference for other attempts to manage the potential and risks of AI systems; it is a sprawling mix of provisions that aims to buttress key EU regulatory interests, such as product health and safety/consumer protection/liability allocation, as well as defend fundamental rights (for a full discussion, see M. Almada and N. Petit, 'The EU AI Act: A Medley of Product Safety and Fundamental Rights?', *Robert Schuman Centre for Advanced Studies Research Paper* No. 2023/59 (18 October 2023), 1–27. Time will tell if it is successful and fit for purpose.

[5] Furthermore, 'Generative AI is the next step in artificial intelligence. You can train it to learn human language, programming languages, art, chemistry, biology, or any complex subject matter. It reuses training data to solve new problems. For example, it can learn English vocabulary and create a poem from the words it processes. Your organization can use generative AI for various purposes, like chatbots, media creation, and product development and design'. Amazon Web Services, 'What Is Generative AI?', https://aws.amazon.com/what-is/generative-ai/?nc1 = h_ls (accessed 28 April 2024).

generally. Directors need to be fully dedicated to this exercise, or risk possibly being replaced or held criminally or civilly liable for failures and resultant damages.

We believe that generative AI tools pose both major risks and opportunities for corporate leaders in running the multinational corporation and that AI will increasingly be considered by institutional investors, legislators and judges as an important component part of defining 'success' when judging such leaders' decision-making, both *ex ante* (in corporate planning and set-up of compliance/monitoring systems) and *ex post* (if and when something has gone wrong). Corporate leaders will need to get ready for a new and more aggressive global atmosphere where they will probably be required in multiple situations under regulatory guidance and governance/compliance best practices to show that have factored 'good AI' into their operations and decisions, as well as 'AI negatives' that could be full of risks, from relatively minor ones, right up to material ones for entire industries, markets or even humanity as a whole. AI avoidance by boards of directors and executive 'C-Suiters' is no longer an option. Instead, informed, diligent and purposeful adoption is the best course of action. Generative AI is increasingly becoming a key component of corporate decision-making and oversight, and all data points to it tremendously increasing over the next decade or so. Another related issue to watch is the evolution of quantum computing, which will only lead to an exponential increase in generative AI power[6] and, we believe, in its opportunities and risks from a corporate governance perspective.

Expectations by key investors and other stakeholders is rapidly evolving, such that directors and executives (as 'good stewards' of corporate value over time) need to already be establishing policies and processes to deal with generative AI risk, but also evaluating how generative AI can be used to improve corporate strategies and competitiveness; in sum, we are in the middle of a process that is redefining what it means to be that 'good steward', and not everything is clear as yet.

Ultimately, the 'buck stops' with boards and executive teams as the responsible decision-makers for managing AI risks concerning all manner of issues: discrimination/bias, cybersecurity/data security, privacy, confidentiality, trade secrets, quality control, competition issues, insurance matters, as well as the risk of AI malfunctions, 'hallucinations' and eventual manipulative or misleading behaviours; the list could go on. This is why we believe directors and executive officers need to go back to the deepest roots of company law governing not just the legal but also the ethical/moral aspects of their role as guarantors of corporate integrity and of the corporate system, applying principles such as care, diligence, loyalty, candour, transparency and good faith in all their decisions regarding generative AI.

21.2 BOARD COMPOSITION, FUNCTIONING AND DUTIES IN LIGHT OF ARTIFICIAL INTELLIGENCE

Boards will increasingly need to have AI-competent, and more generally technologically competent, directors as part of their composition. Of course, this depends on a given company's industry: in some industries, having at least basically AI-competent directors would be sufficient, whilst in others, especially in the technology industries, most or all directors should have directors with varying levels of AI preparedness.[7]

[6] See discussion, e.g., in M. Gschwendtner, H. Soller and S. Zingg, 'Combining Quantum and AI for the Next Superpower', *Nature Reviews Electrical Engineering* (30 April 2024).

[7] Certain companies that depend on AI and similar technology (like quantum computing) might have large or majority of its board or executive team that is AI or otherwise technology savvy. For example, Quantinuum Group, the world's largest integrated quantum computing company with major AI-related business interests, is currently weighing an IPO

As generative AI-related hard law and soft law initiatives gain increasing relevance over the next couple of years, we believe that expectations concerning having at least a number of AI-competent directors and executives will grow, and current best practices or reference standards will be reinterpreted (or specifically updated) to include AI and other new technologies. For example, the UK Corporate Governance Code 2024 includes a principle regarding board composition and evaluation, noting that 'The board and its committees should have a combination of skills, experience and knowledge'.[8]

This, of course, follows similar evolutions impacting global good governance over the past two decades, whereby including directors/executives with financial and accounting, and later compliance-related experience and expertise has become generalised.[9]

Beyond the makeup of corporate boards and executive teams, there is the question that has arisen recently of advocating for the naming of AI applications or some form of 'digital persons' or 'electronic persons' as board members or of the executive team. The EU considered the impact of this in a major background study regarding AI and civil liability, eventually concluding that 'electronic personhood' could be understood in a number of ways.[10] The EU study considered 'electronic personhood' as the acknowledgement of individual rights of the AI system and decided it was a 'radical inadmissibility' and that 'there are no technological, philosophical, nor [sic] legal reasons to deem machines as neither equal to human beings, nor belonging to an intermediate category to be distinguished between the two'.[11] However, when considering giving AI actors some kind of corporate or similar legal personhood, the EU study concluded that there may be cases where it might be sensible to attribute to the AI system a form of legal personhood, either by giving it a type of corporate legal personhood or by creating a different principle of bespoke legal personhood for an 'electronic person' pursuant to a new regulation.[12] This conflicts with earlier EU studies which recommended denying the awarding of electronic personhood, so it seems that the debate will continue. However, we suspect that, depending on technological advances, some kind of limited and functional corporate 'electronic personhood' will eventually be recognised for AI use at the board level or otherwise, in order to ensure liability and accountability to public policy goals.

We think that having a generative AI system as an 'AI person' of some sort serving on a board as an independent and autonomous actor could be significantly risky from a liability point of view,[13] for any damages stemming from erroneous or rebellious/non-conforming decisions made, as well as from a reputational and more general ethical point of view. Many people find the concepts of 'corporate legal personality' and the limited liability springing therefrom to be

(US listing) with a multi-billion-dollar valuation, has a top management team made up of mainly people with technology/science backgrounds: www.quantinuum.com/company/about (accessed 31 January 2025).

[8] UK Corporate Governance Code 2024, UK FRC (January 2024, effective in 2025), 11.

[9] For example, Sections 406 and 407 of the US Sarbanes–Oxley Act of 2002 require a company to disclose whether it has at least one 'audit committee financial expert' serving on its audit committee and, if so, the name of the expert and whether the expert is independent of management. A company that does not have an audit committee financial expert must disclose this fact and explain why it has no such expert. This requirement could be adapted in many legal systems to the presence of an 'AI systems expert' on the board and its pertinent committees.

[10] 'Artificial Intelligence and Civil Liability (July 2020) Legal Affairs', Study requested by the JURI committee, European Parliament, Policy Department for Citizens' Rights and Constitutional Affairs Directorate-General for Internal Policies, 9–10.

[11] *Ibid.*, 36–38.

[12] *Ibid.*, 42–44.

[13] *Pace* Mika, apparently the world's first AI CEO, 'Mika, World's First AI Robot, Is Now a Luxury Brand's CEO – News18' (13 November 2023) *OECD.AI Policy Observatory*, https://oecd.ai/en/incidents/50121 (accessed 1 May 2024).

problematic, unethical, unjustified and a multifaceted risk for stakeholders and, at times, society as a whole. By putting generative AI system digital persons on boards, there is a risk of reducing the truly human elements of the board/executive team and its workings, as well as the level of human oversight and human accountability, as well as trust – all ingredients that are absolutely fundamental for the long-term sustainable workings of corporations as key tools for creating human well-being. Diluting the human element in top management could also have ethical and reputational impacts on the willingness of governments and citizens to accept the principles and assumptions of law and practice that are necessary for the use of the corporate form in the integrated system of global trade and finance that we currently depend on. The oft repeated fear or concern regarding unregulated corporate power, 'Did you ever expect a corporation to have a conscience, when it has no soul to be damned, and no body to be kicked?',[14] would take on a new level of concern with non-human corporate persons (as 'mere creatures of the law'[15]) being run by other non-human 'electronic persons'. Thus, any foray of generative AI systems into the boardroom or executive management would need to be properly thought out and discussed (at both public and specific enterprise levels), highly regulated and adequately monitored, with functioning accountability measures.

21.2.1 *Board Service Providers as a Generative AI Governance Solution?*

An idea that we believe merits a second look in light of the impact of AI on board functioning and expectations, would be the optional use of independent professionalised board agencies/consultancies, which would serve on the board and use AI.[16] These would be made up of corporate and industry experts who would oversee any use of AI for the client corporation's decision-making. Indeed, about a decade ago, US corporate law experts Stephen Bainbridge and M. Todd Henderson advocated for that to become a part of the US corporate governance playbook.[17] Calling such agencies 'board service providers' (BSPs), they argued that engaging BSPs to provide director services, instead of individuals, would increase board functionality and accountability, and be attractive for both investors and the courts. They envisioned potential economies of scale and scope in the nascent 'board services industry', with beneficial risk pooling, and use of wide-ranging talent/expertise. They argued this would mean more transparent board performance and better market pricing of corporate governance, leading to increased reputational strength pertaining to board decisions, and, in sum, overall better corporate governance. This proposal intrigued us back then, but we believe that maybe such a proposal's time has come with the advent of AI's growing presence in the boardroom. Ultimately, in light of the myriad complex risks attending to use of AI, especially from a legal, reputational and technical oversight perspective, greater specialisation and harnessing of a mix of diverse human experts and even 'value-proven' generative AI tools under the aegis of a professionalised BSP could be a valuable solution. It would be for large multinationals, but also especially for smaller or mid-sized entities that lack access to more sophisticated advisors. Of course,

[14] Edward Thurlow, former Lord High Chancellor of Great Britain, as quoted in Archibald Alison, *History of Europe: From the Fall of Napoleon in 1815 to the Accession of Louis Napoleon in 1852*, Vol. 1 (Edinburgh: Blackwood and Sons, 1852), 56.

[15] *Trustees of Dartmouth College v. Woodward*, 17 U.S. (4 Wheat.) 518 (1819).

[16] Of course, in many US and other jurisdictions, the law would have to be amended to provide for some kind of non-physical person, whilst in many others, such organisational directors are permitted, so long as there is actual human oversight.

[17] Stephen M. Bainbridge and M. Todd Henderson, 'Boards-R-Us, Reconceptualizing Corporate Boards' (2014) 66 *Stanford Law Review*, 1051 *et seq.*

we believe that it would be positive to have just one of these BSPs per board – any more would potentially lead to conflicts and deadlock – whilst in some cases, a 'second opinion' BSP could be engaged for conflicted or otherwise complex transactions.

Thus, we think that eventually some form of AI board/executive role would be possible, but in all cases it would have to have human oversight and responsibility, ideally both a physical person or persons to manage such AI board/executive tool and a corporate person who would vet and control such physical persons (as well as insure against and provide a liability backstop in the event that both the AI and the human monitors fail in some way). However, this might best occur within the protections of using generative AI systems in boards under the aegis of a new type of BSP, as proposed by Professors Bainbridge and Henderson.

At a minimum, corporate codes of ethics, conduct governing boards or executive officer teams will need to be substantially updated to handle the legal and ethical issues that generative AI may have on their decision-making processes and corporate governance. Whilst we believe this is/will be a practical requirement more generally, it certainly does and will continue to receive significant attention under the evolving EU AI framework. For example, under the Ethics Guidelines for Trustworthy AI put out by the Independent High-Level Expert Group on Artificial Intelligence, there is significant focus on business leaders ensuring that AI use in their organisations meets guidelines on transparency, societal and environmental well-being, accountability, having proper human agency and oversight protections, being technically robust and safe, respecting privacy and data governance and being attentive to diversity, fairness and non-discrimination principles.[18] These guidelines also note that companies and their stakeholders can (and should, in light of the final provisions of the EU AI Act[19]) integrate them (and their goal of trustworthy AI) into their key corporate documents, including codes of ethics or conduct, charters of corporate responsibility and key performance indicators.[20] Thus, we presume that over time, ethical, responsible and sustainable AI use must become part and parcel of the 'tone at the top', as well as the structures and processes guiding corporate governance. With the expected significant increase in organisational use of all sorts of generative AI products, 'trustworthy AI' will become a key ingredient, a *sine qua non* for global legal and ethical standards of 'good corporate governance'.

In a related vein, the EU generative AI framework we alluded to above draws heavily from OECD efforts to provide best practice and ethical principles for the development and use of AI systems, especially the Organisation for Economic Co-operation and Development (OECD) AI Principles contained in the Recommendation of the Council on Artificial Intelligence, which focuses on a human-centric approach to trustworthy AI.[21] As with many areas of business

[18] 'Ethics Guidelines for Trustworthy AI', Independent High-Level Expert Group on Artificial Intelligence, European Commission, 8 April 2019, 15.

[19] Which, inter alia, mandates (Art. 16) having an organisational quality management system in place which complies with Art. 17; Art. 17 provides that such system (at least as regards 'high-risk AI' systems) must be documented in a systematic and orderly manner, with written policies, procedures and instructions, and with 'a strategy for regulatory compliance, including compliance with conformity assessment procedures and procedures for the management of modifications to the high-risk AI system', techniques, procedures and systematic actions to be used for the control and design verification of the high-risk AI system, techniques, procedures and systematic actions to be used for the development, quality control and quality assurance of the high-risk AI system, examination, test and validation procedures to be carried out before, during and after the development of the high-risk AI system. EU AI Act, 13 March 2024, ss. 16–17. All this will clearly involve significant board/executive team input, training and continuous oversight.

[20] 'Ethics Guidelines for Trustworthy AI', Independent High-Level Expert Group on Artificial Intelligence, European Commission, 8 April 2019, 22.

[21] OECD, Recommendation of the Council on Artificial Intelligence, OECD/LEGAL/0449, OECD Legal Instruments, 2019, 1–12.

governance and compliance issues, the OECD has become a key reference point for other transnational and national regulators and standard setters. Therefore, we believe that these OECD ethical AI recommendations will be important for corporate leadership globally, and will have to be integrated with (and will impact the interpretations and understandings of) other key OECD efforts at good governance and compliance that boards and executives around the world use to inform their codes, policies, best practices and decision-making (such as the OECD Guidelines for Multinational Enterprises on Responsible Business Conduct).[22]

21.3 HOW AI MAY IMPACT DECISION-MAKING ON STRATEGIC CORPORATE TRANSACTIONS, AS WELL AS CORPORATE PURPOSE AND STAKEHOLDER ISSUES

21.3.1 *Director and Officer Duties When Making Strategic Corporate Decisions*

We believe that increasing use of generative AI will impact and ultimately reinvigorate the traditionally recognised statutory and fiduciary duties of directors and officers. For example, the Business Judgement Rule (BJR) in the United States, Australia and other jurisdictions which expressly recognise this equitable, judicially applied abstention doctrine may need to be updated in light of AI use by the board and by the company more generally. The BJR is possibly the most important standard of judicial review under corporate law in the litigation-heavy United States. It protects a decision of the board or officers from more rigorous fairness review ('entire fairness') under Delaware law unless a well-pleaded complaint provides sufficient evidence that directors or officers have breached their fiduciary duties, or that the decision-making process was inadequate and fundamentally unfair, such as with a conflict of interest or a lack of decisional independence.[23] It is an elemental and wide-ranging 'safe harbour' to be applied to most corporate decisions, large and small.

For example, if we consider the Australian business judgement rule,[24] which in our estimation is a well-drafted statutory expression of the civil duties of care, loyalty and diligence as reflected in case law, we see a number of points where generative AI may play a role in interpretation of whether such requirements were actually met. In that act, for all business decisions, directors or officers are required to exercise their powers and discharge their duties with a reasonable person's degree of care and diligence, in light of the specific corporation's circumstances, as well as subject to the peculiarities of the actual office and responsibilities occupied by such director or officer. Such are assumed to meet their legal requirements so long as they make the judgement in *good faith* for a proper purpose, and do not have a material personal interest in the subject matter of the judgement, and *inform themselves* about the subject matter of the judgement to the extent they reasonably believe to be appropriate, and rationally believe that the judgement is in the corporation's best interests. While there are nuanced differences and particularities between this rule and those in other jurisdictions where the rule

[22] See, generally, OECD, *OECD Guidelines for Multinational Enterprises on Responsible Business Conduct* (Paris: OECD Publishing, 2023), 1–79, as well as the related 'OECD Due Diligence Guidance for Responsible Business Conduct' (2018); also, we believe that other OECD recommendations would be affected, such as those regarding compliance and bribery (OECD 'Good Practice Guidance on Internal Controls, Ethics, and Compliance', 2010, 1–4).

[23] *Cede & Co. v. Technicolor, Inc.*, 634 A.2d (Del. 1993), 345, 361.

[24] *Corporations Act 2001*, Sect. 180(1)–(3).

is explicitly recognised, such as the United States (especially in Delaware) or Spain, we believe they all would be materially impacted by generative AI use.[25]

It would seem to us that the major impact that this could have on moulding the future of the various business judgement rules would relate to the requirement to inform oneself before making a business judgement, as well as consider the particulars of a given company's industry and circumstances. All this would affect the meaning of 'diligence' in managing decisions relating thereto. For example, informing oneself under Delaware law implies a duty of care which requires that directors inform themselves adequately as to all reasonably attainable material facts concerning a given decision prior to taking actions based on that decision.[26] Of course, the amount, kind and quality of material information that was available back in 1985 is vastly different from that which was available in 2005. Today in 2025, with the reality of 'Big Data', the use of advanced generative AI systems and the promise that more, much more, computational power is coming our way over the next few years, especially in light of quantum computing advances, it should be clear that BJR information expectations are much greater, and that all this additional information must be properly integrated into board decision-making processes. As mentioned above, such information provides key insights into all manner of material issues that boards need to decide upon: the true value of an acquisition target, the capital markets and accuracy of estimated proceeds by doing an IPO[27] now rather than later, the adequacy of executive pay packages to attract and keep the best management personnel, the prospects of success of a number of promising anti-cancer pharmaceuticals, the true value of potential cyberattack risks, the reality of long-term employee and pensions liabilities to global corporate groups, the accuracy of the annual accounts and ESG[28] commitments of a potential investee, and so on and so forth. Almost every fact that has been recognised as a material issue for the life of a company can be made much more transparent now, and looking into the future, than before. Thus, questions of whether the business judgement rule should be applied to a given board decision will increasingly turn on whether the information obtained and then pondered by the board was sufficient: Were all potential value-added generative AI tools put to use by the humans responsible for making the decisions?

We also see that generative AI could influence the functioning of the system of corporate checks and balances, at least in the US. In the United States, there is a more stringent judicial review of corporate decisions which, due to actual or potential conflicts of interest in which a board majority is interested or will receive material benefits from the decision, a director has pecuniary incentives contrary to the company, or a conflicted director or dominating shareholder controls the board as a whole, are subject to higher or 'entire fairness' review by courts (often in Delaware).[29] Usually,

[25] This notable innovation was introduced into Spanish law in 2014, in Art. 226 of Law 31/2014, which amended the *Ley de Sociedades de Capital* (Joint Stock Corporations Law): *Protección de la discrecionalidad empresarial. 1. En el ámbito de las decisiones estratégicas y de negocio, sujetas a la discrecionalidad empresarial, el estándar de diligencia de un ordenado empresario se entenderá cumplido cuando el administrador haya actuado de buena fe, sin interés personal en el asunto objeto de decisión, con información suficiente y con arreglo a un procedimiento de decisión adecuado.* [Our translation: Protection of business judgement. In the area of strategic and business decisions, subject to corporate business judgement, the standard of diligence of an orderly businessman shall be deemed to be met when the director has acted in good faith, without a personal interest in the matter being decided, having obtained sufficient information to make such decision, and in accordance with an appropriate decision-making procedure.]

[26] See, e.g., *Smith v. Van Gorkom*, 488 A.2d 858, 872 (Del. 1985), *Aronson v. Lewis*, 473 A.2d 805 (Del. 1984), 473, *Cede & Co. v. Technicolor Inc.*, 634 A.2d 345, 367, 368 (Del. 1993) (noting that 'the directors individually and the board collectively [must] inform themselves fully and in a deliberate manner before voting as a board upon a transaction as significant as a proposed merger or sale of the company').

[27] Initial public offering on a regulated stock market.

[28] Environmental, social and governance.

[29] See, e.g., *Weinberger v. UOP, Inc.*, 457 A.2d (Del. 1983) 701 and *Unocal Corp. v. Mesa Petroleum Co.*, 493 A.2d (Del. 1985) 946.

the potentially conflicted parties must show that the decision subject to review is fair, as to both process and price.[30] Indeed, this type of review is extremely pertinent to all manner of mergers, acquisitions, and corporate reorganisations, and the cases have been applied to other material corporate transactions as well, (often additionally involving securities law fraud issues and parallel securities class actions by shareholders). Therefore, to put the burden on shareholders challenging such transaction(s), boards very often set up a 'Special Committee' of independent directors, legal counsel, investment bankers and others tasked with managing the entirety of transactional planning and execution. Showing that the financials and price calculations are reasonable and defensible is often at the crux of the decision (and whether it has a 'fair process' and 'fair price'). We believe that here, the use of generative AI systems to buttress fair pricing calculations or those of business and market risks (which feed into pricing calculations) is a necessary practice that can and should increasingly help identify positive and justifiable transactions and broad decision-making that is generally in shareholders' financial interests – the key focus of corporate purpose. In the notable 2012 *Americas Mining Corporation (In re Southern Peru Copper)* case from Delaware, the Delaware Supreme Court affirmed a decision which awarded damages of US$2 billion and US$300 million in attorneys' fees. There, a group of 'stellar', supposedly independent directors pressured the Special Committee's financial expert, Goldman Sachs, in order to push through a conflicted acquisition by the parent New York Stock Exchange-listed company at the behest of its majority shareholders, for – in hindsight – an exorbitant price. Neither Goldman, nor the independent directors, nor the lawyers checked the strident efforts of the majority shareholders to mould the financial calculations to their liking. With certain generative AI systems available even today, applying 'Big Data' to similar companies and historic commodities prices, especially of copper, the long, slow manipulation of the pricing process would, in our estimation, have been thwarted (and if not thwarted outright, would be transparently ridiculed at the litigation stage by financial or industry expert witnesses who would roundly show how unfair the price was). We can also imagine that other business risks that could impact key pricing processes in large corporate transactions would be subject to greater and more accurate scrutiny. In sum, generative AI will help large, material corporate transactions become more transparent, fairer, and better executed, ideally *ex ante* during the negotiations, structuring and execution of such transactions; and if not, *ex post* in ever more brutally accurate litigation post-mortems of such corporate decision-making processes.

21.3.2 *Stakeholder Issues*

While one of company law's perennial great debates, that of the fundamental purpose of the corporation (the basic dichotomy between shareholder governance and some version of stakeholder governance), has seen a tremendous amount of interest and attention (and marketing), if not yet hard law legislation, in more stakeholder-oriented models,[31] this has very much been accentuated with the rise of ESG investing in the last several years. While all this has gone on, there are still thoughtful debates about the true duties and extent of this evolution, with a number of experts arguing that ESG or stakeholder governance is not efficient, is difficult to

[30] *Ibid.*

[31] For example, see the Business Roundtable's 2019 redefinition of the purpose of a corporation, advocating to move beyond shareholder primacy models to run their businesses to the benefit of all stakeholders – workers, customers, communities, suppliers, the environment, and shareholders. Business Roundtable statement: 'Business Roundtable Redefines the Purpose of a Corporation to Promote "An Economy That Serves All Americans"' (19 August 2019).

implement and manage, and is easily manipulated for purposes of greenwashing or covertly acting in the real interests of management.[32]

Whilst we do not have the space or inclination to enter into an extended consideration of this debate here, at the end of the day, the corporate governance world, when considering it at a global level, will have to deal with the legal and ethical implications of generative AI systems. That is unavoidable. Further, we believe that it is also unavoidable that in dealing with AI, boards and executive teams will necessarily become more stakeholder-oriented, especially in light of the actual risks arising under AI system use (e.g., consumer, worker, children, patient rights, competitor and investor rights, to name a few). Such interests are already, and will continue to be, the focus of major hard law projects, soft law guidelines and litigation. The EU AI Act and the guidance coming out of UN initiatives and the OECD are significantly stakeholder-oriented, with a key focus on businesses' ethical duties to a wide-range of stakeholders. While there is consideration of potential AI system impact on the profitability of a given company (and thus on shareholder value), it is equally or even more the case that the evolving compliance and oversight duties to be imposed on corporate boards will be significant, and demand much more board attention to stakeholders as a whole.

We should also briefly consider how the UK Companies Act and its 'Enlightened Shareholder Value' approach evidenced in the codified general duties of directors[33] could be impacted by generative AI use. While so much more could be written on this, let us just make a few initial considerations: the Section 172 duty to promote the success of the company, the Section 173 duty to exercise independent judgement and the Section 174 duty to exercise reasonable care, skill and diligence.

In Section 172, there is a requirement for directors to have regard to the interests of a laundry list of stakeholders when choosing among a number of options that would be in the best interests of the members and the company's success. Generative AI systems can and will increasingly be used to prove the discharge of this duty. Having done the due diligence of 'considering the effect on' stakeholders such as workers (maybe through financial analysis as to how to maximise the saving of jobs, or human resources in identifying other jobs for dismissed workers, both in the corporate group or elsewhere), communities (AI systems used to measure human trafficking or negative social externalities[34]) and the environment (for example., AI's help with environmental impact studies), AI could also aid suppliers, for example (such as by streamlining supply chains and green logistics); and there are many other potential uses to show that a board is acting for the long-term success of the company. Of course, all of this will help boards provide evidence to strategic institutional investors (many of whom have integrated ESG analytics of their investees) that they do, in fact and not just in word, properly consider stakeholder interests; this will in turn assist in the long-term building up of the reputational strength of the company.

[32] See, e.g., the discussion in S. Bainbridge, 'Why the Business Roundtable CEOs Should Have Stayed the Course', Ch. 10 in *The Profit Motive Defending Shareholder Value Maximization* (Cambridge: Cambridge University Press, 2023), 125–168.

[33] UK Companies Act 2006, c. 46, Part 10, Ch. 2 The general duties – ss. 172 *et seq.*

[34] This would apply to AI use to streamline company operations in some way and to where the AI is often part and parcel of the main products or services offered. This would be extremely pertinent in certain industries, such as 'Big Tech' or social media companies where the negative impacts on, for example, youth mental health are hotly debated today, and litigated. Witness the forty-two US state attorneys general who sued Meta Platforms and others in federal and state courts alleging the group 'knowingly designed and deployed harmful features on Instagram and its other social media platforms that are purposefully addictive for children and teens'. See, e.g., US N.D. Cal. Case 4:23-cv-05448, filed 24 October 2023.

For the Section 173 duty to exercise independent judgement, it is really about directors having to make their own judgements and not indiscriminately following others (including an AI system) without considering the interests of the company; the director must exercise independent judgement for the company's benefit. Ultimately, as the solicitor general stated in testimony before the House of Lords:

> The duty is about directors having to make their own judgments and not follow blindly the views of another without considering the interests of the company. In other words, the role of a director is to exercise independent judgement for the benefit of the company. That is what we expect directors to do. It is surely right that they should have that obligation, given that it is what they were appointed to do.[35]

Directors may delegate their functions in accordance with the articles, and this duty does not prevent a director from relying on the advice or work of others; however, ultimately the final judgement is the director's responsibility.[36] We believe that use of advanced AI systems to inform and advise on key decisions would fall squarely within these principles. Of course, the director (or officer) is not expected to do everything on their own, and in certain situations they may actually breach their duty if they fail to take appropriate advice. However, as with all professional advice, slavish reliance is unacceptable, and obtaining such advice does not absolve a director from exercising their personal judgement.[37] Again, we believe that it is pertinent to set out the boundaries for use of AI by the board itself, such that it may become best practice or otherwise required in certain decisions (similar to the common requirement for boards to obtain a financial valuation before finalising mergers and acquisitions). In the end, each individual director will have to properly and critically reflect upon all advice proffered when making a key decision, whether it is from a qualified human person, such as a lawyer or a financial specialist, or from a qualified generative AI tool.

In Section 174 as regards the exercise of reasonable care, skill and diligence, we believe that in some types of financial transactions and as regards certain industries, the use of generative AI systems by board members and officers will become increasingly expected; as well, much of our discussion above concerning the interpretation of board diligence in using information available to make well-thought-out decision under the business judgement rule is pertinent here too. However, there is also always the problem of explaining exactly why you, as company director, have deferred to the advice of an AI system that may have 'black box' problems of explainability or 'hallucinations', among other negatives. A director could be challenged in a court or arbitral proceeding or by a prosecutorial or regulatory agency to explain the 'why'/reasoning behind that director's blind delegation of a key decision that otherwise cannot be traced and explained properly by the AI tool. This same problem appears where the same AI tool provides apparently different or contradictory results or recommendations based on the same data inputted.

A complete and well-defined observation of this industry-level risk applicable to purveyors and users of AI systems was made by former industrial generative AI and quantum computing specialist, Zapata Computing Holdings:

[35] UK Parliament, HC Official Report 2006, col. 599.

[36] Lords Grand Committee 2006, col. 282 (CA 2006 Duties of Company Directors, Ministerial Statements, DTI, June 2007, 9).

[37] See *Madoff Securities International Limited (In Liquidation) v. Raven & others* (2013) EWHC 3147 (Comm). Directors were not found in breach of duty for attaching great weight to Bernard Madoff's opinion as to the best interests of the company, since at the time (pre-scandal), they had no reason to question his competence, integrity or motives.

> Generative AI is about creating numerical models from training data and then sampling from those models to generate new data. This process is inherently complex with many opportunities for flaws. Even with excellent training data and strong application, these models are non-deterministic, meaning they can give different outputs for the same inputs at different times. All of these factors can lead to false predictions and incorrect outputs. Additionally, many implementations of these techniques are not explainable, meaning a person is unable to clearly explain the reason why a model provided a certain output. This unpredictability could deter potential customers from purchasing our solutions. For these reasons, the impact of generative AI may be far more limited than analysts currently predict following the release of ChatGPT and other well-known generative AI programs.[38]

Here we have one of the great difficulties of AI use in key corporate decisions. Ultimately, the director or executive had better be capable of separately explaining a convincing rationale for a given business decision recommended by a generative AI tool. However, technically, explainability remains a significant challenge in many contexts[39]. After considering the issues and discussing them at length with data/computing experts, we believe that it is clear that this challenge (explainability) must include boards and executive teams as crucial and active participants, willing to put in the time, effort and treasure as part of integrated multidisciplinary teams of digital and other technical experts, lawyers, finance experts, shareholder representatives and others, depending on the industry involved.[40] Indeed, specialised consultancies or certification bodies may arise, and may be arising already, to permit these processes to advance and to ultimately provide some level of comfort or certification for such generative AI use.

Furthermore, use of generative AI tools capable of doing deep due diligence, data gathering, retrieval and verification, such as financial and human relationship mapping[41] could certainly impact other codified director duties, such as the Section 175 duty to avoid conflicts of interest, the Section 176 duty not to accept benefits from third parties, and the Section 177 duty to declare interest in proposed transaction or arrangement.[42]

Thus, while we believe that certain AI tools (also in the form of 'electronic persons') may soon become expected best practice as part of the evaluation, and valuation, processes behind key board and executive decisions, such as major investments, mergers/acquisitions, market listings, loans, key expenditures, sales of material assets, and so on, nonetheless, as the EU has

38 Zapata Computing Holdings Inc., Form S-1 Registration Statement, filed with the US SEC on 23 April 2024, 'Risks Related to our Business and Industry', 34. Zapata subsequently ceased operations on 7 October 2024, as reported in its Form 8-K – Current report: SEC Accession No. 0000950170-24-114391, filed on 11 October 2024.

39 For a solid discussion of the issues, see, e.g., S. Ali et al., 'Explainable Artificial Intelligence (XAI): What We Know and What Is Left to Attain Trustworthy Artificial Intelligence' (2023) 99 *Information Fusion* 101805. Indeed, we are discussing a specific project with a number of AI technical experts to better connect, through evidence and data subject to a new certification process, AI use in a given business or commercial context to legal or best practice requirements regarding oversight, explainability and safety.

40 In fact, this is the approach recommended by the OECD: 'AI actors should ensure traceability, including in relation to datasets, processes and decisions made during the AI system lifecycle, to enable analysis of the AI system's outcomes and responses to inquiry . . . AI actors should, based on their roles, the context, and their ability to act, apply a systematic risk management approach to each phase of the AI system lifecycle on a continuous basis to address risks related to AI systems, including privacy, digital security, safety and bias'; see Section 1.3 (Transparency and Explainability) and Section 1.4 (Robustness, Security and Safety), Recommendation of the Council on Artificial Intelligence, *OECD Legal Instruments*, last amended on 8 November 2023.

41 See, e.g., Taskade, www.taskade.com/generate/agency-workflows/conflict-of-interest-checks-workflow (accessed 1 May 2024); and M. Kunova, 'How AI Can Help Journalists Track MPs Financial Interests: A New Tool That Uses Generative AI to Help Analyse Who Pays Members of the UK Parliament May Soon Be Available to Newsrooms' (5 December 2023), www.journalism.co.uk/news/how-ai-can-help-journalists-track-mps-financial-interests-/s2/a1094609/ (accessed 1 May 2024).

42 UK Companies Act 2006, 2006 c. 46, sections 175–177.

recognised, there must always be human oversight that monitors and critically analyses what is being done by the AI tool. In this case, that would be similar to traditional directors' or officers' use of experts (legal, financial, accounting) when making material corporate decisions. For example, there is ample case law in the United Kingdom and elsewhere that provides critical practice guidance and limitations on use of expert opinion: ultimately, the director or executive must take responsibility for such decisions and cannot avoid liability for wrong or even disastrous decisions. The physical person must be attentive to the expert and trust therein would be subject to a continuous critical oversight and analysis (looking for red, or even yellow, flags as to the actual functioning of such tools).[43]

For example, generative AI may impact stakeholder issues in the German and German-influenced systems, where workers' representatives serve on the supervisory board of the two-tier board system under 'co-determination' or co-decision-making laws. This special feature means that worker interests are not only defended under labour law, but also within the company law system.[44]

The fact is that as generative AI is increasingly rolled out in many industries, including traditionally important ones for the German economy, such as automobiles, chemicals and machinery, there will be a significant, potentially adverse impact on both the number and quality of such traditional German manufacturing/industrial jobs. Therefore, dealing with this wave of uncertainty over the coming years, in Germany and possibly abroad,[45] will be a major challenge for German multinationals' supervisory boards (along with government and union actors) under the co-determination system.[46] Indeed, many jobs globally in a wide range of industries are at risk of being replaced or partially curtailed. A March 2023 Goldman Sachs study calculated based on data for occupational tasks that roughly two-thirds of current jobs in the United States and Europe are exposed to some degree of AI automation and that generative AI could substitute up to a quarter of current work; based on global extrapolation of the study's findings, the Goldman researchers estimate that generative AI could replace the equivalent of 300 million full-time jobs.[47] Indeed, a number of German experts in co-determination foresee that in light of the current and prospective AI challenges to German corporate governance, employee co-determination[48] as a whole can and must be robustly applied to minimise risks and fully take advantage of the benefits of AI in the company, in such a way that accords with workers' rights, under German and other national laws and European rules and principles (such as the European Pillar of Social Rights), even though in

[43] See *Madoff Securities International Limited (In Liquidation) v Raven & others* (2013) EWHC 3147 (Comm).

[44] Co-determination includes company supervisory board co-determination, workplace co-determination with works' councils and trade union collective bargaining rights. Together, these three pillars comprise a robust system impacting company decision-making and management. See E. Klengel and J. Wenckebach, 'Artificial Intelligence, Work, Power Imbalance and Democracy – Why Co-determination Is Essential' (2021) 14(2) *Italian Labour Law e-Journal*, 161.

[45] Some German multinationals, such as BASF SE, provide board worker representation/co-determination rights to all or some of their foreign workforce, as well as their German employees: see www.basf.com/global/en/who-we-are/sustainability/we-value-people-and-treat-them-with-respect/employees/employee-representatives.html (accessed 26 April 2024).

[46] In fact, this role is foreseen by the OECD in Section 2.4 (Building Human Capacity and Preparing for Labour Market Transformation), Recommendation of the Council on Artificial Intelligence, *OECD Legal Instruments*, last amended 8 November 2023.

[47] 'Global Economics Analyst, 'The Potentially Large Effects of Artificial Intelligence on Economic Growth (Briggs/Kodnani)', *Goldman Sachs Economic Research*, 26 March 2023, 1.

[48] Klengel and Wenckebach, 'Artificial Intelligence', 161.

some experts' opinion, the EU AI Act does not go far enough in protecting worker interests from the EU social pillar perspective.[49]

Finally, in our estimation, another investor-related impact of generative AI use on corporate governance on the global level is that the current notion of 'stewardship' (that over the past fifteen years or so,[50] has notably influenced institutional investor interaction with corporate investees, and especially the latter's board and executive teams), will increasingly integrate good practice/law and ethics on generative AI use as a key metric when overseeing investee governance and deciding on *ex ante* and *ex post* efforts to engage with investee boards/executives. This would especially be pertinent as regards Principle 1 of the UK Stewardship Code 2020.[51] The next version of the Code may well explicitly take on board British, European and US regulations and best practice as regards board oversight of AI.[52] Thus, the role of institutional investors in setting the expectations for investee board/executive use of generative AI will be notable, as it has been with the focus on ESG metrics and sustainability by corporates over the past few years. The impact of large 'socially responsible investors', pension funds, sovereign investment funds and more general 'ESG funds' has been significant. Ethically and profitably managing the risks and opportunities of AI at the highest corporate levels will dovetail with ESG/ethics and sustainability metrics already imposed by many of the largest institutional (and other) investors. For example, the world's largest single investor and trailblazer on ESG/CSR (corporate social responsibility), human rights and environmental sustainability issues, the Norway Fund, has been focusing more recently on its AI use internally and in its investees, considering especially consumers' interests and how AI may affect industries such as healthcare, finance and 'big tech'.[53] The fund's CEO Nicolai Tangen noted the importance of all investee firms in its portfolio engaging constructively with AI, since it has immense possibilities to drive productivity and efficiency, whilst becoming a crucial business tool, like power, computers or the internet.[54] Indeed, as he noted in a key policy document put out by the fund that: 'We consider key elements of responsible AI to include: i) board accountability, ii) transparency and explainability, and iii) robust risk management processes that look beyond traditional business risks and address privacy, security, non-discrimination, and human oversight and control.'[55] Large influential investors like the Norway Fund should be closely watched to see how their increase in expectations leads to practical implementation of AI management at many of the world's largest corporate board and executive teams.[56] As with many governance and compliance matters over

[49] *Ibid.*, at 158, 165.

[50] Such as with the UK Stewardship Code 2020 (current version issued by the UK Financial Reporting Council).

[51] '[Signatory institutional investors] purpose, investment beliefs, strategy and culture enable stewardship that creates longterm value for clients and beneficiaries leading to sustainable benefits for the economy, the environment and society.' UK Financial Reporting Council, *UK Stewardship Code 2020*, 8, www.frc.org.uk/library/standards-codes-policy/stewardship/uk-stewardship-code/. In light of the width and breadth of AI's potential impacts on business functioning and the policy objectives of major legislation like the EU AI Act, this principle would be very difficult to respect without a robust AI focus within the investor, as well as among the investees.

[52] In light of the fact that the new UK Corporate Governance Code was recently issued in early 2024, the process of preparing the next version of the UK Stewardship Code is well underway. See UK FRC, 'Statement: FRC Policy Update – Launch of the UK Stewardship Code 2020 Review', 27 February 2024.

[53] Gwladys Fouche, 'Norway Wealth Fund to Firms: Use AI, but Do It Responsibly', *Reuters*, 15 August 2023.

[54] *Ibid.*

[55] Nicolai Tangen, Carine Smith Ihenacho and Corporate Governance Team, 'Responsible Artificial Intelligence: Our View on Responsible Artificial Intelligence (AI)', Norges Bank Investment Management (The Norway Fund), 15 August 2023.

[56] *Ibid.* Stating: 'As a financial investor, we will work at the market level to support the ongoing development of international standards and regulation that impact the companies we invest in, integrate risks and opportunities into our portfolio management, and engage with companies on responsible development and use of AI.'

the past two decades, it is our view that large public institutional investors have been and will continue to be activists, in *ex ante* efforts to decide in whom to invest and in efforts to influence governance once having done so, and in *ex post* accountability actions, especially US-based securities class actions and shareholder derivative lawsuits.

Therefore, balanced, legal and ethical generative AI adoption and risk management by boards and executive teams, especially but not exclusively at the world's largest corporate groups, will not be an isolated exercise, but rather a multilateral effort between and among corporate directors and officers themselves, their major institutional investors, and key legislative and regulatory bodies (such as the EU and the US SEC [Securities and Exchange Commission]). Other stakeholders in this roll-out or implementation of AI into the heart of corporate governance include key international organisations such as the OECD, UN entities (such as the International Labour Organization and the UN Global Compact), corporate insurers, proxy advisors and rating/certification agencies, director organisations, as well as the corporate legal academy and the corporate bar, especially in the United States. The results of this multilateral exercise, which may be several years away, will be a true twenty-first-century, integrated view of what 'good corporate governance' can and should look like in light of AI.

21.4 COMPLIANCE, OVERSIGHT AND CORPORATE REPORTING: A NEW CHAPTER ON GLOBAL OVERSIGHT WITH AI

As generative AI-related initiatives become increasingly impactful over the next couple of years, we additionally expect that interpretations and understandings concerning 'good oversight' of compliance by boards and executive teams will be transformed, and that those directors/executives who are AI-competent will have to (along with the rest of their boards and executive teams) reimagine a '360 degree' compliance and ethics programme for their corporate groups that is AI-proof and fit for purpose at a time of potentially great AI disruption to markets, whereby stakeholders such as workers, consumers, investors, regulators and prosecutors, to name just a few, will be eager to scrutinise corporate groups' approach to using and monitoring AI.

On a positive note, we have observed the increasing use by multinational businesses of generative AI to do legal compliance due diligence, especially in the human rights and modern slavery or supply chain due diligence fields.[57] This has occurred over the past couple of years, in part in order to deal with the explosion of national and EU laws relating to corporate human rights and other ESG due diligence and associated requirements. A partial list thereof includes the UK Modern Slavery Act 2015,[58] the US Uyghur Forced Labor Prevention Act,[59] the EU Supply Chain Due Diligence Directive,[60] France's Duty of Vigilance Law,[61] Germany's Supply Chain Legislation,[62] the California Transparency in Supply Chains Act,[63] and many others.

57 See, e.g., N. Coca, 'AI Is Helping Brands Address Forced Labor in Supply Chains' (14 September 2023), https://sustainable brands.com/read/supply-chain/ai-helping-brands-address-forced-labor-supply-chains (accessed 1 May 2024); see also OECD Business and Finance Outlook 2021, 'AI in Business and Finance 3. Human Rights Due Diligence through Responsible AI', www.oecd-ilibrary.org/sites/31e7edcc-en/index.html?itemId = /content/component/31e7edcc-en#section-d1e6399 (accessed 1 May 2024)

58 2015 c. 30.

59 135 Stat. 1525 (23 December 2021).

60 2022/0051(COD): Proposal for a Directive of the European Parliament and of the Council on Corporate Sustainability Due Diligence and amending Directive (EU) 2019/1937.

61 *LOI n° 2017-399 du 27 mars 2017 relative au devoir de vigilance des sociétés mères et des entreprises donneuses d'ordre.*

62 *Gesetz über die unternehmerischen Sorgfaltspflichten in Lieferketten* (in effect from 1 January 2023, published 22 July 2021).

63 Senate Bill 657, January 2012.

On the other side of the coin, many of the largest global institutional investors are increasingly using generative AI to decide in which companies to invest and then to monitor and ensure proper levels of stewardship over actual and potential investees. Much of this in turn is driven by these investors attempting to ensure their own bona fide ESG credentials vis-à-vis the companies they invest in. For example, for quite some time, the Norway Fund, has been a leader in extensively using AI for due diligence on its actual and potential investees and in pushing all corporate leaders to use AI responsibly, in the development and use thereof.[64] The prominence that the Norway Fund gives to AI in both its responsible use and expectations on use by others as part and parcel of its ESG and ethical vision, shows that 'AI transparency and sustainability' is well on its way to becoming a key component of corporate ESG, or sustainability measures more generally.

Therefore, our view is that generative AI systems used for corporate governance and compliance and general ESG/sustainability issues are going to continue to increase due to raised expectations by businesses' largest investors, lenders/financiers, regulators, their insurers, and ESG or sustainability-related certification bodies. This increase in demand is leading to many new AI applications and service providers; it is a great time to get into the market. One example of this is provided by Altana AI, which provides generative AI solutions for corporates, especially as regards supply chain due diligence, and whose clients include, among others, Maersk, Merck, Boston Scientific, and US Customs & Border Protection.[65]

As mentioned above, current best practices or reference standards will be reinterpreted (or specifically updated) to include AI and other new technologies. Another example from the UK Corporate Governance Code 2024 is the principle that, 'The board should establish and maintain an effective risk management and internal control framework, and determine the nature and extent of the principal risks the company is willing to take in order to achieve its long-term strategic objectives'[66] and a related provision to 'carry out a robust assessment of the company's emerging and principal risks. The board should confirm in the annual report that it has completed this assessment, including a description of its principal risks, and an explanation of how these are being managed or mitigated. The board should explain what procedures are in place to identify and manage emerging risks'.[67]

These emerging UK understandings of board risk assessment and management will dovetail significantly with the roll-out of the EU AI Act and its requirements, especially the extensive quality management system requirements covering providers of high-risk AI systems, which must be systematically documented in an orderly manner, with written policies, procedures and instructions, as well as testing and auditing on AI use at every step of the process.[68] All of this combined will undoubtedly, in our view, impact, on a day-to-day basis, board structuring, management and monitoring of AI and other technology issues in a focused way, one not heretofore expected.

More generally, and depending on the emerging risk of AI use by companies and their top management over the next few years, certain current national laws and legal frameworks will be

[64] 'Responsible Investment – [Norway] Government Pension Fund Global 2023', Norges Bank Investment Management (Oslo, 7 February 2024), 5 and elsewhere.

[65] 'Altana applies artificial intelligence to billions of public and non-public data points to deliver the only dynamic, intelligent map of the global supply chain: the Altana Atlas. Our AI platform provides governments, the biggest logistics providers, and the most important global businesses with unprecedented supply chain visibility and insights.' See https://altana.ai/about (accessed 1 May 2024).

[66] UK FRC, UK Corporate Governance Code 2024 (January 2024, effective 2025), 13.

[67] *Ibid.* at 14.

[68] Art. 17 of the EU AI Act, 217.

repurposed to deal with generative AI risks. The anti-bribery/corruption global framework is highly instructive, as is health and safety legislation (workers, clients, etc.). Of course, we might need new bespoke laws at national level to focus top management/corporate governance attention and accountability on AI. Certainly, the EU AI Act will be a first major step, and it will be a good and necessary exercise over the next several years to see how it impacts European companies and most other large multinationals, due to the 'Brussels effect'.

In the end, a rich, hard and soft law AI-oriented governance ecosystem can, and must, develop: it should include efforts at the national, transnational and global levels. We believe that it would be worth considering a multi-layered approach to the problem of AI risk management and compliance, following the global anti-corruption blueprint: (i) an international 'high-level' treaty (in the vein of the UN Convention against Corruption); (ii) an OECD 'practical' convention for implementation at the national level and copious guidelines/guidance and country enforcement monitoring;[69] (iii) possibly regional treaties/cooperation to buttress efforts and especially cross-border investigations and enforcement;[70] (iv) key national laws with significant accountability measures for both corporations and their top management and agents;[71] and (v) best practice providers and certifiers (Transparency International, the ISO, and private providers, industry groups, ISS [Institutional Shareholder Services], S&P Global Consulting & Advisory[72]).

Of course, due to the potential extent of damage with generative AI risk, we believe any such national laws governing business enterprises, and the quality of top management's corporate governance and compliance oversight, should contain a corporate 'failure to prevent' offence, such as that contained in the UK Bribery Act 2010[73] and in the newly implemented UK Economic Crime and Corporate Transparency Act 2023.[74] The crucial consideration with these strict liability 'failure to prevent' offences is the availability of an 'adequate procedures' defence. These detailed procedures would need to be the product of an extensive, global and continuously updated set of international best practices (for new AI technologies and emerging risks), obligations and suggestions, all with a bespoke industry focus.

21.4.1 *Delaware 'Caremark' Shareholder Derivative Suits*

One concrete area of contemporary compliance and oversight law in the United States, specifically in the world of Delaware corporate law and governance, that we believe will be used as an accountability mechanism for generative AI misuse by corporate groups and their directing minds will be the so-called *Caremark* cases and their related and evolving duty of oversight under Delaware law, as a part of the fiduciary duties of loyalty and good faith (and ultimately also of care). In the seminal *Caremark* decision from 1996,[75] a Delaware court outlined conditions for a corporate director's breach of their fiduciary duty of loyalty for

69 As does the Convention on Combating Bribery of Foreign Public Officials in International Business Transactions (OECD, adopted by the Negotiating Conference on 21 November 1997).

70 For example, the Inter-American Convention against Corruption (adopted by the Organization of American States in March 1996) and the African Union Convention on Preventing and Combating Corruption (adopted on 11 July 2003).

71 For example, the US Foreign Corrupt Practices Act of 1977, the UK Bribery Act 2010, the French *Sapin II*, Law No. 2016-1691 (enacted December 2016), Brazil's Clean Companies Act (*Lei da Empresa Limpa*, Law No. 12.846/2013).

72 Of course, Institutional Shareholder Services (ISS), S&P and other rating/certifying agencies would have to ramp up their AI expertise and capabilities; other, newer ratings providers could emerge.

73 2010 c. 23, section 7 (Failure of commercial organisations to prevent bribery).

74 2023 c. 56, section 199 (Failure to prevent fraud: fraud offences).

75 *In re Caremark International Inc. Derivative Litigation*, 698 A.2d 959 (Del. Ch. 1996).

corporate oversight failures. Known as the *Caremark* test, a director's lack of oversight may breach their fiduciary duty of loyalty and good faith if directors 'utterly failed to implement any reporting or information system or controls or having implemented such a system or controls, consciously failed to monitor or oversee its operations, thus disabling themselves from being informed of risks or problems requiring their attention'.[76] The *Caremark* court and those interpreting it since then have also made it clear that a key part of a director's fiduciary duty requires implementing and overseeing compliance programmes. There are a number of pertinent recent *Caremark* cases, but we believe the most informative, for purposes of analysing future applications on directors and companies suffering AI-related problems, is the 2021 Boeing Company case, where 737 MAX aeroplanes manufactured by Boeing crashed on two occasions (first in Indonesia and then in Ethiopia) in 2018 and 2019, killing everyone onboard – hundreds of people.[77] In the *Boeing* case and similar recent *Caremark* cases, ultimately directors (and potentially officers) are liable if the compliance failure related to some aspect that 'was essential and mission critical' to the company's business (in this case, aeroplane construction), whereby the board's oversight function must be more rigorously exercised, especially where such are central safety and legal compliance issues facing the company.[78] In Boeing's case, the court found that the corporate group surprisingly lacked any functional, integrated, board-level process to oversee aeroplane safety (in design and monitoring), and thus there was a significant risk of liability for the board.[79]

Applying *Caremark* standards to boards or executive teams of corporate groups where generative AI is somehow 'mission critical' to the safe and legal functioning of the business, and where AI-related compliance systems are either utterly absent (but also such systems need to be integrated and fit-for-purpose) or top management, especially key technology people, consciously fail to monitor or oversee its operations, there could be management liability. Of course, this is civil in nature, but would be public and reputationally damaging (as it certainly was for management of the Boeing company); and this would materially impact stock prices. Indeed, the facts underlying a *Caremark* case in Delaware usually support parallel US securities law shareholder class actions relating to companies not having provided all material information about how company compliance and risk were managed, as well as parallel SEC or Department of Justice fraud investigations and charges/suits.[80]

Thus, to take the *Caremark* and related legal risks seriously, experts are already recommending that boards/executive teams of corporates with AI 'mission-critical' compliance/safety risks take preventive actions, such as evidencing board responsibility for managing AI risk (whether the full board or existing/new committees), include AI issues on meeting agendas and in all pertinent board minutes. In addition, as mentioned elsewhere herein, they should choose one or more directors who have AI expertise or training (and use AI external consultants, as appropriate), and designate a dedicated executive officer to have the primary responsibility for AI oversight and risk management.[81]

[76] *Stone v. Ritter*, 911 A.2d 362, 370 (Del. 2006).

[77] *In re The Boeing Company Derivative Litigation*, No. 2019-0907-MTZ (Del. Ch. 7 September 2021).

[78] *Ibid.*, at 70–71.

[79] *Ibid.*, at 12–15.

[80] Based on, e.g., US Securities Exchange Act of 1934: Rule 10b-5 – Employment of Manipulative and Deceptive Devices: 'It shall be unlawful for any person . . . To make any untrue statement of a material fact or to omit to state a material fact necessary in order to make the statements made, in the light of the circumstances under which they were made, not misleading'.

[81] This might be the CTO (Chief Technology Officer) or even the CCO (Chief Compliance Officer) or CECO (Chief Ethics and Compliance Officer) with an adequate AI/technology background.

As with any aspect of a corporate compliance programme, these cannot be 'paper tigers' or mere window-dressing. There needs to be a solid, functioning reality. Therefore, directors need to be familiar with company-critical AI risks and the corporate resources available to deal with them, with the whole AI pipeline covered. There also need to be regular reports to the entire board by executives of significant AI incidents or investigations. Additionally, proper systems to manage and monitor AI compliance/risk management,[82] for example functional policies and procedures (to deal with generative AI incident response, input from whistleblowers, and AI-vendor risk), will be needed, including training for all (from top management on down).[83] Thus, AI risks fit nicely into the wide-ranging and detailed '360 degree' global corporate compliance approach that has evolved piecemeal over the past thirty years or so, such that the aphorism, '*Plus ça change, plus c'est la même chose*'[84] comes to mind.

21.4.2 *Maybe a New, Fit-for-Purpose Compliance Accountability Civil Lawsuit Is Needed?*

We are of the opinion, in light of the uncertainty as to the real extent of AI-related risks (and considering the massive growth over the past two decades in corporate liability issues under the umbrella of compliance[85]), and convinced of the need for more accountability for AI failures,[86] that a new and simplified accountability lawsuit for compliance matters should be considered.

We believe that the new and evolving director and officer duties regarding AI risk compliance have already, or will shortly become, so wide-ranging and capable of damaging corporate value that we need new bespoke accountability mechanisms for boards, ideally something that large institutional investors, especially those who are state-related or socially responsible investors (SRIs), would welcome, as these are the more active ones who traditionally expect expanded or enhanced *Caremark* duties from their investee boards, and who often act as class representatives on compliance-related litigation, at least in the United States. Thus, we would propose a 'new improved' *Caremark* suit that we would call a 'Compliance Accountability Suit for Enforcement' (CASE).[87]

This new suit would procedurally simplify the bringing of good-faith and properly evidenced *Caremark*-style derivative suits by shareholders (or possibly other materially affected stakeholders) who are especially focused on cleaning up corrupt or poorly managed companies that failed to control 'mission critical' risks, such as their use of generative AI.[88]

[82] Which will be fundamental for dealing with the EU AI Act and its requirement of organisational quality management systems under Art. 17 therein.

[83] Lawrence Cunningham et al., 'Generative Artificial Intelligence and Corporate Boards: Cautions and Considerations', Harvard Law School Forum on Corporate Governance (21 June 2023), https://corpgov.law.harvard.edu/2023/06/21/generative-artificial-intelligence-and-corporate-boards-cautions-and-considerations/ (accessed 30 April 2024).

[84] Approximately, 'The more things change, the more they stay the same'.

[85] Including, but not limited to, bribery/corruption, data management and privacy, human rights in supply chains, fair competition, accounting and financial controls and auditing.

[86] Also, as an *ex ante* incentive to take AI compliance seriously; indeed, the OECD mentions that as a key policy goal: 'AI actors should be accountable for the proper functioning of AI systems and for the respect of the above principles, based on their roles, the context, and consistent with the state of art.' AI actors include corporations and their top management. See 1.5 (Accountability), Recommendation of the Council on Artificial Intelligence, OECD Legal Instruments, last amended on 8 November 2023.

[87] See discussion generally in Patrick J. O'Malley, *Directors' Duties and Corporate Anti-Corruption Compliance: The 'Good Steward' in US and UK Law and Practice* (Cheltenham: Edward Elgar, 2021), 215 *et seq.*

[88] *Ibid.*

While our initial thoughts would be to study the implementation of this in Delaware and other US states, it would be good if other global common law jurisdictions (especially the United Kingdom[89]) or even civil law countries that are comfortable with adapting US or UK compliance and accountability structures, such as France (which already has a *ut singuli* shareholder derivative lawsuit, albeit one that is rarely made use of).[90] Of course, whilst the 'CASE' would be an *ex post* tool, the fact remains that a lot of what needs to be done with generative AI risk and corporate compliance/liability limitations is really *ex ante* work planning for potential 'mass AI damages events'.

21.5 EXPANDED CORPORATE LIABILITY ISSUES: AI-SPECIFIC *EX ANTE* AND *EX POST* RISKS

It is clear that general liability concerns for companies will mushroom in the next few years, based, inter alia, on generative AI providing services to consumers, suppliers and clients. The issue is that such AI does not work as planned or promised, or is defective and causes economic, physical or reputational damage to clients or third parties, or in the worst case, that such AI independently decides to do something illegal, improper, destructive or otherwise problematic causing damage (physical, financial, reputational or moral).

Depending on a corporate group's industry,[91] there could be multiple risks: design and use, *ex ante* and *ex post* measures, dealing with risks of AI malfunctions, design defects (poor design) and eventually 'rebellious' autonomous or self-aware AI tools potentially causing large-scale damage, such as mass torts or mass fraud or other illegal activities.[92] This may take on special significance the closer we get to systems functioning as 'artificial general intelligence' (AGI), even though experts differ about when such a function will arise (or if it has already arisen). In addition, corporations could be liable for AI-generated violations of intellectual property rights, or could directly or indirectly expose them to liability for defamation (libel/slander) if their systems are used to make the problematic statements.

As a result of this significant potential increase in civil and criminal liability for companies and their groups (as well as other generative AI-related matters where, even today, liability would clearly lie), it falls ultimately to company boards and executive teams to be heavily focused on the ways in which generative AI systems could cause damage – to shareholders, to financial and other products and services markets, to competitors, to IP rights holders, to the environment, to human health, to civil and human rights – and the resulting civil and/or criminal liability that could be attributed to the company, its group, its employees and other agents, and to themselves as 'top management'. Granted, the standards for corporate and top management liability vary

[89] E.g., under Part 11 Chapter 1 of CA 2006, which was designed to provide a transparent and accessible mechanism by which shareholders can if necessary bring an action in the name of the company against directors for breach of the general director duties set out in Part 10 Chapter 2 of CA 2006. To date, UK courts have been demanding in their scrutiny of such shareholder suits. See the court's denial to give leave to continue a claim thereunder in *ClientEarth v. Shell Plc & Ors*, [2023] EWHC 1897 (Ch), paras. 1–7.

[90] See arts. 225-120, 225–252 *et seq.* of the French *Code de commerce*, www.legifrance.gouv.fr/codes/texte_lc/LEGITEXT000005634379/ (accessed 30 April 2024).

[91] While we suspect few industries would be exempt, some of the riskier ones we can imagine would be fintech (algorithmic trading, etc.), medtech, pharma, arms/weapons systems, engineering-dependent industries generally, social media and online content providers, and aerospace.

[92] Of course, this includes all manner of malicious use of generative AI, which can be weaponised to carry out cyberattacks, the spreading of misinformation and improper surveillance or industrial espionage. These often may also be intertwined with extensive AI geopolitical and commercial competitiveness risks. The possibilities for misuse are immense, and the extent of this is not entirely clear as yet.

from jurisdiction to jurisdiction, with probably the greatest risk of civil lawsuits being borne by corporate groups doing business in the United States, under its very wide-ranging standards of criminal, civil and administrative liability based on the principle of *respondeat superior.* Additional criminal and civil risks for companies and personally for their top decision-makers appears to lie in the United Kingdom[93] and many European countries, where both company and top manager/director would be criminally liable for outcomes leading to workers' or others' deaths or health problems based on company operations.[94] Boards will probably also have to prepare to deal with a new European Commission proposal for a directive on adapting non-contractual civil AI liability rules,[95] which will aim to complement and modernise EU liability rules specific to AI-caused damage. Whilst still being debated, a previous draft would have created a rebuttable 'presumption of causality', eased the burden of proof for victims to establish damage caused by an AI system and given national courts powers to order evidence disclosure regarding high-risk AI systems suspected of having caused damage.[96] This may have major ramifications for businesses using AI in any way, and would certainly condition proper corporate governance of AI issues.

While the need by corporations to cover poorly designed, functionally defective AI is ever present in current governance debates, the question of 'rogue AI' has not been a focus of this chapter, due to space constraints. This is a significant mid- to longer-term issue that directors and executive teams need to consider regarding corporate liability (and their own personal liability as well): how will their governance and compliance systems deal with 'rogue AI' systems? Certainly, corporate insurance providers could be a valid solution for corporate boards trying to manage their generative AI risk,[97] but will coverage be sufficient for some of the potential large-scale damage from a 'mass AI damages event'? Ultimately, to do so, corporate AI insurers will need to take on a key role.[98] As with many other key corporate compliance issues, they will have the power over boards to incentivise and mould the behaviour of their insured companies, helping with sustainable and safe AI integration into business operations and managing/mitigating the potential risks of damage. Thus, insurers will also play a key role in helping boards handle AI-inflicted damage better, both from a preventive and an *ex post* compensatory perspective, and, ultimately, insurance will be a key buttress to AI regulation.[99] In our view,

[93] For example, the UK Corporate Manslaughter and Corporate Homicide Act could be used against the company itself for 'AI-attributable deaths' of workers, customers, suppliers or other third parties if the way in which its activities are managed at senior level (board) causes a death and is a gross breach of a duty of care to the deceased; UK Corporate Manslaughter and Corporate Homicide Act 2007, c. 19. Furthermore, under the same facts, top managers and others can be prosecuted for gross negligence manslaughter/culpable homicide and for health and safety offences; Ministry of Justice (circular): 'Understanding the Corporate Manslaughter and Corporate Homicide Act 2007', October 2007. We think that this law (and corollary personal liability health and safety laws) can and will be used against gross negligence in the design and deployment of generative AI systems.

[94] For example, see the 2011 Italian court ruling on voluntary homicide, whereby ThyssenKrupp's CEO for Italy was sentenced to sixteen and a half years prison due to charges concerning the death of seven Turin steel mill workers in December 2007. 'ThyssenKrupp CEO for Italy Convicted on Deaths', IndustriaALL Global Union, 20 April 2011.

[95] 'Proposal for a Directive of the European Parliament and of the Council on adapting non-contractual civil liability rules to artificial intelligence', the 'AI Liability Directive', Brussels, 28 September 2022, COM(2022) 496, 2022/0303 (COD).

[96] See originally proposed AI Liability Directive, 1. Subject Matter and Scope (Article 1), 11. The proposal was withdrawn in Feb. 2025 as part of the EU Commission's 2025 work program (Commission Press Release, Brussels, 12 Feb. 2025).

[97] Martin Eling, 'Research: How Insurance Can Mitigate AI Risks', The Brookings Institution, 7 November 2019, www.brookings.edu/articles/how-insurance-can-mitigate-ai-risks/ (accessed 1 May 2024); and Angela Puga Garcia, 'Insurance Companies, a Key Player in Mitigating the Risks of Artificial Intelligence', MAPFRE (28 June 2023), www.mapfre.com/en/insights/innovation/insurance-companies-risks-artificial-intelligence/ (accessed 1 May 2024).

[98] Anat Lior, 'Insuring AI: The Role of Insurance in Artificial Intelligence Regulation' (2022) 35(2) *Harvard Journal of Law & Technology*, 468 *et seq*.

[99] *Ibid.*, at 469–470.

corporate insurers need to be included as key stakeholders, working closely with top management and regulators in discussing workable solutions, if we hope to have sustainable corporate governance of AI. Finally, as with many areas of global corporate compliance today, the role of whistleblowers will be fundamental, as they have shown to be with everything from corporate tax compliance, to securities law, anti-bribery and even problematic social media mental health and safety issues.[100]

In the end, we can foresee that there may be corporate civil and criminal AI-related liabilities that cannot be properly covered by a 'corporate AI-related malefactor', since the potential damages may easily outstrip even a large corporation's assets. What can be done to cover a potential 'mass AI damages event' impacting investors, consumers, patients or others? For the largest identified potential generative AI risks, those that are 'too big to handle' for corporate management, we are of the opinion that there needs to be a damage remedy system in place. This could be publicly and/or privately financed, could involve the largest insurers, or the charging of a small, but generalised, 'AI tax' that would be put in a prospective victim reparation fund, and so on. Whilst we have not had space to deal with the worst of potential AI risks here, and may need to revisit this in the future, the fact is that such scenarios remain a distinct possibility. It may be that, since corporate AI-related liability could potentially be so extensive (and indeed would put companies out of business), there may well be the need to manage generative AI risks as we do nuclear energy, with a global AI regulator like the International Atomic Energy Agency and coordinated national and/or industry-specific agencies providing a robust and aggressive AI risk-management ecosystem.

21.5.1 *Note on Tools for AI Corporate Liability Risk and Accountability: US Securities Class Actions*

Generative AI risk will also be front and centre for corporate boards and executive teams as they manage securities law disclosure and compliance risks, especially for listed companies in the US markets, where the US securities class action is a potent accountability tool. If a board puts out false or misleading statements of fact or omits certain information about AI use, there could be (depending on the extent and types of damages), both public and private enforcement actions. Listed corporations and their boards now need to have a high level of transparency to avoid '10b-5 liability' under the general anti-fraud provision of the federal securities laws[101] and need to be candid about generative AI risks,[102] meaning that top management must run the entire global group accordingly: quality due diligence means quality disclosure, meaning less liability and enforcement risk (for all key affected stakeholders: corporations themselves, their boards/officers, underwriters and other financial intermediaries, auditors and accountants, and, at times, major shareholders, among others).

Indeed, at least one AI-related US securities class action (of many currently pending) has already been filed by investors in relation to alleged faulty generative AI safety technology: Evolv Technologies Holdings, Inc., a 'leader in Artificial Intelligence ("AI")-based weapons detection

[100] For example, under the massive whistleblower programme under s. 922 of the Dodd–Frank Wall Street Reform and Consumer Protection Act (Pub. L. No. 111-203, 124 Stat. 1376 (2010)), which includes the payment of bounties, US officials have obtained large numbers of pertinent tips regarding many types of corporate compliance violations from around the world: see www.sec.gov/whistleblower (accessed 1 May 2024).

[101] Section 10(b) and Rule 10b-5. 17 C.F.R. § 240.10b-5.

[102] For example, in Microsoft's 2021 Annual Report, there was a risk factor warning that, 'AI algorithms may be flawed. Datasets may be insufficient or contain biased information . . . If we enable or offer AI solutions that are controversial because of their impact on human rights, privacy, employment, or other social issues, we may experience brand or reputational harm.' Microsoft Corporation, Form 10-K (fiscal year ended 30 June 2021), PART I, Item 1A, 28.

for security screening to stop shootings and terrorist attacks' and its board/executive management were recently sued for allegedly materially false and/or misleading statements and omissions that overstated the efficacy of its products, and hid the lack of effectiveness of its AI products with regard to detecting knives and guns, which led to an increased risk of undetected weapons entering locations such as schools; and that it deceived the general public, its customers and its investors regarding the effectiveness of its products.[103] Thus, the full range of lawsuits against companies and their entire top management for "AI-washing", the overselling of the capabilities of their generative IA products (or of their AI use to generate increased profits) and the dangers associated with their use, will be on full display over the next few years. Corporate boards and their governance systems need to be ready to defend against such securities class actions, and prevention though compliance is, in our estimation, the best shield.

21.5.2 *A Sarbanes–Oxley Style Certification Regime for Generative AI and Related Issues*

Because of this risk and its impact on investors, one potential concrete tool to cover generative AI risks in corporations would be potentially requiring enhanced securities law disclosures under US, EU or other major regulatory systems. Transparency with accountability is important, and boards are beginning to act accordingly. For example, in the United States, if needed, US securities laws could be updated with a general 'Securities Regulation AI Reform Act', which would include, inter alia, extensive and enhanced new SEC AI disclosure rules covering AI/ cybersecurity-risk disclosures. This would dovetail with disclosure and other requirements under new EU sustainability rules, and especially with the EU AI Act and eventually some form of an EU AI Liability Act. The proposed US update could also, in our opinion, potentially build on the model of auditing effectiveness of corporate internal controls over financial reporting under Section 404 Sarbanes–Oxley Act model.[104] In a similar fashion to those required under Section 404, there could be AI-related requirements for certifications regarding AI risks and auditing for public companies' annual reports, which would include a company's own assessment of internal control over AI issues, an auditor's certification, and CEO and maybe CTO (Chief Technology Officer) personal certification about the quality and adequacy of AI controls. The AI auditors would have to have true generative AI expertise for the certification to have any real value in the eyes of investors and regulators. Possibly, there could be an AI version of the Sarbanes–Oxley provision which introduced the PCAOB (Public Company Accounting Oversight Board)[105] to oversee the audits of public companies in order to protect investors and further the public interest in the preparation of informative, accurate, and independent audit reports. The PCAOB also registers public accounting firms that prepare audit reports, sets auditing and related attestation, quality control, ethics and independence standards, inspects registered public accounting firms' audits and quality control systems, and investigates and disciplines registered public accounting firms for legal or professional ethical violations.[106] A similarly structured body could be set up for generative AI and related technological matters,[107] and such a body in the United States could globally coordinate with other similar national or regional bodies, for example at the international level (the OECD, or the ESMA[108]). We believe that this would

[103] See complaint, *Raby v. Evolv Technologies Holdings, Inc. f/k/a NewHold Investment Corp. et al*, Docket No. 1:24-cv-10761 (D. Mass. (Boston)) Case #: 1:24-cv-10761.
[104] Section 404(b) of the Sarbanes–Oxley Act (2002) (15 U.S.C. 7262(b)).
[105] See Title I – Public Company Accounting Oversight Board, Sarbanes–Oxley Act (2002) (15 U.S.C. 7262(b)).
[106] See https://pcaobus.org/about (accessed 1 May 2024)
[107] A 'Public Company AI & New Technologies Oversight Board'.
[108] European Securities and Markets Authority.

immensely aid boards and executive teams in the proper governance of AI matters in a transparent and more coordinated way, both nationally and globally.

21.6 CONCLUSION

At the end of the day, from both a legal[109] and best practices[110] perspective, as well as from a practical management one, key corporate decisions concerning governance (from material transactions, to compliance and day-to-day activities) will still depend on *human oversight* and the *human element of due diligence*, monitoring and digesting the information and data that other humans and machines provide. At a basic level, members of the board and executive team will add generative AI to an already expansive set of tools (financial, technical and legal) to help with key decision-making; but in the end, the 'human hunch factor'[111] about the company and people on the other side of the negotiating table will remain foremost in deciding whether to proceed with a given key transaction. The maxim, backed up by case law in many jurisdictions, of 'There's no such thing as a dummy director'[112] is truer than ever if we begin to look at the expected evolution of generative AI and corporate use thereof. Directors and officers need to be intellectually and critically engaged in good faith with the oversight and strategic duties that they hold due to their key positions of responsibility in the modern corporation.

All told, the human, face-to-face element will remain fundamentally important, both practically and due to the fact that all legal and ethical efforts to deal with generative AI we have seen prioritise human oversight and the human factor in everything from design to use. AI tools can certainly help with certain due diligence (for suppliers, joint venture or strategic partners, acquisition targets, investment decisions, executive arrangements, and basically with all contracts-based decision-making), and will continue to evolve in their utility and capabilities, but the basic origin of the decision will and should remain tempered by human chains of trust that bind together people, companies and other stakeholders in the global web of commerce and finance. AI and other new technologies should strengthen those chains of trust, both internally (within an organisation's board or executive team) and externally (with transactional counterparties, such as international joint venture partners). Whether this actually occurs is the task at hand for all those who believe that 'good corporate governance' is a key ingredient of measuring the 'common good' in today's interdependent world.

[109] See, e.g., EU AI Act, para. 66, which states, 'Requirements should apply to high-risk AI systems as regards risk management, the quality and relevance of data sets used, technical documentation and record-keeping, transparency and the provision of information to deployers, *human oversight*, and robustness, accuracy and cybersecurity. Those requirements are necessary to effectively mitigate the risks for health, safety and fundamental rights', 65. Emphasis added.

[110] Section 1.2 (Human-centred values and fairness), Recommendation of the Council on Artificial Intelligence, OECD Legal Instruments, last amended 8 November 2023.

[111] In law, this sense comes closest in our estimation to the French criminal rule of '*Intime conviction*' (gut feeling or deep conviction) that judges use when assessing guilt or innocence under Articles 427 and 353 of the '*Code de procédure pénale*': '"Deep conviction" is a method of judging that takes into account the reality and subjectivity of the act to be judged and the person involved, by giving judges access to all means of proof: verbal, scientific and psychological.' [Our translation]. J. M. Fayol-Noireterre, 'L'intime conviction, fondement de l'acte de juger' (2005) 7(127) *Informations sociales*, 46–47.

[112] *Francis v. United Jersey Bank*, 432 A.2d 814 (N.J. 1981).

22

Generative AI and Criminal Guilt

When No One Meant to Harm

Beatrice Panattoni

22.1 INTRODUCTION

The recent advancements in the field of AI have opened the opportunity to delegate fractions of activities to artificial systems. Specifically, with large language models (LLMs), the generation of human language can be executed by AI systems designed for this purpose. The outcomes of these systems range from written language to images and videos. The effectiveness of the contents artificially generated by LLMs is related to their abilities to process natural language, synthesize and reason about facts, as well as problem-solve within abstract topics. AI systems that use LLMs "understand" the (contextual, however probabilistic) meaning of natural language.[1]

Equipped with this new set of abilities, the artificial generation of content entails delegating significant fragments of socially relevant behaviors to AI systems. Their autonomous execution of the tasks assigned implies that these systems can actively intervene in the world. They manifest a form of "behavior." However, it is a behavior without intelligence, without understanding or cognitive abilities.[2] As "actors," generative-AI autonomous functioning can generate relevant harms, raising the question of who will answer for perceived "algorithmic misbehavior." However, given the shared-agency context where generative AI systems operate, which include multiple components and actors, generative AI-related harms are not simply the result of a "behavior," but rather of an "interaction." To mention a few: interactions with designers, with users, and with the social environment where the AI is supposed to operate.

When stating that the harm is the result of an interaction, we are not simply looking at the sum of multiple behaviors, but the qualities of the relations that keep the behaviors interacting with each other. These interactions can be "malicious" if they are purposely designed or actualized to cause intentional harm. These interactions can be "dangerous" if they are designed or actualized lawfully but remain capable of causing unintentional harm.

Both malicious *and* dangerous interactions, and the harms they cause, might be relevant under criminal law. This chapter suggests a possible categorization of generative AI-related harms based on the distinction between intentional and unintentional harm. It then outlines the

[1] Harry Surden, 'ChatGPT, Artificial Intelligence (AI) Large Language Models, and Law' (2024) 92 *Fordham Law Review* 1940–1970 at 1951.

[2] Luciano Floridi, 'AI as *Agency without Intelligence*: on ChatGPT, Large Language Models, and Other Generative Models' (2023) 36 *Philosophy & Technology* 3–7 at 4.

consequences they might raise relating to responsibility attribution. The chapter's focus is primarily on the issues related to unintentional harm, since they pose the most challenging scenario when it comes to criminal law. Can we find guilt when harms are the result of a lawful interaction gone bad? If so, can or should criminal law have a role in the set of tech policies related to generative AI?

22.2 GENERATIVE AI AND CRIMINAL LAW

In the case of generative AI-related harms, the areas where criminal law might play a role can be categorized based on whether a human agent acted with criminal intent or not. The first area of interest includes all the interactions purposely directed to committing a crime, which this chapter will label as "malicious interactions." The second area of interest encompasses interactions that occur within a lawful context but have the potential to cause significant harm, which this chapter will label as "dangerous interactions."

22.2.1 *Generative AI-Related Malicious Interactions*

Considering that criminal phenomena involving generative AI systems have started to appear in recent times, rather than verifying which specific criminal offenses might apply in this context, this chapter will highlight, from a criminological perspective, the categories of interactions and the areas of crime that might find, in theory, a connection with generative AI. This approach will allow us to maintain a cross-border perspective, without needing to base the analysis on a specific criminal justice system (which will remain the next needed step in the future developments of this field of study). Without presuming to be exhaustive, when there is a human agent who participates with criminal intent, the following malicious interactions with generative AI can be outlined:

(a) Support to realize content-related criminal offenses, by intentionally producing and using artificially generated illegal contents.
(b) Support to realize other crimes, by aiding or facilitating criminal activities.

Generative AI can be used or designed to create harmful content, whose creation itself, or whose dissemination might be forbidden in most criminal justice systems. The range of contents that can be created is significantly wide. It can include terrorist content, image-based sexual abuse, child pornography, and harmful speech (which can be relevant under criminal law, for instance, in case of some categories of discrimination-based discourse, incitement to crime, defamation).[3] Taking as a case study a well-known chat-based LLM, GPT-4, OpenAI published a report on the safety challenges presented by the model, where they described the results of their adversarial testing processes, called "red teaming."[4] The list of harmful content that might be generated by

[3] See Peter Henderson, Tatsunori Hashimoto and Mark Lemley, 'Where's the Liability in Harmful AI Speech?' (2023) 3 *Journal of Free Speech Law* 561–605 at 563; Nedjma Ousidhoum et al., 'Probing Toxic Content in Large Pre-Trained Language Models', in *Proceedings of the 59th Annual Meeting of the Association for Computational Linguistics and the 11th International Joint Conference on Natural Language Processing* (Online. Association for Computational Linguistics, 2021), pp. 4262–4274; Laura Weidinger et al., 'Taxonomy of Risks Posed by Language Models' in *Proceedings of the 2022 ACM Conference on Fairness, Accountability, and Transparency* (Online: Association for Computing Machinery, 2022), pp. 214–229.

[4] Red teaming is defined as "a structured effort to find flaws and vulnerabilities in a plan, organization, or technical system, often performed by dedicated 'red teams' that seek to adopt an attacker's mindset and methods." See OpenAI, 'GPT-4 System Card', 23 March 2023, p. 5, available at https://cdn.openai.com/papers/gpt-4-system-card.pdf.

LLMs include: advice or encouragement for self-harm behaviors; graphic material such as erotic or violent content;[5] harassing, demeaning, hateful content;[6] apology or incitement to terrorist activities.

Furthermore, fake artificially generated content is raising significant concerns in the current debate, even though it is based on a different sub-category of generative AI, called generative adversarial networks (GANs).[7] In this area, a primary threat regards the so-called deep nudes, namely the use of deep fakes to perpetrate crimes of non-consensual pornography.[8] Although deep nudes are undoubtedly a criminal law concern, the broader category of deep fakes outlines a more problematic area from a criminal law standpoint, since it is questionable whether and to what extent behaviors involving disinformation campaigns and propaganda should be criminalized. Nevertheless, LLMs amplify the range and severity of harms related to these phenomena, which can be realized not only through the generation of deep fakes, but through several operations (such as spreading of polarized content). Generative AI systems can be used for disinformation campaigns at scale,[9] and, more broadly, for covert or deceptive efforts to influence the opinions of a target audience, called "influence operations,"[10] able to cause manipulative effects, such as alter the electoral and democratic process, or exploit cognitive vulnerabilities of users.[11]

The second area of malicious interactions involves the aiding role that generative AI might have as a supporter or facilitator of crime. Considering the GPT-4 system card previously mentioned,[12] two different forms of aid might surface: (a) aid in the preparatory phase of a crime, through the gathering of content useful for planning a crime (such as information for developing unconventional weapons) or through the gathering of instructions for finding illegal content; (b) aid in the execution phase of a crime (for example, LLMs can be used to find alternative, purchasable chemicals used in criminal activities). A relevant area of interest might be the area of cybercrime. LLMs can be used to realize or improve social engineering attacks (drafting phishing emails) or hacking attacks (explaining system or code vulnerabilities).

[5] As happened in the case of *Dungeons & Dragons*, released by Utah-based gaming company Latitude, where the inclusion of the GPT-3 technology led to inappropriate game plotlines (disturbing stories, including sex scenes involving children). See Jahnavi Sivaram et al., 'Adversarial Machine Learning: The Rise in AI-Enabled Crime and its Role in Spam Filter Evasion' (2023) 2 *Computer Fraud & Security* 1–8 at 3.

[6] Harmful content is also one of the risk areas classified in one of the taxonomies available in the literature. See Weidinger et al., 'Taxonomy of Risks', 216.

[7] Invented by Google researcher Ian Goodfellow. See Ian J. Goodfellow et al., 'Generative Adversarial Nets' in Zoubin Ghahramani et al. (eds.), *Neural Information Processing Systems Conference* (Online: NeurIPS Proceedings, 2014), pp. 1–9, available at https://proceedings.neurips.cc/paper_files/paper/2014. In the literature, see Will Knight, 'Real or Fake? AI Is Making It Very Hard to Know', *MIT Technology Review*, 1 May 2017.

[8] See Mary Anne Franks and Ari Ezra Waldman, 'Sex, Lies, and Videotape: Deep Fakes and Free Speech Delusions' (2019) 78 *Maryland Law Review* 892–898.

[9] See Bobby Chesney and Danielle Citron, 'Deep Fakes: A Looming Challenge for Privacy, Democracy, and National Security' (2019) 107 *California Law Review* 1753–1820; Sarah Kreps, R. Miles McCain, and Miles Brundage, 'All the News That's Fit to Fabricate: AI-Generated Text as a Tool of Media Misinformation' (2022) 9 *Journal of Experimental Political Science* 104–117.

[10] See Josh A. Goldstein et al., 'Generative Language Models and Automated Influence Operations: Emerging Threats and Potential Mitigations' (2023) Joint report with Georgetown University's Center for Security and Emerging Technology OpenAI and Stanford Internet Observatory, 1–82, available at https://arxiv.org/abs/2301.04246. Influence operations are defined as "covert or deceptive efforts to influence the opinions of a target audience."

[11] See Daniella DiPaola and Ryan Calo, 'Socio-Digital Vulnerability' (2024), 1–12, available at https://ssrn.com/abstract=4686874; Rostam J. Neuwirth, *The EU Artificial Intelligence Act. Regulating Subliminal AI Systems* (London: Routledge, 2022).

[12] OpenAI, 'GPT-4 System Card', 6–14.

The same threats are outlined by Europol in a recent report, which states how LLMs can be used to learn about crime, ranging from how to break into a home, to cybercrime and child sexual abuse.[13] A specific concern remains the fight against terrorist attacks, since the model can be used to gather more information that may facilitate terrorist activities, such as terrorism financing or anonymous file sharing.[14]

The malicious interactions with generative AI will determine a direct criminal responsibility of the human agents who purposely committed the crime, either by designing the system to realize one of the activities mentioned or by using it to the same end. Therefore, in terms of responsibility attribution, these cases are less challenging. Although some grey areas remain. For instance, there could be arguments in favor of the responsibility of those actors who purposefully design and make available online generative AI platforms that enable users to realize criminal activities (such as platforms to create non-consensual deep nudes). In these cases, where the creation of such platforms is not criminalized itself, the crime would not be directly realized by the providers, but they might be held responsible as accomplices in the crime committed by their users.[15]

22.2.2 *Generative AI-Related Dangerous Interactions*

The picture becomes very different when shifting the focus to the position of different actors in the interaction: the supply chain operators of a generative AI system that is lawfully put online or on the market. The umbrella term "operator," keeping as a reference the definitions provided by the EU AI Act (AIA), includes different categories of actors. Namely, operators are considered as follows: "providers," those that develop, place on the market, and put into service an AI system; "deployers," those that use an AI system under their authority in the exercise of a professional activity; "distributors," all the other remaining actors that participate in the supply chain of an AI system, and make it available on the market.[16]

From the perspective of these actors, generative AI-related harms are unintentional, and the interactions are no longer considered malicious, but dangerous. In other words, they present the probability of the occurrence of severe harms.[17] Unintentional harms awaken the preventive function of criminal law. The legal response to unintentional harm does not end in punishing the agent that caused the harm, but it widens to providing the means to avoid the harm. However, these are unstable grounds for criminal law. The need to reassure against the insecurity created by the risks of harm might create a rise in punitiveness and an expansion of the penal

[13] While all the information provided is freely available online, the possibility to use the model to provide specific steps by asking contextual questions means it is much easier for malicious actors to better understand and then carry out various types of crime. See Report Europol, 'ChatGPT. The Impact of Large Language Models on Law Enforcement', Europol Public Information, 27 March 2023.

[14] Ibid.

[15] The responsibility of actors who purposefully design and make available online Generative AI platforms that enable users to realize criminal activities relates to the broader topic of platform liability regimes, which is very different if we consider the EU or the US legal system. Among the comparative studies on the topic, see Giancarlo Frosio (ed.), *Oxford Handbook of Online Intermediary Liability* (Oxford: Oxford University Press, 2020).

[16] Article 3 nn. 3, 4, 7, 8, Regulation (EU) 2024/1689 of the European Parliament and of the Council of 13 June 2024 laying down harmonized rules on artificial intelligence (Artificial Intelligence Act).

[17] Definition of risk provided by the AIA. According to Art. 3(1a), "risk" "means the combination of the probability of an occurrence of harm and the severity of that harm."

state, which clashes with the legitimacy of criminal law as a modern, liberal institution.[18] Therefore, we need to stay on the fine line between avoiding broad new criminalization to prevent criminally relevant harms and filling gaps in the attribution of responsibility for those harms.

The responsibility gaps created by technology developments are the result of an old issue, defined as the "dilemma of control," that society faces when attempting to predict the social consequences of a technology.[19] The control of technology has proven to be a very difficult task because of its unanticipated social consequences. Narrowing our focus from the broadly harmful social consequences that a technology might have on society to the consequences that can be qualified as specific harms to a person or to a public interest, the risk-based approach is an attempt to address the "dilemma of control."

This chapter approximately summarizes dangerous interactions into three main groups:

(a) Risks of harms related to users' misuse.
(b) Risks of harms related to artificial emergence.
(c) Risks of harms related to overreliance.

The first group corresponds to the misuses listed in the previous paragraph, whereas the last two groups create the more complex scenarios, where generative AI-related harms cannot be traced back to a human agent who interacted with criminal intent. Society might face, on the one hand, harms directly caused by the generative AI system without any user behind it (harmful AI content), and, on the other hand, harms that the generative AI system contributed to causing with the participation of a human agent who acted without criminal intent (negligent AI content).

"Harmful AI contents" might be generated by emergent interactions, where "emergence" states the ability of AI to perform unpredictable behaviors.[20] For instance, harmful content might be the result of the "hallucinations" of LLMs. There have already been cases where LLMs fabricated offensive false claims against a person, falsely accusing him of a crime,[21] or cases where LLMs "degenerate into offensive language from seemingly innocuous prompts."[22] Furthermore, in cases of generative AI implemented beyond the task of content generation, new areas of risks might be created by new emergent behaviors, when the model is set to "accomplish goals which may not have been concretely specified or appeared in the training."[23]

Closer to the present might be cases of overreliance of users on "negligent AI content," where the harm is the result of a dangerous interaction between the generative AI and a "negligent" user. Since generative AI systems might provide part of the knowledge used in decision-making processes, if it provides manipulative information, it might encourage people to commit self-harm or it might violate their self-determination,[24] whereas if it provides neutral, but false,

[18] See Henrique Carvalho, *The Preventive Turn in Criminal Law* (Oxford: Oxford University Press, 2017); Andrew Ashworth, Lucia Zedner, and Patrick Tomlin (eds.), *Prevention and the Limits of the Criminal Law* (Oxford: Oxford University Press, 2013); Massimo Donini and Massimo Pavarini (eds.), *Sicurezza e diritto penale* (Bologna: Bologna University Press, 2011).

[19] David Collingridge, *The Social Control of Technology* (New York: St Martin's Press, 1980).

[20] Ryan Calo, 'Robotics and the Lessons of Cyberlaw' (2015) 103 *California Law Review* 513–564 at 538.

[21] See Eugene Volokh, 'Large Libel Models? Liability for AI Output' (2023) 3 *Journal of Free Speech Law* 489–558 at 563.

[22] Weidinger et al., 'Taxonomy of Risks', 216. See also Samuel Gehman et al., 'Real Toxicity Prompts: Evaluating Neural Toxic Degeneration in Language Models', in Trevor Cohn, Yulan He, and Yang Liu (eds.), *Findings of the Association for Computational Linguistics* (Online: Association for Computational Linguistics, 2020) pp. 3356–3369.

[23] OpenAI, 'GPT-4 System Card', 15.

[24] See E. Atillah, 'Where's the Liability in Harmful AI Speech', *Euronews*, 31 March 2023; B. Perrigo, 'The New AI-Powered Bing Is Threatening Users. That's No Laughing Matter', *Time*, 17 February 2023.

misleading, or poor-quality information to a user who acts based on that information, the result of the interaction might cause harm to the user or to others.[25] For instance, generative AI is used to design proteins and inform patients in the healthcare sector,[26] which might cause injuries due to the health professionals' overreliance on the AI outputs.[27]

Each dangerous interaction might raise different modes of responsibility attribution. In scenario (a), where there is an interaction with a malicious user, the possibility to resort to doctrines of complicity might become relevant, holding the operators of the generative AI responsible for participating in the users' crimes, whether there is an omissive contribution (failure to avoid the user's crime), or an active contribution (development or putting into service of the generative AI through which the user committed the crime).[28]

In scenarios (b) and (c), where malicious users' interactions are lacking, the operator might be directly responsible for the harm realized, whether there is an omissive interaction (failure to avoid the harm), or an active interaction (development or putting into service of the generative AI which caused the harm). However, all these cases reveal several shortcomings, as the next section explores.

22.2.2.1 Omissive Interactions

In case of omissive contributions or interactions, the operators cannot be held responsible unless the legal systems provide for duties to act which hold them responsible for preventing harms from happening (either in the case of user misuses or of emergence or overreliance). It is questionable whether and which operators might have a duty to protect or a duty to control over a source of danger (*Garantenstellung*) because of their activity. Society cannot expect the operators to act to avoid every harm that might be related to the generative AI system that they develop, place online, or deploy. This scenario would hardly comply with a socially expected level of care or diligence. Moreover, in most cases, considering the context of autonomous and active interactions from which the harms originate, the operators might not have foreseen the harm, and they might not have the material possibility to intervene to avoid the harm from occurring. A further argument for distancing from this hypothesis is that omission liability is controversial in many criminal justice systems, given the moral distinction between acts and omissions and the downsides that the commission-by-omission model presents in complying with a strict legal certainty standard.[29]

[25] See Jane Bambauer, 'Negligent AI Speech: Some Thoughts about Duty' (2023) 3 *Journal of Free Speech Law* 344–362 at 349. The author suggests considering the following hypotheticals: "(A) AI tells an adult that it is safe to eat a mushroom that is actually toxic. (B) AI tells a child that it is safe to eat a mushroom that is actually toxic. (C) AI tells an adult how to alter a drug therapy to address or avoid side effects, resulting in harm from the primary disease."

[26] See Mohammed AlQuraishi, 'Machine Learning in Protein Structure Prediction' (2021) 65 *Current Opinion in Chemical Biology* 1–8; Sanjay Chakraborty et al., 'An AI-Based Medical Chatbot Model for Infectious Disease Prediction' (2023) 11 *IEEE Access* 128469–128483.

[27] "Negligent AI contents" are classified as "Misinformation Harms" and "Human-Computer Interaction Harms" by Weidinger et al., 'Taxonomy of Risks', 218.

[28] Outside of the intentional participation in the users' crime, the possibility to lower the subjective requirement to reckless behaviors remains. However, recklessness as a standard for complicity is controversial throughout criminal justice systems. See James G. Stewart, 'Complicity', in Markus D. Dubber and Tatjana Hörnle (eds.), *The Oxford Handbook of Criminal Law* (Oxford: Oxford University Press, 2014), p. 557. For this reason, negligent as a standard for complicity in others' intentional crime should also be excluded.

[29] See Kai Ambos, 'Omission?', in Kai Ambos, Antony Duff, Julian Roberts, Thomas Weigend, and Alexander Heinze (eds.), *Core Concepts in Criminal Law and Criminal Justice* (Cambridge: Cambridge University Press, 2020), vol. I, pp. 17–53.

To follow this path, policies would need to distinguish the positions of the different operators involved (providers, deployers, distributors) and their normatively expected capability to act to avoid generative AI-related harms. However, to date, neither EU nor US law regulates positive obligations that might be associated with a duty to act of generative AI operators.

Considering the EU context, the AIA qualifies generative AI within the broader category of general-purpose AI (GPAI),[30] which is regulated by a specific chapter (Chapter V). According to Article 53, the legal obligations for GPAI providers mostly entail ensuring detailed technical and informational documentation. In case of GPAI that pose a "systemic risk," namely if the GPAI has high-impact capabilities (automatically presumed if the model's training involves more than 10^25 floating-point operations), further obligations must be carried out by the providers. They must conduct model evaluations, including adversarial testing (red teaming), assess and mitigate systemic risks, document and report incidents to the AI Office, and ensure adequate cybersecurity protection (Article 55 AIA). None of these obligations entails a duty to act.

The scenario might have been different if the set of obligations required for high-risk AI systems had been extended to GPAI. Here, an interesting concept is "reasonably foreseeable misuse," namely "the use of an AI system in a way that is not in accordance with its intended purpose, but which may result from reasonably foreseeable human behavior or interaction with other systems, including other AI systems" (Article 3(13) AIA). The risk of reasonably foreseeable misuse is included in the set of risks that providers of high-risk AI systems must address through the implementation of a risk management system (Article 9 AIA). However, these obligations do not apply to GPAI.

A different option might be resorting to another EU regulation, the Digital Service Act (DSA), which regulates intermediaries' liability. Since the regulation imposes a set of obligations to ensure that intermediaries remove illicit content from their services, the normative behaviors expected of generative AI providers could be expanded to include those obligations as well. In the context of generative AI, content moderation obligations and notice-and-takedown procedures might have significant benefits. Nevertheless, it is not clear yet whether generative AI might fall within the scope of the DSA, depending on whether generative AI platforms might be qualified as "hosting providers" or "search engines."[31]

In the United States, generative AI operators' liability will have to deal with the debate on Section 230 of the Communications Decency Act and the immunity regime that it provides. Generative AI-related harms might become a new problematic chapter in the extensive use of the defense provided by Section 230.[32]

22.2.2.2 Active Interactions

Generative AI operators' responsibility for active contributions or interactions also presents several setbacks. One of them involves the problem of causation. The harms that result from all three dangerous interactions could be difficult to trace back to a single and specific operator's

[30] According to recital n. 99 of the AIA: "Large generative AI models are a typical example for a general-purpose AI model, given that they allow for flexible generation of content, such as in the form of text, audio, images or video, that can readily accommodate a wide range of distinctive tasks."

[31] Scholars suggest that generative AI platforms might fall within the category of "hosting providers" or "search engines." See Laureline Lemoine and Mathias Vermeulen, 'Assessing the Extent to Which Generative Artificial Intelligence (AI) Falls Within the Scope of the EU's Digital Services Act: An Initial Analysis' (2023) 1–18, available at https://ssrn.com/abstract=4702422.

[32] See Henderson et al., 'Where's the Liability in Harmful AI Speech', 582; Bambauer, 'Negligent AI Speech', 347.

behavior, because of the "failures of causation" that characterize the AI context.[33] Notwithstanding, even if a solution to the problem of causation is found, this path might lead to overcriminalization of "neutral behaviors," such as the putting into service of a generative AI system used to commit crime.[34] The merely material and objective contribution of making available the technical means to the realization of a user's crime cannot alone legitimize a judgment of blameworthiness.

Moreover, the relevant behaviors might be different depending on the specific generative AI systems deployed as services or products. An approximate distinction can be drawn between open-source generative AI models, namely fully public models which can be downloaded and used by malicious actors, and generative AI platforms, such as chat-based generative AI. In the first case, harms caused by users' misuses of the model overstep the designers' ability to monitor them, whereas in the second case they stay under the operator's monitoring ability.

In case of harms related to emergence or overreliance, a direct responsibility of the operator for an active interaction in causing the harm has the same drawbacks. Even if the operator interacted recklessly, it will be highly challenging to ascertain a causality chain between the harm and the operator's behaviors. However, despite the limits related to causation, the main challenge that characterizes all the hypotheses of responsibility for unintentional harm concerns the problem of guilt.

22.3 GENERATIVE AI AND GUILT: WALLS OR DOORS?

Generative AI-related harms stem from a system dynamic, driven by interactions among various actors. The combination of interactions challenges the paradigm of "control" by a single actor over the whole actualization of the system's functioning, as the many-hands problem outlines.[35] Since the liberal model of criminal law has individual autonomy at its core, when control is challenged, guilt is also challenged.

The field of generative AI and criminal law, outside of the scope of malicious interactions, needs to address this challenge. The requirement of guilt can be seen in a limiting and confining function (a "wall"), which is used to state that where guilt cannot be found, neither can criminal responsibility be attributed. However, in a changing social context, such as the one where artificial and human agents interact with each other, guilt can also be an adapting concept (becoming a "door"). On the one hand, in the first perspective, guilt in the context of generative AI confines criminal law to punishing only intentional malicious interactions (either as use, development, or deployment of generative AI), whereas the area of dangerous

33 See Yavar Bathaee, 'The Artificial Intelligence Black Box and the Failure of Intent and Causation' (2018) 31 *Harvard Journal of Law & Technology* 922–927.

34 Among Italian scholars, this position is shared by the first comments on generative AI and criminal law. See Gaia Fiorinelli, 'Il concorrente virtuale: la prevenzione dell'uso di catgut per finalità criminali tra etero- e auto-regolazione' (2023) 2 *Rivista italiana di medicina legale* 361–378 at 370.

35 The fragmentation of control relates to the many-hands problem, or organizational black boxes, originally studied in relation to the moral responsibilities of political office holders and public officials working in large government bureaucracies (see Dennis Thompson, 'Moral Responsibility of Public Officials: The Problem of Many Hands' (1980) 74 *American Political Science Review* 905–916). The problem of many hands has been a feature of cyber and IT law since its beginning. See Helen Nissenbaum, 'Accountability in a Computerised Society' (1996) 2 *Science and Engineering Ethics* 25–42, at 28. Now "the introduction of AI makes the 'problem of many hands' more acute"; see Filippo Santoni de Sio and Giulio Mecacci, 'Four Responsibility Gaps with Artificial Intelligence: Why they matter and How to Address Them' (2021) 34 *Philosophy & Technology* 1057–1084; Monika Simmler, 'Responsibility Gap or Responsibility Shift? The Attribution of Criminal Responsibility in Human–Machine Interaction' (2023) *Information, Communication & Society* 1–21, www.tandfonline.com/doi/full/10.1080/1369118X.2023.2239895.

interactions is left to other branches of law, such as tort law. On the other hand, in the second perspective, if certain dangerous interactions create too high and diffuse a danger to individuals and society, the question of which kind of guilt can be found in those interactions might open new areas for criminal law.

Instead of looking at the issue from two different perspectives (one negative and one affirmative), the field of generative AI and criminal law might be pictured as a set of closed doors.

22.3.1 *The Natural Person behind the AI: Closed Door*

The traditional allocation of guilt in facing AI-related harms is problematic. Criminal culpability and AI raise several collision points related to multiple factors, such as the distance between human behaviors and their results (determined also by the many-hands problem),[36] the failures of causation, and the challenged foreseeability of harm.[37] The control of the users and of the actors who stand behind the technology is limited and compromised by the shared-agency dimension; that is, if we follow the traditional perspective that devises responsibility attribution starting from the harm instead of from the interactions.

These collision points are not a prerogative of the field of AI-related harms. They are linked to a well-known phenomenon. The use of preventive criminal law to mitigate the risks of our contemporary and complex society is a feature of a longstanding debate related to whether and to what extent criminal law can be used to regulate the harms generated by the risk society, which is now the algorithmic society.[38] The analysis of the broader evolution of criminal law in the risk society provides a lens through which we can examine the inadequacy of the traditional punitive paradigm when applied to risks associated with generative AI. Specifically, the conventional model of person–action–harm fails to adequately address the complexities inherent in situations where harms arise from systemic processes rather than the actions of individual human agents. In other words, assigning direct personal responsibility to a singular human agent for harms resulting from systemic risks poses significant challenges, as elaborated upon in the chapter, particularly concerning questions of culpability. To regulate the harms related to the risks of the algorithmic society, it is not enough to consider the behavior of the single human agent alone. In these cases, guilt will likely close the door, limiting criminal law only to the punishment of intentional criminal behavior.

Alternatively, should we opt to adhere to the conventional punitive paradigm, it may be necessary to analyze the roots and conditions of the interaction. By disentangling the behaviors of generative AI operators from subsequent interactions between AI systems and users, there

[36] See previous footnote.

[37] In analyzing the challenges that AI will pose to criminal culpability, scholars have focused primarily on how these issues will arise in the field of robotics. See Sabine Gless, Emily Silverman, and Thomas Weigend, 'If Robots Cause Harm, Who Is to Blame? Self-Driving Cars and Criminal Liability' (2016) 19 *New Criminal Law Review* 412–436; Monika Simmler and Nora Markwalder, 'Guilty Robots? – Rethinking the Nature of Culpability and Legal Personhood in an Age of Artificial Intelligence' (2019) 30 *Criminal Law Forum* 1–31. In the Italian literature, see Federico Consulich, 'Flash Offenders. Le prospettive di accountability penale nel contrasto alle Intelligenze Artificiali devianti' (2022) 3 *Rivista Italiana di Diritto e Procedura Penale* 1015–1055; Carlo Piergallini, 'Intelligenza artificiale: da "mezzo" ad "autore" del reato?' (2020) 4 *Rivista Italiana di Diritto e Procedura Penale* 1745–1772.

[38] The debate on criminal law in the risk society has drawn the attention of EU scholars since the end of last century. Among the vast number of contributions, a text that collects the Italian and German contributions on the subject is Luigi Stortoni and Luigi Foffani (eds.), *Critica e giustificazione del diritto penale nel cambio di secolo. L"analisi critica della Scuola di Francoforte* (Milano: Giuffrè, 2004).

emerges the possibility of employing criminal law to address novel forms of omission, such as intentional or reckless omission to comply with prescribed safety measures (that is, failure to comply with specific obligations, such as non-delegable duties, transparency obligations, or failure to provide the competent authorities with the required information).[39] However, in addition to the concerns that arise from the use of preventive criminal law, this approach might have collateral effects, disincentivizing progress and investment, as operators might restrict their activities out of fear of facing severe punishments. It would also need to coordinate with the administrative sanctions that might already be regulated in case of violation of legal obligations, for instance by EU law.[40]

Furthermore, the scope and content of the standard of care in the field of generative AI have not yet been established, and will depend on the set of safety standards required by the industry, since best practices will likely be insufficient. Resorting only to self-regulation does not appear to be a sufficient alternative, since delegating altogether the process of selecting the policies and measures for harm prevention to the private sector might raise concerns related to legal certainty. Moreover, certain measures (such as labeling unlawful content into pre-established categories) might be more efficient if based on an active collaboration with public authorities.

22.3.2 *Generative AI and Criminal Law: Whether to Open the Door*

While the door is open for using criminal law to address malicious interactions, this chapter has highlighted various setbacks to using criminal law for dangerous interactions. Given this scenario, the question then becomes whether the context of dangerous interactions might need criminal law.

Excluding criminal law completely from the set of policies related to dangerous interactions is an inadequate long-term strategy. Using the lens of the harm principle or the theory of the legal good (*Rechtsgutstheorie*), it becomes essential to assess the nature of harms and risks related to generative AI. They include not only the harms originating from the offenses targeted for prevention (such as the most serious content-related offenses), but they also extend to the risks related to the delegation of content generation to artificial agents in the information society. The ability to generate information can have significant effects not only on individuals but also on society. This creates a base of legitimacy for criminal law, if limited only to the most serious wrongdoings and the most serious harms (in compliance with the *ultima ratio* principle). As the chapter attempted to demonstrate, engaging in information-generating activities with artificial agents in a shared-agency context can lead to the emergence of social conflicts, manifested in the form of dangerous interactions, which include (it is worth remembering) also the prevention of malicious interactions. The normative regulation and protection of a sector of social life as highly relevant as the generation of information may ultimately necessitate criminal protection involvement in the long term.[41] However, the condition for such involvement

[39] See Consulich, 'Flash Offenders', 1015; Fiorinelli, 'Il concorrente virtuale', 373.

[40] The AIA provides for specific administrative fines in case of violation of the legal obligations required to providers of GPAI. However, these fines can be enforced only by the European Commission. According to Article 101 of the AIA: "The Commission may impose on providers of general purpose AI models fines not exceeding 3 % of their total worldwide turnover in the preceding financial year or 15 million EUR, whichever is higher, when the Commission finds that the provider intentionally or negligently: (a) infringed the relevant provisions of this Regulation."

[41] The approach that moves from "sector of protections" instead of "single rights protection" is outlined, among Italian scholars, by Giovanni De Francesco, *Programmi di tutela e ruolo dell'intervento penale* (Torino: Giappichelli, 2004), pp. 51–55.

is that social conflicts translate into substantial wrongdoings. The question at issue then becomes whether generative AI deployments can indeed result in substantial wrongdoing. Although this possibility exists, given that generative AI opens the possibility for causing widespread and diffuse damage, as well as for facilitating the realization of criminal activities by simplifying their preparation or execution, it is premature to provide a definitive answer. Nevertheless, the question must be posed, and it will require finding an answer by examining the evolution of the sector and the framework of policies aimed at regulating it with an open-ended perspective, which might resort to the blurring boundaries between criminal punishment and administrative or regulatory offenses.

At this stage, the chapter merely suggests that, in the context of generative AI and dangerous interactions, following a completely non-criminal approach, which involves civil litigation and administrative regulation, may prove insufficient in the long term. This approach would narrow the legal response to the perspective of harm mitigation, whereas criminal law aims to establish an institutional normative order aimed at protecting social values. The function of censuring and discouraging wrongdoing, which implies "should not do,"[42] entails state intervention into individual freedoms that extends beyond providing a remedy to the victim for the invasion of protected interests.[43] The punitive and preventive functions, therefore, require that the distribution of responsibility in cases of serious harms relevant under criminal law follows its stricter standards, both substantively and procedurally, while granting certain protections for the defendant. In the case of generative AI-related risks, especially in the case of emergence and overreliance, a non-criminal approach may lead to a situation where a crime occurs, and criminal law falls short because it has become challenging to find the guilty mind. However, the result of interactions remains a crime, and possibly, when behaviors become interactions within a system, a "guilty system" can be identified.[44] According to this perspective, the attribution of responsibility must not address a gap but rather a shift.[45]

In addition, there are pragmatic considerations to ponder. Generative AI holds the potential to either facilitate or contribute to relevant harms, which may manifest with increased rapidity upon deployment of artificial agents, challenging investigation activities. Relying solely on retrospective measures to prosecute malicious uses may prove ineffective or unsustainable. The prospect of intervening during stages that precede interactions (design or online availability) or during interactions themselves (deployment) presents an opportunity to address social conflicts as they arise, preempting their escalation into broader and diffuse harms. Involvement during these phases could equip criminal law with valuable tools for regulating conflicts. For instance, civil courts lack the authority to order defendants to perform positive acts to avoid or to mitigate punishment, such as implementing reactive compliance efforts. Lastly, given the diffuse nature of risks associated with generative AI, it prompts inquiry into the adequacy of entrusting the legal response to harms solely to private citizen initiatives, without a structured intervention of the state, especially in cases where there is no victim, and the harm caused is against collective and public interests.

[42] See Andrew Ashworth, *Positive Obligations in Criminal Law* (London: Hart, 2013), p. 10.

[43] Ibid., p. 8.

[44] Responsibility attribution in the case of behaviors that become interactions within a system may be based on hybrids that blur legal forms. For instance, by blurring the boundaries between criminal and regulatory law and between criminal and civil law. See Ashworth, *Positive Obligations*, 28.

[45] Simmler, 'Responsibility Gap or Responsibility Shift?', 18.

22.4 CONCLUSION

If we consider the possibility of integrating criminal law into the regulation of generative AI-related interactions, the fundamental question concerns which policy would best justify criminal coercion. The answer to this question is contingent upon both the theory of attribution and the nature of the punishment that will be selected.

Instead of dissembling the "interactions" of the shared-agency context, a way to stay within them is to follow one of the suggestions raised in the literature, namely to resort to corporate criminal responsibility instead of human agents' criminal responsibility in the context of AI.[46] Expanding or amending corporate criminal law might be a possibility to explore further,[47] in cases where a relevant harm occurs due to the intentional or reckless noncompliance with the standard of care required of the corporation which interacted in the relevant processes of proving and deploying the generative AI system. The deterrence and prevention raised from a possible affliction to the economic interests of companies might help in enhancing corporate collaboration in the AI industry, without being solely driven by market pressure.[48]

In these instances, legislators may need to ponder whether to open the door of criminal law or not. However, a prerequisite for pursuing this course of action involves determining how to preserve culpability in the context of AI-related harms, firstly, by underscoring the possibility to devise frameworks for accountability within a shared-agency context (a context of emerging social institutions);[49] secondly, by assessing the scope and content of non-criminal regulatory measures pertaining to affirmative obligations. Additionally, a prerequisite entails a comprehensive understanding of the precise nature of harms potentially engendered by generative AI, encompassing both qualitative and quantitative dimensions, from social, legal, and technical standpoints. Until then, we face a wall with many closed doors. But the doors exist. Whether and which one we want to leave closed or to start opening remains a political choice.

[46] See Mihailis E. Diamantis, 'Algorithms Acting Badly: A Solution from Corporate Law' (2021) 89 *George Washington Law Review* 801–856. Among Italian scholars, see Vincenzo Mongillo, 'Corporate Criminal Liability for AI-Related Crimes: Possible Legal Techniques and Obstacles' (2023) 1 *International Review of Penal Law* 77–90.

[47] This hypothesis will have a different outlook depending on the civil law or common law legal systems where it applies. In common law jurisdictions, it will engage with the doctrine of vicarious liability, while in civil law contexts, it will focus on organizational culpability. For a comment on both theories, see Cristina De Maglie, 'Models of Corporate Criminal Liability in Comparative Law' (2005) 4 *Washington University Global Studies Law Review* 547–566.

[48] As outlined also by OpenAI researchers. See Amanda Askell, Miles Brundage and Gillian Hadfield, 'The Role of Collaboration in Responsible AI Development' (10 July 2019), https://arxiv.org/abs/1907.04534.

[49] See Anna Beckers and Gunther Teubner, *Three Liability Regimes for Artificial Intelligence. Algorithmic Actants, Hybrids, Crowds* (Oxford: Hart, 2021). They theorize an "institutional turn" in the law of digital liability. Particularly interesting is the concept of "socio-digital institution" and "hybrids" as legal entities (with strong analogies with organizations).

PART IV

The Use of Generative AI in Legal and Related Sectors

23

Automating Legal Tasks

LLMs, Legal Documents, and the AI Act

Rūta Liepiņa, Francesca Lagioia, Marco Lippi, Przemysław Pałka, Hans-Wolfgang Micklitz, and Giovanni Sartor

23.1 INTRODUCTION

In recent years a major development has taken place in the AI domain, namely the move from predictive AI to generative AI.[1] Until recently, the focus was on developing AI systems as 'prediction machines', trained to make targeted suggestions for new cases (e.g., clinical diagnosis based on an X-ray scan, or a creditworthiness assessment based on the financial profile of a user). Generative AI aims rather to create new data, similar to the objects – text, images, videos – on which the system has been trained.

The breakthrough has come with large language models (LLMs), such as GPT (generative pre-trained transformer) models, consisting of huge and complex neural networks, including billions of parameters (links between neurons). Such networks have been pre-trained on a large corpora of text data collected from the web and from any other source. They have shown an amazing capacity to generate different kinds of texts, according to users' input and requests (named prompts). LLMs have been rapidly followed by systems dealing with other media, such as images and video, and finally by multimedia systems.

As the law deals with language, and indeed legal practice involves the analysis and generation of multiple kinds of written documents, it is no surprise that the AI and law community has joined legal practitioners in embracing the LLM revolution. The present challenge is how to expand current AI and law models with LLMs capabilities. This presupposes an understanding of the new opportunities and shortcomings of LLMs in comparison with earlier approaches.

We would like to thank the funding organisations that have partly funded this research. Liepiņa, Lagioia, Sartor, and Micklitz: European Research Council (ERC) Project 'CompuLaw' (Grant Agreement No. 833647) under the European Union's Horizon 2020 research and innovation programme. Lagioia, Sartor, and Micklitz: CLAUDETTE IV, founded by the EUI Research Council for founding. Sartor, Lagioia: PNRR – M4C2 – Investimento 1.3, Partenariato Esteso PE00000013 – 'FAIR – Future Artificial Intelligence Research' – Spoke 8 'Pervasive AI', funded by the European Commission under the NextGeneration EU programme. Lagioia: the EQUAL (EQUitable ALgorithms) PRIN 2022. A research project funded by the EU Commission under the NextGenerationEU programme and the Italian Ministry of Education, University and Research. (Ref. prot. n.: 2022KFLF3E-001 – CUP J53D23005560001). Sartor: PRIMA – PRivacy Infringements Machine-Advice (Ref. prot. n.: 20224TPEYC – CUP J53D23005130001). A research project funded by the EU Commission under the NextGenerationEU programme and the Italian Ministry of Education, University and Research. Pałka: The research leading to these results has received funding from the National Science Centre, Poland, project No. 2022/45/B/HS5/01419, titled 'Consumer Law and the Attention Economy'.

[1] Ashish Vaswani et al., 'Attention Is All You Need' (2017) 30 *Advances in Neural Information Processing Systems* 1.

Here, we will focus on the use of AI (augmented through LLMs) for consumer empowerment and privacy protection. In particular, we examine how our CLAUDETTE system could be enhanced through LLMs.[2] On this basis, we also investigate what new legal issues can emerge in the context of the AI Act (AIA) and related regulations.

The chapter is structured as follows: Section 23.2 describes the current landscape of how LLMs are changing the legal analytics tasks as compared to other AI approaches. Section 23.3 introduces a case study of LLMs' potential to change the analysis of terms of services (ToS) and privacy policies and compares these models to the supervised machine-learning approaches and results obtained so far. Finally, Section 23.4 analyses the legal obligations of such an AI system under the new AI Act and other European Union legislation.

23.2 LARGE LANGUAGE MODELS

In this section, we explore the advances in natural language processing (NLP), following the introduction of LLMs relevant to legal tasks. To provide some background, text processing has evolved from basic models, centred on word frequencies and string comparisons, to the advanced analysis facilitated by the advent of deep learning, capable of analysing complex texts.[3] The deep learning approaches, fuelled by the availability of large-scale datasets and advancements in computational resources, enabled the development of more robust and scalable NLP models. Techniques such as word embeddings, recurrent neural networks, and more generally transformer architectures revolutionised tasks like language modelling, machine translation, and information retrieval.[4]

The introduction of generative AI further advanced the capabilities of NLP, by empowering machines to generate human-like text and engage in more complex tasks related to natural language understanding, such as question-answering and dialogue. LLMs, underpinned by the development of transformer architectures, reached a significant milestone in NLP, enabling machines to understand and produce language at an unprecedented level. LLMs are trained on huge amounts of text data which enables them to capture long-range dependencies within text and generate coherent content, such that the generated texts are closely related to each other. This is usually done by models that predict the next word based on the previously generated words, so the generated content is grammatically correct and consistent. These recent breakthroughs have created new opportunities for analysing texts through prompt-based queries.

Although the primary objective of LLMs lies in text generation, recent studies demonstrate that these models can accomplish a wide range of tasks, such as information retrieval, summarisation, sentiment classification, predictions, legal opinion drafting, multiple-choice questions, rules application, and more.[5] LLMs performance is on a par or better than the earlier AI approaches. All such tasks can be effectively reformulated into a text-to-text format, thus

[2] Marco Lippi et al., 'CLAUDETTE: An Automated Detector of Potentially Unfair Clauses in Online Terms of Service' (2019) 27 *Artificial Intelligence and Law* 117.

[3] Kevin D. Ashley, *Artificial Intelligence and Legal Analytics: New Tools for Law Practice in the Digital Age* (Cambridge University Press 2017).

[4] Amirsina Torfi et al., 'Natural Language Processing Advancements by Deep Learning: A Survey' (2021), https://export.arxiv.org/pdf/2003.01200.

[5] Jaromir Savelka et al., 'Can GPT-4 Support Analysis of Textual Data in Tasks Requiring Highly Specialized Domain Expertise?', in *Proceedings of the Sixth Workshop on Automated Semantic Analysis of Information in Legal Text* (ASAIL 2023), https://ceur-ws.org/Vol-3441/paper1.pdf.

rendering them amenable to resolution, through text generation and potentially becoming the '*de facto* solution for the majority of text-related problems', including legal analytics.[6]

23.2.1 *Information Retrieval*

Full-text information retrieval is the process of searching and retrieving relevant documents from a collection of text documents, based on the content of the documents themselves, rather than just metadata or keywords.[7] It involves analysing and comparing the entirety of the text content to satisfy user queries or information needs. Given the exponential increase in the number and length of regulations and case law, such systems are highly useful in legal practitioners' day-to-day work. They can be compared to search engines, such as Google and Bing, but for specialised, not general, information. For instance, a user might ask to retrieve all decisions related to data protection breaches, based on the General Data Protection Regulation (GDPR) Article 22, or to find cases based on party names, such as *Smith v. Smith*. Popular commercial information retrieval services include Westlaw[8] and LexisNexis[9] in the United States and the Unite Kingdom, where the user can enter their queries in free text to search for relevant cases, statutes, and other legal documents available in the system databases.

Even though commercial service providers do not share much technical information, the task of information retrieval has been established as one of the core areas of AI and law research.[10] So far, such research has been done by combining various term-based methods, like text pre-processing, feature selection (such as citations of other cases or reference to rules), measuring the frequency of such words and features, and applying an inverted index to retrieve and rank the documents containing the words and features given in the query.[11] Given the complexity of legal language and documents, the frequency measures alone are often insufficient for retrieving legally relevant and meaningful information. Researchers have experimented with enhancing the information retrieval capabilities by using ontologies,[12] citation analysis,[13] and vector space models.[14] However, various limitations remain with this and similar approaches, most of which hinge on the lack of semantic understanding of the legal texts.[15]

6 Yutao Zhu et al., 'Large Language Models for Information Retrieval: A Survey' (2023), https://arxiv.org/pdf/2308.07107.

7 Ashley (n. 3).

8 https://legal.thomsonreuters.com/en/westlaw

9 www.lexisnexis.com/en-us/gateway.page

10 Mi-Young Kim, Juliano Rabelo, and Randy Goebel, 'Statute Law Information Retrieval and Entailment', *Proceedings of the Seventeenth International Conference on Artificial Intelligence and Law* (ICAIL 2019), ACM, New York, NY, USA; Rachayita Giri et al., 'Approaches for Information Retrieval in Legal Documents', 2017 *Tenth International Conference on Contemporary Computing (IC3)* (IEEE, 2017); Peter Jackson et al., 'Information Extraction from Case Law and Retrieval of Prior Cases' (2003) 150 *Artificial Intelligence* 239; Jaromír Šavelka and Kevin D. Ashley, 'Legal Information Retrieval for Understanding Statutory Terms' (2021) 30 *Artificial Intelligence and Law* 30.

11 W. Bruce Croft, Howard R. Turtle, and David D. Lewis, 'The Use of Phrases and Structured Queries in Information Retrieval', *Proceedings of the 14th Annual International ACM SIGIR Conference on Research and Development in Information Retrieval, Association for Computing Machinery (ACM), Chicago, Illinois, USA* (ACM, 1991).

12 Manavalan Saravanan, Balaraman Ravindran, and Shivani Raman, 'Improving Legal Information Retrieval Using an Ontological Framework' (2009) 17 *Artificial Intelligence and Law* 101.

13 K. Raghav, P. Krishna Reddy, and V. Balakista Reddy, 'Analyzing the Extraction of Relevant Legal Judgments Using Paragraph-Level and Citation Information' (2016) AI4JC *Artificial Intelligence for Justice* 30.

14 Keet Sugathadasa et al., 'Legal Document Retrieval Using Document Vector Embeddings and Deep Learning', in *Intelligent Computing: Proceedings of the 2018 Computing Conference, Volume 2* (Springer, 2019).

15 Carlo Sansone and Giancarlo Sperlí, 'Legal Information Retrieval Systems: State-of-the-Art and Open Issues' (2022) 106 *Information Systems* 101967.

Finding relevant information in the text can also be done with LLMs. The advantage of these models, compared to the previous methods, lies in their ability of advanced semantic analysis, use of context information and further personalisation of the answers.[16] LLMs can improve information retrieval by enhancing various steps in the process. It is typical for users to give short and rather vague terms in their search entries – for example, stabbing case in Glasgow, or human rights violations. Such instructions are not sufficiently informative and the retrieval model might struggle in picking out the most relevant cases. LLMs can improve the search in two ways: first, by enhancing the query based on its knowledge about the content of documents, and second, by implementing the querying in a conversational search (as exemplified by the ChatGPT application).[17] Further improvements can be achieved by careful prompt engineering – for example, by setting constraints for LLMs to only use the text found in the original documents, without adding any further information. This aims to reduce the risk of hallucinations (LLM-generated text that is nonsensical, irrelevant, or, even more dangerously, inaccurate or fictional), often deviating significantly from the desired output or context. Different types of hallucinations can be distinguished. Intrinsic hallucinations pertain to the outputs of LLMs that conflict with the source content, while extrinsic hallucinations refer to the LLM generations that cannot be verified from the source content. A further distinction can be made between factual hallucinations – outputs that are either inconsistent with real-world facts or potentially misleading – and faithfulness hallucinations – outputs that are not aligned with the user's instructions.[18] The research on how to mitigate such risks is ongoing. See, for example, the efforts by the Free Law Project, which introduced a citation lookup and verification API (application programming interface), which is built on its public access database of nearly 10 million citations, to check whether the cases mentioned by LLMs correspond to real ones.[19]

Another persisting challenge with using LLMs for legal document analysis is the length of such documents. Court cases can vary between a couple and a few dozen pages. The context window that LLMs can process is expanding every month, but handling very long documents still remains an open issue.

Moreover, information retrieval is an essential component of question-answering systems, as it allows the information sought by the user to be provided and integrates it into a conversational search platform.[20] Studies implementing LLMs for question-answering focus not only on the information retrieval, but also on validation and correction of the produced outputs, to improve the reliability and trust of such systems for professional use.[21]

23.2.2 *Summarisation*

In the era of an unprecedented information overload, clear and accurate summaries of legal documents are invaluable, both for legal professionals and the general public. Such summaries

[16] Zhu et al. (n. 6).

[17] Mi-Young Kim et al., 'Legal Information Retrieval and Entailment Using Transformer-Based Approaches' (2024) 18 *Review of Socionetwork Strategies* 1.

[18] Lei Huang et al., 'A Survey on Hallucination in Large Language Models: Principles, Taxonomy, Challenges, and Open Questions' (2023), *ACM Transactions on Information Systems*, ACM New York.

[19] https://free.law/2024/04/16/citation-lookup-api

[20] Zhu et al. (n. 6).

[21] Cheol Ryu et al., 'Retrieval-Based Evaluation for LLMs: A Case Study in Korean Legal QA', *Proceedings of the Natural Legal Language Processing Workshop 2023* (ACL Anthology, 2023); Antoine Louis, Gijs van Dijck, and Gerasimos Spanakis, 'Interpretable Long-Form Legal Question Answering with Retrieval-Augmented Large Language Models', *Proceedings of the AAAI Conference on Artificial Intelligence* (AAAI Press, 2024).

also provide value for information retrieval, as they can give more context to the ranked documents and help to choose the most relevant ones for the given query.

Automatic summarisation often faces a bottleneck in capturing semantic meaning and contextual understanding. Traditional methods, such as statistical or rule-based techniques, may struggle to generate coherent and contextually relevant summaries, due to limitations in understanding the nuances of human language.[22] These approaches often rely heavily on surface-level features – such as word frequency or sentence position or location in the text – which may not adequately capture the essence of the original text. As a result, the generated summaries may lack coherence, miss important details, or not accurately reflect the intended meaning of the source text. Generally, one can distinguish two approaches to the summarisation task: *extractive* and *abstractive*.[23] Extractive methods rely on selecting important sections in the text and including them word-for-word in a summary. In contrast, abstractive techniques attempt to generalise such a content and generate a summary based on the original text while not necessarily directly quoting it. These summaries are easier to read, as they provide a coherent account of the information rather than a collection of potentially poorly interlinked sentences.

LLMs have the potential to significantly improve the quality and informational value of summaries due to their abilities in capturing the semantic meaning of words and the complex relationships between them. Zhang and colleagues show impressive results of using summarisation of news articles.[24] A handful of early studies test LLMs on summarising legal judgments. Deroy, Ghosh, and Ghosh[25] compared LLMs (DaVinci and GPT-3.5) to pre-trained abstractive summarisation models (Legal Pegasus and LegLED) and some extractive models for summarising Indian court decisions. The results were evaluated against the gold standard summaries written by legal experts, showing that LLMs provide very promising results but do not yet outperform the domain- and task-specific models on the relevant metrics. The limitations of abstractive summaries include incomplete sentences/words, multiple sentences being merged meaninglessly, and more serious errors like inconsistencies and hallucinations. For example, the study shows error analysis where essential information such as dates, party names, and other facts do not correspond to the original text. Moreover, there are unresolved issues with the evaluation of abstractive (generative) summaries, since the errors introduced by hallucinations are difficult to spot. The authors suggest continuing quality checks by human domain experts, while the work on the automated quality check is still in progress.

Other studies show better performance, which might depend on the chosen field of law. For example, the Prodigit project tested the GPT summarisation capabilities on tax law judgments in Italy. The summaries were evaluated by tax law experts (judges and lawyers) based on the summary form, completeness, coherence, and overall quality.[26] LLM summaries were shown to

[22] Paheli Bhattacharya et al., 'A Comparative Study of Summarization Algorithms Applied to Legal Case Judgments', *Advances in Information Retrieval: 41st European Conference on IR Research, ECIR 2019, Cologne, Germany, April 14–18, 2019, Proceedings, Part I 41* (Springer, 2019).

[23] Ani Nenkova and Kathleen McKeown, 'A Survey of Text Summarization Techniques' in Charu C. Aggarwal and ChengXiang Zhai (eds.), *Mining Text Data* (Springer, 2012), 43; Wafaa S El-Kassas et al., 'Automatic Text Summarization: A Comprehensive Survey' (2021) 165 *Expert Systems with Applications* 113679.

[24] Tianyi Zhang et al., 'Benchmarking Large Language Models for News Summarization' (2024) 12 *Transactions of the Association for Computational Linguistics* 39.

[25] Aniket Deroy, Kripabandhu Ghosh, and Saptarshi Ghosh, 'How Ready Are Pre-Trained Abstractive Models and LLMs for Legal Case Judgement Summarization?' (2023) *Proceedings of the Third International Workshop on Artificial Intelligence and Intelligent Assistance for Legal Professionals in the Digital Workplace* (LegalAIIA, 2023), CEUR-WS, https://ceur-ws.org/Vol-3423/paper2.pdf.

[26] Thiago Dal Pont et al., 'Legal Summarisation through LLMs: The PRODIGIT Project' (2023), https://arxiv.org/pdf/2308.04416.

outperform those generated by other NLP approaches.[27] The project also tested the legal user preference between extractive and abstractive summaries, and flowing text versus issue-based summaries, where abstractive issue-based summaries were clearly preferred. Another recent study shows how LLMs are great candidates for summarisation tasks in low-resource domains (in this context, low resources refer to publicly available judgments), as they perform well in few-shot and zero-shot learning conditions.[28]

23.2.3 *Other Legal Analytics Tasks*

Although the LLM advancements are relatively recent, several studies have emerged testing the capabilities of these models in legal analytics beyond the information retrieval and summarisation tasks.[29]

Focusing on the LLM text generative powers, Lam and colleagues propose practical methods for improving contract drafting using LLMs, suggesting 'prompt writing' techniques to enhance coherence in generated contract clauses. They also explore the feasibility of using on-premises LLMs such as 'Vicuna' as privacy-conscious alternatives, alongside proposing an evaluation approach leveraging traditional AI and sentence transformers, to ensure generated clauses meet legal standards and accuracy requirements.[30]

A recent study by Vats and colleagues evaluates the effectiveness of LLMs in legal predictions, specifically focusing on statute prediction and judgment prediction tasks using Indian Supreme Court cases.[31] They find that while LLMs demonstrate strong performance in statute prediction, their accuracy diminishes in judgment prediction compared to standard models, with explanations generated by LLMs being of moderate to decent quality. Additionally, the study highlights concerns regarding gender and religious biases in LLM-predicted results and includes ethical considerations from a senior legal expert regarding the deployment of LLMs in critical legal tasks.

Lastly, LLMs have also been challenged to pass the bar exam in the United States.[32] The exam includes multiple choice questions, an open-ended multi-state essay exam and a multi-state performance test. In multiple choice tests, GPT-4 excels and surpasses human test takers, while in the other tests, it shows average or good results. A similar study has been repeated in Brazil.[33]

This section demonstrates the growing abilities of LLMs in handling legally relevant text analysis tasks. The rapid progress in this field means that in the near future we will see more

[27] The NLP approaches used: latent semantic analysis, Lex-Rank, TextRank, Luhn, Natural Language Toolkit.

[28] Shuaiqi Liu et al., 'Low-Resource Court Judgment Summarization for Common Law Systems' (2024) 61(5) *Information Processing & Management* 103796.

[29] Savelka et al. (n. 5).

[30] Kwok-Yan Lam, Victor C. W. Cheng, and Zee Kin Yeong, 'Applying Large Language Models for Enhancing Contract Drafting', *Proceedings of the Third International Workshop on Artificial Intelligence and Intelligent Assistance for Legal Professionals in the Digital Workspace* (LegalAIIA 2023) (CEUR-WS, 2023), https://ceur-ws.org/Vol-3423/paper7.pdf.

[31] Shaurya Vats et al., 'LLMs – the Good, the Bad or the Indispensable? A Use Case on Legal Statute Prediction and Legal Judgment Prediction on Indian Court Cases', *The 2023 Conference on Empirical Methods in Natural Language Processing* (ACL Anthology, 2023), 12451.

[32] Michael Bommarito and Daniel Martin Katz, 'GPT Takes the Bar Exam' (2022) https://arxiv.org/pdf/2212.14402; Daniel Martin Katz et al., 'GPT-4 Passes the Bar Exam' (2024) 382 *Philosophical Transactions of the Royal Society A* 20230254.

[33] Pedro Miguel Freitas and Luís Mendes Gomes, 'Does ChatGPT Pass the Brazilian Bar Exam?', *EPIA Conference on Artificial Intelligence* (Springer, 2023).

novel studies. These results have also sparked debates around the benchmark design in AI and law. What could serve as the best test for LLM abilities in law?[34]

23.3 NATURAL LANGUAGE PROCESSING FOR ADMINISTRATIVE OVERSIGHT AND DETECTING INFRINGEMENTS

In the last decades, AI has been pervasively used for the large-scale analysis of user-related data, enabling a set of market and data practices that have been – and still are – constantly exposing consumers and citizens to risks and threats.[35] We get used to, and even resigned to, businesses monitoring our activities, analysing our data, and sometimes even influencing our decisions. AI is frequently perceived as a weapon wielded by businesses and criticised for enabling these practices. Over time, various regulations have been enacted to protect consumers and data subjects,[36] which are currently being put under pressure. It is within this context that we envisioned a paradigm shift: in the era where the power of suppliers is boosted by AI, regulation and public enforcement must be complemented by technologies empowering citizens. Therefore, scholars advocated for AI to align with consumers, citizens, and their organisations, to detect violations, resist potential abuses, inform the public, and exercise an effective counter-power.[37]

Among others, a key area for AI benefiting civil society is the analysis of textual documents. Over the years, a large amount of literature has demonstrated the effectiveness of NLP tools in analysing corpora of relevant documents in the legal domain,[38] aiding in comprehension and assessment. Examples include summary generators,[39] document completeness checkers,[40] and ontologies.[41]

In the realm of consumer and data protection law, NLP-based services can be deployed with the goal of analysing massive amounts of information made available to consumers and data subjects and providing help in understanding this information and making a legal assessment. In the last few years, several projects and tools have emerged with these goals in mind. Relevant examples include systems that summarise legally relevant documents[42] and combine reviews, compare prices, and enable consumers themselves to coordinate their actions. These tools could

[34] Zhiwei Fei et al., 'Lawbench: Benchmarking Legal Knowledge of Large Language Models' *Proceedings of the 2024 Conference on Empirical Methods in Natural Language Processing (EMNLP)* (ACM, 2024); Ilias Chalkidis, 'ChatGPT May Pass the Bar Exam Soon, but Has a Long Way to Go for the LEXGLUE Benchmark' (2023), https://ar5iv.labs.arxiv.org/html/2304.12202.

[35] Dirk Helbing, *Societal, Economic, Ethical and Legal Challenges of the Digital Revolution: From Big Data to Deep Learning, Artificial Intelligence, and Manipulative Technologies* (Springer, 2019).

[36] Iain Ramsay, *Consumer Law and Policy: Text and Materials on Regulating Consumer Markets* (Bloomsbury, 2012); Margot E. Kaminski, 'Binary Governance: Lessons from the GDPR's Approach to Algorithmic Accountability' (2018) 92 *Southern California Law Review* 1529.

[37] Marco Lippi et al., 'The Force Awakens: Artificial Intelligence for Consumer Law' (2020) 67 *Journal of Artificial Intelligence Research* 169.

[38] Livio Robaldo et al., 'Introduction for Artificial Intelligence and Law: Special Issue "Natural Language Processing for Legal Texts"' (2019) 27 *Artificial Intelligence and Law* 113.

[39] Razieh Nokhbeh Zaeem, Rachel L. German, and K. Suzanne Barber, 'Privacycheck: Automatic Summarization of Privacy Policies Using Data Mining' (2018) 18 *ACM Transactions on Internet Technology (TOIT)* 1.

[40] Elisa Costante et al., 'A Machine Learning Solution to Assess Privacy Policy Completeness: (Short Paper)', *Proceedings of the 2012 ACM Workshop on Privacy in the Electronic Society* (ACM, 2012), www.researchgate.net/publication/262278232_A_machine_learning_solution_to_assess_privacy_policy_completeness.

[41] Alessandro Oltramari et al., 'PrivOnto: A Semantic Framework for the Analysis of Privacy Policies' (2018) 9 *Semantic Web* 185.

[42] Zaeem, German, and Barber (n. 39).

contribute to new markets where consumers use digital agents to negotiate, form coalitions, and make collective purchasing decisions. Methods for data extraction and analysis can also be beneficial to civil society, for example in identifying discriminatory practices in areas such as credit lending, employment, and the provision of social benefits.[43] NLP can also be used to identify cases where unnecessary or excessive data is collected.[44] Finally, these models can be used for the analysis and validation of the content of textual documents. For instance, consumers typically do not read and are often unable to negotiate contractual terms and data practices implemented by traders. As a result, legal regulations have been put in place to structure and limit the content of these documents. Systems able to analyse contracts and privacy policies and evaluate their legal compliance can assist society by identifying unfair and unlawful clauses.

23.3.1 *The Case of CLAUDETTE and Classical NLP Models*

Significant strides have been made in the context of the CLAUDETTE project,[45] aimed at automating the detection of (potentially) unfair and unlawful clauses in online ToS and privacy policies.[46] Like most of the NLP approaches developed for legal documents, CLAUDETTE is based on the supervised learning paradigm: to detect an (un)fair clause, the system needs to be provided with examples of both lawful and unlawful clauses. To this aim, a corpus consisting of 50 ToS has been initially annotated (and further expanded to 150 documents in subsequent studies) by legal experts and then used as a training set. The problem of detecting potentially unfair clauses was framed as a sentence classification task, treating each sentence independently. To exploit contextual information, when aiming to classify a given sentence, the previous and next sentences were also used as input to the classifier. Different classic machine-learning approaches were tested and compared, including support vector machines (SVM), convolutional neural networks (CNN), and long–short term memory networks (LSTM).[47] The system pipeline consisted of a segmentation phase, which split the document into sentences, a tokenisation phase to identify tokens (words), and a syntactic parsing phase to extract parse trees. In the original paper describing the CLAUDETTE tool,[48] all these parts were implemented using the Stanford CoreNLP tool, which was state-of-the-art at the time, based on statistical learning techniques.[49] In order to process the lexical content and the grammatical structure of sentences, we relied on classical models, such as bag-of-words (BoW) and tree kernels (TK). The first one treats a document, or a piece of text such as a sentence, as a collection of words, disregarding the order in which they appear but considering their frequency. For instance, in document classification, the frequency of each word in a document is used to represent its content. Some context can be considered by also taking into account bi-grams and tri-grams of consecutive words (for example, 'at any time' or 'user account'). These kinds of features are used to capture lexical

[43] Salvatore Ruggieri, Dino Pedreschi, and Franco Turini, 'Integrating Induction and Deduction for Finding Evidence of Discrimination' (2010) 18 *Artificial Intelligence and Law* 1.

[44] Balazs Bodo et al., 'Tackling the Algorithmic Control Crisis – The Technical, Legal, and Ethical Challenges of Research into Algorithmic Agents' (2017) 19 *Yale Jourla of Law & Technology* 133.

[45] http://claudette.eui.eu/.

[46] Lippi et al. (n. 2).

[47] Ibid.

[48] Ibid.

[49] Christopher D. Manning et al., 'The Stanford CoreNLP Natural Language Processing Toolkit', *Proceedings of 52nd Annual Meeting of the Association for Computational Linguistics: System Demonstrations* (ACL Anthology, 2014).

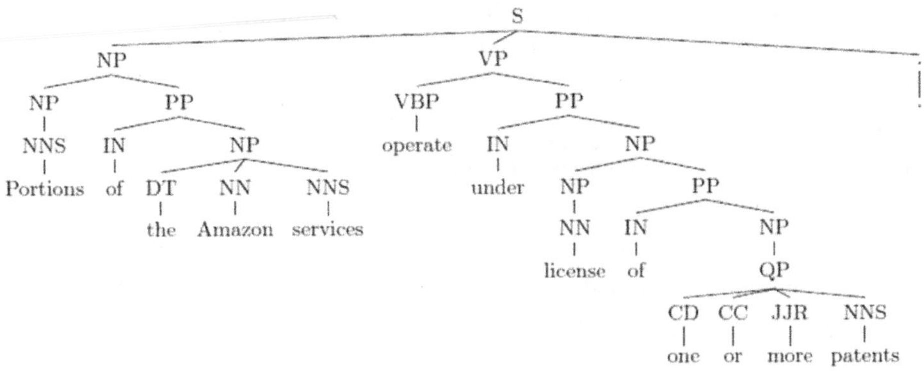

FIGURE 23.1 Constituency parse tree for a sentence in the CLAUDETTE corpus
Source: Marco Lippi et al., 'CLAUDETTE: An Automated Detector of Potentially Unfair Clauses in Online Terms of Service' (2019) 27 *Artificial Intelligence and Law* 117.

information: similar sentences contain the same words (or bi-grams, tri-grams). The second representation, the TK, computes a similarity between the structure of sentences. Each sentence is represented by a tree, named constituency parse tree, which encodes the grammatical structure of the sentence (an example is given in Figure 23.1). The similarity score computed by TK takes into account the number of common substructures (named fragments) between two sentences. With these representations, the idea of supervised learning is that the labelled clauses in the training set can instruct CLAUDETTE on how certain textual forms correspond to specific legal classifications, namely the category to which a clause belongs (e.g., jurisdiction, limitation of liability) and the assessment of its (un)fairness. The training algorithm 'teaches' the system to make assessments similar to those encountered in the training set, providing criteria and mechanisms to make the correct inference. For example, the following clause (from Amazon's terms of service, 30 May 2017 version) is considered to be potentially unfair for the consumer, as it states conditions for unilateral termination from the provider: 'The licenses granted by Amazon terminate if you do not comply with these Conditions of Use or any Service Terms.'

Experimental results show that CLAUDETTE correctly detected around 80 per cent of the potentially unfair clauses in each category, ranging from a minimum 72.7 per cent in the case of arbitration clauses, up to 89.7 per cent in the case of jurisdiction clauses. These results were obtained on a classical cross-validation procedure, in which the system is tested on data that is not seen during model training or calibration. Further studies were conducted to assess the capability of CLAUDETTE to generalise to contracts belonging to sectors not seen during the training set[50] or even to languages other than English.[51]

A similar approach was applied to scrutinising privacy policies under the GDPR,[52] albeit with less conclusive outcomes due to the intricate, incomplete, and vague nature of such policies. One of the earliest challenges encountered in the assessment of privacy policies was that the

[50] Agnieszka Jablonowska et al., 'Assessing the Cross-Market Generalization Capability of the CLAUDETTE System' in Erich Schweighofer (ed.), *Legal Knowledge and Information Systems – JURIX 2021: The Thirty-Fourth Annual Conference, Vilnius, Lithuania, 8–10 December 2021* (IOS Press, 2021), https://doi.org/10.3233/FAIA210318.

[51] Andrea Galassi et al., 'Unfair Clause Detection in Terms of Service across Multiple Languages' (2024) 32 *Artificial Intelligence and Law* 1.

[52] Giuseppe Contissa et al., 'Automated Processing of Privacy Policies Under the EU General Data Protection Regulation' (2018) 313 *Frontiers in Artificial Intelligence and Applications* 51.

analysis of single sentences has proven insufficient to determine their defectiveness under the GDPR. There was the need to link multiple pieces of information spread across several sentences.[53]

23.3.2 *The Changing Landscape: The Advent of LLMs*

As for consumer contracts and privacy policy analysis, we can envision three main tasks where LLMs can support citizens and their organisations in monitoring market and data practices: (i) the retrieval of information from the relevant documents; (ii) the assessment of their legal compliance; and (iii) their generation in a structured machine-human-readable format.

23.3.2.1 Information Retrieval and Question-Answering

The first application of LLMs to the analysis of ToS and privacy policies (PPs) concerns the possibility of retrieving relevant information on market and data practices. This setting exploits the capacity of LLMs to digest information in complex documents, understand natural language questions, and provide comprehensible answers.

In the context of the CLAUDETTE project, we decided to verify whether and to what extent LLMs can answer consumers' questions.[54] Given the numerous challenges that emerged in the analysis of PPs based on classical NLP models, we decided to focus on these documents, rather than on contracts. A number of empirical legal studies have demonstrated that consumers do not read privacy policies and, even when they do, they are unable to obtain meaningful information. Indeed, privacy policies are often ineffective due to their excessive length and complexity,[55] vagueness, and lack of the necessary information.[56] In a world of human-only interpreters, there is certainly a trade-off between comprehensiveness and comprehensibility of privacy policies, leading to the actual policies not containing enough information for users to learn anything meaningful. Indeed, only privacy policies too long to be humanly readable can precisely describe the intended data processing. We argued that this trade-off no longer exists where LLMs are able to extract tailored information from fully comprehensive privacy policies.

To verify our hypothesis, we ran an experiment as a proof of concept to test to what extent the consumer-facing versions of ChatGPT 3.5 and 4 may correctly answer users' questions regarding the content of fully comprehensive privacy policies. To do so, we designed a format for a fully comprehensive privacy policy. Accordingly, we drafted a mock policy of a hypothetical food delivery company, from which all the required and necessary information can be easily extracted by human readers. We identified six questions that a consumer might reasonably be interested in: (i) the categories of data concerned; (ii) the purposes of processing of the user's email address and (iii) geolocation; (iii) the recipients of the geolocation information; (iv) the types of data processed on the basis of consent and for what purposes; (v) the categories of data shared with

[53] Liepina Ruta et al., 'GDPR Privacy Policies in Claudette: Challenges of Omission, Context and Multilingualism', *CEUR Workshop Proceedings* (Sun SITE Central Europe/RWTH Aachen University, 2019).

[54] Przemysław Pałka et al., 'No More Trade-Offs. GPT and Fully Informative Privacy Policies' (2023), https://arxiv.org/pdf/2402.00013.

[55] Yannis Bakos, Florencia Marotta-Wurgler, and David R. Trossen, 'Does Anyone Read the Fine Print? Consumer Attention to Standard-Form Contracts' (2014) 43 *Journal of Legal Studies* 1; Jonathan A. Obar and Anne Oeldorf-Hirsch, 'The Biggest Lie on the Internet: Ignoring the Privacy Policies and Terms of Service Policies of Social Networking Services' (2020) 23 *Information, Communication & Society* 128.

[56] Giuseppe Contissa et al., 'Claudette Meets GDPR: Automating the Evaluation of Privacy Policies Using Artificial Intelligence' (2018) https://papers.ssrn.com/sol3/papers.cfm?abstract_id=3208596.

Facebook; and (vi) whether the company shares the user's personal data with insurers. We tested the ChatGPT versions 3.5 and 4 question-answering performance by designing two prompts, one short and one long – the latter aimed at mitigating hallucinations, unwarranted simplification (listing only some answers, preceded by phrases like 'for example' or 'such as'), and unwarranted text generation (adding information that the user did not ask for, such as advice that one should carefully read the laws). We designed an experimental setting based on four scenarios: (1) GPT 3.5, short prompt; (2) GPT 3.5, long prompt; (3) GPT 4 short prompt; (4) GPT 4 long prompt. For each setting, we repeated the test five times with two independent accounts, for a total of ten runs. We here provide an example of a long prompt used in our experiment: we specifically ask GPT to provide answers based solely on the content of the provided document, without summarisation or inferences.

> What types of data are processed on the basis of consent, and for what purposes? In answering the question please rely solely on the information included in the text and not your knowledge from other sources; please read the document carefully and mention everything, do not omit any information included in the text; please do not shorten or simplify the answers by inserting elements like 'for example', 'including' or 'such as'; please limit your answer strictly to what I am asking about and refrain from giving me advice or informing me about things I have not asked about.

Results show that this is a promising path. As part of our experimental work, we plan to expand the mock privacy policy and the number of documents to be assessed, test different LLMs, including open-source LLMs; and explore the use of API to test whether this would produce a performance improvement and to create further controls for the quality of the answers. In particular, it is necessary to study the robustness of the model to different prompts and queries. Hallucination is also clearly a major issue since one possible drawback is that the LLM provides, as justifications for its answers, explanations that are not grounded in the given document.

23.3.2.2 Legal Assessment

The second application of LLMs within this context is to contribute to the legal assessment of contracts and privacy policies, with regard to different categories of potentially (un)fair and (un) lawful clauses, similar to our experiment in the CLAUDETTE project (Section 23.3.1). For this task we envision a three-step process: (i) fine-tuning the model; (ii) specifying the concept of a(n) (un)lawful clause, for each relevant category (e.g., limitation of liability and jurisdiction), through prompt design; and (iii) the prompt-based activation of the model, supplemented with the relevant specification.

The first step, the fine-tuning, is aimed at training the model to capture complex language patterns and nuances in ToS and privacy policies and to understand their structure and semantics. To this end, a large dataset of relevant documents is needed, possibly covering and representing the diverse set of relevant services and market sectors. The CLAUDETTE corpora, containing 142 ToS and 100 privacy policies, covering nine market sectors,[57] can serve as an initial seed for this scope. Note that this step is not mandatory, as the LLM could be used 'as is', without the need to further specialise.

57 Francesca Lagioia et al., 'AI in Search of Unfairness in Consumer Contracts: The Terms of Service Landscape' (2022) 45 *Journal of Consumer Policy* 481.

The second step, the specification of (un)lawful elements through prompt design, is aimed at guiding the model to classify text related to (un)lawful clauses. These prompts should provide (i) clear instructions of what constitutes an (un)lawful clause and (ii) a set of positive and negative examples associated with how the model should respond in each case. On the one end, providing LLMs with examples is necessary for training the model to identify and differentiate between lawful and unlawful clauses. For example, by presenting a(n) (un)lawful clause followed by a prompt asking the model to classify such a clause as (un)lawful. The same is true for teaching the system how to distinguish between different categories of clauses (such as limitation of liability clauses versus jurisdiction clauses). On the other end, examples of both relevant and irrelevant portions of text may be needed to instruct the LLM on how to distinguish between relevant and irrelevant information. As an example, consider the following prompt:

> *Clauses that indicate conditions for content removal are potentially unfair, whereas clauses stipulating that the service provider may remove content in his full discretion, and/or at any time for any or no reasons and/or without notice nor possibility to retrieve the content are clearly unfair. For example, the following clause is potentially unfair for content removal:*
> 'We can remove any content or information you post on COMPANY if we believe that it violates this Statement or our policies'.
> *whereas the following one is clearly unfair:*
> 'In all cases, COMPANY reserves the right to remove or disable access to any User Content for any or no reason, including but not limited to, User Content that, in COMPANY's sole discretion, violates the Agreements. COMPANY may take these actions without prior notification to you or any third party'.

Note that this step also requires an iterative improvement process where the model is continuously refined based on feedback from legal experts. For instance, if the model misclassifies a clause, provide corrective feedback, explaining why the classification is incorrect. This helps the model learn from its mistakes and improve over time. Moreover, it might be necessary to regularly update the prompt-based specifications of unfair clauses to incorporate new knowledge and address emerging challenges.

The third step, prompt-based testing, is aimed at validating the model on a separate dataset to assess its performance in detecting (un)lawful clauses, through classical evaluation metrics (such as precision and recall). Here is an example of prompt to be used as a query for testing, given that the previous prompt had been provided as context:

> *Is this clause fair, potentially unfair or clearly unfair?*[58]
> 'If you select a username or similar identifier for your account or COMPANY, we reserve the right to remove or reclaim it if we believe it is appropriate (such as when a trademark owner complains about a username that does not closely relate to a user's actual name)'.

Compared to the use of classical NLP methods, relying on LLMs is clearly less time- and labour-intensive, as this approach does not require the time-consuming phase of creating a large labelled training set. However, LLMs will only reduce but not rule out entirely the need for legal expert involvement. Indeed, they still play a crucial role for the specification of (un)lawful

[58] Here is the answer provided by the demo web interface of ChatGPT, on 21 April 2024: 'The clause you provided falls into the category of potentially unfair. While it does provide some justification for content removal (such as in cases of trademark infringement), it lacks specificity about the criteria for removal. The phrase "if we believe it is appropriate" leaves room for interpretation and potential abuse of power by the service provider. This ambiguity could result in arbitrary removal of content without clear guidelines or recourse for users. Therefore, it could be considered potentially unfair.'

elements through prompt design and the ex post evaluation of the model outputs and provide the necessary feedback and indications for adjustments. The latter point would be particularly relevant not only in case of misclassification, but even more in case of hallucination, which would be a major problem within this setting. In addition, it has to be remarked that classical NLP approaches only depend on the training data and the chosen learning algorithm so that the model always gives the same answers when provided the same query. On the other hand, LLMs, given their inherent non-deterministic nature, may provide different answers when fed with slightly different (or even identical!) prompts and queries. A very recent work has shown that the performance of LLMs for legal tasks without adequate prompting (e.g., zero-shot learning) is still far from ad hoc classification systems.[59]

23.3.2.3 Document Drafting and Generation

One of the primary tasks of LLMs is to model the generation of language. The possibility to apply this new technology to contract and privacy policy drafting is currently overlooked in the literature, but we argue that it could significantly enhance the work of legal professionals. In this vein, a few studies have recently motivated the idea of using LLMs as AI-based assistants for legal writing,[60] though without a specific focus on this kind of document.

In the case of generation or drafting, the interaction with the LLM is slightly different from the previously discussed scenarios, because we are asking neither to answer questions or retrieve information from a document nor to perform a classification task regarding a document (or part thereof). Here, the document is to be generated. The aim is to produce a document with a certain style and with specific content, based on the indications provided by the user. In the case of contracts and privacy policies, a suitable form of interaction that we envisage consists in feeding the LLM with a list of items that should be covered by the final document, with the recommendation to write the clauses with a clear and not vague language, and to be compliant with a set of regulations. Such regulations will likely be provided by the user via prompting, in the form of context for the LLM. The list of items to be included in the final policy could be formulated using a standardised template with a specific format, and the LLM could be instructed to process (and thus to produce) separate paragraphs one at a time: for example, in the case of privacy policies, they could be the categories of data, the purpose and the legal basis for its processing. Note that, within this context, fine-tuning could also be performed beforehand, in order to specialise the LLM in the legal language.

Clearly, the set of machine-generated documents and clauses may not meet the context-specific requirements and circumstances, thus requiring the user to identify possible mistakes, discrepancies between the user's request and the generated text, hallucinations, as well as any missed or extraneous aspects. Therefore, the contribution of legal experts still remains crucial to customise and refine the documents and to provide feedback to the model. Once the possible issues in the generated clauses are identified, legal experts may intervene by directly revising either the model prompt or the clauses, to ensure legal accuracy and quality.

59 Ilias Chalkidis, 'ChatGPT May Pass the Bar Exam Soon, but Has a Long Way to Go for the Lexglue Benchmark' (2023), https://arxiv.org/pdf/2304.12202.

60 Jonathan H. Choi et al., 'ChatGPT Goes to Law School' (2021) 71 *Journal of Legal Education* 387; Teresa Phelps and Kevin Ashley, '"Alexa, Write a Memo": The Promise and Challenges of AI and Legal Writing' (2022) 26 *Legal Writing: Journal of the Legal Writing Institute*. 329.

23.4 CLAUDETTE UNDER THE AI ACT

In addition to the new capacities and possibilities offered to projects like CLAUDETTE by the emergence of GenAI, another tectonic change has occurred: the European Union has adopted the AI Act.[61] A comprehensive regulation on placing AI systems on the market might have significant consequences for the development and widespread adoption of systems like CLAUDETTE by civil society or administrative agencies. In this last substantive section of the chapter, we analyse these consequences and discuss, first, what rules of the AI Act apply to systems like CLAUDETTE and, second, whether to assess this positively or negatively.

In short, under the AIA, systems like CLAUDETTE will not be considered high-risk, with the sole exception of when they are used by judicial authorities or in alternative dispute resolution (ADR)/online dispute resolution (ODR).[62] For this reason, we also discuss three other sets of rules that are strongly connected to the AIA, namely the DSA (Digital Services Act) Regulation 2022/2065[63] and the DA (Data Act) Regulation 2023/2854,[64] as well as those on collective redress Directive 1828/2020 on Representative Action,[65] on Transborder Cooperation Regulation 2017/2394,[66] and those on alternative and online dispute resolution, Directive 2013/11 ADR,[67] Regulation 524/2013 on ODR[68] (both under revision).[69]

Other than in situations such as the usage by judicial authorities or ADR/ODR, systems like CLAUDETTE will be considered low-risk if they are intended to interact directly with natural persons[70] and minimal risk in all the other scenarios. This means that all other actors – researchers, civil society, law firms, scammers, or even administrative authorities – will be free to use systems like CLAUDETTE without the need to comply with any rules of the AI Act and without the regulatory scrutiny of the oversight bodies. This situation has both bright and dark sides.

On the one hand, regulatory freedom will enable benevolent actors, such as consumer organisations and even proactive companies, to use technological advances with considerable freedom. They will be able to experiment with their development and deployment as they are

61 Regulation (EU) 2024/... of the European Parliament and the Council laying down harmonized rules on artificial intelligence [2024] OJ (AI Act or AIA).

62 AIA, Annex III, 8(a).

63 Regulation (EU) 2022/2065 of the European Parliament and of the Council of 19 October 2022 on a Single Market for Digital Services and amending Directive 2000/31/EC (Text with EEA relevance), OJ L 277, 27 October 2022, pp. 1–102.

64 Regulation (EU) 2023/2854 of the European Parliament and of the Council of 13 December 2023 on harmonised rules on fair access to and use of data and amending Regulation (EU) 2017/2394 and Directive (EU) 2020/1828 (Data Act), OJ L, 2023/2854, 22 December 2023, ELI: http://data.europa.eu/eli/reg/2023/2854/oj

65 Directive (EU) 2020/1828 of the European Parliament and of the Council of 25 November 2020 on representative actions for the protection of the collective interests of consumers and repealing Directive 2009/22/EC (Text with EEA relevance) OJ L 409, 4 December 2020, pp. 1–27.

66 Regulation (EU) 2017/2394 of the European Parliament and of the Council of 12 December 2017 on cooperation between national authorities responsible for the enforcement of consumer protection laws and repealing Regulation (EC) No. 2006/2004 (Text with EEA relevance), OJ L 345, 27 December 2017, pp. 1–26.

67 Directive 2013/11/EU of the European Parliament and of the Council of 21 May 2013 on alternative dispute resolution for consumer disputes and amending Regulation (EC) No. 2006/2004 and Directive 2009/22/EC, OJ L 165, 18 June 2013, pp. 63–79.

68 Regulation (EU) No. 524/2013 of the European Parliament and of the Council of 21 May 2013 on online dispute resolution for consumer disputes and amending Regulation (EC) No. 2006/2004 and Directive 2009/22/EC, OJ L 165, 18 June 2013, pp. 1–12.

69 Proposals of 17 October 2023, https://commission.europa.eu/live-work-travel-eu/consumer-rights-and-complaints/resolve-your-consumer-complaint/alternative-dispute-resolution-consumers.

70 AIA, Art. 50.1.

now. The same is true for providers of ODR, on which the DSA heavily relies through the promotion of competition.[71] On the other hand, this creates a space for nefarious actors – such as scammers or law firms seeking easy profit – to operate without transparency or oversight. One might also wonder whether public authorities developing CLAUDETTE-like systems should be obliged to meet transparency requirements.

23.4.1 *The Place of CLAUDETTE under the AI Act*

The AI Act is constructed on the so-called risk-based approach.[72] Consequently, even though the high-level definition of an AI system is quite broad and encompasses a wide range of software applications, the specific rules that apply to AI systems differ based on the level of risk that a given system belongs to. The core of the regulation applies to the systems classified as high-risk. Under the AI Act, these are either (safety components of the) products covered by the European Union harmonisation legislation listed in Annex I or systems listed in Annex III. Systems like CLAUDETTE can only belong to the latter category, and the only possible area there is the administration of justice.[73] Consequently, and somewhat paradoxically, whether a system like CLAUDETTE will be considered high-risk will depend neither on the system's characteristics nor on the actual risk posed by its usage but, rather, on *who* uses it.

A system belonging to the high-risk category comes with many due diligence obligations to providers and deployers, concretised in Chapters II and III of the AIA. Out of the many, the technical documentation[74] seems to be most relevant when it comes to CLAUDETTE's promoted law enforcement strategies. Enforcement agencies and attorneys preparing litigation would need access to the technical documentation. However, it is difficult to imagine many uses in which courts could find systems like CLAUDETTE directly useful. Courts usually act in reaction to the parties' lawsuits and work with claims provided in such documents rather than analysing terms of service or privacy policies in general. Overburdened courts might feel tempted to use AI to reduce their workload and speed up the procedures on conflicts between private parties (business-to-business and business-to-consumer), though.

There are many other possible scenarios one can imagine when different actors deploy systems like CLAUDETTE. For example, most directly, consumer protection agencies or data protection authorities – with the competence to scrutinise contracts or privacy policies in abstract – can deploy such systems in search of unfair clauses or other violations of positive law. Law firms might use them to automate the generation of such documents, but also in search of 'leads', potential clients whose services can be offered. One could imagine such a system deploying a crawler, traversing the web in search of documents violating some laws, automatically notifying the businesses that some compliance problem has been detected and offering services such as preparing amendments. The line between a corporation doing this as a legitimate business (arguably when there is indeed a violation of the law) and a scammer (when, for example, they are lying about the violation) is thin and not always clear.

[71] DSA, Art. 21.

[72] Giovanni De Gregorio and Pietro Dunn, 'The European Risk-Based Approaches: Connecting Constitutional Dots in the Digital Age' (2022) 59 *Common Market Law Review* 473; Michael Veale and Frederik Zuiderveen Borgesius, 'Demystifying the Draft EU Artificial Intelligence Act – Analysing the Good, the Bad, and the Unclear Elements of the Proposed Approach' (2021) 22 *Computer Law Review International* 97.

[73] Annex III, 8(a).

[74] AIA, Art. 11 in combination with Annex IV.

In all these scenarios, systems like CLAUDETTE will be considered either low-risk – and then only required to inform the natural persons they interact with that they are AI systems – or minimal risk. In the last case, not only will they not be governed by the rules of the AIA, but the member states will be prevented from unilaterally considering them high-risk, as the legal basis for the regulation is Article 114 Treaty on the Functioning of the European Union (TFEU).

23.4.2 *Consequences of the EU Collective Action Rules on CLAUDETTE and the AIA, DSA, and DA*

Projects like CLAUDETTE are particularly enticing for consumer agencies and consumer organisations. The AI Act, the DSA, and the DA are added to the long list of EU directives and regulations in Directive 1828/2020,[75] where consumer agencies and consumer organisations are granted the right to launch an action for injunction, a kind of stop-order mechanism, or to claim collective compensation against infringements of EU law. Here the conflict is not one between two contracting parties but on the legality of business practices, typically the fairness of contract terms, commercial practices (advertising and sales promotion), and data privacy policies, fields in which CLAUDETTE type of projects are most advanced and where the fairness test has to be made *in abstracto* – whether the business practices abide by the law and not whether an individual company has infringed the law to the dismay of an individual consumer or customer. The inclusion of the AI Act and the DSA broadens the scope of potential collective actions considerably. For instance, it would be possible for the agencies and the consumer organisations to argue that the provider and the deployer of high-risk AI systems are infringing their due diligence obligations under Chapters II and III or that the providers and deployers of low-risk AI systems are infringing the transparency requirements in Chapter IV, provided they affect the collective interests of consumers.

The broad scope of application as well as the abstract character of the infringement provides space to facilitate the abstract control of illegal business practices to CLAUDETTE-like projects.[76] To the best of our knowledge, none of the consumer organisations in the EU has developed a CLAUDETTE type of system or has been testing CLAUDETTE as it stands. The situation is different for consumer agencies. In 2022 the European Commission launched a tender, which enabled the Polish Authority for Competition and Consumer Protection to develop an automated control of unfair terms, similar to the open-source CLAUDETTE.[77] There are a couple of legal questions which arise provided the qualified entities would systematically and strategically use CLAUDETTE type of systems not only to control unfair terms but to challenge the legality of due diligence obligations.

Directive 1828/2020 introduces a twofold distinction about the legal requirements the qualified entities have to respect to be granted legal standing. Suppose the qualified entity is a consumer organisation. In that case, legal standing is tied to compliance with a whole range of requirements which has to ensure that the civil society organisation represents the legitimate interests of consumers, requirements which do not apply to consumer agencies. These requirements, however, only concern cross-border actions, not national ones. There are member states, like Germany, that feared that other member states might be too generous in granting national consumer organisations

[75] AIA, Art. 110, DSA, Art. 90, DA Art. 48.
[76] Eliza Mik, 'Caveat Lector: Large Language Models in Legal Practice' (2024) 19(2) *Rutgers Business Law Review* 70.
[77] https://uokik.gov.pl/download/27227, 76.

standing, thus enabling a kind of 'litigation industry' through the back door. Whilst the fear mainly results from collection compensation claims, barring US-type class actions, the limitations equally affect mere actions for an injunction against, for instance, providers of AI systems. Directive 1828/2020 does not deal with business organisations as qualified entities, although such type of actions exist in some of the member states, in particular when it comes to unfair commercial practices, where there is equal space for CLAUDETTE-like projects.

The EU and the member states, it is obvious, tend to trust public agencies more than civil society organisations in the 'correct' use of collection actions. Unlike for energy, finance, telecommunications, and transport, EU law does not oblige member states to establish a consumer agency. However, Regulation 2017/2394 obliges the member states to designate the cooperation in cross-border enforcement to a national public agency that is ultimately responsible. However, neither the AIA nor the DSA has been added to the list of EU laws where the regulation applies, contrary to the DA.[78] Therefore national consumer agencies, which are competent for the enforcement of consumer laws, inter alia unfair terms and unfair commercial practices, are excluded from the enforcement of the AIA and the DSA. Both leave the designation of the competent national authorities to the member states. None of the member state authorities, competent under DSA, empowers national consumer agencies unless consumer law is one of the different fields of competence.[79] The national authorities in charge of the AIA are not yet known, but the outcome will be similar.

The strong reliance on national agencies, consumer agencies, and those designated under the AIA and the DSA begs the question whether national agencies that are ready to develop CLAUDETTE-type AI systems could be legally obliged by their member states to disclose information on the technology used and the safeguards taken – something similar though at a lower level to the registration of high-risk AI systems.[80] There is a tension between the full harmonisation approach in the AIA and the minimum harmonisation approach in Directive 1828/2020 and Regulation 2017/2394. The AIA would hinder the member states from laying down transparency requirements unilaterally, whereas the EU rules on collective action left their regulatory sovereignty untouched.

Last but not least, the minimal risk of CLAUDETTE type of projects may quickly turn into a disadvantage. The more successful CLAUDETTE-type projects might become, the more data is integrated, the more fields of law are covered, the more likely it might be that businesses that are confronted with efficient CLAUDETTE-based law enforcement tools will test the degree to which the AI Act can be used to hinder their use by consumer agencies and consumer organisations.

23.4.3 *Consequences of the EU ADR/ODR Rules on CLAUDETTE and the AIA/DSA*

The AI Act puts the judiciary and alternative dispute resolution on an equal footing. The EU is currently revising the ADR Directive and has proposed to repeal the ODR Regulation and replace it with a mere recommendation.[81] These amendments have to be read in the context of the DSA, which obliges the large and very large online platforms and search engines to develop appropriate dispute settlement procedures to directly solve conflicts between them and the

[78] DA, Art. 47.
[79] https://digital-strategy.ec.europa.eu/en/policies/dsa-dscs.
[80] AIA, Art. 71.
[81] C(2023) 7019 final Commission Recommendation of 17 October 2023 on quality requirements for dispute resolution procedures offered by online, marketplaces and EU trade associations, https://commission.europa.eu/document/download/c075baaa-f3eb-4899-8c55-4efb82b4254f.

recipients, which include individuals and entities that have submitted notices on illegal content.[82] The DSA lays down rather broad standards, which cannot be compared with the much more sophisticated and detailed rules in the ADR Directive – neither the present one nor the proposed revision.[83] Each ODR system has to be certified by the national authorities. The rather loose framework offers freedom for the providers of online services to develop innovative approaches, which might rely on AI systems to solve conflicts on the legality of the content. There is ample evidence that the number of ODR systems will explode in the next few years. There will be competition between them, and between national certification bodies and the ODR providers. In countries like South Korea, ODR systems are already fully operational. If the ODR providers use AI – and this is what can be expected – the full machinery on high-risk AI systems in the AI Act will be set in motion. The due diligence obligations under Chapters II and III on providers, deployers, distributors, and importers, and possible exemptions which might reduce the burden[84] as well as the registration duties will be implemented through algorithms.[85] This scenario will lead to further complications if the chosen variant of the ODR must be regarded as generative AI.

23.5 CONCLUSIONS

The aim of this chapter was to survey the ways in which the emergence of generative AI, specifically large language models such as GPT, is and could be affecting the long-standing attempts to automate various legal tasks. Having discussed the pre-GenAI advancements in NLP, aimed at information retrieval or summarisation, we have presented in detail the CLAUDETTE Project striving to automate the evaluation of consumer contracts and privacy policies. Further, we have discussed how LLMs entering the scene change this landscape. Finally, we looked at the place of projects like CLAUDETTE in the EU's recently adopted AI Act and related regulations.

Without a doubt, LLMs constitute a revolution for research in AI and law, as well as for legal practice and legal tech. Many tasks that previously could not be automated soon will be; many will be cheaper to automate, and for many that automation will be of higher quality. This is both good and bad news. On the one hand, civil society and oversight bodies will be able to lower the costs of their operations, thereby increasing the chances of actually helping consumers. On the other hand, nefarious actors will also benefit from lower costs, while one can expect even more text generated in the process of compliance.

Ultimately, one should bear in mind that even though generative AI is the latest iteration of the AI revolution, not all legal tasks will necessarily be best automated using these methods. Moreover, one should remember that, as a general rule, humans tend to overestimate technological change in the short term and underestimate it in the long term. This means that certain hopes for automation might not materialise in a year or two, though the landscape of legal tech will continue to change significantly and look very different in a decade from now. Whether the recently adopted AI Act will prove a good instrument in guiding these changes remains to be seen.

82 This is not the place to discuss the relationship between DSA Art. 21, the ADR Directive, and the proposed recommendation.

83 COM/2023/649 final, 17 October 2023, Proposal for a Directive of the European Parliament and of the Council amending Directive 2013/11/EU on alternative dispute resolution for consumer disputes, as well as Directives (EU) 2015/2302, (EU) 2019/2161, and (EU) 2020/1828, https://eur-lex.europa.eu/legal-content/EN/TXT/PDF/?uri=CELEX:52023PC0649.

84 AIA, Art. 6(3).

85 AIA, Arts. 49 and 71.

24

LawGPT

LLMs under Legal Services Regulation

Martin Ebers

24.1 INTRODUCTION

24.1.1 *Impact of LLMs on the Legal Services Market*

Generative AI (GenAI), especially large language models (LLMs) and applications – such as OpenAI's ChatGPT, Microsoft's Copilot, Google's Gemini, Meta's LLaMa, and others (e.g. BLOOM, Ernie 3.0 Titan, Anthropic's Claude 2) – have the potential to disrupt the legal profession unlike any other technology before them.

The public release of ChatGPT in November 2022[1] ushered in a new era of technological advancement, transforming and reshaping many industries across the world. The application quickly gained global attention, becoming the fastest growing internet app of all time within a month of its release.[2]

Since then, the legal profession has been one of the industries to experience significant change, as GenAI has the potential to redefine established processes while improving and expediting the delivery of legal services. According to Goldman Sachs Research,[3] analyzing databases detailing the task content of over 900 occupations, roughly two-thirds of US occupations are exposed to some degree of automation by AI, with the estimate that one-fourth of current work tasks can be automated by AI. Surprisingly, the report estimates that legal (44 percent) and administrative (46 percent) professions will be particularly affected, rather than sectors such as production (9 percent), transportation (11 percent), or sales (31 percent).

This chapter was finalized in early July 2024. Legislation, case law, and papers published after this date have not been taken into account; in particular, American Bar Association, Standing Committee on Ethics and Professional Responsibility, Formal Opinion 512, Generative Artificial Intelligence Tools, July 29, 2024, available at www.americanbar.org/content/dam/aba/administrative/professional_responsibility/ethics-opinions/aba-formal-opinion-512.pdf. All internet sources referred to were last accessed on July 1, 2024.

[1] ChatGPT 2 was released on 14 February 2019 while the enhanced version 4 was released on 14 March 2023.

[2] The Guardian, 'ChatGPT Reaches 100 Million Users Two Months after Launch' (2 February 2023), available at www.theguardian.com/technology/2023/feb/02/chatgpt-100-million-users-open-ai-fastest-growing-app.

[3] Jan Hatzius et al., 'The Potentially Large Effects of Artificial Intelligence on Economic Growth' (2023), available at www.gspublishing.com/content/research/en/reports/2023/03/27/d64e052b-0f6e-45d7-967b-d7be35fabd16.html.

Similarly, a study published by LexisNexis in March 2023[4] showed that 36 percent of lawyers in the United States already use GenAI for research (59 percent), drafting documents (45 percent), writing emails (38 percent), understanding new legal concepts (25 percent), and document analysis (23 percent).

Based on interviews with 700 lawyers in law firms, legal departments, and legal service providers in the United States and nine European countries – the United Kingdom, Germany, the Netherlands, Italy, France, Spain, Poland, Belgium, and Hungary – the *Future Ready Lawyer Study 2023* by Wolters Kluwer[5] presents very similar results: 73 percent of the lawyers surveyed expect to use GenAI in their law firm. Almost half of all lawyers (43 percent) see GenAI as an opportunity, while one in four (25 percent) see it as a threat and a further quarter (26 percent) perceive GenAI as both an opportunity and a threat.

Legal education is also undergoing a dramatic change. According to the LexisNexis report, 44 percent of law students already use GenAI tools. Other papers have shown that GPT-4 is capable of passing the Uniform Bar Exam in all three components (Multistate Bar Exam, Multistate Essay Exam, and Multistate Performance Test).[6]

24.1.2 *Open Questions*

AI powered solutions are capable of speeding up legal work – leading to a more efficient use of human resources and time. However, they raise a number of ethical, regulatory, and societal issues that require detailed consideration. Some risks became apparent immediately after the launch of ChatGPT. Two lawyers in New York were ordered to pay $5,000 for submitting non-existent judicial opinions with fake quotes and citations created by ChatGPT, and for sticking to the fake opinions even after judicial orders called their existence into question.[7] Quite understandably, the story raised critical questions about the use of AI in the practice of law and beyond. Is it appropriate for lawyers to use LLMs (such as ChatGPT) in legal practice? What obligations do lawyers have if they would like to rely on LLMs? Are lawyers who use LLMs fully responsible for their potential errors? How can clients be protected from harms and risks of LLMs? Does the provision of an LLM constitute a case of unauthorized practice of law?

The present chapter explores these and other questions by taking a comparative legal look at US and EU law and model rules. First, an overview is given of the use of LLMs in the legal sector as well as their advantages and risks (Section 24.2). This is followed by an analysis of the question as to whether the deployment of LLMs by non-lawyers can be classified as an unauthorized practice of law (24.3). Thereafter, the chapter discusses the professional rules of conduct of lawyers and law firms in the use of LLMs (24.4) as well as the recently adopted AI Act of the European Union and its potential impact on the legal tech industry (24.5). A concluding section summarizes the main findings and points out open questions (24.6).

[4] LexisNexis, 'Generative AI & the Legal Profession 2023 Survey Report' (2023), available at https://lnlp.widen.net/s/mvgdgfhkdb/2023-gen-ai-full-survey-report.

[5] Wolters Kluwer, 'Future Ready Lawyer' (2023), available at www.wolterskluwer.com/en/know/future-ready-lawyer-2023#download.

[6] D. M. Katz et al., 'GPT-4 Passes the Bar Exam' (2023) 382 *Philosophical Transactions of the Royal Society* A, available at https://ssrn.com/abstract=4389233. Critically discussed by E. Martínez, Re-evaluating GPT-4's Bar Exam Performance' (2024) *Artificial Intelligence and Law*, available at https://doi.org/10.1007/s10506-024-09396-9.

[7] *Mata v. Avianca, Inc.*, 1:22-cv-01461-PKC (S.D.N.Y.).

Further issues arising from the use of LLMs in law firms and legal departments – including the question of when the use of LLMs violates data protection law,[8] copyright law,[9] consumer protection law,[10] or anti-discrimination law,[11] and under what conditions deployers or users of LLMs are liable[12] – are addressed in other chapters of this book.

As (legal) applications based on ChatGPT and other generative AI systems advance rapidly, a caveat is proposed. This chapter does not attempt to provide any definitive answers as to how LLMs can or may be used in the legal sector or what the future regulatory framework will look like. Rather, the primary aim of this study is to contribute to the discussion on principles and guidelines for the responsible use of LLMs and other AI tools in the legal field.

24.2 LLMS IN THE LEGAL SECTOR

24.2.1 *Use Cases*

AI has brought significant changes in the legal sector, revolutionizing how legal professionals undertake their tasks and responsibilities. Trained on vast datasets of legal documents and case histories, machine learning (ML) algorithms have demonstrated efficacy in legal research, contract analysis, and predictive analytics. More recently GenAI applications, especially LLMs, have added another dimension to how lawyers utilize AI. While traditional AI tools specialize in data analysis, pattern recognition, and predictive analytics, LLMs have remarkable abilities to generate human-like text from the input they receive. This innovation could revolutionize the way lawyers approach tasks such as drafting legal documents and contracts or formulating nuanced legal arguments.

Generally, lawyers and non-lawyers can use LLMs for legal purposes in different ways. First, LLMs – such as ChatGPT or CoPilot – can be used directly to perform specific legal tasks. As such, many tutorials[13] and courses[14] have been designed on how to formulate legal prompts for optimal results. On the other hand, a growing number of LLMs on the market are specially trained with legal data and optimized for use in the legal sector, such as Harvey,[15] CoCounsel,[16] Spellbook,[17] Lexion,[18] AnyLawyer,[19] Lexis+AI,[20] KL3M,[21]

[8] See Chapter 15 by Hannah Ruschemeier and Chapter 16 by Elana Zaide.
[9] See Chapter 17 by Bruce Boyden, and Chapter 18 by Christoph Rademacher and Wanru Cai.
[10] See Chapter 20 by Cristina Poncibò.
[11] See Chapter 14 by Riccardo de Caria.
[12] See Chapter 7 by Teresa Rodriguez de las Heras Ballell.
[13] See Daniel Schwarcz and Jonathan Choi, 'AI Tools for Lawyers: A Practical Guide' (2023), available at https://papers.ssrn.com/sol3/papers.cfm?abstract_id=440401.
[14] See PwC, 'Legal Prompt Engineering: Die Brücke zwischen GenAI und juristischer Praxis' (2024), available at https://legal.pwc.de/de/services/legal-prompting.
[15] www.harvey.ai.
[16] CoCounsel, 'Meet CoCounsel – The World's First AI Legal Assistant' (2023), available at https://casetext.com/blog/casetext-announces-cocounsel-ai-legal-assistant
[17] 'AI Contract Drafting & Review' (*Spellbook*), available at www.spellbook.legal/
[18] 'The Fastest Way to Get Contracts Done Right' (*Lexion*), available at www.lexion.ai/
[19] 'AI (ChatGPT) for Lawyers – Home' (*AnyLawyer*), available at www.anylawyer.com/
[20] 'Lexis+ AI®' (*Lexis+ AI | AI Legal Assistant by LexisNexis*), available at www.lexisnexis.com/en-us/products/lexis-plus-ai.page
[21] KL3M (Kelvin Legal Large Language Model) was released in February 2024. It claims to be the first legal LLM to be trained from scratch on a proprietary dataset of legal, financial and general domain text; see www.273ventures.com/kl3m-the-first-legal-large-language-model/

and companies like JUNE[22] and JustInLegal,[23] that have integrated LLMs into their software.[24]

Law firms and legal departments can use LLMs for a variety of purposes, in particular information retrieval, e-discovery and legal research, document generation, and speech-to-text tools and chatbots to communicate with clients. Other use cases are currently being tested, such as AI agents designed to perform various tasks autonomously. Due to the dynamic development, the following overview can only provide a small selection of possible use cases.[25]

Information Retrieval and e-Discovery

As information retrieval and e-discovery tools, LLMs can be used to determine and clarify relevant facts and other circumstances of a case.[26]

Document Analysis and Classification

Also, they can assist users in document analysis and classification,[27] such as contracts, briefs or other court documents, memoranda, or reports.[28] Often, these tools classify the document or its parts (at different levels, such as paragraphs, sentences, or phrases) according to one or more characteristics.[29] Such characteristics include grammatical roles of words or sentences, language, content of a word or document, or the existence of a certain (unfair) clause.[30] Besides classical document classification, software tools can also be used for file version tracking,[31] detection of language errors, as well as for compliance checks regarding state law and company policies.[32]

Information Extraction

Another use of LLMs is in information extraction comprising all use cases that extract valuable insights from a body of text, such as persons and locations, keywords and key phrases, monetary amounts, dates, points of time, relations, or even the text of specific contractual provisions such as a term of a lease contract.[33] Classification and extraction

[22] 'Legal AI & Automation' (*JUNE*), available at www.june.de/

[23] Justin Legal, 'Die Erste E-Akte Mit Chatgpt-Funktionen für Anwaltskanzleien' (*Justin Legal*, 4 January 2023), available at https://justin-legal.com/ChatGPT

[24] For an overview of legal AI applications that have been trained with Chinese LLMs: Lai J et al., 'Large Language Models in Law: A Survey' (arXiv.org, 26 November 2023), available at https://arxiv.org/abs/2312.03718

[25] For a comprehensive overview see Stephen Meisenbacher et al., 'Legal AI Use Case Radar 2024 Report' (Technical University of Munich, July 2024), available at https://mediatum.ub.tum.de/doc/1748412/1748412.pdf.

[26] Daniel Jurafsky and James Martin, 'Speech and Language Processing: An Introduction to Natural Language Processing, Computational Linguistics, and Speech Recognition' (draft ms, 3 February 2024), available at https://web.stanford.edu/~jurafsky/slp3/ed3book.pdf, chapter 23.1.

[27] Matthias Grabmair in Martin Ebers (ed.), *StichwortKommentar Legal Tech: Recht, Geschäftsmodelle, Technik: Alphabetische Gesamtdarstellung* (Nomos, 2023). Dokumentenanalyse No. 8.

[28] CCBE/ELF, 'Guide on the Use of Artificial Intelligence-Based Tools by Lawyers and Law Firms in the EU' (2022), 25, available at www.ccbe.eu/fileadmin/speciality_distribution/public/documents/IT_LAW/ITL_Reports_studies/EN_ITL_20220331_Guide-AI4L.pdf.

[29] Ibid.

[30] Marco Lippi et al., 'CLAUDETTE: An Automated Detector of Potentially Unfair Clauses in Online Terms of Service' (2019) 27 *Artificial Intelligence and Law* 117.

[31] Davide Gianfelice et al., 'Modificatory Provisions Detection: A Hybrid NLP Approach', *Proceedings of the Fourteenth International Conference on Artificial Intelligence and Law* (ICAIL, 2013), 43–52, available at https://doi.org/10.1145/2514601.2514607.

[32] Monica Palmirani et al., 'Hybrid AI Framework for Legal Analysis of the EU Legislation Corrigenda', in Erich Schweighofer (ed.), *Legal Knowledge and Information Systems* (IOS Press, 2021), p. 68 et seq.

[33] CCBE/ELF (n. 28) 26.

tools often rely on each other. While a classification tool determines the relevance of a provision (for example, identifying if a contract is a lease agreement), an extraction tool labels those relevant provisions (such as those containing lease amounts, and extracts and displays the amount).[34]

Contract Review, Analysis, and Life Cycle Management

A particular successful use case is in contract review, analysis, and life cycle management. LLMs and other AI systems can automatically search thousands of contracts for insights; classify contracts, extract key information, retrieve defined terms and definitions from the contract, guide their users to review, redline, and negotiate contracts based on historical data analysis, precedents, and playbooks to predict the best terms and conditions, and manage the entire lifecycle of a contract.[35] Beyond the capability to speed up due diligence, contract review, and research processes, these tools also help to maintain accuracy across large volumes of documents. The integration of LLMs into legal document analysis processes increases workflow efficiency and effectiveness. This enables legal professionals to keep their focus on more strategic tasks.

Legal Research

By identifying relevant legislation, and finding and evaluating case law, LLMs can also help with legal research.[36] Where they provide summaries of relevant judgments, it becomes possible to obtain an overview of the entire body of case law in a short span of time.[37]

In addition, LLMs can be used to check how relevant a particular judgment is to a case.[38] These can then be used to develop a more fundamental understanding of the legal issues. For example, questions can be asked about the specific laws that were relevant to the court's decision[39] and how the court applied those laws in the specific case.[40]

Semantic Search and Argument Mining

Moreover, LLMs can be used for semantic search and argument mining. Semantic searches provide the best ways to retrieve text based on the intended meaning of the query – for instance, searches that rely on layers of meaning beyond the surface of the text, or argument mining – which involves finding arguments in natural language texts, finding typical schemes of argumentation and visualizing argumentation – including arguments in a given field, and assisting in the verification of lines of arguments or making summaries of argumentation. Thus, LLMs can help find lines of reasoning present in briefs and judicial decisions written in natural language and can help uncover deeper structures in judicial decisions, such as the kind of evidence needed to prove a statement of a particular fact.[41]

34 Ibid.

35 Monish Darda, 'How AI Is Reshaping Contract Management', *The AI Journal* (3 April 2024), available at https://aijourn.com/how-ai-is-reshaping-contract-management/#:~:text=Generative%20AI%20in%20Contract%20Management&text=Combined%20with%20the%20data%20in,in%20efficiency%20and%20decision%2Dmaking; Nick Noonan, 'Creative Mutation: A Prescriptive Approach to the Use of ChatGPT and Large Language Models in Lawyering' (2023), available at https://papers.ssrn.com/sol3/papers.cfm?abstract_id=4406907, 10 et seq.

36 Schwarcz and Choi (n. 13), 7.

37 Grabmair (n. 27), 10 et seq.

38 Schwarcz and Choi (n. 13), 13 et seq.

39 Ibid.

40 Ibid.

41 CCBE/ELF (n. 28), 31.

Document Generation

Another important area where LLMs are used is document generation. LLMs can create new documents from scratch, summarize long documents, or enrich existing documents by inserting valuable information. In the legal domain, this functionality is particularly useful for drafting emails, contracts, legal memos, motions, briefs, pleadings, and memoranda of law.[42]

In the past, law firms often used rule-based techniques, especially template engines to create contracts and other documents by selecting pre-written templates and filling them out with individual information. Although machine learning methods for contract generation are not yet mature enough for widespread use,[43] modern LLMs have greatly improved their generative capabilities in recent years and are often used to produce new texts quickly, or to summarize, simplify, refine, paraphrase, or translate existing texts.

Speech-to-Text Tools and Chatbots

Speech-to text tools can convert live speech and verbal instructions and commands into written text. These tools can be used for dictation, transcription or for voice assistants (chatbots)[44] – dialogue or conversational systems that simulate human conversational skills to a certain degree.[45]

Chatbots can be integrated into a law firm's website or appear as a point of contact for the lawyer on social media or messaging platforms.[46] They can be used to communicate directly with a client to collect their individual information.[47] They can also be used to draft and send emails to new clients, to provide them with basic (legal) information, and to create documents based on the "interview" previously conducted. Chatbots can also be used by law firms for online marketing purposes. In addition to introducing potential clients to the firm's website, blog, and any other online presence, chatbots can be used to present users with a direct opportunity to subscribe to the platform's client lists or become followers, depending on the platform.[48]

24.2.2 *Opportunities*

Generative AI has propelled legal services into an era of new opportunities to reshape traditional practices and improve operational efficiencies at pace with the evolving demands of our data-driven society. LLMs used in the legal sector can help to reduce costs and speed up workflows by increasing efficiency in processes.[49] In addition, LLMs have the potential to produce output that is more consistent and coherent, compared to humans.[50] Given that the use of LLMs can

[42] Ibid., 21 et seq.
[43] Meisenbacher et al. (n. 25), 20.
[44] CCBE/ELF (n. 28), 33.
[45] Ibid., 34.
[46] Ibid.
[47] Christoff Hamm, Benno Heussen and Hans-Ulrich Büchting, *Beck'sches Rechtsanwalts-Handbuch* (11th ed., C. H. Beck, 2016), § 64 Rn. 57.
[48] CCBE/ELF (n. 28), 34.
[49] Lauren Martin et al., 'Better Call GPT: Comparing Large Language Models Against Lawyers', available at https://arxiv.org/html/2401.16212v1#S3; Eliza Mik, 'Will LLMs Replace Lawyers?' (13 July 2023), available at https://elizamik.medium.com/llms-will-not-replace-lawyers-d491e7c655ca.
[50] CCBE/ELF (n. 28), 11.

compensate for a lack of personnel and financial capacity, smaller law firms now have the opportunity to compete with larger law firms.[51]

These findings are also confirmed by a new report which surveyed around 200 law firms around the world, representing nearly 100,000 legal professionals.[52] According to the report, most lawyers (87 percent) agreed that implementing AI will streamline repetitive tasks and productivity. In addition, more than half of the respondents (56 percent) agreed that AI provides an opportunity to reduce human error.

24.2.3 *Legal Hallucinations, Biases, Discrimination*

On the other hand, there are also negative impacts associated with the rise of generative AI in legal practice. While its transformative potential can bring many positive developments, its application must take into account a number of complex considerations which, if overlooked, may hinder progress or compromise integrity.

First, it is important to note that the fact that LLMs can generate text does not mean they understand it. They can only predict words, not comprehend user input. Given that most tasks performed by lawyers require comprehension, common sense, legal knowledge, and critical thinking, this deficiency in comprehension can have a very negative effect.[53] LLMs often "hallucinate" – they produce nonsensical or factually incorrect output, as in the case of *Mata v. Avianca*.[54] Since they do not understand the content, they cannot distinguish the possible from the impossible.

A recently published study by the Stanford RegLab and the Institute for Human-Centered AI (HAI)[55] shows the result of tests on GPT 3.5, Llama 2, and PaLM 2 with more than 200,000 queries to investigate the phenomenon of so-called hallucinations in typical legal tasks. Those results were sobering. According to the study, hallucination rates in response to specific legal queries ranged from 69 to 88 percent for state-of-the-art language models.

The performance of LLMs deteriorated in more complex tasks that require a flexible understanding of legal issues or the interpretation of legal texts. In addition, it was found that case law from lower courts – such as district courts – was subject to more frequent hallucinations than case law from higher courts – such as the Supreme Court. There were also differences between individual LLMs. For example, ChatGPT 3.5 generally performed better than other models. Still, it showed certain inclinations – for example, favoring well-known judges or certain types of cases. It tended, as an instance, to indicate that Judge Joseph Story had written many more opinions than he actually did.

The study also looked at the phenomenon of so-called contrafactual bias – the tendency to assume that a factual premise in a query is true, even if it is flatly wrong. For example, if you ask why a particular judge expressed a dissenting opinion in a particular case, a model might fail to second-guess whether this judge in fact dissented. This phenomenon can be observed particularly in LLMs like ChatGPT 3.5, which often provided credible responses to queries based on

[51] Ibid.

[52] Michał Jackowski, Michał Araszkiewicz, and Martin Ebers, 'First Global Report on the State of AI in Legal Practice' (2024) 3 *LegalTech Zeitschrift (LTZ)* 226.

[53] Mik (n. 49).

[54] *Mata v. Avianca, Inc.*, 1:22-cv-01461-PKC (S.D.N.Y.).

[55] Stanford HAI, 'Hallucinating Law: Legal Mistakes by Large Language Models Are Pervasive' (Stanford HAI, 2024), available at https://hai.stanford.edu/news/hallucinating-law-legal-mistakes-large-language-models-are-pervasive.

false premises. In contrast, Llama 2 frequently rejected false premises, but sometimes mistakenly denied the existence of actual cases or justices.

Another Stanford HAI paper – evaluating Thomas Reuters' and LexisNexis' GenAI software – claims that Lexis+ AI provides accurate (correct and grounded) responses on 65 percent of queries, while Ask Practical Law AI refuses to answer queries 62 percent of the time and responds accurately just 18 percent of the time. When looking solely at responsive answers, Thomson Reuters' system hallucinates at a similar rate to GPT-4, and more than twice as often as Lexis+AI.[56] However, in response, Thomas Reuters refuted that the researchers used *wrong data* and *a wrong model* (Ask Practical Law AI instead of Westlaw's AI-Assisted Research tool) for the study, which led to the low performance.[57] Subsequent tests by the HAI team indicated that Westlaw's results were even worse – with a 33 percent hallucination rate, above Practical Law's 17 percent.[58] While Thomas Reuters has continued to insist that an internal testing of the AI-Assisted Research shows "an accuracy rate of approximately 90% based on how our customers use it," they also admit that it can occasionally produce inaccuracies.[59] In an interview in June 2024, Jeff Pfeifer (LexisNexis' CPO for North America and the United Kingdom) further argues that Stanford HAI deliberately crafted the queries in their study to *confuse* the system – admitting, however, inaccuracies, and affirming that "customers can still find it useful."[60] This debacle leaves lawyers and other customers with questions as to what accuracy means, and whether these LLMs can – generally speaking – be trusted.

In addition, LLMs can produce responses littered with biases, exclusion, discrimination, and hate speech.[61] Given that they are fed with huge amounts of text and learning during (largely unsupervised) training, such data may contain racist, antisemitic, Islamophobic, or otherwise discriminatory evaluations.[62] Biased training data may produce output that excludes certain communities or present systems that perform better for some social groups than for others.[63]

24.2.4 *Transparency, Data Protection and Cybersecurity, IP Rights*

LLMs also bring challenges in terms of explainability and transparency. To properly evaluate AI-generated content, lawyers need to understand how the system derives a particular output from the input it receives. However, this is highly challenging due to the inherent opacity of deep neural networks that form the basis of LLMs. Accordingly, explainable AI (XAI) methods focus on "permutation feature importance" (finding out which variables in the dataset a model

[56] Artificial Lawyer, 'Problematic Stanford GenAI Study Takes Aim at Thomson Reuters, LexisNexis' (Artificial Lawyer, 24 May 2024), available at www.artificiallawyer.com/2024/05/24/problematic-stanford-genai-study-takes-aim-at-thomson-reuters-lexisnexis/.

[57] Artificial Lawyer, 'Stanford GenAI Study Debacle: Thomson Reuters Replies' (Artificial Lawyer, 24 May 2024), available at www.artificiallawyer.com/2024/05/24/stanford-genai-study-debacle-thomson-reuters-replies/.

[58] Artificial Lawyer, 'Stanford HAI Tests Westlaw, but the GenAI Results Look Worse' (Artificial Lawyer, 30 May 2024), available at www.artificiallawyer.com/2024/05/30/stanford-hai-tests-westlaw-but-the-genai-results-look-worse/.

[59] Artificial Lawyer, 'Thomson Reuters Contradicts Stanford GenAI Study: We Are 90% Accurate' (Artificial Lawyer, 10 June 2024), available at www.artificiallawyer.com/2024/06/10/thomson-reuters-contradicts-stanford-genai-study-we-are-90-accurate/.

[60] Artificial Lawyer, 'AL Interview with Jeff Pfeifer: Lexis AI Henchman, That Stanford Study' (Artificial Lawyer, 13 June 2024), available at www.artificiallawyer.com/2024/06/13/al-interview-with-jeff-pfeifer-lexis-ai-henchman-that-stanford-study/.

[61] J. A. Omiye et al., 'Large Language Models Propagate Race-Based Medicine' (2023) 6 *npj Digital Medicine*, 195, available at https://doi.org/10.1038/s41746-023-00939-z.

[62] Laura Weidinger et al., 'Ethical and Social Risks of Harm from Language Models' (2021), 9 et seq., available at https://arxiv.org/abs/2112.04359.

[63] Ibid., 9 et seq.

particularly relies on for its decision) as well as on "counterfactual explanations" to provide information on how a slight change in the input data could have led to a different decision.[64] Further investigation is needed to find out whether these methods also work for LLMs used in the legal field.

Other issues, not discussed in this chapter, but in other chapters of this book, concern data protection and cybersecurity, especially as legal practice is laden with a series of private information of individuals and businesses. Confidentiality, privacy, and security can be breached if systems leak sensitive information or are hacked.[65] This raises the question of whether entering clients' personal data into a LLM violates data protection law or a lawyer's duty of client confidentiality. Additionally, it is controversial under what circumstances the output of an LLM violates existing copyrights and to what extent "new" outputs of an LLM system are copyright protected.

24.2.5 *Status Quo Bias, Anchor Effect, Automation Bias*

There is also the risk of overreliance due to various psychological factors.

First of all, the fluency with which LLMs present information creates the illusion of relevance, correct information, plausibility, and credibility. This makes it harder to detect falsehoods.[66] Second, LLMs encourage "status quo bias," where people are often reluctant to deviate from a proposed decision. This is worsened if such a decision requires additional justification.[67] Closely related, LLMs can also trigger the so-called anchor effect – that is, the tendency to over-rely on the first piece of information offered (the "anchor") when making decisions.[68] Finally, there is the phenomenon of "automation bias" – the presence of a high degree of trust in the supposed "infallibility" of technical systems.[69] Conflicting information is not taken into account, even if it is the correct option. As such, there is a risk that a lawyer will have inhibitions about deviating from the proposal of an AI system.

24.2.6 *Socioeconomic Implications*

The use of generative AI in the legal sector also has a number of socioeconomic consequences.

Clearly, LLMs are already changing existing workflows in law firms and legal departments. While existing jobs will transform and some are likely to disappear, new areas of practice and professions will emerge.

The use of LLMs and other AI systems in law firms will also affect the structure of law firms – as a study by the Boston Consulting Group and Bucerius Law School already predicted back in

64 Umang Bhatt et al., 'Explainable Machine Learning in Deployment' (2019), 1 et seq., available at https://arxiv.org/abs/1909.06342.

65 Weidinger et al. (n. 62), 18 et seq.

66 Mik (n. 49).

67 W Samuelson and R Zeckhauser, 'Status Quo Bias in Decision Making' (1988) 1 *Journal of Risk and Uncertainty* 7, available at https://doi.org/10.1007/BF00055564; Datenethikkommission, 'Opinion of the Data Ethics Commission' (2019), 213, available at www.bmi.bund.de/SharedDocs/downloads/EN/themen/it-digital-policy/datenethikkommission-abschlussgutachten-lang.pdf;jsessionid = CA15CF16DE6453BAE812C620F9018688.live881?__blob = publicationFile &v = 5.

68 Charvi Rastogi et al., 'Deciding Fast and Slow: The Role of Cognitive Biases in AI-Assisted Decision-Making' (2022) 6 *Proceedings of the ACM on Human-Computer Interaction*, CSCW1, 2, available at https://doi.org/10.1145/3512930

69 Cordula Kupfer et al., 'Check the Box! How to Deal with Automation Bias in AI-Based Personnel Selection' (2023) 14 *Frontiers in Psychology* 2.

2016.[70] Here, law firms are gradually restructured from a pyramid (with many junior associates at the bottom and a few partners at the top) to a more rocket-shaped structure (with fewer junior associates and associates per partner and a larger group of non-lawyers, namely paralegals, legal project managers, and legal technicians).

Another factor that should not be underestimated is the growing dependence on Big Tech. Developing, refining, and deploying LLMs require a significant financial investment that many law firms cannot afford.[71] Only a few companies have the computing power, capacity, and capital to develop powerful LLMs. Based on this, large tech companies with huge datasets, computing resources, and engineering skills can centralize power in their hands.[72] Companies developing LLMs for the legal sector, as well as law firms and legal departments using these tools, are therefore heavily dependent on the big players. This raises the question of how the rule of law and the legal system in general can be protected and how society can be involved in the development, deployment, and evaluation of these systems to ensure that they are consistent with democratic and constitutional values.[73]

24.2.7 *Evaluation*

In summary, while the use of LLMs in the legal sector has many benefits, it is important to also consider the risks that accompany such uses. To ensure that legal advice remains appropriate, lawyers must review and critically reflect on the output of such LLMs.

Law firms are aware of the current risks. A recent report which surveyed about 200 law firms globally revealed that most firms are cautious about implementing AI. According to the report, 58 percent of firms have chosen to pilot AI solutions before full adoption, while 50 percent of companies are monitoring the implementation of these tools very closely.[74] When asked about the challenges of implementing AI, the survey also revealed a high level of concern about the legal aspects surrounding LLMs and other AI systems. The most frequently cited challenges were legal issues (legal liability and regulation – 80.2 percent of respondents chose this answer), privacy and security (66.8 percent), and the accuracy and reliability of AI (63.9 percent).

24.3 LLMS AS UNAUTHORIZED PRACTICE OF LAW?

One of the most pressing issues surrounding the use of LLMs for legal activities is how to protect consumers and other clients from false or inaccurate legal advice. One of the legal tools that come into play in this regard is the unauthorized practice of law (UPL), which is used by many jurisdictions to protect clients from fraudulent, negligent, or incompetent legal services. Accordingly, the question arises as to whether LLMs used for legal activities can be classified as UPL and thus prohibited.

After a brief comparative overview of the regulation of legal services (Section 24.3.1), the following observations analyze why LLMs pose a challenge to the UPL doctrine (Section

[70] Christian Veith et al., 'How Legal Technology Will Change the Business of Law' (2016), available at http://media-publications.bcg.com/How-legal-tech-will-change-business-of-low.pdf

[71] CCBE/ELF (n. 28), 12.

[72] Trang Anh, 'CHATGPT: What Legal and Ethical Issues Do You Need to Know?' (AstraIA Gear, 22 January 2023), available at www.astraiagear.com/2023/01/22/chatgpt-what-legal-and-ethical-issues-do-you-need-to-know/.

[73] M. Ebers, 'Legal Tech and EU Consumer Law', in L. diMatteo et al. (eds.), *The Cambridge Handbook of Lawyering in the Digital Age* (Cambridge University Press, 2021).

[74] Jackowski et al. (n. 52), 226.

24.3.2). Then, UPL cases involving software systems used for legal purposes in both the United States (Section 24.3.3) and Germany (Section 24.3.4) will be examined in more detail, before drawing general conclusions as to why UPL is an inadequate tool for protecting clients from hallucinating LLMs (Section 24.3.5).

24.3.1 *The Regulation of Legal Services: A Short Comparative Overview*

Worldwide, there are significant differences in the way legal services are regulated. As the UK Competition & Markets Authority (CMA) points out in a report, these differences include, inter alia,[75] what types of legal activities are exclusively reserved for lawyers and how they are carried out, whether nonlawyers are allowed to operate in the legal services sector, and whether nonlawyers can own and manage law firms.

The European Union has not yet succeeded in harmonizing the professional rules for lawyers either. Differences in the professional rules across EU countries exist most notably with regard to the question whether nonlawyers are allowed to provide out-of-court legal advice. In this respect, a study published by Claessens and colleagues on the legal situation in the (then) twenty-seven member states is particularly revealing.[76] According to this study, fifteen member states consider out-of-court "legal advice" to be an activity reserved for lawyers. In the remaining twelve countries, on the other hand, "legal advice" per se does not seem to be subject to the legal services regulations.

In the United States, on the other hand, all fifty states and the District of Columbia prohibit the UPL,[77] following Rule 5.5 of the Model Rules of Professional Conduct of the American Bar Association (ABA),[78] which, among other things, prohibits lawyers from practicing in a jurisdiction in which they are not licensed. However, there is little guidance as to what does and does not fall within the definition of UPL.[79]

24.3.2 *LLMs as a Challenge for UPL Regulation*

Most of the companies offering LLMs are software providers that are not licensed to practice law. This raises the question as to whether this constitutes a case of UPL. Typically, jurisdictions that prohibit or restrict out-of-court legal activities by non-licensed people distinguish between (unregulated) legal information and (regulated) legal advice.

Legal information is often perceived as public good that should be accessible for everyone.[80] Generally, it is described "as generic, not addressing the particular circumstances of the

[75] Competition & Markets Authority (CMA), 'Legal Services Market Study' (2016) CMA Final Report Appendix I (International Comparison), 1.

[76] S. J. Claessens et al., 'Evaluation of the Legal Framework for the Free Movement of Lawyers' (2012), 40–42, available at www.ccbe.eu/fileadmin/speciality_distribution/public/documents/FREE_MOVEMENT_OF_LAWYERS/FML_Reports___studies/EN_FML_20131125_Study_on_the_Evaluation_of_the_Legal_Framework_for_the_Free_Movement_of_Lawyers__PanteiaMaastricht_University_.pdf.

[77] Susan D, Hoppock, 'Enforcing Unauthorized Practice of Law Prohibitions: The Emergence of the Private Cause of Action and Its Impact on Effective Enforcement' (2007) 20 *Georgetown Journal of Legal Ethics* 719, 722.

[78] Model Rules of Professional Conduct, American Bar Association, available at www.americanbar.org/groups/professional_responsibility/publications/model_rules_of_professional_conduct/.

[79] Ed Walters, 'Re-regulating UPL in an Age of AI' (2024) 8 *Georgetown Law Technology Review* 316, 323 et seq., available at https://ssrn.com/abstract=4822750.

[80] Judith Bennett et al., 'Current State of Automated Legal Advice Tools' (2018) *University of Melbourne Networked Society Institute Discussion Paper* 1/2018, 16.

individual," whereas legal advice "is more tailored and specific to the needs of the consumer."[81] Accordingly, printed legal materials, such as directions and how-to manuals, are usually not considered legal advice. This is also applicable to general instructions on how to file a lawsuit or explaining court requirements for documents requesting relief.[82] A non-lawyer may also publish and sell legal sample forms or DIY legal kits, and provide general instructions for filling out forms – provided that no advice is given.[83]

Legal advice, on the other hand, is tailored to the individual circumstances and needs of the client. Typically, it involves analyzing a set of facts and advising a person to take a specific course of action based on the applicable law. Examples of activities that constitute providing legal advice include (i) selecting, drafting, or completing legal forms, documents, or agreements tailored to a person's particular situation; (ii) representing a person before a court; (iii) negotiating legal rights on behalf of a person; and (iv) predicting the outcome of a legal dispute.[84]

Legal technology – in particular LLMs – is disrupting these boundaries. The more sophisticated applications become, the more difficult it is to draw a sharp line between legal information and advice, between standardized and tailored forms of communication, and between products and services. As software companies increasingly offer applications that can be used for legal purposes, it becomes very likely that this will cross into the territory of providing legal advice.

Against this background, state bar associations and regulators all over the world have filed actions against legal tech companies for the "unauthorized practice of law."

24.3.3 *The Legal Situation in the United States*

24.3.3.1 The LegalZoom Saga

An example of this is LegalZoom,[85] a leading legal document service in the United States, which provides customers with downloadable forms and internet-mediated walk-throughs of questionnaires and flow charts related to their legal problems. LegalZoom does not claim to provide its users with a lawyer, but rather with "legal information" in the form of a sophisticated series of forms and queries.[86] That notwithstanding, its business model led to widespread concerns as to whether it was engaging in UPL.[87] This resulted in a dispute with the North Carolina State Bar Association for several years,[88] and other legal disputes with competitors and customers.

[81] Jeff Giddings and Michael Robertson, 'Informed Litigants with Nowhere to Go: Self-Help Legal Aid Services in Australia' (2001) 26(4) *Alternative Law Journal* 184.

[82] See Judicial Council of California, 'Legal Advice vs. Legal Information' (2003), available at www.courts.ca.gov/documents/mayihelpyou.pdf.

[83] Derek Denckla, 'Nonlawyers and the Unauthorized Practice of Law: An Overview of the Legal and Ethical Parameters' (1999) 67(5) *Fordham Law Review*, 2591.

[84] Bennett et al. (n. 80), 15.

[85] Website 'LegalZoom', available at www.legalzoom.com.

[86] See Lauren Moxley, 'Note, Zooming Past the Monopoly: A Consumer Rights Approach to Reforming the Lawyer's Monopoly and Improving Access to Justice' (2015) 9(2) *Harvard Law & Policy Review*, 553; see also Catherin Lanctot, 'Does Legalzoom Have First Amendment Rights? Some Thoughts About Freedom of Speech and the Unauthorized Practice of Law' (2011) 20(2) *Temple Political & Civil Rights Law Review*, 257.

[87] See Emily McClure, 'LegalZoom and Online Legal Service Providers: Is the Development and Sale of Interactive Questionnaires that Generate Legal Documents the Unauthorized Practice of Law?' (2017) 105(3) *Kentucky Law Journal*, Article 5; Thomas Spahn, 'Is Your Artificial Intelligence Guilty of the Unauthorized Practice of Law? (2018) 24(4) *Richmond Journal of Law & Technology*, 1.

[88] *LegalZoom.com v. N.C. State Bar*, No. 11CVS15111, 2011 WL 8424700 (N.C. Super. Ct. 30.9.2011).

The main question was whether the offer produced by the document generator constituted an impermissible legal service within the meaning of Article 5.5(b) ABA Model Rules. US courts held that this was indeed the case.[89] Yet, in other jurisdictions, courts found that LegalZoom was not engaging in the unauthorized practice of law.[90] The dispute with the North Carolina State Bar ended on a conciliatory note. In 2016, the state passed a new law. Now, if a provider offers a consumer access to interactive software that generates a legal document based on the consumer's answers to questions posed by the software, it is not considered practice of law.[91]

24.3.3.2 Regulatory Sandboxes

Additionally, some US states have established regulatory sandboxes – for example, the states of Utah and Arizona. Under these pilot programs, certain rules of the applicable ABA Model Rules were suspended for a trial period to test innovative forms of legal services.[92] This allowed applicants to seek approval to experiment with new legal business models and approaches.[93] Utah recognized the opportunity to expand the types of legal providers in 2020 when its Supreme Court approved a "sandbox" where nonlawyers could provide legal services and operations.[94] Arizona, on the other hand, in 2021 repealed Rule 5.4(b) ABA Model Rules which prohibits partnerships between nonlawyers and lawyers, where any part of their work involves the practice of law.[95] California also considered a "regulatory sandbox" model. However, in August 2022, the state legislature passed a bill restricting "regulatory sandbox" initiatives.[96]

24.3.3.3 The DoNotPay Case

Another interesting case concerns DoNotPay – a US company offering AI systems to provide users with free legal advice on minor issues such as traffic tickets or refunds. From February 2023, the company wanted the AI system to go beyond just giving advice, and communicate directly with clients in the courtroom via a Bluetooth headset, telling them what to say. However, after several bar associations threatened legal action, DoNotPay quashed the plan.[97]

Various lawsuits have been filed against DoNotPay. Notably, on March 3, 2023, Jonathan Faridian (named plaintiff) filed a class action in the Superior Court of California, San Francisco

[89] *Janson v. LegalZoom.com Inc* 802 F. Supp. 2d 1053, 1065 (W.D. Mo. 2011). LegalZoom settled that case; see Martin Bricketto, 'LegalZoom Settles with Class over Legal Service Fees' (Law360, 2011), available at www.law360.com/articles/266603/legalzoom-settles-with-class-over-legal-service-fees, https://perma.cc/L9MV-586Z.

[90] *Medlock v. LegalZoom.com Inc* 2012-208067, 2013 S.C. LEXIS 362, 26–27 (S.C. 2013).

[91] NC Gen Stat § 84-2.2 (2016).

[92] 'Arizona and Utah Opened the Door, but Firms Remain Skeptical of Alternative Business Structures' (Law.com, 14 February 2023), available at www.law.com/americanlawyer/2023/02/14/arizona-and-utah-opened-the-door-but-firms-remain-skeptical-of-alternative-business-structures/?slreturn = 20240624200311.

[93] Ibid.

[94] Sam Skolnik and Melissa Stanzione, 'Utah Oks Pathbreaking Pilot on New Legal Service Models' (Bloomberg Law, 2020), available at www.bloomberglaw.com/bloomberglawnews/business-and-practice/X8U3RG24000000?bna_news_filter = business-and-practice#jcite.

[95] Joel Truett, 'Goodbye Rule 5.4: Legal Ethics Change in Arizona' (2021) *Arizona State Law Journal*, available at https://arizonastatelawjournal.org/2021/04/19/goodbye-rule-5-4-legal-ethics-change-in-arizona/.

[96] Reuters, 'California Lawmakers Pull Plug on Legal Industry Reforms', *Reuters* (26 August 2022), available at www.reuters.com/legal/legalindustry/california-lawmakers-pull-plug-legal-industry-reforms-2022-08-26/.

[97] USA Today, 'First AI Robot Lawyer: DoNotPay' (USA Today, 9 January 2023), available at https://eu.usatoday.com/story/tech/2023/01/09/first-ai-robot-lawyer-donotpay/11018060002/.

County, against the service.[98] He alleged that the defendant had engaged in "unlawful, unfair, and/or fraudulent business practices" in violation of California's Unfair Competition Law. The complaint highlighted DoNotPay's display of the slogan "The World's First Robot Lawyer" on its website, along with snapshots marketing other services such as "Defamation Demand Letters," "Create a Power of Attorney," and "Sue Anyone in Small Claims Court" and a clickable button entitled "Solve This Problem For Me." Faridian argued that DoNotPay was being misrepresented as a lawyer.[99]

Also, recently, the dismissed petition for pre-action discovery in New York State Supreme Court, New York County – *Tewson v. DoNotPay* – focused on the other part of the robot-lawyer slogan, suggesting that the app is not really a robot and claiming that "DoNotPay does not actually have any AI or 'robot' undergirding its system."[100]

24.3.4 *The Legal Situation in Germany*

24.3.4.1 The Smartlaw Case

Similar developments have occurred in Germany. Most notably, in 2019, the Regional Court of Cologne[101] banned Smartlaw,[102] an online contract/document generator developed by Wolters Kluwer. The software guides users through a series of questions and uses the feedback to customize a contract based on different templates. The user enters information in a form and answers simple, closed-ended questions. Smartlaw then instantly generates contracts or letters as PDF or Word documents. The Smartlaw generator was initially advertised as a low-cost, print-at-home alternative to a lawyer. The plaintiff, the Hanseatic Bar Association of Hamburg, regarded this to be UPL.

The Regional Court of Cologne agreed with this assessment. According to the Court, the drafting of legally compliant contracts is a "legal service" that can only be provided by lawyers under the German Act on Out-of-Court Legal Services. Section 2(1) of the Act defines a "legal service" as "any activity relating to the concrete affairs of others as soon as it requires a legal assessment of the individual case."[103] According to the Regional Court of Cologne, this is the case with the Smartlaw document generator, because the software is highly individualized and goes far beyond classic handbooks.

Later, this decision was overturned by the Higher Regional Court of Cologne[104] and by the Federal Court of Justice (Bundesgerichtshof; BGH).[105] According to the BGH, there is no legal service in the sense of Section 2(1) RDG if the software does not take into account the individual case, but only considers fictitious individual cases using automated questions and

98 *Jonathan Faridian v. DoNotPay, Inc.* (Superior Court of California, County of San Francisco, 3 March 2023), Case No CGC-23-604987.

99 K. Niven, 'DoNotPay Cases Underscore Hurdles for AI-Fueled Legal Help' (Frankfurt Kurnit Klein + Selz PC, 5 April 2023), available at www.law360.com/pulse/articles/1593612/donotpay-cases-underscore-hurdles-for-ai-fueled-legal-help.

100 Tewson petition available at https://s3.documentcloud.org/documents/23609120/tewson-donotpay.pdf.

101 Landgericht Köln, Judgment of 8 October 2019, 33 O 35/19, ECLI:DE:LGK:2019:1008.33O35.19.00.

102 Website 'SmartLaw', available at www.smartlaw.com.

103 Translation provided by Ute Reusch, available at www.gesetze-im-internet.de/englisch_rdg. The German version of Section 2(1) Act on Out-of-Court Legal Services (R echtsdienstleistungsgesetz , RDG) reads as follows: "Rechtsdienstleistung ist jede Tätigkeit in konkreten fremden Angelegenheiten, sobald sie eine rechtliche Prüfung des Einzelfalls erfordert."

104 Oberlandesgericht Köln, judgment of 19 June 2020, 6 U 263/19, ECLI:DE:OLGK:2020:0619.6U263.19.00.

105 BGH, judgment of 9 September 2021, I ZR 113/20, NJW 2021, 3125.

answers (Q&As) and templates.[106] Although the decision has been heavily criticized,[107] the ruling has created legal certainty for simple rule-based systems, based on templates.

24.3.4.2 Unclear Legal Situation Regarding LLMs

However, this line of argument does not apply to LLMs because they work differently from rule-based contract generators such as Smartlaw. While the Smartlaw document generator works with templates, LLMs generate text according to probability criteria, and are able to calculate the likelihood that one word will be followed by another. The results are constantly regenerated and are not preprogrammed, unlike rule-based contract generators. Also, unlike rule-based contract generators, LLMs can recognize patterns in the data.[108]

With this in mind, it is currently unclear whether LLMs used for legal activities can be considered UPL and thus prohibited. According to one view, automated services provided by LLMs do not constitute an "activity" within the meaning of Section 2(1) RDG (*Rechtsdienstle istungsgesetz*), as LLMs have a high degree of automation, so that their actions cannot be traced back to a person in a concrete case.[109] In addition, users do not expect to receive legal services, as LLMs are not usually advertised as providing them.[110] For these two reasons, LLMs should not be classified as legal services requiring a license. This has been countered in the literature with the argument that the activity of an LLM can always be traced back to the provider, since AI systems cannot yet make their own decisions independently of human programming.[111]

The opposing view therefore considers it possible that the use of LLMs could be qualified as legal services, depending on the user's prompt.[112] If the user asks for general legal information, there can be no activity related to the "concrete affairs of others." However, the situation is claimed to be different if the prompt relates to a specific matter. If the user asks the LLM an individual legal question, then the answer given by the LLM also relates to this specific question. Therefore, a "concrete affair" within the meaning of Section 2(1) RDG should be assumed. Disclaimers stating that the LLM only provides general information and does not offer legal services should also be disregarded.[113] The protection of consumers and other clients under the RDG is said to be necessary precisely because LLMs may provide erroneous results that are not recognizable to a layperson.

If this interpretation is followed, LLMs would have to be banned in Germany. Nonetheless, it is still unclear under German law whether LLMs used for legal activities qualify as a legal service that can only be provided by lawyers and not by software companies, since the courts have not yet ruled on this question.

[106] Martin Huff, 'Smartlaw berät nicht' (Legal Tribune Online, 2021), available at www.lto.de/recht/juristen/b/bgh-urteil-izr11320-vertragsgenerator-smartlaw-keine-unzulaessige-rechtsdienstleistung-rak-hamburg-rdg-legal-tech.

[107] Markus Hartung, 'Smartlaw und GPT-3' (2022) 1 *LegalTech Zeitschrift (LTZ)* 63; Viktoria Kraetzig and Lina Krawietz, 'Vertragsgeneratoren als Subsumtionsautomaten' (2022) 3 *Recht Digitalb (RDi)* 145; Reinhard Singer, 'Vertragsgeneratoren als "smarte" Formularhandbücher? – Erweiterte Betätigungsfelder für nichtanwaltliche Dienstleister nach dem "Smartlaw"-Urteil des BGH und ihre Grenzen' (2022) *Recht Digitalb (RDi)* 53; Christoph Thole, 'Anmerkung zu BGH, Urteil vom 9.9.2021 – I ZR 113/20' (2021) 74 *Neue Juristische Wochenschrift* 3125.

[108] Frank Remmertz, 'Rechtsdienstleistungen durch Large Language Models (LLMs)' (2023) 3 *Recht Digitalb (RDi)* 402 et seq.

[109] M. Hartung, 'Smartlaw, ChatGPT und das RDG' (2023) 3 *Recht Digitalb (Rdi)* 209, 215.

[110] Ibid., 216.

[111] Remmertz (n. 108) 404.

[112] A. Nickl, 'ChatGPT als Rechtsdienstleister?' (2023) 26 *MMR (Zeitschrift fur IT-Recht und Recht der Digitalisierung)* 328, 332; Remmertz (n. 108), 404.

[113] Remmertz (n. 108), 406.

24.3.5 *Evaluation*

The cases discussed above show that LLMs raise a number of new questions and challenges for regulators. How far can we stretch existing rules to accommodate new forms of delivery? At what point does an LLM move from information to advice? Does the distinction between (unregulated) information and (regulated) legal advice make sense at all? Does the use of LLMs and other AI systems alter the ultimate purpose of legal services regulation? Are the objectives of that regulation still valid? Are the right rules in place, in the right form? Is there too much regulation of certain forms of legal services and underregulation of others? How can we justify the current regulatory monopoly of lawyers over legal advice in a technology-driven world? Should the law be reformed to address the risks identified in the use of AI-based legal services (access to justice, choice and information, quality, fairness, redress, and representation)?

All of these issues will need to be addressed in the future. Most importantly, regulators will have to consider that the legal frameworks for UPL in many countries – including the United States and Germany – rely primarily on personal expertise for licensing requirements, mandating that lawyers graduate from a law school, pass the state's bar exam, and pass the state's character and background check. However, such requirements cannot guarantee that the output generated by the software will be of sufficient quality. After all, the quality of an algorithmic legal service is primarily determined by the software and the training data, not by the competence of the person using it. Even if a software provider were licensed to practice law, this would not guarantee that consumers and other clients seeking legal advice would be protected. Therefore, regulators need to consider alternative measures, in particular product-related approval procedures and certification schemes, that verify the quality of the software and, in particular, of the training data.

24.4 LLMS AND RULES OF PROFESSIONAL CONDUCT

24.4.1 *Overview*

The use of LLMs for legal purposes also raises a number of unresolved issues under the existing codes of professional conduct. However, it is currently unclear what lawyers, law firms, and legal departments need to consider when using LLMs.

24.4.1.1 Principles and Guidelines for the Use of LLMs

Around the world, there are already a number of initiatives dealing with the use of AI in the legal market in general or with LLMs in particular:

- The "Task Force on Responsible Use of Generative AI for Law" – founded by the US law journal *MIT Computational Law Report* – was established to develop principles and guidelines on ensuring the professional and responsible conduct of legal professionals in the application and use of generative AI for law and legal processes.[114] This task force specifically works toward the development of concrete principles and guidelines for determining how generative AI can be used or misused in the legal field. To this end,

[114] 'AI for Law – MIT Computational Law Report' (MIT Computational Law Report), available at https://law.mit.edu/ai#:~:text=The%20purpose%20of%20this%20Task,for%20law%20and%20legal%20processes.

they published an initial draft set of guidelines in mid-2023. Based on seven core principles, these guidelines set out the legal obligations that must be noted when using LLMs.[115] Building on this, a working group of the State Bar of California recently adopted a practical guide for the use of generative AI in legal practice.[116] The New York State Bar Association's Task Force on AI also recently commented on this topic.[117]

- In 2022, the Council of Bars and Law Societies of Europe (French: Commission de Conseil des Barreaux européens, CCBE) and the European Lawyers Foundation (ELF) published "Guide on the Use of Artificial Intelligence-Based Tools by Lawyers and Law Firms in the EU,"[118] which provides information on how lawyers can use the opportunities provided by AI tools and how such tools could help the business processes of small firms.
- A year later – in 2023 – the European Bars Federation published the guide "European Lawyers in the Era of ChatGPT."[119] This contains guidelines on how lawyers should take advantage of the opportunities offered by LLMs and generative AI.
- Other bar associations have also drawn up guidelines for dealing with the use of LLMs in legal practice. For instance, the New South Wales Bar Association has recently approved guidelines on "Issues Arising from the Use of AI Language Models (including ChatGPT) in Legal Practice."[120]

None of these principles and guidelines are legally binding. Thus, how lawyers may use LLMs and other AI systems will ultimately depend on the applicable rules of professional conduct and their interpretation.

24.4.1.2 Interpreting the Existing Rules of Professional Conduct

In this section, we discuss two sets of rules in more detail: the American Bar Association Model Rules of Professional Conduct (ABA Model Rules) and the Charter of Core Principles of the European Legal Profession of the Council of Bars and Law Societies of Europe (CCBE) (CCBE Charter).

The ABA Model Rules were originally adopted by the House of Delegates of the American Bar Association in 1983 and last amended in August 2023. Generally, the ABA Model Rules are

[115] These principles include: (1) Duty of confidentiality to the client in all usage of AI applications; (2) Duty of fiduciary care to the client in all usage of AI applications; (3) Duty of client notice and consent to the client in all usage of AI applications; (4) Duty of competence in the usage and understanding of AI applications; (5) Duty of Fiduciary Loyalty to the client in all usage of AI applications; (6) Duty of regulatory compliance and respect for the rights of third parties, applicable to the usage of AI applications in your jurisdiction(s); (7) Duty of accountability and supervision to maintain human oversight over all usage and outputs of AI applications.

[116] The State Bar of California Standing Committee on Professional Responsibility and Conduct, 'Practical Guidance for the Use of Generative Artificial Intelligence in the Practice of Law' (2023), www.calbar.ca.gov/Portals/0/documents/ethics/Generative-AI-Practical-Guidance.pdf.

[117] New York State Bar Association, 'Report and Recommendations of the Task Force on Artificial Intelligence' (April 2024), available at https://nysba.org/app/uploads/2022/03/2024-April-Report-and-Recommendations-of-the-Task-Force-on-Artificial-Intelligence.pdf.

[118] CCBE/ELF (n. 29).

[119] European Bars Federation, 'European Lawyers in the Era of ChatGPT: Guidelines on How Lawyers Should Take Advantage of the Opportunities Offered by Large Language Models and Generative AI' (June 2023), www.fbe.org/wp-content/uploads/2023/06/European-lawyers-in-the-era-of-ChatGPT-FBE-Guidelines-on-how-lawyers-should-take-advantage-of-the-opportunities-offered-by-large-language-models-and-gene-kopia.pdf.

[120] NSW Bar Association, 'Issues Arising from the Use of AI Language Models (including ChatGPT) in Legal Practice' (12 July 2023), https://inbrief.nswbar.asn.au/posts/9e292ee2fc90581f795ff1df0105692d/attachment/NSW%20Bar%20Association%20GPT%20AI%20Language%20Models%20Guidelines.pdf.

not legally binding. However, they are intended to be a guideline for state regulators of the legal profession to adopt. As mentioned before, all fifty states and the District of Columbia have adopted legal ethics rules partly based on the ABA Model Rules.[121]

The aim of the CCBE Charter is to express the common ground which underlies all the national and international rules governing the conduct of European lawyers – even though the regulation of the legal profession is not necessarily uniform in jurisdictions within Europe.[122] To this end, the Charter contains a list of ten principles common to the whole European legal profession. These are based on the national professional rules from states throughout Europe, the CCBE's Code of Conduct for European Lawyers and other principles.[123]

Neither the ABA Model Rules nor the CCBE Charter *explicitly* regulates the use of LLMs or other AI systems. However, many of the existing principles and rules can be interpreted to guide lawyers in the use of LLMs and other AI systems.

24.4.2 *Duty of Fiduciary Care, Loyalty, and Truthfulness to the Client*

The duty of fiduciary care, loyalty, and truthfulness is recognized in both the ABA Model Rules and the CCBE Charter.[124] Both sets of rules require a lawyer to act with reasonable diligence and promptness in representing a client. Moreover, a lawyer must act with commitment and dedication to the interests of the client and with zeal in representing them.[125]

24.4.2.1 Standard of Care in the Use of New Technologies

New technologies, such as LLMs, affect the level of the required standard of care. On the one hand, new technologies may lead to new errors – so that their use may be considered a breach of the duty of care. This may occur, for instance, if a lawyer fails to check the results produced by an LLM and uses incomplete, incorrect, or otherwise unlawful LLM output. On the other hand, new technologies may help to prevent errors – and aid the advancement of the standard of care. In these cases, the decision not to use them could also be considered a breach of the duty of care.

In Germany, case law suggests that the use of new technology in the event of errors is more likely to be considered a breach of the standard of care than the failure to use it. For example, according to the Federal Court of Justice, a lawyer breaches the standard of care if they rely on an electronic calendar without manually checking deadlines.[126] In such cases, if a lawyer misses a deadline, they cannot excuse themselves by claiming that it would have been unreasonable to check the deadlines manually in mass proceedings.[127] In contrast, the Federal Court of Justice ruled that lawyers do not have an unwritten legal obligation to use their electronic mailbox,[128]

121 American Bar Association, 'Alphabetical List of Jurisdictions Adopting Model Rules' (17 August 2018), available at www.americanbar.org/groups/professional_responsibility/publications/model_rules_of_professional_conduct/alpha_list_state_adopting_model_rules/.

122 AE Davis and M Hartung, 'The Impact of Generative AI on the Legal Practice: Some Ethical and Professional Considerations' (2024) 2 *Transatlantic Law Journal* 106.

123 CCBE/ELF (n. 28), 6–7.

124 See Rule 1.3 ABA Model Rules; Principle (e) CCBE Charter.

125 Rule 1.3 ABA Model Rules.

126 BGH 28 February 2019, III ZB 96/18, NJW 2019, 1456 (1457).

127 BGH 23 June 2020, VI ZB 63/19, NJW 2020, 2641 (2642).

128 As of January 1, 2022, lawyers are required to submit documents to the courts electronically. The case decided by the BGH concerned the time before such a statutory obligation existed.

even if other means of communication (such as fax machines) do not work.[129] For LLMs, it is therefore likely that the courts in Germany (and probably also elsewhere) will require a manual review of the output.

In the United States, Rule 1.1 of the ABA Model Rules requires a lawyer to provide competent representation to a client – where competent representation consists of "the legal knowledge, skill, thoroughness and preparation reasonably necessary for the representation." In addition, Comment 8 to Rule 1.1 expressly imposes a duty on a lawyer to keep up with the changes in technology that impact the practice of law.[130] Nevertheless, it is highly unlikely that the use of LLMs will be considered necessary for the practice of law at this time. Although they are becoming more common, LLMs are far from being as widely adopted as specialized platforms such as Lexis or Westlaw. Besides, ten states have not yet adopted Comment 8.[131]

In the medium term, however, there may even be an obligation on lawyers to use LLMs to competently complete certain tasks for clients. Where the performance of LLMs and other AI systems is significantly better than that of lawyers, the required standard of care is uncertain – as it is likely to evolve with technological advancements. Based on this, the failure to use these new technologies could then be considered a breach of duty.

24.4.2.2 Standard of Care in the Use of LLMs

At present, a strict standard of care must be applied – especially given that LLMs currently still produce many inaccurate results.

An attorney who fails to fact-check or verify citations from LLM results is in breach of the duty of fiduciary care. This also applies to attorneys who use LLMs to review or draft contracts without regard to their defensibility or accuracy. Lawyers are also prohibited from accepting the output of generative AI that makes recommendations or decisions that are contrary to the best interests of the client. To avoid these negative consequences, lawyers must critically review, validate, or correct the output of generative AI. They must ensure diligence and prudence with respect to facts and law by maintaining existing fact-checking practices.

24.4.2.3 Duty of Competence in the Usage and Understanding of LLMs

Clearly, lawyers using LLMs cannot effectively act with due diligence in representing a client, unless they are competent in the use and understanding of LLMs. Rule 1.1 ABA Model Rules and Principle (g) CCBE Charter both require lawyers to possess the requisite professional competence – in particular the legal knowledge, skill, thoroughness, and preparation – reasonably necessary for the representation. As noted above, Comment 8 to Rule 1.1 ABA Model Rules further states that a lawyer "should keep abreast of changes in the law and its practice, including the benefits and risks associated with relevant technology." More specifically, the comments to Principle (g) CCBE Charter state that a lawyer "should be aware of the benefits and risks of using relevant technologies in his or her practice."

Thus, lawyers need to understand the workings and limitations of LLMs. As the California State Bar's "Practical Guidance for the Use of Generative Artificial Intelligence in the Practice

[129] BGH 17 December 2020, III ZB 31/20, NJW 2021, 390.

[130] Sara Khan and Elizabeth Powers, 'Efficiency, Ethics, and Algorithms: The Implications of AI on the Legal Profession and the ABA Model Rules' (2023), 13, available at https://ssrn.com/abstract=4461276 or http://dx.doi.org/10.2139/ssrn.4461276.

[131] Ibid., 22.

of Law" points out, before using LLMs, lawyers should understand "to a reasonable degree how the technology works, its limitations, and the applicable terms of use and other policies governing the use and exploitation of client data by the product."[132]

24.4.3 *Duty of Confidentiality in the Client–Lawyer Relationship*

Lawyers are also bound by the duty of confidentiality and professional secrecy.[133] Accordingly, they must make reasonable efforts to prevent the inadvertent or unauthorized disclosure of, or unauthorized access to, information relating to the representation of a client.[134]

It is important to remember that chatbots usually store data from users' prompts.[135] It is also critical to note that service providers may have a provision in their terms and conditions that allows them to share such information with third parties or to use the prompts to retrain their models. Law firms themselves may train a model based on client data in their possession. They may then allow a third party to copy the trained model data and use it for their own purposes.[136] As a result, lawyers will need to anonymize or pseudonymize the information in their prompts. Alternatively, they could obtain the client's consent (for example, through the retainer agreement) before entering the client's information into an LLM.

A number of providers are currently attempting to ensure that data protection principles are respected when personal data is entered and processed in a chatbot – both technically and contractually. This has been done, for example, by anonymizing or pseudonymizing the data, or even by concluding appropriate contracts. However, it is currently uncertain whether lawyers can rely on information from such providers.

24.4.4 *Duty of Client Notice and Client's Consent to the Usage of LLMs*

Another issue that remains to be resolved is the extent to which lawyers must inform clients about the use of LLMs and whether they must obtain a client's consent.

In the United States, Rule 1.4 ABA Model Rules establishes a duty of reasonable communication between the lawyer and the client that is necessary for the client's effective participation in the representation. Specifically, paragraph (a)(2) of this rule requires the lawyer to reasonably consult with the client about the means to be used to achieve the client's objectives. Thus, it appears that a lawyer must inform the client about the use of LLMs to the extent that such use materially affects the lawyer's practice and the client's interests. Such communication should also include the risks and limitations of the LLM(s) being used. On the other hand, it is not necessary to provide a detailed description of the system's features or even to disclose the computer code, as such clarification may be beyond the client's understanding and may not necessarily affect their legitimate interests.[137]

Whether law firms are also required to obtain the client's informed consent for the use of AI applications is unclear. Neither the ABA Rules nor the CCBE Charter explicitly contain such a requirement. However, to be on the safe side, it might be advisable for law firms to specifically

[132] California State Bar (n. 116), p. 3.
[133] Rule 1.6 ABA Model Rules; Principle (b) CCBE Charter.
[134] Rule 1.6 ABA Model Rules.
[135] Christina-Maria Leeb, *Digitalisierung, Legal Tech und Innovation* (Duncker & Humblot, 2019), 272.
[136] CCBE/ELF (n. 28), 48.
[137] Martin Ebers, 'Transparenz und Erklärbarkeit', in *Stichwortkommentar Legal Tech* (1st ed., Nomos, 2023), para. 45; MIT, Task Force in Responsible Use of Generative AI for Law (n. 115), 4.

address in their terms the responsible use of LLMs, particularly in cases where the use of this technology has a substantial impact on the case. If necessary, an amended engagement letter could also be agreed upon with the client.

24.4.5 *Duty to Supervise Assisting Lawyers and Nonlawyers*

Lawyers also have a professional duty to supervise both lawyers and nonlawyers who assist them in the provision of legal services, to ensure that their conduct complies with the Rules of Professional Conduct. In 2012, the ABA clarified that the rule even applies when non-human assistance is involved. Based on this, the duty to supervise could apply to the use of generative AI tools. In addition, any language produced by generative AI must be reviewed for accuracy by a responsible human using authoritative legal sources.[138]

There are several preventive measures that can be taken to avoid breaches of due diligence in the use of LLMs by employees. First, firms can require that the technology used by lawyers in the firm must be preapproved by the firm (partners, chief information officer, and so on).[139] Second, it is important that employees are properly informed. All employees should be adequately trained and made aware of the risks of using LLMs. They should be informed that some data may not be processed or that automated decisions are generally not permitted. In addition, law firms should implement governance frameworks or develop policies on the responsible use of LLMs. This will help to identify, mitigate, and correct any breaches of due diligence early on. In order to monitor compliance with all due diligence obligations, it is also advisable to maintain adequate documentation of the use of LLMs.

24.4.6 *Advertising LLM-Based Legal Services*

Lawyers who advertise their LLM-based legal services must comply with certain advertising rules. According to Rule 7.1 ABA Model Rules, a lawyer shall not make a false or misleading communication about the lawyer or the lawyer's services. Similarly, Principle 2.6 CCBE Charter requires lawyers who inform the public about their services to ensure that the information is accurate and not misleading.

This was precisely the problem in the DoNotPay case discussed above.[140] This service was advertised as "The World's First Robot Lawyer," although the system was neither a lawyer nor a robot.[141]

Additionally, a commercial practice may also be considered misleading if a lawyer – using LLMs – claims that their services are "faster," "cheaper," or "better" than those of other providers, without being able to prove that this is actually the case. Blanket claims using buzzwords – such as "automated contract creation by artificial intelligence" – may also be considered misleading if the provider is actually just assembling text modules based on a simple if–then scheme.[142]

138 Rules 1.1, 1.3 and 5.3 ABA Model Rules; Principles (d), I and (g) CCBE Charter; Janine Cerny, Steve Delchin, and Huu Nguyen, 'Legal Ethics in the Use of Artificial Intelligence', 4 et seq., available at www.squirepattonboggs.com/-/media/files/insights/publications/2019/02/legal-ethics-in-the-use-of-artificial-intelligence/legalethics_feb2019.pdf.

139 According to a recently published study, which surveyed approximately 200 law firms worldwide representing approximately 100,000 lawyers, 49.5 percent of respondents believed that the use of LLMs in law firms should be approved internally; Jackowski et al. (n. 52), 226.

140 See above, Section 24.3.3.3.

141 Tewson (n. 100).

142 Michael Beurskens, 'So gut wie ein Anwalt? – Chancen und Grenzen der Werbung für Legal Tech Angebote' (2022) 1 *LegalTech Zeitschrift (LTZ)* 208 et seq.

24.4.7 *Evaluation*

Law firms and legal departments are expected to double-check the output of an LLM even if it seems plausible at first glance. Since AI applications often provide incorrect or incomplete answers, the output generated by the LLM should only serve as a starting point.

As a result, it is doubtful whether LLMs will make legal work more efficient.[143] Ultimately, the use of LLMs makes sense especially in areas where the risk of incorrect results is tolerable, or where it is more efficient to check the generated result than to produce it manually. Against this background, LLMs are probably not suitable for simple, highly standardized texts. In such cases, conventional templates may provide more reliable results. Furthermore, the use of LLMs to generate new text is particularly useful where there is a need to produce individualized text that cannot be produced by templates.

A recent report on the state of AI in legal practice shows that lawyers are quite aware of the risks. When asked what resources law firms need to successfully implement AI in their organizations, most (61.7 percent) of the more than 200 firms surveyed globally agreed that it is necessary to develop internal policies and guidelines for the use of AI and to provide additional training and education for both for lawyers and nonlawyers (52.2 percent).[144]

24.5 IMPACT OF THE EUROPEAN UNION'S AI ACT ON LEGAL LLMS

Finally, there is the question of how the recently published AI Act[145] will affect the legal tech market, and in particular LLMs used in the legal market.

24.5.1 *Broad Definition of AI and Risk-Based Approach*

According to Article 3 No. 1 AI Act, an AI system is "a machine-based system that is designed to operate with varying levels of autonomy and that may exhibit adaptiveness after deployment, and that, for explicit or implicit objectives, infers, from the input it receives, how to generate outputs such as predictions, content, recommendations, or decisions that can influence physical or virtual environments."

Since this definition does not specify the degree of autonomy and adaptation, almost all software applications seem to be covered, especially since – as Recital 12 AI Act clarifies – not only machine learning approaches, but also logic- and knowledge-based approaches that infer from encoded knowledge or symbolic representation of the task to be solved[146] are included.

However, this does not mean that all legal tech applications are subject to strict regulations. Rather, the AI Act has a risk-based approach.[147] While AI systems with unacceptable risk are prohibited, general-purpose AI (GPAI) models and high-risk AI systems must meet mandatory

[143] Mik (n. 49).

[144] Michał Jackowski and Michał Araszkiewiecz (eds.), 'LLI Whitepaper: First Global Report on the State of Artificial Intelligence in Legal Practice' (2023), 37, https://10.0.148.135/5501c854-14eb-4529-b6b9-44343e477f44.

[145] Regulation (EU) 2024/1689 of the European Parliament and of the Council of 13 June 2024 laying down harmonised rules on artificial intelligence and amending Regulations (EC) No. 300/2008, (EU) No. 167/2013, (EU) No. 168/2013, (EU) 2018/858, (EU) 2018/1139, and (EU) 2019/2144 and Directives 2014/90/EU, (EU) 2016/797 and (EU) 2020/1828 (Artificial Intelligence Act), OJ L 2024.

[146] According to Recital 12 AI Act only systems "based on the rules defined solely by natural persons to automatically execute operations" are excluded.

[147] Critically: Martin Ebers, 'Truly Risk-Based Regulation of Artificial Intelligence – How to Implement the EU's AI Act' (2024) *European Journal of Risk Regulation* 1–20, https://papers.ssrn.com/sol3/papers.cfm?abstract_id=4870387.

requirements before they can be placed on the market. Additionally, the AI Act establishes transparency requirements for certain AI systems such as chatbots and GenAI. All other systems, by contrast, are not subject to any specific regulation.

24.5.2 *Classification of LLMs Used for Legal Purposes*

24.5.2.1 Prohibited AI Practices

LLMs (generally) do not fall under the prohibitions of Article 5 of the AI Act, because they are not designed to manipulate or exploit natural persons, nor are they typically used to identify or categorize persons.

24.5.2.2 General-Purpose AI Models

The provisions of Article 51 ff. AI Act on General Purpose AI models only apply to providers of these models (OpenAI/Microsoft, Google, Meta, Anthropic), but not to their deployers (for example, lawyers using ChatGPT).

Companies that distribute software applications based on LLMs that are optimized for use in the legal field (such as Allen & Overy with ContractMatrix) are also not subject to the GPAI rules of the AI Act, because as soon as an LLM is trained or optimized for specific purposes, it is no longer to be considered a GPAI, since in this case the software – as Article 3 No. 63 AI Act requires – ceases to display "significant generality and is capable of competently performing a wide range of distinct tasks regardless of the way the model is placed on the market and that can be integrated into a variety of downstream systems or applications."

24.5.2.3 High-Risk AI Systems

Under the AI Act, LLMs that are developed for the legal market and used by law firms are not regarded as high-risk AI systems. Annex III of the AI Act primarily covers applications that are used by public authorities in sensitive areas, such as essential public services (healthcare, social services), law enforcement, migration, asylum, and border control.

In the area of administration of justice, Annex III.8a qualifies AI systems as high-risk only when they are "intended to be used by a judicial authority or on their behalf to assist a judicial authority in researching and interpreting facts and the law and in applying the law to a concrete set of facts, or to be used in a similar way in alternative dispute resolution."

This raises the question of how to determine the intended purpose of an AI system. If the purpose (also) depends on how a system is used in practice, an AI system such as ChatGPT (as well as software systems developed for the legal market in general) could be considered high risk under Annex III.8.a when used by courts to research/interpret facts or law, even if such a system has not been developed specifically for the judiciary. This would have far-reaching consequences, as providers might refrain from offering their software systems to the judiciary altogether if this is the only way to avoid classification as a high-risk system.

However, as Article 3 No. 12 AI Act clarifies, the "intended purpose" is to be determined according to the use "for which an AI system is intended by the provider, including the specific context and conditions of use, as specified in the information supplied by the provider in the instructions for use, promotional or sales materials and statements, as well as in the technical documentation." Providers, therefore, can specify through their operating instructions, technical documentation, and advertising and sales material that the LLM is intended for use only by law firms and private companies, but not by courts.

24.5.2.4 Other AI Systems

Ultimately, the only relevant provisions of the AI Act regarding LLMs used by law firms and legal departments are those contained in Article 50(1) AI Act for interactive AI systems and Articles 50(2) and 50(4) subparagraph 4 AI Act for GenAI. In contrast, the transparency obligations for emotion recognition systems (Article 50(3) AI Act) and deep fakes (Article 50 (4) subparagraph 1 AI Act) are still of minor importance for the legal sector and will therefore not be discussed in the following.

24.5.3 *Transparency Obligations for Certain AI Systems*

24.5.3.1 Transparency Obligations for Interactive AI Systems

Article 50(1) AI Act establishes special transparency obligations for providers of AI systems intended to interact directly with natural persons – that is, legal chatbots including Q&A applications. According to Article 50(1) AI Act, providers of these systems must ensure that these systems are designed and developed in such a way that those affected are informed that they are dealing with an AI system, unless this is obvious from the point of view of a natural person who is reasonably well-informed, observant, and circumspect, taking into account the circumstances and the context of use.

According to Article 3 No. 2 AI Act, a provider is a person who develops an AI system or a GPAI model or who has an AI system or a GPAI model developed, and places it on the market or puts it into service under its own name or trademark. Therefore, both providers of GPAI models (such as OpenAI with ChatGPT) and companies that develop LLMs specifically optimized for the legal sector (such as Harvey) must comply with the transparency obligations set out in Article 50(1) AI Act.

Law firms, on the other hand, are not subject to the transparency obligations of Article 50(1) AI Act, as they are only deployers – persons using an AI system (Article 3 No. 3 AI Act). However, as discussed above,[148] the rules of professional conduct may oblige law firms to disclose the use of LLMs to their clients.

24.5.3.2 Transparency Obligations for GenAI Systems

Transparency obligations also apply to providers of GenAI systems that, like LLMs, generate synthetic content (such as text). According to Article 50(2) AI Act, providers must ensure that the output of such a system is marked in a "machine-readable format and is detectable as artificially generated or manipulated." According to Recital 133 AI Act, such techniques include "watermarks, metadata identifications, cryptographic methods for proving provenance and authenticity of content, logging methods, fingerprints." However, the obligations do not apply to the extent that AI systems perform "an assistive function for standard editing or do not substantially alter the input data provided by the deployer or the semantics thereof." Since Article 50(2) AI Act only

[148] See Section 24.4.4.4.

imposes obligations on providers but not on deployers of GenAI systems, law firms are again not subject to these obligations.

The only transparency obligations directly applicable to law firms are those set forth in Article 50(4) subparagraph 2 AI Act. According to this provision, deployers of an AI system that generates or manipulates text which is "published with the purpose of informing the public on matters of public interest" are required to disclose that the text has been artificially generated or manipulated. What constitutes a matter of "public interest" is unclear. In principle, this could include general legal information published on a lawyer's website or in a newsletter.[149] However, even in this case, deployers are exempted from disclosure if the "AI-generated content has undergone a process of human review or editorial control and where a natural or legal person holds editorial responsibility for the publication of the content" (Article 50(4) subparagraph 2, 2nd sentence, AI Act). Law firms are therefore not required to disclose if they review AI-generated text and are editorially responsible for it.

24.5.4 *Relationship of the AI Act to UPL and the Rules of Professional Conduct*

Another question concerns the relationship of the AI Act to UPL and the rules of professional conduct. Does the direct applicability (and primacy) of an EU regulation over national law mean that the AI Act takes precedence over national rules on UPL and the professional codes of conduct, so that the use of an AI system that complies with the AI Act cannot be prohibited under national law?

In our opinion, the answer to this question is clearly no.[150] Since the AI Act does not regulate aspects of UPL or professional conduct of lawyers, it cannot displace national rules in this field, especially since relevant EU directives are based on the principle of mutual recognition of the different rules of professional conduct.[151] Conversely, a violation of the AI Act, in particular of the transparency obligations set out therein, could very well constitute a violation of the duty to conscientiously practice the profession in accordance with Section 43 of the Federal Lawyers' Act (BRAO).[152]

24.5.5 *Evaluation*

The AI Act will be directly applicable in all EU member states as of August 2, 2026.[153] Judicial and administrative authorities using AI applications must carefully check whether the provisions of the AI Act on high-risk AI systems apply to them and what requirements arise from this. Additionally, the AI Act foresees far-reaching obligations for providers of GPAI models (such as OpenAI) and LLM providers (such as Harvey). Law firms using LLMs to provide legal services are, on the other hand, only subject to minor transparency obligations.

[149] Further: Frank Remmertz, 'Legal Tech-Update im anwaltlichen Berufsrecht und im RDG' (2024) 3 *LegalTech Zeitschrift (LTZ)* 95, 100, according to which even advertising texts written by lawyers can fall under the provision.

[150] Martin Ebers, 'Die KI-Verordnung ante portas: Ein neuer Rechtsrahmen für Legal Tech?' (2024) 1(2) *LegalTech Zeitschrift (LTZ)* 1, 2; Remmertz (n. 149), 99.

[151] According to EU directives, a lawyer who provides services in another member state has to abide by two sets of rules: the rules of professional conduct of the host member state and those set by their home member state (so-called double deontology or Kumulationsprinzip); see Art. 4 Lawyers' Services Directive 77/249/EEC and Art. 6(1) Lawyers' Establishment Directive 98/5/EC.

[152] Remmertz (n. 149), 100.

[153] Art. 113 AI Act. Some provisions of the AI Act will apply even earlier (from February 2, 2025), such as the prohibitions in Art. 5 AI Act.

Accordingly, the Act will probably not have any significant impact on the market for legal services. However, in that respect it must be clarified whether the use of LLMs constitutes a case of UPL and what obligations arise for lawyers using LLMs under the existing rules of professional conduct

24.6 OUTLOOK

The advent of modern AI-powered LLMs is changing the delivery of legal services at a rapid pace, leading at the same time to a significant disruption of the legal services market. On a daily basis, new startups in legal tech spring up, introducing novel legal tech solutions, improved legal workflows, new business models, and increased interest in legal tech investments. In the United States alone, venture funding for legal tech startups was approximated at $700 million between January 2023 and February 2024, whereas the total legal tech market in the United States was estimated to be (approximately) $13 billion in 2023 growing at around 3.5 percent compounded annual growth rate (CAGR), and is expected to surpass $15 billion by 2026 – all heavily influenced by the recent advances in generative AI, particularly LLMs.[154]

In view of this dynamic situation, the foregoing analysis could only offer an incomplete snapshot of the many issues surrounding the use of legal LLMs – how LLMs are currently being used for legal purposes, including their benefits and risks (see Section 24.2); whether the use of LLMs can be considered unauthorized practice of law; whether UPL rules can protect consumers and other clients from hallucinatory LLMs (see Section 24.3); what law firms and legal departments need to do under existing rules of professional conduct when using LLMs for legal purposes (see Section 24.4); and how the EU's AI Act will impact legal LLMs (see Section 24.5).

Two key insights from this study stand out: First, the analysis of UPL rules in both the United States and Germany has shown that UPL rules are inadequate tools for protecting clients from hallucinatory LLMs. Based on this finding, it is suggested that legislators should consider alternative means – for instance, product-related approval procedures and certification schemes to audit the quality of the (legal) software and (in particular) of the training data. Second, the use of LLMs in the provision of legal services raises a number of unresolved issues under the existing rules of professional conduct. Here, it is currently unclear what standard of care and duty of competence is required when using LLMs, how confidentiality in the client–lawyer relationship is to be protected, and whether lawyers need to inform clients about the use of LLMs.

In light of these developments, it is encouraging to see the growing consensus within the legal tech community on the necessity for standards, benchmarks, and unified approaches to legal LLMs.[155] This collaborative effort, supported by law firms, bar associations, and regulators, will provide essential guidance on the ethical and effective use of LLMs in legal practice.

154 Megan Ma et al., *Generative AI Legal Landscape 2024* (Stanford Law School, March 2024), available at https://law.stanford.edu/publications/generative-ai-legal-landscape-2024-2/.

155 Richard Tromans, 'Why We Need Standards for Legal GenAI' (Artificial Lawyer, 1 July 2024), available at www.artificiallawyer.com/2024/07/01/why-we-need-standards-for-legal-genai/; N.N., 'GenAI Benchmarks Initiative – Key Points from First Meeting' (Artificial Lawyer, 6 August 2024), available at www.artificiallawyer.com/2024/08/06/genai-benchmarks-initiative-key-points-from-first-meeting/.

25

Generative AI and Article 6 of the European Convention on Human Rights

The Right to a Human *Judge?*

Mimi Zou and Ellen Lefley

25.1 INTRODUCTION

The public launch of ChatGPT in December 2022 sparked widespread excitement and concern about AI's potential and risks. The powerful capabilities of the latest generative AI models have captured public attention. For every article or social media post praising AI as a revolutionary solution to major challenges, there is another warning of its existential threat to humanity. Policymakers across various sectors are grappling with the same question: how can we harness the transformative benefits of AI while mitigating its risks?

The justice sector is no exception to the impact of AI. Regardless of whether one views AI as a transformative opportunity or an existential threat, it is essential to anticipate how new and emerging AI technologies are changing the justice system. Generative AI is already being used in courtrooms worldwide, with lawyers and self-represented litigants using chatbots and other AI tools for research and drafting submissions. Judges, judicial officers, and support staff are also increasingly utilising AI tools in their work, with judicial guidelines issued in several jurisdictions since 2023.[1]

For some, there has been a strong desire for the adoption of AI in the justice sector due to longstanding concerns about the inaccessibility of justice and the significant inequality between those who can afford lawyers and those who cannot. Consequently, even though not all risks have been identified, tested, or assessed, there is a compelling attraction to using AI chatbots for legal advice and drafting, as they are arguably far better than having no assistance at all.

The authors would like to thank Katherine Willetts of the University of New South Wales, Sydney for her invaluable research assistance, as well as Herbert Smith Freehills LLP for their pro bono research support in conducting initial scoping research on this topic.

[1] See Courts and Tribunals Judiciary, 'Artificial Intelligence (AI) – Judicial Guidance' (Judicial guidance in the UK on the use of AI in courts, 12 December 2023), www.judiciary.uk/guidance-and-resources/artificial-intelligence-ai-judicial-guidance/; Courts of New Zealand, 'Guidelines for Use of Generative Artificial Intelligence in Courts and Tribunals' (Judicial guidance in New Zealand on the use of AI in courts, 2023), www.courtsofnz.govt.nz/going-to-court/practice-directions/practice-guidelines/all-benches/guidelines-for-use-of-generative-artificial-intelligence-in-courts-and-tribunals/; Hong Kong Judiciary, 'Use of Generative AI for Judges and Judicial Officers and Support Staff of the Judiciary' (Judicial guidance in Hong Kong on the use of AI in courts, 2024), www.judiciary.hk/doc/en/court_services_facilities/guidelines_on_the_use_of_generative_ai.pdf.

Access to justice issues extend beyond just the affordability of legal advice. With record levels of court backlogs,[2] it has been a common occurrence for people to endure years-long delays in their cases. Looking to the immediate future, as more people are assisted by generative AI tools to understand, articulate, and assert their legal rights, the irony is that increasing access to advice may exacerbate the problem of delay. Indeed, the already overrun resources of the justice system may be stretched further, creating even greater strain. Therefore, the complexity of these challenges focuses our attention not only on how generative AI can help the public to help identify and express their legal problems, but also how it can assist in resolving them. This includes broader consideration of generative AI's role in dispute prevention, as well as alternative dispute resolution (ADR) and court proceedings.

Importantly, the potential for people to have legal problems resolved primarily or entirely by AI systems in the judicial setting is one that stirs up considerable debate. The Council of Europe's Ethical Charter on the use of AI in judicial systems identified one of the core principles to be respected as the need to ensure 'guarantees to the right of access to the judge'.[3] The Council of Bars and Law Societies of Europe also published in May 2023 a policy statement on AI and the justice system, stating 'a right to a human judge should be guaranteed at all stages of the proceedings'.[4]

On 13 March 2024, the European Parliament adopted the Artificial Intelligence Act (AI Act).[5] The AI Act came into effect in August 2024, marking the first legal regulation of AI in the EU. Annex III, Article 8(a) of the AI Act classifies certain judicial use of AI as 'high-risk':[6]

> 8. Administration of justice and democratic processes:
> (a) AI systems intended to be used by a judicial authority or on their behalf to assist a judicial authority in researching and interpreting facts and the law and in applying the law to a concrete set of facts, or to be used in a similar way in alternative dispute resolution;

This is elaborated in Recital 61:

> Certain AI systems intended for the administration of justice and democratic processes should be classified as high-risk, considering their potentially significant impact on democracy, the rule of law, individual freedoms as well as the right to an effective remedy and to a fair trial. In particular, to address the risks of potential biases, errors and opacity, it is appropriate to qualify as high-risk AI systems intended to be used by a judicial authority or on its behalf to assist judicial authorities in researching and interpreting facts and the law and in applying the law to a concrete set of facts . . . The use of AI tools can support the decision-making power of judges or

2 UK government statistics show delays have increased since the pandemic rather than recovered. For example, the average time for civil small claims to reach trial in England and Wales was 39 weeks in September 2019, which rose quickly to above 50 weeks during the pandemic. This figure has since reached 55.4 weeks in September 2023. See His Majesty's Courts and Tribunal Services, 'HMCTS Management Information' (National data on workloads and timeliness, His Majesty's Government, 2024), www.gov.uk/government/collections/hmcts-management-information. For criminal justice delays, see also National Audit Office, 'Reducing the Backlog in the Crown Court Report – Value for Money' (UK report on the Ministry of Justice court backlogs, 24 May 2024), www.nao.org.uk/reports/reducing-the-backlog-in-the-crown-court/.

3 Principle One of the Council of Europe, 'European Ethical Charter on the Use of Artificial Intelligence in Judicial Systems and Their Environment' (Adopted at the 31st Plenary Meeting of the European Commission for the Efficiency of Justice in Strasbourg, 3–4 December 2018), at 8.

4 Council of Bars and Law Societies of Europe, 'CCBE Statement on the Use of AI in the Justice System and Law Enforcement' (25 May 2023), at 1, www.ccbe.eu/fileadmin/speciality_distribution/public/documents/Statements/2023/EN_ITL_20230525_CCBE-Statement-on-the-use-of-AI-in-the-justice-system-and-law-enforcement.pdf.

5 Regulation (EU) 2024/1689 of the European Parliament and of the Council of 13 June 2024 Laying down Harmonised Rules on Artificial Intelligence, *OJ L* 2024/1689.

6 Annex III lists high-risk AI systems, pursuant to Article 6(2) of Regulation (EU) 2024/1689.

judicial independence, but should not replace it: the final decision-making must remain a human-driven activity.

In this context, a crucial question arises as to how judicial use of AI, especially considering the rapid advancements in generative AI, affects the right to a fair trial. This chapter examines the right to a fair trial as outlined in Article 6 of the European Convention on Human Rights (ECHR),[7] an international human rights treaty that covers forty-six countries in Europe and has given rise to an extensive body of case law. Various issues related to the interpretation and application of Article 6 of the ECHR emerge from this examination. Notwithstanding the AI Act's declaration that 'the final decision-making must remain a human-driven activity', our main concern in this chapter is whether Article 6 actually recognises the right to a human judge, with a focus on the civil limb of Article 6.

In addressing this concern, our analysis points to the lack of attention to date to the principle of human dignity in interpreting Article 6 of the ECHR in the context of judicial AI. We argue that human dignity necessitates a deeper understanding of Article 6, recognising the intrinsic value of human judgement, empathy, and the importance of being heard and respected by the decision-maker. Given courts are public institutions and the ultimate authority in resolving civil disputes, we find that a dignity-based interpretation of Article 6 includes the right to a human judge.

Our chapter is structured as follows. Section 25.2 analyses the potential implications of using generative AI in the civil justice system for key aspects of Article 6 of the ECHR. These include the right and access to a court within a reasonable time, the impartiality and independence of the judiciary, procedural fairness, and the right to a reasoned judgment. Although existing case law does not explicitly recognise a right to a human judge, Section 25.3 explores a richer understanding of Article 6 through the lens of human dignity. We conclude that this perspective gives rise to an interpretation of Article 6 that supports the right to a human judge. We also suggest how AI systems should be deployed in civil justice to complement, rather than undermine, human dignity.

While there are various definitions of 'generative AI', our working definition refers to AI systems that generate content, typically in the form of text, images, or other data, based on patterns learned from large datasets. These systems include different models – perhaps the most well-known at the time of writing are large language models (LLMs), on which applications like ChatGPT are based. Yet we do not consider it helpful to limit our analysis to the generative AI models available at the time of writing. Ever-increasing claims are being made about the latest models' capabilities and the reliability of their outputs, sometimes contradictorily even within the same company.[8] We therefore consider a prudent approach that takes into account the following:

(i) We cannot predict the scientific breakthroughs that will support new LLMs or alternative generative AI models in the near future, let alone over the next twenty years.

[7] European Convention for the Protection of Human Rights and Fundamental Freedoms, as amended by Protocols Nos. 11 and 14, ETS 5, 4 November 1950.

[8] At the launch of Meta's new LLM, Llama 3, in April 2024, Meta's head of global affairs, Sir Nick Clegg, said it had 'vastly improved capabilities like reasoning'. However, Meta's Chief Scientist Yann LeCunn has made clear his alternative modelling research – so-called world-modelling – is progressing precisely because an LLM is not reasoning: 'it certainly appears to most people as reasoning – but mostly it's exploiting accumulated knowledge from lots of training data'. See Hannah Murphy and Cristina Criddle, 'Meta AI Chief Says Large Language Models Will Not Reach Human Intelligence', *Financial Times*, 22 May 2024, www.ft.com/content/23fab126-f1d3-4add-a457-207a25730ad9.

(ii) Even if new models are released that claim to 'understand' or 'reason', we cannot equate these models with human understanding and reasoning.[9] It is important to consider the motivations of companies that may exaggerate their models' capabilities.[10]
(iii) Advancements in the development and deployment of this technology in courts will continue to appeal to those seeking solutions for an under-resourced and backlogged justice system.

If an AI-powered chatbot were used to determine a list of small claims today, it would be unsurprising to find some errors in its outputs. These erroneous outputs would be relatively straightforward to analyse: their unreasonable and arbitrary nature is very likely to breach an individual's right to a reasoned judgment under Article 6 of the ECHR. However, a more challenging scenario is when generative AI systems produce outputs in judicial processes that fall within a range of legally plausible outcomes – our focus here is on the impact of such a scenario on Article 6.

25.2 ARTICLE 6 OF ECHR AND IMPLICATIONS OF GENERATIVE AI

25.2.1 *Why Article 6 of the ECHR?*

As a preliminary point, it is important to explain why Article 6 of the ECHR, and human rights law more generally, deserves our focus in the context of analysing the impact of generative AI on civil justice. Ethical guidelines of the use of AI issued by numerous international organisations have consistently referred to the importance of the protection of fundamental rights generally[11] and the right to a fair trial specifically – for example, one of the key principles of the European Ethical Charter on the use of AI in Judicial Systems and Their Environment refers to the need to ensure that the use of AI does not 'undermine . . . the right to a fair trial'.[12]

In Europe, enforceable legal standards for automated data processing exist within data protection law. Article 9 of the Council of Europe's Convention 108+ secures the right for an individual 'not to be subject to a decision significantly affecting him or her based solely on an automated processing of [their personal] data without having his or her views taken into Consideration'.[13] This was then developed by the EU, first in its now invalid 1995 Data Protection Directive[14] and later in Article 22 of the General Data Protection Regulation

[9] For example, in September 2024, OpenAI released beta o1 advanced reasoning large language models which are 'designed to reason about hard problems using broad general knowledge about the world'. See OpenAI Platform, 'Reasoning Models' (Website, 2024), https://platform.openai.com/docs/guides/reasoning/reasoning.

[10] A Microsoft report in March 2023 titled 'Sparks of Artificial General Intelligence: Early Experiments with GPT-4' sparked criticism for creating such hype. An AI scientist unaffiliated with the study was quoted calling Microsoft's report an example of 'big companies co-opting the research paper format into PR pitches'. See Darren Orf, 'AI Has Evolved to Reason Like Humans, Scientists Say', *Popular Mechanics*, 16 May 2023.

[11] See, for example, Principle One of the Council of Europe, 'European Ethical Charter on the Use of Artificial Intelligence in Judicial Systems and Their Environment', at 7; United Nations Educational, Scientific and Cultural Organisation, 'Recommendations on the Ethics of Artificial Intelligence' (Adopted at the 41st session of the General Conference of the United Nations Educational, Scientific and Cultural Organization (UNESCO) meeting in Paris, 9–24 November 2021) at 28.

[12] Principle One of the Council of Europe, 'European Ethical Charter on the Use of Artificial Intelligence in Judicial Systems and Their Environment', at 8.

[13] Article 9(1)(a) of the Convention for the Protection of Individuals with regard to Automatic Processing of Personal Data (CETS No. 108).

[14] Directive 95/46/EC of the European Parliament and of the Council of 24 October 1995 on the protection of individuals with regard to the processing of personal data and on the free movement of such data, *OJ L* 281.

(GDPR).[15] Article 22 of the GDPR gives data subjects 'the right not to be subject to a decision based solely on automated processing [of their personal data], including profiling, which produces legal effects concerning him or her or similarly significantly affects him or her'.

Data protection laws, however, have their limitations for addressing potential risks arising from the judicial use of AI. Firstly, data protection laws are only engaged when a natural person's personal data is being processed. One can think of many types of civil disputes that involve non-personal information, such as a factual dispute where the data processed concerns the accounts of small businesses or a legal dispute involving the interpretation of case law. Secondly, data protection provisions only prohibit fully automated decision-making, and do not address the use of *assistive* generative AI (and provide no protection against it). Thirdly, there are broad exceptions in data protection law that require a rights framework to navigate. Both Convention 108+ and the GDPR permit exceptions to the prohibition on automated decision-making, as long as they safeguard the data subject's 'rights, freedoms, and legitimate interests' and 'respect the essence of fundamental rights and freedoms and constitute a necessary and proportionate measure in a democratic society'.[16] Therefore, in our analysis of the judicial use of generative AI, data protection law does not provide a complete answer.

Elsewhere in EU law, the impact on the right to a fair trial is explicitly referred to in the AI Act's reference in Annex III, Article 8(a) in the context of the use of AI in judicial decision-making as 'high-risk'. As discussed earlier, AI systems used by or on behalf of judicial authorities to assist in researching, interpreting, and applying the law to specific facts are classified as 'high-risk'. This classification is driven by concerns regarding the risks of biases, errors, and lack of transparency involved in such deployment of AI systems.[17]

However, Article 6(3) of the AI Act provides exceptions to the high-risk classification, namely where a high-risk AI system referred to in Annex III 'does not pose a significant risk of harm to the health, safety or fundamental rights of natural persons, including by not materially influencing the outcome of decision making'. According to the second subparagraph of Article 6(3), this exception applies to situations in which:

(a) the AI system is intended to perform a narrow procedural task;
(b) the AI system is intended to improve the result of a previously completed human activity;
(c) the AI system is intended to detect decision-making patterns or deviations from prior decision-making patterns and is not meant to replace or influence the previously completed human assessment, without proper human review; or
(d) the AI system is intended to perform a preparatory task to an assessment.

The AI Act does not define further the circumstances in which these relatively broad exceptions could apply. Potentially significant risks can still flow from such 'exceptions', when generative AI is applied in the judicial function to perform narrow procedural tasks (e.g. automated draft generation for routine court orders), improve previously completed human activity (e.g. AI enhancement of judicial opinions), detect decision-making patterns (e.g. generative analysis of judicial decision trends), and perform preparatory tasks (e.g. AI-generated case summaries and research memos). The application of 'exceptions' to high-risk AI is

[15] Regulation (EU) 2016/679 of the European Parliament and of the Council of 27 April 2016, *OJ L* 119.

[16] See Article 9(2) and 11(1) of Convention 108+. Article 22 (2)(b) and (3) of the GDPR indicates that data controllers themselves must safeguard rights, freedoms, and legitimate interests when they are making automated decisions under a contract or subject to consent. If it is pursuant to a member state law to which the controller is subject, the law itself must lay down suitable measures to safeguard the data subject's rights and freedoms and legitimate interests.

[17] Recital 61 of the Regulation (EU) 2024/1689.

complicated by the technology's capabilities, which are advancing quickly and continuously. What constitutes a 'narrow' task or 'preparatory' work when an AI can generate complex, nuanced text that mimics human-created content? Moreover, the cognitive impact of interacting with AI-generated content in judicial work is not yet fully understood.

As generative AI capabilities rapidly advance, there is a real risk that systems initially classified as exceptions under the AI Act could evolve to have more significant impacts, necessitating ongoing scrutiny. Overall, the provisions of the AI Act, despite their emphasis on human-driven decision-making, leave room for interpretation and potential loopholes. The AI Act may therefore be insufficient to ensure appropriate safeguards and oversight of high-risk AI systems used in judicial settings. This is where existing human rights frameworks provide important protections in addressing such gaps. Indeed, Preamble 6 of the AI Act requires that the use and regulation of AI be consistent with other fundamental rights and freedoms.

Therefore, in assessing the impact of judicial AI, we pay specific attention to Article 6(1) of the ECHR. Article 6(1) concerns the right to a fair trial in line with the rule of law in democratic societies. The text of Article 6(1) ECHR reads:

> In the determination of his civil rights and obligations or of any criminal charge against him, everyone is entitled to a fair and public hearing within a reasonable time by an independent and impartial tribunal established by law. Judgement shall be pronounced publicly but the press and public may be excluded from all or part of the trial in the interests of morals, public order or national security in a democratic society, where the interests of juveniles or the protection of the private life of the parties so require, or to the extent strictly necessary in the opinion of the court in special circumstances where publicity would prejudice the interests of justice.

Uses of generative AI in judicial functions and court processes raise a range of issues relating to four important aspects of Article 6(1) of the ECHR, which we examine in this section: (i) right and access to a court; (ii) independence and impartiality; (iii) procedural fairness; and (iv) right to a reasoned judgment. We note that the actual and potential impacts of generative AI deployment are likely to vary across different types of civil cases. As such, while we examine these aspects of Article 6(1) in light of potential opportunities and concerns, our analysis is by no means exhaustive, especially given the ongoing development and deployment of generative AI tools.

25.2.2 *Right of Access to a Court*

Perhaps the most appealing argument for those advocating for greater use of AI in the civil justice system concerns a central tenet of Article 6(1), which is access to a court. This mandates the provision of an effective judicial recourse for litigants to assert their civil rights.[18] The right of access to a court must be 'practical and effective', and not 'theoretical and illusory'.[19] In specific circumstances, the practical and effective nature of this right may be impaired, for instance, by the prohibitive cost of the proceedings in view of the individual's financial capacity, or by issues relating to time limits, including strict deadlines or prolonged appeal processes.[20]

Importantly, the right to access a court includes having one's case heard 'within a reasonable time'. This explicit requirement under Article 6 is based on the 'importance of administering

[18] *DH and Others v. the Czech Republic* [2007] ECHR 57325/00 (13 November 2007) § 49.
[19] *Bellet v. France* [1995] ECHR 23805/94 (4 December 1995) § 38.
[20] *Melnyk v. Ukraine* [2006] ECHR 23436/03 (28 March 2006) § 26.

justice without delays which might jeopardise its effectiveness and credibility'.[21] The European Court of Human Rights (ECtHR) has pointed out that excessive delays in the administration of justice have affected public confidence in the judicial system and seriously jeopardised the rule of law on which the ECHR was based.[22] Given the significant backlogs of cases that many courts face,[23] it is unsurprising that the European Ethical Charter on the use of AI in Judicial Systems and Their Environment has encouraged the application of AI to improve judicial efficiency and quality.[24] It is here that generative AI can make a difference in expediting the resolution of civil claims, reducing the costs of accessing a court, and alleviating the main barriers that may inhibit individuals from accessing the courts within a reasonable timeframe.

Generative AI-powered chatbots and virtual assistants can provide tailored information, resources, and guidance to court users, and even generate and draft relevant legal documents. Such LLM-based tools can offer invaluable support in navigating court processes and initiating or responding to legal proceedings promptly, particularly for self-represented litigants. The transcription capabilities of generative AI models potentially enable high-quality and efficient record-keeping of court proceedings, ensuring real-time documentation and facilitating post-hearing analysis. Furthermore, improved language accessibility for court users arises from LLMs' powerful translation capabilities and the ability to simplify complex legal language. By streamlining various court processes, generative AI can potentially reduce the overall cost and duration of legal proceedings, enabling many individuals to access a court within a reasonable timeframe.

The above applications of generative AI in civil justice processes are unlikely to be controversial, though they are not without concerns. In addition to data security and privacy issues, it is crucial to ensure fair and equitable access for all court users. Disparities in access could worsen existing inequalities in the justice system, undermining trust in the judiciary and confidence in the legal process, which is already difficult to navigate for many people worldwide.[25]

The more contentious landscape concerns the integration of generative AI in judicial decision-making, tapping into its immense potential in expediting fact-finding, legal analysis, and research, potentially alleviating significant case backlogs and reducing onerous judicial workloads.[26] The use of AI in this context necessitates careful consideration of its impact on various aspects of the right to a fair trial, such as those as examined below. A primary concern is the potential for AI-generated errors, such as hallucinations and bias built into AI systems, to

[21] *H. v. France* [1989] ECHR 5856/72 (24 October 1989) § 58; *Vernillo v. France* [1991] ECHR 11889/85 (20 February 1991) § 38.

[22] *Vanden Kerkhof v. Belgium* [2023] ECHR 13630/19 (5 September 2023).

[23] This ongoing problem for courts has led the European Commission for the Efficiency of Justice to develop and adopt a new tool to reduce the backlogs of court cases. See further European Commission for the Efficiency of Justice (CEPEJ), 'The CEPEJ Adopts Its "Backlog Reduction Tool": A New Roadmap for Identification and Addressing Structural Delays in Court Proceedings' (16 June 2023), www.coe.int/en/web/cepej/-/the-«backlog-reduction-tool»-the-cepej-s-new-roadmap-to-national-judicial-systems-for-identification-and-addressing-structural-delays-in-court-proceedings.

[24] Council of Europe, 'European Ethical Charter on the Use of Artificial Intelligence in Judicial Systems and Their Environment', at 5.

[25] JUSTICE, Preventing Digital Exclusion from Online Justice (April 2018), https://files.justice.org.uk/wp-content/uploads/2018/06/06170424/Preventing-Digital-Exclusion-from-Online-Justice.pdf; Victor D. Quintanilla, Kurt Hugenberg, Margaret Hagan, Amy Gonzales, Ryan Hutchings, and Nedim Yel, 'Digital Inequalities and Access to Justice', in David Freeman Engstrom (ed.), *Legal Tech and the Future of Civil Justice* (Cambridge University Press, 2023) 225–250.

[26] Sir Geoffrey Vos, 'Speech by the Master of the Rolls to the Bar Council of England and Wales' (20th Annual Law Reform Lecture at Lincolns Inn on Thursday 21 June 2023, Courts and Tribunals Judiciary, 18 July 2023), www.judiciary.uk/speech-by-the-master-of-the-rolls-to-the-bar-council-of-england-and-wales/.

cause delay and prolong court proceedings. These risks pose a potential obstacle to the right of access to a court, as they may introduce uncertainties and inaccuracies into the judicial process, risking the erosion of public trust in the legal system. Recognising the risks arising from AI-generated errors, judicial guidelines for the use of AI in court in the United Kingdom have specifically recommended that AI should not be used by judicial officers for legal research that cannot be independently verified.[27]

25.2.3 *Independence and Impartiality*

Independence and impartiality, as enshrined in Article 6 of the ECHR, are fundamental pillars of the judiciary. The principles are intricately connected and underpin essential democratic and rule of law principles.[28]

First, the independence of a 'tribunal' (terminology in Article 6 that covers a range of court-like institutions) from the executive and the parties is assessed by reference to the manner of appointment of the tribunal's members, the duration of the term of office of its members, the existence of guarantees against outside pressures, and whether the tribunal presents an appearance of independence.[29]

Generative AI has the potential to meet the demands of independence by being designed and operated externally to the executive or litigating parties. At present, much of the technological developments in AI occur in the private sector. While this private-sector development could potentially insulate AI systems from direct governmental influence, it also introduces new concerns. The risk of indirect influence through funding, development priorities, or data selection in AI training cannot be overlooked. Such influences, even if unintended, could undermine both the actual independence of AI-driven or AI-assisted judicial processes and the public perception of that independence.

To address these concerns and maintain the integrity of judicial independence, robust safeguards and transparency measures are crucial. One approach is to mandate transparent development processes for any AI systems intended for use in courts. This transparency could include full disclosure of funding sources, development methodologies, and design specifications, including open access to the training data. This would serve a dual purpose: it would allow for public scrutiny of potential influences on the AI system, and it would provide a new framework for assessing the 'appointment' and 'tenure' of AI in judicial roles – concepts that traditionally apply to human judges but need reinterpretation for AI systems.

However, implementing such measures is not without challenges. The private companies developing these AI systems may resist, citing concerns about trade secrets and competitive advantages. This resistance highlights the tension between the need for transparency in judicial processes and the proprietary nature of cutting-edge generative AI technology. Albeit not generative AI, the use of the COMPAS algorithm in the United States is a salient example. Developed and sold by a private company, originally Northpointe now Equivant, the COMPAS algorithm gives defendants a risk score, to be used by judges in the context of criminal sentencing and bail decision-making. Its methodology is a trade secret. The proprietary nature of the tool means judges cannot evaluate how the risk scores are determined or how factors are weighed to produce the risk score. This had led legal commentators and appeal judges to express

[27] Courts and Tribunals Judiciary, 'Artificial Intelligence (AI) – Judicial Guidance', at 6.
[28] *Kleyn and Others v. the Netherlands* [2003] 39343/98, 39651/98, 43147/98, 46664/99 (6 May 2003) § 192.
[29] *Langborger v. Sweden* [1989] 11179/84 (22 June 1989) § 32; *Kleyn and Others v. the Netherlands* § 190.

concern about the judicial competence in interpreting the outputs of such systems, and the independence and impartiality of the resulting judicial risk assessment exercise, when incorporating such technology.[30] Such concerns appear to be well-founded, given the evidence of discrimination against Black defendants, who are more likely to be falsely identified as high risk, while white defendants are more likely to be falsely identified as low risk.[31]

Turning to the requirement of impartiality under Article 6, a tribunal must be free from prejudice and bias. This is assessed in two steps. First, a subjective test necessitates that the tribunal be free from bias or prejudice in each case regarding the conviction of behaviour of a particular judge. Second, an objective test requires that the tribunal takes sufficient steps to exclude legitimate doubt of its impartiality.[32] Together, then, the requirement of independence and impartiality puts demands on tribunals to not only be free from prejudice, bias, and to be independent from the executive and the parties, but also to take steps to avoid the appearance of not having impartiality or independence.

The use of AI in judicial decision-making is sometimes represented as an opportunity to minimise human bias and prejudice, giving rise to perceptions of impartiality. However, this purported objectivity is over-simplified. AI systems are subject to human bias due to numerous points of human contact during their design, development, maintenance, and use.[33] As just one example during use, phrasing of questions or prompts can skew the outputs generated.[34] Bias and prejudice may also emerge from the training data and data sources available for the training of LLMs. This includes the use of training data that features historical bias and/or inequalities or is missing important data points.[35] As discussed further in Section 25.3, the risk of AI bias may not only undermine judicial impartiality but may also give rise to the potential of more exaggerated forms of discrimination, objectification, and dehumanisation of individuals before the court.

25.2.4 *Procedural Fairness*

Procedural fairness is a multifaceted requirement of Article 6(1). As a starting point, the principle of legal certainty constitutes one of the basic elements of the rule of law underpinning procedural fairness.[36] The use of generative AI in judicial decision-making may help to improve consistency in outcomes in similar cases, drawing on vast data related to judicial trends.

Another key component of procedural fairness encompasses the right of parties to present observations which they regard as relevant to their case. Generative AI tools can support the

[30] 'State v. Loomis' (2017) 130 *Harvard Law Review* 1530.

[31] Julia Angwin, Jeff Larson, Surya Mattu, and Lauren Kirchner, '"Machine Bias" and "How We Analysed the COMPAS Recidivism Algorithm"', *Propublica* (23 May 2016).

[32] *Wettstein v. Switzerland* [2000] 33958/96 (21 December 2001) § 43; *Micallef v. Malta* [2009] 17056/06 (15 October 2009) § 93.

[33] Aziz Z. Huq, 'A Right to a Human Decision' (2020) 10(3) *Virginia Law Review* 611–688 at 646–648.

[34] Law Council of Australia, 'Human Rights and Technology' (Submission to the Australian Human Rights Commission in response to its 'Human Rights and Technology Issues Paper', 2018) at 14, https://lawcouncil.au/publicassets/85d805e0-14d8-e811-93fc-005056be13b5/3533%20-%20Human%20Rights%20and%20Technology.pdf.

[35] Carston Orwat, 'Algorithmic Discrimination from the Perspective of Human Dignity' (2024) 12 *Social Inclusion*, https://doi.org/10.17645/si.7160; Felicity Bell, Lyria Bennett Moses, Michael Legg, Jacob Silove, and Monika Zalnieriute, 'AI Decision-Making and the Courts: A Guide for Judges, Tribunal Members and Court Administrators' (Australiasian Institute on Judicial Administration, 2022), at 2.

[36] *Beian v. Romania* (no. 1) [2007] 30658/05 (6 December 2007) § 39; *Lupeni Greek Catholic Parish and Others v. Romania* [76943/11] (29 November 2016) § 116.

preparation and presentation of submissions, arguments, and evidence brought forward by parties. Generative AI has capacities to produce and summarise case law, explanations, and articles to support the communication of legal knowledge in accessible forms to litigants. This can clarify an understanding of what might be relevant to bring forward as a litigant in a civil matter. These uses of generative AI may be of particular benefit in the context of fairness for those litigants who may be illiterate or do not speak English.

Procedural fairness also involves the appropriate consideration of the observations by the court and hence requires courts to conduct proper examinations of submissions, arguments, and evidence adduced by the parties.[37] The use of generative AI tools by judicial decision-makers in the consideration of submissions, arguments, and evidence adduced by parties raises challenging questions. One concern here (also discussed earlier) is that data processing in AI systems can be impacted by bias in ways that perpetuate or create discriminatory outcomes.[38]

Another possible concern is the so-called relationality gap between AI systems and humans. That is, AI knowledge is abstract and language-driven while human knowledge and interactions are rooted in a relational experience of the world.[39] This connects back to the classic syntax and semantic discussion as put forward by John Searle,[40] and since reconsidered in the context of symbol grounding problems and AI learning.[41] In the context of our discussion, these issues may provide justification for limitations on the use of generative AI in civil justice processes. For instance, in family law, the use of generative AI may require training data beyond the body of statute and case law to adjudicate cases that consider the sensitivity of matters where parties are particularly vulnerable.

A potential safeguard against concerns for discrimination or the relationality gap include human involvement and constant appraisal and refinement of programming in generative AI. There is additional potential benefit here of maintaining trust in the justice system and 'social legitimacy' of AI-informed decisions by keeping humans in the loop.[42] However, it is also worth considering that even with human involvement, perceptions that AI-generated content is objective and accurate may mean people might not appropriately scrutinise automated decisions.[43] Related to the idea of deference to generative AI on matters is a question about whether generative AI has legal authority comparable to that of a human judge, and therefore whether generative AI can act meaningfully within the obligations imposed by Article 6 as a judicial decision-maker.[44]

[37] *Donadze v. Georgia* [2006] 74644/01 (7 March 2006) § 35; *Kraska v. Switzerland* [1993] 13942/88 (19 April 1993) § 30; *Van de Hurk v. the Netherlands* [1994] 16034/90 (19 April 1994) § 59; *Perez v. France* [2004] 47287/99 (12 February 2004) § 80.

[38] United Nations Educational, Scientific and Cultural Organisation, 'Recommendations on the Ethics of Artificial Intelligence' at 20; Council of Europe, 'European Ethical Charter on the Use of Artificial Intelligence in Judicial Systems and Their Environment' at 8.

[39] Emily Bender, 'Resisting Dehumanisation in the Age of "AI"' (2024) 33(2) *Current Directions in Psychological Science*, https://doi.org/10.1177/09637214231217286.

[40] John R. Searle, 'Minds, Brains, and Programs' (1980) 3(3) *Behavioral and Brain Sciences* 417–424.

[41] See Steven Harnad, 'The Symbol Grounding Problem' (1990) 42 *Physica D: Nonlinear Phenomena* 335–346.

[42] Sofia Olhede and Patrick Wolfe, 'The Growing Ubiquity of Algorithms in Society: Implications, Impacts and Innovations' (2018) 376(2128) *Philosophical Transactions. Series A, Mathematical, Physical, and Engineering Sciences* 20170364, https://doi.org/10.1098/rsta.2017.0364.

[43] Elena Abrusci and Richard Mackenzie-Gray Scott, 'The Questionable Necessity of a New Human Right against Being Subject to Automated Decision-Making' (2023) 31(2) *International Journal of Law and Information Technology* 114–143 https://doi.org/10.1093/ijlit/eaad013.

[44] Tania Sourdin, 'Judge v Robot? Artificial Intelligence and Judicial Decision-Making' (2018) 41(4) *UNSW Law Journal* 1114.

25.2.5 *Right to Reasoned Judgment*

Article 6 of the ECHR imposes an obligation on courts and tribunals to provide sufficient reasons for their decisions, that is, 'adequately state the reasons on which their [judgments] are based'.[45] Such reasons demonstrate to the parties that their case has been actually 'heard'.[46] It also affords a party the opportunity to challenge and appeal a decision, with the possibility of having an appellate body review the decision.[47] The European Court of Human Rights has explained: 'The right to be heard therefore includes not only the possibility to make submissions to the court, but also a corresponding duty of the court to show, in its reasoning, the reasons for which the relevant submissions were accepted or rejected.'[48] Nevertheless, this does not require courts to give a detailed answer to every argument,[49] and the extent of the duty to give a reasoned decision will vary according to the nature of the decision.[50] Overall, this guarantee of a reasoned decision ensures judicial transparency, protects individuals against arbitrariness, and upholds the administration of justice.

Beyond the potential for drafting judgments, generative AI applications may also be used by judges to support fact-finding. For instance, a Dutch judge has used ChatGPT to assist in estimating the lifespan of solar panels in a civil matter.[51] Unlike an expert witness or a specific information source, such a fact-finding exercise may be difficult to reconstruct for the purposes of transparency. In addition to accuracy concerns, it also poses challenges for the ability of litigants to respond to the 'facts' sourced from generative AI.

At the time of writing, the United Kingdom's guidelines on the judicial use of AI notes that generative AI does not necessarily provide convincing or accurate legal analysis or reasoning.[52] Similarly, the judicial guidelines in the state of Victoria, Australia make it clear that 'Generative AI and Large Language Models create output that is not the product of reasoning. Nor are they a legal research tool. They use probability to predict a given sequence of words. Output is determined by the information provided to it and is not presumed to be correct'.[53]

An area of scepticism relates to the ability of generative AI to participate in the kind of reasoning required of judicial decision-making; that is, not merely deductive decisions based on facts and logic but involve discretionary decisions that include reflection on social values and the incorporation of 'soft decision-making factors' including intuition and inductive reasoning.[54] Due to the aforementioned relationality gap and the practical reality that generative AI seems unable to utilise factors such as compassion in reasoning, generative AI may well be

45 *Hirvisaari v. Finland* (2001) ECHR 49684/99 (27 September 2001) § 30.

46 *Fomin v. Moldova* (2012) ECHR 36755/06 (11 January 2012) § 31.

47 Ibid.

48 Ibid.

49 *Van de Hurk v. the Netherlands* [1994] ECHR 16034/90 (19 April 1994) § 61; *Case of Perez v. France* [2004] ECHR 47287/99 (12 February 2004) § 81.

50 *Ruiz Torija v. Spain* [1994] ECHR 18390/91 (9 December 1994) § 29; *Hiro Balani v. Spain* [1994] ECHR 18064/91 (9 December 1994) § 27.

51 See the civil law case of CLI:NL:RBGEL:2024:3636 (2024) § 5.7.

52 Courts and Tribunals Judiciary, 'Artificial Intelligence (AI) – Judicial Guidance', at 6.

53 Principle 8 of the Supreme Court of Victoria, 'Guidelines for Litigants: Responsible Use of Artificial Intelligence in Litigation' (Supreme Court of Victoria, May 2014), www.supremecourt.vic.gov.au/forms-fees-and-services/forms-templates-and-guidelines/guideline-responsible-use-of-ai-in-litigation.

54 Luís Greco, 'Judicial Power without Judicial Responsibility: The Case against Robot Judges', in Dário Moura Vicente, Rui Soares Pereira, and Ana Alves Leal (eds.), *Legal Aspects of Autonomous Systems. ICASL 2022. Data Science, Machine Intelligence, and Law* (Vol. 4., Springer, 2024), https://doi.org/10.1007/978-3-031-47946-5_12; Australian Law Reform Commission, 'Technology: What It Means for Federal Dispute Resolution' (Issues Paper No. 23, 1998), at 101.

inappropriate in decision-making especially in areas like family law where oral evidence and witness demeaner can provide insights. By contrast, generative AI may be a tool for reasoning in commercial civil matters, where chronologies and decisions are often recorded in paper trails. An option here may be to 'apportion discrete types of judicial decision-making to human actors based on subject matter or legal issues which raise particular justice concerns'.[55]

A key concern is also a lack of transparency and explainability associated with the 'black box' characteristics of AI decision-making, which can defy the idea of a 'reasoned decision'. This can invoke a transparency gap in which it may be impossible for humans to reconstruct and access the grounds on which AI came to a decision or output.[56] Explainability describes how much of AI reasoning can be accessible and is comprehensible if it is indeed accessible.[57] As captured by Greco's critique of 'robo-judges': 'For insofar as algorithms function as black boxes, they deny individuals any justification for the outcome adversely impacting them. Put plainly, individuals are denied the very thing that constitutes the lawfulness of the results affecting them, the thing that distinguishes the decision from a fiat pronouncement.'[58]

To address the 'black box' problem, there have developments in explainable AI research which aims to create understandable AI models that can shed light on their decision-making processes.[59] Whether in fully automated systems or as support tools in judicial decision-making, the ability to explain the actions of generative AI tools is crucial for the right to a reasoned decision. There can be technical safeguards such as requiring the disclosure and independent verification of the underlying AI models, as well as procedural safeguards for litigants to be able to respond and challenge elements of the decision generated by AI.

Despite the safeguards and interpretations developed around Article 6, a crucial question remains unresolved in the face of advancing AI: does the right to a fair trial inherently encompass a right to a human judge? While Article 6 has been interpreted to guarantee various aspects of a fair trial, including access to a court, independence, impartiality, procedural fairness, and the right to a reasoned decision, it has not explicitly addressed the nature of the decision-maker itself. As AI systems become increasingly sophisticated and their potential role in judicial processes expands, this gap in our interpretation of Article 6 becomes more pressing.

25.3 AI DECISION-MAKING IN COURTS: THE RIGHT TO A HUMAN JUDGE?

We have identified in Section 25.2 the safeguards in Article 6 which can be found explicitly listed in the article as well as extrapolated by the ECtHR. Unsurprisingly, the 'humanness' of the judge is not one of these safeguards. Over the past seventy-five years, it has not needed to be. Instead, Article 6 has been exercised in the face of threats which we already know about from centuries of human-driven justice, including inaccessible courts, corrupt judiciaries, opaque reasoning, and unfair procedures. We have shown that generative AI provides fresh challenges to these existing threats but may also provide some new opportunities to counter them.

[55] Tania Sourdin, 'Regulating Judge Artificial Intelligence (AI)', in Dário Moura Vicente, Rui Soares Pereira, and Ana Alves Leal (eds.), *Legal Aspects of Autonomous Systems. ICASL 2022. Data Science, Machine Intelligence, and Law* (Vol. 4, Springer, 2024), https://doi.org/10.1007/978-3-031-47946-5_13.

[56] Huq, 'A Right to a Human Decision', at 636.

[57] Elena Abrusci and Richard Mackenzie-Gray Scott, 'The Questionable Necessity of a New Human Right against Being Subject to Automated Decision-Making'.

[58] Greco, 'Judicial Power without Judicial Responsibility'.

[59] See Chapter 2 in this *Handbook*: 'Unleashing Creative Potential: Nurturing Trustworthy Generative AI' by Zijie Huang. See further Johannes Schneider, 'Explainable Generative AI (GenXAI): A Survey, Conceptualization, and Research Agenda', 15 April 2024, https://arxiv.org/html/2404.09554v1.

Yet the above analysis is incomplete, since generative AI, and AI more broadly, pose an additional threat to justice which requires considered analysis: the risk of dehumanisation in the context of AI judicial decision-making. We situate 'the right to a human judge' not as a novel idea to the corpus of human rights jurisprudence but advocate for a 'thick' reading of Article 6 which is underpinned by the principle of human dignity. In this section, we go on to argue that this dignity-informed interpretation of Article 6 can be used to elucidate a right to a human judge implicit in Article 6. Dignity must also be a guiding principle in which all AI systems can be integrated into the justice system.

25.3.1 *The Threat of Dehumanisation*

First, we must establish what we mean by 'dehumanisation'. This concept is detected in various guises in the literature examining the 'datafication' of society – that is, the abstraction of the world and its phenomena, including humans and their characteristics, experiences, and behaviours, into quantifiable and analysable data.[60] Vociferous data acquisition by powerful actors has been described as 'echo[ing] imperialist modes of accumulation'.[61] The increasing access to and use of data by powerful actors, either state bodies or multinational corporations, has been criticised for its intrusive nature through surveillance and commodification of private human experience, which manifests as a form of dehumanisation.[62]

Dehumanisation also underlies discussions of the discriminatory impacts of data-driven algorithms, including the ways in which certain groups are treated, excluded, and marginalised. For example, in the case of predictive policing algorithms, studies have pointed out that biased data is created through patterns of concentrated police powers and surveillance on majority Black and racialised communities. Such data leads to discriminatory outcomes that are then used to justify and perpetuate over-policing of those communities.[63]

As Deborah Raji points out, the dehumanisation occurs not only in the discrimination itself but also in the fiction of 'the data does not lie' and the purported accuracy or 'ground truth' in datasets that contain those biases.[64] Raji considers examples such as Google Image search results for 'healthy skin' that show only light-skinned women or ImageNet-trained models that label her (as a Black person) a 'bad person', a 'drug addict', or a 'failure'. She observes: 'data sets so specifically built in and for white spaces represent the constructed reality, not the natural one. To have accuracy calculated in the absence of my lived experience not only offends me, but also puts me in real danger'.[65]

60 See the definition of Mayer-Schönberger and Cukier: 'to datafy a phenomenon is to put it in quantified form so that it can be tabulated and analyzed'. Viktor Mayer-Schönberger and Kenneth Cukier, *Big Data: A Revolution That Will Transform How We Live, Work and Think* (John Murray, 2013), p. 78.

61 Jathan Sadowski, 'When Data Is Capital: Datafication, Accumulation, and Extraction' (2019) 6(1) *Big Data & Society*, https://doi.org/10.1177/2053951718820549, citing Jim Thatcher, David O'Sullivan, and Dillon Mahmoudi, 'Data Colonialism through Accumulation by Dispossession: New Metaphors for Daily Data' (2016) 34(6) *Environment and Planning D: Society and Space* 990–1006; Rosa Luxemburg, *The Accumulation of Capital* (Monthly Review Press, 1951).

62 Jose van Dijck offers a critical interpretation of datafication as 'a means to *access* … and *monitor* people's behavior'. See Jose van Dijck, 'Datafication, Dataism and Dataveillance: Big Data between Scientific Paradigm and Ideology' (2014) 12(2) *Surveillance & Society* 197–208 at 198. See also Shoshana Zuboff, *The Age of Surveillance Capitalism* (Profile Books, 2019).

63 Rashida Richardson, Jason Schultz, and Kate Crawford, 'Dirty Data, Bad Predictions: How Civil Rights Violations Impact Police Data, Predictive Policing Systems, and Justice' (2019) 94 *New York University Law Review* 192–233.

64 Deborah Raji, 'How Our Data Encodes Systematic Racism', *MIT Technology Review*, 10 December 2020, www.technologyreview.com/2020/12/10/1013617/racism-data-science-artificial-intelligence-ai-opinion.

65 Ibid.

The above examples point to another potential type of dehumanisation, connected to but distinct from discrimination: stripping the person of their individuality and autonomy. As Tennison has observed in the justice context, 'data by its nature flattens and categorises people, and isn't good at capturing complex contexts and nuance'.[66] If being treated humanely is to be treated as an individual, then people can be dehumanised in being not treated as individuals with autonomy and free will, but as categories. In other words, the use of generative AI in judicial decision-making may abstract and objectify people into 'algorithmic categories'.[67]

The potential dehumanisation brought by the deployment of generative AI in the justice system is linked to the question of its 'understanding' of the outputs that it is producing or approaching something like 'reason'.[68] It has been stressed that LLMs do *not* exhibit natural language understanding.[69] However, coherence is in the eye of the beholder. While LLMs may not 'understand' what the sequences of words mean, or have any intent to communicate, that does not stop humans' predisposition to interpret meaning and intent *into* what they listen to or read.[70] Anthropomorphising the output risks lulling the user into forgetting they are the only one in the conversation who is imbuing meaning. A potential aspect of dehumanisation could arise here, from the inherent deception of the interaction, should the human interpret coherence in the machine which has none.

In the context of judicial decision-making, socio-legal and psychological research on procedural justice offers valuable insights into how individuals experience and perceive judicial processes. An individual's 'satisfaction' with their experience of court is not merely determined by the verdict or outcome of their case. Instead, it is more directly linked to their perceptions of how fair the *process* itself was.[71] This insight is consistent across age, gender, education level, income, ideological beliefs, or ethnicity. In contrast, ideas of what constitutes a fair *outcome* in any given case can vary widely between different demographic groups.[72] Furthermore, court users' perceptions of fairness are shown to impact the legitimacy attributed to the institutions involved, and the likelihood of people accepting outcomes that are unfavourable to them.[73] In this context, Tyler identifies four factors that are important to individuals when they are subject to decision-making by an authority, and what it means to be treated fairly and 'humanely':

66 Jenni Tennison, 'Future of Courts' (Panellist remarks given at an event sponsored by the Nuffield Foundation and Legal Education Foundation in collaboration with UCL Faculty of Laws, Connected by Data, 14 May 2024), https://connectedbydata.org/events/2024-05-14-future-of-courts.

67 Yuval Shany, 'The Case for a New Right to a Human Decision under International Human Rights Law' (4 October 2023), http://dx.doi.org/10.2139/ssrn.4592244, at 38; Abrusci and Scott, 'The Questionable Necessity of a New Human Right against Being Subject to Automated Decision-Making'.

68 Jacob Browning and Yann LeCun, 'AI and the Limits of Language', *Noema Magazine*, 23 August 2022, www.noemamag.com/ai-and-the-limits-of-language//.

69 Emily Bender and Alexander Koller, 'Climbing towards NLU: On Meaning, Form, and Understanding in the Age of Data' (Proceedings of the 58th Annual Meeting of the Association for Computational Linguistics, Association for Computational Linguistics Anthology, July 2020), https://aclanthology.org/2020.acl-main.463/.

70 Ibid. See further Bender and colleagues, who coined the term 'stochastic parrots' to describe the way in which LLMs 'haphazardly [stitch] together sequences of linguistic forms … according to probabilistic information about how they combine, but without any reference to meaning'. Emily Bender, Timnit Gebru, Angelina McMillan-Major, and Shmargaret Shmitchell, 'On the Dangers of Stochastic Parrots: Can Language Models Be Too Big?' (Proceedings of the 2021 ACM Conference on Fairness, Accountability, and Transparency, 1 March 2021), https://doi.org/10.1145/3442188.3445922.

71 Tom Tyler, 'Introduction', in Tom Tyler (ed.), *Procedural Justice: Volume I. Procedural Justice and the Dynamics of Authority* (Ashgate, 2005), pp. xii–xiii.

72 Ibid., xv.

73 Ibid., xii; John Thibaut and Laurens Walker, *Procedural Justice: A Psychological Analysis Hillsdale* (Lawrence Erlbaum, 1975).

(i) the opportunity for individuals to express their views during the decision-making process (participation or voice);
(ii) unbiased decision-making (neutrality);
(iii) being treated with respect (respect); and
(iv) are willing to help and support them (trustworthiness).[74]

Considering these factors, we identify below some potential risks of dehumanisation should generative AI increasingly replace the functions of a human judicial decision-maker.

25.3.1.1 Voice

First, the concept of participation, or 'voice', is crucial to one's perception of fairness in judicial proceedings. It allows individuals to feel heard and to contribute their perspective to the decision-making process. However, the use of generative AI in this context presents significant challenges. While generative AI can process and analyse input, generating human-like responses, it cannot genuinely 'understand' in the way a human judge can. The output, while seemingly natural, is generated based on patterns in the training data rather than genuine understanding. The richness of tone, emotion, context, and cultural nuances that humans naturally perceive and interpret are processed by generative AI without true comprehension. This fundamental limitation of generative AI systems undermines the essence of participation.

Moreover, generative AI may give an illusion of a seemingly meaningful dialogue, asking follow-up questions and exploring various aspects of a case. However, this interaction is fundamentally different from a conversation with a human judge. The AI's responses, while potentially relevant and articulate, are generated based on statistical patterns from processing large amounts of data and executing complex algorithms. Without true understanding or empathy, the application of generative AI in judicial processes can lead to a false sense of the individual being heard. This can potentially be more dehumanising than no interaction at all.

An additional reflection emerges from potential differences in cultural communication and expression styles across Europe. There is an emerging body of research that identifies the problem of bias in relation to how generative AI outputs around non-Western cultural contexts entail 'superimposed Western interpretations of those contexts'.[75] Such models may struggle to accurately respond to diverse cultural contexts, potentially leading to misunderstandings or misrepresentations in communications with individuals from non-Western communities.

25.3.1.2 Neutrality

Generative AI models are trained on vast datasets of human-generated content. These datasets inevitably contain biases present in society, which the AI may amplify in its outputs. Unlike human judges, who can be trained to recognise and mitigate their biases, generative AI systems

[74] Steven Blader and Tom Tyler, 'A Four-Component Model of Procedural Justice: Defining the Meaning of a "Fair" Process' (2003) 29 *Personality and Social Psychology Bulletin* 747–758, 748–749; Tom Tyler, 'Procedural Justice and the Courts' (2007) 44 *Court Review* 26–31.

[75] Dan M. Kotliar, 'Data Orientalism: On the Algorithmic Construction of the Non-Western Other' (2020) 49(5) *Theory and Society* 919. See further Sourojit Ghosh, Pranav Narayanan Venkit, Sanjana Gautam, Shomir Wilson, and Aylin Caliskan, 'Do Generative AI Models Output Harm while Representing Non-Western Cultures: Evidence from A Community-Centered Approach' (paper accepted at 7th AAAI/ACM Conference on AI, Ethics, and Society, 21–23 October 2024), https://arxiv.org/pdf/2407.14779.

may perpetuate and even exacerbate biases without the ability to self-reflect or adjust based on changing and nuanced ethical considerations.

The concept of neutrality in judicial decision-making goes beyond mere absence of bias. It requires a nuanced understanding of context and an ability to recognise and account for one's own limitations. There is a common misconception that empathy is at odds with impartiality. However, empathy is better understood as 'our capacity to better comprehend – through both knowledge and feeling – another's perspective by trying to view the world from that person's position, rather than simply observing another's position from where we stand'.[76] Sourdin highlights the underlying importance of the emotional authority of judges in moral decision-making which allows judges to respond to parties in ways that uphold compassion and underscore fundamental rights of dignity.[77] While generative AI can produce empathetic-sounding language, it is not capable of understanding the lived experiences that shape an individual's actions and circumstances.

Building on this, we argue that neutrality in judicial decisions require a deep understanding of societal norms, cultural contexts, and evolving social values. Generative AI is unable to achieve this level of understanding of changing social changes and emerging ethical considerations. This can result in decisions that fail to account for the current social and human context.

25.3.1.3 Respect

The element of respect in judicial proceedings encompasses more than just polite treatment; it involves recognising the inherent dignity of each individual and acknowledging their rights and humanity throughout the process. While generative AI can be programmed to acknowledge individual circumstances and experiences, it cannot truly recognise the unique human dignity of each person. This lack of genuine recognition can be particularly damaging in cases involving sensitive or traumatic experiences, where human understanding and compassion are crucial.

Human judges can adapt their communication style based on the needs and capabilities of the individuals appearing before them. Judicial styles can vary – for example, some judges may be more 'responsive' than others and/or 'show more emotion and compassion or be oriented towards therapeutic justice'.[78] Nevertheless, the absence of personal interactions with a human judge presents a risk of 'dehumanising' communication. Generative AI, despite its ability to produce varied language, lacks the intuitive ability to truly adapt its communication style to the emotional and cognitive needs of diverse individuals. The technology is, after all, selecting the statistically more likely word among different options. For example, it may end up using overly technical language when describing personal and emotional matters, which can contribute to a sense of being treated as a 'case' rather than a person.

25.3.1.4 Trustworthiness

Trustworthiness involves not just the reliability of decisions, but also the perception that the judiciary is able to support those who are subject to its authority. The introduction of generative AI into judicial decision-making poses several challenges to building and maintaining this trust.

[76] Rebecca K. Lee, 'Judging Judges: Empathy as the Litmus Test for Impartiality' (2014) 82 *University of Cincinnati Law Review* 145–206. On the importance of humility to the role of the judge, see also Sir Mark Hedley, *The Modern Judge: Power, Responsibility and Society's Expectations* (Jordan Publishing, 2016).

[77] Sourdin, 'Regulating Judge Artificial Intelligence (AI)'.

[78] Sourdin, 'Judge v Robot?'

While generative AI may provide 'explanations' for its decisions, these explanations are generated post hoc and may not reflect the actual pathways by which the decision was made, which can potentially eroding users' trust in the process. The complex neural networks behind advanced AI models are often opaque, even to their creators. It is unsurprising that explainable AI has become a significant area of research among legal AI researchers.[79] Their 'black box' characteristics make it difficult to truly understand how and why certain decisions were made. AI researchers have further pointed out the significant challenges of testing and evaluating LLMs due to the 'sheer scale of data and training, plus the proprietary nature of LLMs'.[80]

Where there are inaccuracies produced by generative AI, such errors in a judicial context could have severe consequences and significantly undermine trust in the system. The potential for these errors, even if they are rare, can make it difficult for individuals to fully trust decisions flowing from generative AI-driven judicial processes.

Moreover, AI systems cannot be held accountable for their decisions in the way human judges can. Unlike human judges who can be questioned, challenged, and held personally accountable for their decisions and reasoning, it is doubtful that AI systems possess moral culpability.[81] This diffusion of responsibility can further erode users' trust in the judicial system. The use of generative AI here requires serious rethinking of judicial accountability and responsibility. When problems arise in the process, to whom (or what) do we attribute responsibility?[82] As Greco highlights, this issue is not one to be taken lightly, especially considering the potential use of generative AI in decision-making may represent a 'historically unprecedented detachment of the exercise of power from individual responsibility'.[83]

Overall, the potential dehumanising effects of the use of AI in judicial decision-making are multifaceted and can significantly undermine the right to a fair trial. Considering this threat, we argue that the principle of dignity should underpin a 'thick' interpretation of the protections offered by Article 6.

25.3.2 *Protection from Dehumanisation: Human Dignity and Article 6 of the ECHR*

The concept of 'human dignity' became prevalent in international human rights legal instruments after the atrocities of the Second World War.[84] The Preamble of the UN Charter in 1945 cites the 'untold sorrow to mankind' of the world wars alongside its statement of purpose: to 'reaffirm faith in fundamental human rights, in the dignity and worth of the human person'.[85] Similarly, the Universal Declaration of Human Rights (UNHR) in 1948 recognises in its

[79] See, for example, Joe Collenette, Katie Atkinson, and Trevor Bench-Capon, 'Explainable AI Tools for Legal Reasoning about Cases: A Study on the European Court of Human Rights' (2023) 317 *Artificial Intelligence* 103861; Ashley Deeks, 'The Judicial Demand for Explainable Artificial Intelligence' (2019) 119 *Columbia Law Review* 1829.

[80] Ananya, 'AI's Understanding and reasoning skills can't be assessed by current tests', *Science News*, 10 July 2024, www.sciencenews.org/article/ai-understanding-reasoning-skill-assess.

[81] It is outside the scope of this chapter to discuss the philosophical debates on whether autonomous AI has moral responsibility. A good discussion of relevant issues can be found in Mihaela Constantinescu, Constantin Vică, Radu Uszkai, and Cristina Voinea, 'Blame It on the AI? On the Moral Responsibility of Artificial Moral Advisors' (2022) 35 *Philosophy and Technology* 1–26, https://doi.org/10.1007/s13347-022-00529-z.

[82] For more discussion, see Greco, 'Judicial Power without Judicial Responsibility'.

[83] Ibid.

[84] Christopher McCrudden, 'Human Dignity and Judicial Interpretation of Human Rights' (2008) 19(4) *European Journal of International Law* 655–724 at 667.

[85] Paragraph 2 in the Preamble of the Charter of the United Nations, 1 UNTS XVI, 24 October 1945.

Preamble 'barbarous acts which have outraged the conscience of mankind',[86] before asserting the 'inherent dignity and the equal and unalienable rights of all members of the human family'.[87] It also goes further than the UN Charter and dedicates its first article to dignity: 'All human beings are born free and equal in dignity and rights. They are endowed with reason.'

Human dignity maintains its prevalence in human rights instruments throughout the second half of the twentieth century. The 1976 International Covenant on Civil and Political Rights states that rights 'derive from the inherent dignity of the human person', and that the recognition of 'inherent dignity' and of 'the equal and inalienable rights of all members of the human family' is the 'foundation of freedom, justice and peace in the world'.[88] Further, in more specific international human rights legal instruments, for example those aimed at children or people with disabilities,[89] human dignity remains a ubiquitous concept.

While it was unusual for the drafters of the ECHR not to cite human dignity explicitly in 1950,[90] a careful reading of the Convention reveals its implicit presence.[91] The Preamble directly invokes the UDHR, which was only a few months old when the ECHR was being drafted. Indeed, many of the ECHR drafters had also drafted the UDHR, and the Convention was in many ways a *continuation* of their work, not a separate project. The Preamble of the ECHR goes on to state as its purpose not to rewrite or replace the UNDR, but rather to 'take the first steps for the collective enforcement of certain of the rights stated in the Universal Declaration'. The UNDR is therefore not superseded but rather incorporated as the foundation of the ECHR, the latter seeking make the human dignity and rights in the former practically enforceable. The ECtHR has repeatedly agreed with this view and found that 'human dignity and human freedom' are the 'very essence' of the ECHR.[92]

While human dignity is relevant to the ECHR, how to apply the principle can sometimes be unclear. McCrudden has argued that dignity as a standalone right is too vague.[93] The fact that the drafters of the ECHR did not explicitly include dignity as a standalone right may reinforce this view. Instead, it is more useful to consider it as a fundamental principle underlying the interpretation of specific rights within the ECHR. In this sense, the principle of dignity can support the interpretation of other rights, including their scope and application, having what has been called an 'indirect legal effect'.[94]

We consider this function of human dignity to be particularly apt to the ECHR when understanding it as a living instrument. As Sir Humphrey Waldock (former President of the

86 Paragraph 2 of the Universal Declaration of Human Rights, 217 A (III), 10 December 1948.

87 Ibid., Paragraph 3.

88 Paragraphs 2 and 3 of the Preamble of the International Covenant on Civil and Political Rights, United Nations, Treaty Series, Vol. 999, p. 171, 16 December 1966.

89 Sebastian Heselhaus and Ralph Hemsley, 'Human Dignity and the European Convention on Human Rights', in Paolo Becchi and Klaus Mathis (eds.), *Handbook of Human Dignity in Europe* (Springer, 2019) pp. 1–24.

90 In fact, the word 'dignity' was included for the first time in the Convention in 2002 upon the introduction of Protocol 13 on the abolition of the death penalty. The Preamble states at Paragraph 1: 'everyone's right to life is a basic value in a democratic society and that the abolition of the death penalty is essential for the protection of this right and for the full recognition of the inherent dignity of all human beings'.

91 Jean-Paul Costa has also argued that the absence of human dignity is due to technical and practical alignments of the ECHR rather than its irrelevance to the ideas that underpinned it. See Jean-Paul Costa, 'Human Dignity in the Jurisprudence of the European Court of Human Rights', in Christopher McCrudden (ed.), *Understanding Human Dignity – Proceedings of the British Academy* (Vol. 192, Oxford University Press, 2013) pp. 393–402, at 394.

92 *Christine Goodwin v. UK* [2002] 28967/95 (11 July 2002) § 90.

93 McCrudden, 'Human Dignity and Judicial Interpretation of Human Rights'.

94 Heselhaus and Hemsley, 'Human Dignity and the European Convention on Human Rights', quoting Lennart von Schwichow, 'Die Menschenwürde in der EMRK', in W. Marauhn (ed.), *Jus Internationale et Europaeum* (Vol. 123, 2016).

Court) once put it: 'The meaning and content of the provisions of the ECHR will be understood as intended to evolve in response to changes in legal or social concepts.'[95] This approach is particularly valuable when faced with novel contexts, such as the integration of AI into judicial processes. Human dignity can serve as a guiding principle, ensuring that the interpretation of evolution of rights remains consistent with the ECHR's core values.

In delving deeper into the interpretative value of the principle, McCrudden has identified a minimum core of three elements making up a substantive idea of dignity. The first, the 'ontological claim', is that every human being possesses an intrinsic worth, merely by being human. The second is that this intrinsic worth should be recognised and respected by others, and some forms of treatment by others are inconsistent with, or required by, respect for this intrinsic worth. This is the 'relational claim'. The third is the recognition that 'the state should be seen to exist for the sake of the individual human being, and not vice versa (the limited-state claim)'.[96]

While McCrudden himself still finds dignity to have an 'impossible vagueness' in the diversity of contextual meanings that it can take on, he agrees with Clapham that there are four values to which dignity seems particularly closely and consistently related: (1) the prohibition of all types of inhuman treatment, humiliation, or degradation by one person over another; (2) the assurance of the possibility for individual choice and the conditions for each individual's self-fulfilment, autonomy, or self-realisation; (3) the recognition that the protection of group identity and culture may be essential for the protection of personal dignity; (4) the creation of the necessary conditions for each individual to have their essential needs satisfied.[97]

Given these potential threats to human dignity, we propose a 'thick' interpretation of Article 6 of the ECHR, guided by the principle of human dignity. This interpretation would: (1) recognise the intrinsic worth of everyone appearing before a court, ensuring that they are treated as unique human beings rather than mere data points; (2) guarantee meaningful participation in the judicial process, including the ability to be truly heard and understood; (3) ensure that decisions are made with genuine understanding of the human context, including cultural and personal factors; (4) maintain transparency and explainability in the decision-making process, allowing individuals to understand and potentially challenge the reasoning behind judgments; and (5) preserve moral accountability in the judicial system, recognising that justice is fundamentally a human concept that requires human understanding and responsibility.

Based on these considerations, we argue that a dignity-informed reading of Article 6 implicitly secures the right to a human judge. This interpretation recognises that the essence of a fair trial, as envisioned in the ECHR, relies on human judgment, empathy, and understanding that cannot be fully replicated by AI systems.

25.3.3 *Potential Counterarguments*

While the case for a human judge based on dignity is strong, several counterarguments merit consideration. First, it may be argued that respecting human dignity includes respecting an

[95] Sir Humphrey Waldock, 'The Evolution of Human Rights Concepts and the Application of the European Convention on Human Rights', in André Gros and Paul Reuter (eds.), *Mélanges offerts à Paul Reuter: le droit international: unité et diversité* (Pedone, 1981), 547.

[96] McCrudden, 'Human Dignity and Judicial Interpretation of Human Rights'.

[97] Ibid., at 686, citing Andrew Clapham, *Human Rights Obligations of Non-State Actors* (Oxford University Press, 2006), at 545–546.

individual's choice to have their case decided by an AI if they prefer. Second, as discussed earlier in Section 25.2, the current human-based judicial system often results in significant delays and unequal access to courts. An AI-based system, especially using generative AI, could potentially offer quicker, more affordable, and more consistent access to justice. Finally, some would argue that human judges are susceptible to various biases, which can compromise the fairness of trials. AI systems, if properly designed, could potentially reduce certain types of bias, thereby enhancing the dignity of all parties by ensuring more equitable treatment.

While these counterarguments raise valid points, they do not necessarily negate the need for human judges. Instead, they highlight the need for a nuanced approach that balances various aspects of human dignity. We propose the following considerations. First, rather than replacing human judges with AI, efforts should focus on addressing and mitigating human biases through training, diverse judicial appointments, and accountability measures. Second, AI can be valuable in automating non-judicial tasks, providing research assistance, and identifying potential biases or inconsistencies for human review. This approach preserves human judgment while leveraging AI's strengths. Third, for cases where parties might prefer a more automated or rapid process, improving access to ADR mechanisms (where informed consent can be obtained) could provide options without compromising the core judicial system. We note that the AI Act refers to the use of AI in ADR, with Recital 61 providing that 'AI systems intended to be used by alternative dispute resolution bodies for [the purposes of the administration of justice and democratic processes] should also be considered to be high-risk when the outcomes of the alternative dispute resolution proceedings produce legal effects for the parties'. Fourth, whether AI is used in supporting roles or in ADR, emphasis should be placed on transparency and explainability of AI-assisted processes, ensuring that human dignity is respected through the informed participation of all stakeholders. Finally, the integration of AI into any part of the judicial system should be subject to ongoing ethical review, with a focus on preserving human dignity in upholding the right to a fair trial.

Dignity is particularly important in the context of interactions between the civil justice system and marginalised and vulnerable populations. For instance, the European Commission Strategy for the Rights of Persons with Disabilities 2021–2030 and the Directive (EU) 2019/882 on the accessibility requirements for products and services specifically emphasise the importance of accessibility of use of technology for people living with disabilities or functional limitations.[98] In this context, the use of generative AI in courts or in parties' preparation for judicial proceedings must consider the accommodation and support of needs associated with the disabilities that people may live with. Here assistive AI technology, designed to support people with specific disabilities to promote dignity, independence, and facilitate participation, may be used to support their access to courts.[99] The deployment of generative AI in this context would recognise the importance of human interaction (including interaction with a human judge) in facilitating access and supporting access to justice for marginalised groups in an inclusive way, which is underpinned by respect for dignity of all.

[98] See Directive (EU) 2019/882 of the European Parliament and of the Council of 17 April 2019 on the accessibility requirements for products and services, *OJ L* 151.

[99] Mihalis Kritikos, 'Assistive Technologies for People with Disabilities: Part IV: Legal and Socio-ethical Perspectives' (Scientific Foresight Unit (Science and Technology Options Assessment) of the European Parliamentary Research Service, 2018) at 4, www.europarl.europa.eu/RegData/etudes/IDAN/2018/603218/EPRS_IDA(2018)603218(ANN4)_EN.pdf.

25.4 CONCLUSION

The United Nations Educational, Scientific and Cultural Organization's Recommendations on the Ethics of Artificial Intelligence reiterates that in interactions with AI, humans 'should never be objectified nor should their dignity be otherwise undermined, or human rights and fundamental freedoms violated'.[100] The principle of human dignity, deeply rooted in international human rights law and implicitly present in the ECHR, provides a crucial guiding framework for interpreting the right to a fair trial under Article 6 of the ECHR in the face of technological advancements. This necessarily implies a right to have one's case heard and decided by a human judge. While generative AI presents significant opportunities to enhance certain aspects of the right to a fair trial, its implementation must be carefully managed to avoid the risks of dehumanisation. The right to a fair trial is fundamentally about ensuring justice for human beings, by human beings. A dignity-centred interpretation of Article 6 strongly suggests the need to preserve human judges at the core of the judicial process in the age of AI.

[100] United Nations Educational, Scientific and Cultural Organisation, 'Recommendations on the Ethics of Artificial Intelligence', at 18.

26

Generative AI in Public Administration

Sophie Weerts

26.1 INTRODUCTION

In January 2024, the European Commission (EC) stated: "The advent of generative AI marks a transformative shift: unprecedented possibilities for supporting our staff, reducing administrative burden, and enhancing quality and impact of the Commission's work."[1] The Court of Justice of the European Union (CJEU) also emphasized that in the future, all staff members could benefit from an AI-powered virtual assistant, AI avatars could be used to deliver internal training and to produce didactic materials, and the case management system (SIGA) could be completed with capabilities for generating classification indicators and case correlation.[2] Such discourses echo the narratives of global consultancy firms and other organizations concerning the need to modernize the functioning of governments through innovative artifacts.[3] Generative AI should change ways of working by eliminating repetitive tasks, reducing the risk of human error, saving time in file processing, improving services for users, and supporting workers in processing individual requests and their integration into the organization.[4]

Generative AI appears to offer a new lever for re-enchanting public administration, having the potential to contribute to a new turn in the project of "reinventing government" through

[1] European Commission, 'Communication to the Commission, Artificial Intelligence in the European Commission (AI@EC) A strategic vision to foster the development and use of lawful, safe and trustworthy Artificial Intelligence systems in the European Commission' (Brussels, 2024), p. 2.

[2] Court of Justice of the European Union, 'Artificial Intelligence Strategy' (2023), available at https://curia.europa.eu/jcms/upload/docs/application/pdf/2023-11/cjeu_ai_strategy.pdf (last consulted 16 January 2025).

[3] McKinsey & Company, 'Deploying Generative AI in US State Governments: Pilot, Scale, Adopt', February 2024, available at www.mckinsey.com/industries/public-sector/our-insights/deploying-generative-ai-in-us-state-governments-pilot-scale-adopt (last consulted 21 May 2024); World Government Summit and Accenture, 'Generative AI & Government: How Can Government Agencies Responsibly Navigate the AI Landscape to Implement High Impact Generative Solutions?', February 2024, available at www.worldgovernmentsummit.org/observer/reports/2024/detail/generative-ai-government-how-can-government (last consulted 21 May 2024).

[4] World Economic Forum, 'Jobs of Tomorrow: Large Language Models and Jobs, White Paper', September 2023, available at www.weforum.org/publications/jobs-of-tomorrow-large-language-models-and-jobs/ (last consulted 21 May 2024); N. B. Martin, E. Brynjolfsson, and A. Korinek, 'Machines of Mind: The Case for an AI-Powered Productivity Boom', Brookings, 10 May 2023, available at www.brookings.edu/articles/machines-of-mind-the-case-for-an-ai-powered-productivity-boom/ (last consulted 21 May 2024).

technology.[5] Since the 1990s, the deployment of the internet and the development and implementation of information technology in government has been expected to improve access and use of government services[6] and reframe bureaucracy for "e-government" or "smart government."[7] In this regard, and from a public administration perspective, AI and big data have already opened the door to "new public analytics," an innovative way of renewing public administration.[8] The deployment of generative AI systems could then be the ultimate stage in this digital transformation of public administration, but users may not understand their disruptive effects on administrative organizations and power.

From practical and scholarly perspectives, use cases are generally recent, poorly documented, and occasional. Literature on generative AI in public administration and administrative law is also in its infancy.[9] In that context, this chapter aims to explore how public administration regulates the deployment of generative AI through the analysis of regulations and policies of the United States and the European Union, both key players in technology and regulations of AI and sharing a common legal basis (the rule of law).[10] It focuses on internal administrative issues, echoing one of the two dimensions that have shaped the division between public administration studies and administrative law.[11] Adopting a regulation studies perspective, this explorative analysis sheds light on the approaches to regulating the development and deployment of generative AI in public administration. It also illuminates not only the key legal issues that the deployment of such technology poses in public administration but also the main administrative values and principles that need to be guaranteed.

In the following sections, we first provide some background about public administration, administrative law, and technology (Section 26.2). Next, we map the US and EU regulatory instruments adopted in the context of the deployment of generative AI, distinguishing between command-and-control, preventive, and experimental measures (Section 26.3). Such mapping will then enable us to identify not only the legal issues established by authorities but also the intentions pursued in terms of deployment, as well as the values and principles promoted by the administrative and legislative authorities (Section 26.4). To conclude this explorative study, we formulate some potential research avenues (Section 26.5).

5 The 'reinventing government' project was driven by US Presidency Office and supported by private companies such as IBM. D. F. Engstrom and D. E. Ho, 'Algorithmic Accountability in the Administrative State' (2020) 37 *Yale Journal on Regulation* 800, at 802

6 In the United States and in European member states, the movement starts in the 1990. See e.g., H. Margetts, 'The Automated State' (1995) 10 *Public Policy and Administration* 88–103.

7 T. Mettler, 'The Road to Digital and Smart Government in Switzerland', in A. Ladner, N. Soguel, Y. Emery, S. Weerts, and S. Nahrath (eds.), *Swiss Public Administration: Making the State Work Successfully* (Cham, 2019), 175–186; A. Kankanhalli, Y. Charalabidis, and S. Mellouli, 'IoT and AI for Smart Government: A Research Agenda' (2019) 36 *Government Information Quarterly* 304–309; C. Valli Buttow and S. Weerts, 'Open Government Data: The OECD's Swiss Army Knife in the Transformation of Government' (2022) 14 *Policy & Internet* 219–234.

8 K. Yeung, 'The New Public Analytics as an Emerging Paradigm in public Sector Administration' (2022) 27 *Tilburg Law Review* 1–32.

9 T. Cantens, 'How Will the State Think with ChatGPT? The Challenges of Generative Artificial Intelligence for Public Administrations' (2024) *AI & Society* 1–12, https://doi.org/10.1007/s00146-023-01840-9 (last consulted 21 May 2024).

10 See G. Napolitano, 'The Rule of Law', in Peter Cane et al. (eds.), *The Oxford Handbook of Comparative Administrative Law* (2020; online ed., Oxford Academic, 2020); J. S. Bell, 'Comparative Administrative Law', in M. Reimann and R. Zimmermann (eds.), *The Oxford Handbook of Comparative Law* (2019; online ed., Oxford Academic, 2019).

11 G. E. Metzger, 'Administrative Law, Public Administration, and the Administrative Conference of the United States' (2014) 83 *George Washington Law Review* 1517.

26.2 PUBLIC ADMINISTRATION, ADMINISTRATIVE LAW, AND TECHNOLOGY

Before exploring the regulatory responses put in place for generative AI in public administration and the resulting key legal issues and principles, this section briefly sheds light on two aspects: the classic or traditional activities for a public administration (Section 26.2.1), and the current and potential use of generative AI for pursuing administrative activities and their deployment scenarios (Section 26.2.2).

26.2.1 *Administrative Activities*

Public administrations are pursuing administrative action in various fields of governmental activities (e.g., policy- and lawmaking, social benefits, education, justice, law enforcement, tax, transport, energy, and border controls). To act in these areas, public administration must have the legal authority (the legal basis condition, which is consubstantial with the idea of the rule of law). Public administration must be able to deploy human resources (civil servants), financial resources, and material resources (for example, buildings, computers, or internet access).

Public administration activities can fit into three categories: (quasi-) legislative lawmaking, (quasi-) judicial making, and a last group that we will call "non-legally binding activities." In legislative or quasi-legislative lawmaking, the administration contributes to the rulemaking process through preparatory work, delegated rulemaking, and implementation. In this regard, the output of public administration is preparing statutes and implementing them through delegated binding acts. Legal rules govern all these activities. For example, US and EU rules and policymaking processes require public consultation (for legislative acts) or notice-and-comment procedures (for agency regulations) as a preparatory step of the legislative process. They also establish (with diverse levels of obligation) the adoption of an evidence-based approach, encouraging or imposing *ex ante* and *ex post* legislative evaluations.

In the quasi-judicial function, public administration exercises the adjudication function of a department or agency. This type of activity develops in the wake of social benefits and the regulation of economic activities. In this framework, the output of public administration will be the adoption of individual decisions, such as granting subsidies, authorizing the opening of regulated activities, or placing products on the market. Decision-making activities have a binding effect on others and are governed by legal rules to prevent arbitrariness and ensure accountability in decision-making. European and US public administrations are bound by the principles of the right to an effective remedy and fair trial (e.g., Art. 47 EU Charter on Fundamental Rights and the US due process[12]).

The last group of activities covers an array of factual situations and declarative actions with a guiding or coordinating function. This broad category brings together acts and activities that are not legally binding for people outside the administration. It covers purely material activities, such as building a road, watering a park, publishing press releases and information campaigns, or using software. It also includes an important variety of governance frameworks and documents produced in the context of pursuing administrative actions such as policies, plans, strategies, and other guidelines. Additionally, it contains preparatory, interpretative, confirmatory, and

[12] M. Finck, 'Automated Decision-Making and Administrative Law', in Peter Cane et al. (eds.), *The Oxford Handbook of Comparative Administrative Law* (2020; online ed., Oxford Academic, 2020), p. 664; D. K. Citron, 'Technological Due Process' (2007) 85 *Washington University Law Review* 1249.

informative measures (e.g., concerning a civil servant's answers to a citizen). Some of these actions have an internal administrative effect on civil servants' work (e.g., an information notice) as well as that of agencies and authorities, such as a plan or strategy that guides the organization's action. From an external point of view, they do not have a binding effect on people outside of the administration. They remain, in principle, outside the scope of judicial review of public administration.[13]

Technology deployment and use can be categorized as falling into the "nonbinding act" but technological tools can also be viewed as a means of implementing each of the situations described in the three categories. They can then have legal and ethical effects depending on the context of their deployment. Such an internal approach may explain why administrative law principles seem superseded by public and ethical values in the context of digital transformation. Nonetheless, this internal – and implementation – dimension does not mean that administrations should not comply with the obligations of administrative law in their organization and functioning. Administrations are bound by the principle of legality and the public interest. As soon as the implementation measure restricts a human right, the administration needs a legal basis for using the technology.[14]

26.2.2 *Development and Use of Generative AI and Deployment Scenarios*

Because information technology is first a question of internal organization, generative AI systems – used as a tool or service – can be viewed as sociotechnical means with the potential to contribute or carry out various administrative activities. Generative AI systems can help civil servants complete their tasks of law-, policy-, and decision-making. For example, California asked technology companies to propose generative AI tools that could help California reduce traffic jams and make roads safer for pedestrians, cyclists, and scooter riders.[15] Spain and Denmark are considering using generative AI as a tool for regional languages in their policy of promoting less-used languages.[16] The EC has developed a tool known as "etranslation." Additionally, the Commission and the Court intend to deploy many AI solutions. The EC projects the use of AI tools to enhance "document summarisation capabilities, streamlining the preparation of briefings and responses to questions" to introduce "a conversational platform that supports non-classified human-like dialogues" and to provide "services to leverage the vast data, information, and knowledge base that the administration has across various business areas."[17] The EC is also exploring generative AI and large language model (LLM) technologies to help case handlers deal with complaints in shorter time spans by providing "smart search," or semantic search capabilities, and "smart drafting," allowing for the reuse of past replies from similar complaints.[18] The CJEU hopes that all staff members could benefit from an AI-powered

[13] However, non-binding acts are sometimes reviewed by courts. In this regard, the CJEU upholds the action of annulment against non-binding measures if these measures have an obligatory legal effect on the interest of a private person or a legal effect vis-à-vis third parties. See C-294/83, *Les Verts v. Parliament* [1986] ECLI:EU:C:1986:166.

[14] T. Tanquerel, *Manuel de droit administratif* (Schulthess, 2018), p. 242.

[15] S. Fox Sowell, 'California Seeking Generative AI Ideas to Help Lighten Traffic Jams', STATESCOOP, 12 January 2024, available at https://statescoop.com/california-traffic-jams-generative-ai/ (last consulted 21 May 2024).

[16] IBM Newsroom, 'IBM and the Government of Spain Collaborate to Advance National AI strategy and Build the World's Leading Spanish Languages AI Models', 5 April 2024, available at https://newsroom.ibm.com/2024-04-05-IBM-and-The-Government-of-Spain-Collaborate-to-Advance-National-AI-Strategy-and-Build-the-Worlds-Leading-Spanish-Language-AI-Models (last consulted 21 May 2024).

[17] European Commission, 'Communication to the Commission, Artificial Intelligence in the European Commission (AI@EC)', p. 7.

[18] Ibid.

virtual assistant, AI avatars could be used to deliver internal training and to produce didactic materials, and SIGA will be able to generate classification indicators and case correlation.[19] These projects show that generative AI tools will permeate all types of administrative activities, from supporting staff in their tasks of preparing binding and nonbinding acts to engaging with the public. In this sense, generative AI tools can be described as human-enhancing technologies, particularly in the context of performing public tasks. However, questions arise about the trade-offs concerning expertise and technological solutions and the effects of this broad use on society and administrative legal principles that were developed to guarantee accountability and prevent arbitrary action from public administration.

Deploying generative AI to pursue administrative action can result in three scenarios. The first occurs when, in the scope of their administrative tasks, agents use a "public" generative AI system (a solution accessible to everyone either free of charge or for a fee), such as ChatGPT or Bard. A second scenario occurs when the public authority purchases access to an LLM-based tool from a third party that fine-tunes the AI system based on the needs and data of the user – the administration. For example, in the United States, the Defense Department tested a generative AI tool (Acqbot) to help agencies write contracts and speed up the federal acquisition process, developed by a private company.[20] The last scenario happens when the administration develops its own generative AI system. For example, the IT unit of the Directorate-General for Translation of the European Commission developed tools based on LLMs such as eSummary and eBriefing.[21] eSummary is built on an open-source LLM that is accessible on HuggingFace. eBriefing uses commercial LLMs to increase the robustness of the tool. Such generative AI systems can take the form of chatbots: the French AI chatbot, Albert, supports civil servants in their daily tasks;[22] the Portuguese Sigma chatbot responds to citizens;[23] and soon the AI chatbot Aristotle should answer French students. These examples show that some of these tools are only for internal use (e.g., eSummary and eBriefing, Albert), while others are accessible to citizens (e.g., Sigma).

Each scenario depends on political choices. From this perspective, scenario 3 requires human, financial, and computing resources. It requires a model, meaning a neural network architecture including, for instance, transformers, autoencoders, generative adversarial networks, and/or diffusion models that have learned patterns from a large set of data. Alternatively, it may use an open-source model that is fine-tuned on internally collected and preprocessed training data as well as internal technical expertise. Such a scenario implies financial investment and a long-run perspective on technology and public administration. It is also strongly aligned with digital sovereignty for public administration, a key challenge in terms of cybersecurity and industrial policy for governments. Scenario 2 follows the commercial logic of the software world between off-the-shelf or tailored solutions, meaning a readily available solution designed for a larger user base. These solutions are mainly based on private actors and are market-oriented. They involve outsourcing human and technical requirements and imply very limited control of the administration over its tool, which the contractual provisions and conditions of use of the service provider regulate. Scenario 1 echoes the data platform model already put in place by

[19] Court of Justice of the European Union, 'Artificial Intelligence Strategy'.
[20] See https://acqbot.com/ (last consulted 21 May 2024).
[21] See https://language-tools.ec.europa.eu/ (last consulted 21 May 2024).
[22] R. Koller, 'Comment a été développée Albert, l'IA générative de l'Etat français', *ICT Journal*, 26 April 2024, available at www.ictjournal.ch/news/2024-04-26/comment-a-ete-developpee-albert-lia-generative-de-letat-francais (last consulted 21 May 2024).
[23] See www.ama.gov.pt/web/english/citizen-portal (last consulted 21 May 2024).

social media companies, in which services are free in return for users' data. It does not require any specific financial, human, or IT resources, but it does not protect confidentiality, personal data, or copyrights. In terms of cybersecurity, every scenario carries a different distribution of risks and perspectives on dangerous "backdoors" for unauthorized actors, and usage is without guarantee. Additionally, it entails specific risks concerning the training data (internal and external) that may negatively impact the model's performance.

At the end of this first section, we must remember that the deployment of generative AI in public administration needs to be considered an aspect of the non-legally binding measures that an administration can put in place. Generative AI can be used for various purposes and can contribute to lawmaking, decision-making, or policy adoption and implementation activities. It is therefore likely to have a legal effect on people outside the administration, and its use may require regulatory or even legislative measures to ensure that with such technological means, the public administration remains faithful to the fundamental administrative law principles of legality, transparency, accountability, prohibition of arbitrariness, equality, good faith, and proportionality. In the following section, we analyze how generative AI has been regulated so far in US and European institutions.

26.3 REGULATORY APPROACHES FOR THE DEPLOYMENT AND USES OF GENERATIVE AI

In this section, we analyze the United States' and European Union's regulatory measures adopted in the aftermath of the public availability of ChatGPT in November 2022. From a legal perspective, authorities have responded using various types of regulatory instruments. In this context, we classify the sets of measures in three approaches: command-and-control, preventive, and experimental approaches. By regulatory measures, we refer to all kinds of rules – legal or not – requiring administrations to comply with certain procedures regarding implementing such technology in public administrations.[24] Considering that US states were the first to regulate the deployment and use of generative AI systems in their administration, we start with the US (Section 26.3.1), and then we explore the EU's responses (Section 26.3.2).

26.3.1 *The United States of America*

In the United States, both levels of government adopted regulatory measures incorporating a continuum of responses, from prescriptive to experimental solutions. Considering that the United States was the first to address the question of deploying generative AI in state departments and agencies, we start by analyzing their executive orders (Section 26.3.1.1), and then we analyze the federal response (Section 26.3.1.2).

26.3.1.1 Regulating Generative AI in States

The scope of analysis is limited to the first eight states that in 2023 regulated the deployment of AI by administrative bodies with executive orders: Kansas (July 25), Wisconsin (August 23), California (September 6), Oklahoma (September 25), Virginia (September 29), Pennsylvania

[24] E. Fisher and S. A. Shapiro, *Administrative Competence: Reimagining Administrative Law* (Cambridge University Press, 2020).

(September 29), New Jersey (October 10), and Oregon (November 28).[25] Not all executive orders specifically mention generative AI or provide the same degree of precision regarding the regulatory measures put in place. For this reason, we concentrate on Kansas, California, Pennsylvania, Oklahoma, and New Jersey. The content analysis of the executive orders reveals a diversity of measures.

First, the executive orders include a series of measures that can be categorized as command-and-control. In this regard, only Kansas' and Pennsylvania's executive orders contain direct injunctions regarding the use of generative AI. Kansas policy establishes situations in which the use of AI must be limited, stating that AI output "shall not be assumed to be truthful, credible, or accurate, be used to issue official statements (i.e., policy, legislation, or regulations), be treated as the sole source of reference, be solely relied upon making final decisions, [or] be used to impersonate individuals and organizations." Providing restricted information in Kansas legislation or copyright and property materials is also prohibited when interacting with generative AI.[26] Contractors must disclose their utilization or integration of generative AI in their programs.[27] They cannot use restricted information or other confidential data in generative AI queries for building and training proprietary generative AI programs unless explicitly approved by the agency head in consultation with the chief information security officer.[28] Other measures are oriented toward prevention. The preventive approach requires, for example, conducting a preliminary assessment, the review of responses generated from generative AI outputs by a "knowledgeable human,"[29] or, when using generative AI tools, agency external-facing services or dataset inputs or outputs shall disclose the use of AI and what bias testing was done, if any.[30] Finally, other measures express an experimental approach. In this regard, some executive orders encourage state agencies to pilot generative AI projects and explore new ways of utilizing technology to improve services and administration.[31]

Executive orders covering AI also share a common concept regarding the need to set one or several governance bodies to monitor AI systems and generative AI. They put in place governance bodies (such as AI task forces or generative AI governance boards), regulatory bodies (AI council), or mandated state agencies.[32] These bodies play various roles in terms of implementing measures to ensure information, training, planning, and evaluation. In this context, some

[25] At the end of 2023, Georgia also fixed standards for responsible AI use, which covers generative AI. It includes questions of public procurement, bias and discrimination, accuracy and appropriateness of generative AI outputs, data protection, safety and security guidelines. Available at https://gta-psg.georgia.gov/psg/artificial-intelligence-responsible-use-ss-23-002 (last consulted 4 October 2024). The regulatory movement regarding generative AI governance in public administration continues in 2024 notably with Minnesota, Washington, and Idaho.

[26] Kansas, Generative Artificial Intelligence Policy, approved in 25 July 2023, available at www.kslegislature.gov/li_2024/b2023_24/committees/ctte_jt_it_1/documents/testimony/20230823_03.pdf (last consulted 17 January 2025), 9.2.3. and 9.2.5.

[27] Ibid., 9.2.7.

[28] Ibid., 9.2.8.

[29] Ibid., 9.2.1.

[30] Pennsylvania, EO 2023-19, 'Expanding and Governing the Use of Generative Artificial Intelligence Technologies within the Commonwealth of Pennsylvania', available at www.oa.pa.gov/Policies/eo/Documents/2023-19.pdf (last consulted 21 May 2024).

[31] Ibid., section 4; State of California EO N-12-23, available at www.gov.ca.gov/wp-content/uploads/2023/09/AI-EO-No.12-_-GGN-Signed.pdf (last consulted 21 May 2024), sections 3f, 3g.

[32] New Jersey, Executive Order n. 346, available at https://nj.gov/infobank/eo/056murphy/pdf/EO-346.pdf (last consulted 21 May 2024). The New Jersey's EO charged the office of information technology to develop a policy to govern and facilitate the use of AI by executive branch departments and agencies and to evaluate tools and strategies to improve government services through AI (10.c). The office of innovation shall develop a training program for staff members (10.d).

bodies must gather information about emerging technologies, assess their impacts on vulnerable communities, or collect salient cases.[33] Some executive orders require the governance bodies to update knowledge among civil servants.[34] They are charged to draft new guidelines regarding public procurement – and, if the executive order did not include such rules, for the use of generative AI tools.[35] Some also command the administration to adopt a comprehensive approach regarding generative AI, from the design, development, and procurement to the deployment of generative AI tools.

26.3.1.2 Regulating Generative AI in the Federal Government

On October 30, 2023, President Biden signed Executive Order (EO) 14110, regulating the use of AI systems and generative AI in departments and agencies,[36] in response to the scattered responses of US federal agencies. Between the submission of this chapter and its publication, Executive Order 14110 issued by President Biden was revoked by his successor, President Trump, on January 23, 2024.[37] This new situation opens the door to legal uncertainty regarding the development and use of generative AI in the federal administration. By repealing EO 14110, the new EO "American Leadership in AI" removes the legal basis for all executive actions – policies, directives, regulations, orders and other measures taken by agencies – notably, the OMP guidance and the OMB Memorandum advancing governance, innovation, and risk management for agency use of AI. The new EO also requires the special advisor for AI and crypto, the assistant to the president for science and technology, the assistant to the president for national security affairs, and the heads of relevant agencies "to identify any actions taken under Executive Order 14110 that are or may be inconsistent with, or present obstacles to, the policies set forth in Section 2 of that order, and to take steps to remedy them." However, the criteria for such an assessment are rather vague ("maintaining and enhancing America's global leadership in AI to promote human flourishing, economic competitiveness, and national security"). Ultimately, as national security remains a motive, it is unlikely that President Trump's administration will not implement any regulatory approach. However, the preventive approach that dominates risk analysis obligations could be abandoned or recalibrated in accordance with the

[33] The New Jersey EO charged its AI task force to studying emerging AI technologies in order to issue findings on the potential impacts of these technologies on society and offer recommendations to identify government actions appropriate to encourage the ethical and responsible use of AI technologies (1).

[34] State of Oklahoma, EO 2023–24, 25 September 2023, available at www.sos.ok.gov/documents/executive/2084.pdf (last consulted 21 May 2024); State of California EO N-12-23, available at www.gov.ca.gov/wp-content/uploads/2023/09/AI-EO-No.12-_-GGN-Signed.pdf (last consulted 21 May 2024), Section 5, State of Oregon, EO n. 23–26, available at www.oregon.gov/gov/eo/eo-23-26.pdf (last consulted 21 May 2024), (7.a); Pennsylvania, EO 2023-19, 'Expanding and Governing the Use of Generative Artificial Intelligence Technologies' (4.a.6).

[35] State of Oklahoma, EO 2023–24, 25 September 2023, available at www.sos.ok.gov/documents/executive/2084.pdf (last consulted 21 May 2024).

[36] Executive Order No. 14110, 88 Fed. Reg. 75191 (1 November 2023), available at www.federalregister.gov/documents/2023/11/01/2023-24283/safe-secure-and-trustworthy-development-and-use-of-artificial-intelligence (last consulted 21 May 2024). The EO does not apply to the government accountability office, the federal election commission, the governments of the District of Columbia and of the territories and possessions of the United States, and their various subdivisions and the government-owned contractor-operated facilities, including laboratories engaged in national defense research and production activities. for security reasons (44 U.S.C. 350 (1)). In this framework, the scope of application covers executive departments, public corporations, and other establishments in the executive branch of the government and the Executive Office of the President. It also included independent regulatory agencies such as the Federal Trade Commission or the Consumer Product Safety Commission (44 U.S.C. 350 (5)). AI in national security is governed by Section 10 (i) EO 13960.

[37] www.whitehouse.gov/presidential-actions/2025/01/removing-barriers-to-american-leadership-in-artificial-intelligence/ (last consulted 21 May 2024).

interests to be protected (national security versus civil rights). For example, due to privacy and security concerns, the Environmental Protection Agency did not permit its employees to use generative AI tools for official use.[38] However, the Defense Department was testing a generative tool to help agencies write contracts and speed up the federal acquisition process. In this context, the president's executive order adds its own new regulatory layer to a range of legislative and executive documents on AI, such as the Blueprint for an AI Bill of Rights and the National Institute of Standards and Technology (NIST) AI Risk Management Framework.[39] Moreover, two internal documents extend the executive order on the issue of the deployment and use of generative AI in federal departments and agencies: the Office Personnel Management Guidance on Responsible Use of Generative Artificial Intelligence for the Federal Workforce[40] and the Memorandum Advancing Governance, Innovation, and Risk Management for Agency Use of Artificial Intelligence of the Office of Management and Budget (OMB).[41] In this subsection, we limit our analysis to the executive order and the two last documents. Additionally, in the federal EO, we find the three regulatory approaches – command-and-control, preventive, and experimental – that we identified at the state level.

The federal executive order poses no general ban or block on using generative AI in federal departments and agencies (Section 10, f, i). However, the Office of Personnel Management (OPM) offers general guidance on using generative AI in the logic of command-and-control. It includes principles such as "Do not input non-public information into public GenAI interfaces"; "Do not leave GenAI technology to operate autonomously without human accountability and control"; "Review all AI-generated materials, including sources cited, to check that they are valid, accurate, complete, and safe"; "Do not tamper with or attempt to turn off guardrails against unsafe, offensive, misleading inputs or outputs of GenAI systems"; and "Follow your agency's policy on when and how to disclose uses of GenAI."[42]

More broadly, the federal executive order requires that federal agencies adopt a risk-averse approach when deploying AI systems if they impact the rights and safety of the public. It contains

[38] K. Borgardus, 'EPA Blocks Employee Use of ChatGPT', *Politcopro*, 5 February 2023, available at https://subscriber.politicopro.com/article/eenews/2023/05/02/epa-blocks-employee-use-of-chatgpt-00094868 (last consulted 21 May 2024).

[39] AI was on the political agenda at the end of the 2010s and was defined in Section 238(g) of the John McCain National Defense Authorization Act for fiscal year 2019. The US Congress put in place a National AI advisory committee. The Office of Management and Budget (OMB) was required to issue guidance to federal agencies and to create an AI Center of Excellence within the General Services Administration (AI in Government Act, 2020). The Congress also adopted the AI Training Act (Artificial Intelligence Training for the Acquisition Workforce, PL 117-207) to help train federal employees on AI's capabilities and risks and the Advancing American AI Act (James M. Inhofe National Defense Authorization Act for Fiscal Year 2023, PL 117-263 (Title LXXII, subtitle B) to encourage agency AI-related programs and initiatives to enhance US competitiveness in terms of innovation and entrepreneurship. The first steps were dedicated to building the general governance of AI with the National AI Advisory Committee and Center of Excellence and focused on the government and not on private companies, with the adoption of the AI in Government Act. Two executive orders were already adopted – Executive Order 13859, 'Maintaining American Leadership in Artificial Intelligence' 19 (2019) and EO 13960, 'Promoting the Use of Trustworthy Artificial Intelligence in the Federal Government' (2020), translating the ethical principles of the OECD recommendation – but they were partially implemented. This last one was updated by the NIST AI 100-1 for generative AI and the secure software development framework for generative AI and for dual-use foundation models.

[40] Office of Personnel Management, Responsible Use of Generative Artificial Intelligence for the Federal Workforce, available at www.opm.gov/data/resources/ai-guidance/ (last consulted 21 May 2024).

[41] Office of Management and Budget, Memorandum for the Heads of Executive Departments and Agencies, M-24-10, Advancing Governance, Innovation, and Risk Management for Agency Use of Artificial Intelligence, available at www.whitehouse.gov/wp-content/uploads/2024/03/M-24-10-Advancing-Governance-Innovation-and-Risk-Management-for-Agency-Use-of-Artificial-Intelligence.pdf (last consulted 21 May 2024).

[42] Office of Personnel Management, Responsible Use of Generative Artificial Intelligence for the Federal Workforce.

a series of measures regarding generative IA and the "dual foundation model," which the agencies must develop as part of their regulatory activity. For example, it requires the director of the OMB to provide guidance that "shall specify, to the extent appropriate and consistent with applicable law, ... external testing for AI, including red-teaming for generative AI, to be developed in coordination with the Cybersecurity and Infrastructure Security Agency" (Section 10, b, viii [A]). It shall also include testing and safeguarding against discriminatory, misleading, inflammatory, unsafe, deceptive, unlawful, or harmful outputs for generative AI (Section 10, b, viii [B]) and the steps to watermark or label output from generative AI (Section 10, b, viii [C]). Moreover, the OMB's memorandum provides a list of presumed risks describing when AI can affect safety, such as controlling or meaningfully influencing the outcomes of a series of activities (e.g., dam management, emergency services, electrical grids, transportation, industrial emission, environmental impact control processes) (Appendix I, 1) or when AI can impact rights in controlling or meaningfully influencing the outcomes of activities and decisions regarding individuals (free speech, law enforcement, immigration and asylum, measuring emotions, decisions regarding medical devices, medical diagnosis tools, loan-allocation processes, government benefits, decisions about child welfare or child custody) (Appendix I, 2). Generative AI can be deployed in some of these activity fields. In such a case, agencies must carry out an impact assessment on AI, test the performance of AI in a real context, and obtain an independent evaluation, which must cover the two previous elements (Section 5). For each aspect, the memorandum enumerates a long list of measures. For example, the impact assessment covers the objectives and expected benefits, the potential risks, and the stakeholders that will be most affected. In this respect, it also requires that agencies do not use AI if the benefits do not significantly outweigh the risks (Section 5, c, iv, A, 1). The impact assessment must also include evaluating the quality and adequacy of the data used for the design, development, training, testing, and operation of the AI (Section 5, c, iv, A, 3). In the case of generative AI developed by private actors, agencies may find themselves in a situation in which they do not have access to the data. In this case, they must obtain sufficient descriptive information from the supplier to satisfy requirements for the provenance and quality of the data.

Finally, by adopting an innovation-oriented mindset, the executive order encourages agencies to increase their capacity to successfully and responsibly implement AI, including generative AI, into their operations. To achieve such a goal, agencies must develop an enterprise AI strategy.[43] The EO encourages agencies to provide access to secure and reliable generative AI capabilities for experimental purposes "that carry a low risk of impacting Americans' rights" (Section 10.1, f [i]). It also authorizes "AI red-teaming," which is described as a "structured testing effort to find flaws and vulnerabilities in AI systems, often in a controlled environment and in collaboration with developers of AI" (Section 3, d).

26.3.2 *European Union Institutions*

The institutions of the EU also support the use of generative AI in public administration, and they have adopted AI strategies to advance development and deployment. The European legislator has adopted the AI Act (AIA), which contains provisions applying to private and public actors throughout the AI supply chain. In this context, and considering that the deployment and use of generative AI is part of the internal administration but its framing concerns agents and

[43] Office of Management and Budget, Memorandum for the Heads of Executive Departments and Agencies, M-24-10, Section 1.

services, we focus on the AI strategy and guidelines adopted by the EC and CJEU as well as the AIA.[44] We consider these two key European institutions paradigmatic for understanding how generative AI is regulated in the EU. For the analysis, we follow the same analytical grid distinguishing between command-and-control, preventive and experimental approaches.

From a chronological perspective, internal guidelines regarding the use of public generative AI tools, such as ChatGPT, were the first documents the European bodies adopted.[45] These guidelines are theoretically not legally binding documents. However, they refer to legal obligations and convey injunctions to their staff members in a logic of command-and-control.

The EC and CJEU guidelines show a close similarity.[46] The EC guidelines were first drafted in 2023 by the Information Management Steering Board. The document is designed to help staff assess the risks and limitations of such tools and clearly indicates that these risks and limitations are not necessarily relevant for internally developed generative AI tools. For those, the assessment is regulated by corporate governance for IT systems.

The EC guidelines are described as a "living document" to be updated as needed, taking the AIA into account. It states five rules. First, "Staff must never share any information that is not already in the public domain, nor personal data, with an online available generative AI model," considering that "staff are bound by art. 17 of the Staff Regulations, which forbids the unauthorized disclosure of any information received in the line of duty unless it is already public." Rule 2 requires that "staff should always critically assess any response produced by an online available generative AI model for potential bias and factually inaccurate information key issues for public administration services." Rule 3 is that "staff should always critically assess whether the outputs of an online generative AI model are not violating intellectual property rights, in particular copyright of third parties." According to Rule 4, "Staff shall never directly replicate the output of a generative AI model in public documents, such as the creation of Commission texts, notably legally binding documents." Finally, "Staff should never rely on online available generative AI models for critical and time-sensitive processes."[47]

In the same vein, the CJEU guidelines establish five principles regarding the use of unapproved online available generative AI tools.[48] One principle differs from the EC guidelines. It recommends that "staff members discuss and agree with their colleagues on how to ensure

[44] At the time of writing this chapter, Parliament's IA strategy was not yet public. On 16 April 2024, the DG for Innovation and Technological Support (ITEC) from the European Parliament (EP) adopted the guidelines 'Use of Publicly Available Artificial Intelligence Tools for Parliament Staff'. We got access to this document on the basis of a request for access to public documents. Due to the lack of data, we did not include the European Parliament in our analysis.

[45] European Commission, 'Guidelines for Staff on the Use of Online Available Generative Artificial Intelligence Tools'; Court of Justice of the European Union, 'Staff Guidelines on the Use of Non-approved Online Available Generative Artificial Intelligence (AI) Tools'. We got access to this document on the basis of a request for access to public documents.

[46] Regarding the European Parliament guidelines, the document indicates three principles: (1) Non-disclosure and personal data protection which echoes the rule and principle 1 of the EC and CJEU; (2) Content responsibility (which is similar to rule 4 of the EC); (3) Transparency and Compliance; and (4) Autonomy and Business Continuity, which is close to rule 5 of the EC. The transparency and compliance principle offers the most distinctive dimension from the two other guidelines. It means that Parliament staff must always properly reference sources when making substantial use of generative AI tools, using the disclaimer 'AI-assisted.' The idea of substantial use is defined as the action of 'interpreting data analysis, generating draft legislation, developing hypotheses, etc.' It does not cover using generative AI as a basic author support tool.

[47] European Commission, 'Guidelines for Staff on the Use of Online Available Generative Artificial Intelligence Tools'.

[48] Court of Justice of the European Union, 'Staff Guidelines on the use of non-Approved Online Available Generative Artificial Intelligence (AI) Tools', Directorate General for Information. The qualification if non-approved online available generative AI tools means that an intern body of ECJ can approved such tools and release the injunctions.

human quality control to the information generated via AI tools. They should ensure, through human review, of all outputs based on AI inputs, after careful reflection on the need to use generative AI."[49]

Moreover, in 2024, the two European institutions adopted their own AI strategies. These documents already indicate the preventive approach accompanying AI development. Here, strategy documents are again internal documents that play an organizational role and orient administrative action. They put in place an overarching framework for action inside each institution and specific plans to achieve the desired outcomes. In this regard, both strategies strengthen the IT governance regarding AI, which will play a decisive role in the assessment, implementation, and evaluation of each AI and generative AI system. For example, the European Commission Technology and Cybersecurity Board (ITCB) is in charge of conducting the preliminary assessment of AI initiatives in terms of compliance with ethical, legal, and regulatory requirements.[50] The CJEU added two new bodies responsible for architecture and data governance. The first takes the form of an initiative with the mission of identifying potential areas in which AI tools can bring benefits and to set up pilot projects/prototypes for the use of AI tools to test their benefits.[51] The second structure is a committee that drafts policies and guidelines.[52] Strategies also identified potential new use cases for AI systems within generative AI that can play a determinant role, such as to "support the legislative process, policy monitoring, and responses to parliamentary questions" – in carrying out an impact assessment of major legal proposals, searching and analyzing legislation, assessing the impact of new legislation on existing European and national legislation – or to support legislative (thematic) negotiations or "the drafting of non-sensitive content for briefing, reports, and other documents."[53]

Beyond these administrative documents, the European legislator adopted the AIA,[54] which covers generative AI under a specific regime. The legislative act adds a complex layer of compliance obligations that contribute to this preventive approach. The European regulation also applies to public administration. In this respect, the scope of obligations varies depending

49 Ibid.

50 European Commission, 'Communication to the Commission, Artificial Intelligence in the European Commission (AI@EC)', p. 5.

51 Ibid. At the EC level, the AI@EC network is in charge of identifying AI opportunities and use cases alongside the potential risks and facilitating the exploration of new AI projects services and building and sharing knowledge in the AI area. In the ECJ, the 'AI+ Network' has for its mission 'to detect the areas in which AI tools will bring benefits to current activities.' They will also be 'in charge of the prototypes and/or pilots designated to test the envisaged capabilities and to assess the benefits of their realization' (Court of Justice of the European Union, 'Artificial Intelligence Strategy', p. 20).

52 In the EC, the Interservice Steering Group on AI (ISG-AI) will coordinate and implement AI initiatives and oversee the AI@EC network activities. It will also set policies and frameworks and drafting operational guidelines for using AI in the commission (European Commission, 'Communication to the Commission, Artificial Intelligence in the European Commission (AI@EC)', p. 5). At the ECJ, the AI management board will be in charge of ensuring that the acquisition or creation of any AI tools respects ethical principles and fundamental rights. They will issue an ethical and fundamental rights charter that will be used as based to assess of any decision of acquisition or creation of AI tools. They would also define 'red lines' in case of a high level of risks in the adoption of AI in certain types of business areas or with certain AI tools (Court of Justice of the European Union, 'Artificial Intelligence Strategy', p. 20).

53 European Commission, 'Communication to the Commission, Artificial Intelligence in the European Commission (AI@EC)', p. 9.

54 European Parliament, Corrigendum to the position of the European Parliament Adopted at First Reading on 13 March 2024 with a view to the adoption of Regulation (EU) 2024/ . . . of the European Parliament and of the Council laying down harmonised rules on artificial intelligence and amending Regulations (EC) No. 300/2008, (EU) No. 167/2013, (EU) No. 168/2013, (EU) 2018/858, (EU) 2018/1139, and (EU) 2019/2144 and Directives 2014/90/EU, (EU) 2016/797, and (EU) 2020/1828 (Artificial Intelligence Act) P9_TA(2024)0138 (COM(2021)0206 – C9-0146/2021 – 2021/0106(COD)).

on the context of purpose (high risk or not) and whether the public administration is a provider or only a deployer of a generative AI system.[55]

In the case of developing a generative AI model to carry out an activity that is not categorized as representing a high risk, the administration acts as a provider and has to fulfill a series of obligations. For example, in the case of IT services developing an in-house general-purpose AI system, it "shall ensure that the outputs of the AI system are marked in a machine-readable format and detectable as artificially generated or manipulated," unless the system performs "an assistive function for standard editing or do[es] not substantially alter the input data provided by the deployer or the semantics thereof" (Art. 50 [2], AIA). Except under certain circumstances, and unless the interaction with the machine is obvious, administrations also have to ensure that citizens who interact with the generative AI system are informed in a clear and distinguishable manner of the interaction with a machine (Art. 50 [1] and [3], AIA). Such an obligation should benefit civil servants, who have the right to be informed about the technical means to pursue their public tasks. As providers, administrations have extra transparency obligations in making publicly available a sufficiently detailed summary of the content of the AI model. This summary should include the main data collections or sets that went into training the model (Art. 53 [1] AIA). If administrations want to use a tailored generative AI system or integrate a generative AI model interface in their own AI systems, they also need to show diligence in accessing technical documentation and a comprehensive summary regarding the datasets, unless the AI model is under a free and open access license (Art. 53 [2], AIA). Administrations can also be in the position of deployers when using a generative AI system. In this case, they have to disclose that the text has been artificially generated or manipulated (Art. 50 [4] AIA). However, such an obligation does not apply where the use is authorized by law for criminal prosecution, a human reviews the generated content or takes editorial control, or a natural legal person is responsible for the content's publication.

However, it cannot be denied that generative AI systems could be used to make decisions affecting terms of work or access to essential public services and benefits. They could also contribute to the administration of justice, such as assisting a public authority in interpreting facts and the law. Such purposes fall into the high-risk category established in Annex III; in this circumstance, the compliance obligations could be more difficult to disentangle, but we can identify two options. The first applies when an agent is in the decision loop or editorial role. In that case, one might consider that the generative AI system does not play a determinant role, and there is no need to comply with the specific obligations resulting from the high-risk deployment domain. The second option is based on the assumption that generative AI's impact on decision-making is not incidental, or the decision-making process will not ensure a decisive role for human control,[56] in which case the administration acting as provider will have to comply with a series of obligations. These include implementing a risk management system for monitoring and mitigating risks to which generative AI can contribute, notably fundamental rights (Art. 9, AIA); implementing safeguards regarding data preparation and governance, such as a bias detection process (Art. 10, AIA); keeping up-to-date technical documentation (Art. 11, AIA); and ensuring the tool's accuracy, robustness, and cybersecurity (Art. 15, AIA).

Lastly, the analyzed documents show that the EU and its institutions also want to promote AI innovation through an experimental approach. In this regard, the AIA endorses experimentation

[55] We did not include the hypothesis of general-purpose AI model with systemic risks considering highly hypothetical that a European public administration developed such a high-performance model.

[56] Such a decision-making process could then also present an issue regarding the GDPR, art. 22.

through authorized regulatory sandboxes as a framework for ensuring regulatory oversight and controlled space for experimentation to enhance a notable understanding of the opportunities, emerging risks, and impacts of AI use (Art. 57, AIA). Such an experimental approach is also promoted in the European Court of Justice (ECJ) and EC strategies, indicating a two-stage strategy. The first stage is explorative, meaning that the institutions deploy and test AI solutions in their services. The second is the industrialization phase, which can be deployed when there are positive results.[57] This is the case with GPT Lab at the Directorate-General for Translation and the GPT@JRC and AI sandbox at the Joint Research Centre.[58] Other initiatives could be developed through the work of the AI@EC network. The ECJ also adheres to the experimental approach. It indicates that the last three years comprised an experimentation phase, with thirty projects two-thirds of the way to being viable. The Court relied on an AI+ network and implemented an Innovation Lab where they worked with the industry. However, in the case of a regulatory assessment by the ITCB at the implementation stage, the test protocols are expected to remain at this stage.

Finally, this section shows that there are similarities between the regulatory movement underway in certain American and European Union administrations. The preventive approach is the way forward. It takes the form of a series of compliance measures but also establishes a governance structure dedicated to AI, which is called upon to play a key role in meeting compliance obligations. On this point, the versatility of generative AI technology could complicate the scope of obligations. Moreover, the regulatory effort does not follow the same path. Whereas the EU has adopted a legislative act, the US federal executive order requires US agencies to put in place more than 150 delegated measures.[59] In this regard, the US NIST framework could serve as a landmark implementation tool. The experimental approach illustrates one difference between the United States and the European Union, specifically regarding the EU's regulatory sandboxes. However, both emphasize the experimental approach for testing benefits and risks in real administrative situations. Finally, the most classic regulatory approach – command-and-control – is not absent from the regulation of generative AI in the United States or European Union. However, it is here that the differences are most striking. The measures taken by the two European institutions regarding freely accessible online generative AI show that the scenario 1 hypothesis described in the previous section is not favored in European administrative practice.

26.4 VALUES AND LEGAL ISSUES

The analysis of regulatory measures shows common and similar movements in favor of advancing generative AI in public administration. This section sheds light on three points: the political–economic perspective surrounding generative AI in public administration, the legally and ethically driven values for the deployment and use of generative AI in public administration, and lastly, some key legal issues.

[57] European Commission, 'Communication to the Commission, Artificial Intelligence in the European Commission (AI@EC)', p. 9.

[58] Ibid.

[59] C. Lawrence, I. Cui, and D. Ho, 'The Bureaucratic Challenge to AI Governance: An Empirical Assessment of Implementation at U.S. Federal Agencies' (2023) *Proceedings of the 2023 AAAI/ACM Conference on AI, Ethics, and Society*, pp. 606–652, https://doi.org/10.1145/3600211.3604701.

26.4.1 *Political Economy Perspective*

The United States' and European Union's documents give information regarding possible scenarios to operationalize generative AI advancement in public administration. From this perspective, they illustrate the political economy that underlines the attended administrative turn. For example, state executive orders mention the importance of reviewing regulations on public procurements.[60] The federal documents also emphasize the need to adapt a regulatory framework for acquiring solutions developed by private players. Federal agencies are encouraged to submit proposals to the Technology Modernization Fund to fund projects, particularly generative AI, to support mission execution (Section 10 [g] from the Executive Order). They are encouraged to negotiate "appropriate terms of service with vendors" (Section 10.1, f, [i] from the EO). The General Services Administration, in coordination with other departments, must develop a resource guide to take actions consistent with applicable law to facilitate access to federal government-wide acquisition solutions for specific types of AI services and products, including generative AI solutions (Section 10.1, h from the EO). In addition, the US administration has to develop and publish "a framework for prioritizing critical and emerging technology offerings … starting with generative AI offerings that have the primary focus of providing large language model-based chat interfaces, code-generation and debugging tools, and associated application programming interfaces, as well as prompt-based image generators" (Section 10.1, f[ii] from the EO). In this context, the United States plans to build its administration shift on private (American) solutions. The documents that were analyzed in this research indicate a logic of industrial policy in favor of its own industry.

The EU adopts a more nuanced – or maybe less clear due to the limited documents analyzed – economic approach. In this regard, strategies concerning AI governance for experimenting with in-house solutions and guidelines convey strong caution regarding online-available tools. The AIA also favors open-access models, which benefit from fewer compliance obligations. Considering the current trend toward big data and the computational resources needed for LLMs, it seems unrealistic to imagine that governments do not rely on outsourcing regarding generative AI models, despite the cautionary approach adopted by the internal guidelines with regard to online, freely available generative AI.

26.4.2 *Ethical and Legal Values*

Regulatory documents from the United States and European Union regarding generative AI contain commitments and convey a series of values. Both the US and EU documents emphasize that generative AI should play a supporting role for staff. For the ECJ, generative AI could more precisely enhance the efficiency and effectiveness of administrative and judicial processes. Additionally, it could benefit the ideal of justice in fostering the quality and consistency of judicial decisions and increasing access and transparency for EU citizens; moreover, people with disabilities could benefit from chatbots, virtual assistants, and AI avatars that could support them in their quest for information. The selected documents also convey the human-centric perspective. The EC will refrain from using AI systems that are incompatible with European values or

[60] State of California EO N-12-23, available at www.gov.ca.gov/wp-content/uploads/2023/09/AI-EO-No.12-_-GGN-Signed.pdf (last consulted 21 May 2024), section 3. Pennsylvania, EO 2023-19, Expanding and Governing the Use of Generative Artificial Intelligence Technologies within the Commonwealth of Pennsylvania, available at www.oa.pa.gov/Policies/eo/Documents/2023-19.pdf (last time consulted 21 May 2024), section 4.

that threaten security, safety, health, and fundamental rights. The US federal executive order announces that all existing AI systems should be assessed and dismantled in case of incompatibility with civil rights. In this regard, the selected documents convey administrative and societal commitment.

Regulatory documents are anchored in a series of values, sometimes expressly named, sometimes conveyed through measures. For example, the CJEU indicates that AI systems, particularly generative AI, should comply with fairness, impartiality and nondiscrimination, transparency, traceability, privacy and data protection, human oversight, and continuous improvement.[61]

Pennsylvania's executive order offers another striking example. The document points to values that concern three themes: technology (accuracy, appropriateness, transparency, and accountability), government (proportionality, sensitive information, safety, and security), and citizens (diversity, inclusion, discrimination, equity and fairness, privacy, and protection of personally identifiable information).

Regarding technology design, accuracy means that generative AI tools produce accurate and verifiable information. Appropriateness requires that training and data input into those tools comply with applicable laws, regulations, and policies concerning users' privacy rights and proceed through audit and evaluation of the tools' outputs. Transparency and accountability need to be guaranteed at various stages of AI implementation in a manner that respects and strengthens public trust.

The executive order also reflects a series of key values for the government, such as proportionality, safety and security, adaptability, and efficacy. In this regard, proportionality is described as a means for balancing between developing policies that encourage or control the use of generative AI in a context-specific way and avoiding unnecessarily burdening end users of agencies. Safety and security require the development and implementation of standards, procedures, and policies to safeguard and secure data provided to the state government by individuals and companies. Adaptability means that agencies must establish and maintain agility and willingness, they must also adapt to shifting risks and opportunities. This implies main investments that promote continued research and diligence, engagement with external stakeholders and subject matter experts, and learning from other government partners. Efficacy needs to be reached by improving the delivery of public services to individuals and companies and enabling agencies to be more effective and efficient in their daily work.

Finally, AI advancement needs to comply with civil rights. Generative AI tools must be used in a human-centered and equitable manner; bias must be tested for and protected against so that it does not favor or disadvantage any group over others. Agencies should ensure that they do not unlawfully discriminate against or disparately impact individuals or communities based on or due to ancestry, disability, age, sex, national origin, familial status, race, gender, religious creed, color, sexual orientation, gender identity, or gender expression.

The commitment in favor of a long list of technology, government, and society values does not mean that all values receive the same attention. This commitment can also generate misunderstanding in the administrative context. For example, regulatory measures emphasize transparency in technical documentation and tracing process obligations. However, this understanding of transparency does not completely meet the legal understanding of transparency, which is a key legal value from a rule-of-law perspective. In administrative law, transparency might be understood as the minimal openness process, access to documents, and publications of

[61] Court of Justice of the European Union, 'Artificial Intelligence Strategy', p. 16.

official measures.[62] It is the basis for a whole series of individual rights guaranteeing political participation and protection against arbitrariness (right to an effective remedy and fair trial). In this regard, transparency is intrinsically related to accountability. It has to be respected regardless of the means.[63] The documentation and explanation approach does not resolve the technological opacity, because generated content cannot be completely explained from a technical perspective. The technical understanding of transparency might be insufficient to meet the legal understanding of transparency. This issue has emerged concerning algorithmic tools; alternative options have been debated between fully disclosing training data and source code, ensuring the explainability of the system through procedural guarantees, providing counterfactual explanations, or limiting the machine's autonomy, placing it under the decision-making power of the human.[64] This illustrates the ongoing difficulty of translating legal obligations into technical measures and the risks of departing from fundamental administrative law principles.

26.4.3 *Legal Issues*

The regulatory documents are particularly enlightening in mapping the legal issues at stake when deploying generative AI in public administration, but they leave other possible issues in the shadows.

In this regard, generative AI technology represents a problem regarding secrecy in conducting public affairs and the secret duty of public agents. Moreover, generative AI also represents a risk for civil servants of breaching the law (and violating the principle of legality). All input data – including prompts – is exposed to disclosure risk. Input data can cover all types of data in possession of the public administration (personal and other proprietary data, closed and open government data), and data reuse can be subject to legal requirements (such as personal consent or legal basis). This means that civil servants could commit professional misconduct and be liable for disciplinary or criminal action if protected data is entered into the model.

The second key legal issue is discrimination. Public administration is required to respect the principles of equality and nondiscrimination among individuals. Here again, the large datasets on which generative AI systems are built make the task of combating bias particularly sensitive. Moreover, whatever the contractual arrangements regarding data, there is a risk of bias in the output, jeopardizing impartiality and nondiscrimination principles. Bias and discriminatory behavior are intrinsic characteristics of generative AI models; therefore, complete protection against this problem can be considered a technical challenge. Asserting mechanisms that counter this problem by flagging problematic categorization remains an important technical

[62] H. C. Hofmann, 'General Principles of EU Law and EU Administrative Law' in Steve Peers and Catherine Barnard (eds.), *European Union Law* (4th ed, Oxford University Press, 2023), pp. 212–241.

[63] Finck, 'Automated Decision-Making and Administrative Law'.

[64] E.g., S. Wachter, B. Mittelstadt, and C. Russell, 'Counterfactual Explanations without Opening the Black Box: Automated Decisions and the GDPR' (2018) 31(2) *Harvard Journal of Law and Technology*, https://jolt.law.harvard.edu/assets/articlePDFs/v31/Counterfactual-Explanations-without-Opening-the-Black-Box-Sandra-Wachter-et-al.pdf; M. K. Lee, A. Jain, H. J. Cha, S. Ojha, and D. Kusbit, 'Procedural Justice in Algorithmic Fairness: Leveraging Transparency and Outcome Control for Fair Algorithmic Mediation' (2019) 3 *Proceedings of the ACM on Human–Computer Interaction*, https://doi.org/10.1145/3359284; D. Merigoux, M. Alauzen, and L. Slimani. 'Rules, Computation and Politics. Scrutinizing Unnoticed Programming Choices in French Housing Benefits' (2023) 2(1) *Journal of Cross-disciplinary Research in Computational Law* 19.

problem. Moreover, the possibilities of legal responses to discriminatory algorithmic behavior are scarce due to the difficulties of detecting and acting against it.[65]

Another legal issue for public administration is legal certainty, which requires administrations to act consistently, enabling individuals to regulate their conduct according to the law. It thus protects individuals from contradictory and inconsistent decisions. Legal certainty also guarantees that demands will be addressed within a reasonable time. The potential shortcomings of the AI model due to the data and the design of the algorithms is generally considered a reliability issue.[66] Hallucination and output incoherence might then cause tension with principles of legal certainty and protection of legitimate expectations, both related to the principle of legality.

Furthermore, the case of the acquisition of generative AI systems from private providers poses a risk of administrations becoming strategically dependent on private players and exposing confidential information. Moreover, in the case of an approach based on experimentation, an AI system could be tested before its integration into the organizational process is decided. In such a case, the provider participating in the experiment may have a competitive advantage over other potential providers. These factors show that public administrations also need to critically assess the deployment scenario in the light of public procurement law.

Finally, the use of generative AI tools may also engage an administration's extra-contractual liability, which relies on three conditions: there must be a specific breach, the damage suffered must be real, and there must be a causal link between the breach and the damage. For example, the Tribunal of the European Union ruled that not giving access to an econometric model when it was decisive in an administrative decision and left the administration virtually no room for maneuver constituted a breach of the rights of the defense. Manifest and serious errors in the decision-making process were also considered the causal link between the conduct and the damage.[67] Regarding the issues previously identified and depending on whether it is used by civil servants, generative AI could give rise to the same kind of situation if the administration could not exercise substantial power of appreciation over the output produced by the machine. Subject to establishing the damage, a generative AI tool with a decisive function in a decision-making process to which the data subject does not have access would constitute a breach of procedural rights.[68] In addition, given the opacity of the operation and sometimes fanciful results of large language models, the administration could be accused of using a decision-making process that contains obvious errors.

26.5 CONCLUSIONS

This chapter is intended to offer a first exploratory approach of regulatory measures regarding deploying generative AI in public administration. Such a regulatory perspective was justified by the internal approach that has mainly dominated the literature regarding the deployment of information technology in public administrations. In this context, we selected documents from the United States and the European Union that share common commitments in terms of administrative law ("the rule of law") and for advancing generative AI in their public

[65] A. Beaulieu and S. Leonelli, *Data and Society: A Critical Introduction* (Sage Publications, 2022); F. Pasquale and G. Malgieri, 'Generative AI, Explainability, and Score-Based Natural Language Processing in Benefits Administration' (2024) 2(2) *Journal of Cross-Disciplinary Research in Computational Law*, https://journalcrcl.org/crcl/issue/view/7

[66] L. Floridi, 'AI as Agency without Intelligence: On ChatGPT, Large Language Models, and other Generative Models' (2023) 36 *Philosophy & Technology* 15.

[67] Affaire T-834/17, United Parcel Service/Commission, ECLI:EU:T:2022:84.

[68] Pasquale and Malgieri, 'Generative AI, Explainability, and Score-Based Natural Language Processing'.

administrations. We analyzed these documents through an analytical lens, differentiating between command-and-control, preventive, and experimental approaches. The analysis maps a set of measures echoing these regulatory approaches to ensure trustworthiness concerning AI technology. The documents also show elements that could be part of an industrial policy regarding potential scenarios for advancing generative AI as well as some strong commitments in favor of civil servants and citizens. The analysis reveals complex measures that do not always address key administrative law principles. Moreover, the normative choice for regulating generative AI in public administration confirms that despite such technology's social and environmental impact, its deployment is apprehended from an internal perspective. In this regard, the generative AI moment in public administration will remain a question of public administration studies. From this perspective, leaving the environmental and societal impact of generative AI unexplored confirms this remaining political silo approach regarding public problems and the techno-solutionism perspective on AI technology.

However, explorative analyses do not pretend to offer exhaustive analysis; rather, they help to formulate paths for future research. In this regard, the state of development regarding generative AI limits the scope of our research on policies. Case law will come later, allowing for legal dogmatic analysis. In the meantime, sociolegal studies could be carried out to understand, for example, how civil servants use technology and integrate the principles of good public administration and other legal issues into their use of technology. This aspect should also raise questions regarding the potential deskilling and upskilling effect on civil servants. Furthermore, from a regulation studies perspective, the experimental approach is the next generation of regulatory approaches; its combination with the preventive approach (compliance) will certainly necessitate attention. Preventive measures such as impact assessment are often imperfect tools, including their judicial review, and experimentations could then supplement the previous ones. Finally, the United States and European Union offer a field for investigation and comparison from a public administration perspective. The analysis of the embedded values regarding technology, government, and individuals and their potential translation into administrative measures could help to promote the renewal of administrative law in the digital state.

Printed by Integrated Books International,
United States of America